NATIVE AMERICANS

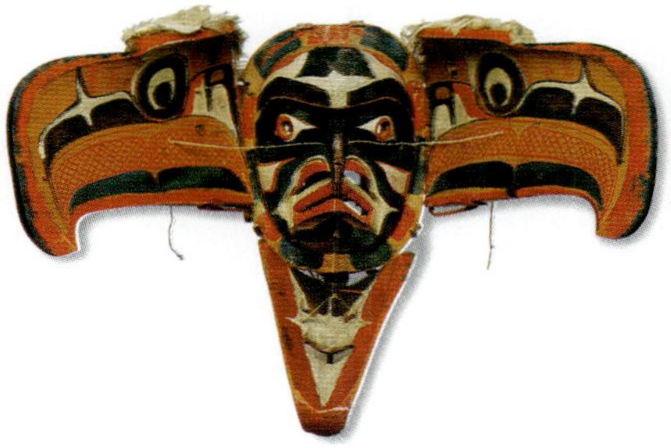

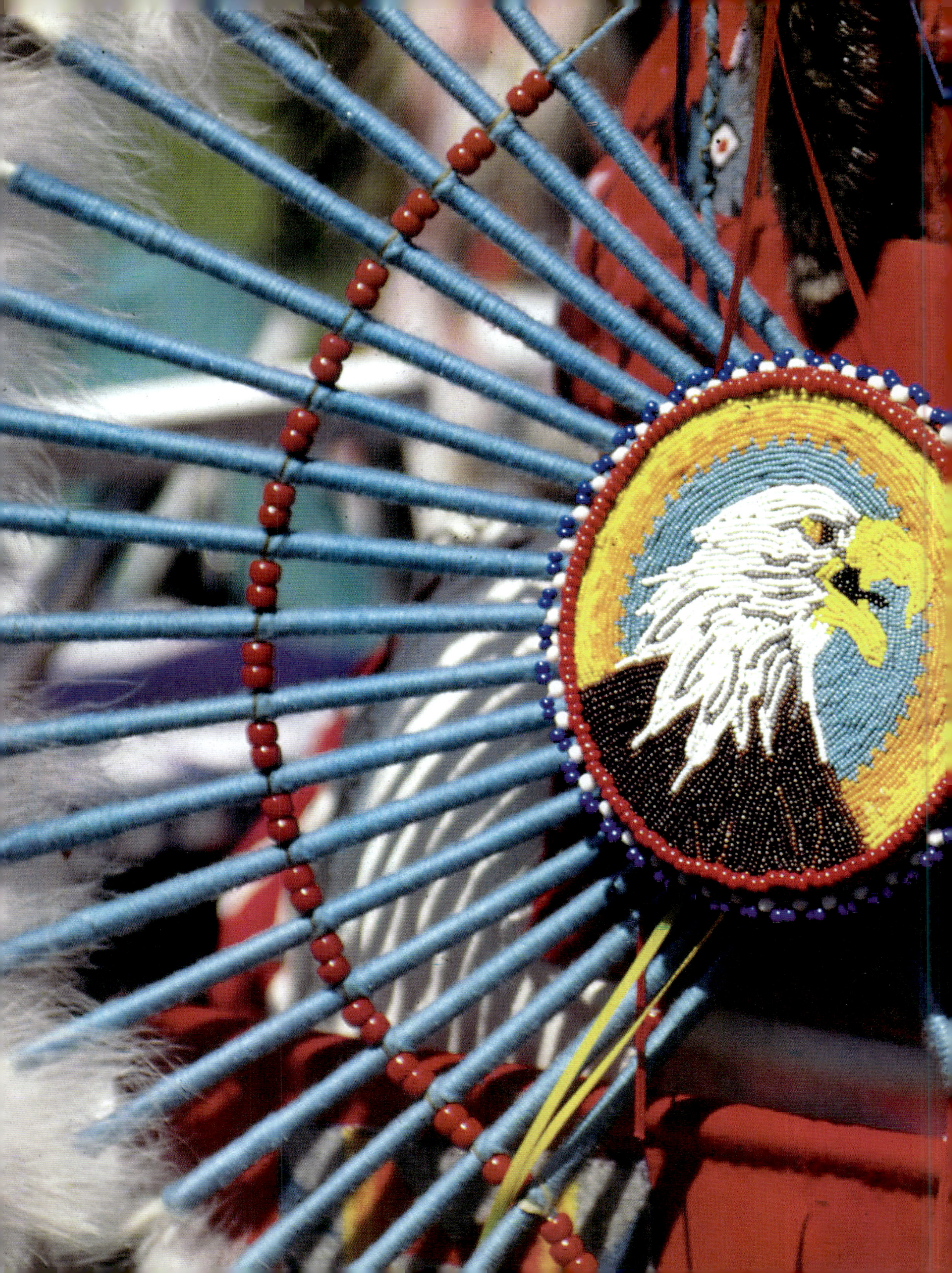

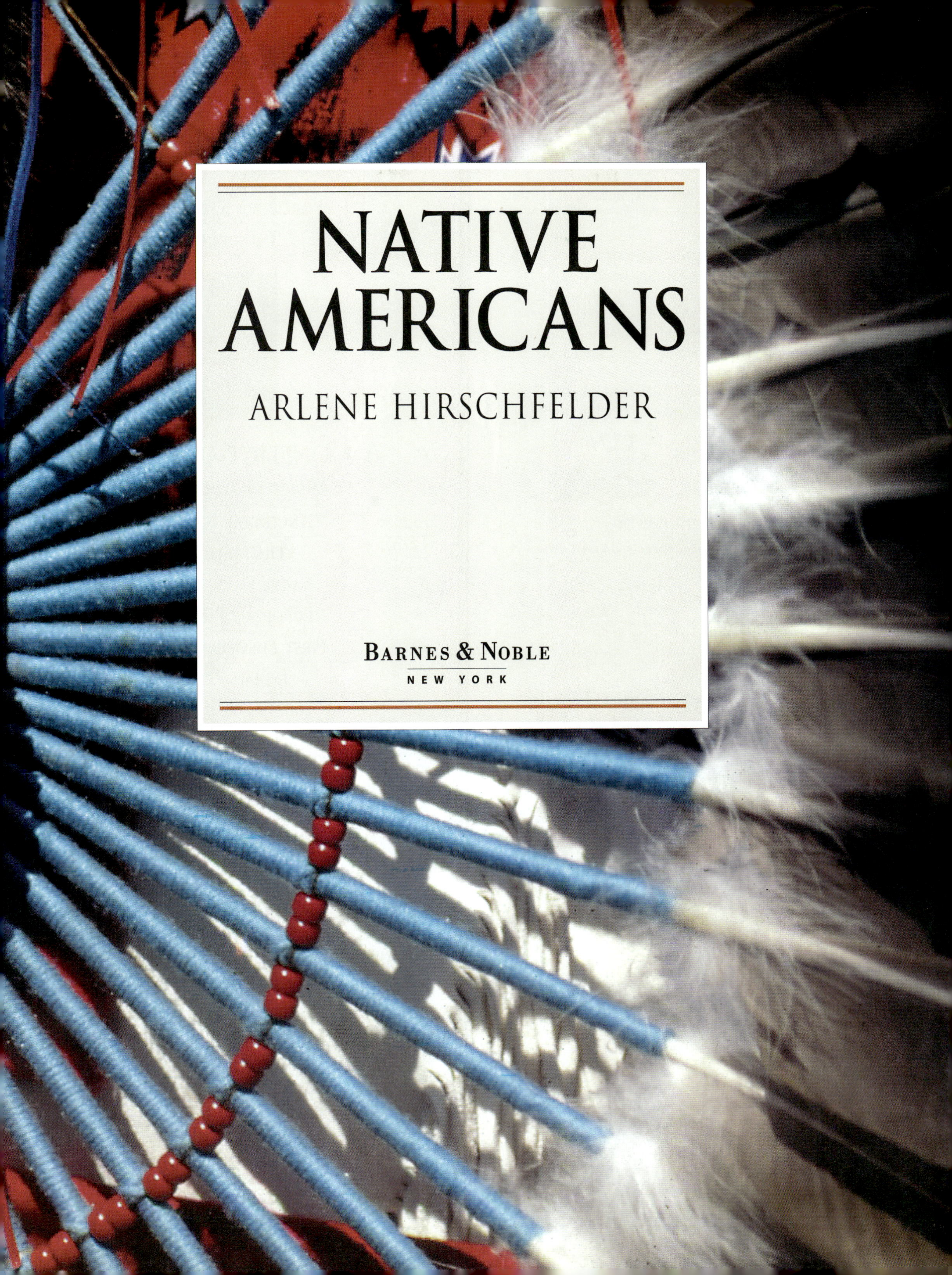

NATIVE AMERICANS

ARLENE HIRSCHFELDER

BARNES & NOBLE
NEW YORK

A portion of the author's royalties will be donated to the Red Rock Foundation, Inc., a Native American nonprofit organization in Arizona.

PROJECT EDITOR Irene Lyford
ART EDITOR Martin Hendry
PICTURE RESEARCHER Fiona Wilson
SENIOR ART EDITOR Alison Lotinga
US EDITOR Barbara Minton
SENIOR MANAGING EDITOR Mary-Clare Jerram
SENIOR MANAGING ART EDITOR Lee Griffiths
DTP DESIGNER Louise Paddick
PRODUCTION MANAGER Mandy Inness

This edition published by Barnes & Noble, Inc., by arrangement of Dorling Kindersley Limited

2006 Barnes & Noble Books

M 10 9 8 7 6 5 4 3 2 1

ISBN-13: 978-0-7607-7842-5

ISBN-10: 0-7607-7842-6

Dorling Kindersley has made every effort to contact copyright holders. We thank the following for allowing us to reprint extracts, and apologize for any omissions:
p.27 Reprinted from *Black Elk Speaks,* by John G. Neihardt, by permission of University of Nebraska Press. Copyright 1932, 1959, 1972, by John G. Neihardt. Copyright © 1961 by the John G. Neihardt Trust. p.61 *The Unjust Society* copyright © 1969 Harold Cardinal. Published in Canada by Douglas & McIntyre in 1997. Reprinted by permission of the publisher. p.127 From *The Arapaho Way: A Memoir of an Indian Boyhood* by Althea Bass. Copyright © 1966 by Althea Bass. Reprinted by permission of Clarkson Potter/Publishers, a division of Random House, Inc. p.147 Reprinted from *Pretty-Shield: Medicine Woman of the Crows* by Frank Bird Linderman. Copyright © Frank Bird Linderman 1932. p.167 Reprinted from *Alcatraz! Alcatraz!: The Indian Occupation of 1969–1971* by Adam Fortunate Eagle. Copyright © Adam Fortunate Eagle 1992. p.181 First published in *Native Peoples Magazine*, 1991. Reprinted by kind permission of the publisher.

Reproduced in Singapore by Colourscan
Printed and bound in China

CONTENTS

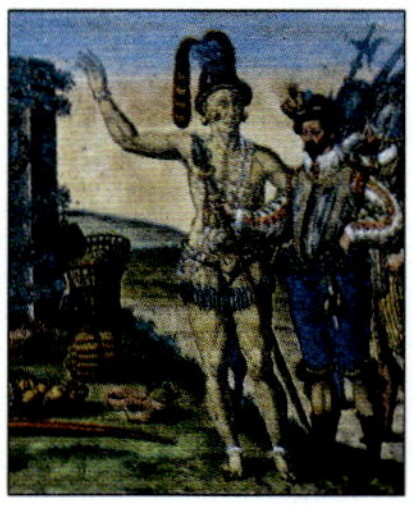

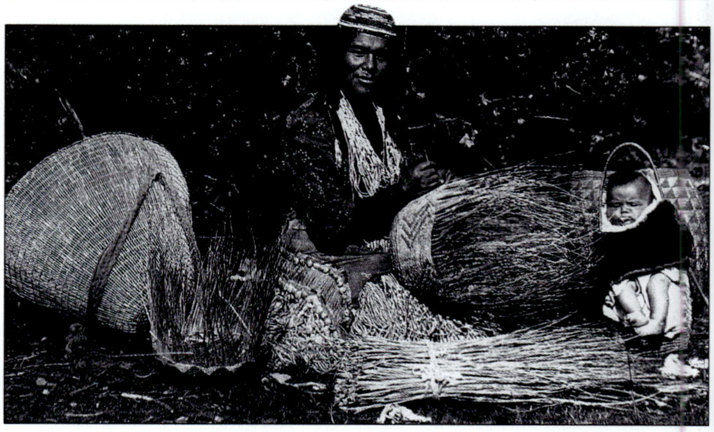

A LIFETIME OF BASKETMAKING
From birth to death, the lives of California Indians were filled with baskets. Women, like this Karok mother pictured here, made baskets for every conceivable purpose.

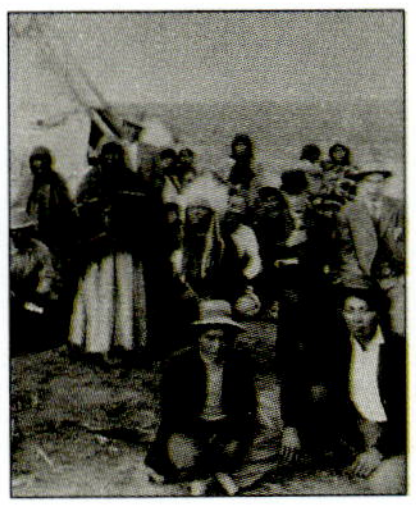

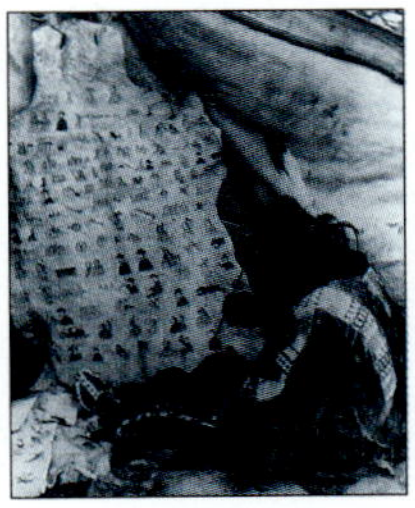

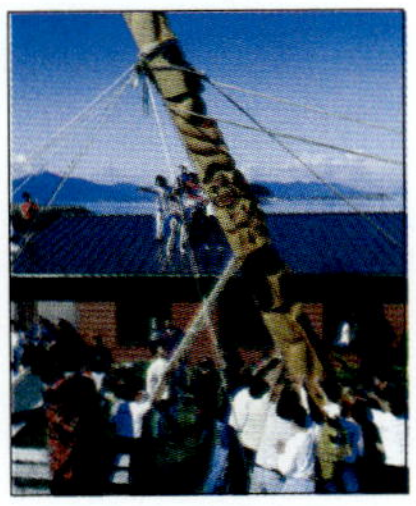

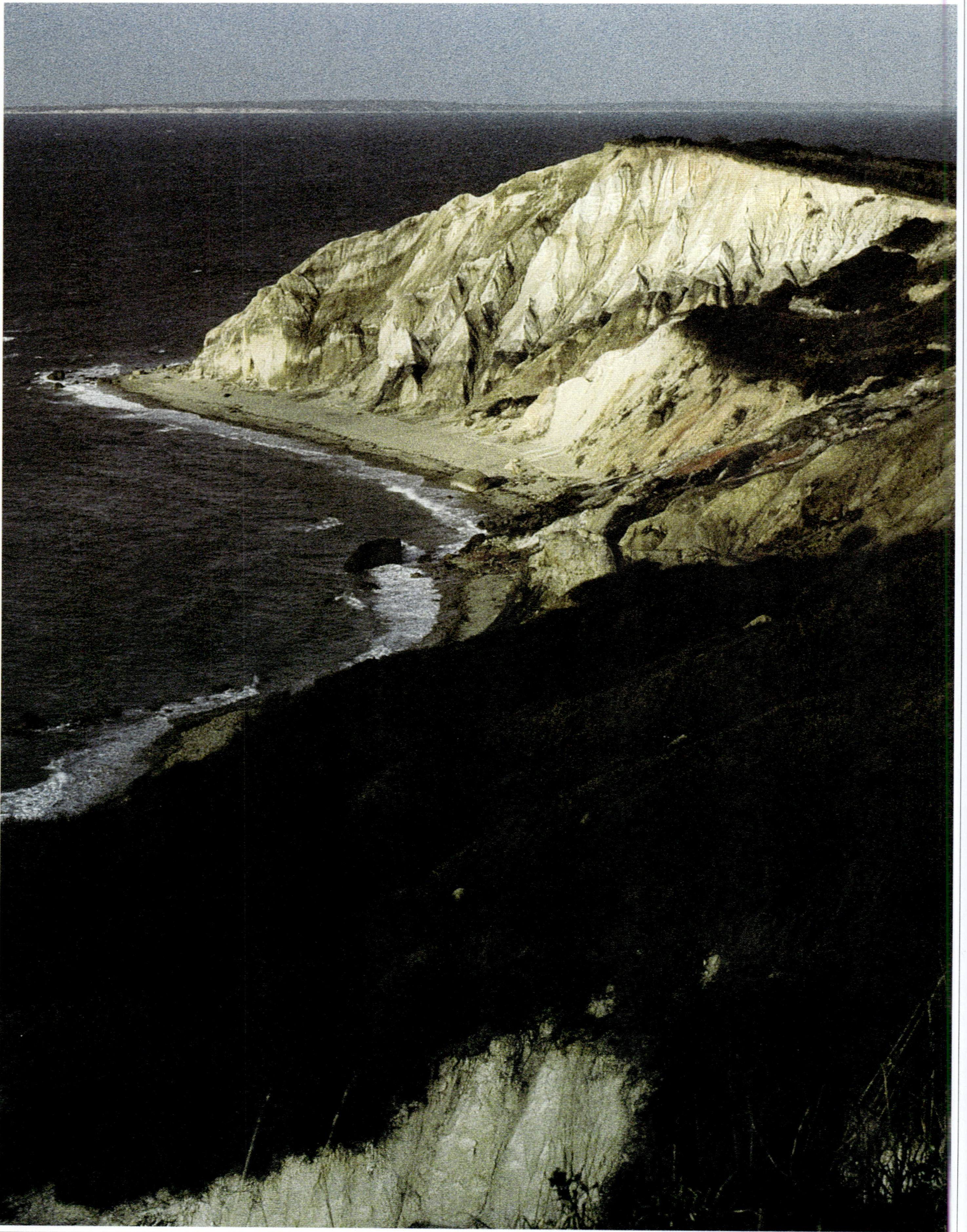

FOREWORD by Beverly Wright

As Chairperson of the Wampanoag Tribe of Gay Head/Acquinnah, I have a selfish reason for accepting the invitation and honor of writing the Foreword to Arlene Hirschfelder's *Native Americans.* It disturbs me that many inhabitants of the US still do not know that Native Americans exist east of the Mississippi River. The Wampanoags are the People of the First Light. Our leader, Massasoit, met the Pilgrims and greeted them in English, saying, "Welcome Englishmen." Our ancestors showed the Pilgrims sustenance methods that allowed them to exist through their first winter. The Wampanoag Tribe was federally recognized in 1987, when the US government sanctioned what we knew all along: we are Native Americans! Today, we are a thriving Indian community on the westernmost end of Martha's Vineyard Island, Massachusetts.

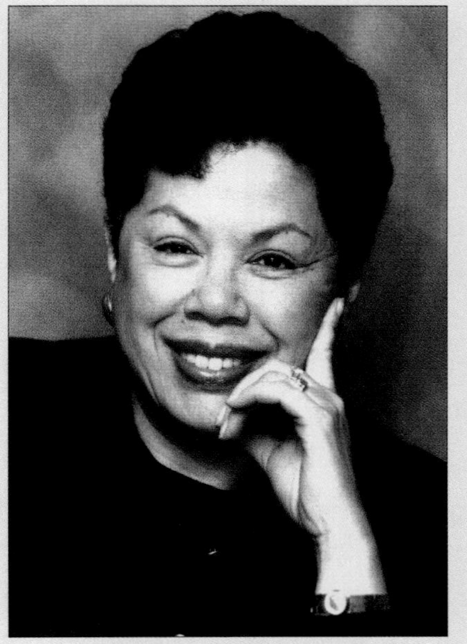

THE PEOPLE OF THE FIRST LIGHT
Aquinnah Cliff in Massachusetts State is a sacred place to the Wampanoag Tribe of Gay Head/Aquinnah, whose Chairperson, Beverly Wright, is pictured above. The Cliff, which is composed of layers of clay, sand, quartz, soil, and lignite, dates back over 100 million years.

Since the first treaty in 1778, the US government entered into over 800 treaties with Indian nations, although the Senate only ratified around 400 of them. Every single treaty has been broken in one way or the other, resulting in the loss to North America's original inhabitants of over 500 million acres (200 million hectares) of land. In exchange, the government promised to provide health care, education, and housing, but Natives today still suffer the highest rate of alcoholism, diabetes, suicide, and heart disease in the US.

Native Americans is an important book because it is told from a perspective that shows Indians, not as savages, but as people with ways that were different from those of the dominant society. I ask that when you are reading this history, you try and see it through the eyes of people who want to preserve Mother Earth for the seventh generation to come; people who want to have a balanced life with self, family, community, and nation; people who believe in the visions of their ancestors; people who respect the four-legged, the winged, and the two-legged; people who gather only what is needed to sustain their families.

Beverly M Wright

INTRODUCTION

THE ORIGINAL INHABITANTS of North America were a diverse, hetergeneous group of people. North of the Rio Grande, which forms the border between Texas and Mexico, at least 400 separate languages were spoken and at least as many distinct societies flourished. These small, independent cultures, with an estimated total population of 7 to 10 million, traded with one another across wide networks. While there were a number of multitribal alliances, such as the Iroquois Confederacy, there were no empires like those of Rome. Leadership derived from ability rather than heredity, and land was "owned" collectively.

Armed conflict occurred in a limited way between tribes, parts of tribes, or between individuals. Battles were fought for a variety of reasons, such as revenge, honor, or the acquisition of horses or other property. Once these objectives were achieved, the reason for fighting no longer existed. Hostilities usually lasted no longer than a few months, with minimal loss of life. Rarely did a conflict between enemy tribes completely wipe out one or the other.

European Arrivals

Conditioned as they were to cultural diversity, Native Americans, whether they lived in what is now Massachusetts, New Mexico, Alaska, or Quebec Province, initially welcomed European newcomers and treated them as guests and trading partners. Most Europeans, however, considered Native people "savages" because they weren't Christian, didn't wear European clothes, didn't live in houses, didn't speak English, Spanish, French, or Russian, and didn't have "proper" customs and institutions. The newcomers neither understood that Natives revered their creation stories (which explain the origins of their people and of every particle on earth and in the sky) not that they performed their own complex religious ceremonies, practiced child-rearing practices that were just as valid as those of Europeans, and ran government by consensus rather than by majority rule.

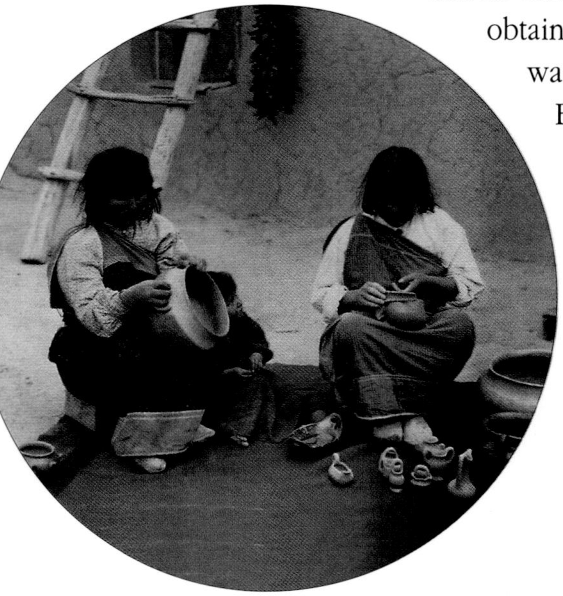

ANCIENT PRACTICES AT ACOMA
The pottery made by Pueblo women possessed great beauty and technical quality. After laboriously gathering and preparing the clay, these Santa Clara women molded pots and other objects by hand, in a centuries-old tradition.

The Seeds of Conflict

During the colonial period, Europeans, who were greatly outnumbered by the Indians and dependent on their cooperation for survival, recognized the sovereignty of Indian governments and dealt with them on a nation-to-nation basis. They traded with the Indians, made treaties, acquired land, and established boundaries. All too often, however, they attempted to change the way of life of the Natives. Spanish conquistadores demanded that Indians provide labor to mine precious metals, while French and English traders and trappers employed them to obtain pelts. Catholic missionaries wanted to convert Indian souls, and English settlers wanted their lands for farming. During the 1600s, unreasonable demands led to bloody wars between Native societies and Europeans and, by the end of the seventeenth century, tribes along the Atlantic seaboard had been destroyed or subjected to the control of European colonists.

Prior to the end of the eighteenth century, European colonists did not interfere, for the most part, in the internal affairs of the tribes, but their presence caused catastrophic change nonetheless. Native Americans were helpless in the face of the diseases that the European explorers, missionaries, and colonists had carried from the "Old World," some tribes losing most of their population within weeks of illness infecting the group. Many leaders and elders died, weakening the governments of different Indian societies. With Native populations dramatically reduced, empty land became available for exploitation and colonization, thus paving the way for European dominance over Native North America.

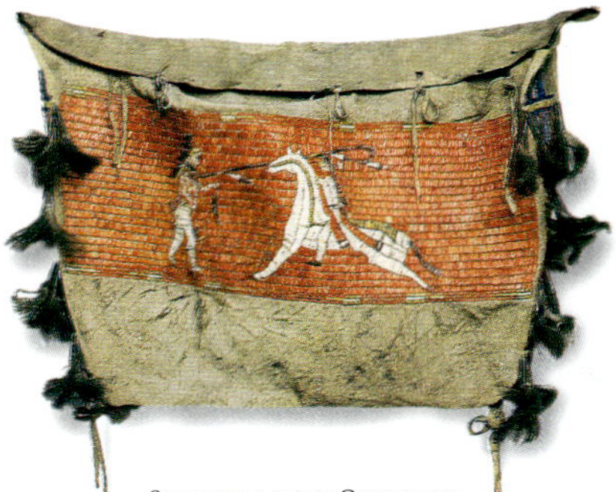

SADDLEBAG WITH QUILLWORK BY PLAINS INDIAN WOMEN

A Struggle for Land

Although the British crown, and later the Americans, established various boundaries on Indian lands beyond which settlers should not advance, encroachment continued because inadequate enforcement failed to stem the tide of settlers moving westward.

At first, treaties with Europeans, and later with Americans, established the precedent that Native Americans lived in recognized nations with aboriginal right of title to land and to control of their own territory. Europeans and Americans, however, wrongly assumed that each tribe had a leader who was empowered to speak for everyone. They did not understand that individuals might be persuaded to sell their own rights to a piece of territory, but that they could rarely negotiate for another's land unless that right had been granted. As a result, negotiations were carried on with the people most willing to cooperate with whites and payments were made to these individuals, who had no authority over the vast homelands in question. Such dealings undermined traditional forms of rule and created internal conflicts among tribal members. The US government also broke treaties whenever it deemed necessary. In 1871, Congress ended the treaty-making system, but voted to uphold previously signed treaties.

In Canada, treaties were signed between the mid-1700s and 1923. No further treaties were negotiated

ESTABLISHMENT OF THE GREAT SIOUX RESERVATION
At an 1868 treaty council at Fort Laramie, in southeastern Wyoming, US commissioners and Lakota leaders, pictured here, established the Great Sioux Reservation. Violation of the Fort Laramie Treaty (which also closed the Bozeman trail and the three forts set up to protect prospectors) precipitated a decade of hostilities on the Northern Plains.

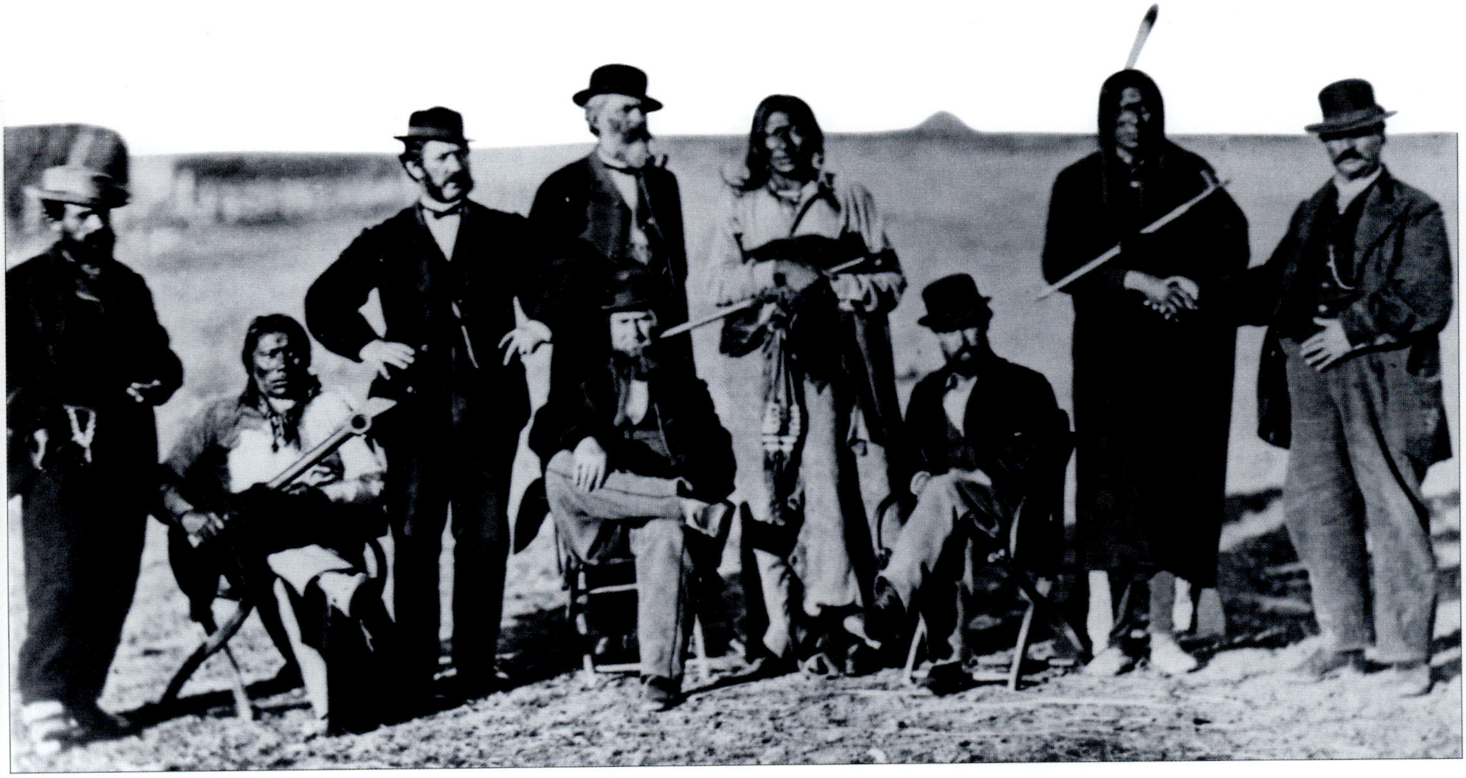

NATIVE NORTH AMERICA

Around 1500, North America was populated by millions of people organized into more than 600 autonomous societies, each with its own way of life. An estimated 500 or more Native languages were spoken in diverse geographic settings. This map illustrates the kinds of dwellings these peoples lived in and the foods they survived on - both important indices of the diversities that existed in Native North America.

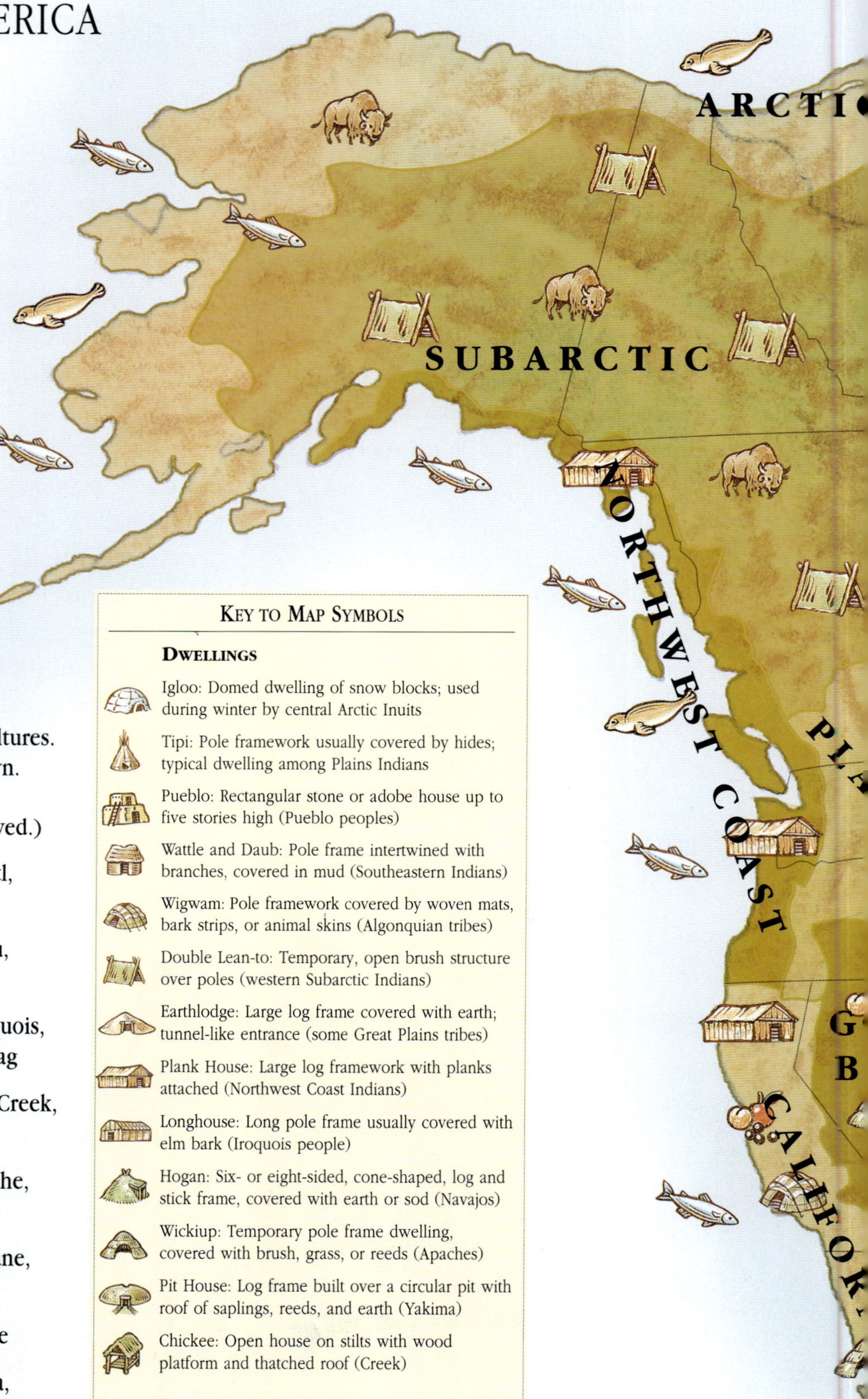

KEY TO MAP SYMBOLS

DWELLINGS

- Igloo: Domed dwelling of snow blocks; used during winter by central Arctic Inuits
- Tipi: Pole framework usually covered by hides; typical dwelling among Plains Indians
- Pueblo: Rectangular stone or adobe house up to five stories high (Pueblo peoples)
- Wattle and Daub: Pole frame intertwined with branches, covered in mud (Southeastern Indians)
- Wigwam: Pole framework covered by woven mats, bark strips, or animal skins (Algonquian tribes)
- Double Lean-to: Temporary, open brush structure over poles (western Subarctic Indians)
- Earthlodge: Large log frame covered with earth; tunnel-like entrance (some Great Plains tribes)
- Plank House: Large log framework with planks attached (Northwest Coast Indians)
- Longhouse: Long pole frame usually covered with elm bark (Iroquois people)
- Hogan: Six- or eight-sided, cone-shaped, log and stick frame, covered with earth or sod (Navajos)
- Wickiup: Temporary pole frame dwelling, covered with brush, grass, or reeds (Apaches)
- Pit House: Log frame built over a circular pit with roof of saplings, reeds, and earth (Yakima)
- Chickee: Open house on stilts with wood platform and thatched roof (Creek)

SUBSISTENCE

- Game
- Cultivated plants
- Fish and shellfish
- Sea mammals
- Wild plants

MAJOR TRIBES AND CULTURE AREAS

The map is divided into ten areas that were occupied by Native peoples with similar cultures. The location of major tribes *c.* 1500 is shown. (Note: data on Great Plains tribes relates to *c.* 1820, when their distinct way of life evolved.)

Northwest Coast: Chinook, Haida, Kwakiutl, Makah, Nootka, Tlingit, Tsimshian

California: Cahuilla, Chumash, Hupa, Maidu, Miwok, Pomo, Yurok

Northeast: Algonquian, Five Nations of Iroquois, Huron, Micmac, Pequot, Shawnee, Wampanoag

Southeast: Cherokee, Chickasaw, Choctaw, Creek, Timucua, Yuchi

Great Plains: Blackfeet, Cheyenne, Comanche, Crow, Osage, Pawnee, Quapaw, Sioux

Plateau: Cayuse, Kootenai, Nez Percé, Spokane, Umatilla, Yakima

Great Basin: Bannock, Paiute, Shoshone, Ute

Southwest: Apache, Havasupai, Navajo, Pima, Rio Grande (Eastern) Pueblos, Western Pueblos

Arctic: Inuits, Aleuts

Subarctic: Carrier, Cree, Chippewyan, Kutchin, Montagnais, Naskapi

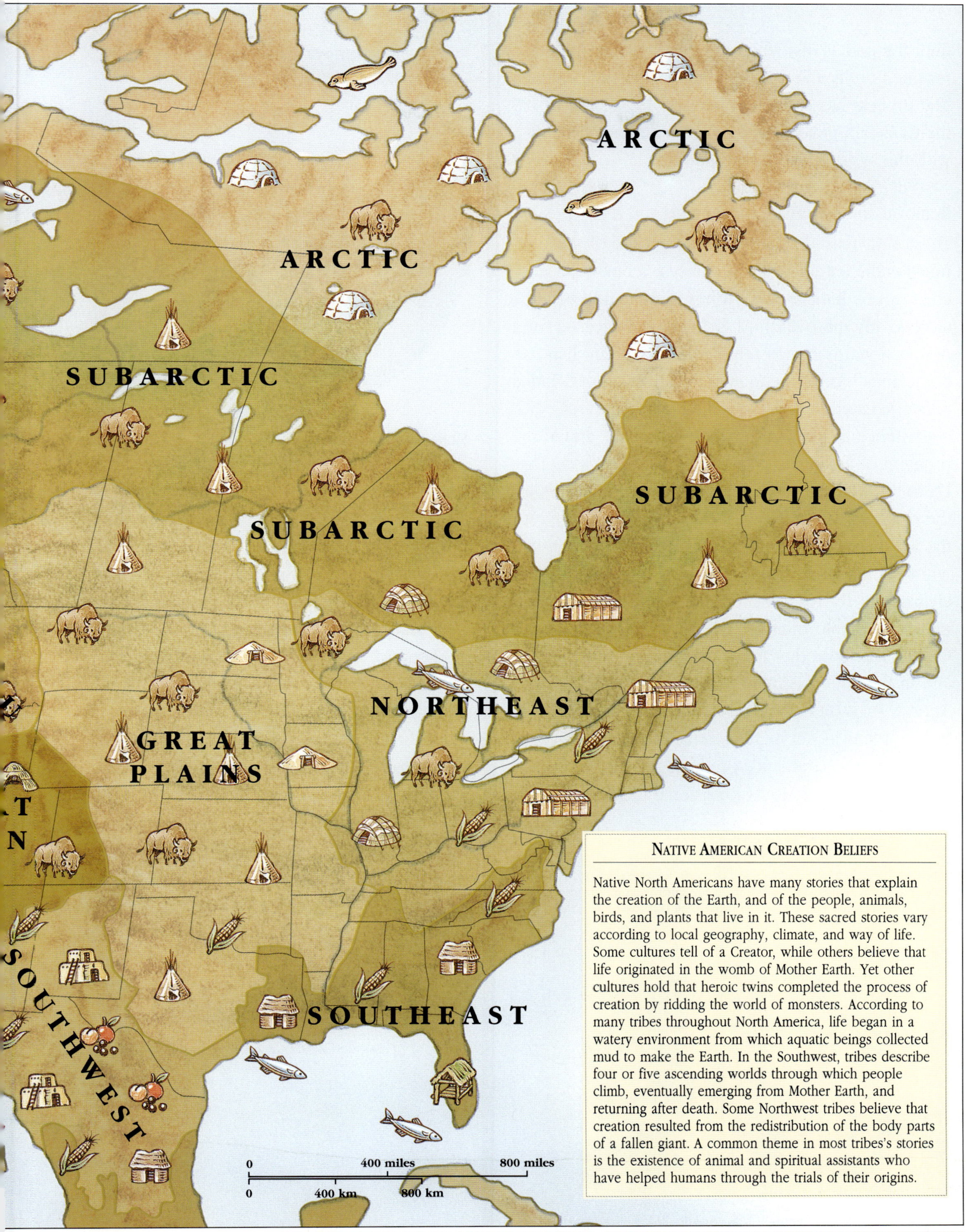

NATIVE AMERICAN CREATION BELIEFS

Native North Americans have many stories that explain the creation of the Earth, and of the people, animals, birds, and plants that live in it. These sacred stories vary according to local geography, climate, and way of life. Some cultures tell of a Creator, while others believe that life originated in the womb of Mother Earth. Yet other cultures hold that heroic twins completed the process of creation by ridding the world of monsters. According to many tribes throughout North America, life began in a watery environment from which aquatic beings collected mud to make the Earth. In the Southwest, tribes describe four or five ascending worlds through which people climb, eventually emerging from Mother Earth, and returning after death. Some Northwest tribes believe that creation resulted from the redistribution of the body parts of a fallen giant. A common theme in most tribes's stories is the existence of animal and spiritual assistants who have helped humans through the trials of their origins.

until the mid-1970s, when the treaty-making process resumed under the government's "claims agreements." The process has continued into the 1990s and, in 1999, the Canadian government signed a landmark treaty with the Nisga'a in British Columbia.

Removal and Assimilation Programs

Tension increased during the first decade of the nineteenth century when Tecumseh, a Shawnee war chief, urged Indians of all tribes to unite and to refuse to cede any more land. After pressure increased for a new national policy to remove Indians from their homelands east of the Mississippi River, the US Indian Office, created in 1824, switched from peaceful coexistence to physical removal of Indians and a program of assimilating them into white society. The US tried to talk tribes into selling their homelands in the Northeast and Southeast by suggesting that west of the Mississippi, in a protected area relatively free of white settlers, they would have time to adjust to white civilization. By 1825, some tribes had voluntarily moved west into Indian Territory (present-day Oklahoma), but other tribes in the Great Lakes area and in the Southeast resisted moving. President Andrew Jackson convinced Congress to pass the Indian Removal Act in 1830, which forced the eviction from their ancestral lands of almost all the Native people east of the Mississippi. Some tribes resisted but, by 1840, about 100,000 Native people had been forcibly removed and relocated to Indian Territory, where missionaries and government officials pursued their goals of "educating" and Christianizing them.

Removal created enormous hardships for Indians. The tribes relocated to the West had to learn to live among the tribes already living there. Removal also intensified the factionalism in tribes between traditionalists, who opposed removal, and those assimilated or progressive Indians who experienced little remorse in leaving their homeland. The relocated tribes also faced hordes of white people streaming onto their lands, accelerated by the 1848 California gold rush, the completion of the transcontinental

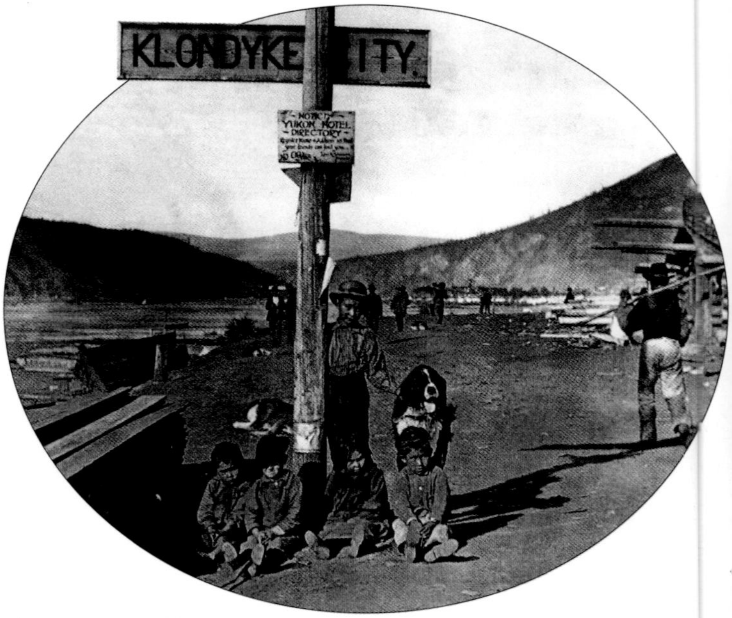

SIGNPOSTING A DREAM
Around 1890, a group of Native children sit, with their dog, by the Klondike City signpost, on the banks of the Klondike River in Yukon Territory, northwest Canada. Gold was discovered in the area in 1896: the subsequent gold rush opened up the Yukon and yielded over $22 million worth of gold in one peak year of production.

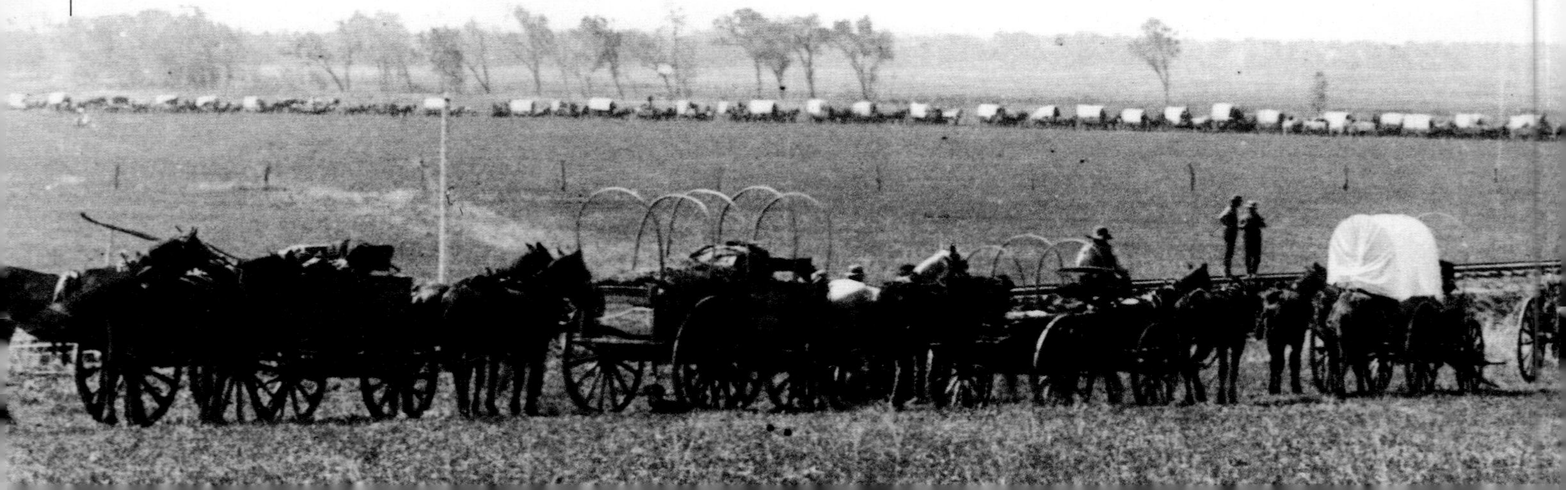

LINING UP FOR LAND IN INDIAN TERRITORY
Around 4,000 covered wagons filled with homesteaders moved up to the starting line for the 1889 land rush following President Benjamin Harrison's proclamation opening up land in Indian Territory for settlement. Photographer William Prettyman caught this picture of wagons lining up to cross the swollen Salt Fork River before the run.

railroad in 1869, and the establishment of forts along the westbound trails. In Canada, gold rushes, railroad building, and disruption of homelands took place later in the century.

Fighting for a Way of Life

The Civil War period, which temporarily slowed down the westward movement of settlers, was disastrous for many Indians, especially those in Indian Territory, who endured civil wars themselves as tribes and individuals disagreed over which side to support.

After the war ended, with increasing numbers of whites encroaching on Native lands, Indians began to retaliate by attacking the trespassers. In response, the US government tried to separate Indians from whites by relocating more tribes to reservations in Indian Territory and turning over reservation administration, at various times, to churchmen, army officers, and Indian agents. The government preferred to resolve the "Indian problem" peaceably by confining Indians to reservations, because waging war was a far more costly option. But more than two decades of incessant and desperate warfare followed as the federal government tried to force western tribes to move to reservations. Tribes in the Southern and Northern Plains, Texas, the Southwest, the Basin-Plateau, and in California fought valiantly to hold on to their traditional homelands and ways of life. By the late nineteenth century, however, more than 100 tribes, reduced in number by warfare and disease, were eventually forced to sign treaties and move onto reservations.

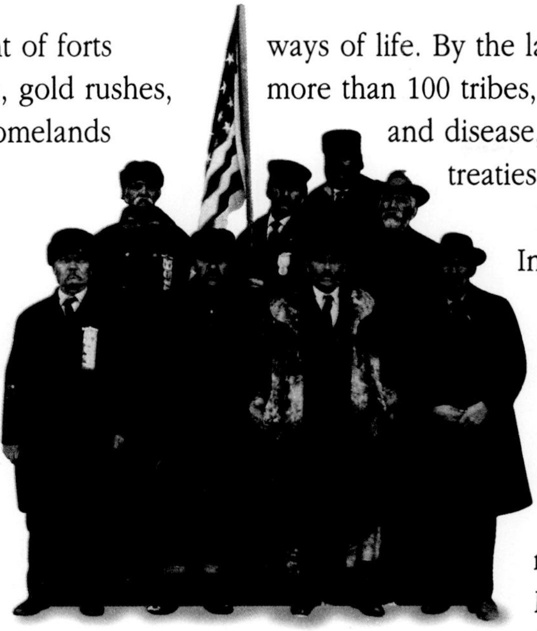

ONEIDA CIVIL WAR VETERANS
The Oneida Indian veterans of the Fourteenth Wisconsin, pictured here, served the Union. At the Battle of Vicksburg in 1863 their sharpshooting silenced a rebel cannon.

In Canada, relations between Indians and whites were marked by considerably less conflict and violence than in the US. Conflicts between settlers and Indians over land were rare, but economic problems plagued many Indians. In 1885, miserable from starvation, the Métis and Cree in Saskatchewan fought Canadian troops. Their revolt, led by Louis Riel, was rapidly crushed and Riel was executed.

Government Attempts to Destroy Native Cultures

Militarily defeated and confined to reservations, Indians were subjected by the US government to programs of cultural assimilation that were designed to end their way of life. Large numbers of Indian youth were removed from their families and communities and placed in federal boarding schools that tried to educate them away from their cultures. The schools reinforced Euro-American history and Christian values, demanded the exclusive use of English, and provided instruction in manual trades and skills. In Canada, also, boarding schools were set up with the same agenda. But, against all odds, most Native children did not reject their origins.

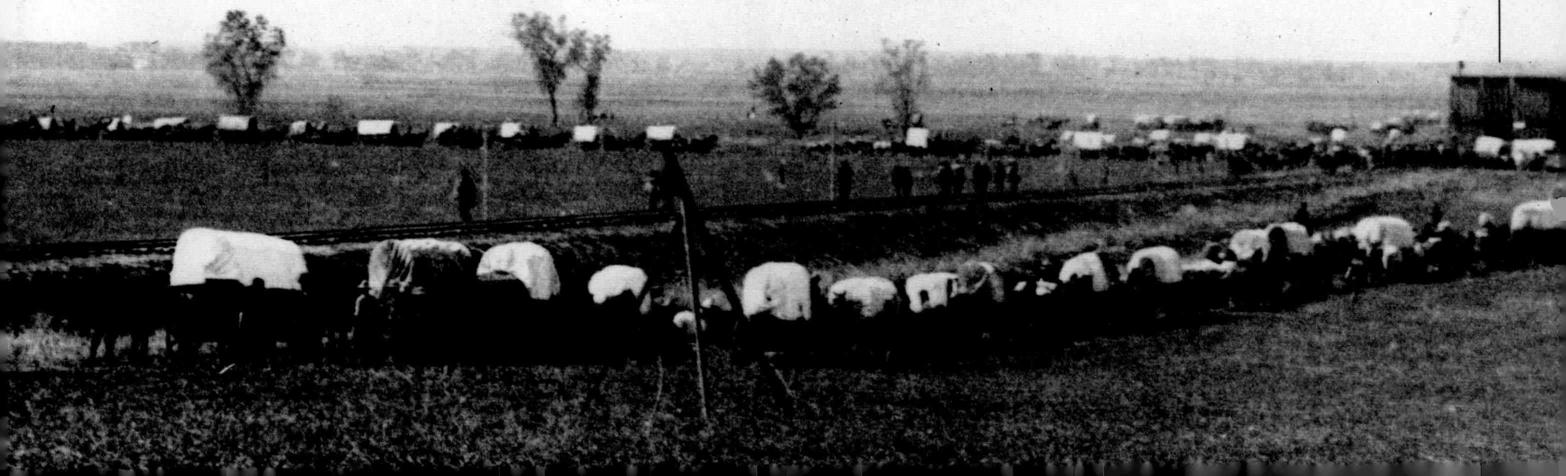

In 1887, the US Congress decided to take even more drastic steps to undermine Native cultures. Reformers in the East and the West felt that too much land had been set aside for Indian use. Eastern reformers convinced themselves that Indian salvation lay in the "civilizing" effects of private property, and argued that privately owned lands were less vulnerable to selfish interests than the commonly held Indian lands. Developers saw, in allotment, possibilities for freeing up more Indian lands. Under the provisions of the General Allotment (or Dawes) Act, which was passed by Congress in 1887 and endorsed by Indian reform organizations, reservation lands owned collectively by tribes were split up into small portions of 160 acres (65 hectares) or less and allotted to families and individual Indians, leaving the "surplus" land to be sold to the US. The act was a disaster for Indians. Much of their best land was leased or sold to whites, sometimes in decidedly shady deals. Before the Dawes Act, Indian tribes collectively owned 140 million acres (56 million hectares) of land. Between 1887 and 1934, when the allotment policy was abandoned, about 90 million acres (36 million hectares) of land had passed out of Indian ownership. Like their lands, the Native population also appeared to be vanishing as their numbers dropped to a low level at the end of the nineteenth century.

From the 1890s into the early twentieth century, reservation conditions were disastrous: on many reservations, Indian leaders were uninterested in leadership, were in jail, or had died; reservation economies depended on land rentals, seasonal labor, and government handouts. Bureau of Indian Affairs agents intruded on the daily routines and personal habits of people in their care, running every aspect of their lives. Indian dress and the wearing of long hair by males was forbidden and religious practices were banned, with offenders sentenced to imprisonment and hard labor. In Canada, too, religious practices

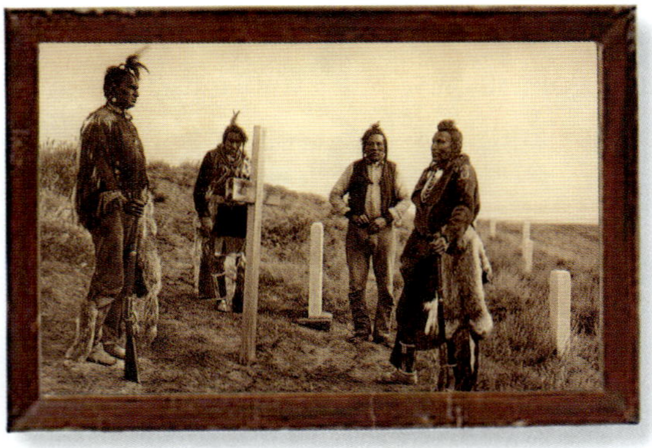

WHERE CUSTER FELL
A group of Indians look at the spot where Lieutenant Colonel Custer is believed to have fallen. Custer was buried on the battlefield but his remains were later reburied at West Point.

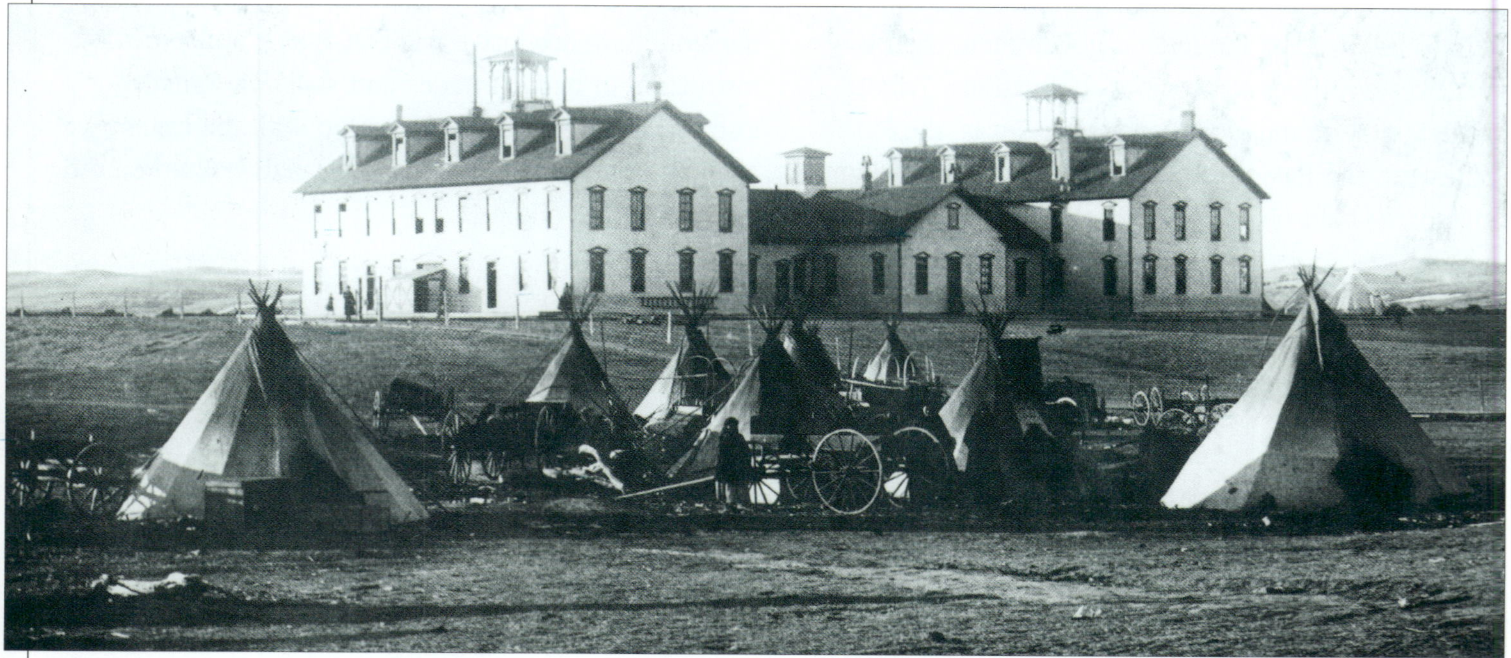

BOARDING SCHOOL AT PINE RIDGE
Federal policymakers came to regard the proximity of boarding schools to Indian communities – such as the Pine Ridge reservation school, pictured here in 1891 – as counterproductive to their aim of assimilating Indian children into white society and began to create off-reservation schools, far away from the children's homes.

were banned. Bureau of Indian Affairs agents established reservation police forces and appointed "chiefs" through whom they governed tribes.

The Indian New Deal

By the 1920s, there was a growing concern that Indian affairs were being mishandled. Tens of millions of acres had passed out of Indian ownership and Indians were impoverished and unhealthy, but their religions and cultures still persisted. In 1934, Congress enacted the Indian Reorganization Act that ended allotment, restored some land to Indian tribes, created a loan fund for economic development, and restored some measure of self-government. World War II interrupted the implementation of these "Indian New Deal" programs and, by the end of the war, federal policy again shifted back to assimilation despite evidence that it had not worked before.

In the 1950s, the US pursued a policy called "termination," which ended the special relationship between selected tribes and the federal government. At the same time, the Bureau of Indian Affairs (*see p.187*) launched a massive program to relocate reservation Indians to urban centers in preparation for dissolving the tribal land base. Relocation became another way for the government to absolve themselves of responsibility for Indians. By the end of the 1950s, Indian resistance and some Congressional opposition caused the government to abandon its termination policy, which had resulted, for Native peoples, in further impoverishment and land loss.

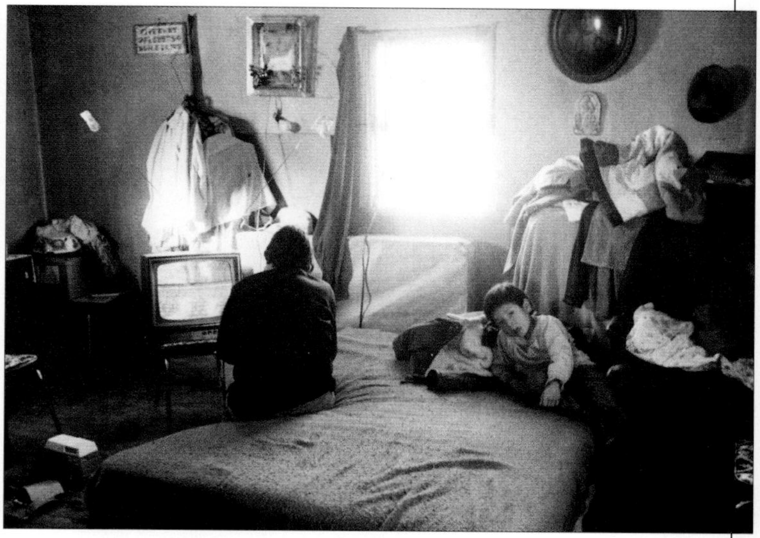

LATE-TWENTIETH-CENTURY RESERVATION LIFE
The Cornelius family, pictured in 1976, lived in the Pine Ridge reservation home of Oliver Red Cloud, one of the descendants of the Lakota leader Red Cloud. Dire economic conditions and inadequate housing characterize reservation life.

Moves toward Self-determination

The termination policy made Indian leaders aware that their property and civil rights were in danger. Growing alarm culminated in the "Red Power" demonstrations of the early 1960s, including fish-ins in the Northwest, the occupation of Alcatraz, the Trail of Broken Treaties, the Wounded Knee takeover, and the Longest Walk.

A renaissance in federal policy, with a shift towards self-determination, saw a corresponding decline in the Red Power movement. In the 1970s, laws were passed denouncing termination. The move toward Native self-determination gained momentum in the 1980s and 90s as Indian attorneys fought for land, for the repatriation of Indian remains, and for the right to regulate and develop reservation resources. Determined to maintain their cultural identities, tribal peoples now run their own schools and colleges, operate hotels and other businesses, write fiction and poetry, and produce and direct films. Most Indian tribes and First Nations are still fighting to determine their own future.

A NOTE ON NATIVE NAMES

This book uses "Native Americans" in its title, but this is not the only correct term to use. "American Indians" and "First Nations" also serve as shorthand for the hundreds of different peoples who have populated North America since long before Europeans arrived. Native peoples prefer to be called by their tribal names – Innu, Navajo, Seminole, and so on.

Spellings of the names of Native nations vary considerably. For example, the Blackfeet in the US prefer this spelling to "Blackfoot," which is more popular in Canada. The Kwagiutls in Canada prefer that spelling to "Kwakiutl," which is more commonly used by writers in the US.

Names for Native peoples also vary. In Canada, the people popularly called "Eskimo" prefer to call themselves "Inuit," that name meaning "people" in the Inuit language. Many in the US prefer "Yupik" or "Yupik Eskimo" – the designation of the Eskimos of southwestern Alaska, who do not have the word "Inuit" in their language. The popular name "Sioux" is often used in treaties and by writers although many of the people to whom the name refers prefer the original "Dakota" (eastern groups) or "Lakota" (western groups).

In this book, however, when space limitations dictate that one name or spelling be chosen over another, we use "Inuit" rather than "Eskimo;" "Blackfeet" rather than "Blackfoot;" and "Kwakiutl" over "Kwagiutl." When possible, the book uses "Dakota" and "Lakota" to differentiate groups.

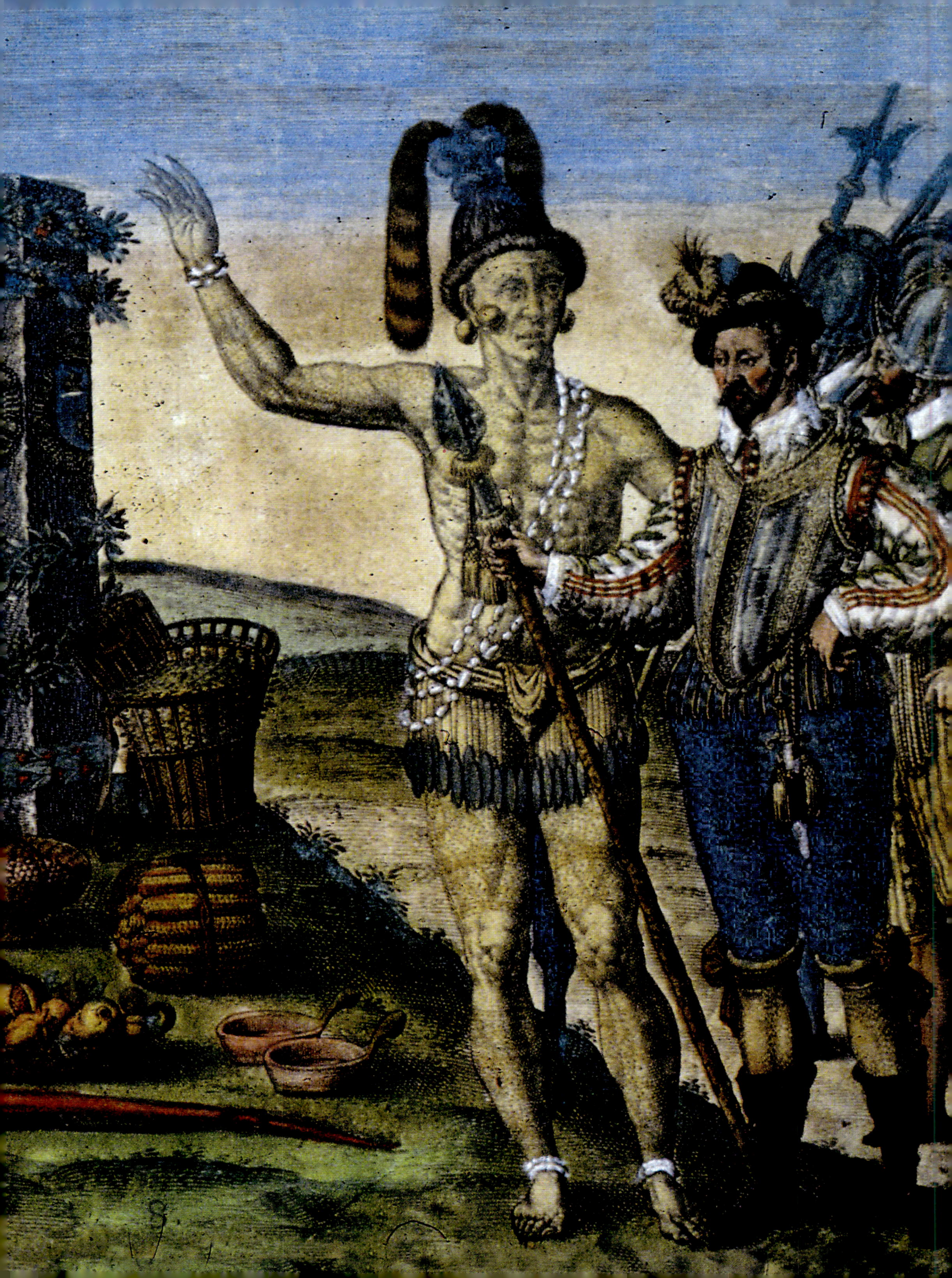

Ancestral Times to 1850s

A CONFLICT OF CULTURES

Encounters between North American Native peoples and Europeans began peaceably, but soon deteriorated as the newcomers sought to conquer the disease-weakened Native populations.

A Friendly Encounter
In this illustration, dated June 1564, Timucua chief Athore and French explorers are pictured in a friendly encounter. Many Timucuas died subsequently from European diseases and military attacks.

Ancestral Native Life

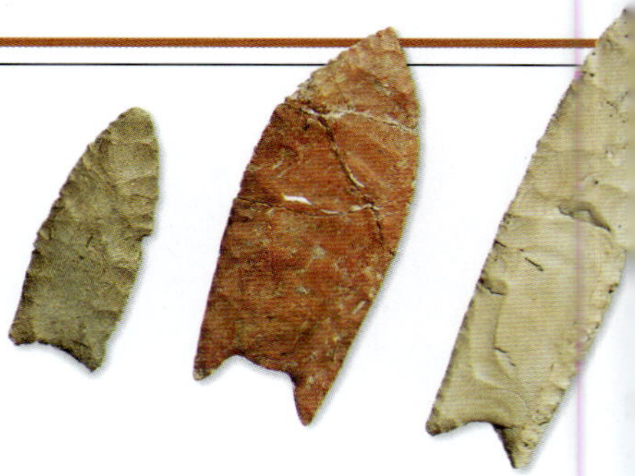

Ice-age Weapon Points
Proof of Ice-age humans in America came in 1926 with the discovery at Folsom, New Mexico, of stone weapon points (center), dating from 10,000 years ago. In 1932, weapon points from an even older period, up to 12,000 years ago (left and right), were unearthed at Clovis, New Mexico.

For at least 30,000 years, long before the first arrivals of Europeans in 1500, ancient Native peoples had populated the North American landscape with a diversity of thriving societies. These first Americans regarded nature as the source of all existence and excelled at exploiting natural resources and adapting to the climates and terrains in which they lived. Many Natives today dispute scientific theories that their ancestors originally migrated across the Bering Sea land bridge from Siberia to Alaska.

Past Times

98,000–28,000 BC
Ancestors of today's Native peoples spread across America

c. **8300 BC**
Hunters trap buffalo (a food source) by driving them over cliffs to their death

c. **5800 BC**
People along Northwest coast eat salmon

c. **2500 BC**
Southeast people make pottery, an advance in food preparation and storage

c. **1000 BC**
Southwest people eat maize

500 BC
Mound-building begins in central Ohio valley and spreads across Northeast and Southeast

Post-AD 800
Northeast people cultivate corn

c. **AD 900**
Anasazis build apartment-like buildings with as many as 800 rooms

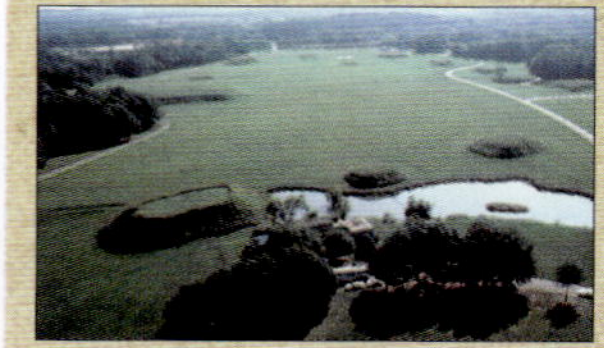

Moundville, Alabama (AD 900–1500)

Some scientists believe that the human history of North America began when small bands of Paleo-Indian hunters made their way across the Bering Sea land bridge from Siberia to Alaska. Eventually these people and their descendants spread throughout North and South America, and they, the scientists say, are the ancestors of all subsequent generations of Native peoples. The best known of the early arrivals are estimated to have occurred between 30,000 and 50,000 years ago, but some archaeologists extend this period back to 100,000 years.

Many Native peoples, however, argue that their ancestors originated in the Americas, and they question the scientists' theories, citing the lack of archaeological evidence, the difficulty of the journey, and the fact that the theory does not fit with tribes' oral accounts of their origins, which have been passed on through the generations. These creation stories describe spirits ascending from the underground or the sea into the world today, and tell of spiritual beings descending from the sky. In such accounts, the spirits often create people after arriving in the present-day world.

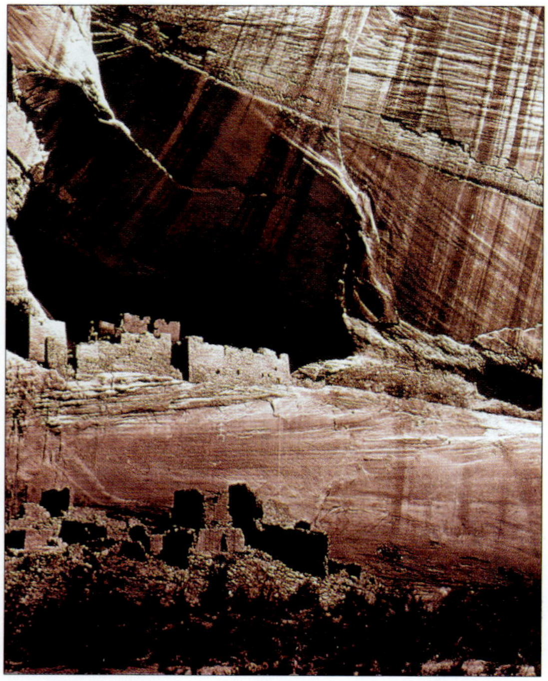

◁ Anasazi Cliff Dwelling
Named the White House Ruin for the white gypsum clay used to coat its upper section, this cliff dwelling, dating from 1000 BC, is one of almost 400 Anasazi settlements in the Canyon de Chelly area of Arizona. The Anasazis worked and slept in multilevel dwellings built beneath the eaves of overhanging rock.

Developing Native Cultures

By AD 1000, Native peoples had established complex societies across North America. Dense populations on the Northwest coast exploited the abundance of sea mammals and fish in the Pacific Ocean and in the tributaries of the

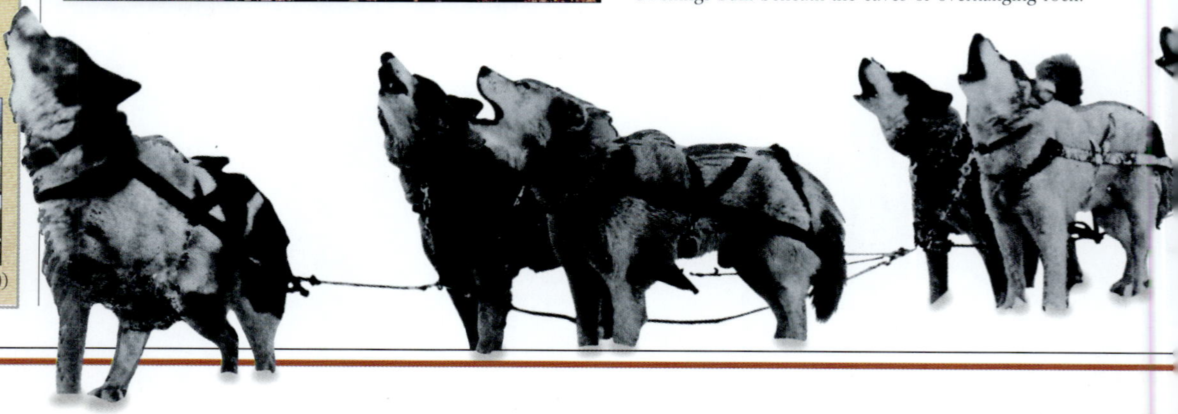

Columbia River. A warm climate promoted the growth of vast forests of giant evergreen trees, which the Natives used to build houses and to construct giant totem poles.

In the deserts of the Southwest, the Natives built apartment-like dwellings and practiced agriculture so successfully that, even in such arid surroundings, they could support sizable populations. In the Arctic, inhabitants adapted remarkably well to the harsh environment, becoming highly skilled hunters and fishermen and relying on sea and land mammals to provide dependable food sources. The forests of the Northeast were a natural resource for Native peoples – wood for houses, boats, tools, and fuel, as well as bark for clothing, roofing, and bedding. These forests also housed game – a source of meat for food, hides for clothing, and bones for tools.

The famous Plains Indian culture evolved in the treeless grassland region only after the arrival of whites. Different kinds of animals, such as buffalo, antelope, deer, elk, and rabbits, lived on the grasslands and provided meat for food as well as hides, bones, and horns for shelter, clothing, and tools.

Natural Spirituality

Religion was the center of existence for these ancient peoples, who constructed their ceremonies and rituals around solstices and equinoxes. They worshiped at natural sacred sites, where they communed with their ancestors and with plants, animals, and spirits. Their daily lives were built around praying to spiritual powers and giving thanks for crop harvests and success in hunting.

HUSKY POWER ▽
For more than 4,000 years, Inuit (Eskimo) people trained dogs to pull their loaded sleds. Known as "huskies," the dogs have a double coat of fur that enables them to live outdoors all year round in the harsh Arctic environment.

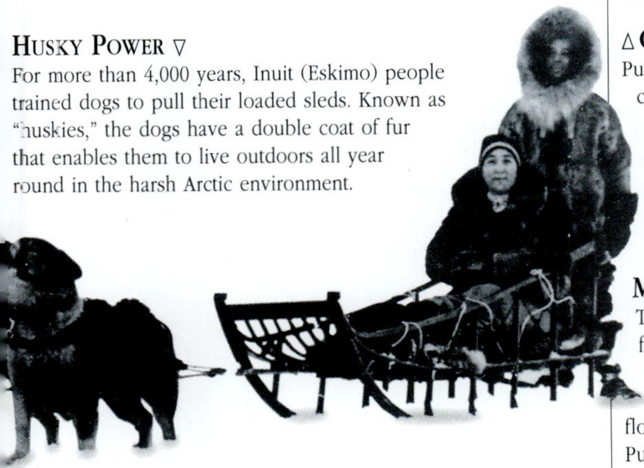

THE PUEBLO PEOPLES

Around AD 800, the Pueblo Indians began to form their distinctive cultures, living in multilevel, apartment-style adobe villages. As well as being gifted potters, they mastered irrigation, allowing them to farm in the arid environment. They also planted crops at the mouths of large washes to capture the runoff from heavy rainfall.

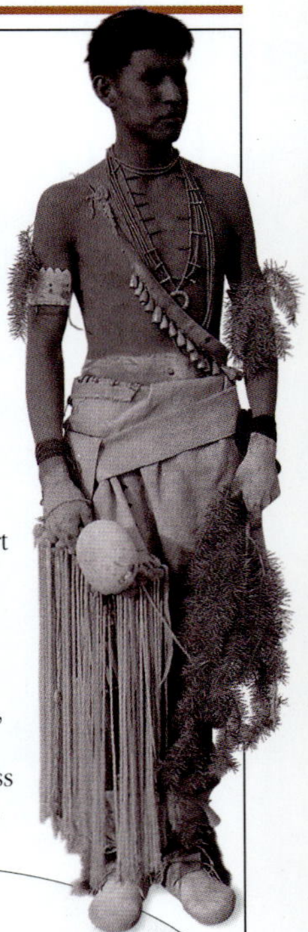

CORN DANCER ▷
In the Corn Dance – part of an annual cycle of communal Pueblo ceremonies reflecting seasonal subsistence activities – corn dancers, like this Cochiti Pueblo man, pray for the success of corn and other crops.

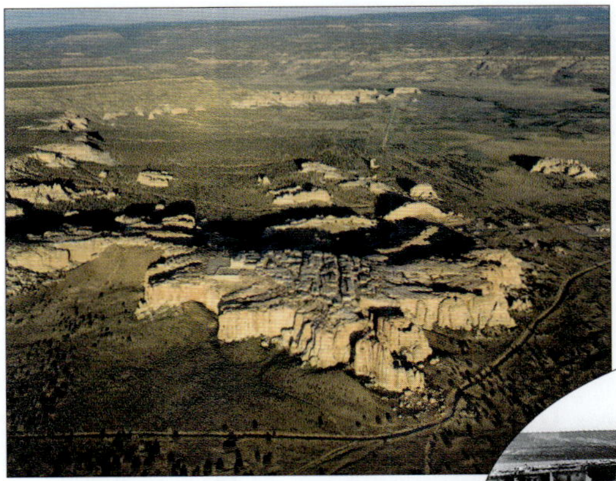

△ SKY CITY
Acoma Pueblo, a multistory complex of stone and adobe, is located on a mesa, or plateau, 365 ft (112 m) above the surrounding valley in present-day New Mexico. Often called Sky City, because of its location atop the high mesa, Acoma is believed to be one of the oldest inhabited sites in the US.

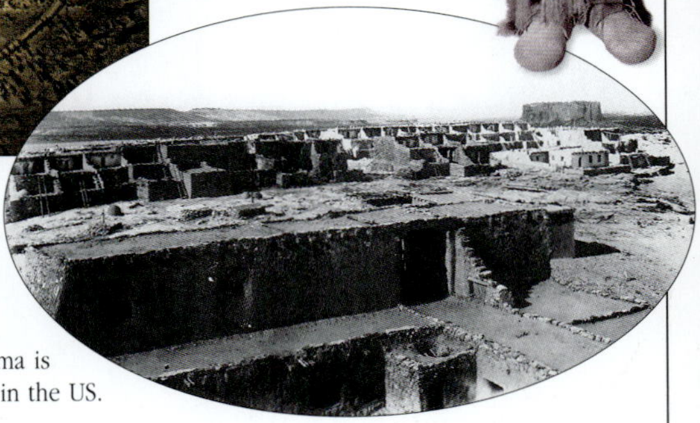

△ ADOBE VILLAGE
In the western Pueblo villages of Acoma, pictured here, wet adobe was used more often as plaster over stone walls than as masonry. In the eastern Pueblos, or Rio Grande communities, adobe bricks set with mud mortar formed the house walls.

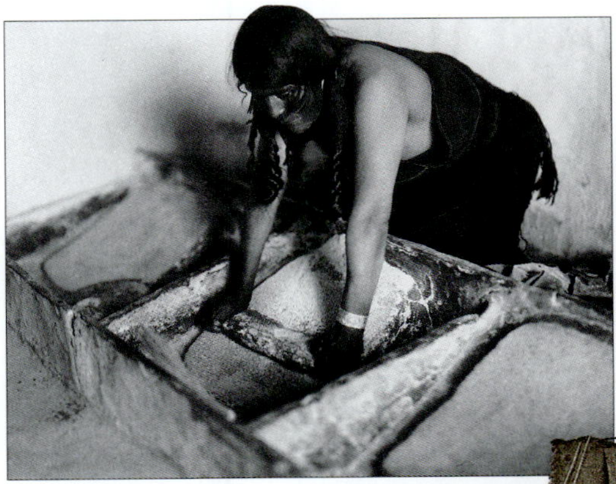

△ GRINDING CORN
Pueblo women spent hours grinding corn at bins holding stones of varying degrees of roughness. After grinding the kernels on the coarse stones, they worked the corn through finer stones until they had obtained a smooth flour.

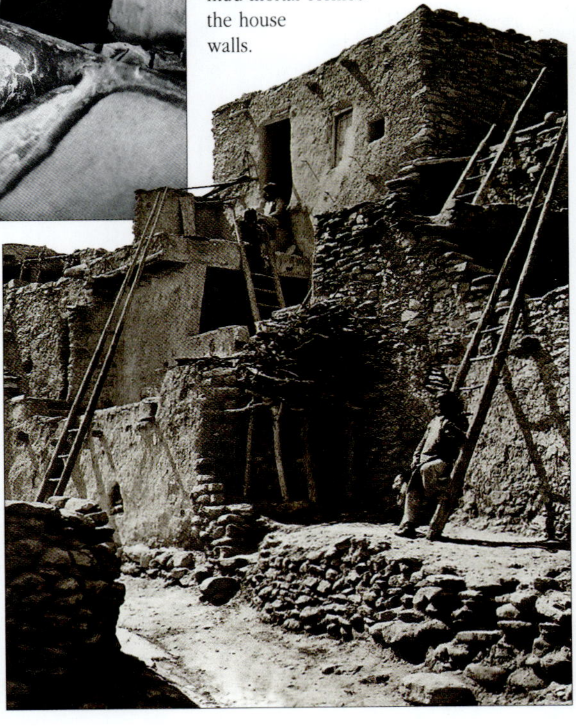

MULTILEVEL LIVING ▷
The homes of Walpi, pictured here, form a village on the first mesa of the Hopi reservation in Arizona, 600 ft (183 m) above the desert floor. Entrance to a traditional Pueblo is via a ladder to the lower rooftop. Shorter ladders lead from there to the upper rooms.

League of the Iroquois

Some time before the mid-fifteenth century, five nations in present-day New York State and Ontario – Mohawk, Oneida, Onondaga, Cayuga, and Seneca (later jointed by the Tuscarora) – united to form the Iroquois Confederacy. Known as Haudenosaunee (People of the Longhouse), the nations form an east-to-west geographic line, just as families were arranged in a longhouse.

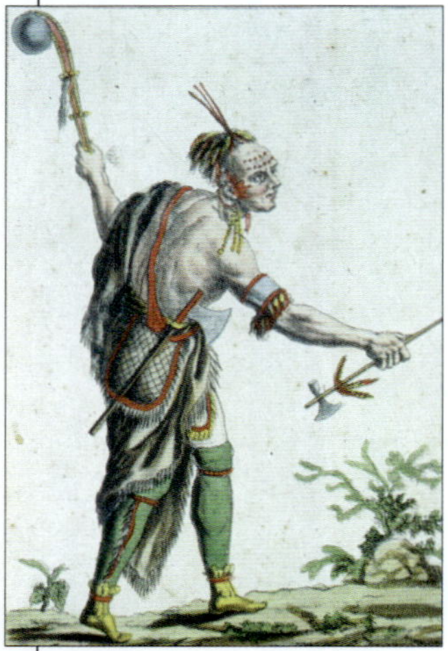

△ **Military Ideal**
Iroquois men gained respect in their society through military exploits. Holding a war club, the Iroquois warrior pictured here represents this ideal.

Woven History ▷
Wampum – tiny white or purple cylindrical beads fashioned from seashells into strings or belts – served as currency and, more importantly, were used to record tribal history and sacred pacts. They played a vital role in diplomacy between the Iroquois and the Europeans.

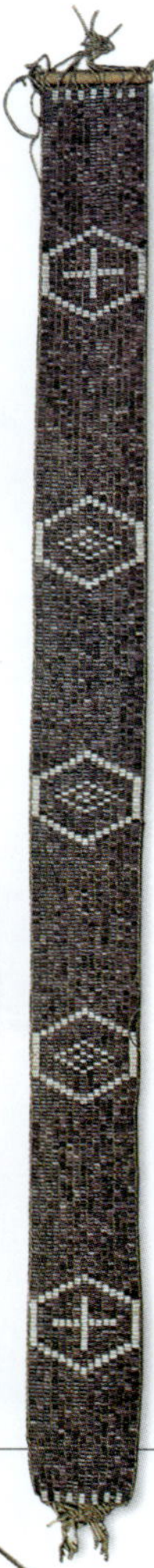

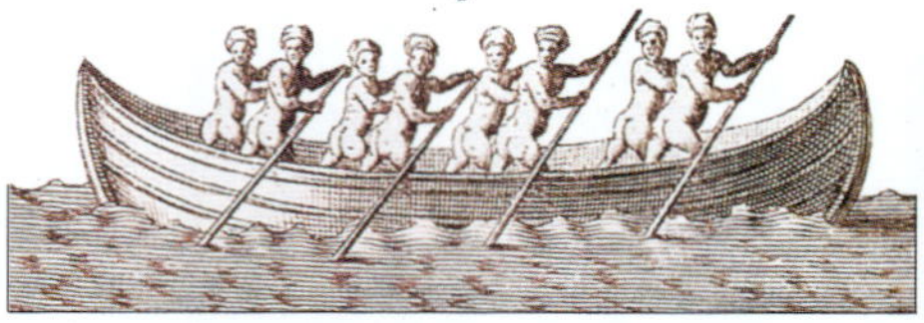

△ **Iroquois Boatmen**
The Iroquois were master boatmen who traveled by canoe to hunt and to make war. Their canoes were made from large logs, which they hollowed out and covered with birch, elm, or spruce bark.

Working the Land ▷
The Iroquois were great farmers, working the soil with stone, bone, antler, and wooden tools. They called their three main crops (corn, beans, and squash) "the Three Sisters." Important religious festivals honored corn as well as other wild plant foods.

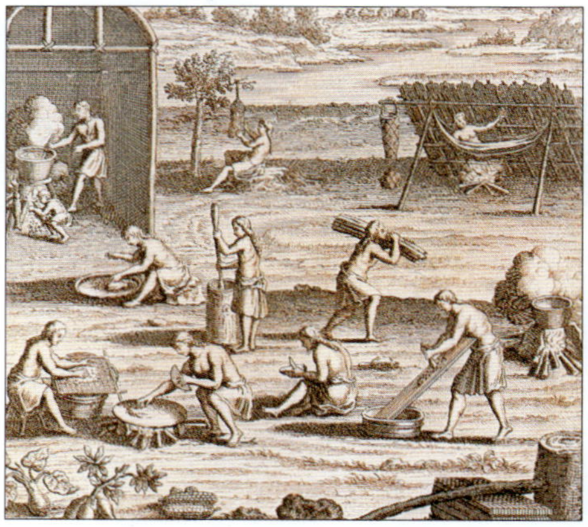

The Haida

The Northwest coast provided an abundant food supply for the Haida, who lived on the Queen Charlotte Islands, off present-day British Columbia. There, they hunted sea mammals, such as seals and fished for cod. In an area well supplied with timber, they built large houses of cedar planks; the door openings faced the sea and one or more totem poles were erected in front of each house.

Family History ▷
Giant totem poles face the sea in the Haida village of Skidegate on the Queen Charlotte Islands. The poles, usually of red cedar, are carved with crest designs that refer to the ancestry of the family whose home they front.

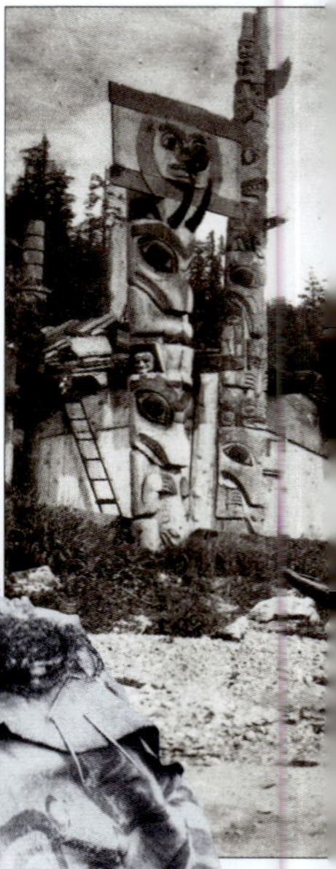

▽ **Tending the Sick**
Intermediaries between humans and the spirit world, Haida shamans performed extraordinary feats, such as controlling the weather and curing illness. Their ritual objects included rattles, masks, and neck rings.

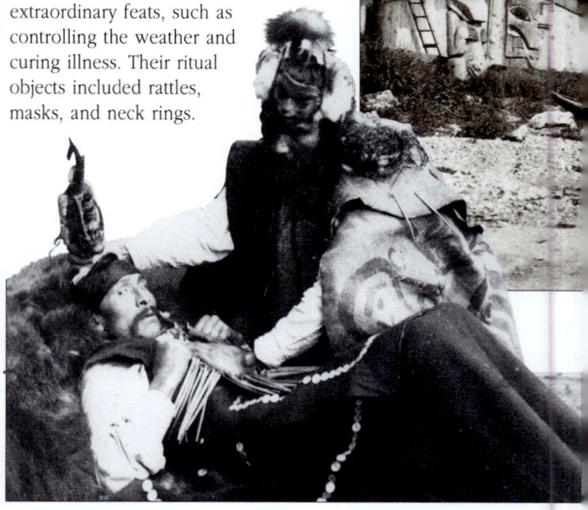

The Blackfeet

One of the most powerful and numerous Indian tribes, the Blackfeet controlled a huge area from the North Saskatchewan River in what is now Alberta, Canada, to the upper Missouri River in present-day Montana. They adapted to a mobile life on the open grasslands, hunting buffalo, their main food source, on foot with stone and bone arrows and lances.

Mobile Homes ▷
Since the Blackfeet lived by hunting, their housing evolved to meet the requirements of a mobile lifestyle. Their portable, cone-shaped tipis were designed to be taken down quickly and transported to new locations as they followed the wandering buffalo herds.

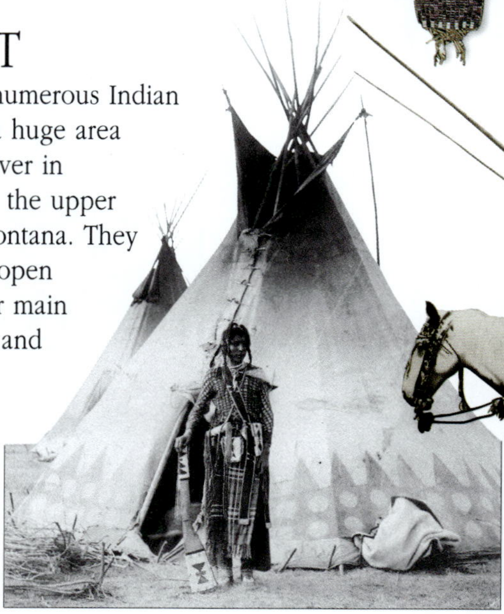

▽ **Transporting Tipis**
Tipi lodge covers were folded and packed on travois – two poles tied together in a "V" shape, and harnessed to sturdy, wolf-like dogs (or sometimes pulled by women.) After acquiring horses, the Blackfeet used larger travois, on which many more supplies could be carried.

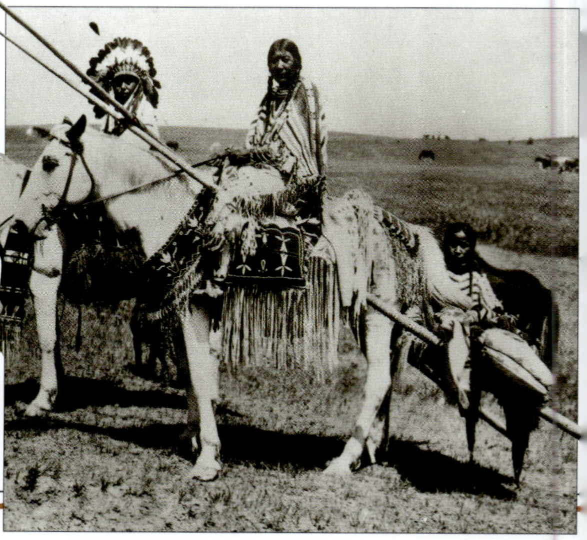

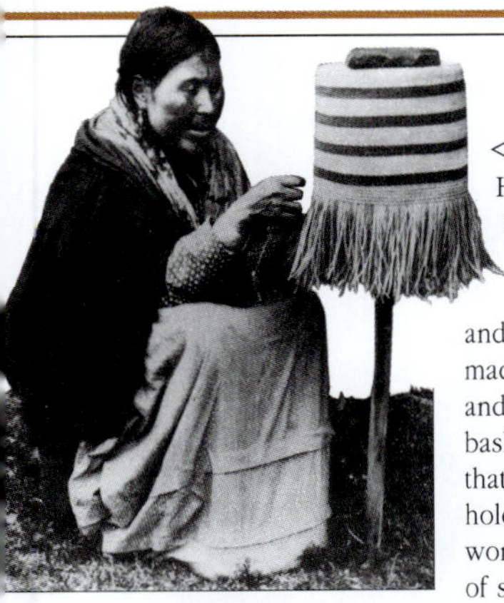

◁ **BASKET MAKING**
Haida girls were taught from an early age to make baskets. Using the roots and inner bark of cedar and spruce trees, the women made mats, screens, cloaks, and rain hats. Some of the baskets were woven so tightly that they were capable of holding water. Here a Haida woman weaves a basket out of strands of cedar root.

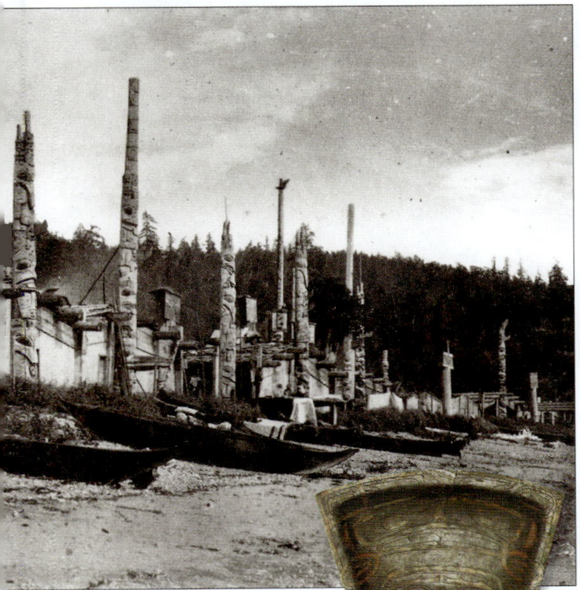

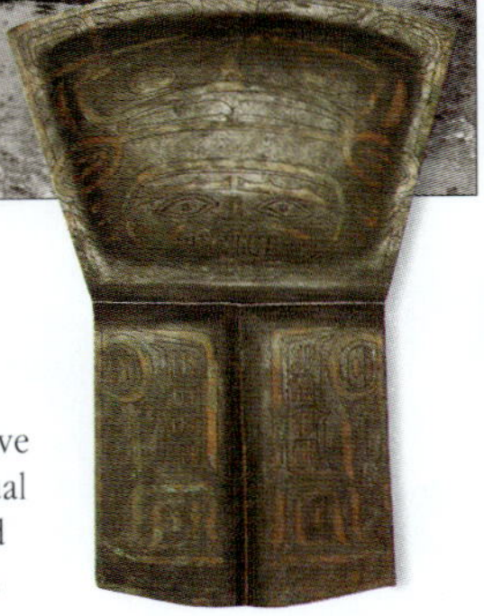

THE PRECIOUS COPPER ▷
The most precious gifts distributed during potlatches (*see p.22*) were "coppers." Originally made from native ore, and later from copper, these ritual objects, owned by chiefs, symbolized the wealth of sea and heavenly light.

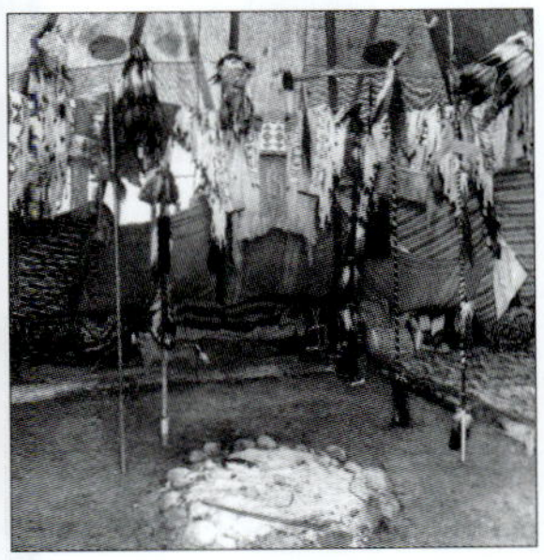

◁ **SETTING UP HOME**
After pitching their large, tall, beautifully proportioned tipis, Blackfeet women hung sacred bundles, then arranged the bed areas, household equipment and utensils, and personal objects.

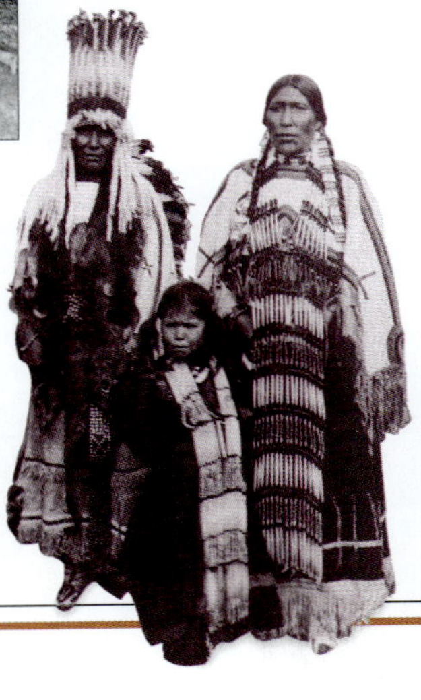

CEREMONIAL DRESS ▷
Wearing the tribe's unique feathered headdress, a Canadian Blackfeet chief poses here with his family in their ceremonial beaded clothing. Dyed quillwork was originally used to decorate buffalo-skin or deerskin shirts, vests, leggings, boots, and moccasins. Even their horse gear was adorned.

THE INUITS

The Inuits, formerly known in Canada as Eskimos (*see p.15*), have lived in Alaska, the Northwest Territories, the provinces of Newfoundland and Quebec, Siberia, and Greenland. In this mostly icebound region, some Inuits hunted walruses, seals, and whales for food, clothing, weapons, tools, and oil for lighting and cooking. Inland, others hunted caribou for meat and materials.

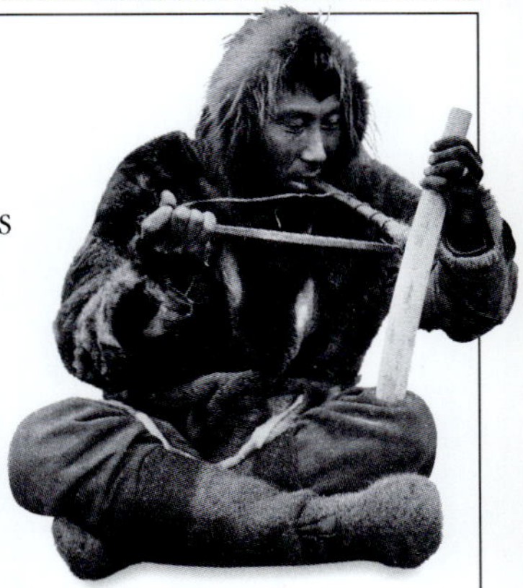

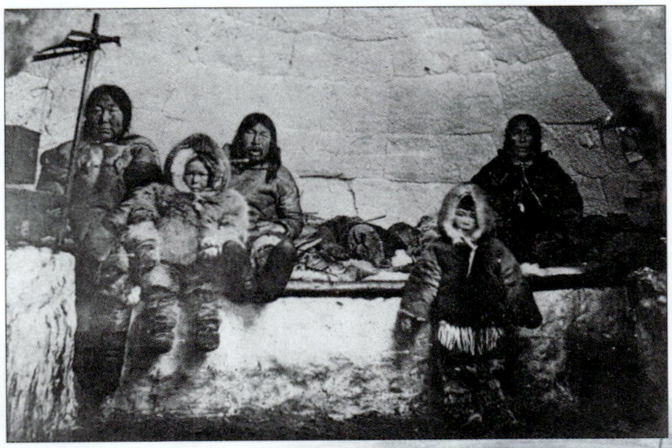

△ **WORKING IN IVORY**
For over 2,000 years, Inuit men have carved ivory walrus tusks into hunting equipment and everyday domestic implements. The carvers made their objects as beautiful as they were functional.

◁ **WINTER SNOWHOUSE**
An Inuit family is pictured here, sitting on a fur-covered ice-bed in their igloo. Snowhouses, used by Central Inuits in winter, were especially warm when oil was burned in stone lamps.

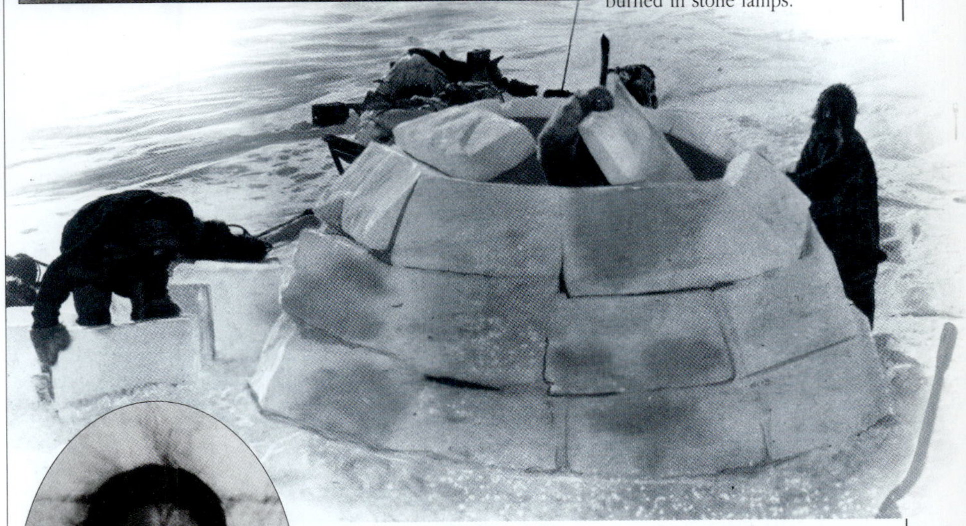

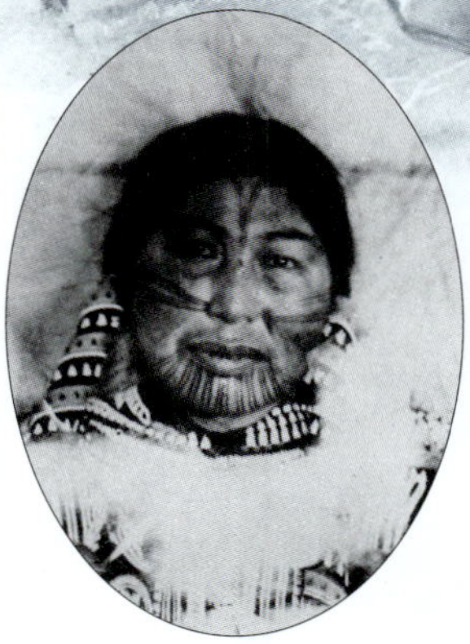

◁ **FACIAL ADORNMENT**
Some Inuit women wore facial tattoos, which were not only thought to enhance female beauty, but signified a woman's readiness to marry and bear children. A common design was lines drawn under the lower lip.

△ **SNOW-BUILDING SKILLS**
To build an igloo, Inuit men had to know snow, how to cut out large blocks with a snow knife, and how to build the blocks into a dome-shaped dwelling. Family members helped, patching gaps in the outer walls with snow.

▽ **WHALERS PUT TO SEA**
Crews prepared all year round for whale hunting They cleaned their harpoons and paddles to avoid offending the whales with shabby equipment; they prepared new skin covers for the boats; and they accumulated food for the crew. After a whale was beached, it was greeted with ceremony and the meat distributed to the community.

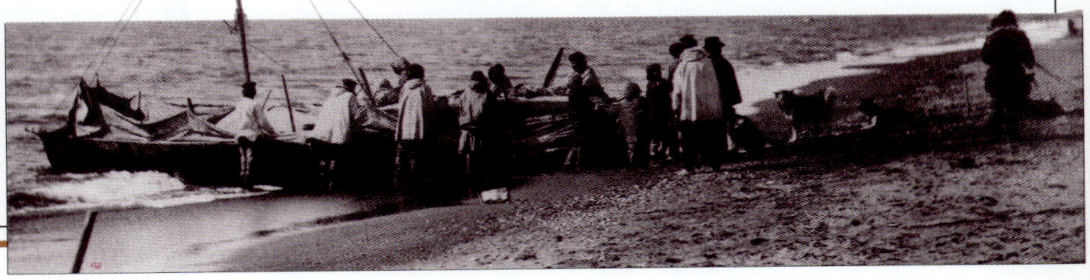

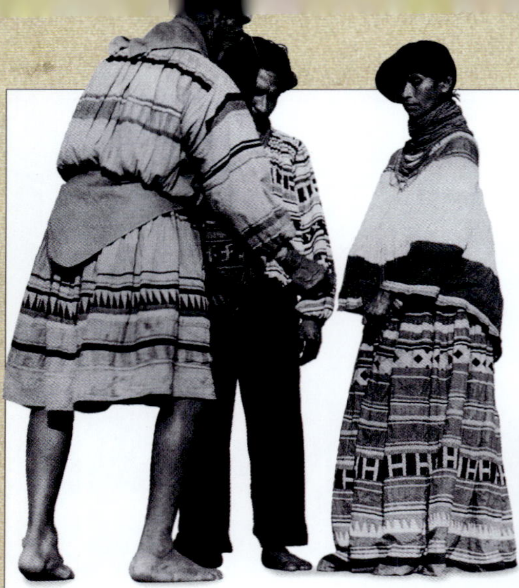

◁A Seminole Marriage

In Seminole tradition, older clan kin arranged marriages for young people. After the couple consented to the union, the groom-to-be gave gifts to his bride's relatives. This couple, wearing distinctive Seminole patchwork clothing, are about to be married.

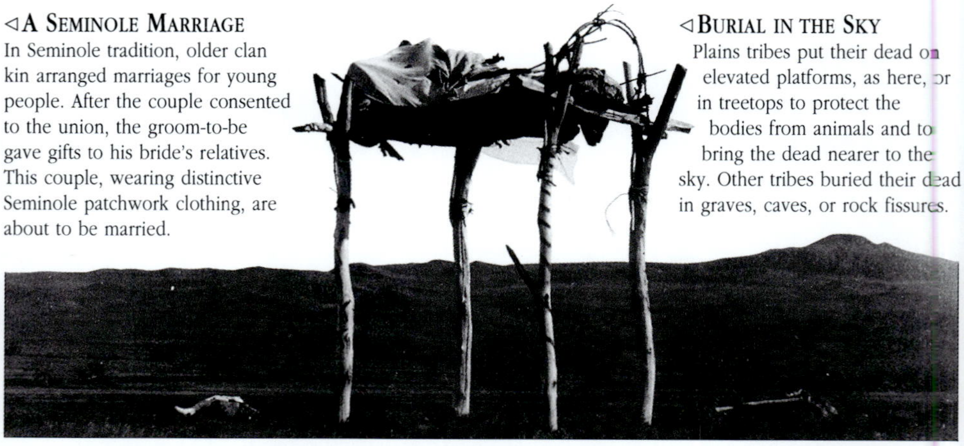

◁Burial in the Sky

Plains tribes put their dead on elevated platforms, as here, or in treetops to protect the bodies from animals and to bring the dead nearer to the sky. Other tribes buried their dead in graves, caves, or rock fissures.

Potlatch at Aleut Bay ▷

At potlatches, guests were seated and given gifts according to their wealth or rank. The more a host gave away, the higher the status he achieved. Hosts who gave everything away were repaid by guests who held another potlatch.

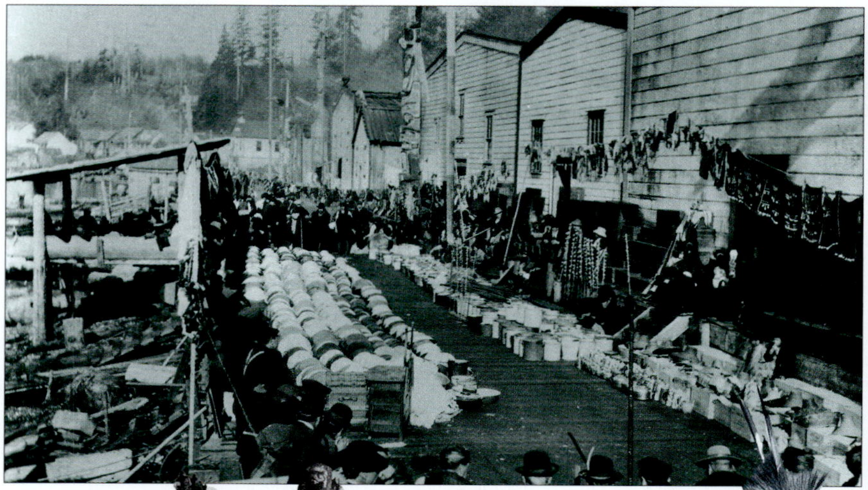

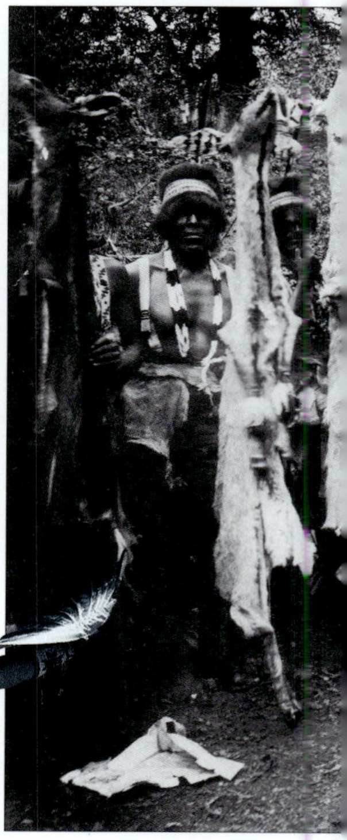

▽Ceremonial Dancers

This 1900 photograph shows potlatch dancers in Alaska wearing their ceremonial clothing and masks. The masks, which have animal or human faces, represent ancestors or guardian spirits.

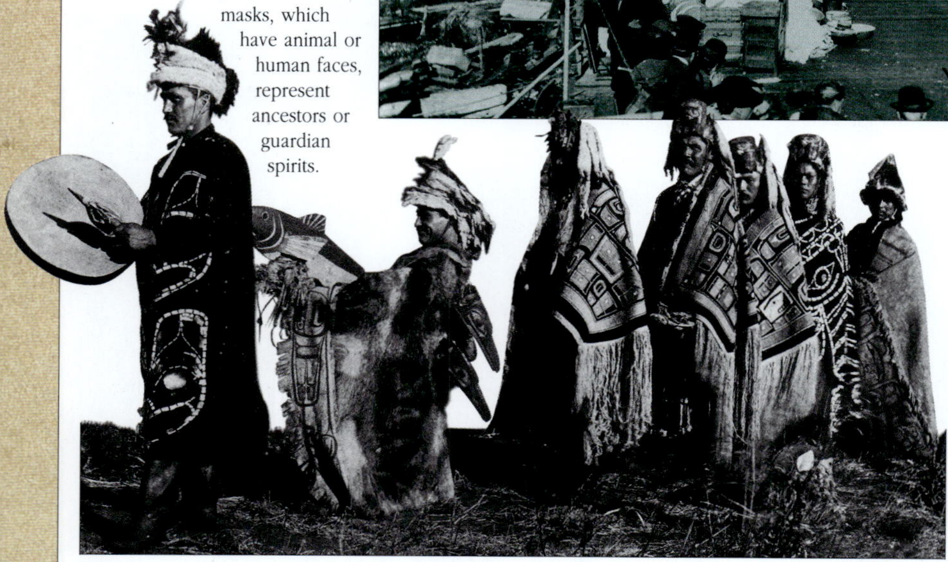

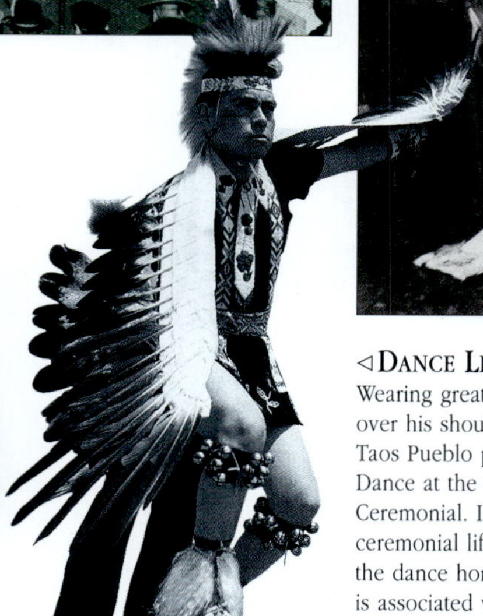

◁Dance Like an Eagle

Wearing great feathered wings over his shoulders, a man from Taos Pueblo performs the Eagle Dance at the Gallup, New Mexico, Ceremonial. Important to the ceremonial life of Pueblo peoples, the dance honors the eagle, which is associated with rain, thunder, lightning, and healing powers.

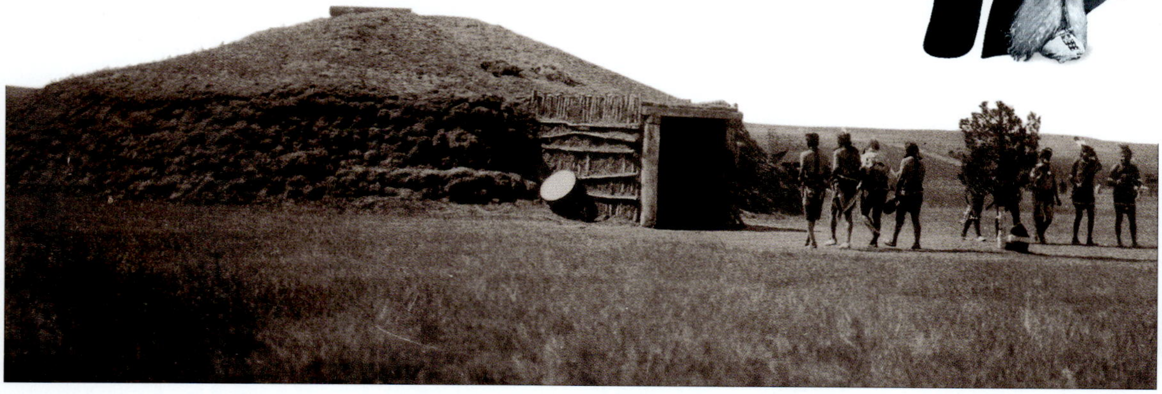

◁To the Sacred Lodge

In this 1908 Edward Curtis photograph, Arikara men walk toward their sacred earth lodge in North Dakota. The holy lodge – a ceremonial structure in which various rites of Mother Corn were performed – mirrored Arikara cosmology. It also played a central role in the traditional stories and rituals of the Mandan, Hidatsa, and Pawnee peoples.

The Spirit World

NATIVE NORTH AMERICA is home to hundreds of religious traditions that have endured despite the long history of forced removals, sacred-site destruction, jailing of Native religious practitioners, and pressure to assimilate by missionaries and governments. Many of these sacred beliefs, ceremonies, and rituals, and much knowledge continue to live on as the heart of Native cultural identity.

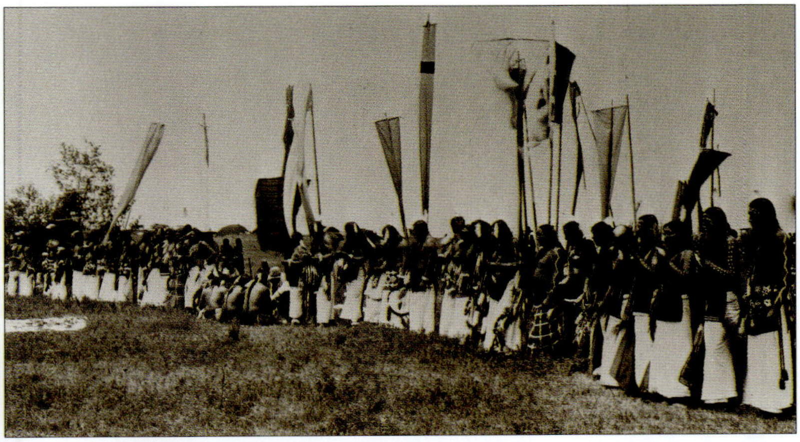

△ PONCA DANCE TO THE SUN
One of the most spectacular ceremonies of Native North America, the Sun Dance (here danced by Poncas) involved fasting and dancing before a sacred pole. The Sun Dance period still is a time for renewing friendships, visiting relatives, holding traditional games, and conducting council meetings.

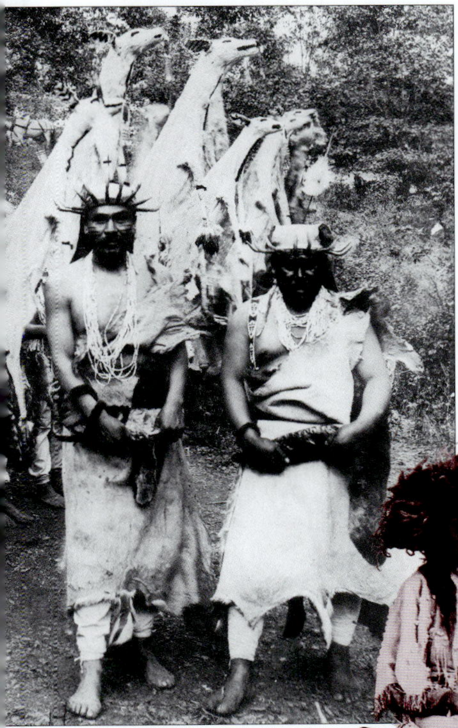

◁ HUPAS' THANKSGIVING
In an autumn ceremony in northern California, lasting 10–16 days, Hupa men, wearing hooked headbands and skins of albino deer, dance at ritually prescribed spots. They give thanks for food, pray for plentiful fish and game, and express gratitude to the Creator for sharing Earthly resources.

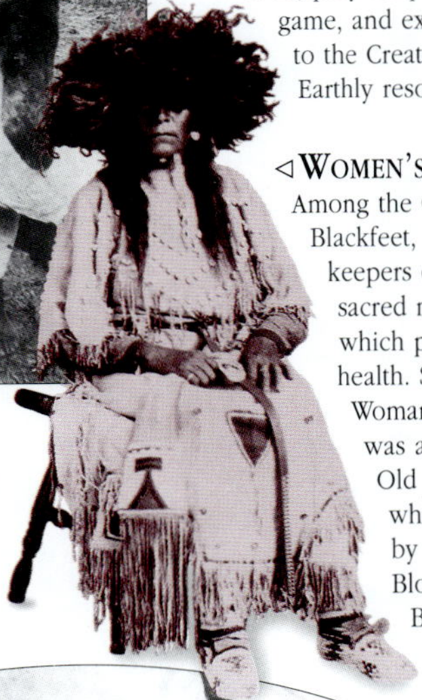

◁ WOMEN'S POWERS
Among the Canadian Blackfeet, women are the keepers of the most sacred medicine bundles, which protect people's health. Snake People Woman, pictured here, was a member of the Old Woman's Society, which was organized by women of the Blood division of the Blackfeet Nation.

▽ CROW TOBACCO SOCIETY
Many tribes communicate with the spirit world through tobacco. The Tobacco Society, a sacred group of men and women among the Crow of Montana, grow a medicinal tobacco that is ritually planted, cared for, and harvested by members of the Society.

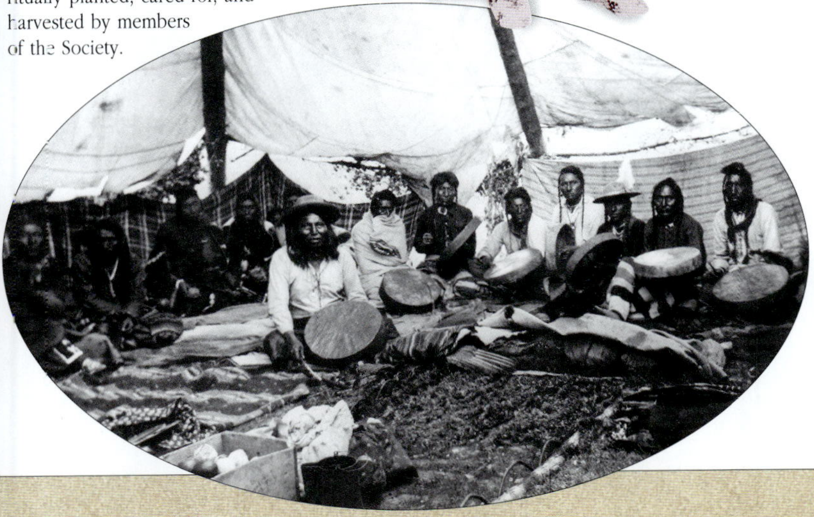

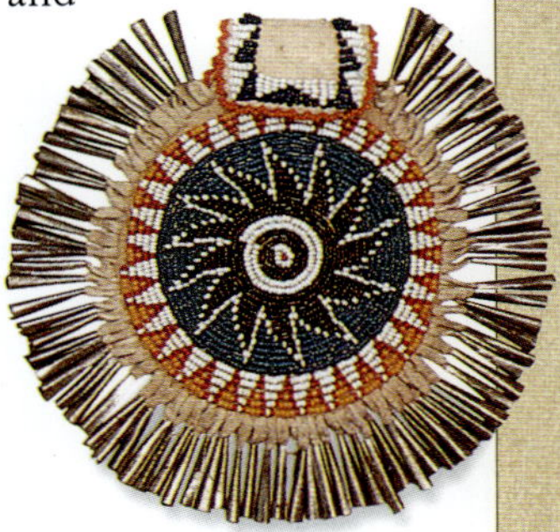

APACHE TOBACCO POUCH

Natives and Christianity

While ancient religions remain strong among some Native people, others practice Christianity exclusively; yet other Native people pray in church and also attend Indian healing ceremonies, finding that both traditions offer spiritual comfort. Some mix Catholicism and ancient rituals; others follow the practices of the Native American Church, which uses peyote as a sacrament.

Ceremonies and Sacred Sites

Each tribe performs ceremonies according to instructions given in sacred "genesis" stories. Some of the most important ceremonies must be conducted at certain sacred places, at specific times of the year. Some mark important events in a person's life; others are performed to heal the sick, renew relationships with spiritual beings, initiate people into religious societies, ensure success in hunting and growing crops, pray for rain, and give thanks for food harvests. Yet more ceremonies are performed in order to ensure the survival of the Earth and all forms of life.

Since time immemorial, Indian religious practitioners have gone to sacred places to pray, fast, make vision quests, receive guidance, and train young people in the spiritual life of the community. In these places, they communicate with ancestors, humans, plants, animals – and especially with the spirits that most often reveal themselves there. Many commercial activities damage the sacred nature of land, however, and, if sacred sites are restricted or destroyed, so too are the religious rituals connected to those places.

"It is a strict law that bids us dance. It is a strict law that bids us distribute our property among our friends and neighbors."

ANONYMOUS KWAKIUTL, *c.* 1886

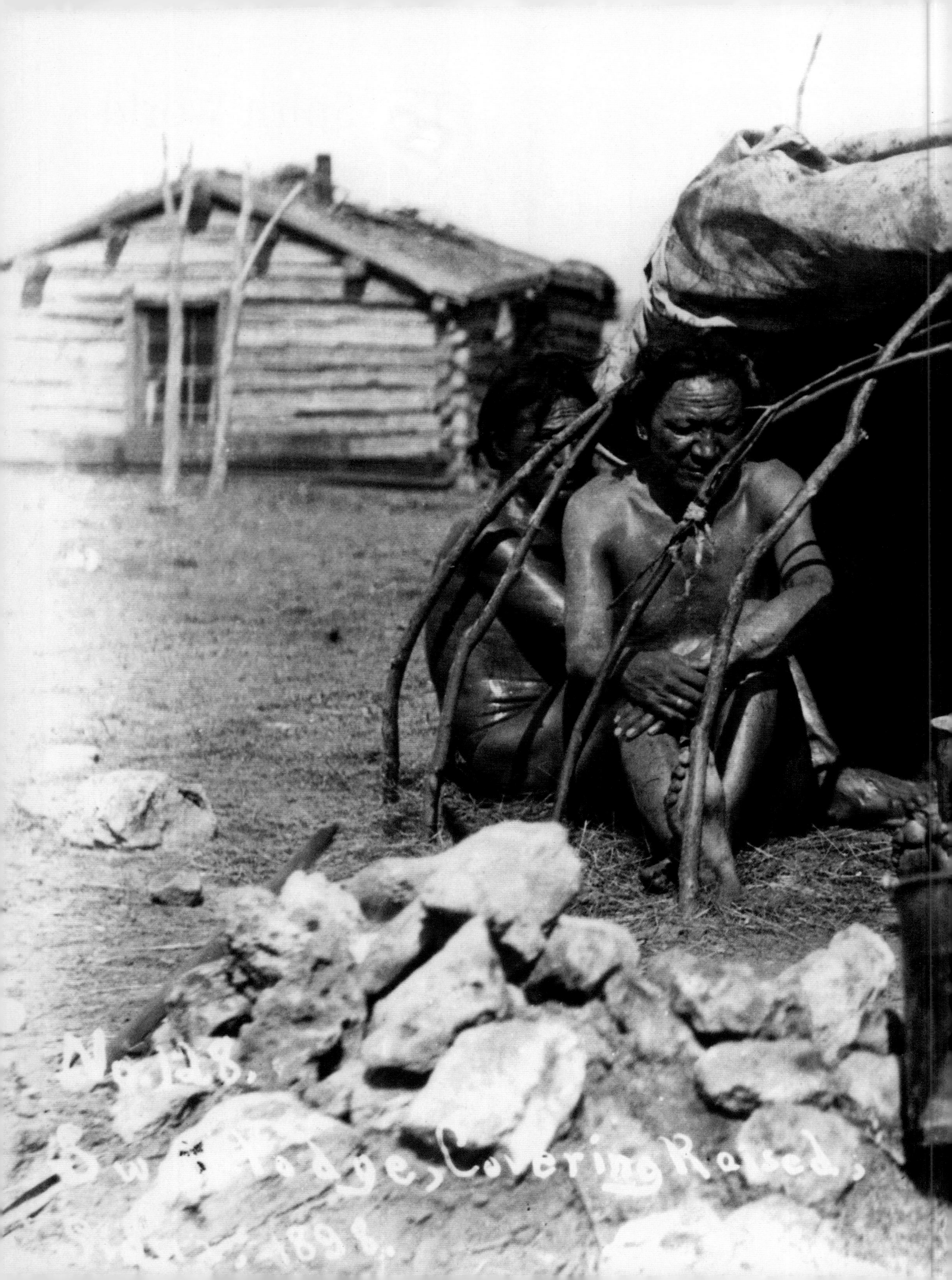
No. 18.
Covering Raised,
1898.

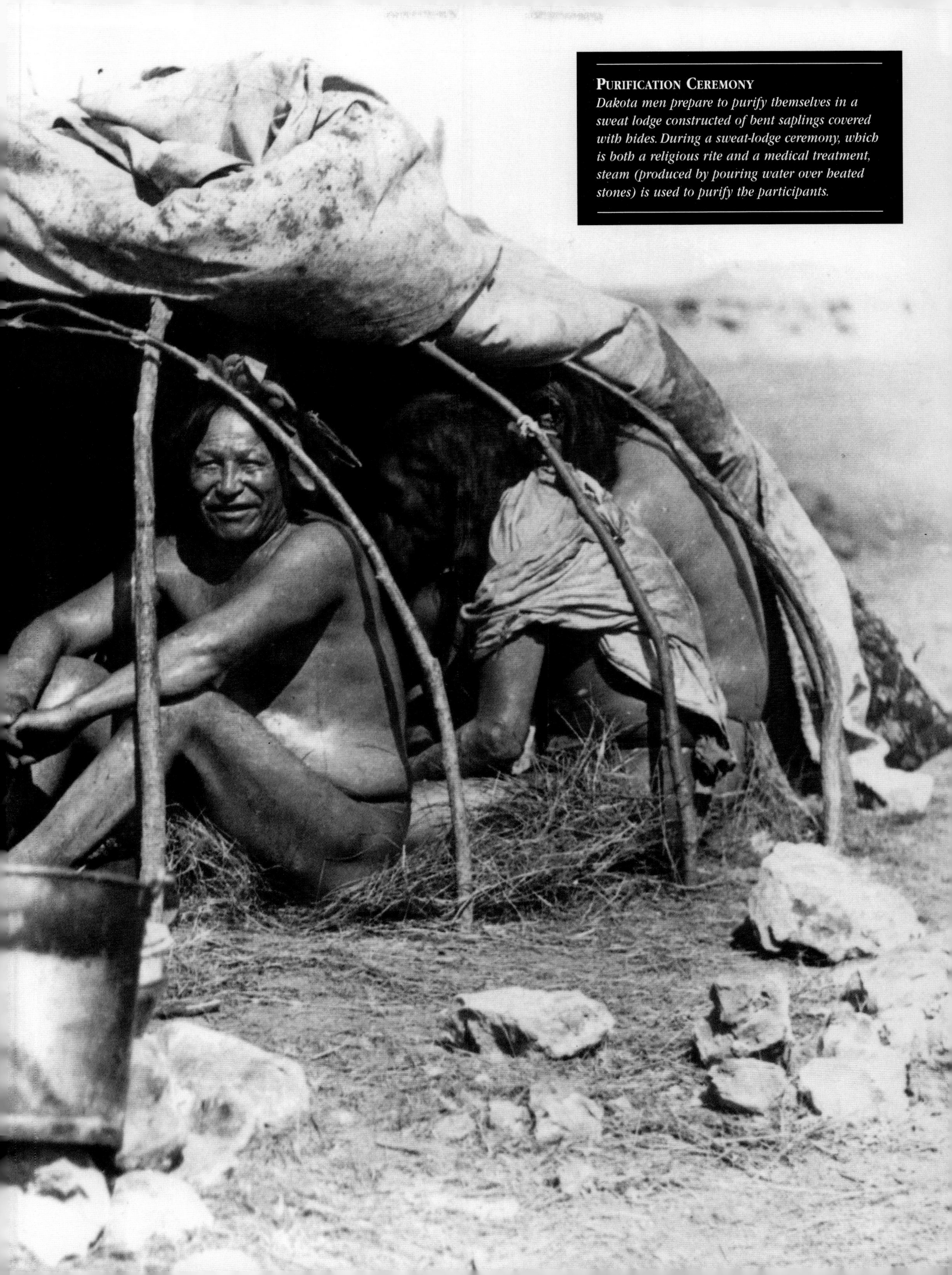

Purification Ceremony
Dakota men prepare to purify themselves in a sweat lodge constructed of bent saplings covered with hides. During a sweat-lodge ceremony, which is both a religious rite and a medical treatment, steam (produced by pouring water over heated stones) is used to purify the participants.

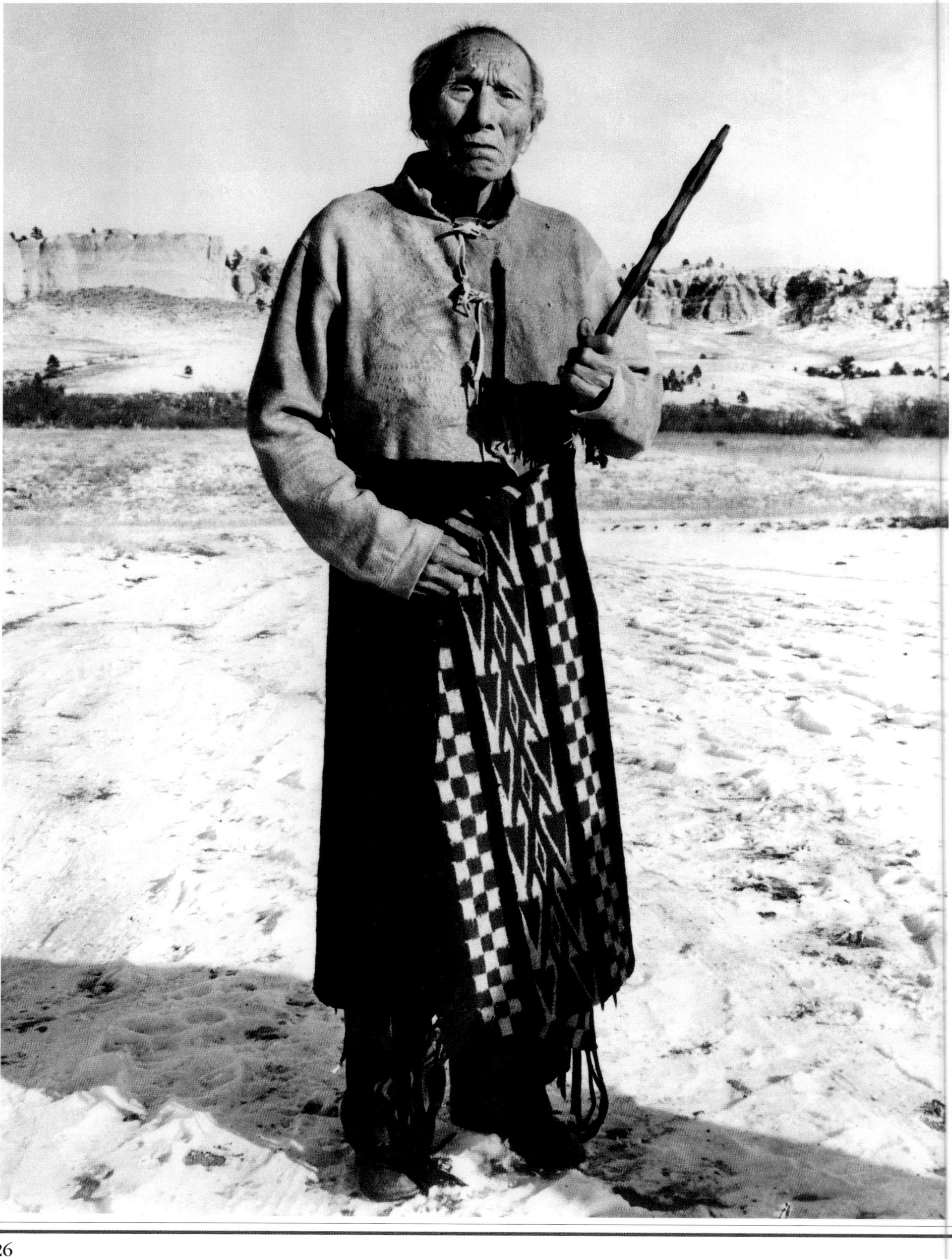

BLACK ELK

1931: ON THE SACRED HOOP OF THE INDIAN NATION

BORN BY THE LITTLE POWDER RIVER IN WYOMING, Oglala Lakota Black Elk (1863–1950) experienced a vision at the age of nine that led to his becoming a medicine man renowned for his spiritual and healing powers. In 1931, Black Elk shared his life story with Nebraska poet laureate John C. Neihardt, describing his participation in the Custer battle, the Ghost Dance religion, and the Wounded Knee massacre. One of the most important books ever written about Native spirituality, *Black Elk Speaks: The Life Story of a Holy Man of the Oglala Sioux* has become the "bible" for young Indians, who look to it for spiritual guidance.

"You have noticed that everything an Indian does is in a circle, and that is because the Power of the World always works in circles, and everything tries to be round. In the old days when we were a strong and happy people, all our power came to us from the sacred hoop of the nation, and so long as the hoop was unbroken, the people flourished. The flowering tree was the living center of the hoop, and the circle of the four quarters nourished it. The east gave peace and light, the south gave warmth, the west gave rain, and the north with its cold and mighty wind gave strength and endurance. This knowledge came to us from the outer world with our religion. Everything the Power of the World does is done in a circle. The sky is round, and I have heard that the earth is round like a ball, and so are all the stars. The wind, in its greatest power, whirls. Birds make their nests in circles, for theirs is the same religion as ours. The sun comes forth and goes down again in a circle. The moon does the same, and both are round. Even the seasons form a great circle in their changing, and always come back again to where they were. The life of a man is a circle ... and so it is in everything where power moves. Our tepees were round like the nests of birds, and these were always set in a circle, the nation's hoop, a nest of many nests, where the Great Spirit meant for us to hatch our children."

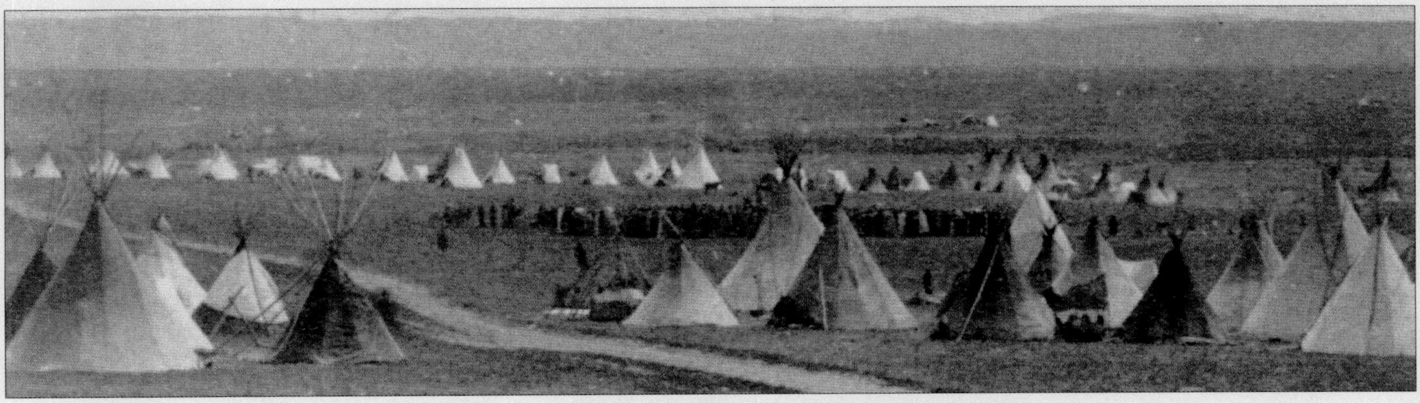

THE NATION'S HOOP: A CIRCLE OF TIPIS

When tribal bands of the Lakota, Cheyenne, or other Plains Indians gathered together as a nation for ceremonies or councils, tipis were placed in a camp circle facing east. The position of each lodge depended on which tribal division, band, clan, or religious association it belonged to.

EUROPEAN PENETRATION

THIS MAP ILLUSTRATES how Native North America was penetrated by six different sovereignties. Early European attempts to establish colonies were unsuccessful but, after 1565, the Spanish, French, English, and Dutch gradually gained footholds on the continent. Over the next 200 years, the strength of the colonies increased as Europeans populated the areas they had settled in the Southeast, Virginia, Pennsylvania, New England, and Quebec, and established outposts in the interior. Russia colonized Alaska during the 1700s, remaining there until 1867 when the US bought the region.

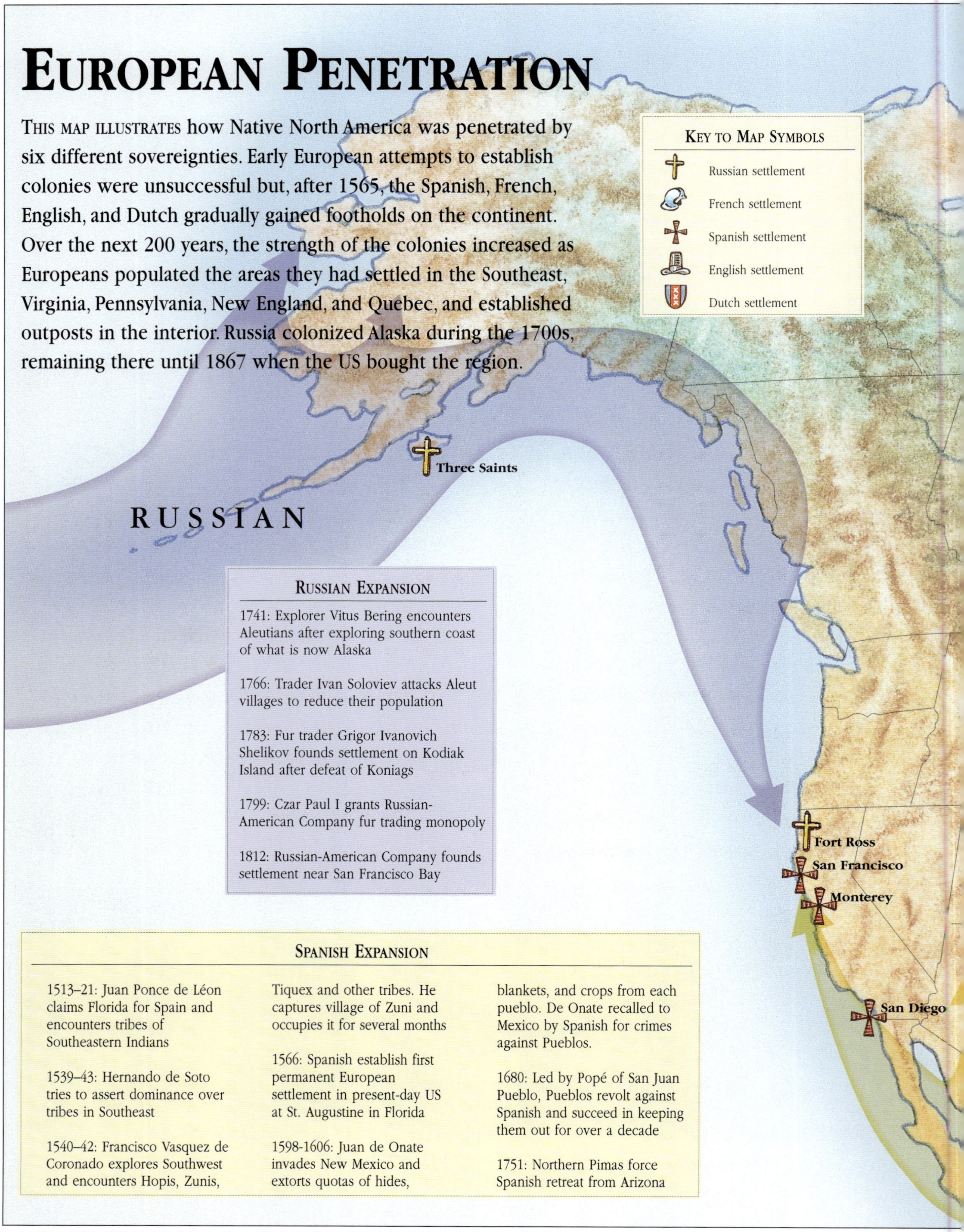

RUSSIAN EXPANSION

1741: Explorer Vitus Bering encounters Aleutians after exploring southern coast of what is now Alaska

1766: Trader Ivan Soloviev attacks Aleut villages to reduce their population

1783: Fur trader Grigor Ivanovich Shelikov founds settlement on Kodiak Island after defeat of Koniags

1799: Czar Paul I grants Russian-American Company fur trading monopoly

1812: Russian-American Company founds settlement near San Francisco Bay

SPANISH EXPANSION

1513–21: Juan Ponce de Léon claims Florida for Spain and encounters tribes of Southeastern Indians

1539–43: Hernando de Soto tries to assert dominance over tribes in Southeast

1540–42: Francisco Vasquez de Coronado explores Southwest and encounters Hopis, Zunis, Tiquex and other tribes. He captures village of Zuni and occupies it for several months

1566: Spanish establish first permanent European settlement in present-day US at St. Augustine in Florida

1598-1606: Juan de Onate invades New Mexico and extorts quotas of hides, blankets, and crops from each pueblo. De Onate recalled to Mexico by Spanish for crimes against Pueblos.

1680: Led by Popé of San Juan Pueblo, Pueblos revolt against Spanish and succeed in keeping them out for over a decade

1751: Northern Pimas force Spanish retreat from Arizona

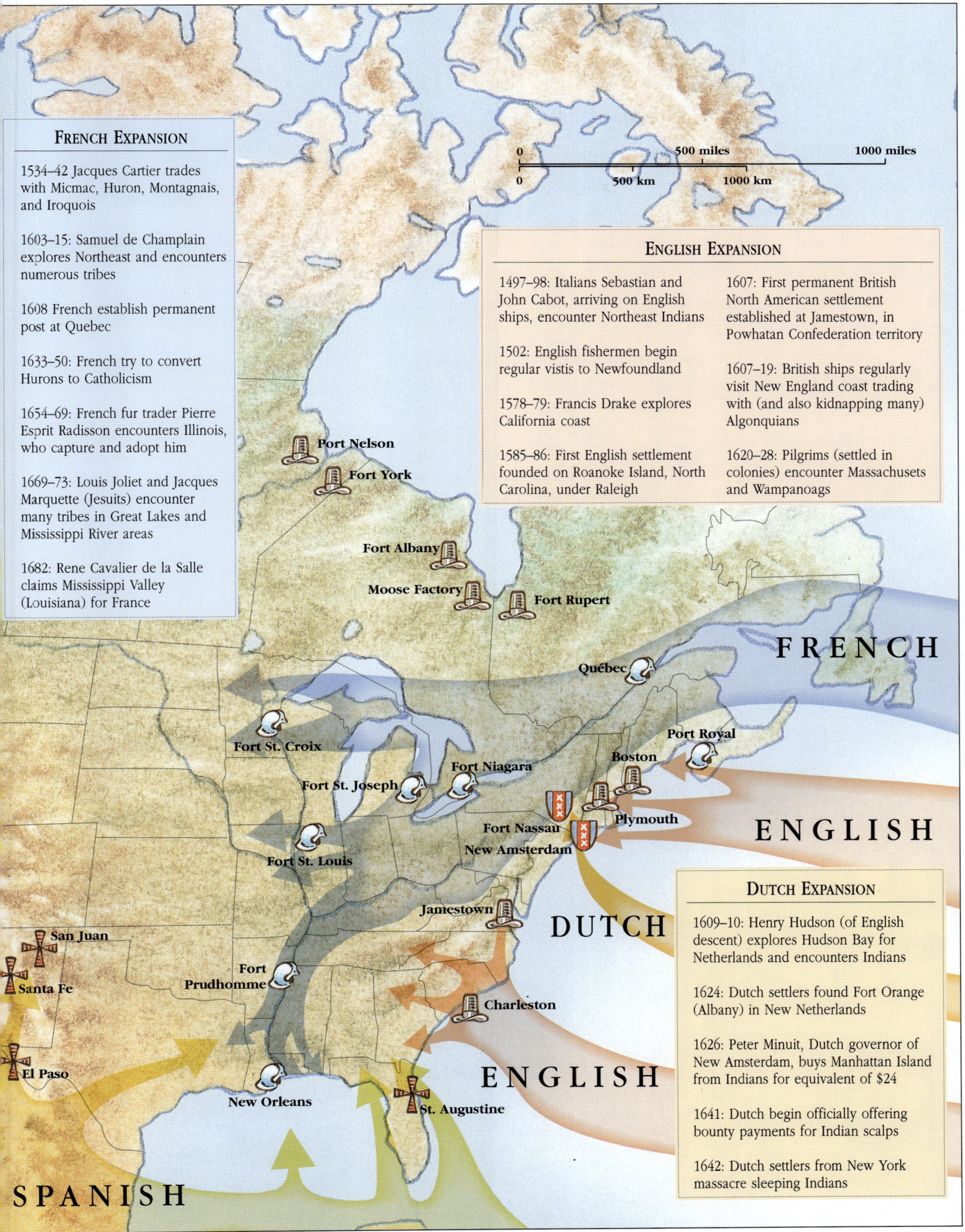

French Expansion

1534–42 Jacques Cartier trades with Micmac, Huron, Montagnais, and Iroquois

1603–15: Samuel de Champlain explores Northeast and encounters numerous tribes

1608 French establish permanent post at Quebec

1633–50: French try to convert Hurons to Catholicism

1654–69: French fur trader Pierre Esprit Radisson encounters Illinois, who capture and adopt him

1669–73: Louis Joliet and Jacques Marquette (Jesuits) encounter many tribes in Great Lakes and Mississippi River areas

1682: Rene Cavalier de la Salle claims Mississippi Valley (Louisiana) for France

English Expansion

1497–98: Italians Sebastian and John Cabot, arriving on English ships, encounter Northeast Indians

1502: English fishermen begin regular vistis to Newfoundland

1578–79: Francis Drake explores California coast

1585–86: First English settlement founded on Roanoke Island, North Carolina, under Raleigh

1607: First permanent British North American settlement established at Jamestown, in Powhatan Confederation territory

1607–19: British ships regularly visit New England coast trading with (and also kidnapping many) Algonquians

1620–28: Pilgrims (settled in colonies) encounter Massachusets and Wampanoags

Dutch Expansion

1609–10: Henry Hudson (of English descent) explores Hudson Bay for Netherlands and encounters Indians

1624: Dutch settlers found Fort Orange (Albany) in New Netherlands

1626: Peter Minuit, Dutch governor of New Amsterdam, buys Manhattan Island from Indians for equivalent of $24

1641: Dutch begin officially offering bounty payments for Indian scalps

1642: Dutch settlers from New York massacre sleeping Indians

FIRST EUROPEAN CONTACTS

WHEN EUROPEAN TRADERS, soldiers, farmers, and townspeople began arriving in North America in the 1600s, Native peoples greeted them with their customary hospitality. But the newcomers were peaceable only for as long as it took them to gain a foothold in the area; then they proceeded to make and break treaties, kill, and steal Indian lands. Although Natives fought back valiantly, a combination of factors – especially the introduction of diseases, such as smallpox, and the power of European firearms – decimated their populations.

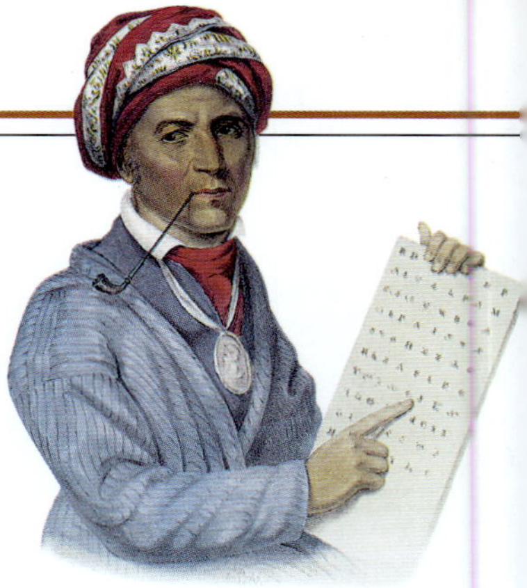

OVERCOMING LANGUAGE BARRIERS
In 1821, Sequoyah, son of a Cherokee woman and a British trader, devised an 86-character syllabary that permitted him to capture all the sounds of the Cherokee language on paper.

EARLY EUROPEAN EXPLORERS

European explorers established contacts with Native peoples from *c.* 1000 onwards. Records from early expeditions provided the first information on tribes.

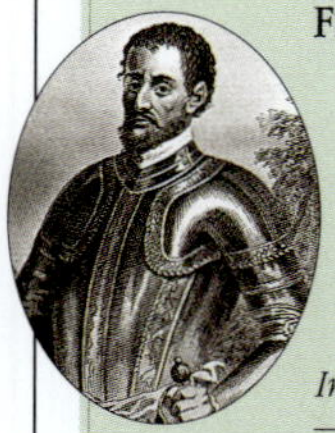

FERDINAND DE SOTO
Spanish explorer de Soto trekked through the Southeast from 1539–42 in search of gold and precious minerals, robbing, sacking, and killing Indians as he went.

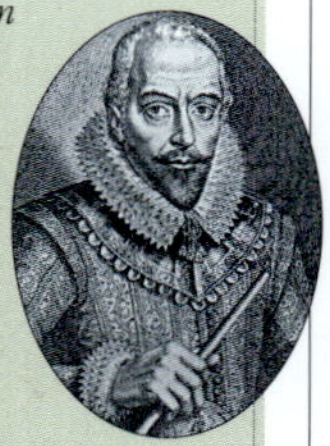

WALTER RALEIGH
In 1585, Raleigh – an English explorer and colonizer – ordered the establishment of a colony on the North Carolina coast. The colony, on Roanoke Island, mysteriously disappeared.

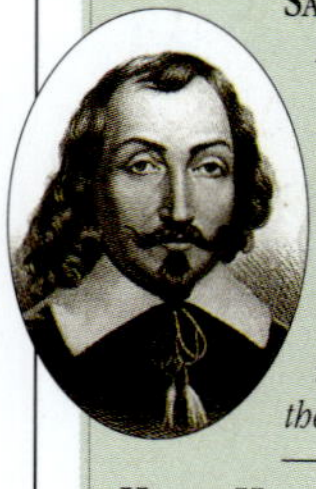

SAMUEL DE CHAMPLAIN
French explorer de Champlain founded the Canadian city of Quebec in 1608 as a center for the Indian fur trade, negotiating trade agreements and military alliances with the local tribes.

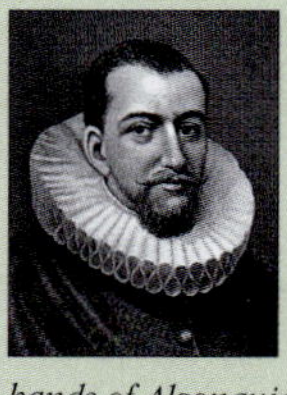

HENRY HUDSON
In 1609, English navigator and explorer Hudson "discovered" the river named after him and claimed the region for the Netherlands. While exploring the Hudson Valley, he traded with bands of Algonquian Indians and brought the furs back to Europe.

REGULAR CONTACT between Europeans and Native peoples began in the early 1500s and continued for a century before permanent European settlements arose. Fishermen from France, Portugal, and the Basque region of Spain visited the Labrador and Newfoundland coasts. Spanish explorers encountered Southeastern tribes, some of whom they captured and sold as slaves. During the sixteenth and seventeenth centuries, Britain, France, Spain, and the Netherlands made inroads into North America, planting their flags in Native soil, overpowering Indians, and proclaiming ownership wherever they set foot.

Europeans on Indian Lands

The various European powers dealt with Indians in different ways. The French, in Canada, were primarily interested in the fur trade and did not require much land; they farmed little of mainland Canada and developed no permanent settlements. As a result, Indian-white relations in Canada remained fairly amicable until the early seventeenth century. The Spanish conquistadors viewed Indians as potential converts to Catholicism and established missions in what are now New Mexico and California. They forced Indians to labor in their gold and silver mines. The Dutch, hungry for furs in the early 1600s, negotiated with Natives for small pieces of land for trading posts and villages. By the 1630s, as furs were depleted in coastal areas, the Dutch turned to agriculture, using force to acquire land. British settlers, who came in the early 1600s, wanted the fertile river valleys that had been cultivated by Indian farmers for centuries. They cut down ancient forests full of game, clearing the land for small homesteads, then for huge plantations. As tribal lands were ruined, Natives were forced to move away or convert to the British lifestyle. In

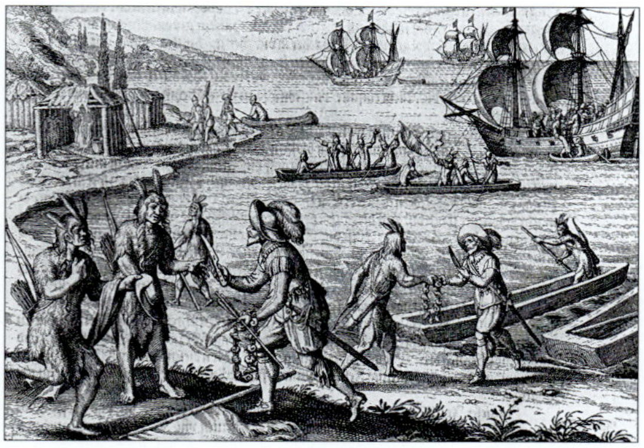

△ GOSNOLD'S ATTEMPT AT SETTLEMENT
In 1602, English explorer Bartholomew Gosnold tried to establish a settlement on the New England coast. Trading peacefully at first with tribes around Cape Cod, he received gifts of cooked fish and tobacco from friendly Wampanoags, pictured in this illustration. The explorer abandoned settlement plans after a dispute over trade objects between his crew and Indians.

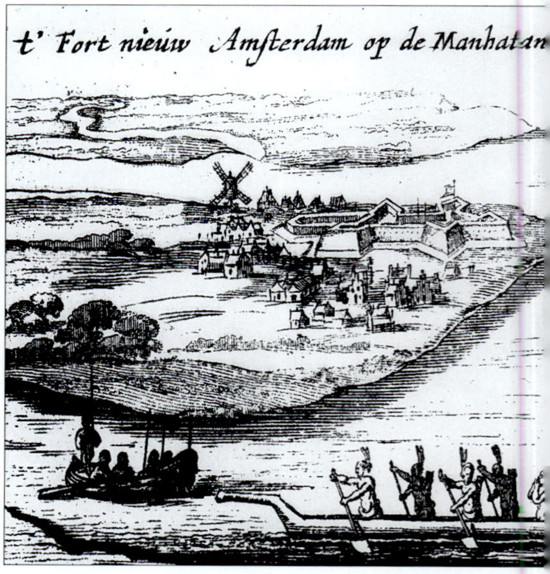

1741, Russian fur traders extended their activities to Alaska, forcing Native men to supply furs, children to prepare hides, and women to become concubines.

Changing Native Lifestyles

For thousands of years, tribes traded turquoise, flint, shells, mica, and other goods, which were carried over Indian trade routes throughout the Americas; but, once Europeans and Indians met and began trading, manufactured goods entered Native cultures, irrevocably altering their lifestyles. The Natives traded animal pelts and skins, which Europeans made into muffs, collars, and felt hats – then fashionable among Europe's upper classes. In exchange, the Indians wanted labor-saving metal tools – hoes, axes, and knives – as well as broadcloths and wool. Eventually, manufactured cloth replaced animal skins; traditional tools made from stone, bone, and wood were replaced by metal implements; and guns replaced bows and arrows. Fierce competition among the European nations led to rivalry among Indian tribes for limited supplies of pelts – a contributory factor in many intertribal conflicts and colonial wars.

From the early seventeenth century through the early nineteenth century, many Natives were displaced from their ancestral homelands in the Northeast and Southeast by wars and takeovers of their lands by white settlers. In 1830, the US Congress passed the Indian Removal Act, which forcibly exiled tribes from their tilled fields, farms, and forests to Indian Territory west of the Mississippi River.

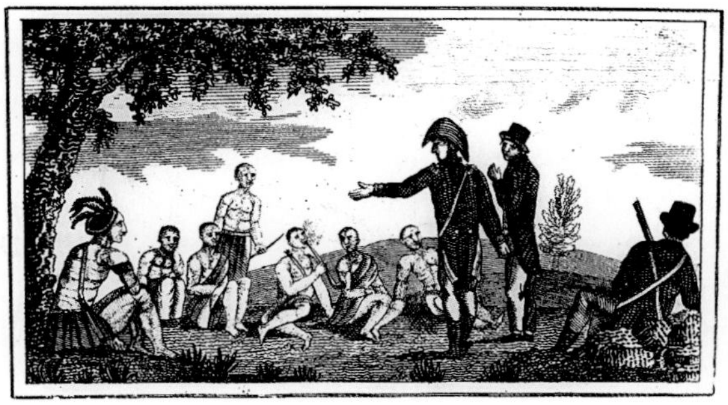

EXPLORING WESTWARDS ▷
In the late 1700s, explorers from the US and Canada progressed westward into vast, unknown regions, surveying coastal areas, rivers, lakes, valleys, and mountain passes. In the course of their travels, most of the explorers made contact with Native populations. Their reports – full of botanical, geological, and other scientific data – also recorded information about the Indian nations they encountered.

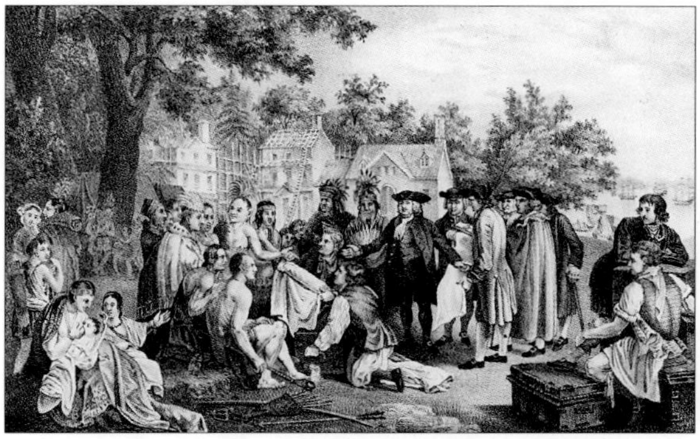

◁ PENNSYLVANIA PEACE TALKS
William Penn, the son of a British admiral and a Quaker, inherited a huge tract of land, most of which now comprises the present state of Pennsylvania. In 1682, Penn negotiated a treaty with chiefs of the Lenni Lenape (Delaware) tribe, and named the colony Pennsylvania. Penn, a religious reformer, pledged peace to the Indian inhabitants of the colony, offering religious freedom to all who lived there. A long period of peaceful relations ensued.

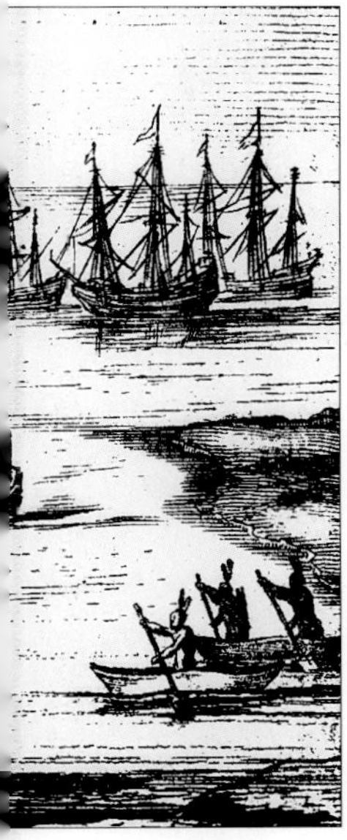

◁ BIRTH OF NEW YORK CITY
This 1651 depiction is the earliest known view of New Amsterdam, which was founded in 1626 by the Dutch West India Company on the southern tip of Manhattan Island. After the area fell to the British in 1664, New Amsterdam became known as New York City.

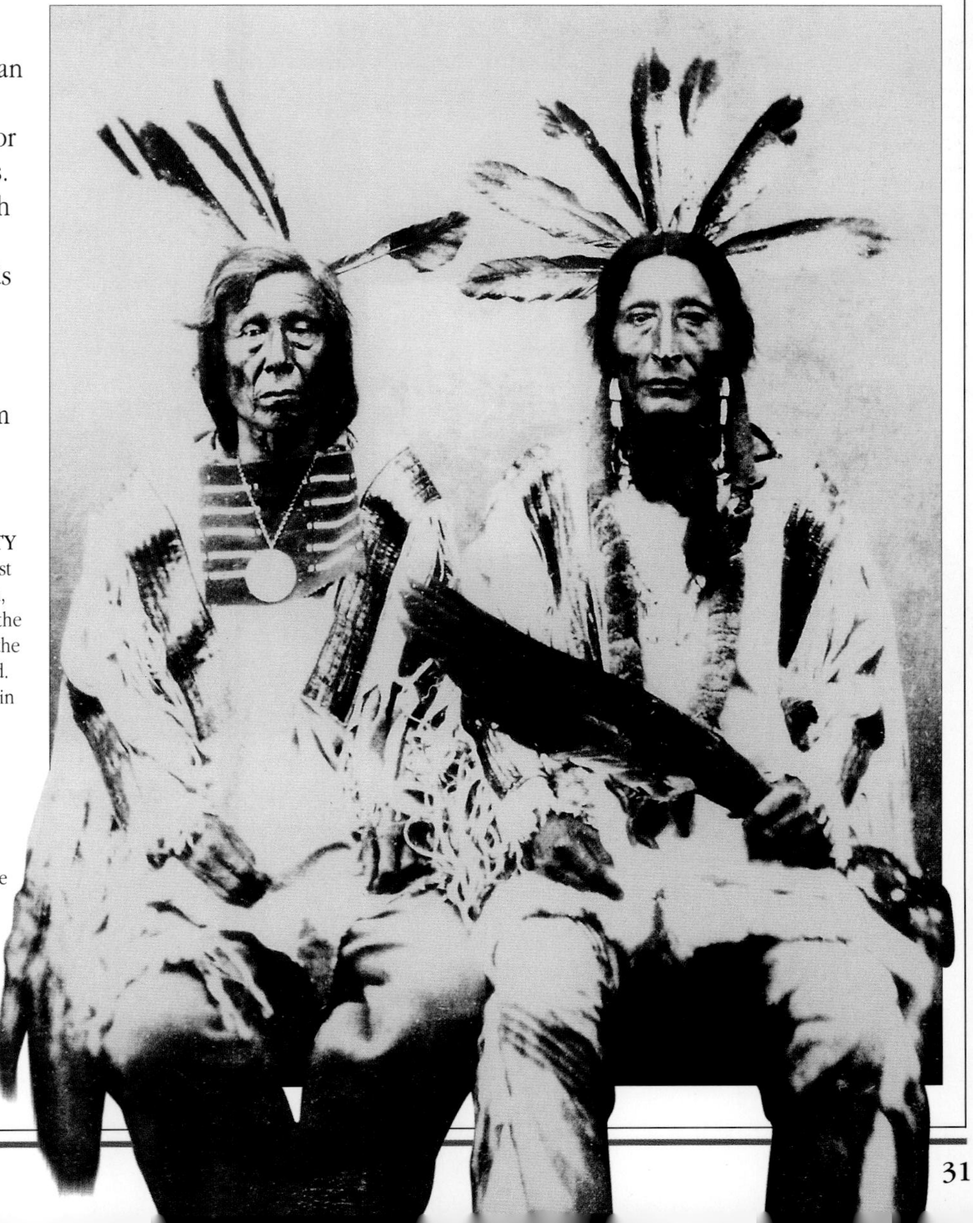

RAVAGED SURVIVORS ▷
Europeans brought to North America diseases to which the Natives had little or no resistance and some tribes were virtually wiped out within weeks of being infected. More Indians died from diseases such as smallpox than from all their warfare with whites. These two Mandans are survivors of a smallpox epidemic.

PARLEYS AND TRADE

Trading for furs with Indian peoples began as soon as colonies were established along the Atlantic coast and, throughout the colonial period and well into the nineteenth century, the fur trade developed into one of the principal business enterprises of North America. Trading benefited Indians for a time, but they became more dependent on European goods for survival after they discarded their own tools and technologies.

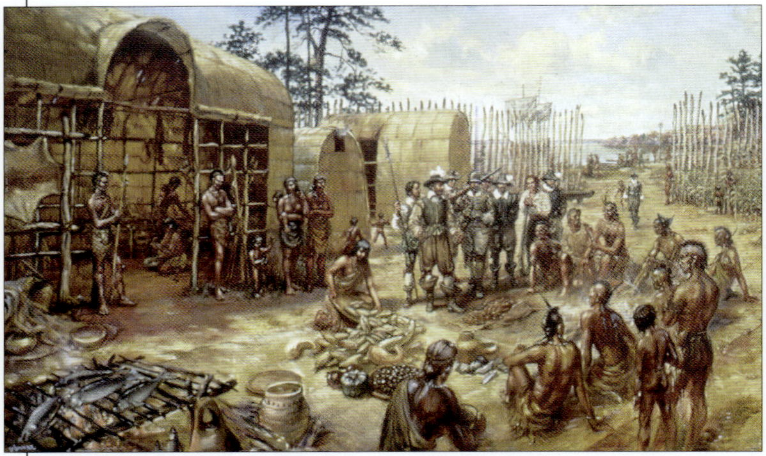

△ RELATIONS WITH POWHATANS
The British, who settled the colony of Jamestown, Virginia, in 1607, constructed a palisaded fort as protection from Indian attacks. But Powhatan Indians traded peacefully with the settlers, bringing them corn and showing them how to build fish weirs and plant vegetables.

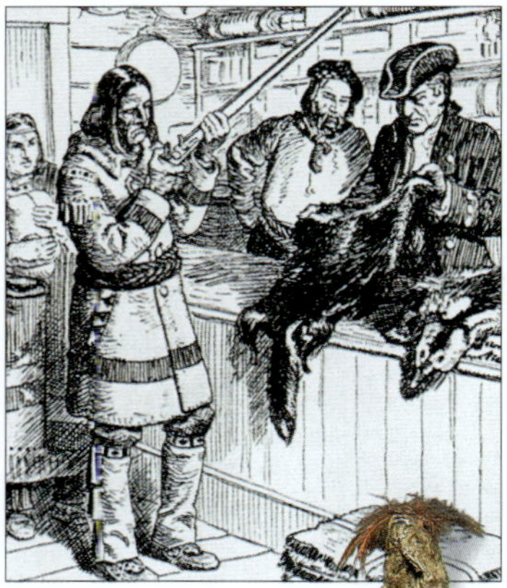

FURS FOR FIREARMS ▷
After eastern tribes had stripped the land of beavers, Hurons, Ottawas, and other tribes, no longer self-sufficient, depended on European goods, particularly firearms for hunting game. In Canada, the French traded muskets for furs with the Indians.

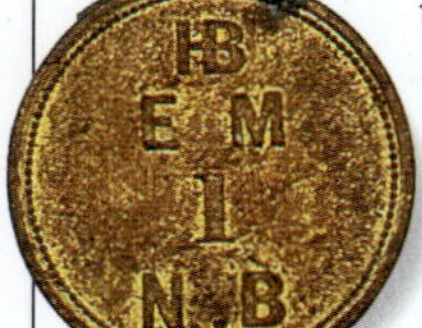

◁ TOKEN VALUE
Brass tokens, which could be used to buy supplies from the Hudson's Bay Trading Company, were given to Indian and white trappers in exchange for beaver skins. The company built forts and trading posts at convenient river mouths.

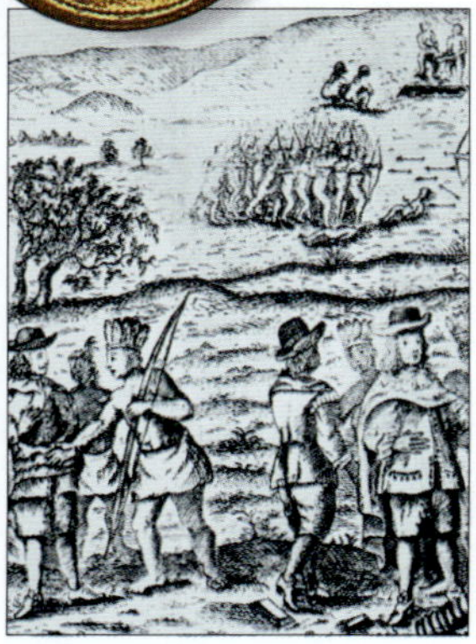

◁ SWEDISH TRADING
In this seventeenth-century sketch, Delaware Indians are depicted negotiating trade agreements with Swedish colonists. The Swedish claimed land along Delaware Bay from 1638 until 1655, when they were ousted by the Dutch.

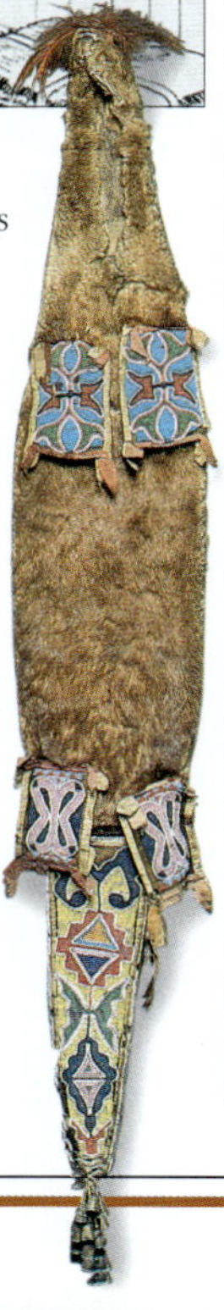

MIDEWININ MEDICINE BAG ▷
This otterskin medicine bag of the Chippewa religious society, the Midewinin, is decorated with dyed porcupine quills and glass beads obtained from European traders.

A WAVE OF CONFLICT

Once they had gained a foothold in North America, Europeans began to engage in bloody conflicts with Natives. Explorers, settlers, and colonial governments made constant, unreasonable demands, using fear and force to get what they wanted. The Natives, inevitably, fought back. One of the early casualties was the Spanish explorer, Ponce de Léon, who was attacked by Florida Indians in 1521 during his mission to acquire slaves.

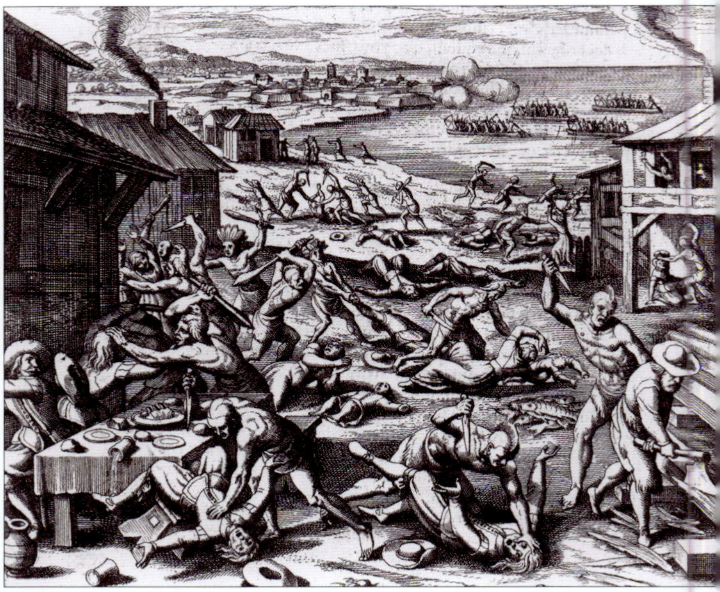

△ POWHATAN WARS
The massacre of 350 Virginians by Powhatan Indians in 1622 was an expression of the hostility and resentments that had built up during the early years of the settlement. British expansion continued after 1622 and new tensions developed, exploding in violence in 1644, when Powhatan Indians once again attacked the Virginia settlement.

SEMINOLE RESISTANCE

Despite signing treaties with the US government in 1823, 1832, and 1833, ceding land and agreeing to move, many Seminoles resisted removal from Florida. This led to the Second Seminole War – by far the bloodiest of the three wars fought in Florida between 1817 and 1858. From 1835 to 1842, the Seminoles, led by Osceola, Billy Bowlegs, and Alligator, fought the US army, but the war was inconclusive and no peace treaty was signed.

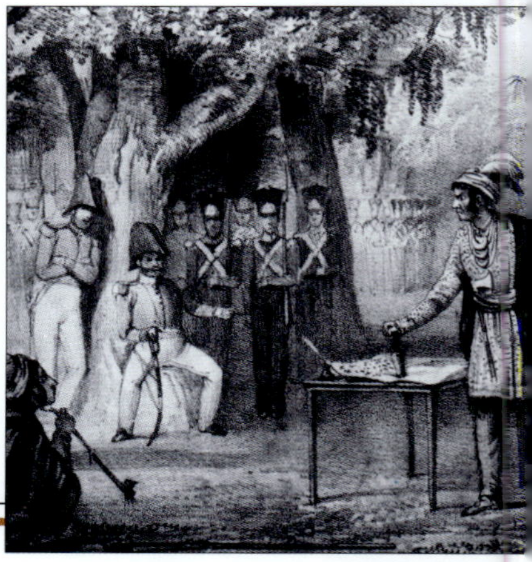

REFUSING TO SIGN ▷
In 1833, Seminole leader Osceola emerged as a powerful voice in the resistance movement against the mandated removal of his people from present-day Florida to Indian Territory, west of the Mississippi. Principal spokesman for the tribe's cause in 1834 negotiations with the government, Osceola was at the forefront again in April 1835, when he is said to have plunged a knife into a treaty that he refused to sign.

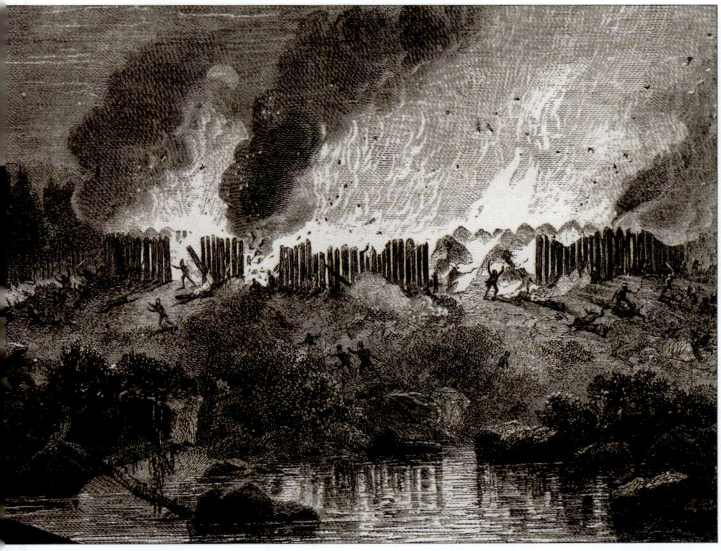

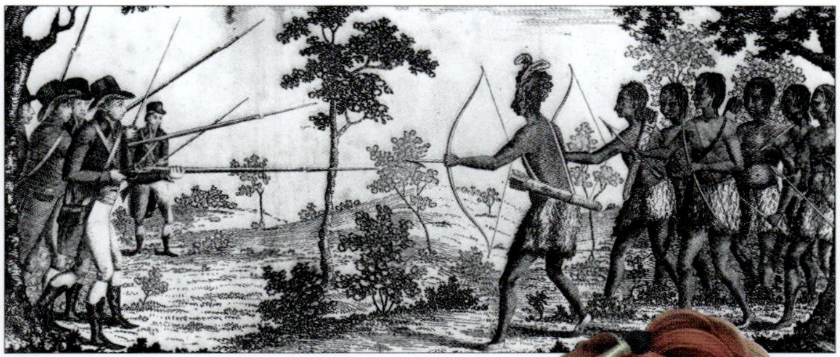

△ DEFIANT KING PHILIP
During 1675–76, the cataclysmic King Philip's War ravaged New England. Wampanoag chief Metacom, whom the British called King Philip, led his tribe and allies in a war against the British, destroying many of their settlements. The war, which cost 600 British and 3,000 Indian lives, ended independent Indian power in New England. Philip was killed by an Indian turncoat, then beheaded.

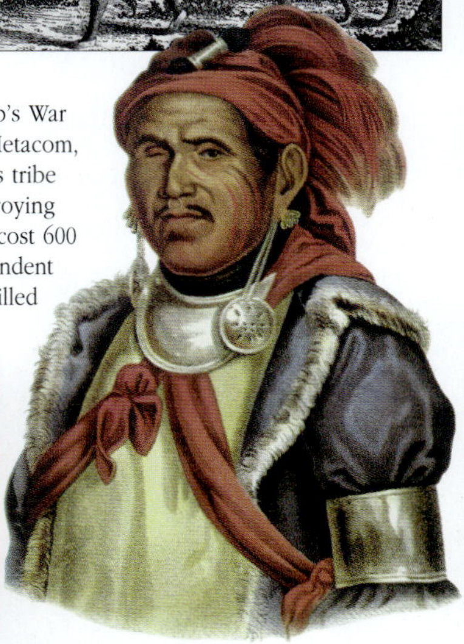

\ PEQUOT MASSACRE
n 1637, Captain John Mason, an nglishman, and allied Indians marched to he principal Pequot village on the Mystic iver, in what is now Connecticut. At awn, when most of the warriors were way from the village, they set fire to 80 vigwams, killing 600–700 inhabitants.

BRADDOCK'S DEFEAT ▷
n 1754, when the French built a fort on erritory claimed by the British colony in /irginia, General Edward Braddock was ent to dislodge them. On 9 July 1755, Braddock, who commanded British and olonial forces totaling 2,500 men, was lefeated by the French and their Indian llies. Braddock and hundreds of his nadequately trained troops were killed.

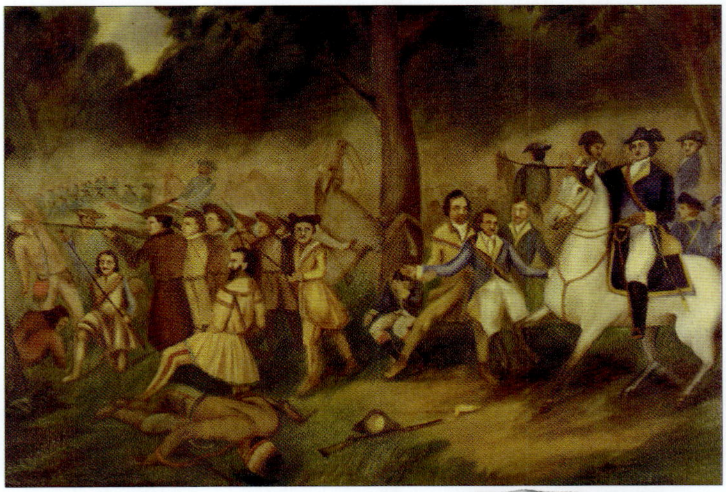

△ A SHAWNEE PROPHET
Tenskwatawa, brother of Shawnee leader Tecumseh, was a prophet who attracted many Indians. When he demanded that tribes abandon white customs and return to those of their ancestors, many Shawnees flocked to his call. In 1808, he established a community of believers in Prophetstown, Indiana Territory – later destroyed by Indiana governor, William Henry Harrison.

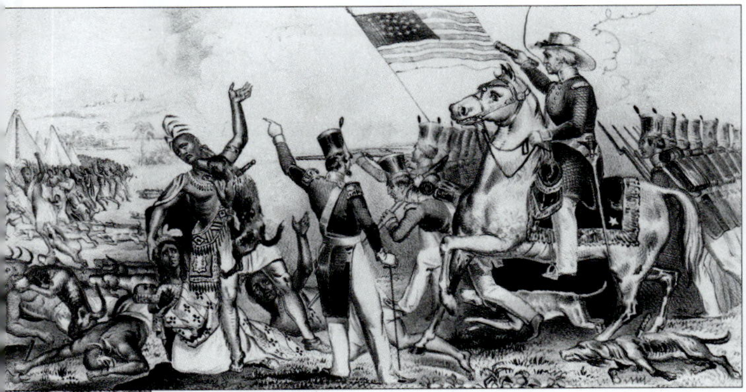

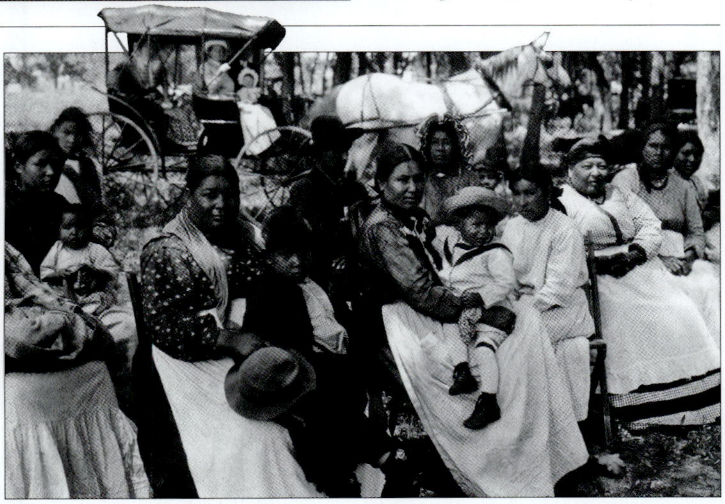

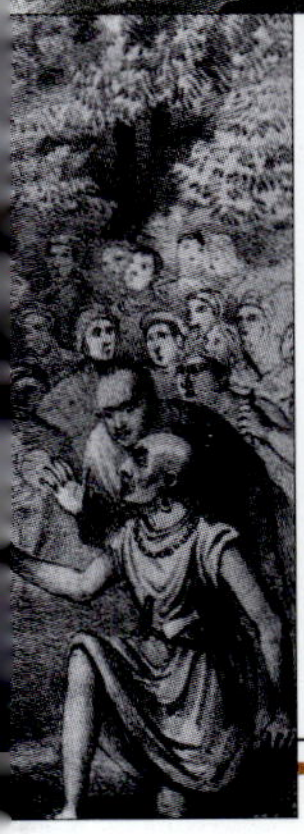

△ COSTLY WAR
During the Second Seminole War, from 1835 to 1842, 200,000 US soldiers fought defiant Seminoles who refused to leave their Florida homeland. The army used bloodhounds to hunt down the Indians, who hid in dense swamp lands where they were virtually undetectable. The troops eventually gave up trying to evict the Indians and withdrew.

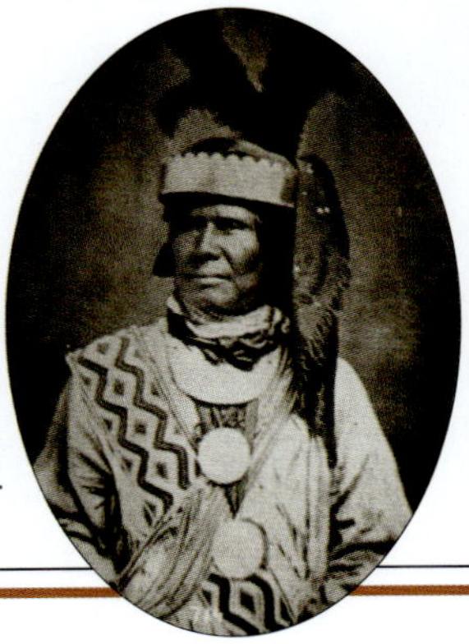

◁ BOWLEGS RESISTS REMOVAL
Chief Billy Bowlegs, who led Seminoles after the death of Osceola, finally agreed to emigrate to Indian Territory in 1858, 16 years after his surrender in 1842, at the end of the Second Seminole War. In the years after his surrender, he gardened a small parcel of land, but its vandalization, in 1855, led to the Third Seminole War.

△ SEMINOLES IN OKLAHOMA
At the end of the Second Seminole War, most of the Seminole tribe were forced to resettle in Indian Territory (now Oklahoma) – a large, unorganized, "permanent" Indian country west of Arkansas, Missouri, and Iowa. Pictured here is a group of Seminole women and children in Wewoka, Oklahoma.

INDIAN REMOVALS

IN 1830, PERSUADED BY President Andrew Jackson, the US Congress passed the Indian Removal Act, which authorized the removal of Indian tribes to a large, unorganized, "permanent" Indian territory west of the Mississippi River (later called Oklahoma.) A removal policy was first suggested in 1803 by President Thomas Jefferson, but subsequent presidents were unwilling to use military force to remove tribes. President Jackson, however, backed the use of force that ultimately expelled about 100,000 Native Americans from their homelands.

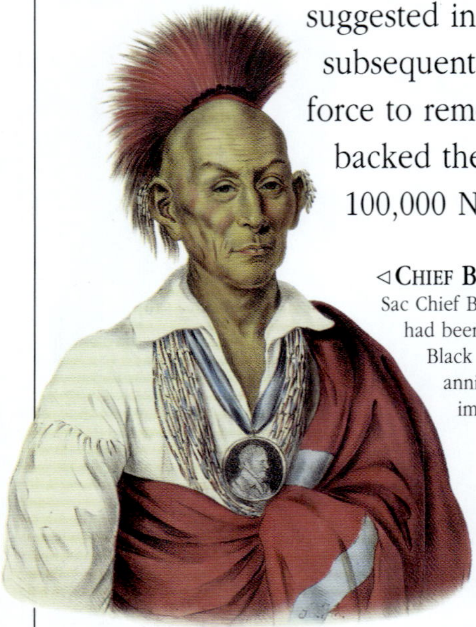

◁ CHIEF BLACK HAWK LEADS RESISTANCE

Sac Chief Black Hawk led a faction of his tribe that resisted removal from lands that had been sold without tribal approval. Forcibly evicted from their homes in 1832, Black Hawk's band eluded the militia for three months until they were nearly annihilated at the battle of Bad Axe. Black Hawk, who surrendered and was imprisoned, was permitted to return to his people, but no longer as a chief.

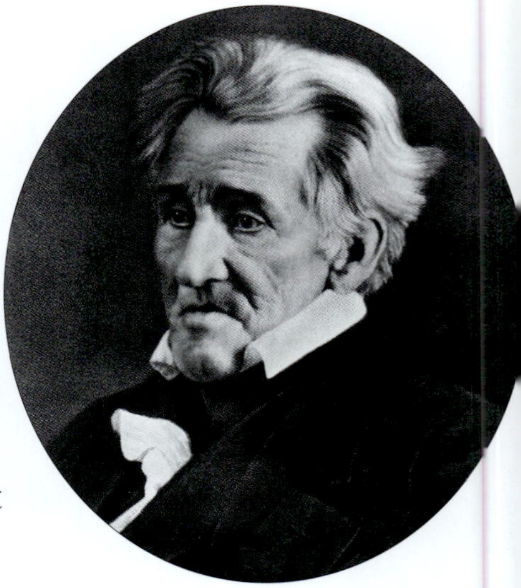

△ JACKSON BACKS REMOVAL

When Andrew Jackson came to office in 1829, he faced a government divided over the Indian removal question. Influenced by the demands of Georgia and Alabama states, Jackson became a major proponent of removal policy.

▽ CHEROKEE TRAIL OF TEARS

During the winter of 1838–39, in what is known as the "Trail of Tears," approximately 16,000 Cherokees were forced to leave their homes in the Southeast and move to Indian Territory. Because of inadequate government preparations, the Indians suffered on their journey from lack of blankets and warm clothing, severe food shortages, and cholera.

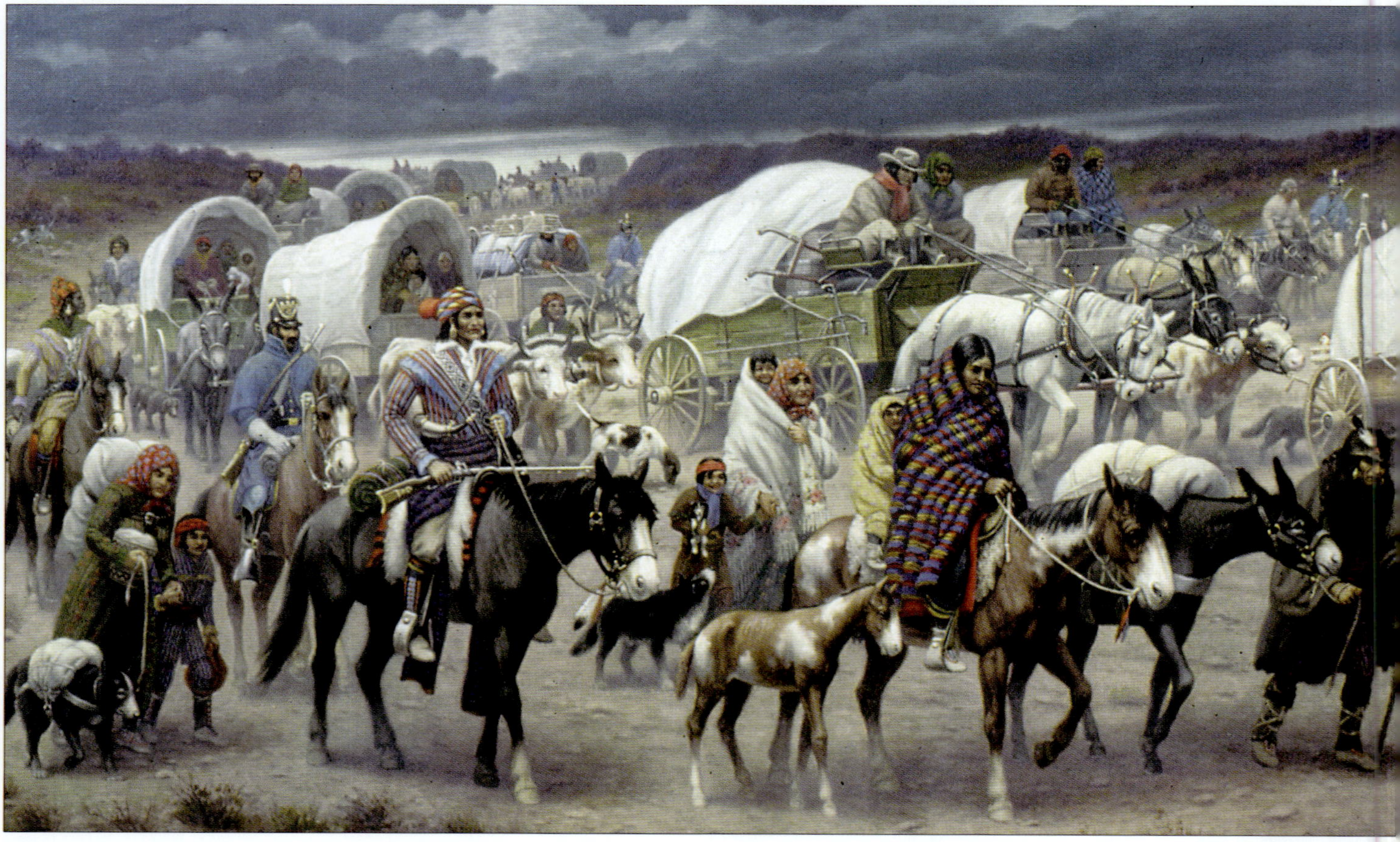

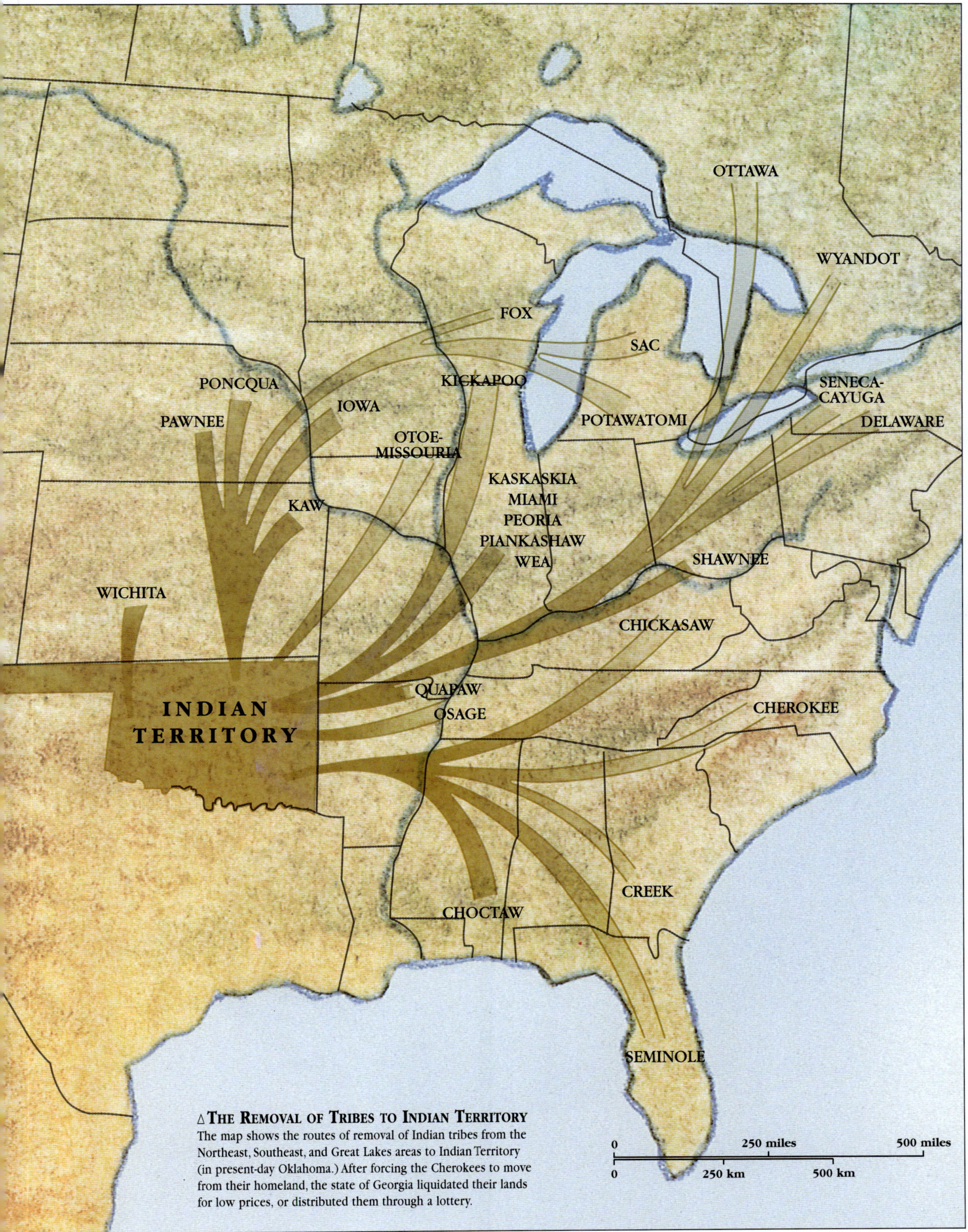

△ THE REMOVAL OF TRIBES TO INDIAN TERRITORY
The map shows the routes of removal of Indian tribes from the Northeast, Southeast, and Great Lakes areas to Indian Territory (in present-day Oklahoma.) After forcing the Cherokees to move from their homeland, the state of Georgia liquidated their lands for low prices, or distributed them through a lottery.

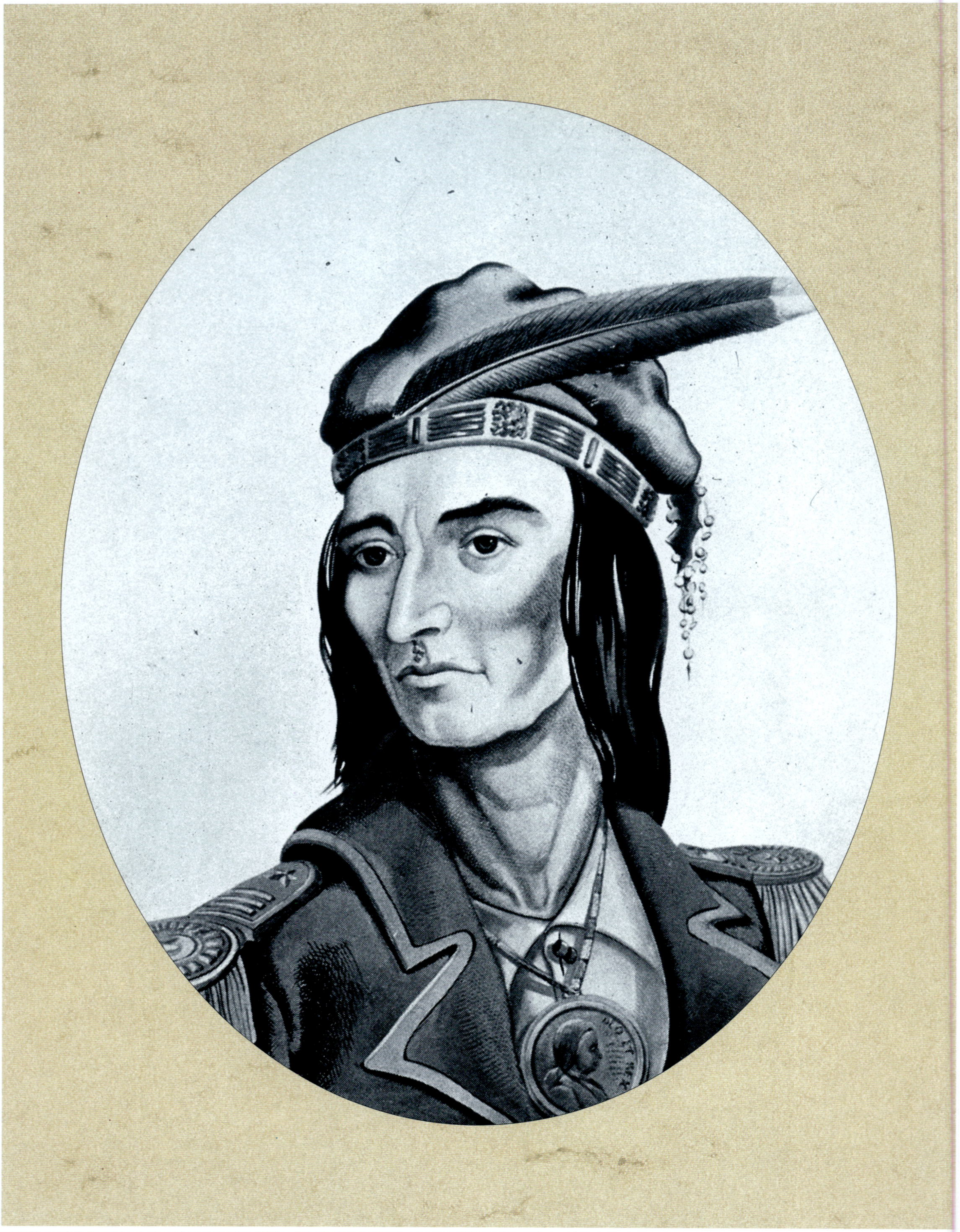

TECUMSEH

c. 1810–11: A CALL FOR INDIAN UNITY

TECUMSEH (*c.* 1768–1813) WAS BORN at a Shawnee village in present-day Ohio. From an early age, he was imbued with the determination to unify Indians in resistance against white encroachment on Native lands, but he failed to create a pan-Indian union. Tecumseh accepted support from the British, who seemed to pose less of a threat than expansionist American colonists, and fought with them against the US in the War of 1812. He was killed at the battle of the Thames in 1813. In *c.* 1810–11, when he was about 42 years of age, Tecumseh spoke to the Osage about uniting Indian people against whites.

"Brothers – We all belong to one family; we are all children of the Great Spirit; we walk in the same path; slake our thirst at the same spring; and now affairs of the greatest concern lead us to smoke the pipe around the same council fire!

Brothers – We are friends; we must assist each other to bear our burdens. The blood of many of our fathers and brothers has run like water on the ground, to satisfy the avarice of the white men. We, ourselves, are threatened with a great evil; nothing will pacify them but the destruction of all the red men.

Brothers – When the white men first set foot on our grounds, they were hungry; they had no place on which to spread their blankets, or to kindle their fires. They were feeble; they could do nothing for themselves. Our fathers commiserated their distress, and shared freely with them whatever the Great Spirit had given his red children. They gave them food when hungry, medicine when sick, spread skins for them to sleep on, and gave them grounds, that they might hunt and raise corn.

Brothers – The white people are like poisonous serpents: when chilled, they are feeble, and harmless, but invigorate them with warmth, and they sting their benefactors to death ....

Brothers – The white men are not friends to the Indians: at first, they only asked for land sufficient for a wigwam; now, nothing will satisfy them but the whole of our hunting grounds, from the rising to the setting sun ....

Brothers – My people are brave and numerous; but the white people are too strong for them alone. I wish you to take up the tomahawk with them. If we all unite, we will cause the rivers to stain the great waters with their blood.

Brothers – If you do not unite with us, they will first destroy us, and then you will fall an easy prey to them. They have destroyed many nations of red men because they were not united, because they were not friends to each other.

Brothers – We must be united; we must smoke the same pipe; we must fight each other's battles; and more than all, we must love the Great Spirit: he is for us; he will destroy our enemies, and make his red children happy."

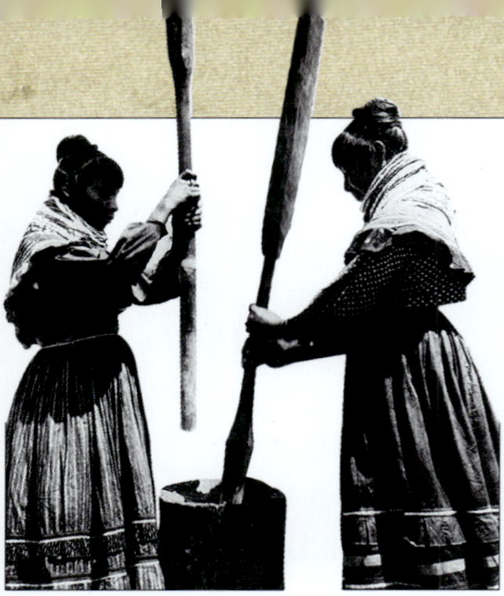

◁ WOMEN GRIND THE CORN
Seminole women in Florida, pictured here at the end of the nineteenth century, made corn meal by grinding the kernels in a hollowed-out tree trunk. Corn was the staff of life for many tribes in the Northeast, Southeast, and Southwest.

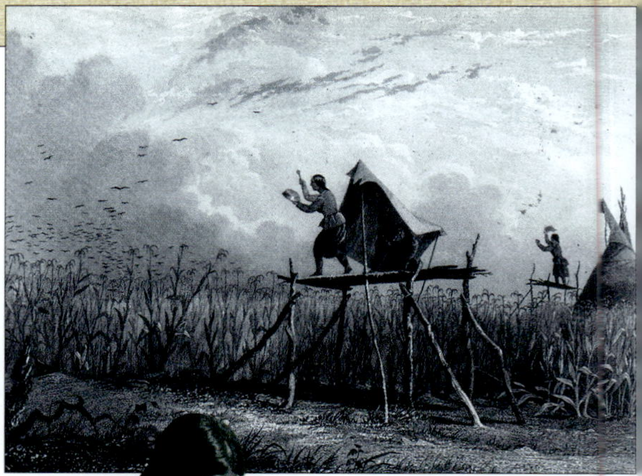

PROTECTING THE CROP ▷
Corn crops were closely guarded. This illustration shows Indian women frightening birds away from a ripening crop. As well as scarecrows flapping their arms in the breeze, children sometimes protected the crops by throwing rocks at rabbits and rodents.

HARVEST HOME ▷
Preparing the food that the men had grown was women's work. Here, a Pueblo woman grinds corn, surrounded by corn and chilies that have been hung up to dry. Crops are difficult to grow in the arid terrain of New Mexico and Arizona, so the harvest was particularly precious.

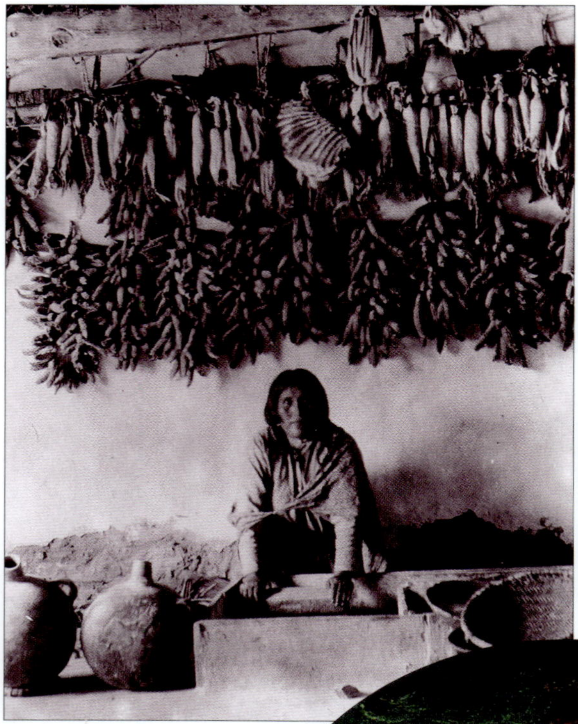

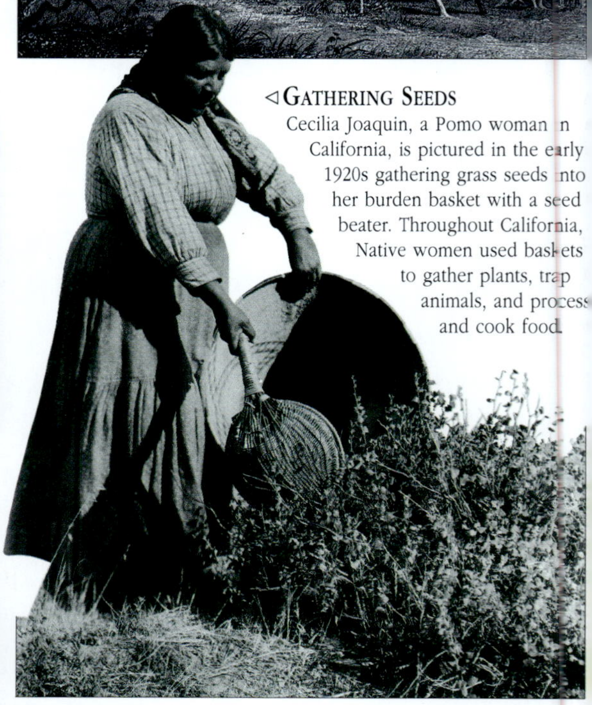

◁ GATHERING SEEDS
Cecilia Joaquin, a Pomo woman in California, is pictured in the early 1920s gathering grass seeds into her burden basket with a seed beater. Throughout California, Native women used baskets to gather plants, trap animals, and process and cook food.

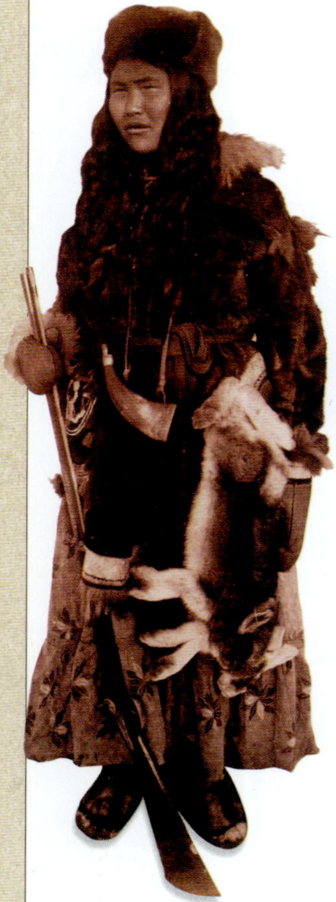

◁ A FEMALE HUNTER
Although the roles of Native men and women followed established rules, in most groups women could take on men's work if they wished. Occasionally, Native women, like the Alaskan Tanana woman pictured, became hunters.

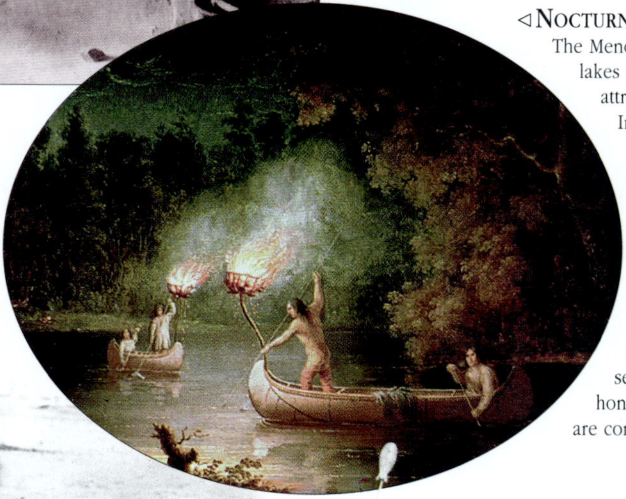

◁ NOCTURNAL FISHING
The Menominees of Wisconsin fished on lakes at night, using iron fire baskets to attract fish to the surface of the water. In this detail from an 1845 painting by Canadian artist Paul Kane, the fishermen are depicted preparing to use spears to catch the fish.

▽ HONORING SALMON
Stan Jones Senior, tribal chairman of the Tulalip in Washington State, here celebrates the first salmon catch of the fishing season in the annual salmon-honoring ceremony. After the rituals are completed, fishing is open to all.

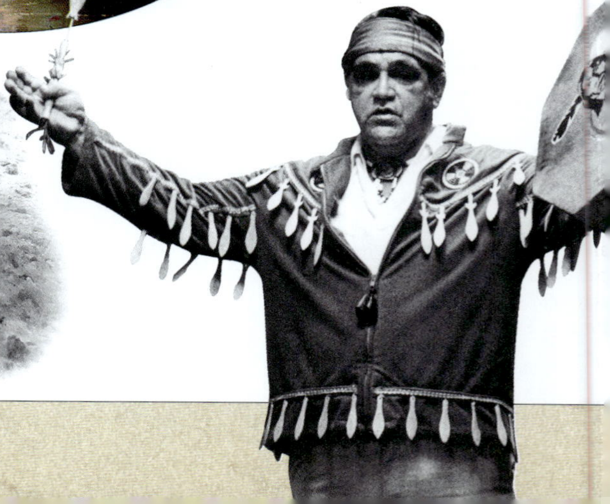

FISHING THROUGH ICE ▷
Enormous effort and endurance were required for winter fishing. Copper Inuit fishermen chipped a hole through 5–6 ft (1.5–1.8 m) of ice, dropped in a line with a barbless hook attached to a fish decoy, then, like this young girl, patiently sat or knelt on the ice, waiting for a catch.

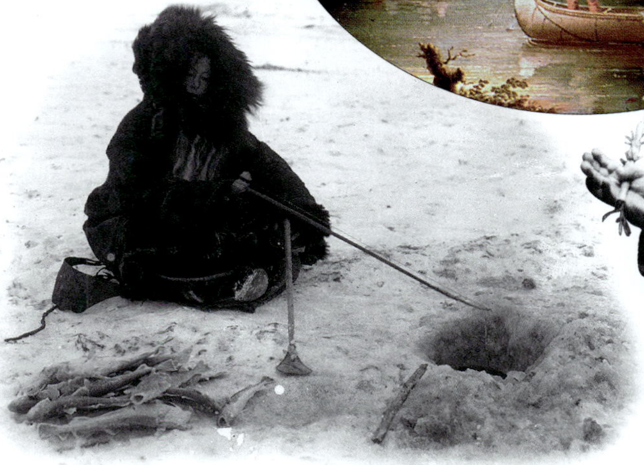

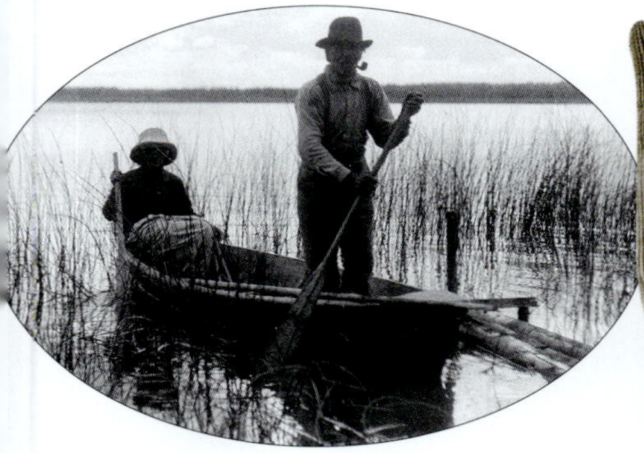

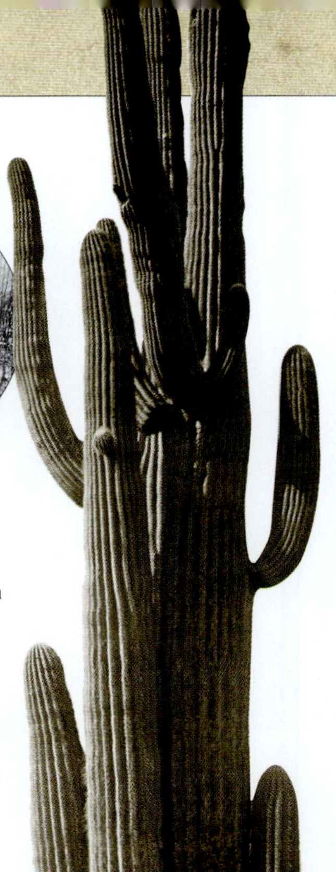

\ Aquatic Yield
\ Chippewa couple at Mille Lacs, Minnesota, gather wild ice *c.* 1920. The ripe grain was beaten from the stalks with ticks, then dried until the inedible hulls could be cracked ree and the loosened kernels winnowed out.

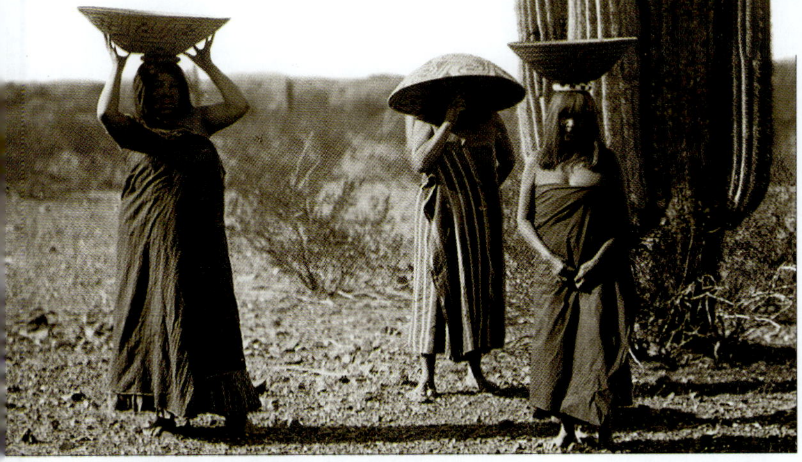

'ruit of the Cactus ▷
Vomen from Arizona's Maricopa tribe stand beside a giant aguaro cactus, holding the bowls they use to gather its dible fruit in early summer. As well as eating the fruit, the 'ohono O'odham brew it into a ritual drink that is used in eremonies to mark the beginning of the rainy season.

Nature's Harvest

Utilizing a remarkable ability to exploit natural resources, Native Americans harvested a wide variety of wild and domesticated plants throughout most of North America: fresh berries to provide energy, and serve as thickeners and flavorings; edible seeds, high in nutritional value; and the roots and tender greens of wild plants, which they parboiled and cooked with meat. In the upper Great Lakes, Indians harvested wild rice – a grass that grows in shallow lakes and provides a nutritious grain staple. In California, camas bulbs and acorns were gathered and made into flour. Corn, beans, and squash became – and continue to be – important domesticated crops throughout North America. Foods were sweetened with wild honey, dried and fresh fruit, and with the maple sugar produced by sugar-maple trees.

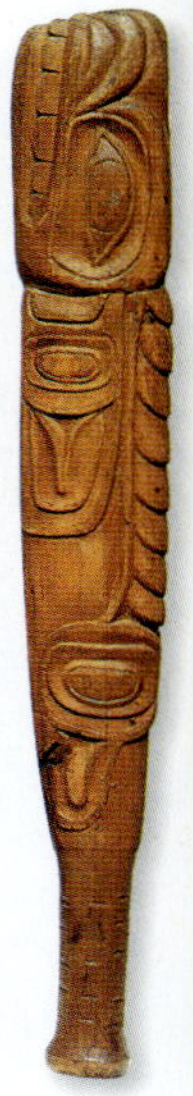

Haida Halibut Club

Abundant Sources of Nutrients

Across North America, deer were plentiful, as were buffalo and antelope in the Great Plains. In the East, lobsters, clams, mussels, bass, and cod provided rich sources of protein while, in the Southeast, Indians ate wild geese and squid. Indians on the Northwest coast smoked salmon and halibut in longhouses, and derived an abundant source of oil from whales and seals. Fat was rendered from the meat of bears, which were common throughout North America.

Food Ceremonies and Rituals

American Indian people, recognizing a social contract between themselves and the animals, fish, birds, and plants that they harvested for food, honored the living things whose lives they took. "First Food" observances were widespread: in the Northeast, the Iroquois and other tribes participated in the Green Corn ceremony and gave thanks for the arrival of strawberries. In the Southwest, corn was honored, while, in the Pacific Northwest, rituals marked the first catch of salmon and other fish. The Inuit celebrated the first deer, seal, whale, or other large animals killed by a young hunter.

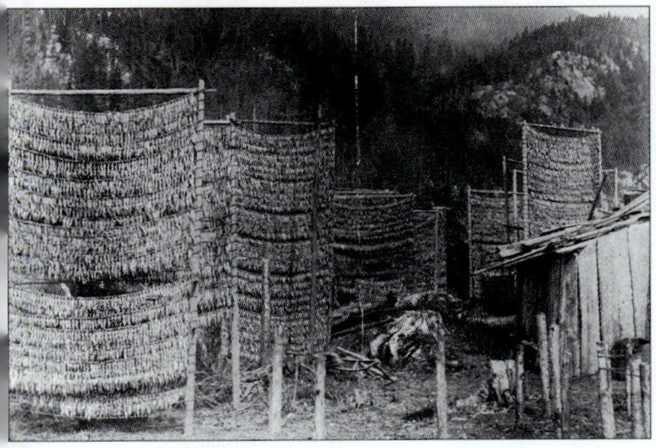

◁ Curing Candle Fish
In British Columbia, Canada, Indian tribes caught eulachon (candle fish) in spring, and preserved some of the catch for winter by drying it on racks in the sun. These tiny fish were prized mainly for their oil – a popular seasoning. They were left to ripen in covered pits for several days, then boiled in water. Once the mixture had settled, the oil was collected off the surface.

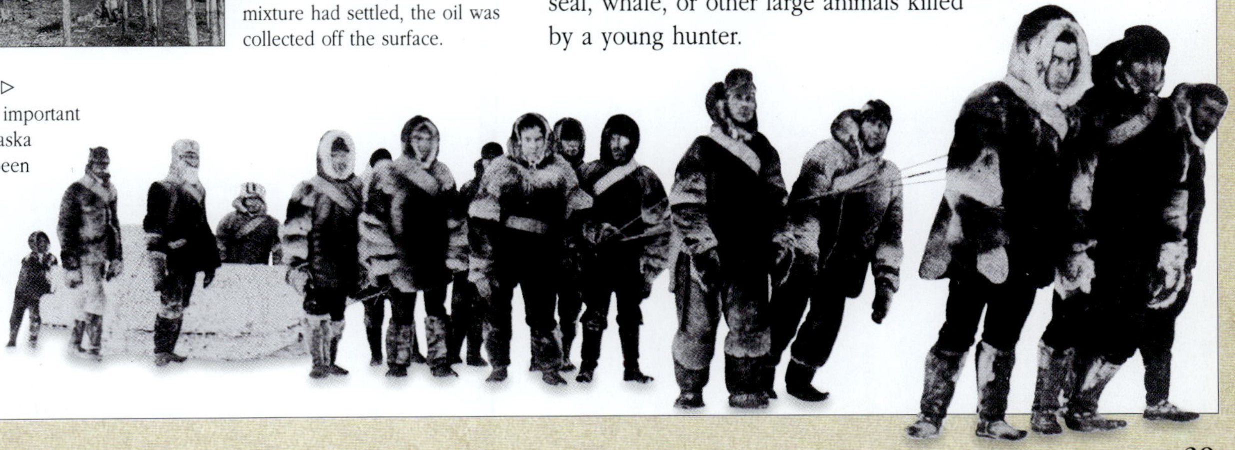

All Hands to the Whale ▷
Whale meat has always been an important source of food to the Inuit in Alaska and Canada. After a whale has been caught, it takes many hands to pull it ashore, as pictured here. Once grounded, it is cut up and distributed to the participating crews and community, according to formal, prescribed rules.

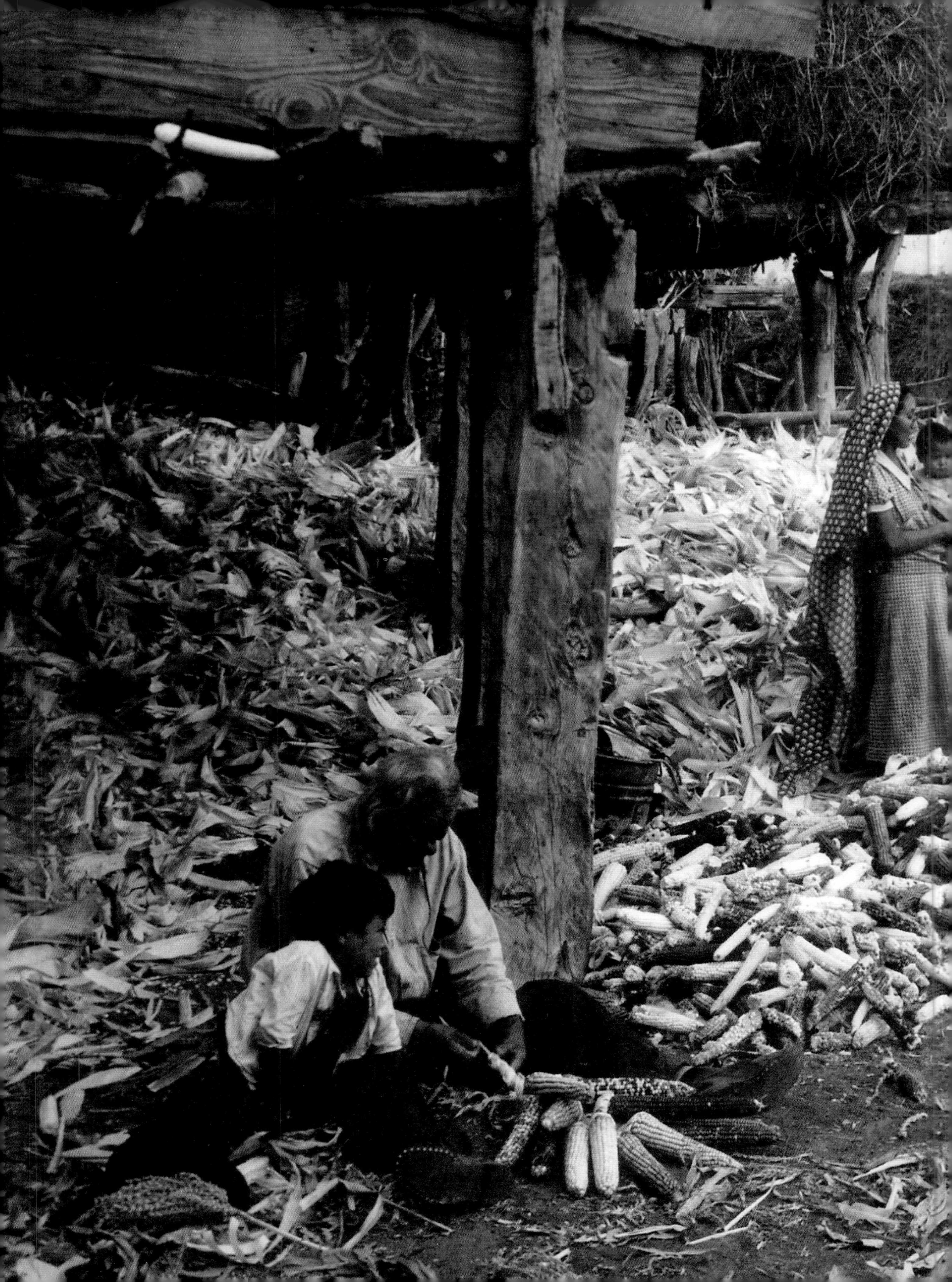

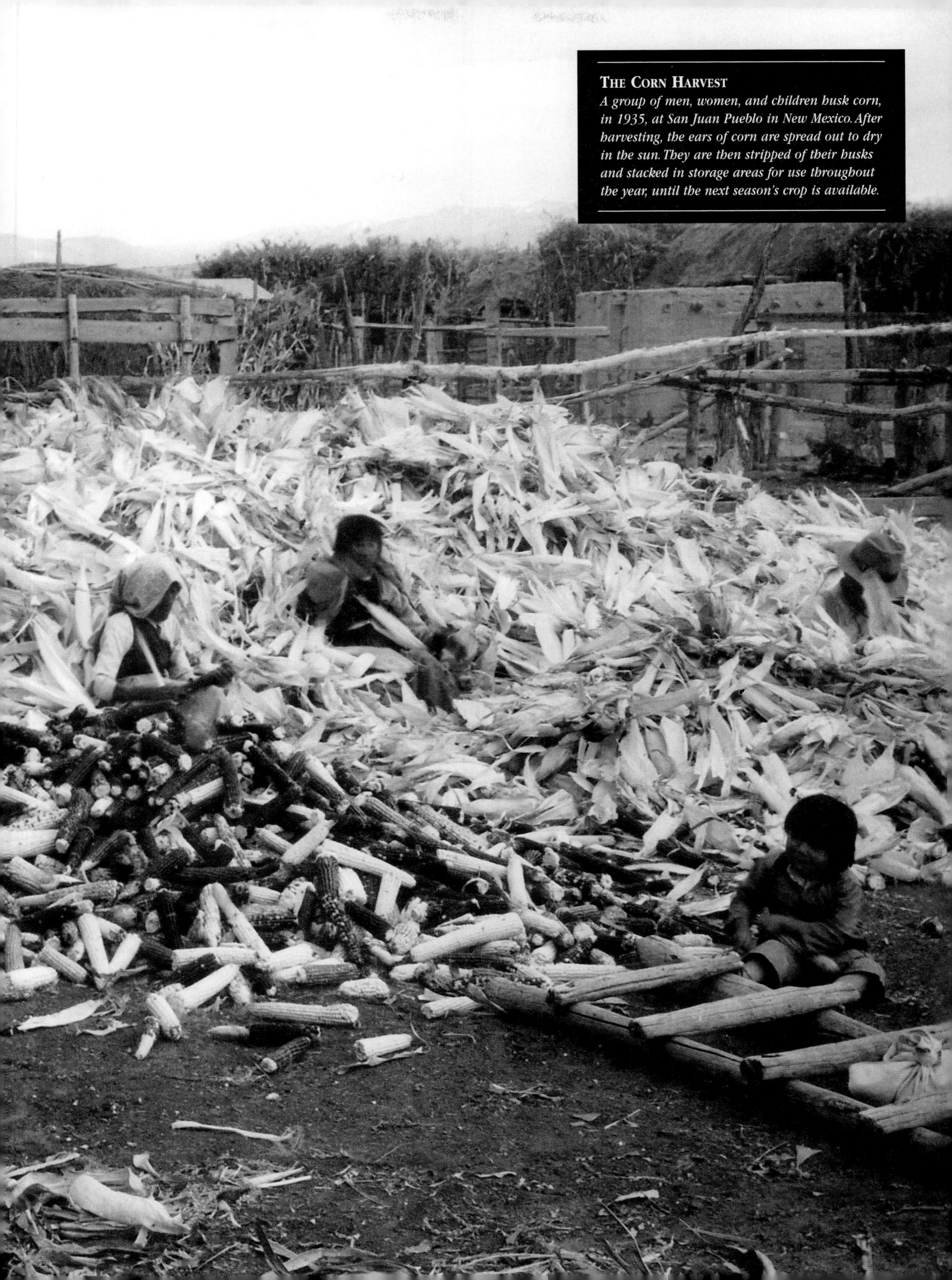

The Corn Harvest
A group of men, women, and children husk corn, in 1935, at San Juan Pueblo in New Mexico. After harvesting, the ears of corn are spread out to dry in the sun. They are then stripped of their husks and stacked in storage areas for use throughout the year, until the next season's crop is available.

INDIAN HOMELANDS DISRUPTED

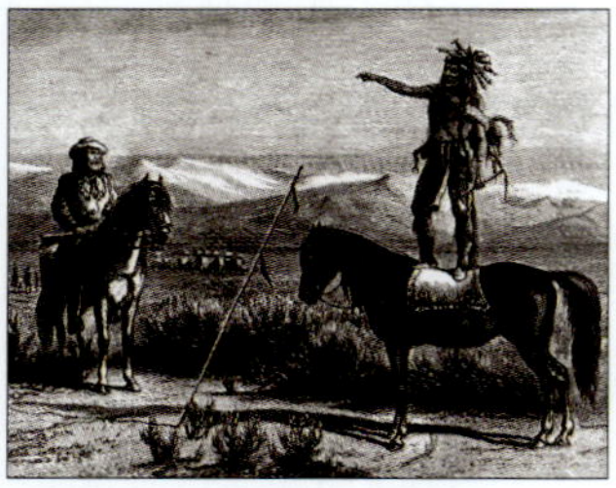

HALTING THE WAGON TRAIN
In this *Harper's Weekly* image, a chief forbids the passage of a wagon train – part of the steady stream of settlers passing through the Great Plains on their way to California and Oregon.

DURING THE MID-NINETEENTH CENTURY, Indians saw thousands of settlers, miners, farmers, and squatters pour onto their tribal lands west of the Mississippi River. The vast influx drastically altered the traditional way of life: the emigrants carried European diseases that caused massive epidemics among tribes; friction developed along travel routes crossing Indian-owned lands; and increasing numbers of settlers killed or drove off the herds of buffalo so vital to Plains Indians' survival. Eventually, troops were deployed to protect travelers and to punish the Natives.

DAKOTA HISTORY RECORDED

Tribal historians reckoned time by recording one outstanding event for each year in their winter counts. The Big Missouri's Winter Count covered 131 years, from 1796 to 1926, in the lives of the Dakota Indians who lived along the Missouri River.

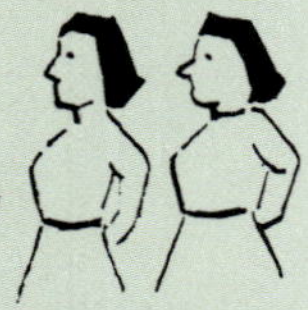

1800
Two friendly white women, dressed in long gowns, arrive among the Dakotas during troubled times. The women were so godlike that the Indians did not harm them.

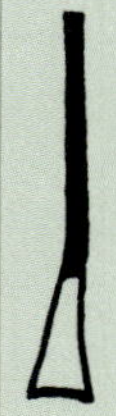

1814
A Pawnee Indian carrying a gun is killed. This was the first time this group of Dakotas had seen such a weapon.

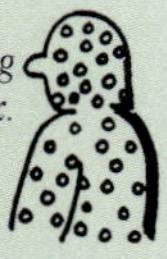

1819
Many Dakotas die during the winter from smallpox. The contagious disease, previously unknown to the group, caused Indian populations to plummet.

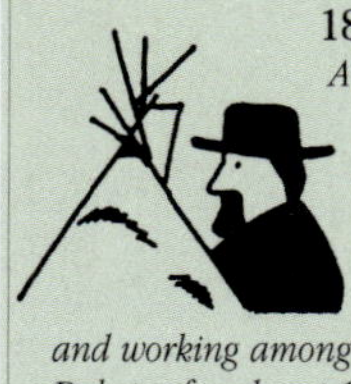

1839
A white trader sets up his store in a tipi. French fur traders had been living and working among this group of Dakotas for almost 100 years.

1861
In 1861, many babies and children die from an unknown disease.

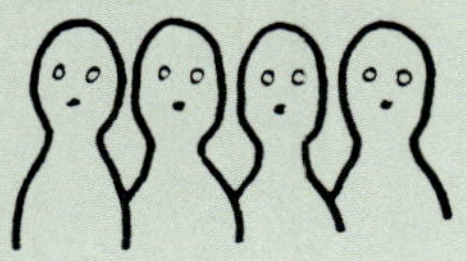

THOUSANDS OF pioneers streamed westward in the 1840s. Mostly white and American-born, from cities on the Atlantic seaboard and villages in the Midwest and Upper South, they traveled over water and land routes, by foot, horse, wagon, or coach. Hoping to better themselves, they hungered for better farms and pastureland and for the fortunes to be made from panning for gold.

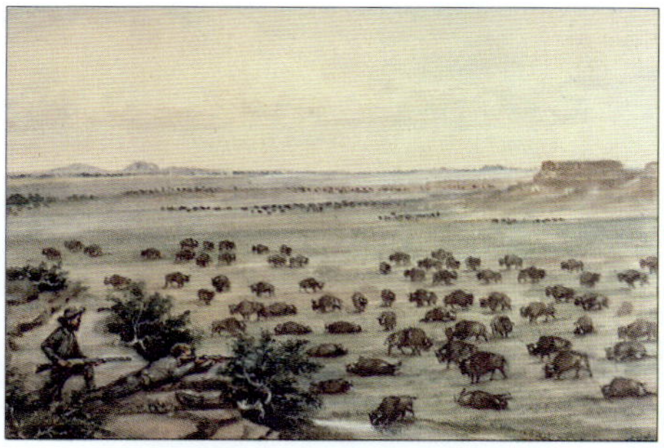

KILLING THE BUFFALO
In the 1850s, white explorers, emigrants, fur traders, and powerfully armed professional hunters pursued buffalo on the Great Plains, without the consent of the Indians whose homeland it was, severely diminishing the Plains Indians' primary means of subsistence.

The emigrants brought with them European diseases to which the Native population had no resistance. In 1833, trappers from the Hudson's Bay Company carried malaria into California's valleys, where the disease wiped out an estimated 20,000 Indians. In the late 1830s, smallpox swept across the Plains from the Missouri River to the Pacific Northwest, and into Canada and Alaska. The disease weakened whole Indian populations shortly before any significant numbers of immigrants arrived.

The gold rush of 1848 brought to California's Sierra Nevadas thousands of gold-struck adventurers, who were intolerant of Native peoples. They pushed them off their lands, preventing them from harvesting acorns or grass seed – their traditional diet. By the 1860s, the Indian population of California had declined by as much as 70 percent.

During the 1850s, an increasing number of forts and military roads began to appear, built to protect the traders, trappers, miners, and squatters. More protection led to yet more white emigration to the West: lumbermen came, who provided wood to build army posts; these, in turn, were supplied with goods by traders; steamboats carried travelers, adventurers, traders, and supplies; and homesteaders staked claims on Indian lands.

The flood of people destroyed traditional Indian homelands. The emigrants harvested precious prairie timber for campfires, and their livestock stripped bare the grasses and destroyed animal habitats and the wild plants upon which the Indians depended for food and medicines. Buffalo, the mainstay of the Plains Indians' lifestyle, were threatened in a variety of ways: Native peoples, forced by their dependence on trade with white settlers, hunted more buffalo for their thick pelts; the throngs of emigrants drove off the buffalo and other wild animals; and the railroads brought white buffalo hunters to the Plains. Drought on the Central Plains, coupled with diseases carried by the emigrants' livestock, added to the decline in buffalo numbers.

In Canada, due to the vast extent of the territory, the relative scarcity of non-Indian settlers, and the rigors of the terrain, westward migration was not a serious problem until the 1870s and 1880s.

Intensifying Conflict

Confrontations rarely occurred between Plains Indians and westbound emigrant wagons

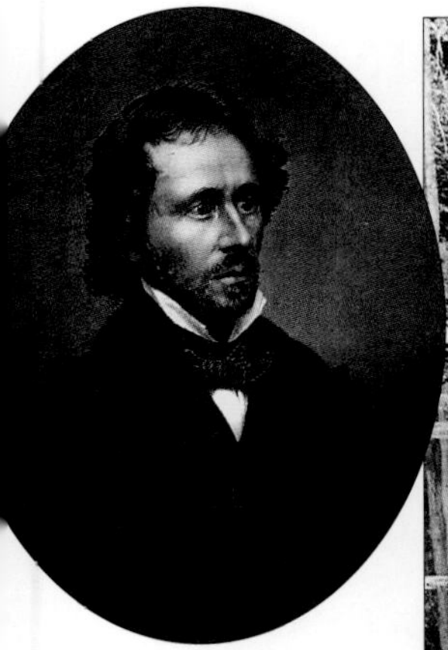

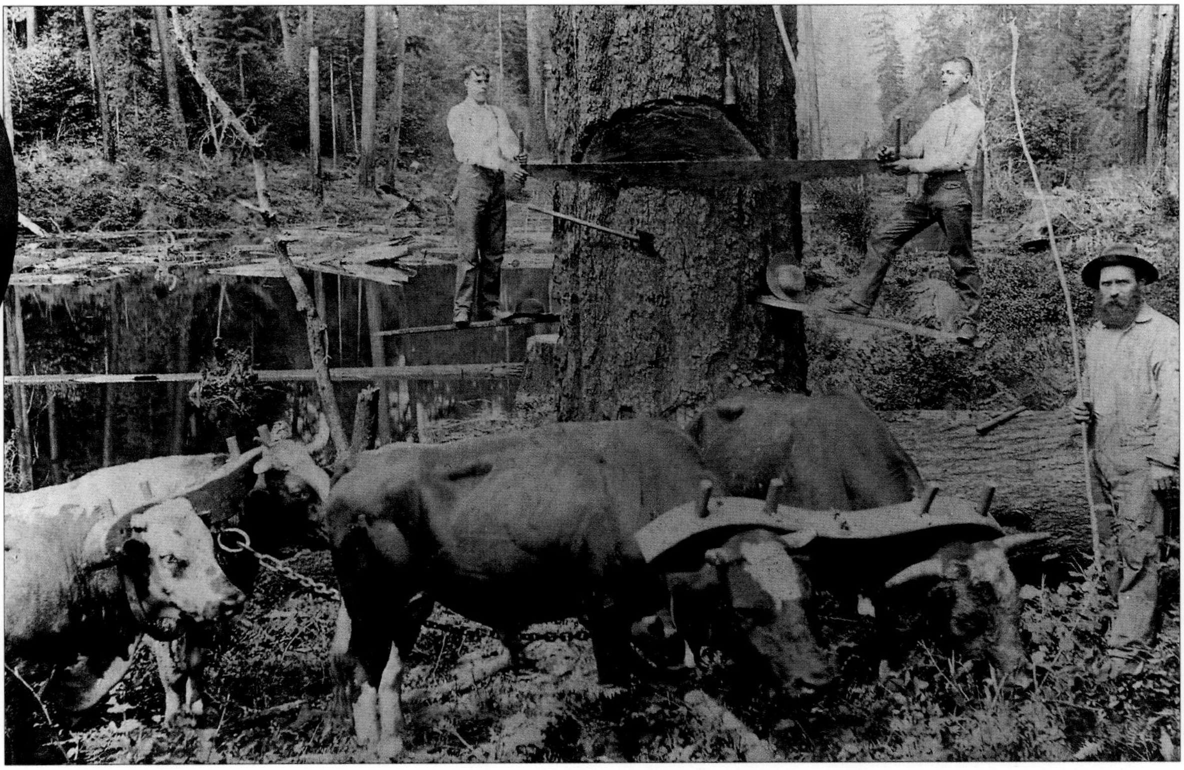

, GO WEST!
)uring the 1840s and 1850s, .merican explorer and map-1aker John Charles Fremont credited as the father of the)regon Trail), led five xpeditions throughout the Vest. Relying on Delaware ndians as hunters and scouts, remont explored thousands of niles of Indian country. His ptimistic reports encouraged nany emigrants to head west.

luring the 1840s, but, during the 1850s and .860s, their interactions became less friendly ınd more dangerous – a situation for which he emigrants shared a major responsibility. Sometimes Indians stole horses or camp equipment, but, more often, they served as guides or traded game for flour, sugar, or other staples. In the absence of government promises o compensate Indians for the destruction of heir resources, Pawnee and other Indian groups levied fees for the wood and grass used by the travelers; but the idea that Indians had any right to claim payments infuriated some emigrants, who refused to pay tributes and eadily instigated skirmishes. These led the Indians to retaliate on subsequent emigrants, which, in turn, caused emigrants to fire on innocent Indians.

Emigrants were largely unaware that Indians might have their own fears of violent encounters. News of approaching wagon trains, however, filled most Natives with dread and apprehension. Paiute Sarah Winnemucca has described how her family were so terrified at the approach of white people that her mother buried her under a sage brush.

As conflicts over land and its resources intensified between settlers and the Plains Indians, trading forts situated along emigrant roads were converted into military posts.

△ LOGGING PARTY
During the 1850s, westbound emigrants cut down and helped themselves to timber along the trails and river banks in Indian territories, paying no heed to who owned the land. Small parties of loggers with only two yoke of oxen, such as the group above, could extract as much as 1 million ft (304,800 m) of lumber in a few weeks.

▽ SETTING UP HOME
After living in tents and wagons, travelers longed for real homes. Some dug out a hillside and moved in with their furniture. Other settlers lived in flimsy shacks; where timber was plentiful, they built log cabins. Those who decided to homestead on the treeless prairies built houses out of large blocks of tough sod, held together with clay, like this one near Coburg, Nebraska.

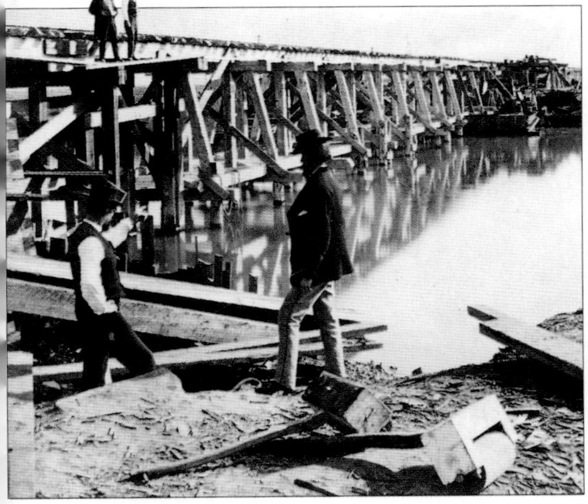

◁ ACCELERATING WESTWARD MIGRATION
Railroads revolutionized travel in North America and promoted westward migration on a grand scale. By the 1850s, trains with reliable locomotives moved over wooden tracks and bridges, carrying settlers onto US Indian lands. This railroad bridge, built over the river at Salt Lake City, Utah, was located near the beginnings of a Mormon community.

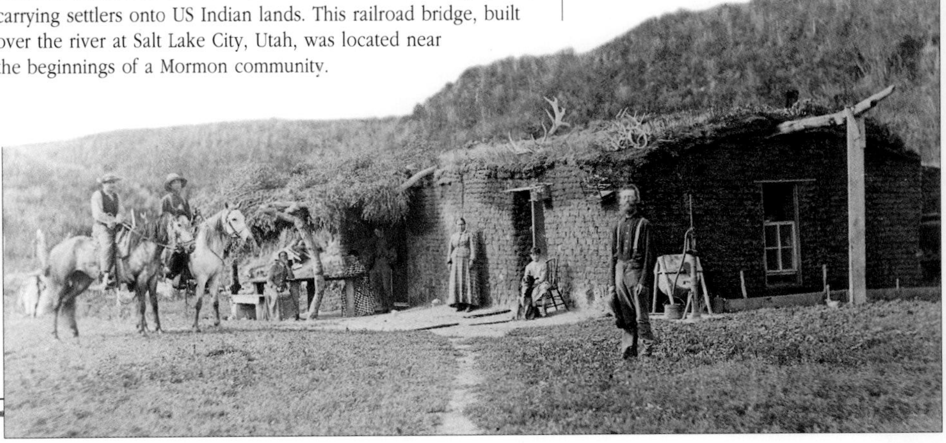

The Rush for Gold

In January 1848, gold was found near Sacramento, California, and by May 1849, 5,000 wagons were heading west on the California Trail. Many of the miners who rushed to the gold fields in the valleys west of the Sierra Nevadas saw the local Native peoples as obstacles and killed them with impunity.

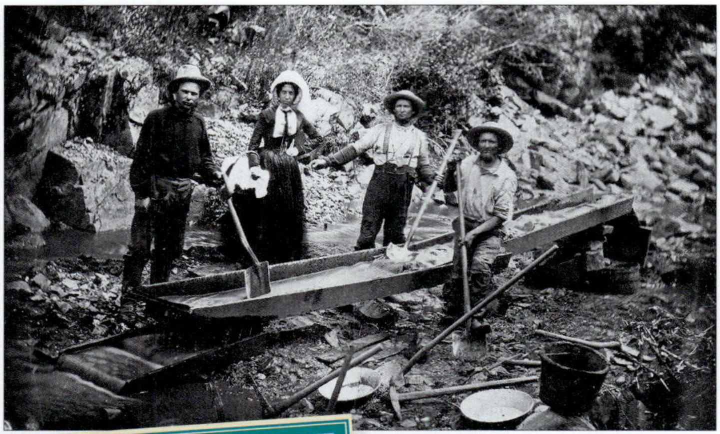

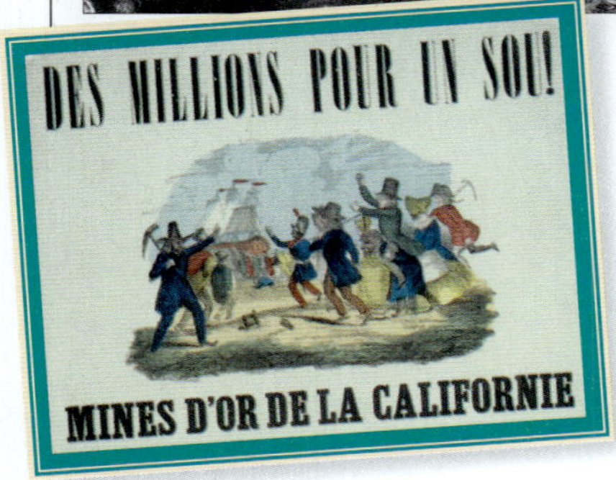

△ Gold Fever
The California Gold Rush attracted thousands of European adventurers in search of easy wealth. Few found it, but some stayed on to become farmers, ranchers, and merchants.

◁ Prospectors Welcome
Would-be prospectors arriving in San Francisco were encouraged in their ambitions by signs in French, English, German, Spanish, and Chinese.

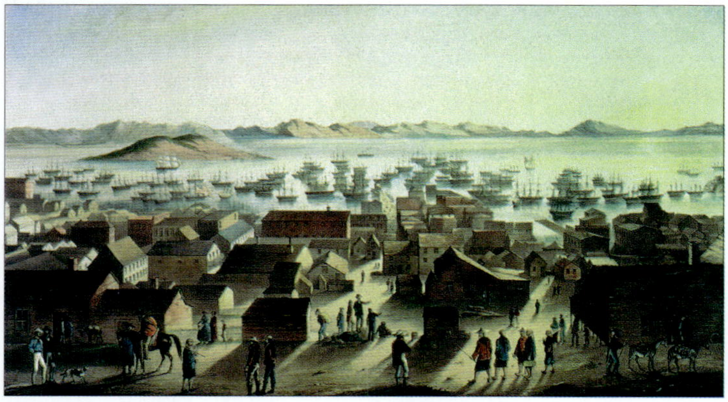

△ San Francisco Booms
In 1849, San Francisco was a bedlam of shacks, tents, gambling halls, and dingy saloons. By 1855, however, dozens of churches and schools had emerged.

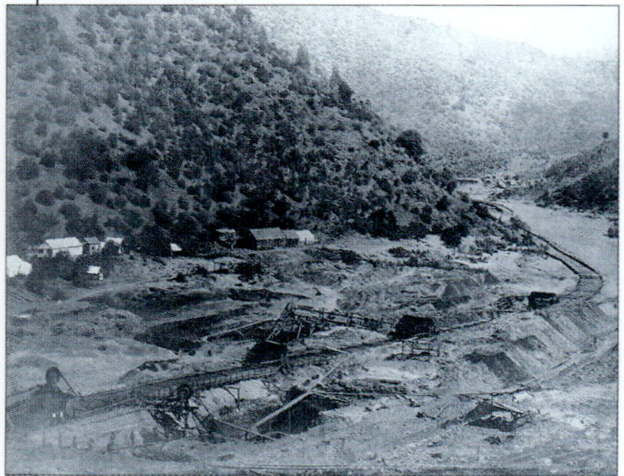

◁ Fishing Threatened
Salmon, a traditional food for local Indians, began to disappear from streams that were silted and dammed by mining activities. Mining also disrupted Indians' hunting and gathering activities.

Blazing the Trail

Originally an Indian trail, and one of the few transcontinental routes, the Santa Fe Trail was used by traders carrying goods from Westport, Missouri, to Santa Fe, New Mexico, primarily from 1821 to 1880. From the 1840s onward, the Oregon Trail carried traffic from the Missouri River to the Pacific Ocean.

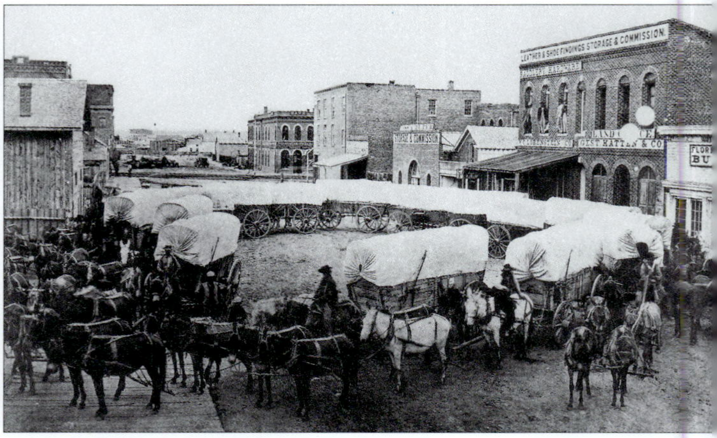

△ Wagons Roll into Denver
By the end of the 1850s, following the discovery of gold in the Rockies in 1858, towns of white emigrants spread throughout the plains and mountains of Colorado. In Denver, Colorado, which became a major town in the West, travelers made wagon repairs and loaded up with supplies from the shops lining its wide streets.

Forts Line the Routes

By the 1840s, there were a few forts along the routes where emigrants could rest, make repairs to their wagons, and buy mules and other supplies. At first, these forts were simply trading posts where Natives and traders met to exchange goods, as well as providing a site for treaty negotiations with Indian tribes. By the 1850s, however, they had become the headquarters for many military campaigns against Indian tribes.

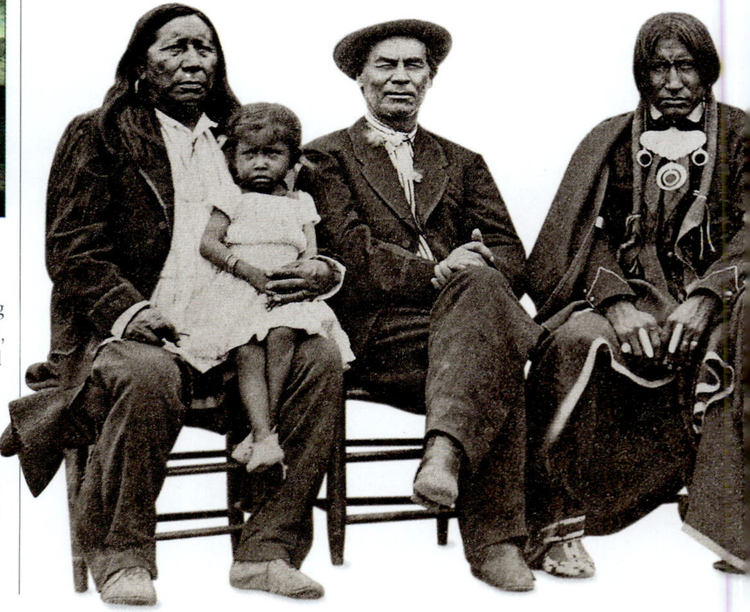

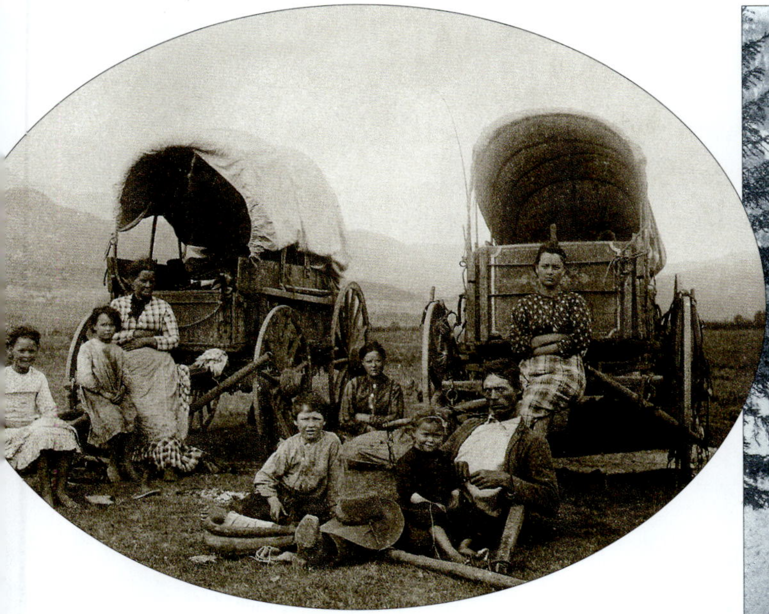

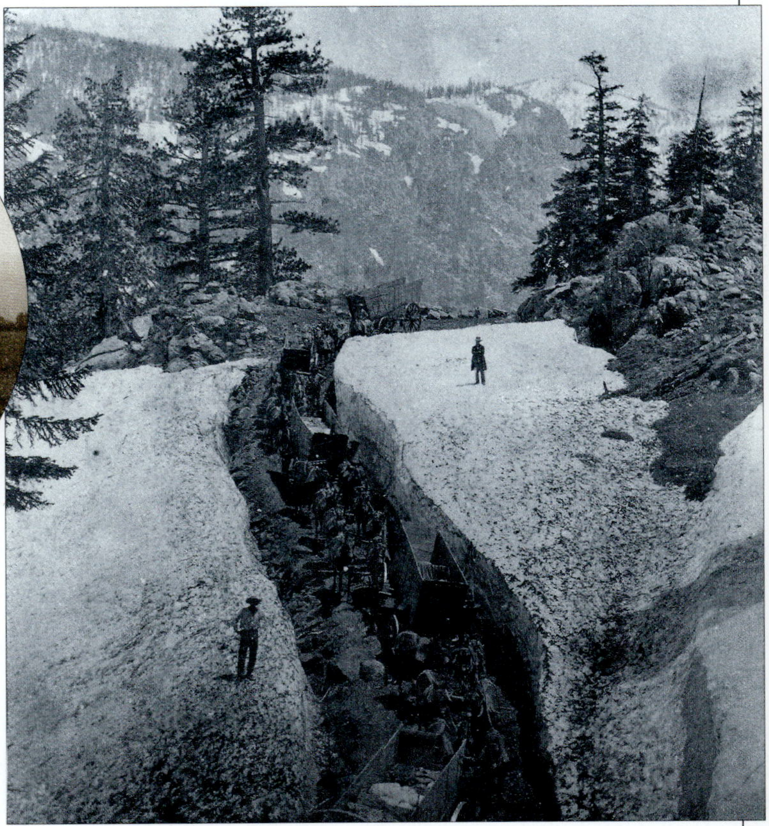

. CAMPING EN ROUTE
ravel was slow and tiring for the migrants journeying west. Rising before unrise each day, they progressed to the ext night's resting place, where animals vere turned loose inside a circle of vagons, cows milked, supplies unloaded, ents pitched, and supper prepared.

A WINTER'S TRAIL ▷
Emigrants raced west, trying to reach their destinations in California and Oregon before the onset of snowstorms in the mountains. On the route pictured here, leading down into Lake Valley, California, from the Sierra Nevadas, travelers battle against deep snow.

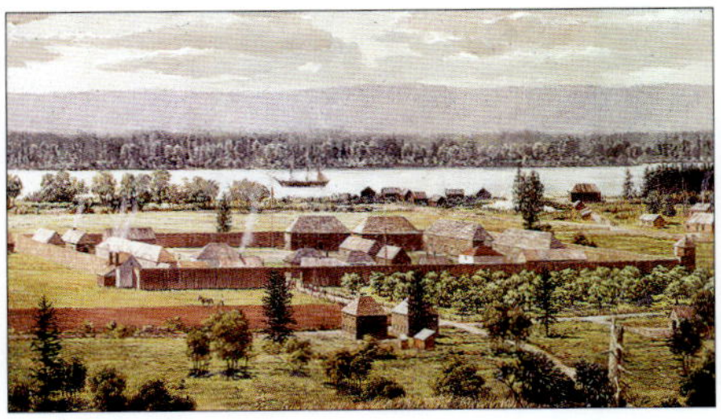

RAIL PROTECTION ▷
uilt in 1824 on the Columbia iver, by the Hudson's Bay ompany, Fort Vancouver was major military headquarters uring the Pacific Northwest ndian wars of the 1850s. The ort's powerful stockade nclosed warehouses, offices, nd dormitories.

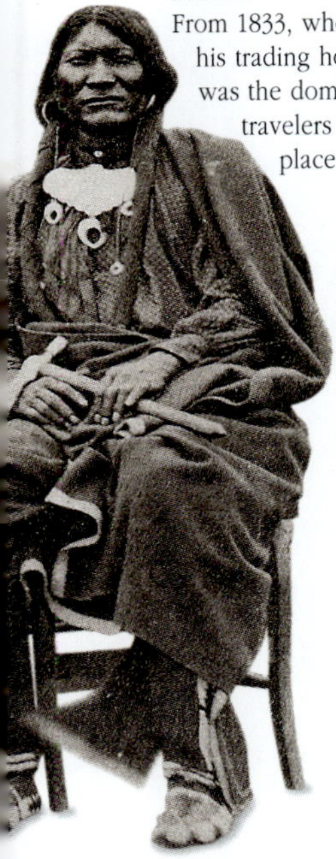

◁ TRADING AT BENT'S FORT
From 1833, when trader William Bent (second from left), constructed his trading houses along the Arkansas River in Colorado, Bent's Fort was the dominant structure in the Southwest. A stopping place for travelers bound for the Rocky Mountains, it was also a gathering place for Indians, who visited the fort to trade and socialize.

"... a desperate war of starvation and extinction is imminent and inevitable, unless prompt measure shall prevent it."

WILLIAM BENT, INDIAN AGENT, WRITING TO THE US COMMISSIONER OF INDIAN AFFAIRS, 1859

YAKIMAS DEFIANT

The Yakima War erupted in eastern Washington and northern Idaho in 1855, when Yakima Indians and warriors from other tribes tried to resist the influx of settlers onto their lands: they were enraged by treaties requiring them to give up their lands and move to a reservation. Yakima Chief Kamiakin's forces were defeated, however, and his brother, Chief Owhi, killed.

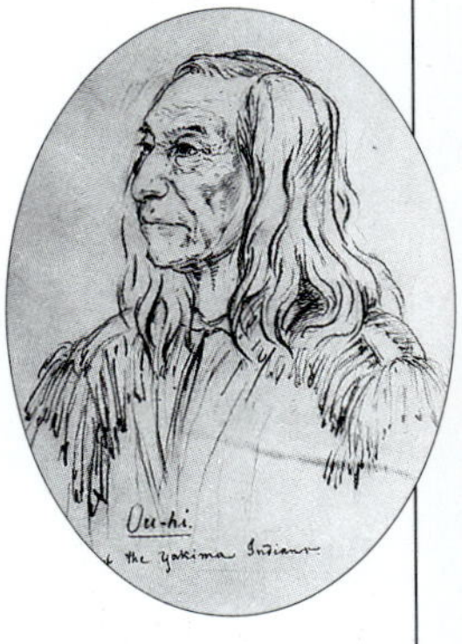

CHIEF OWHI

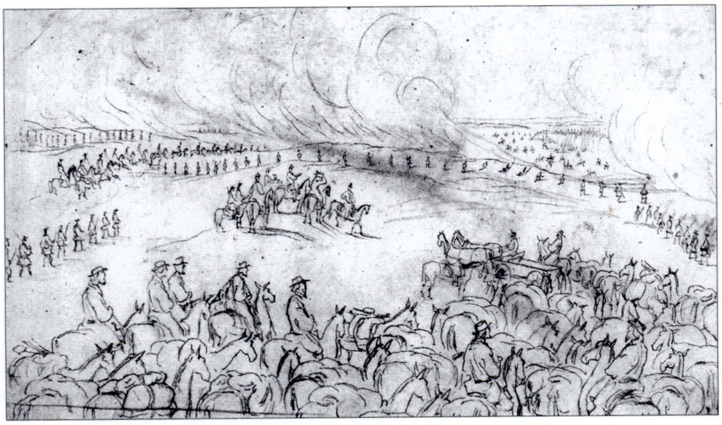

△ GRASS FIRES FAIL
In September 1858, 500 Yakima and allied Indians set grass on fire in an unsuccessful attempt to prevent troops evicting them from their homes. But the troops rode through the smoke, firing on the Indians until they gave up and withdrew from the action.

Opening Up the West

During the 1840s, 1850s, and 1860s, thousands of Americans headed west, their interest stimulated by guide books, news articles, and reports by explorers. Most emigrants chose land routes: between 1840 and 1867, some 350,000 people traveled the overland routes to California or Oregon, while others trekked part of the way to areas such as Colorado and Utah. After 1869, the completion of the trans-continental Union Pacific railroad and the construction of additional railroads brought a steady stream of white settlers westward – and onto Indian lands. This map shows important land routes over which settlers, miners, homesteaders and others journeyed West.

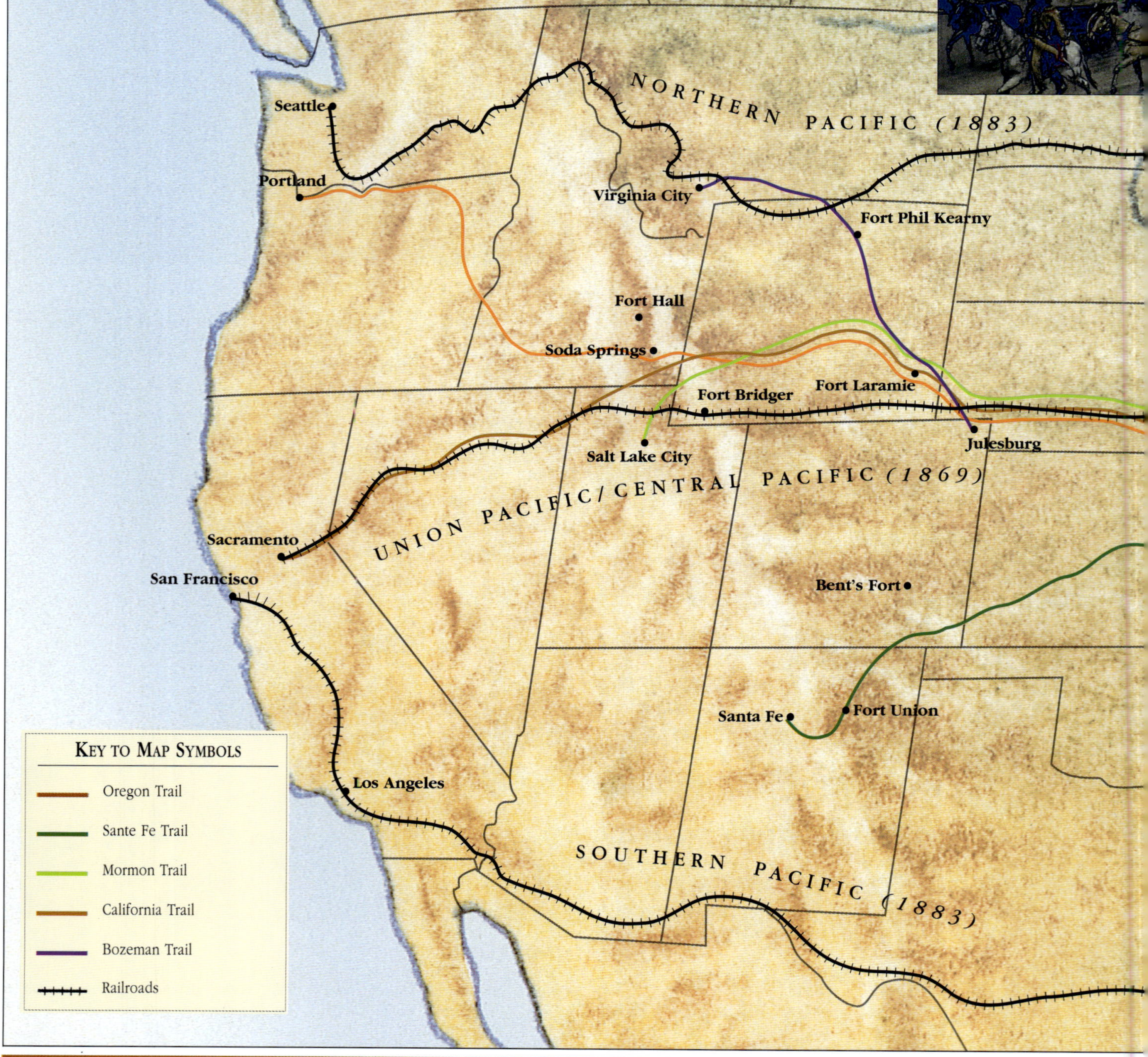

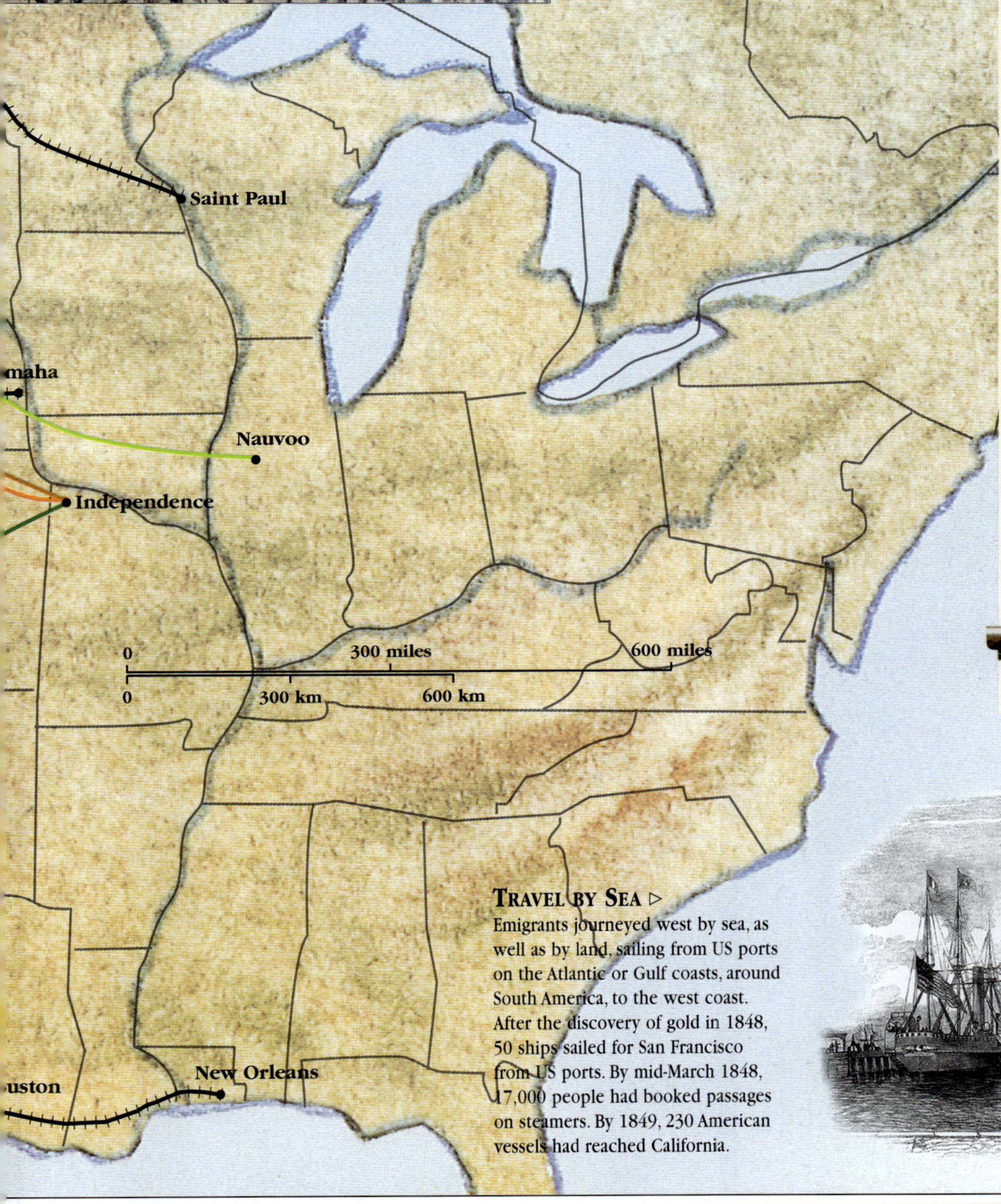

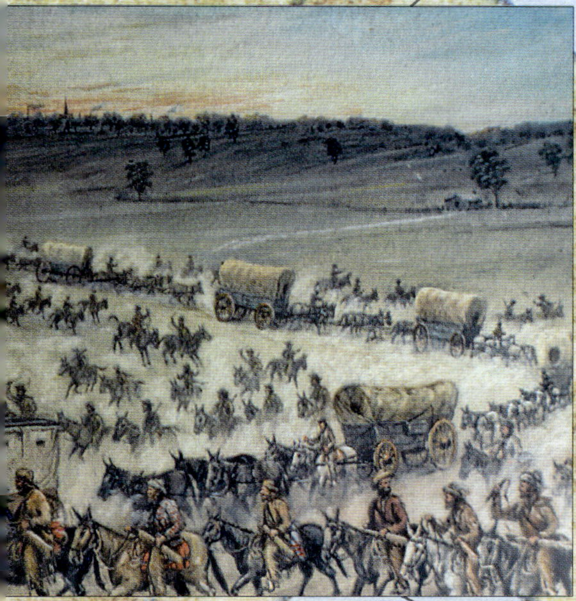

◁ EXODUS TO THE WEST

For many years in the mid-eighteenth century, a stream of emigrants headed West. They gathered in the Missouri towns of Independence, Westport, and St. Joseph, or Council Bluffs in Iowa, and joined wagon trains bound for California or Oregon. A typical train of 50 wagons might stretch for one mile (1.6 km). After the discovery of gold in California in 1848, the stream became a flood: by the end of the year, some 10,000 prospectors had reached California. During one three-week period in spring 1849, nearly 18,000 people headed for the gold fields.

CANADIAN PACIFIC RAILWAY

In 1867, much of Canada's western region was unsettled. In an effort to secure the union of British Columbia with the new confederation, the Canadian government promised the region a trans-Canadian railroad. Work began on the Canadian Pacific Railway (CPR) in 1881 and the track between the east and west coasts was joined in British Columbia in 1885. The CPR, which acquired 25 million acres (10 million hectares) of land, sold any undeveloped land to settlers, so fostering Canada's westward expansion.

ITEMS OF TRADE

Trade with Europeans benefited Native peoples for a time since the goods they received in exchange for beaver pelts eased their existence. Ultimately, however, these items increased their dependence on whites.

FOR ONE BEAVER SKIN A TRAPPER COULD BUY ONE OF THE FOLLOWING:
- ½ lb (23 g) beads
- 1 kettle
- 1 lb (45 g) shot
- 5 lbs (2.25 kg) sugar
- 1 lb (45 g) tobacco
- 12 buttons
- 12 fish hooks

FOR FOUR SKINS A TRAPPER COULD BUY:
- 1 pistol

FOR SIX SKINS A TRAPPER COULD BUY:
- 1 blanket

FOR TWELVE SKINS A TRAPPER COULD BUY:
- 1 rifle

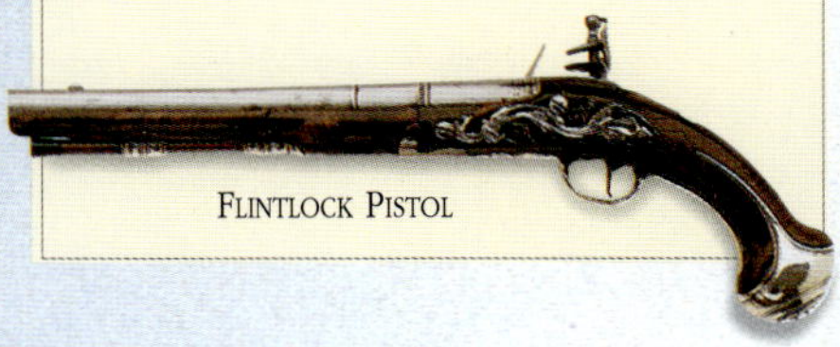

FLINTLOCK PISTOL

TRAVEL BY SEA ▷

Emigrants journeyed west by sea, as well as by land, sailing from US ports on the Atlantic or Gulf coasts, around South America, to the west coast. After the discovery of gold in 1848, 50 ships sailed for San Francisco from US ports. By mid-March 1848, 17,000 people had booked passages on steamers. By 1849, 230 American vessels had reached California.

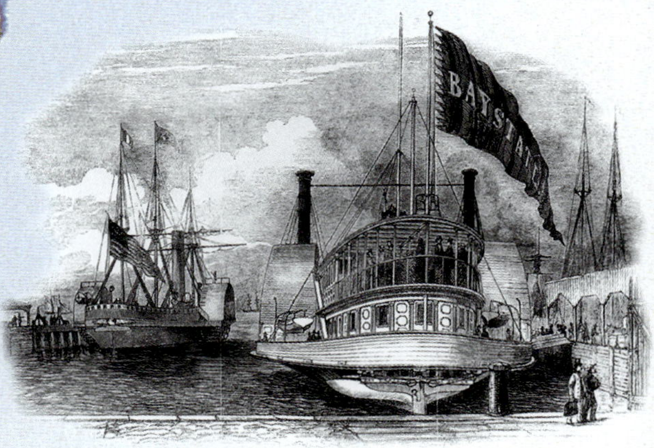

ARRIVAL OF THE MISSIONARIES

BEFORE MISSIONARIES ARRIVED in North America, Indians practiced hundreds of religious traditions, often with elaborate tribal ceremonies, such as the Sun Dance of the Lakota and other Plains peoples, the Kachina dances of the Pueblo peoples, and the Midwinter ceremony of the Iroquois. The British, Spanish, and French missionaries – Catholic and Protestant alike – viewed these ceremonies as heathenistic and contemptible, and tried to force Indians to abandon their practices and convert to Christianity.

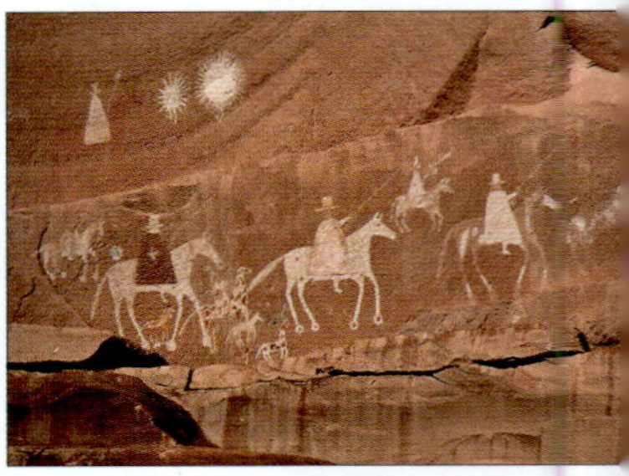

EARLY CHRISTIAN VISITORS
A pictograph on a wall in Canyon de Chelly, Arizona, showing a column of Spanish soldiers and priests, testifies to the arrival of missionaries in the mid-sixteenth century.

A PIONEER MISSIONARY

In 1836, Henry Spaulding set up a mission at Lapwai, Idaho, among the Nez Percé people, who tolerated the Presbyterian missionary. He founded a school where he introduced agriculture, and his wife, Eliza, taught spinning and weaving. Henry later published biblical and other works in the Nez Percé language.

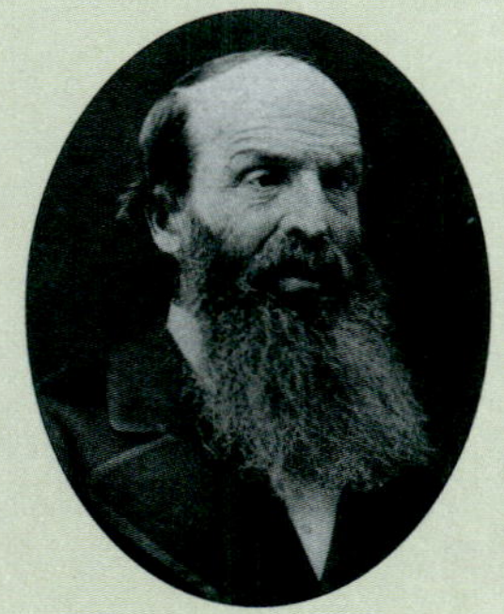

HENRY SPAULDING

WHEN FRENCH PRIESTS first arrived in Canada in the early seventeenth century, and Protestant missionaries in the early nineteenth century, Indians received them as people with spiritual power (as well as suppliers of tools and goods they desired), and some became converts. In Christian villages, like Sillery, Quebec, and Metlakatla, in British Columbia, the Indians lived under the religious, political, and economic control of the missionaries, who tried to persuade them to abandon their traditional beliefs.

Methods of Conversion

From the late 1640s to the 1670s, Puritans in the 13 British colonies founded 14 "praying towns" among southern New England Algonquians. There, potential converts were isolated from unconverted Indians and from the British settlers encroaching on their lands. When it became clear that the Indians were not giving up their own spiritual convictions, the British abandoned efforts at conversion – but not before denouncing Indian beliefs.

The Spanish Franciscan missionaries in the Southwest concentrated Indians in settlements around mission churches, where they worked at digging ditches, building irrigation dams, and tending livestock. In 1769, Father Junipero Serra founded the first of 21 Indian missions along the Californian coast, intending to convert the Indians to Catholicism. Members of the Hupa, Cahuilla, Cupa, and at least 20 other tribes, who volunteered or were forced to live

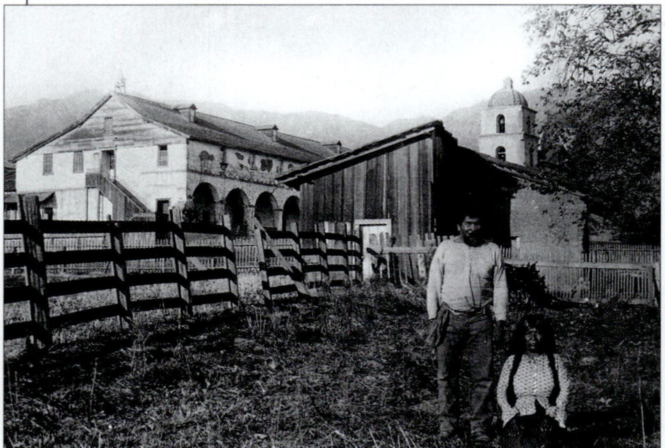

△ REGULAR ATTENDERS
This Chumash Indian couple, pictured in the 1880s, frequented the mission church in Santa Barbara, California, which was founded in 1786. When missions were shut down in 1834, 15,000 Indians were released.

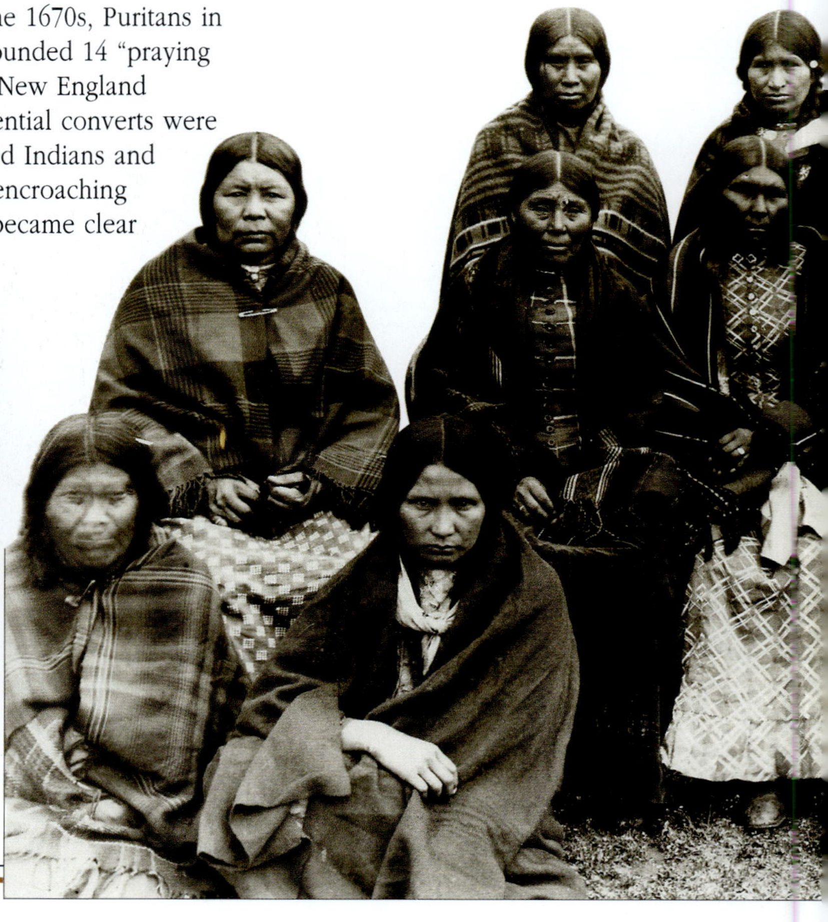

n missions, became known as "mission ndians." In 1834, the Mexican government ecularized the missions, thereby releasing their mmense holdings to land-hungry Mexican itizens. Some converted Indians returned to heir families, but those who had no families eft, or were too ill to travel, or whose dentities had been destroyed, lingered on.

ndian Responses to Missionary Zeal

As the reality of conquest became more real o Indian nations, tribal peoples invited nissionaries into their midst. Open to the pirituality of others and capable of adding to heir spiritual ways without sacrificing their own beliefs, Indians were surprised to discover hat the missionaries required them to give up heir traditional beliefs. Some tribes, such as he Navajos, managed to withstand much of he missionary pressure, while others gave uperficial acknowledgment to the imposed Christian religion but clung to their Indian beliefs. Other Indians believed that conversion o the conqueror's religion was the only way to naintain their existence. Native peoples even participated in the missionizing process, and ome, like Ojibway leader Peter Jones, went on o become missionaries.

> *"... if there is but one religion, why do you White people differ so much about it?"*
>
> RED JACKET'S REPLY TO MISSIONARY CRAM, BOSTON, 1828

Despite their efforts to eradicate Native beliefs, the missionaries failed to suppress traditional religious practices. Many tribal peoples simply preferred their own beliefs and ceremonies to those of the invaders. Missionaries did succeed, however, in dividing tribal societies into converts to Christianity and traditionalists, who were pitted against each other in bitter ideological conflicts.

In 1917, an act separating Church and State formally ended the partnership between federal government and the missionaries – a partnership that had existed since 1819, when, early in the history of the US government, Congress passed the Civilization Fund, which paid various missionary groups to teach the "habits and arts of civilization" to Indians.

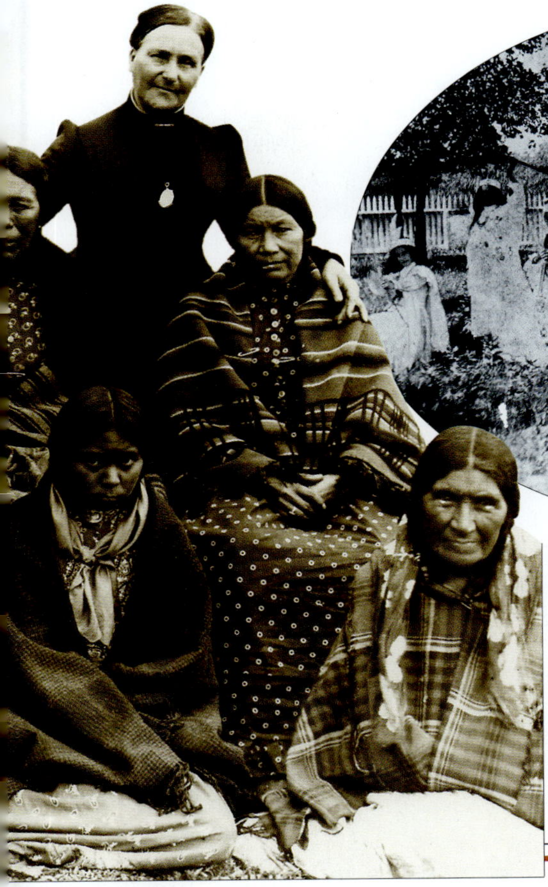

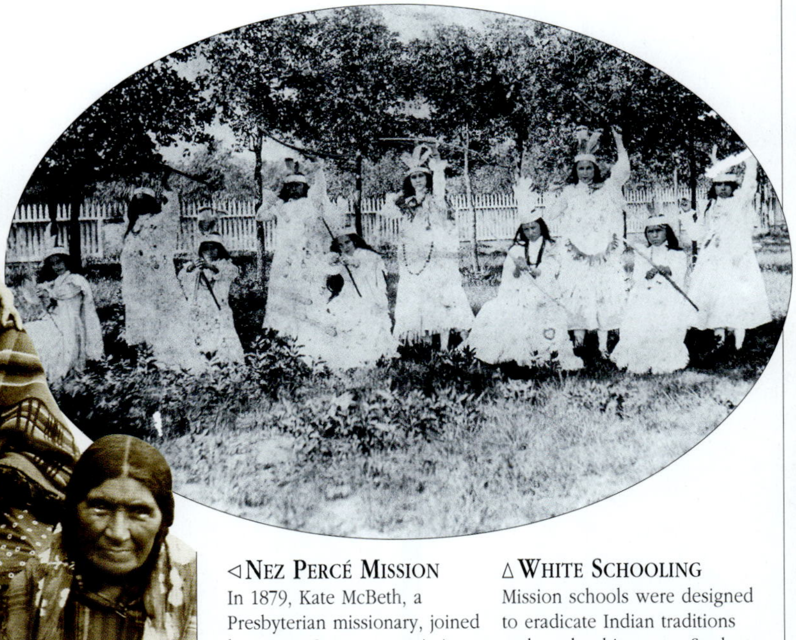

◁ NEZ PERCÉ MISSION
In 1879, Kate McBeth, a Presbyterian missionary, joined her sister, Susan, at a mission serving Nez Percé people. Although Kate believed that the Nez Percé were uncivilized heathens who knew nothing of God, she found them honest, kind, and dignified.

△ WHITE SCHOOLING
Mission schools were designed to eradicate Indian traditions and teach white ways. Students were banned from speaking their own language and taking part in traditional customs. Yet at Emahaka Mission school, girls were dressed as "Indian maidens" to perform in plays.

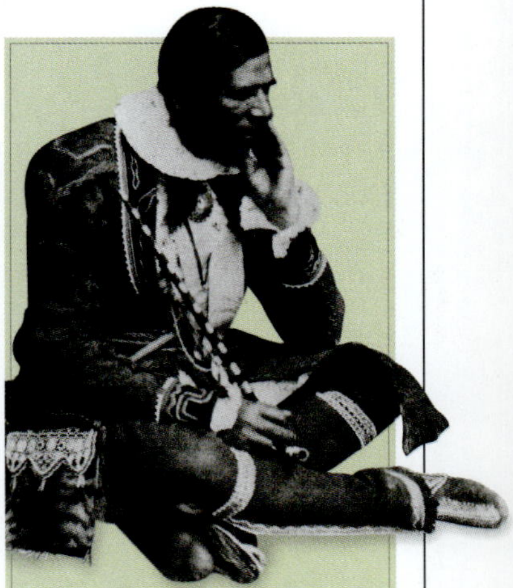

OJIBWAY MISSIONARY

In 1823, Peter Jones, a Canadian Ojibway (Chippewa) leader, was converted to Christianity at a revival meeting. He later became the first Native missionary to the Ojibways. Jones visited Britain on three occasions, delivering sermons and making numerous speeches about North American Indians. The above photograph was taken on 4 August 1845, in Edinburgh, Scotland, during his third visit to Britain.

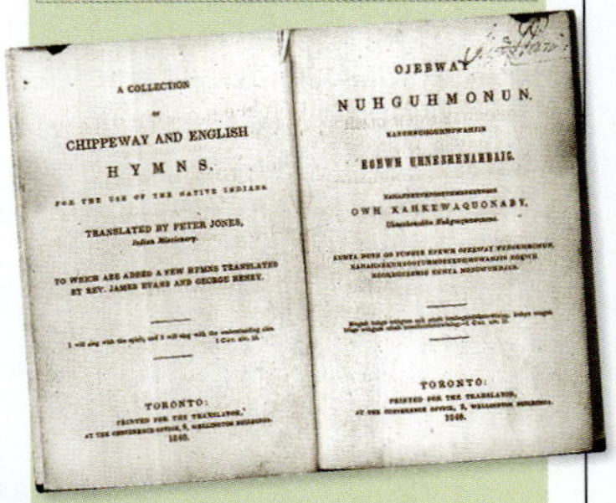

OJIBWAY TRANSLATIONS
Peter Jones's 1840 publication, A Collection of Chippewa and English Hymns, *was reprinted many times.*

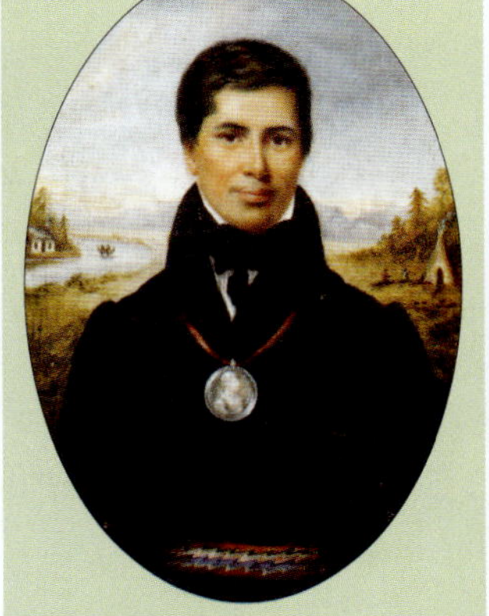

JONES THE FIGHTER
Jones fought long for the land rights of his people, the Mississaugas of Credit River, and for other Ojibway communities in southern Ontario.

All Denominations Arrive

The first missionaries, Spanish Roman Catholics belonging to the Dominican, Jesuit, Franciscan, and Augustine orders, established themselves in Florida, the Southwest, and California, while Jesuits and Récollets pioneered missions in eastern and central Canada. Protestant clergy set out later to convert Indians in the British colonies.

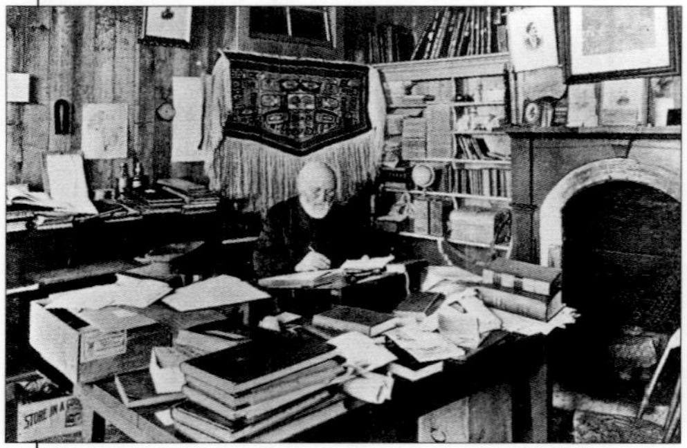

△ **Episcopal Missionary**
William Duncan spent 60 years of his life converting Tsimshian Indians to Christianity and preaching against traditional Tsimshian observances like the potlatch. He founded two Christian communities for his followers, in British Columbia and Alaska.

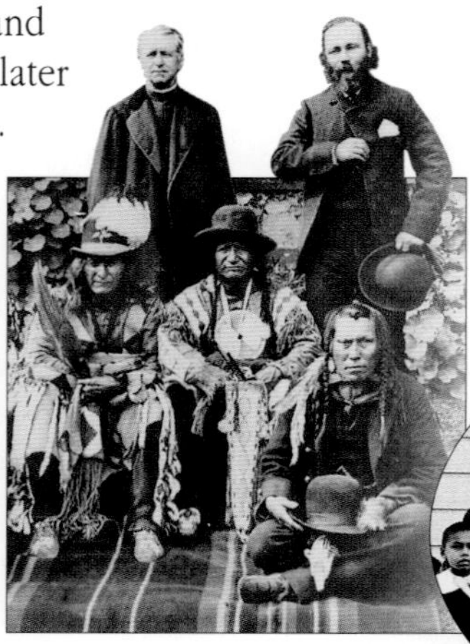

△ **Catholic Converts**
Father Albert LaCombe, one of the first Roman Catholic missionaries sent to the Canadian Northwest, spent his life working with the Blackfeet (seen here with him) and Cree peoples.

Haida Congregation ▷
Reverend Harrison and his wife are pictured, about 1880, behind a group of Haidas, who were members of his congregation at Masset, Queen Charlotte Islands, British Columbia.

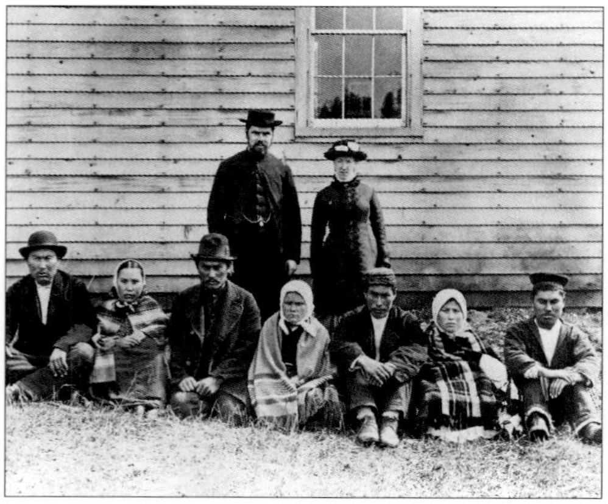

▽ **A Blend of Cultures**
Russian Orthodox missionaries respected Native rituals, accepting members into their missions without requiring radical cultural change. Churches with onion-shaped domes became a familiar sight in Aleutian settlements.

New Ceremonies

Catholic and Protestant missionaries, viewing Native peoples' religious ceremonies and rituals as superstitious, introduced Christian observances, such as mass, Sabbath services, Lenten fasting, baptism, and marriage. These seemed unreasonable to people whose beliefs and traditions were bound up with the growth and harvest of plants and with hunting.

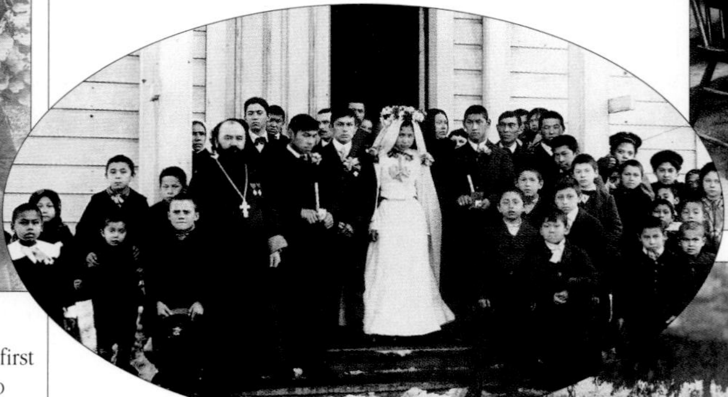

△ **Wedding Vows**
After the Russian Orthodox Church became established, wedding ceremonies replaced traditional Aleutian arranged marriages. This wedding ceremony took place in the Pribilof village of St. Paul.

Open-air Mass ▷
Luiseno and Cupa Indians are seen here taking part in an open-air mass near San Diego around 1910. Indians were used to group ceremonies, but their traditional gatherings involved the exchange of food and other goods in a vital distribution system.

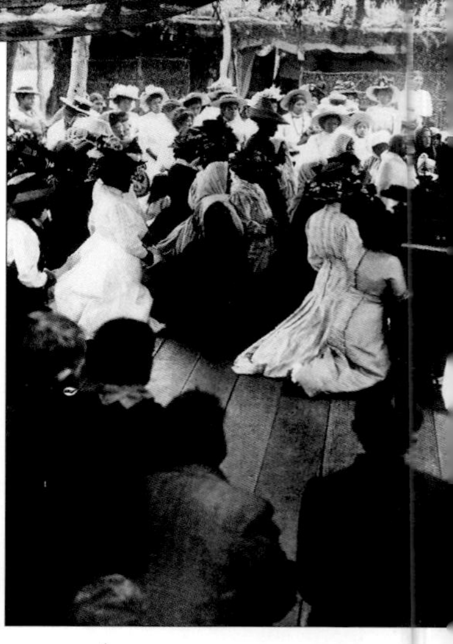

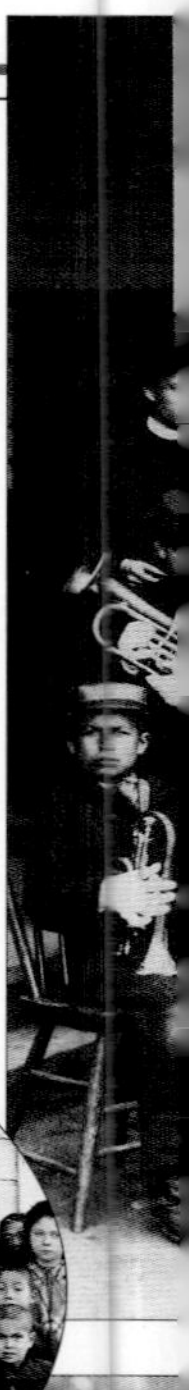

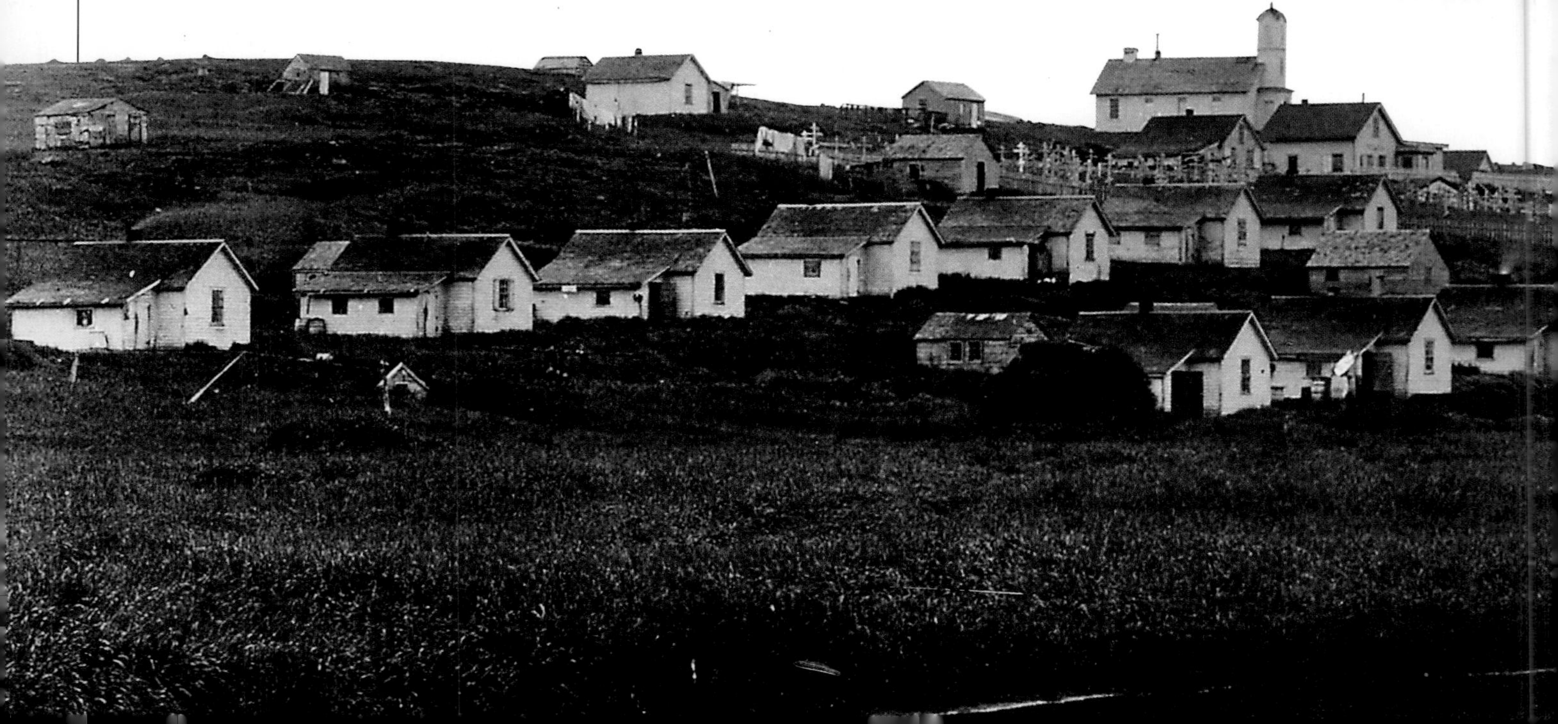

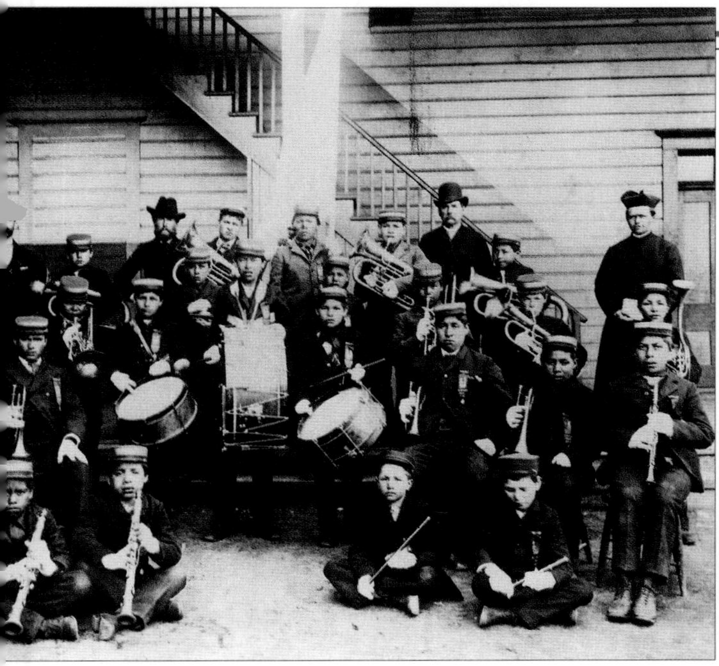

LIFE IN THE SEMINARIES

Life in seminaries revolved around educating the minds, hearts, and souls of Indian children with the aim of obliterating their tribal identities. Efforts to build Christian character included Sunday church services, morning and evening prayers, Bible readings, and memorizing the Ten Commandments, sometimes with no explanation of the meaning behind the phrases.

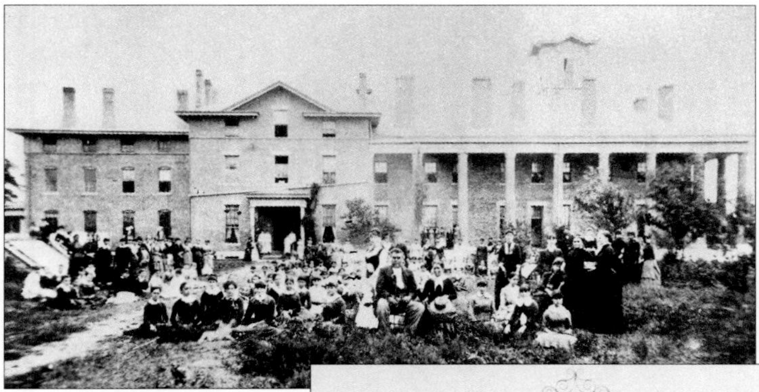

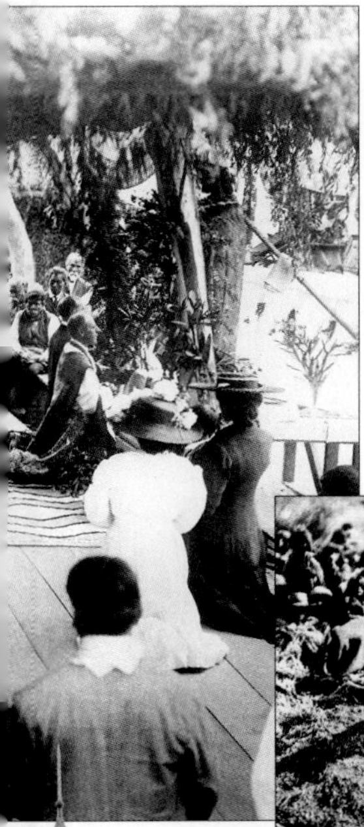

△ **BAND PRACTICE**
A popular feature of many mission schools, bands composed of Indian boys or girls performed at school functions and to entertain local audiences. School officials emphasized the benefits of musical training as a "civilizing" endeavor that "improved" the behavior of Indian youngsters.

▽ **PAIUTE BAPTISM IN UTAH**
During the mid-1850s, missionaries from the Church of Jesus Christ of Latter-Day Saints spread throughout the Ute and Paiute homelands in Utah territory, eager to convert Indians. Pictured here is a Paiute convert being baptized in a Utah pool.

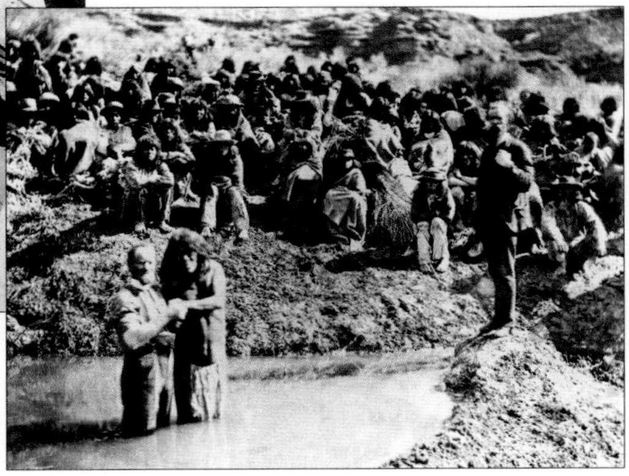

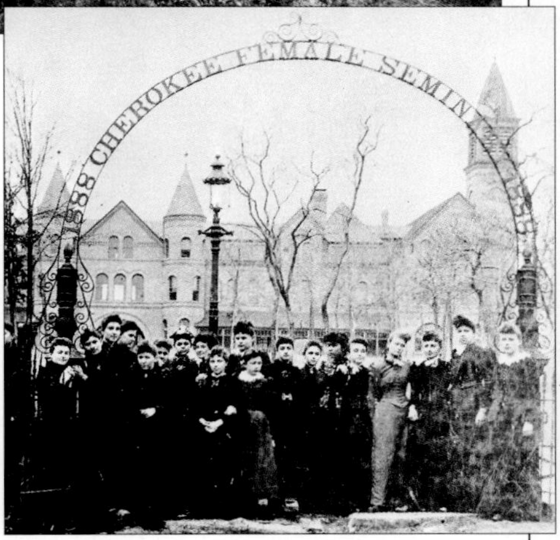

△ **STRICT REGIME**
The lives of boys pictured at the Cherokee Male Seminary were regulated every minute of every day, from the wake-up bell until lights-out. Those who disobeyed the rules might be whipped with a hickory rod.

LEARNING NEW SKILLS ▷
Female Indian students at the Cherokee Female Seminary in Tahlequah, Oklahoma, were instructed in sewing, cooking, canning, laundering, ironing, cleaning, and childcare.

"How they go to work to enslave a free people, and call it religion, is beyond the power of my imagination ..."

WILLIAM APESS, PEQUOT, 1836

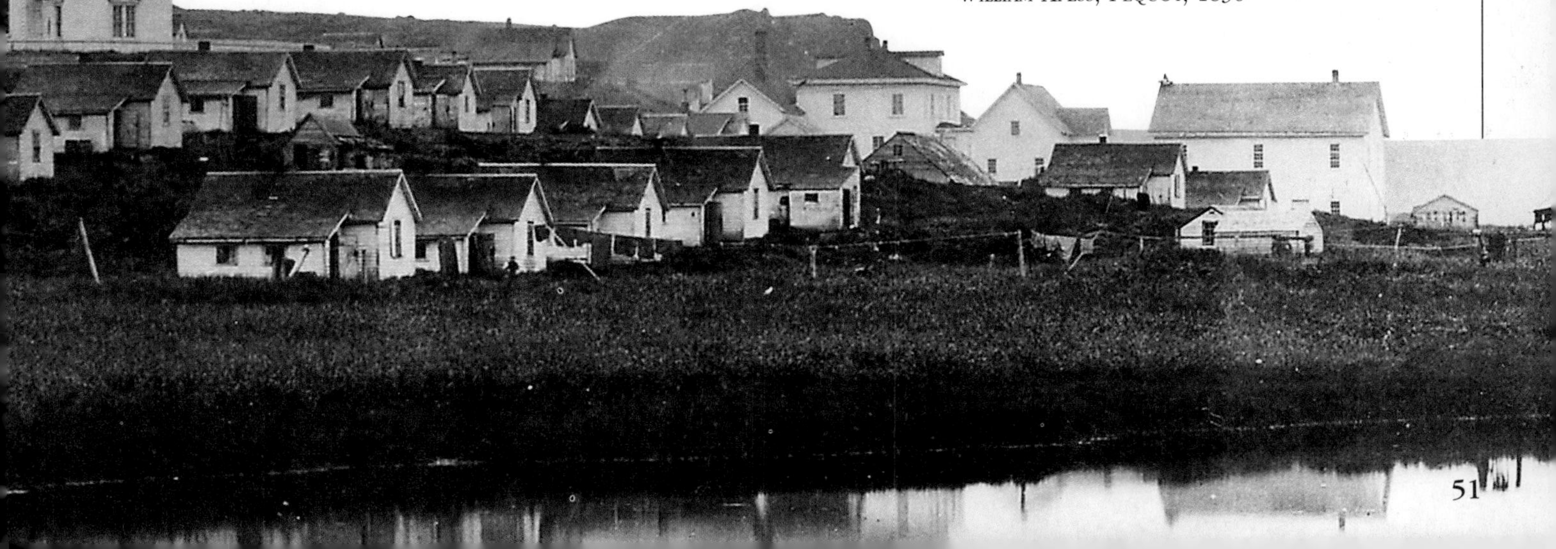

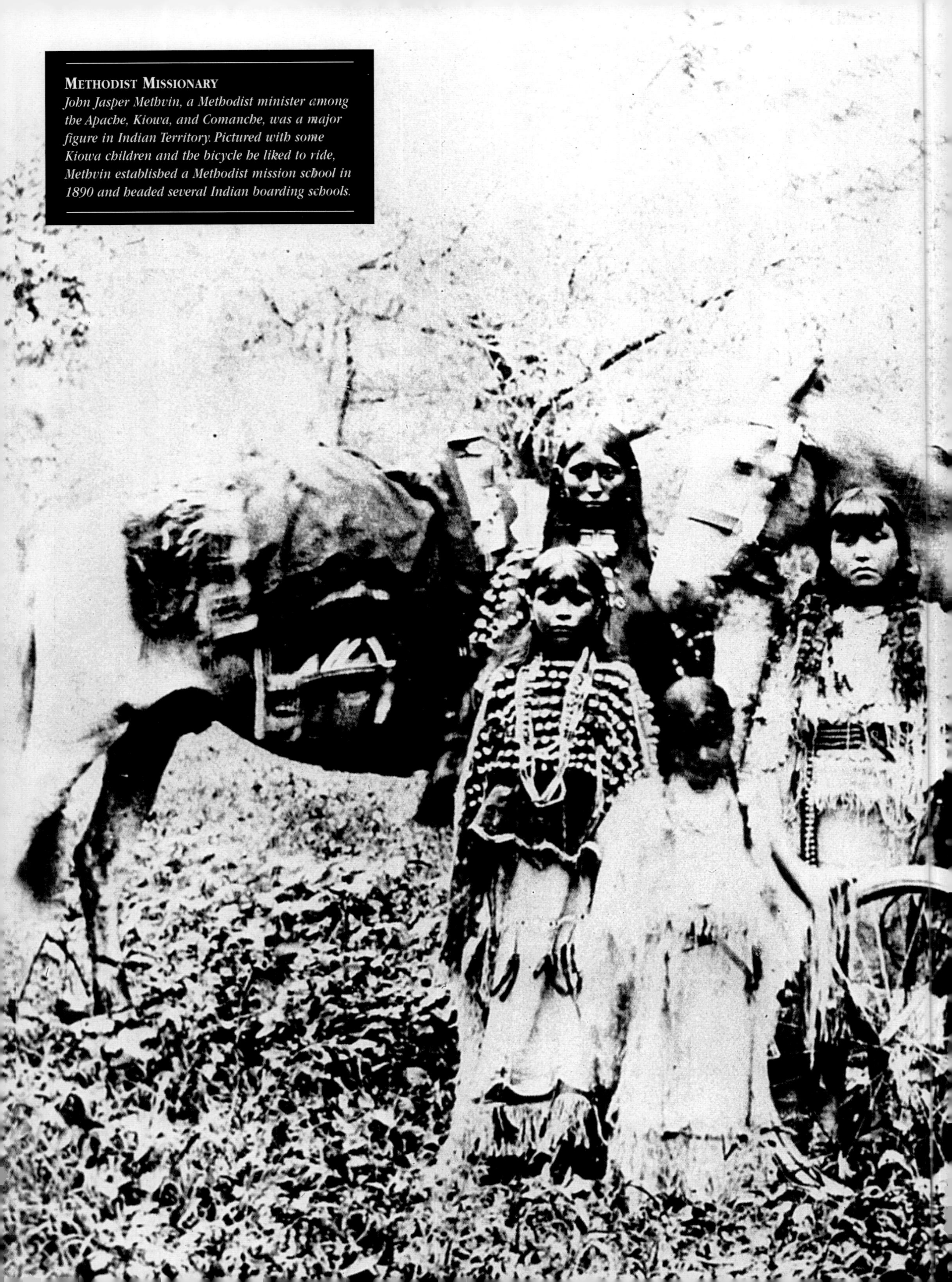

Methodist Missionary

John Jasper Methvin, a Methodist minister among the Apache, Kiowa, and Comanche, was a major figure in Indian Territory. Pictured with some Kiowa children and the bicycle he liked to ride, Methvin established a Methodist mission school in 1890 and headed several Indian boarding schools.

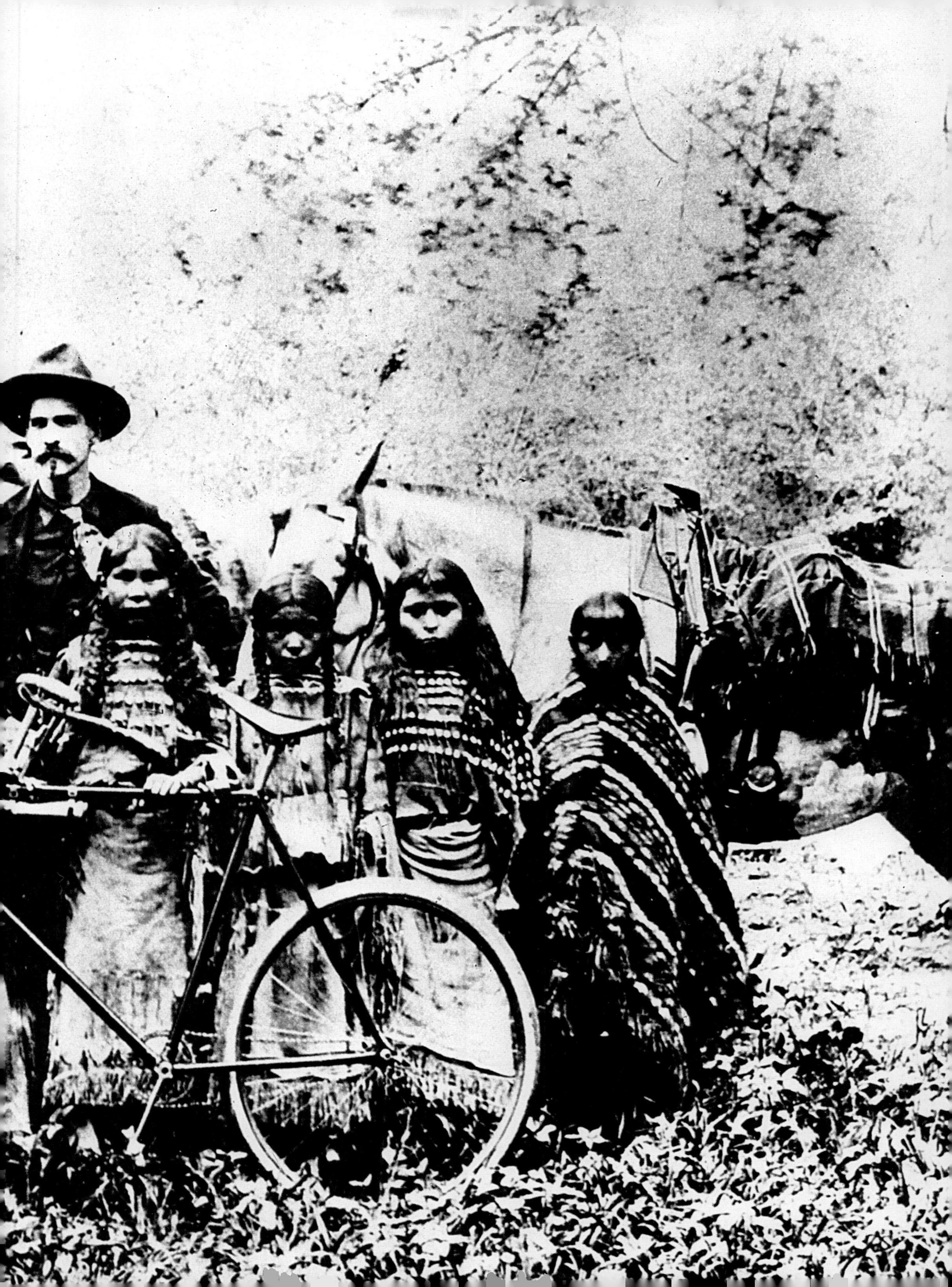

▽ **Baby Transport**
Most women carried their babies, swaddled safe and secure, in cradleboards, leaving their hands free. Made from local materials, these beautiful objects are the personal expressions of their makers.

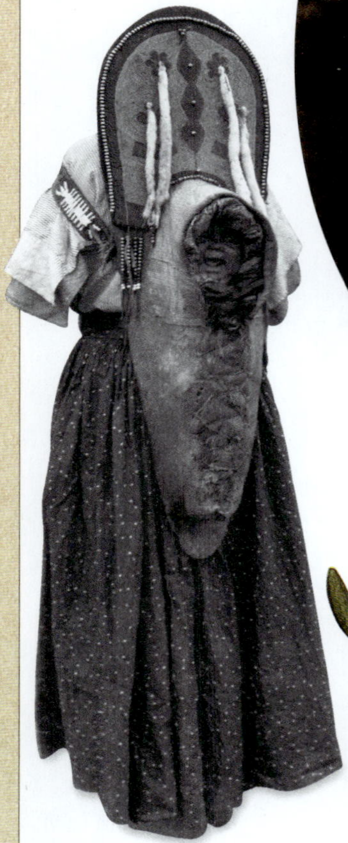

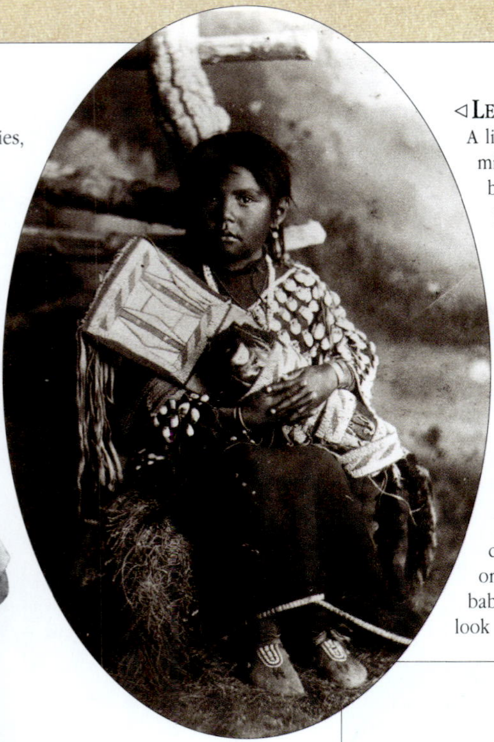

◁ **Learning through Play**
A little girl holds her own miniature cradleboard with a baby doll tucked inside. Girls played at getting married and having families, even learning to make little moccasins for their dolls. Such childhood play prepared and educated girls for future motherhood.

Time for a Nap ▷
In Sitka, Alaska, in 1897, Tlingit basket weavers pose for a photographer while they make spruce-root baskets. A baby sleeps soundly in a cradleboard, propped up beside one of the women. When the baby awakes, he or she can easily look around at the surroundings.

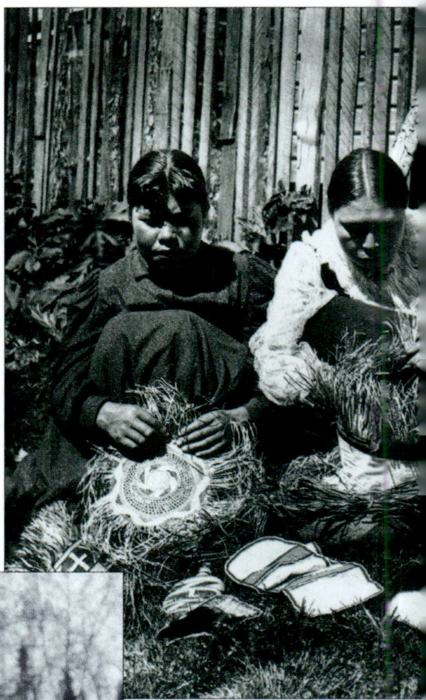

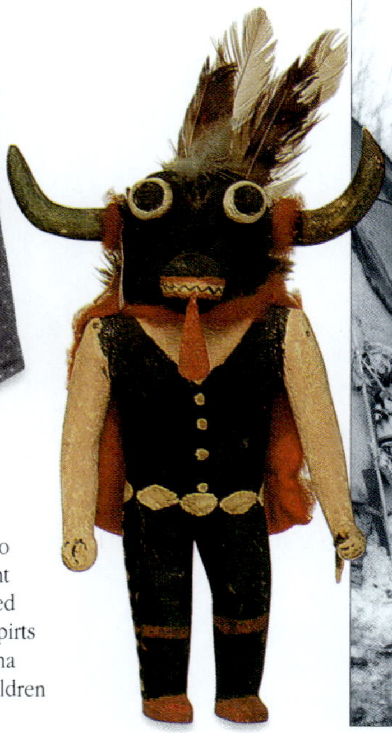

Educational Dolls ▷
Hopi parents gave their children ceremonial gifts of kachina dolls to teach the youngsters what different kachinas look like, the small carved figures representing the kachina spirts who appear in ceremonies. Kachina dolls were hung up where the children would see them constantly.

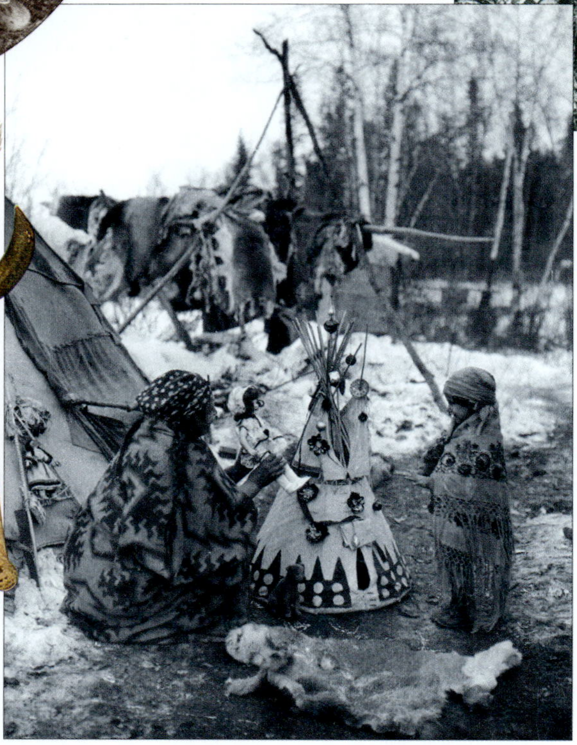

◁ **Playing House**
Girls from the Blackfeet Nation in Montana play house with little tipis made from real buckskin. Their tipis look exactly like the lodges of their mothers and aunts, with the same number of poles. Girls learned to make tipis by the same methods as used by the adult women of the tribe.

▽ **Tipi Training**
A group of Lakota girls in the Dakotas pitched this play tipi village. Every year, when the girls made a tipi, they cut the lodge-skin larger than the previous one until the lodge was finally large enough to sleep in. Apache girls in the Southwest made play wickiups, in which they built fires. Such play prepared girls for future roles and responsibilities.

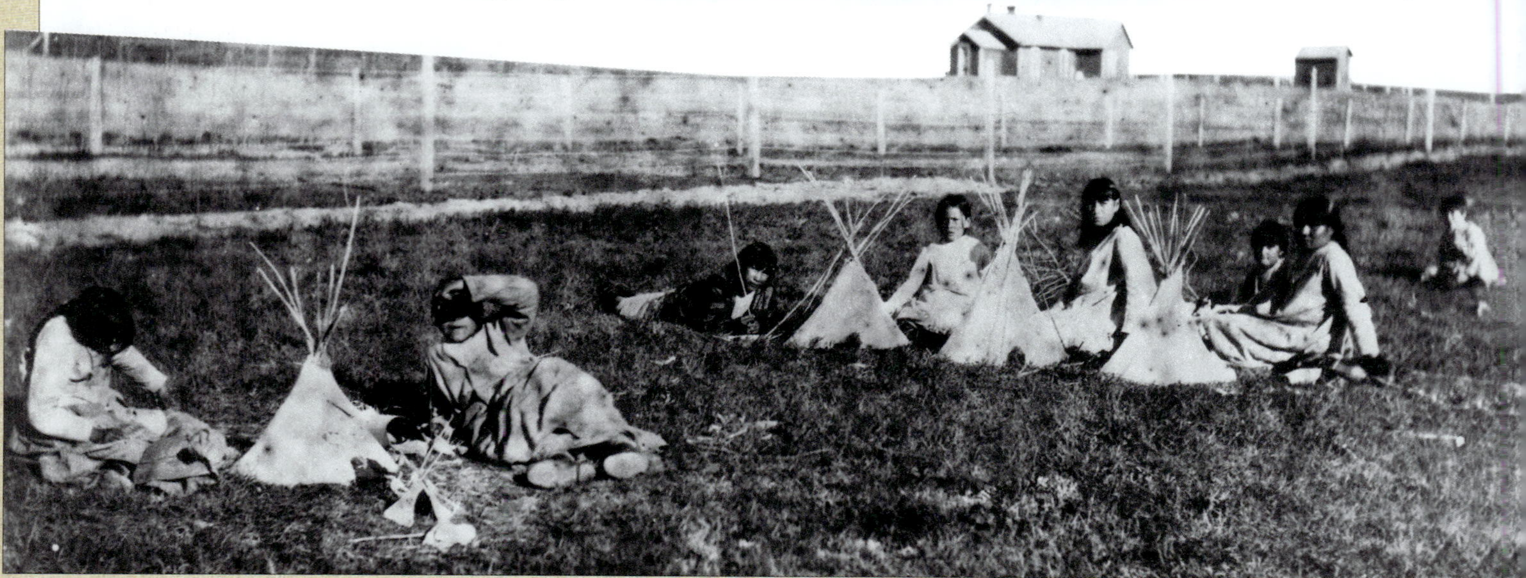

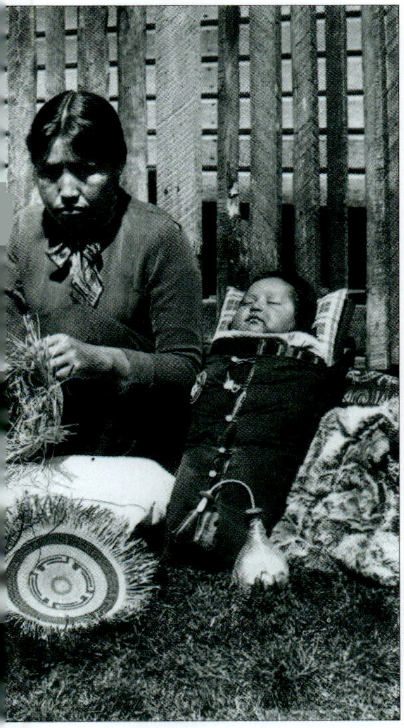

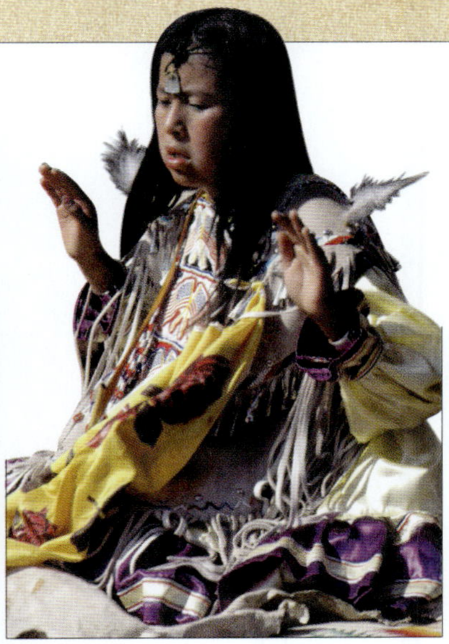

△ PUBERTY CEREMONIES
Rituals for girls on the verge of womanhood took place across Native North America and are still observed among some tribes. Western Apache girls, like the one pictured here, have an elaborate public ceremony with religious rituals, followed by rituals, feasting, social visiting, and dancing, lasting four days.

A Traditional Indian Childhood

DESPITE THE DIVERSITY of Native North American cultures, children were raised in similar ways. Child-rearing emphasized a responsiveness to the wishes of the children rather than schedules based on adult needs. Toilet training began when the child was ready and, in some Native societies, children nursed for as long as five to seven years. Children were free to sleep when tired, eat when hungry, and to engage in physical activities, such as running, swimming, and horse-riding, with minimal adult direction. Seldom punished and rarely coerced by adults, children who called attention to themselves were shamed into conformity by their peers.

Childhood Learning

Children learned through their own observations, relying on nonverbal rather than on verbal directions. Relatives, practiced in the art of noninterference, often stood back, allowing children to explore and experience life on their own, permitting children to make their own decisions – and mistakes. Youngsters also learned from stories told by their grandparents, who were repositories of cultural knowledge and wisdom and who were often the adults who cared for them. Grandparents passed on stories about the histories, cultural traditions, and laws of their peoples – stories that explained how the world and everything in it came to be. The stories taught children the correct way for people to treat one another, especially their obligations to other beings in the world, and contained practical advice such as how to hunt and fish and "recipes" for ways to heal.

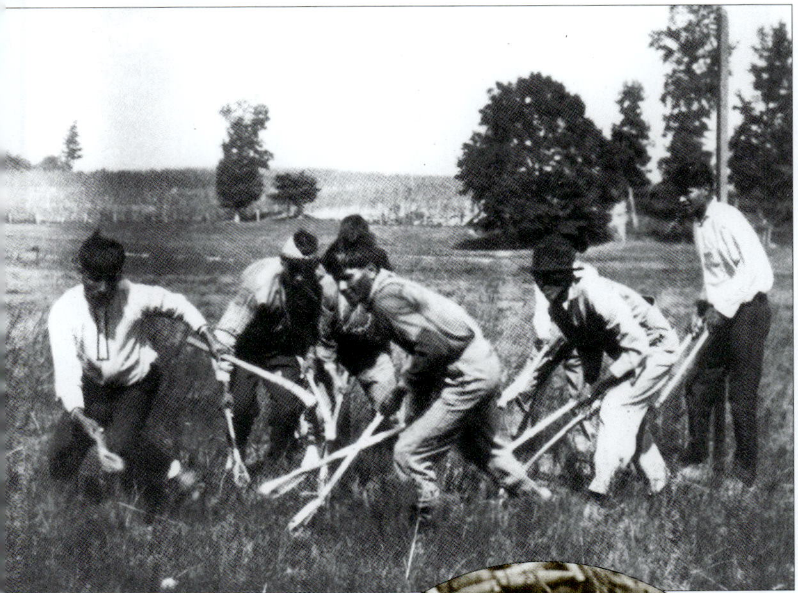

△ MORE THAN A GAME
These Choctaw boys learned how to play lacrosse – a game of great significance in Indian cultures, and believed to have curative powers. Today, lacrosse equipment and players are still ceremonially prepared by a religious practitioner.

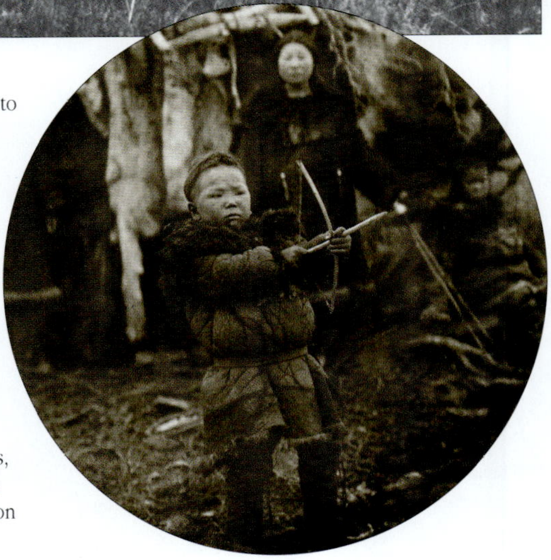

PRACTICING SKILLS ▷
A Koryak boy here practices marksmanship with his miniature bow and arrow. Boys were encouraged to play with slingshots, stilts, darts, and tops to help them develop the speed and coordination required for hunting and warfare.

Public Ceremonies

The importance of children to Native cultures was reflected in the public celebrations of events in the children's lives, such as a child's first steps or first haircut, a girl's first menstrual cycle, or a boy's search for his spiritual helper at puberty. The passage of children into each new stage of development was marked with a public ceremony. Puberty ceremonies, for example, prepared girls for their adult roles as wives and mothers, and boys for their future roles as husbands, providers, and protectors.

Children were given their everyday or ritual names in naming ceremonies. In many tribes, the children were named after distinguished relatives, elders, or ancestors, while some received sacred names following a vision quest.

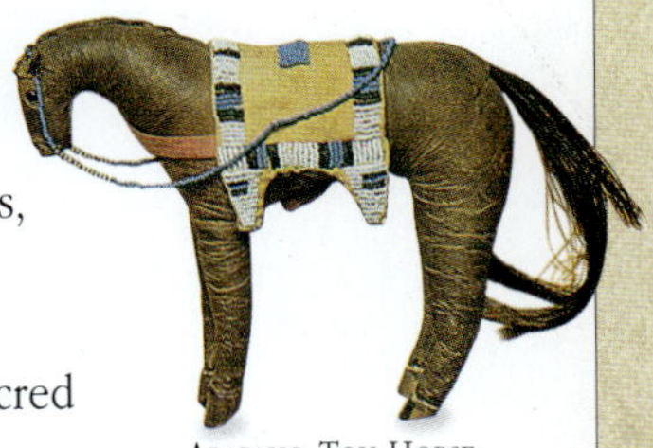

ARAPAHO TOY HORSE

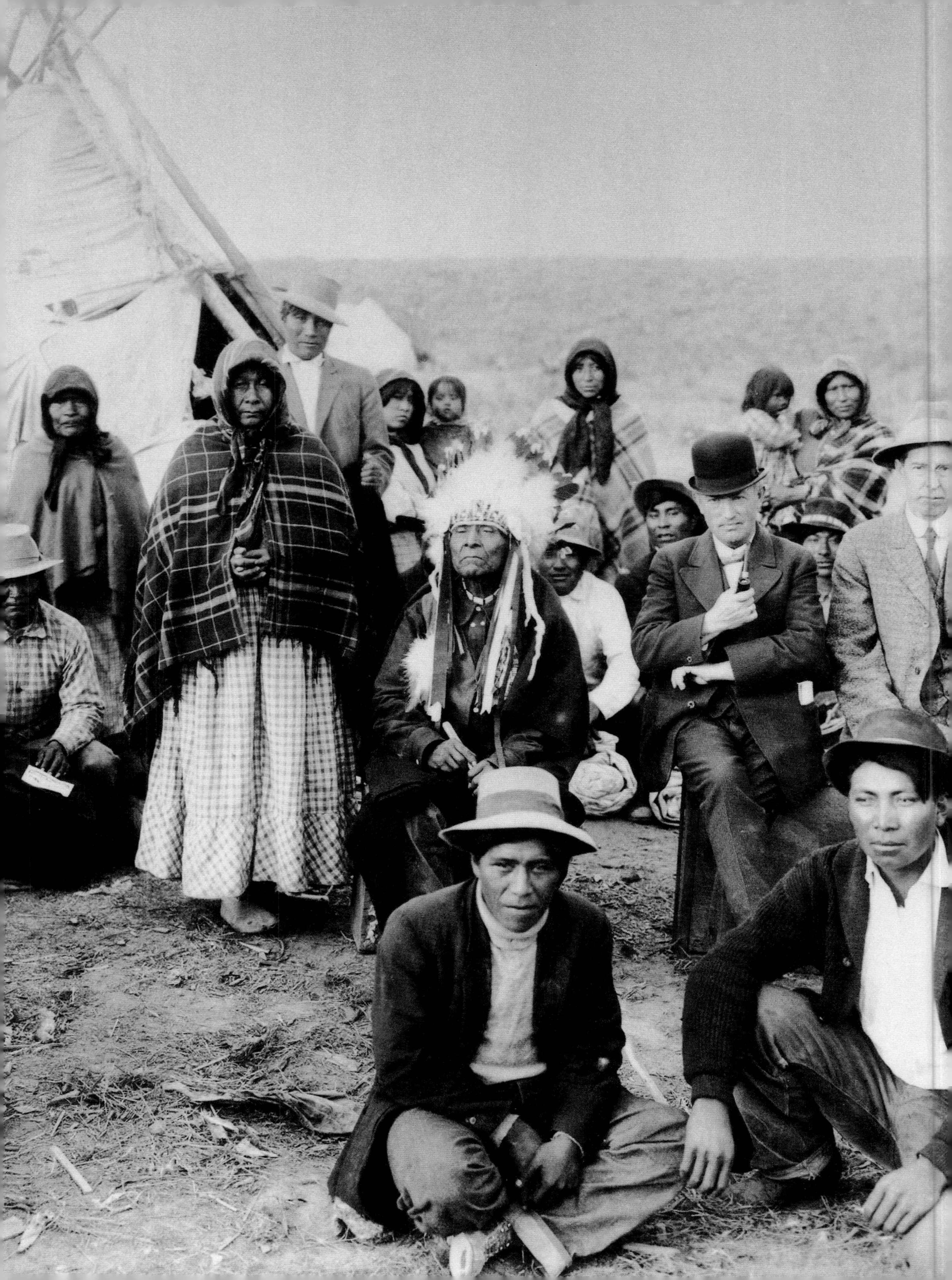

1780s TO 1860s

DISPOSSESSION AND LOSS

Between 1778 and 1868, the US government negotiated hundreds of treaties that deprived Indian nations of large areas of their homelands. A similar process began in Canada in 1850.

POVERTY AND ENFORCED DEPENDENCY
Loss of their homelands undermined Native self-sufficiency, forcing impoverished Indians – like this group of Paiutes – to rely on the treaty annuities that were doled out by government agents.

TIME FOR TALKING

FROM 1778 UNTIL 1871, the treaty was the principal instrument of US government Indian policy: over 370 treaties, 60 percent of which required tribes to give up their homelands to the US, were negotiated and signed between Indian nations and the US government. In Canada, 11 treaties were signed after the First Nations in central Canada (the Assiniboine, Cree, and Ojibway) began negotiating land cession treaties in 1850.

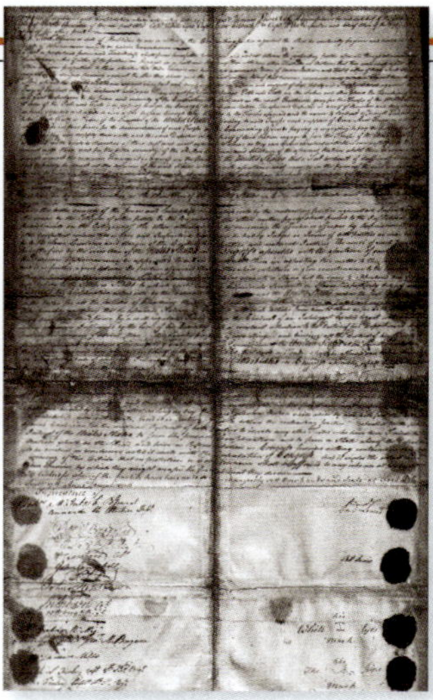

FIRST TREATY
Negotiated by President George Washington, the first treaty was signed on 17 September 1778 between the US government and the Delaware tribe. Then a young country under threat from European powers, the US needed assurances of peace from Indian nations whose governments held the balance of power in colonial America.

MAJOR TREATIES

11 NOVEMBER 1794
Jay Treaty guarantees Six Nations Iroquois the right to pass freely across the US–Canada border

8 JULY 1817
First removal treaty between Cherokee Nation and US cedes land in Georgia to white settlers

17 SEPTEMBER 1851
Fort Laramie Treaty between US and Northern Plains tribes aims to achieve peace between Indians and whites and intertribal peace among Indian signatories

21–28 OCTOBER 1867
Treaty of Medicine Lodge Creek between US and Southern Plains tribes attempts to end hostilities

1 JUNE 1868
Treaty allows 7,000 Navajos to return from New Mexico to reservation on Arizona-New Mexico border

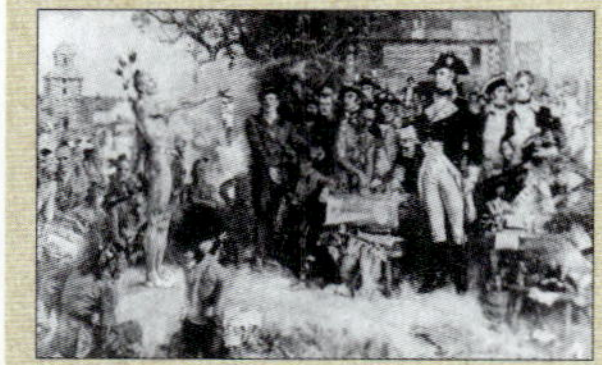

SIGNING AT GREENVILLE
The Treaty of Greenville, signed by 12 tribes on 3 August 1795, placed much of the Ohio Valley in American hands, changing forever tribal boundaries in the area.

THE FIRST TREATY between the US government and Indian nations was signed in 1778 by the Delaware tribe at Fort Pitt, in present-day Pittsburgh, Pennsylvania. From then until August 1868, when the last treaty was negotiated, treaties were signed with over 100 Indian nations, ranging from a couple with the Navajos to over 40 with Potawatomi bands. Congress ended treaty making in 1871, but the law did not repeal or change treaties that had been signed and ratified before that date.

Shifting Bargaining Positions

The first negotiations led to treaties of peace but, as the US grew more powerful, a shift in bargaining positions emerged, concluding in treaties of surrender imposed on militarily defeated tribes. Negotiations were not always conducted in an ethical manner: some treaties were negotiated by only part of the tribe presuming to represent the entire nation. In some cases, many of the tribe were absent, and sometimes a tribe leader was bribed so that he would persuade the tribe to negotiate.

Indian nations were forced to agree to terms that diminished their homelands and their right to govern themselves. In over 230 treaties, Indian nations agreed to give up parts of their homelands. In the 1795 Treaty of Greenville, 12 Indian nations ceded to the US "one piece of land six miles square at the mouth of the

▽ **DELEGATES AT THE WHITE HOUSE**
In this earliest known photograph of a delegation of Indians in Washington, DC, dated 31 December 1857, the Pawnees, Ponca, Potawatomi, and Sac and Fox delegates assemble on the south portico of the White House with government officials.

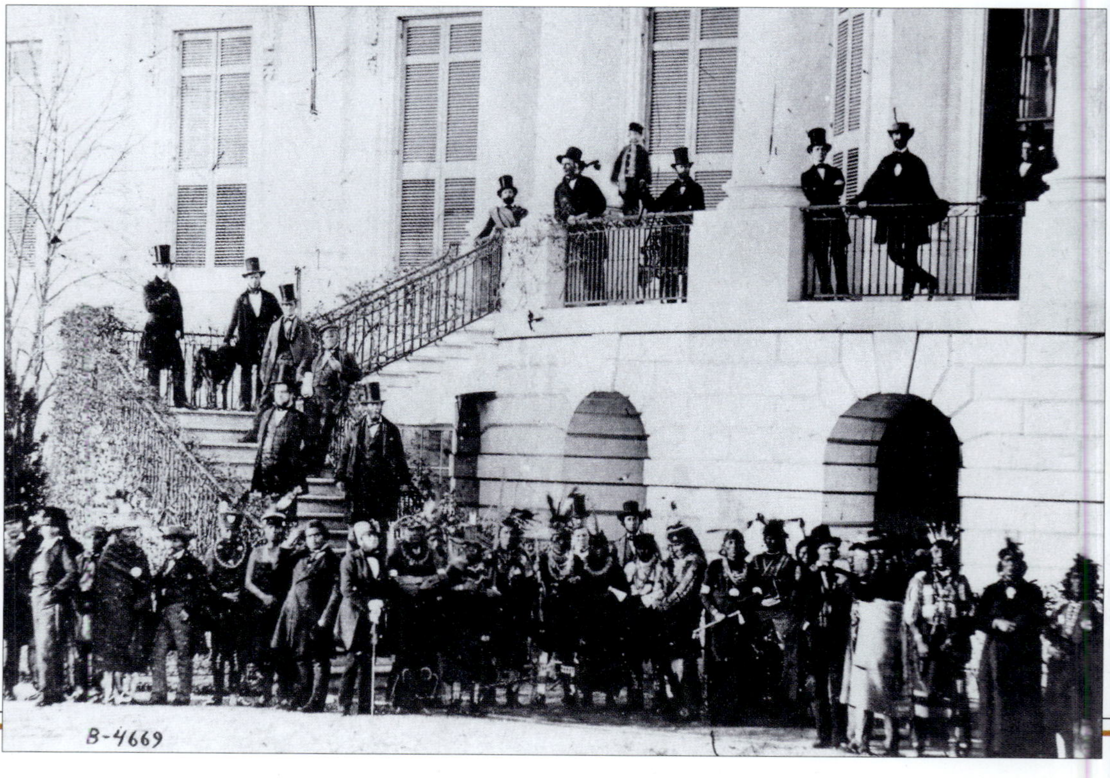

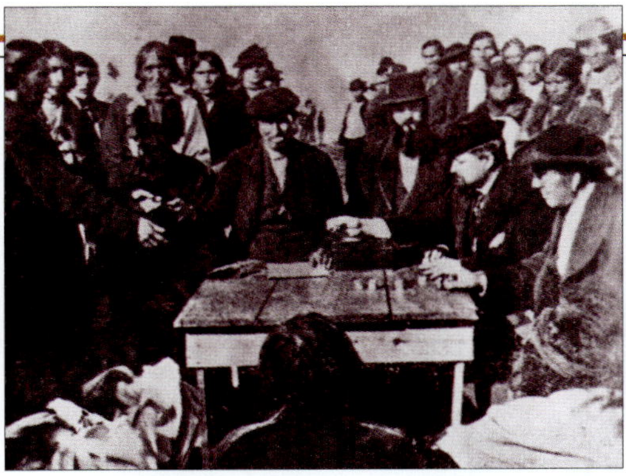

ANNUITY LINE IN LAPOINTE, WISCONSIN
Indians were frequently persuaded to accept treaty terms by promises of "annuities" of money, goods, or both. Chippewa Indians line up here, in 1869, to receive annuity payments.

hicago River." By the arly 1800s, this small hunk of land, called hicago, had become the usiest port in the US. n nearly 80 treaties, ndians agreed to terms hat permitted roads or ailroads to be built cross their lands. In nany cases, the government simply vanted to clear away title to Indian lands so hat settlers could homestead them.

In exchange for Indian land cessions, rights of way for roads and railroads, and exclusive rade agreements, the US government offered noney, food for a specified number of years, education, health provisions, and missionaries. t agreed to permit Indians to hunt, fish, and gather foods or plant crops within ceded erritories as long as they acted "peaceably." In at least two dozen treaties, the government agreed to give Indians land in other locations n exchange for homelands that were ceded.

Negotiations in Canada

Treaty making began with Maritime "Peace and Friendship" agreements during colonial struggles, in which the principals agreed to aid each other in conflict; but no mention was made of land title. The First Nations of central Canada commenced negotiating land cession treaties with the British Crown in 1850. Two treaties at the time, in which the Ojibway gave up land north of Lake Superior and Lake Huron, became models for the later so-called "numbered treaties." After the Northwest Territories and British Columbia joined the Canadian Confederation, a series of treaties – numbered from one to seven – were signed with the Indians in the southern parts of these areas between 1871 and 1877. Four more treaties – numbered eight to eleven – were signed between 1899 and 1923. These, too, covered mostly western Canada.

Treaties were later signed with the Dene Indians covering the western part of the Northwest Territories, but the Maritime Provinces, Quebec, most of the Yukon Territory, and British Columbia were not subject to land-surrender treaties.

All treaties shared a common feature: that the British sovereign, and later the Canadian government, acquired title to vast tracts of land in exchange for the right to fish and hunt in surrendered areas, monetary payments, and provision for the establishment of reserves.

SIGNS AND SIGNATURES

Treaties were legitimized with the signatures, seals, or marks of authorized representatives of the US and Indian nations. The clan signs shown below were drawn by Six Nations (Iroquois) Indians on a treaty they negotiated with William Penn in 1769.

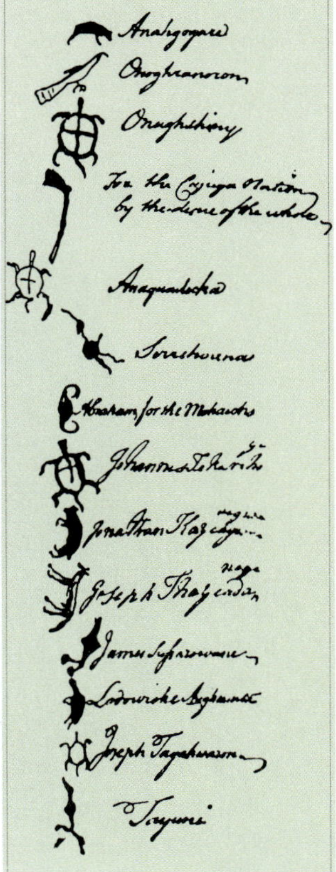

SIGNINGS AT FORT LARAMIE

On 8 September 1851, following a council gathering of some 5,000 Plains Indian representatives at Fort Laramie, the chiefs signed a treaty guaranteeing safe passage for westbound settlers along the Platte River. A further treaty, signed in 1868, brought temporary peace to the Northern Plains.

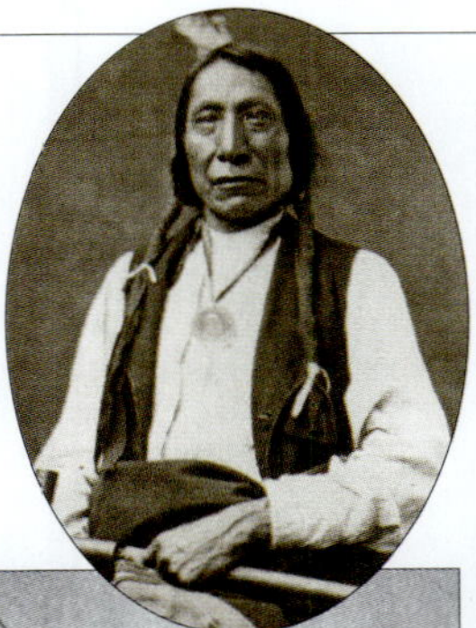

◁ RED CLOUD SIGNS FOR PEACE
Determined to stop traffic on the Bozeman Trail, located in Oglala hunting grounds, Oglala Lakota Chief Red Cloud attacked forts along the route. Once the army had abandoned them, Red Cloud signed the 1868 Fort Laramie Treaty and gave up fighting.

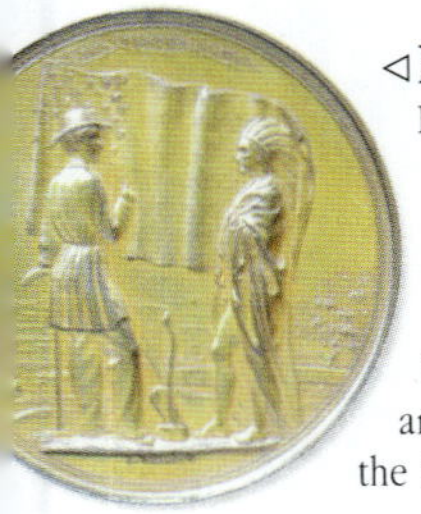

◁ PEACE TOKEN
Indian signatories of the 1851 Fort Laramie Treaty received peace medals that depicted a friendly meeting between white man and Indian on one side, the President on the other.

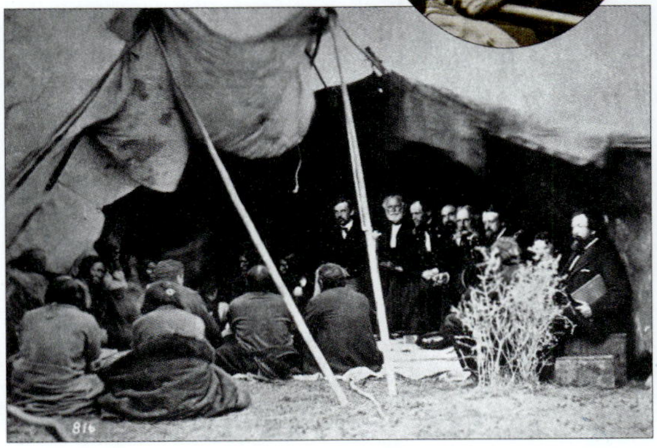

PEACE TALKS AT FORT LARAMIE ▷
In May 1868, General William Tecumseh Sherman and members of the Peace Commission met with Cheyenne and Arapaho Indians at Fort Laramie in an attempt to end Red Cloud's War.

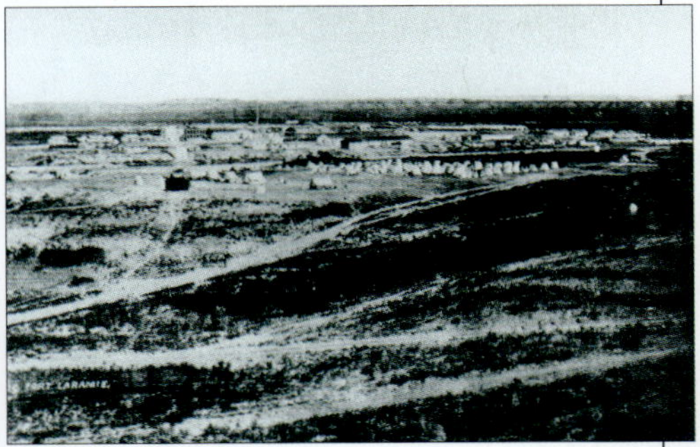

△ TRADING-POST OASIS
Founded in 1834 on the Laramie River, in present-day southeastern Wyoming, the Fort Laramie trading post offered travelers rich grass, cottonwood groves, and clear water on their grueling westbound journey.

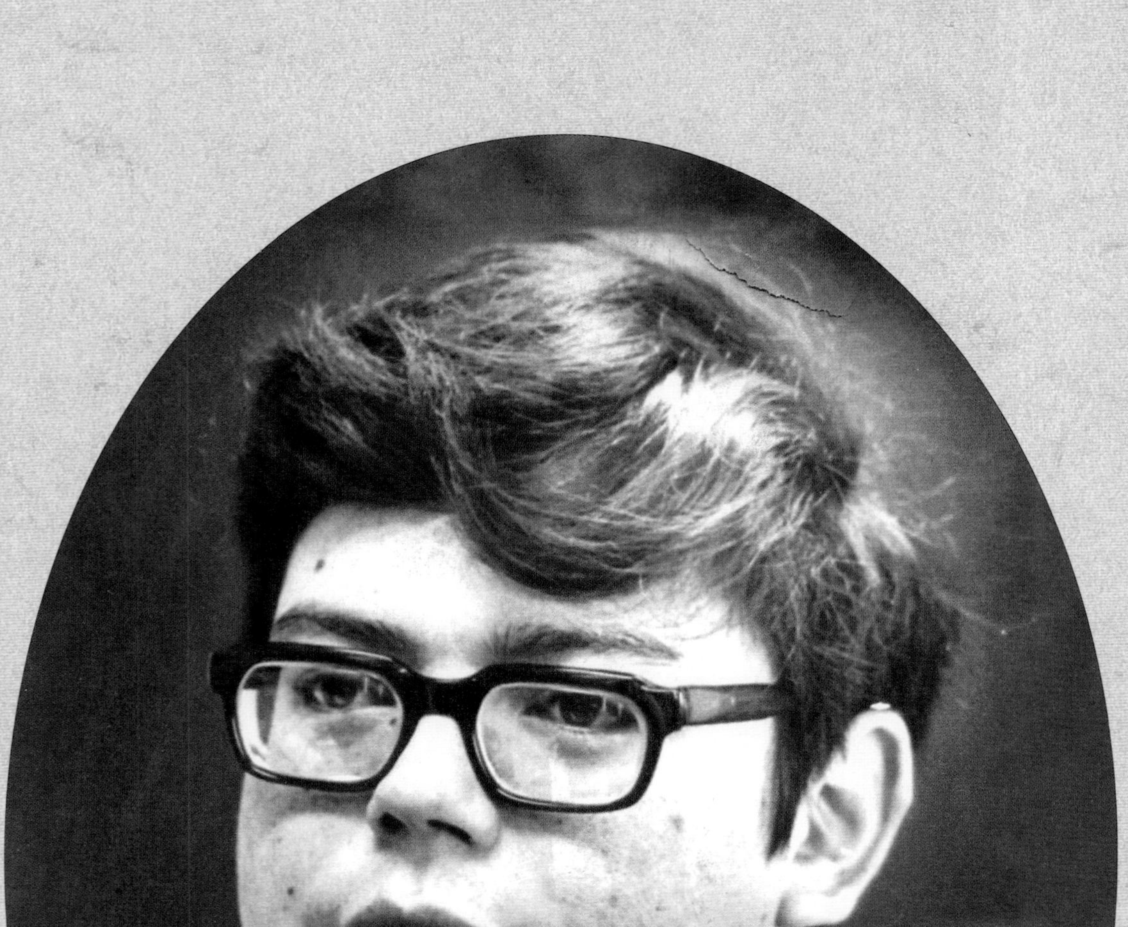

HAROLD CARDINAL

1969: ON THE CANADIAN GOVERNMENT'S BETRAYAL OF INDIAN TREATIES

BORN IN 1945 IN HIGH PRAIRIE, ALBERTA, Cree political leader Harold Cardinal left college in 1967 to pursue Indian politics full time. Within a month of commencing work at the then stagnant Indian Association of Alberta, he was elected to his first of nine terms as president of the Association. This extract is from *The Unjust Society: The Tragedy of Canada's Indians*, published in 1969, in which Harold Cardinal discussed Canadian Indian treaties. In 1977, he wrote *The Rebirth of Canada's Indians* in response to attempts by the Canadian federal government to cast off its legal and moral obligation to Indians.

"To the Indians of Canada, the treaties represent an Indian Magna Carta. [They] are important to us, because we entered into these negotiations with faith, with hope for a better life with honour. The Indians entered into the treaty negotiations as honourable men who came to deal as equals with the queen's representatives .... Our leaders pledged themselves, their people and their heirs to honour what was done to them.

Our leaders mistakenly thought they were dealing with an honourable people who would do no less than the Indians were doing – bind themselves, bind their people and bind their heirs to honourable contracts.

Our people talked with the government representatives, not as beggars pleading for handouts, but as men with something to offer in return for rights they expected. To our people, this was the beginning of a contractual relationship whereby the representatives of the queen would have lasting responsibilities to the Indian people in return for the valuable lands that were ceded to them.

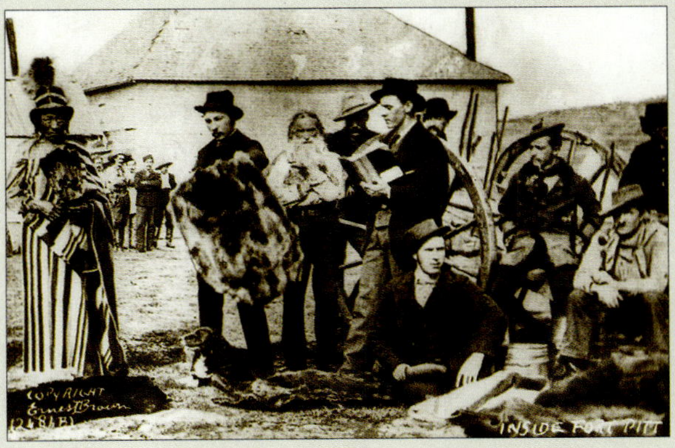

CHIEF BIG BEAR TRADES AT FORT PITT
Cree Indian chief Big Bear began signing treaties with the Canadian Confederation in 1873. He is pictured in 1885, trading at Fort Pitt, Saskatchewan.

The treaties were the way in which the white people legitimized in the eyes of the world their presence in our country. It was an attempt to settle the terms of occupancy on a just basis, legally and morally to extinguish the legitimate claims of our people to title to the land in our country. There never has been any doubt in the minds of our people that the land in Canada belonged to them. Nor can there have been any doubt in the mind of the government or in the minds of the white people about who owned the land, for it was upon the basis of white recognition of Indian rights that the treaties were negotiated. Otherwise, there could have been nothing to negotiate, no need for treaties. In the language of the Cree Indians, the Indian reserves are known as the land that we kept for ourselves or the land that we did not give to the government. In our language, skun-gun."

INDIANS IN THE CIVIL WAR

ROUGHLY 20,000 AMERICAN INDIANS left their homes for the Civil War battlefields, some to side with the victorious North, or Union, while others joined the South, or Confederacy. Whatever their choice, the war was disastrous for Indians: tribes were torn apart, men lost their lives, and, in Indian Territory, homes, barns, stores, and schools were looted and burned. After the war ended, tribes had to repair the bitter factionalism that the conflict had revived.

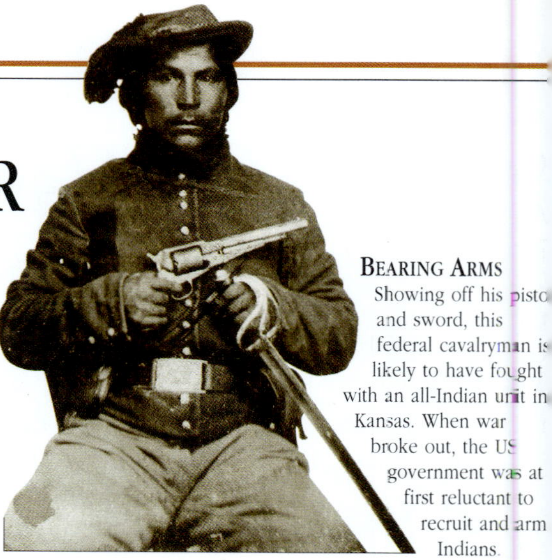

BEARING ARMS
Showing off his pistol and sword, this federal cavalryman is likely to have fought with an all-Indian unit in Kansas. When war broke out, the US government was at first reluctant to recruit and arm Indians.

CIVIL WAR DIARY

12 APRIL 1861
Fort Sumter: first shot of War. Confederacy win

21 JULY 1861
First Bull Run: first battle of war. Confederacy win

17 SEPTEMBER 1862
Antietam: first invasion of North by Lee. Union win

1-3 JULY 1863
Gettysburg: second invasion of North by Lee. Union win

DECEMBER 1862-JULY 1863
Vicksburg: vital supply route for Confederacy. Union win

MAY-SEPTEMBER 1864
Atlanta: important railway route for Confederacy. Union win

9 APRIL 1865
Lee surrenders to Grant. War over

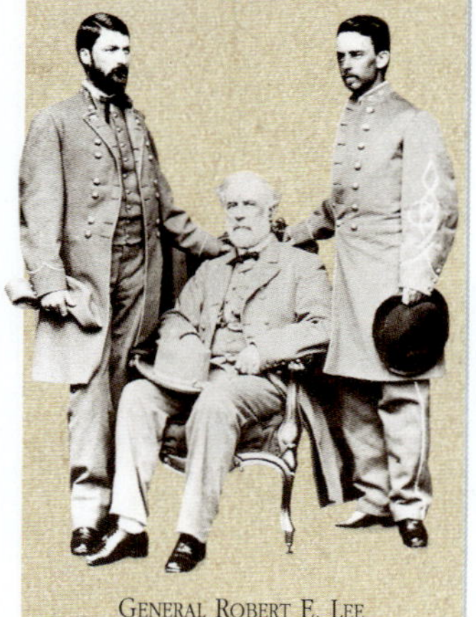

GENERAL ROBERT E. LEE

WHEN THE CIVIL WAR BROKE OUT, the federal government was at first reluctant to enlist Indians on the Union side. In 1862, however, they formed three Union Indian Home Guard regiments for duty in Indian Territory: about 3,500 men from Indian Territory served in these units. Eventually, Indians were recruited in nearly every northern state.

The Confederacy, keen to gain a foothold in Indian Territory, eagerly recruited Indians, too. Albert Pike negotiated treaties with the Cherokees, Creeks, Seminoles, Chickasaws, and Choctaws (the Five Tribes), and with other tribes in Indian Territory, persuading them to support the South despite opposition within each tribe. Altogether around 10,000 Indians in more than 25 separate units were raised by the Confederacy in Indian Territory. The Indian troops took part in some of the principal early battles west of the Mississippi.

After the March 1862 Union victory at Pea Ridge, Arkansas, opened the way for a Union drive into Indian Territory, desolation reigned as Indian fought Indian and Cherokees, Creeks, and Seminoles endured civil wars of their own.

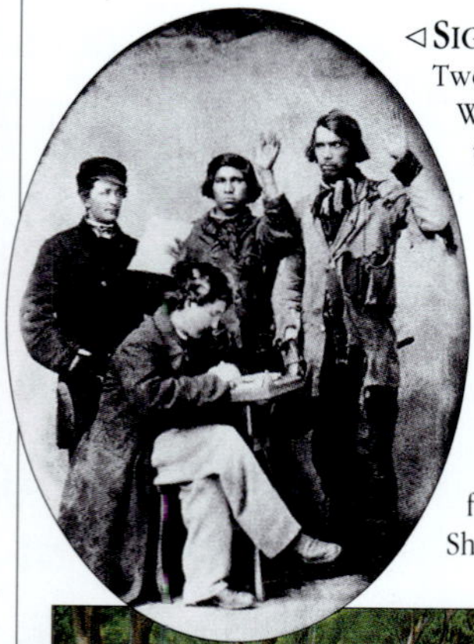

◁ **SIGNING UP FOR THE UNION**
Two Stockbridge Indians from Wisconsin swear allegiance to the Union army, which formed special brigades for thousands of Indians who joined up.

▽ **FIGHTING IN VIRGINIA**
At the Battle of Spotsylvania, in May 1864, five days of inconclusive fighting left many dead, including 12 Ottawa men from the famed First Michigan Sharpshooters' Company K.

The Price of War

By the end of the war, the Five Tribes had lost over 6,000 people out of a total population of over 60,000, the economy of Indian Territory was destroyed, and many Indian families were homeless. Even though as many members of the Five Tribes had served in the Union army as with the Confederates, the US government declared its treaties with the tribes null and void, forcing them to renegotiate and cede the western part of Indian Territory to the US.

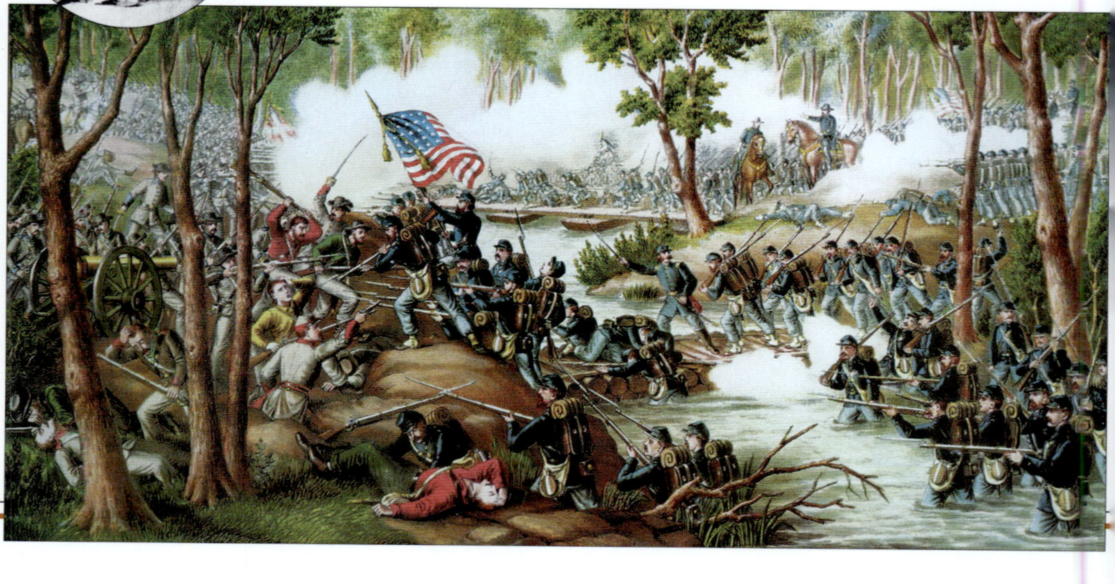

CHEROKEES JOIN LEE

Although the majority of Cherokees favored the Union, Chief John Ross, unable to withstand the pressures of Confederate agents and their Cherokee sympathizers, signed a treaty with the Confederacy. Within a year, Ross – who had served the Cherokees for more than 50 years – fled east. After war's end, he returned and worked at reunifying a defeated, bitterly divided nation.

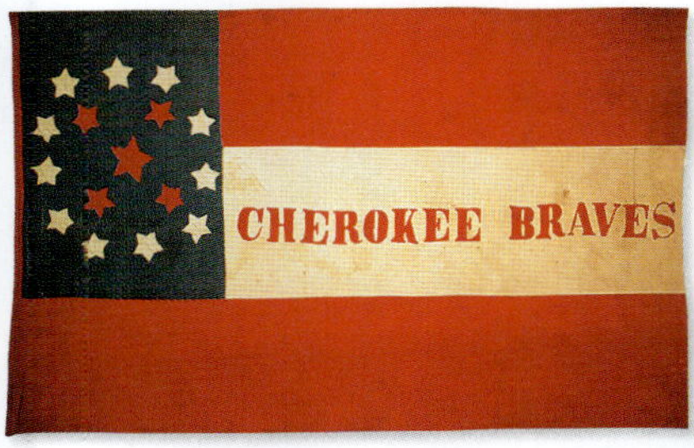

BANNER OF THE FIRST CHEROKEE MOUNTED RIFLES

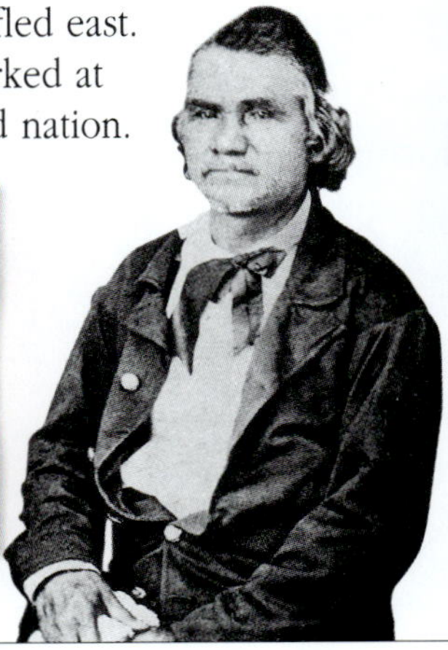

◁ HIGH-RANKING CHEROKEE
Cherokee planter and slaveholder, Stand Watie supported the South and organized a Cherokee Home Guard company. In 1864, the Confederates made him a brigadier general, the only Indian to hold such high rank during the war.

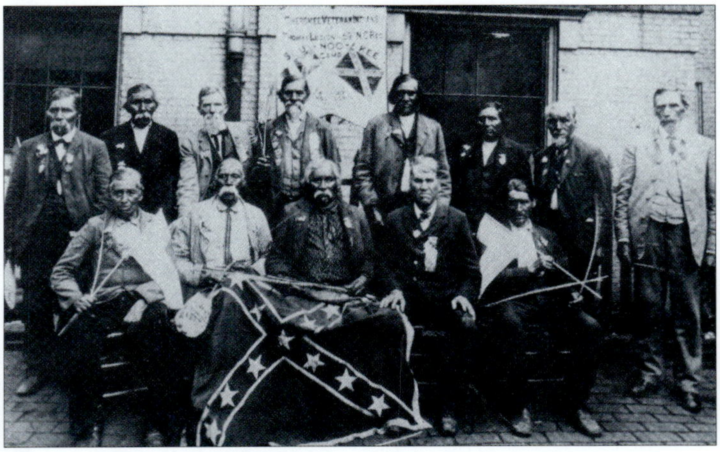

△ THOMAS LEGION VETERANS
In 1862, white trader William Holland Thomas raised four Cherokee companies for his Confederate North Carolina regiment. Known as the "Thomas Legion," the Indians operated in the mountains of North Carolina and Tennessee.

INDIANS SCOUT FOR BOTH SIDES

Indians were used as scouts by both sides: they knew their terrain and how to use topography to advantage in battle, and they were skilled at locating, pinpointing, and reporting on enemy activity without endangering their own troops. One group of Choctaw scouts tracked down Confederate deserters in the Mississippi swamps.

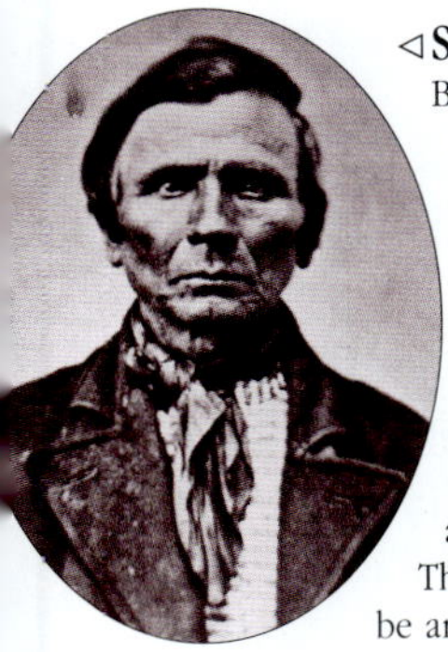

◁ SCOUTING FOR THE UNION
Black Beaver, a member of the Delaware Nation and an accomplished scout, led federal troops to safety from Indian Territory in 1861.

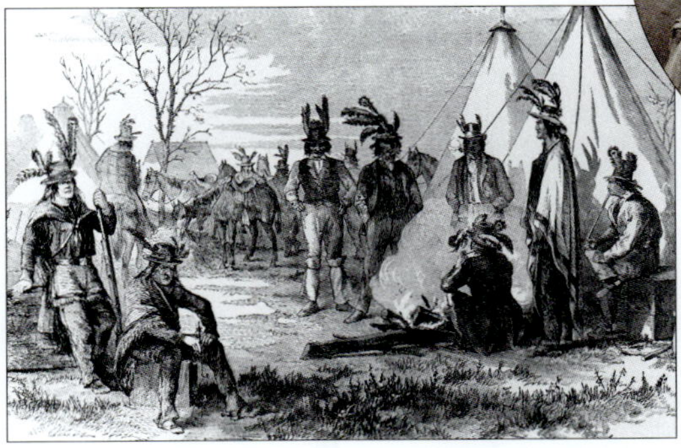

DELAWARE SCOUTS ▷
A group of Delaware scouts, equipped by the US, rest after a mission for the Union army. Their feather headdresses may be an artistic embellishment.

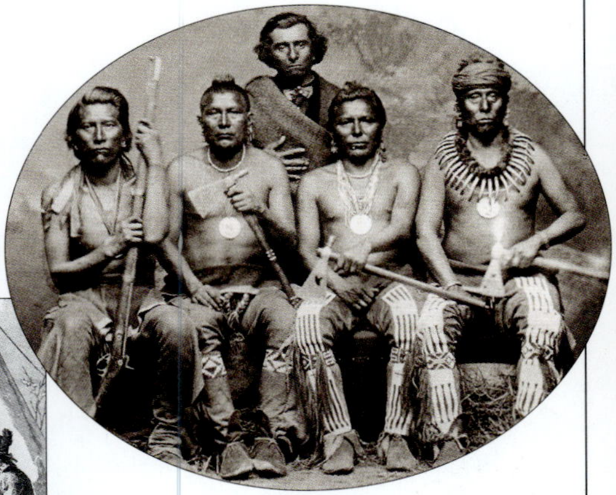

△ PAWNEES' PEACE MEDALS
Pawnee scouts, here displaying government peace medals, helped protect construction workers on the Union Pacific railroad from attacks by Plains Indians, whose traditional life had been disrupted by the expanding railroad system of the 1860s.

TAKING COMMAND

Lieutenant Colonel Ely Parker, a Tonawanda Seneca chief, trained as an engineer and later became a Union officer during the Civil War. In 1864, he became President Grant's military secretary and, in 1869, was appointed Commissioner of Indian Affairs – the first Indian to fill the position.

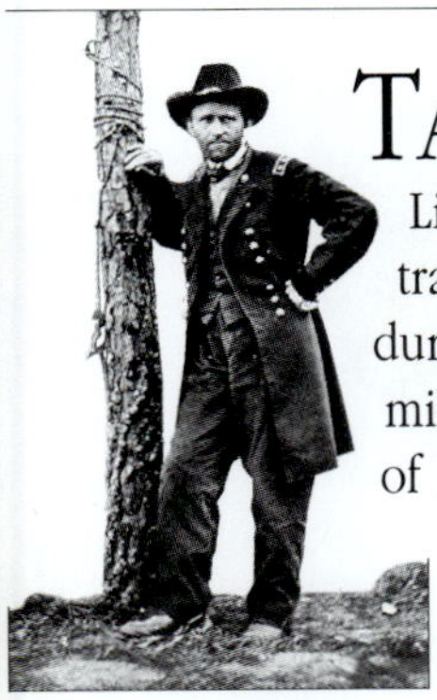

△ ULYSSES S. GRANT
Grant was given command of all Union armies in 1864. Five years later, he became the eighteenth President of the United States.

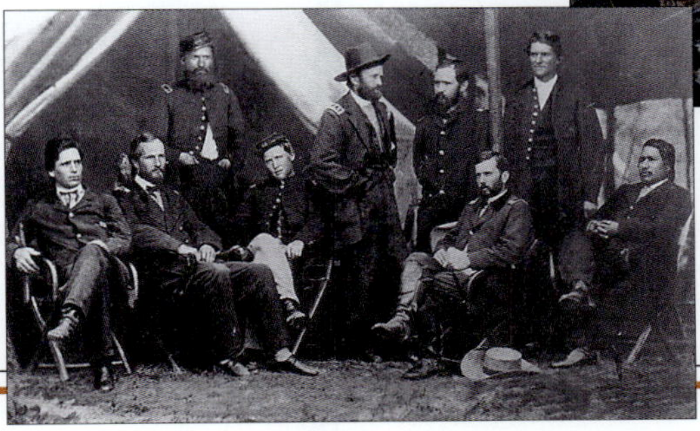

SECRETARY PARKER ▷
Ely Parker (far right) acted as scribe for the surrender of Lee's Confederate army at Appomattox Court House, Virginia, on 9 April 1865, handwriting the official document that ended the war in the East.

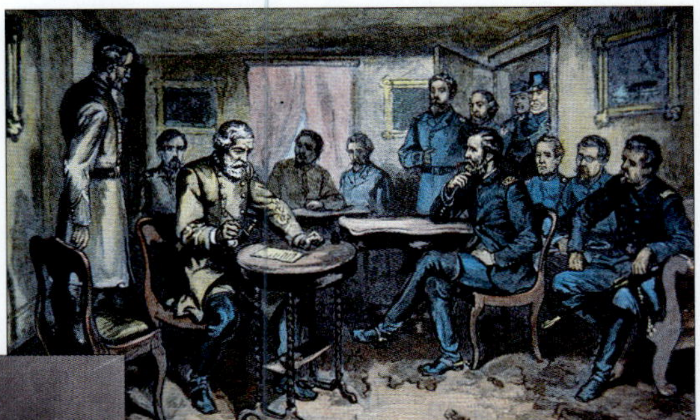

△ SURRENDER OF ROBERT E. LEE
General-in-chief of all Confederate armies for the last few months of a losing war, Lee surrendered to Grant, urging his troops and all southerners to accept the outcome and rebuild their homeland.

THE SANTEE DAKOTA REVOLT

The "Great Sioux Uprising" (involving the Santee Dakota) began in Minnesota at the end of August 1862 when, resentful over the loss of their lands, the disappearance of the buffalo and other game, and the presence of dishonest traders and Indian agents, the Dakotas' pent-up fury finally erupted. In September 1862 the US army put down the uprising, during which hundreds of white people had been killed. On 26 December 1862, 38 Dakotas were hanged at Mankato, Minnesota, in punishment.

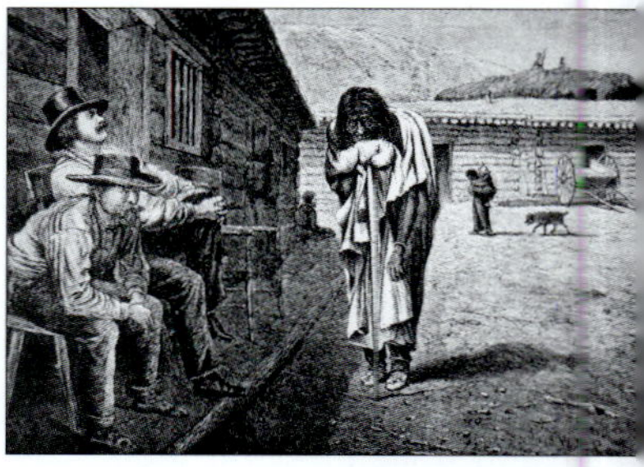

A STARVING PEOPLE
Failure of the summer corn crop led to serious malnutrition among the Santee Dakotas (Sioux), forcing some to eat roots and the shriveled ears of corn, and others their horses and dogs.

INDIAN RESCUER

During the Santee Dakota revolt, Dakota chief Anpetu-Tokeca (also known as John Otherday), who converted to Christianity and adopted white ways, rescued 62 missionaries, traders, and employees. His home and those of other Christian Indians were burned, in reprisal, by Little Crow and his followers.

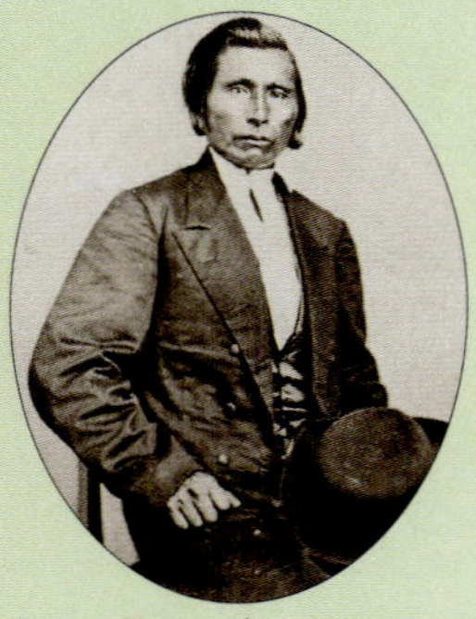

ANPETU-TOKECA (JOHN OTHERDAY)

BY THE TIME of the Civil War, the Santee Dakota in Minnesota had surrendered nine-tenths of their territory and were surrounded by whites, who relentlessly wanted more and more of their land. Corrupt traders, theft, assaults on Dakota women, and loss of game strained to breaking point relations between Indians and whites. Factions within the tribe disagreed on how to deal with the abuse.

Sparking Conflict

In July 1862, the desperately hungry Santees were told that their annuity payments would be delayed because Congress was preoccupied with the Civil War. Even though the agency warehouse was filled with food and supplies, the agent, Thomas Galbraith, refused to distribute anything until the money arrived. Andrew Myrick, a trader who refused the Indians credit, advised Galbraith, "If they are hungry let them eat grass or their own dung." In this tense atmosphere, a minor incident sparked off a major uprising. Returning from an unsuccessful hunt, four young Dakota men found some eggs laid by a settler's chicken. When one taunted another that he was afraid to take even an egg from a white man, the hunters killed five settlers to prove their courage. Little Crow, a prominent Dakota chief was sickened by the incident: he had worked at making himself acceptable to his neighbors by embracing white customs, living in a frame house, farming, and attending church. The killers, however, knowing that there would be reprisals, convinced Little Crow to lead a strike against the whites. Taking the settlers off-guard, the Santees attacked the agency store on 18 August, killing the men, including Myrick who was found with grass stuffed in his mouth They took women and children captive and torched the buildings, then spread out over the countryside, burning settlements, killing as

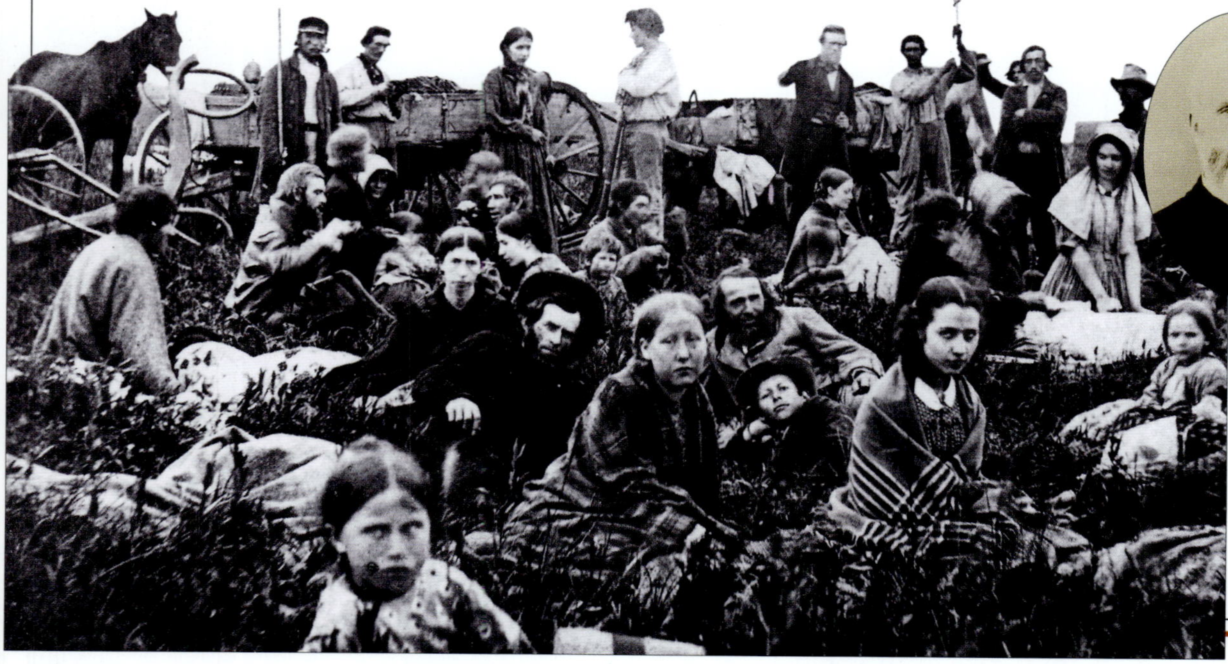

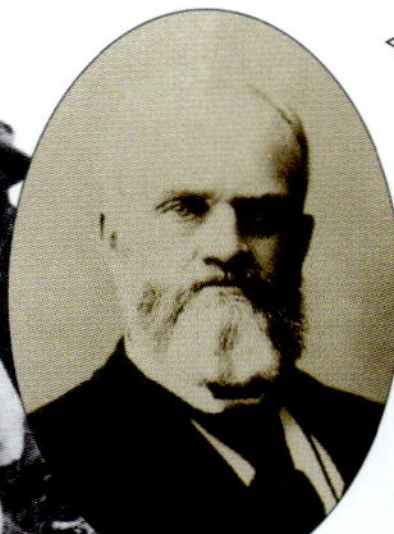

◁ **CORRUPT AGENT**
In 1861, the starving Dakotas appealed to agent, Thomas J. Galbraith, for relief, but he refused to release foodstuffs from the warehouse before treaty-guaranteed money arrived.

◁ **FLEEING THE TROUBLES**
This group of refugees, which included almost 30 women and children and two missionaries, fled the uprising with a horse-drawn buggy and a few oxcarts. They struggled eastwards, with no shelter from the winds and rain, until they reached the town of Henderson.

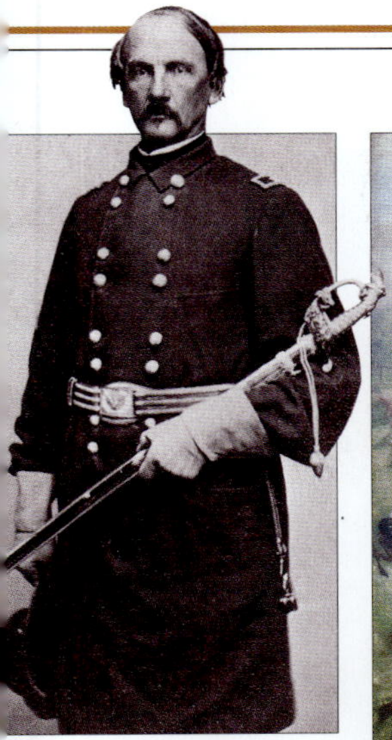

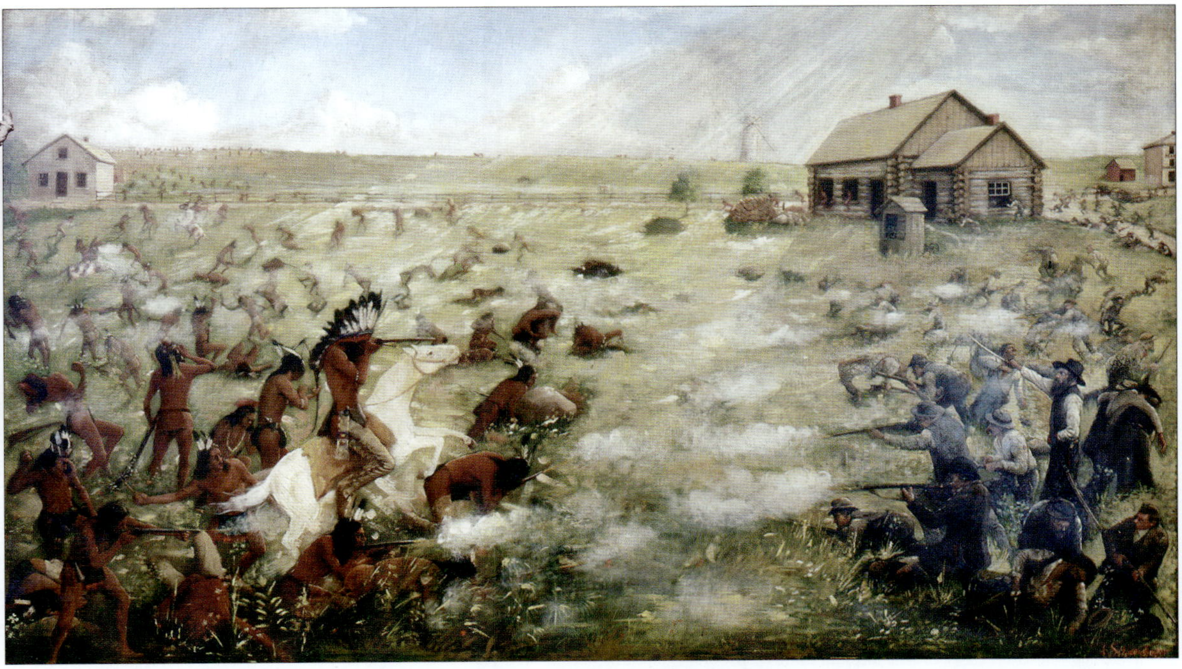

SIBLEY IN CHARGE
enry H. Sibley led Minnesota olunteer militias against the akota Indians besieging Fort idgely. By the time Sibley and is 1,500 men reached the fort, ne Dakotas had withdrawn.

nany as 400 whites the first day, and sending nundreds in panic to Fort Ridgely. Little Crow ed an assault on the fort, but three howitzers cut down 100 of his men. Another group, who tormed the town of New Ulm, were forced to etreat after a day of bitter fighting.

Not all Dakotas looked on whites as enemies: many protected them during the conflict. "Nearly every Indian had a friend he lid not want killed," explained Big Eagle, a Dakota chief, adding, "Of course he did not care about anyone else's friend."

The Minnesota governor sent General Henry H. Sibley into Minnesota with a force of 1,500 men. A detachment of Sibley's troops was attacked by Little Crow's warriors at Birch Coulee and held out for 31 hours until a relief force from the fort arrived and the Indians withdrew. Finally, on 23 September, 700 Santees decided to attack the army camp at Wood Lake, but they were no match for Sibley's troops and their artillery. Scattering in defeat, hundreds of Dakotas either fled to Canada or were captured and imprisoned at Fort Snelling. Hundreds were sentenced to be hanged, but President Lincoln later commuted the sentences for most of the prisoners. On 26 December 1862, 38 Dakotas were hanged simultaneously at Mankato, Minnesota, in the largest mass execution in the US.

△ FIERCE FIGHT AT NEW ULM
Four days after the first battle of New Ulm, a second battle was fought on 23 August 1862, when 650 Dakota warriors, led by Little Crow, attacked the town. New Ulm was ill-equipped for defense as few citizens had guns. They were joined by Judge Charles E. Flandrau and a few veteran Indian fighters, who repelled the Dakotas.

▽ DEFEAT FOR GRANT
One of the fiercest engagements of the Dakota uprising took place on 2–3 September 1862 at Birch Coulee. The Dakotas attacked while Captain Hiram Grant's soldiers were asleep, killing many of their horses, but were forced to retreat after General Sibley sent reinforcements to the scene.

▽ DAKOTA LEADERS
Dakota chiefs Mankato and Big Eagle led the attack on Fort Ridgely with Little Crow. Both fought Sibley's men at Birch Coulee and Wood Lake, where Mankato was killed. Big Eagle was imprisoned for three years.

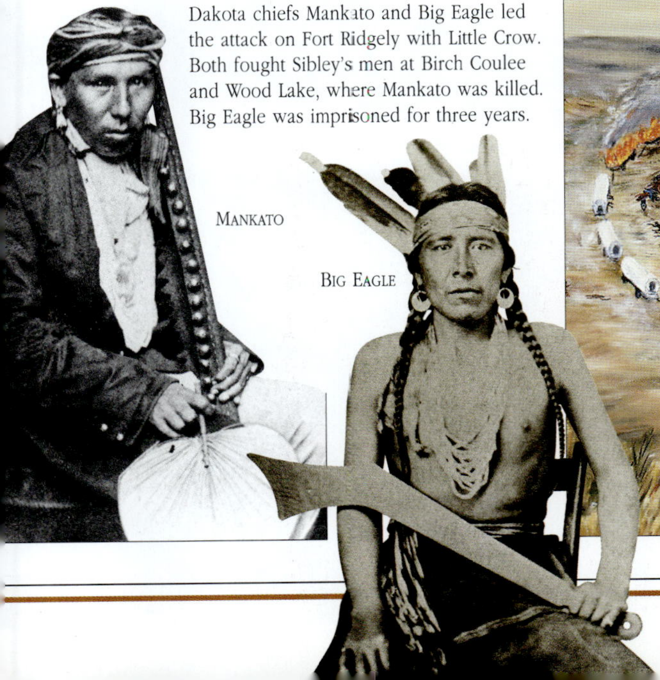

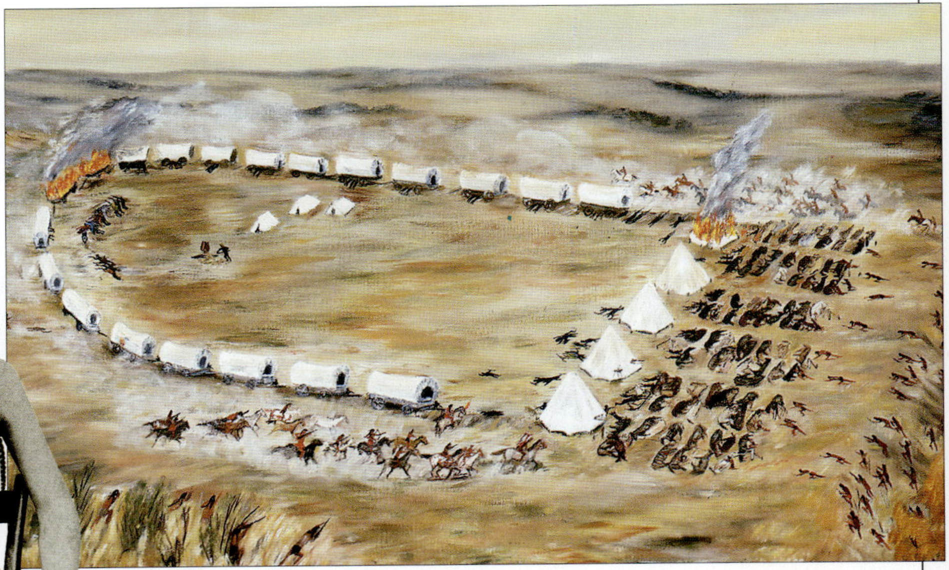

EXECUTIONS ORDERED

Following the Great Sioux (Santee Dakota) uprising, a military tribunal found 307 tribe members guilty of various offenses, on the flimsiest of evidence, and sentenced them to be hanged. President Lincoln called for the trial records and, despite protests by Minnesota officials, reduced the number to 38.

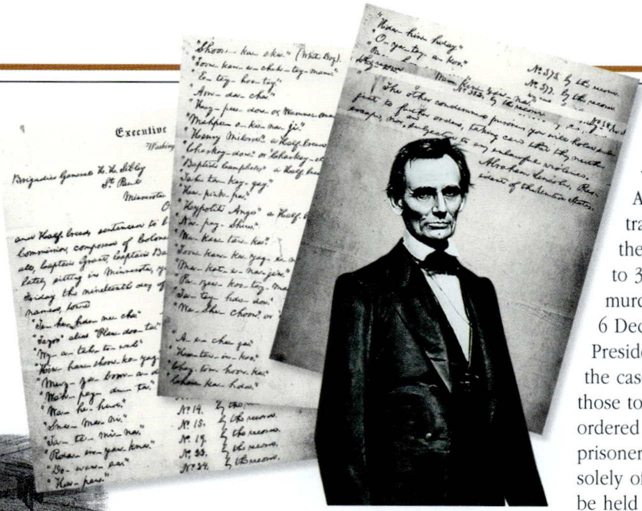

◁ **WARRANTS SIGNED**
After reviewing the trial transcripts, Lincoln reduced the number of condemned to 38 men found guilty of murder and rape. On 6 December 1862, the President hand-wrote a list of the case numbers and names of those to be executed. He then ordered that the other convicted prisoners – those judged guilty solely of participating in battle – be held subject to further orders.

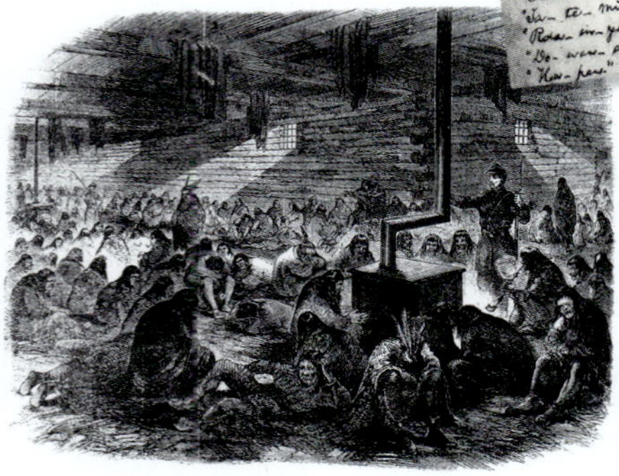

AWAITING THE VERDICT ▷
Guarded by soldiers, Dakota prisoners awaited the decisions being handed down by a five-man military tribunal. They were not allowed to have witnesses or attorneys to explain to them what was going on. Some trials lasted less than five minutes. Of the 392 men tried, 307 were sentenced to death by hanging.

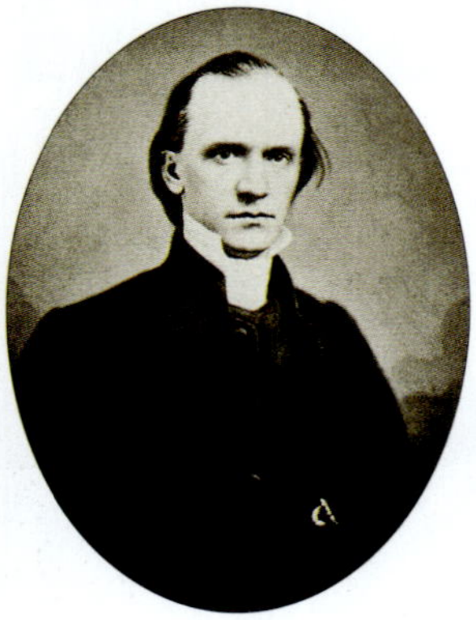

◁ **APPEAL FOR CLEMENCY**
A devoted friend of the Dakotas, Episcopal Bishop Henry B. Whipple appealed to President Lincoln to reprieve the condemned Dakota men. He argued that an unjust government Indian policy and corrupt Indian agents had sparked the violence.

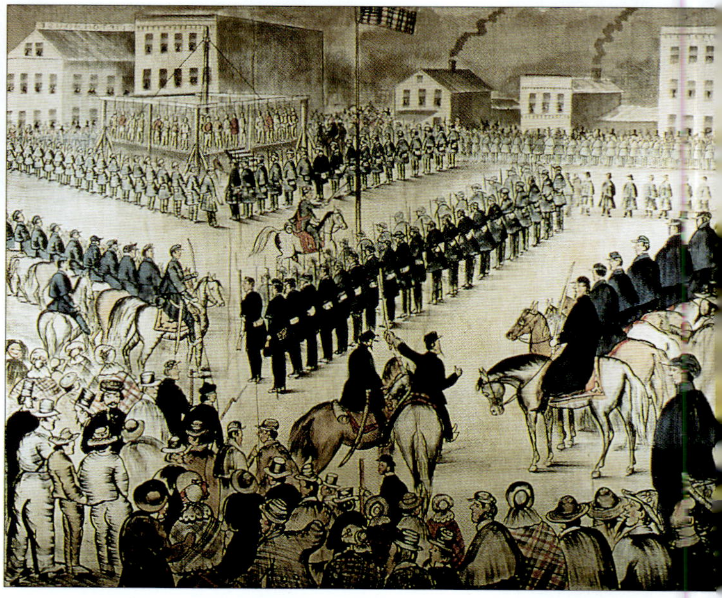

MASS HANGING AT MANKATO ▷
On 26 December 1862, in Mankato, Minnesota, 38 Santee Dakotas were hanged together in public in retribution for the Dakota uprising. The men went to their deaths chanting their death songs and trying to link their bound hands, man to man.

SANTEE DAKOTAS IMPRISONED

Some 1,700 men, women, and children were imprisoned by General Sibley in tipis cramped inside Fort Snelling, outside St. Paul, Minnesota; none of them had been convicted of any crime or brought to trial. Survivors of the internment were eventually sent to a distant reservation in what is now South Dakota. Other prisoners with reduced sentences, including Big Eagle, were imprisoned in Iowa, where nearly half of them died of disease.

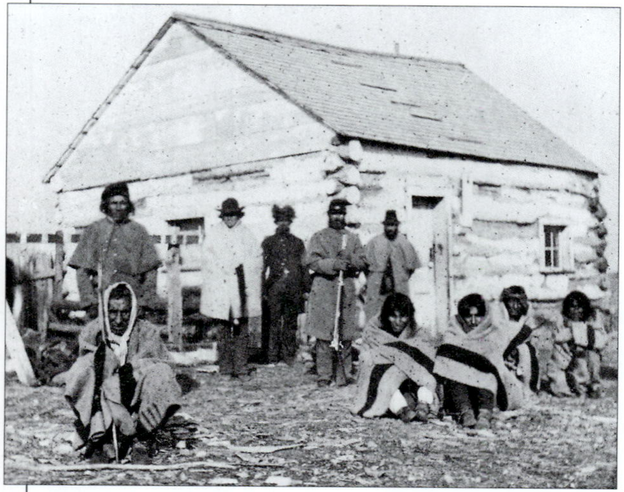

◁ **LOG-CABIN COURTROOM**
Wrapped in blankets, Dakota prisoners sit outside the log cabin that served as a courtroom for about half of the trials. Most of those condemned were convicted for merely being present at the battles of Fort Ridgely, New Ulm, Birch Coulee, or Wood Lake.

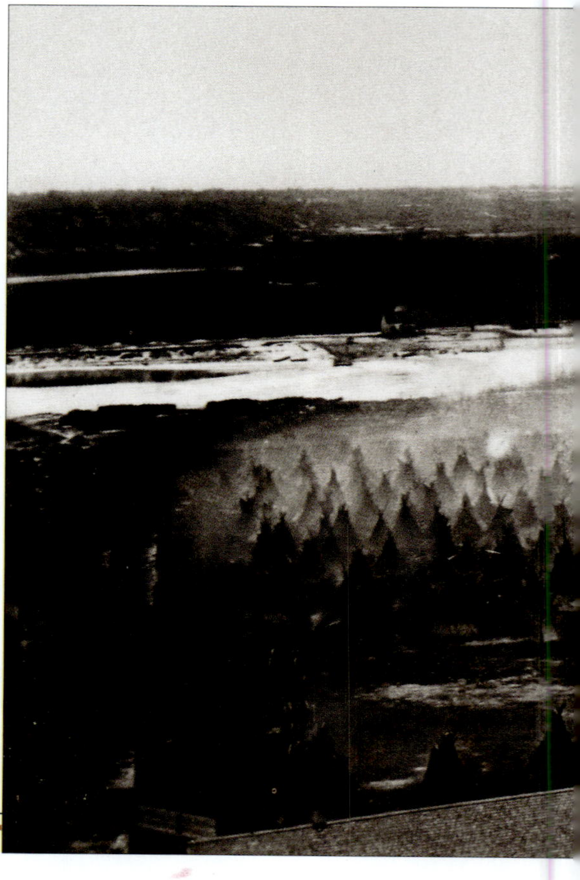

BLEAK INCARCERATION ▷
The Dakotas were confined in an inhospitable fenced camp within Fort Snelling. Established in 1819 at the juncture of the Mississippi and Minnesota Rivers, and located on low-lying fields that turned to mud, the fort provided no protection from icy winter winds.

NO DEAL IN CANADA

.ittle Crow fled to Canada with plans for a mighty
lliance of Dakotas and Lakotas of the Western
'lains, which would march across Minnesota to
eclaim their homeland. Rebuffed by the British
n Canada, who he had hoped would arm his
ndeavor, Little Crow returned to Minnesota.

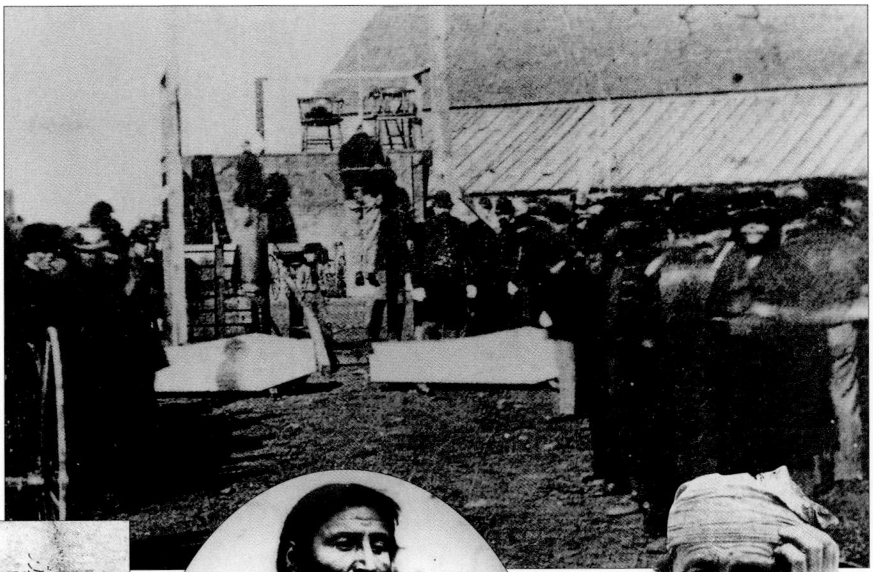

DASHED HOPES
Vhen the Dakotas were beaten t the Battle of Wood Lake, many ed to Canada, believing that the British were beholden to them or their assistance in the War of 812. British Canada in 1862, owever, did not share this view.

RINGLEADERS HANGED ▷
Two of the most wanted chiefs, Shakopee and Medicine Bottle, were tracked to Canada. They were drugged, smuggled across the border, and returned to stand trial. On 11 November 1865, the two were hanged at Fort Snelling.

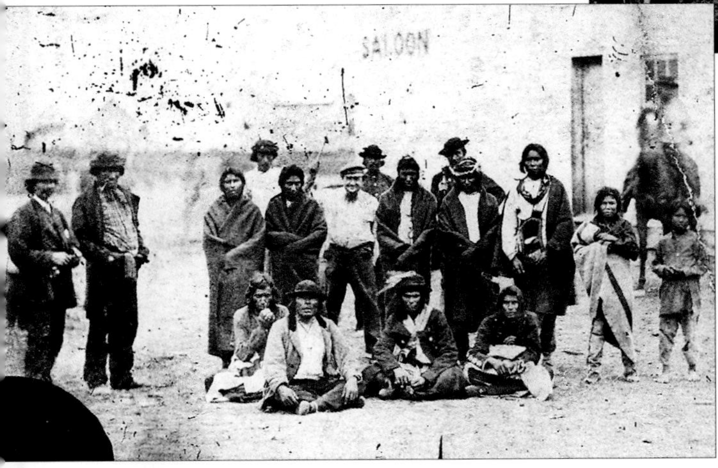

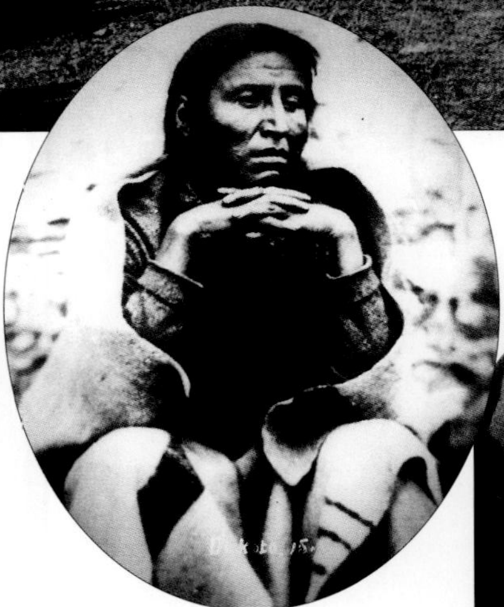

MEDICINE BOTTLE

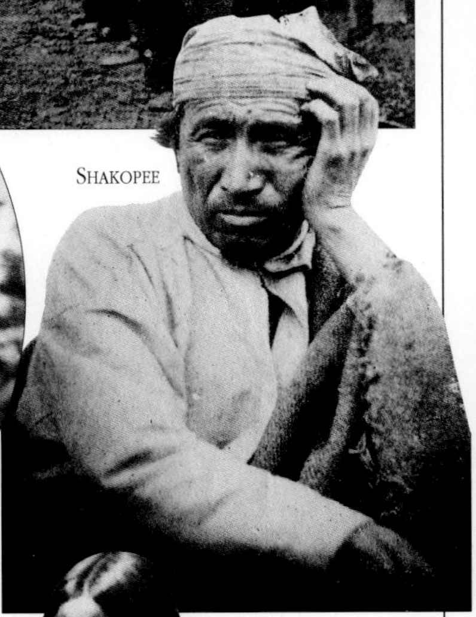

SHAKOPEE

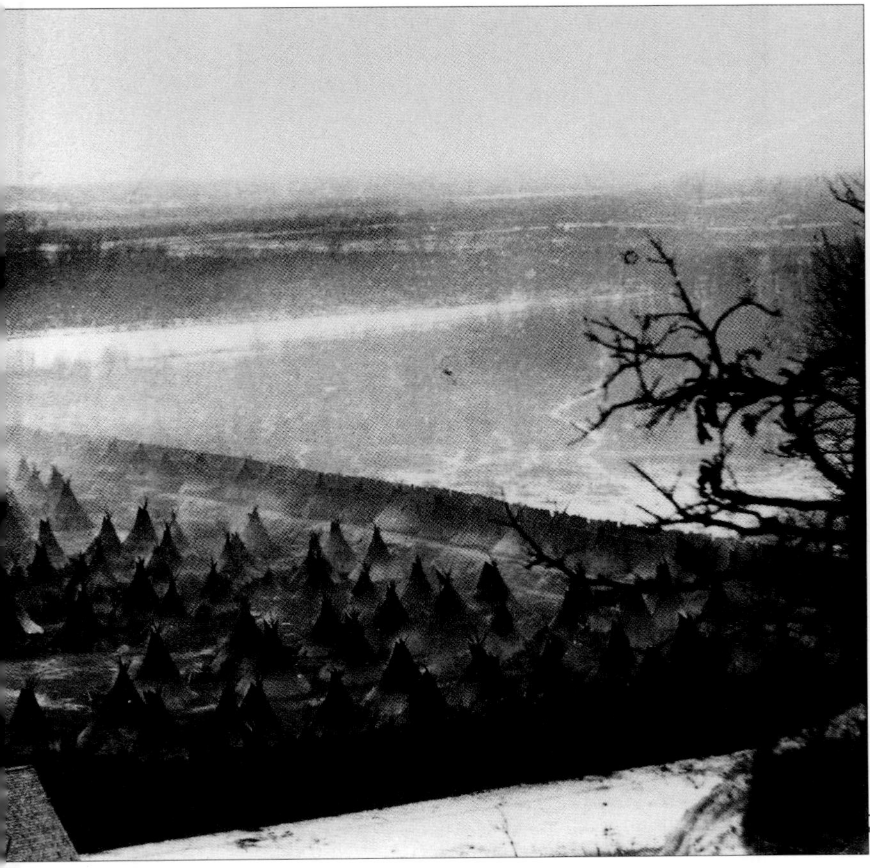

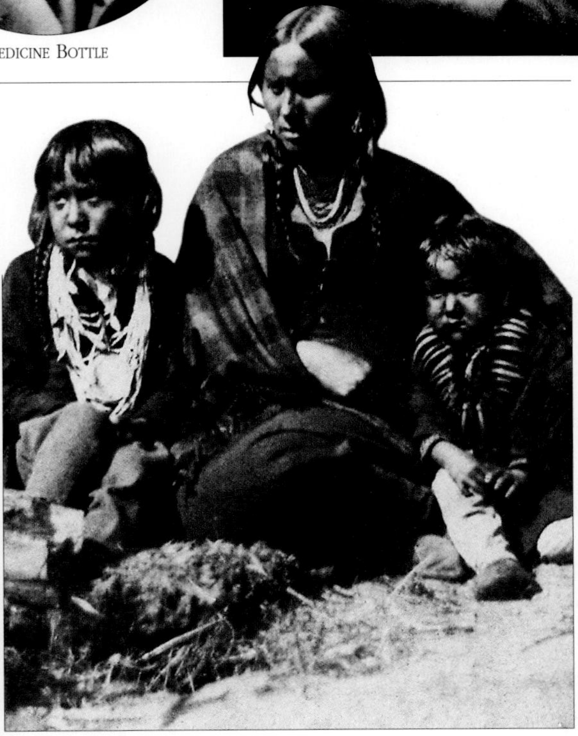

△ LITTLE CROW'S FAMILY HELD CAPTIVE
In 1863, Little Crow's wives and children (above) were imprisoned at Fort Snelling. Other Dakotas, whose homes and farms had been destroyed, entered the stockade for food and shelter. Rations were meager, however, and measles and other diseases were widespread.

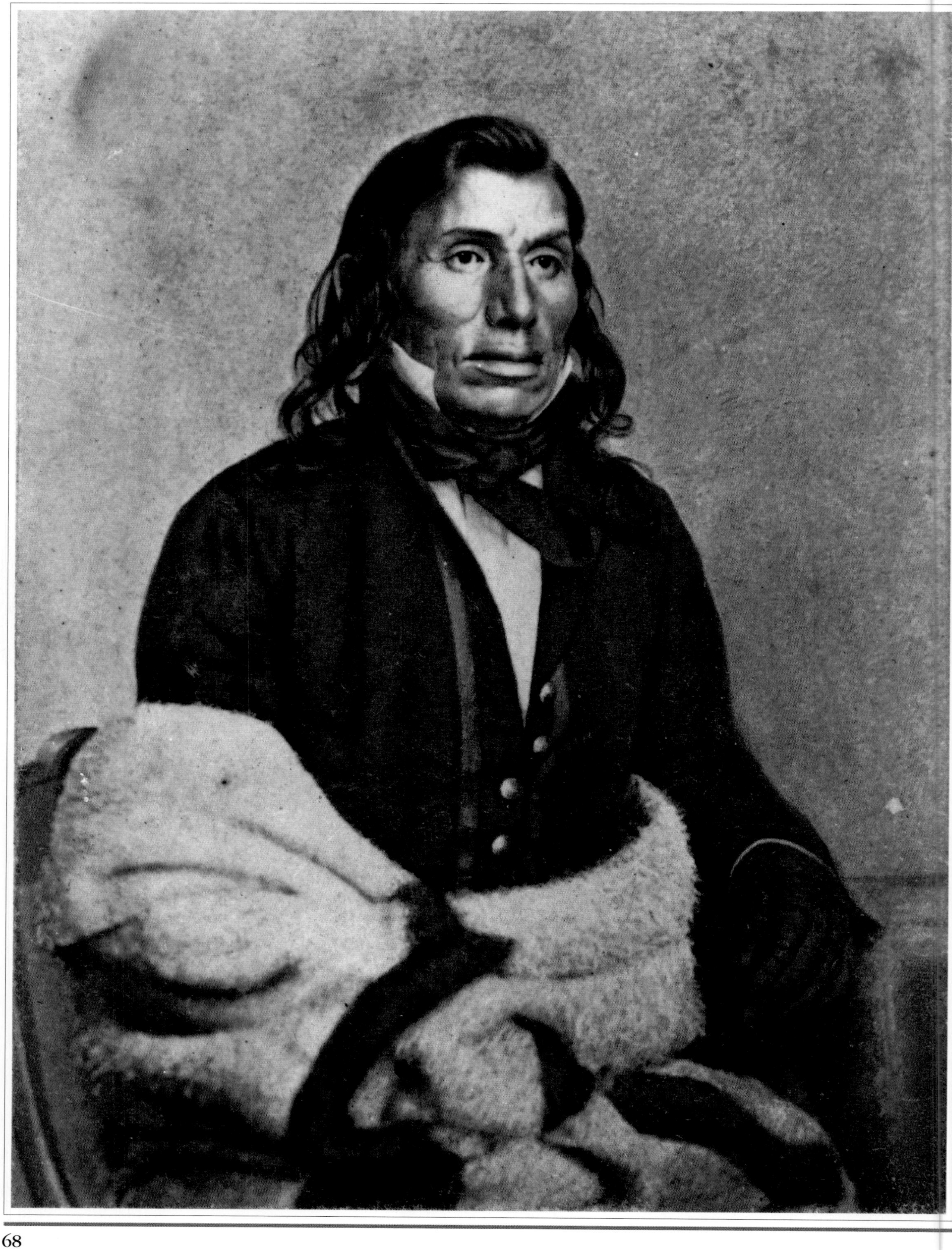

LITTLE CROW

1862: ON AGREEING TO LEAD THE SANTEE RESISTANCE

LITTLE CROW (*c.* 1810–63), A DAKOTA SIOUX, became principal chief of the Mdewakantons in 1834. Although he was condemned by many Dakotas for his adoption of white ways, at the onset of the 1862 uprising, on 18 August 1862, they asked Little Crow to lead them. This excerpt is from the speech he made on that occasion. Little Crow was wounded during the unsuccessful August 1862 attack on Fort Ridgely, which he led, but he survived to fight in most of the Dakotas' ensuing battles. After their defeat in 1862, Little Crow fled to Canada, but returned to Minnesota the following year, and was killed by a settler.

"We are only little herds of buffalo left scattered; the great herds that once covered the prairies are no more. See! – the white men are like the locusts when they fly so thick that the whole sky is a snowstorm. You may kill one – two – ten: yes, as many as the leaves in the forest yonder, and their brothers will not miss them. Kill one, kill two, kill ten, and ten times ten will come to kill you. Count your fingers all day long and white men with guns in their hands will come faster than you can count.

Yes, they fight among themselves [the Civil War] .... Do you hear the thunder of their big guns? No, it would take you two moons to run down to where they are fighting, and all the way your path would be among white soldiers as thick as tamaracks in the swamps of the Ojibways. Yes, they fight among themselves, but if you strike at them they will all turn on you and devour you and your women and little children just as the locusts in their time fall on the trees and devour all the leaves in one day.

You are fools. You cannot see the face of your chief; your eyes are full of smoke. You cannot hear his voice; your ears are full of roaring waters. Braves, you are little children – you are fools. You will die like the rabbits when the hungry wolves hunt them in the Hard Moon of January.

Little Crow is not a coward. He will die with you."

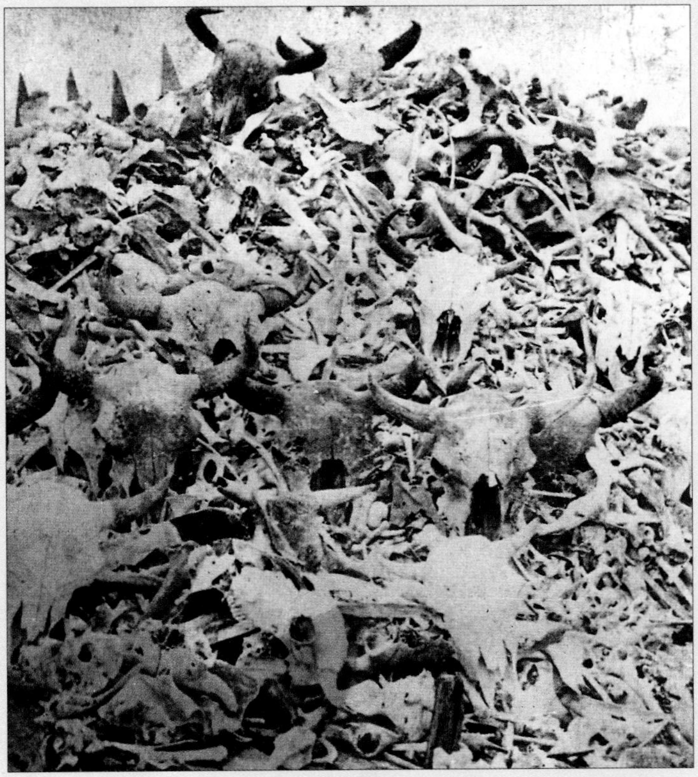

THE END OF A WAY OF LIFE
Throughout the nineteenth century, piles of skulls and bones mounted as white hunters slaughtered buffalo for sport and profit. Throughout the 1800s, Native peoples, too, died in droves from disease, starvation, war, and massacres. The loss of the buffalo ended a way of life for Plains Indians.

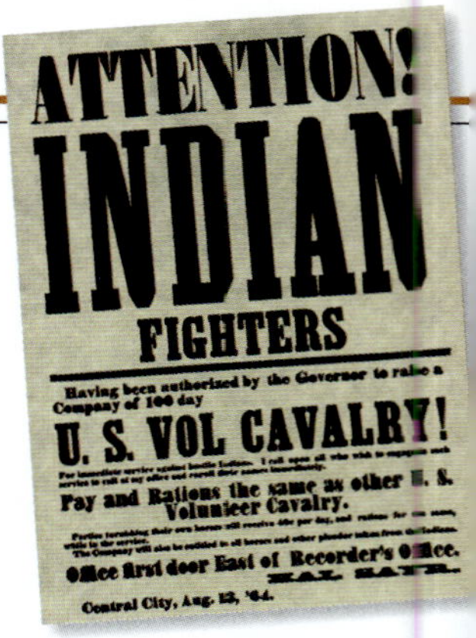

THE "HUNDRED DAZERS"
Recruited by Governor Evans and enlisted for just 100 days, the Third Colorado Cavalry had only one purpose: to fight Indians.

MASSACRE AT SAND CREEK

IN THE FALL OF 1864, 600 peaceful Southern Cheyenne and Arapaho people – two-thirds of them women and children – were encamped on a bend of Sand Creek in southeastern Colorado. There, in late November 1864, a column of 700 heavily armed Colorado militia, led by Indian-hater Colonel John Chivington, caught the village unaware. Showing no mercy, his forces slaughtered over 100 women and children and over two dozen men. The massacre, one of the most atrocious war crimes against American Indians, inflamed Indians throughout the Great Plains.

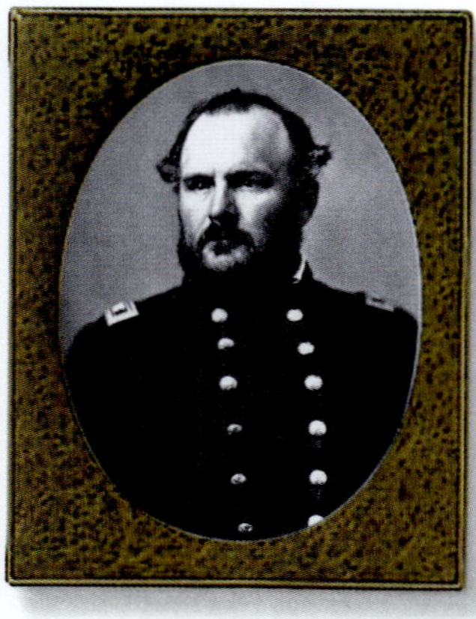

△ **COLONEL JOHN CHIVINGTON**
A hero of the Civil War, Chivington was reviled after his 1864 massacre of peaceful Cheyennes at Sand Creek.

IN THE SPRING OF 1864, the Dog Soldiers, an autonomous military society of Cheyenne warriors, unleashed fierce attacks on whites in Colorado's eastern plains, stealing horses and mules, butchering cattle, and killing dozens of settlers. They no longer subscribed to the accommodation policy of chiefs, like Black Kettle, who had signed an 1861 treaty agreeing to settle on a small reservation, stop hunting, and, with government aid, start planting.

Concerned that the militant Dog Soldiers endangered the majority of Cheyennes who were peaceful, Black Kettle tried and failed to stop their destructive acts. The chief wanted peace and, through the intervention of Major Edward Wynkoop, the sympathetic commander of Fort Lyon in southeastern Colorado, he was granted an audience, in September 1864, with Governor John Evans and Colonel John Chivington, military commander of the territory and a confirmed Indian hater. Evans, however, had no intention of stifling the war frenzy he had whipped up. The Indians were told that those who wanted peace should "submit to military authority" by laying down their arms at a local fort.

The Indians left the meeting and marched to Sand Creek, 40 miles northeast of Fort Lyon, where they planned to talk with Major Wynkoop. The army, however, replaced

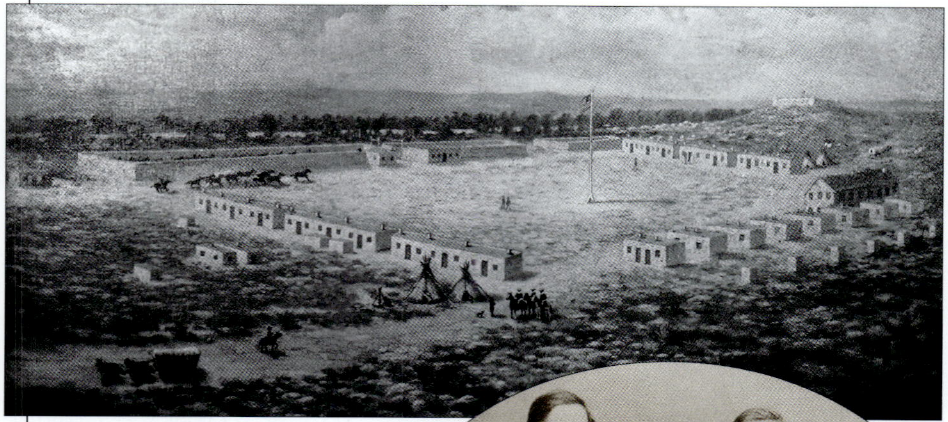

△ **BASE FOR THE MASSACRE**
Armed with four 12-pound mountain howitzers, Colonel Chivington and his troops marched out of Fort Lyon in November 1864 to launch the deadly attack on Cheyennes at Sand Creek.

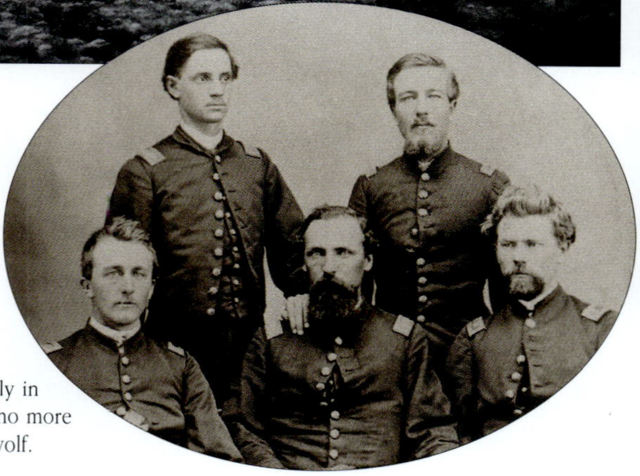

UNDISCIPLINED VOLUNTEERS ▷
Members of the Third Colorado were undisciplined and their officers had no control over them. They were united only in their eagerness to kill Indians, thinking no more of shooting an Indian than of killing a wolf.

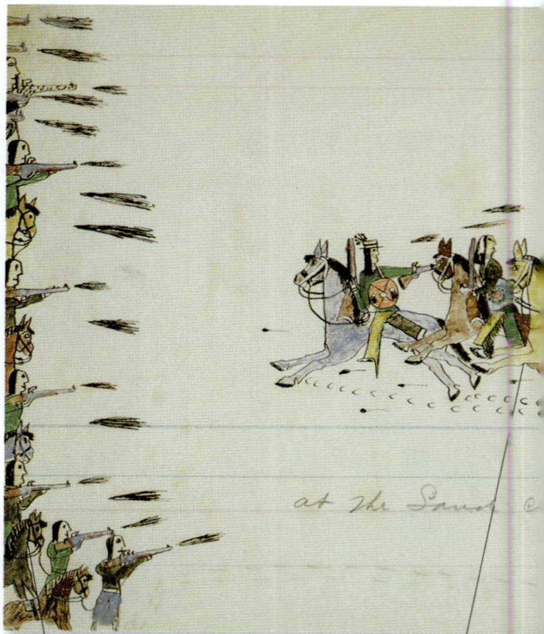

Indians, with rifles blazing, shoot at soldiers (not seen on drawing)

The Cheyennes aim their rifles at the soldiers behind them

Wynkoop with a new post commander, who cut the Indians' rations and demanded the surrender of their weapons.

Massacre at a Peaceful Village

On 29 November 1864, having assembled an army of 700 men at Fort Lyon, Chivington and his troops rode at dawn to Sand Creek, where peaceful Cheyennes had set up camp. A white flag of truce and an American flag flew above Black Kettle's tipi. The fact that the Cheyenne Dog Soldiers were not camped with Black Kettle's group did not stop Chivington from unleashing his attack. After releasing a hail of cannon fire into the village, Chivington's officers lost control of their men, who killed every Indian they could find. At least one officer refused to participate when it became clear that these Indians were peaceful. After six hours, some 150 Indians, mostly women and children, lay dead. Black Kettle survived the slaughter and returned to search for his wife whom he found alive but severely injured.

Coloradans hailed the soldiers, who scalped and mutilated Indian bodies. In Washington, however, news of Sand Creek was poorly received. President Lincoln replaced Evans as Colorado's governor and a Congressional inquiry castigated Chivington for the massacre.

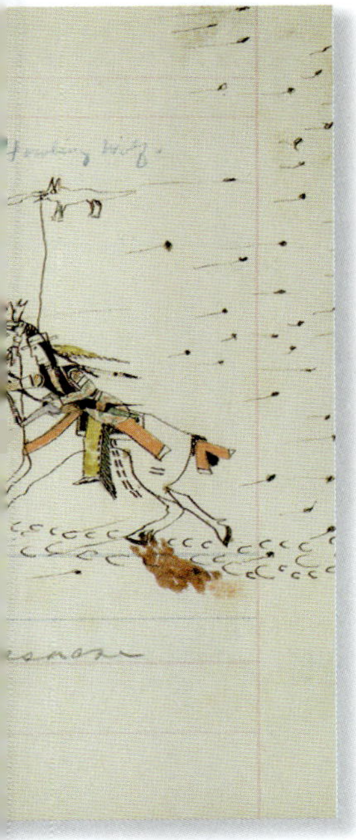

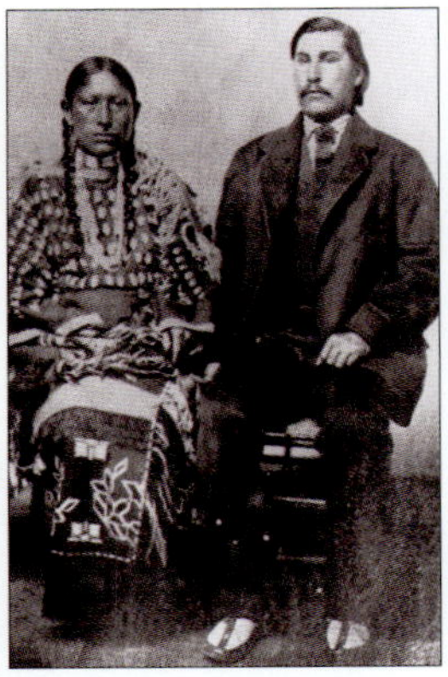

△ EYEWITNESSES
George Bent, the son of well-known fur trader William Bent and his Southern Cheyenne wife, Owl Woman, recorded the Indian side of events at Sand Creek. Here, Bent poses with his wife, Magpie, a niece of Black Kettle.

△ RECORDING THE BATTLE
Southern Cheyenne artist Howling Wolf used a traditional Plains hide painting to record his participation in the battle at Sand Creek. He identified himself in the traditional way by attaching a line from his head to a drawing of a wolf overhead.

DENVER DELEGATION

In September 1864, having gained the Indians' respect and trust, Major Edward Wynkoop, commander of Fort Lyon, led a delegation of Southern Cheyenne and Arapaho leaders, headed by Black Kettle, to Camp Weld, near Denver, to meet with Colorado Governor Evans. Black Kettle greeted Evans in council there with an appeal: "All we ask is that we may have peace with the whites."

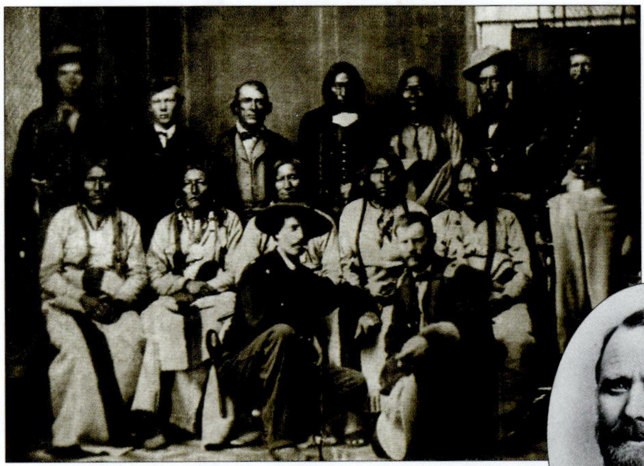

◁ CAMP WELD CONFERENCE
Little was accomplished at the peace conference at Camp Weld in September 1864, but Black Kettle (seated, third from left) and his fellow chiefs, believing that peace had been made, thought that they would be safe in their camp at Sand Creek.

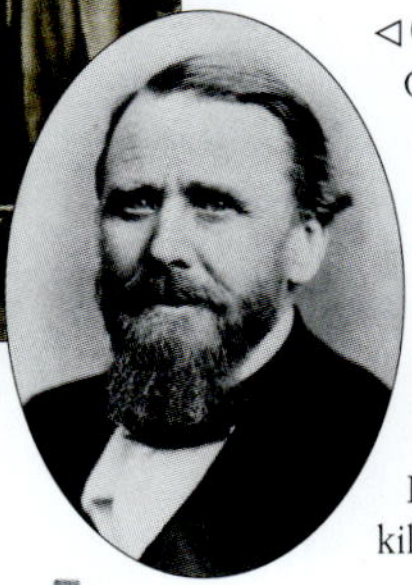

◁ GOVERNOR EVANS
On learning that the Indians sought peace, Evans replied, "But what shall I do with the Third Colorado regiment if I make peace? They have been raised to kill Indians, and they must kill Indians."

▽ PASSING THROUGH DENVER
Two months before the Sand Creek massacre, the Southern Cheyenne and Arapaho Indian delegation passed through Denver on their way to Camp Weld, where the parley was to take place. They traveled past Governor Evans's home, on their right.

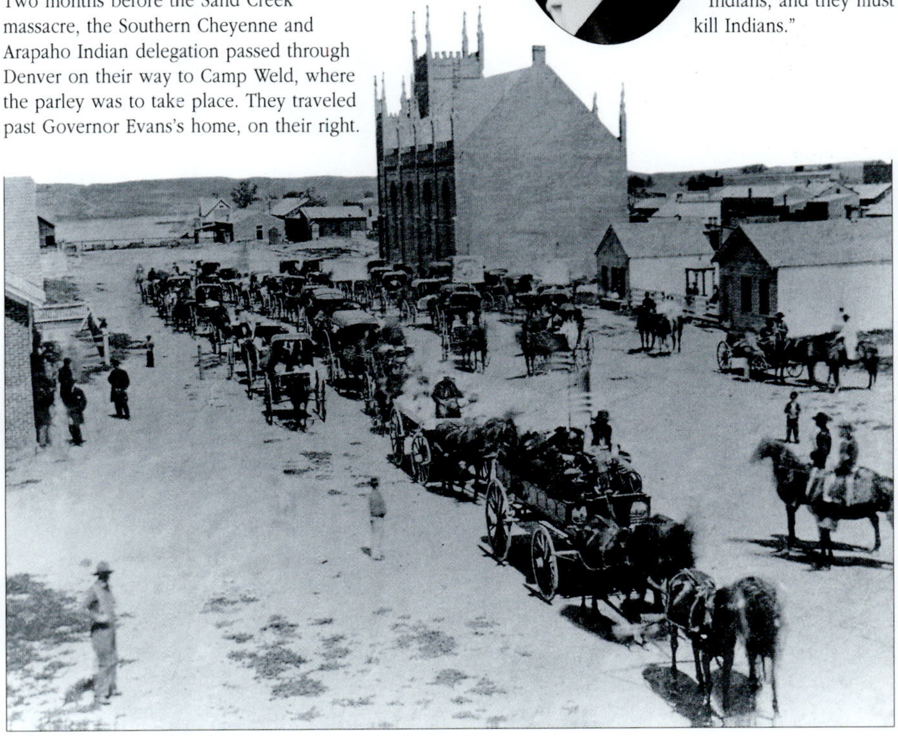

"... I want you to give all the chiefs of the soldiers here to understand that we are for peace, and we have made peace, that we may not be mistaken by them for enemies ..."

BLACK KETTLE TO GOVERNOR EVANS AND COLONEL JOHN CHIVINGTON, DENVER, 1864

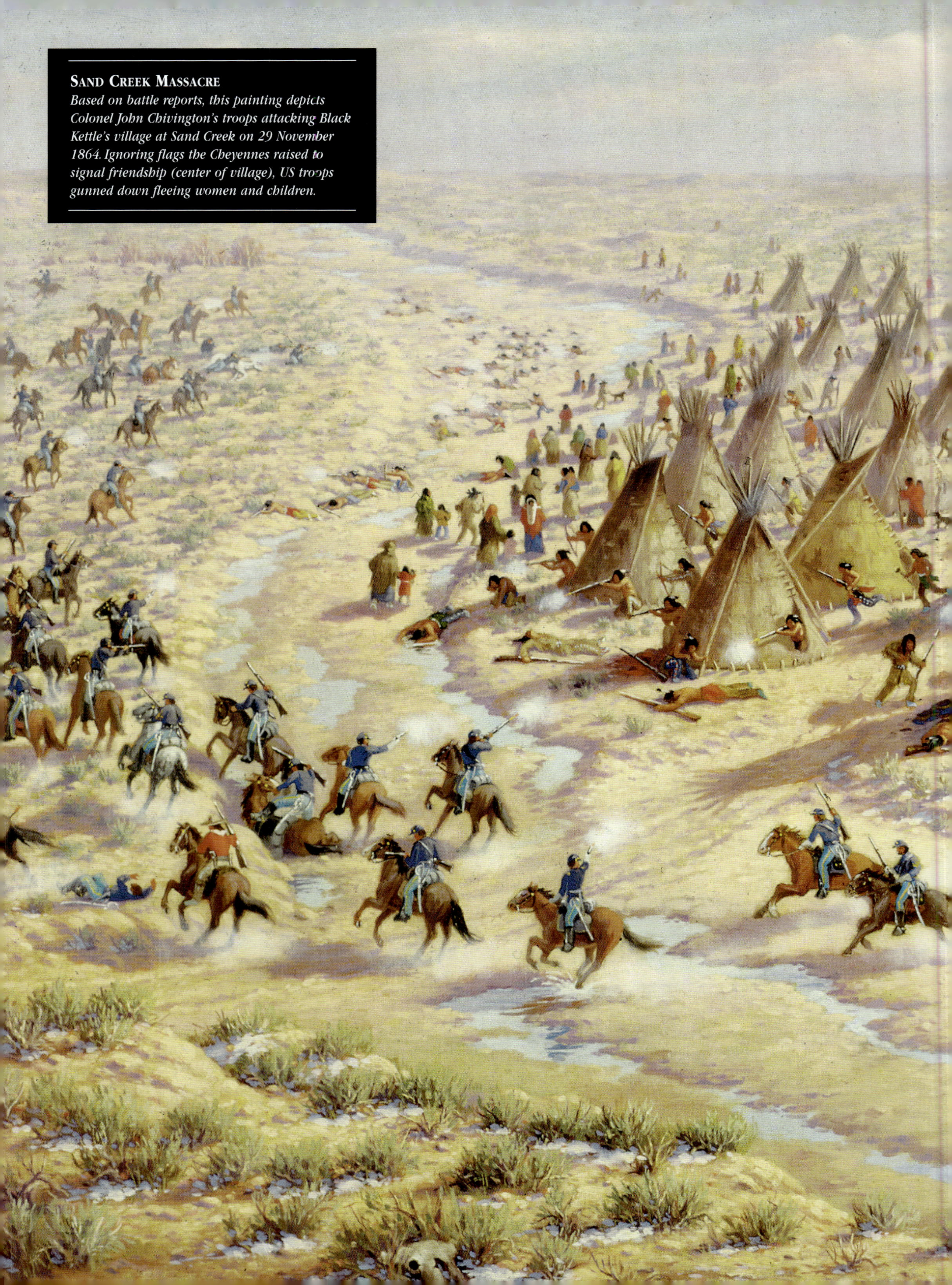

Sand Creek Massacre
Based on battle reports, this painting depicts Colonel John Chivington's troops attacking Black Kettle's village at Sand Creek on 29 November 1864. Ignoring flags the Cheyennes raised to signal friendship (center of village), US troops gunned down fleeing women and children.

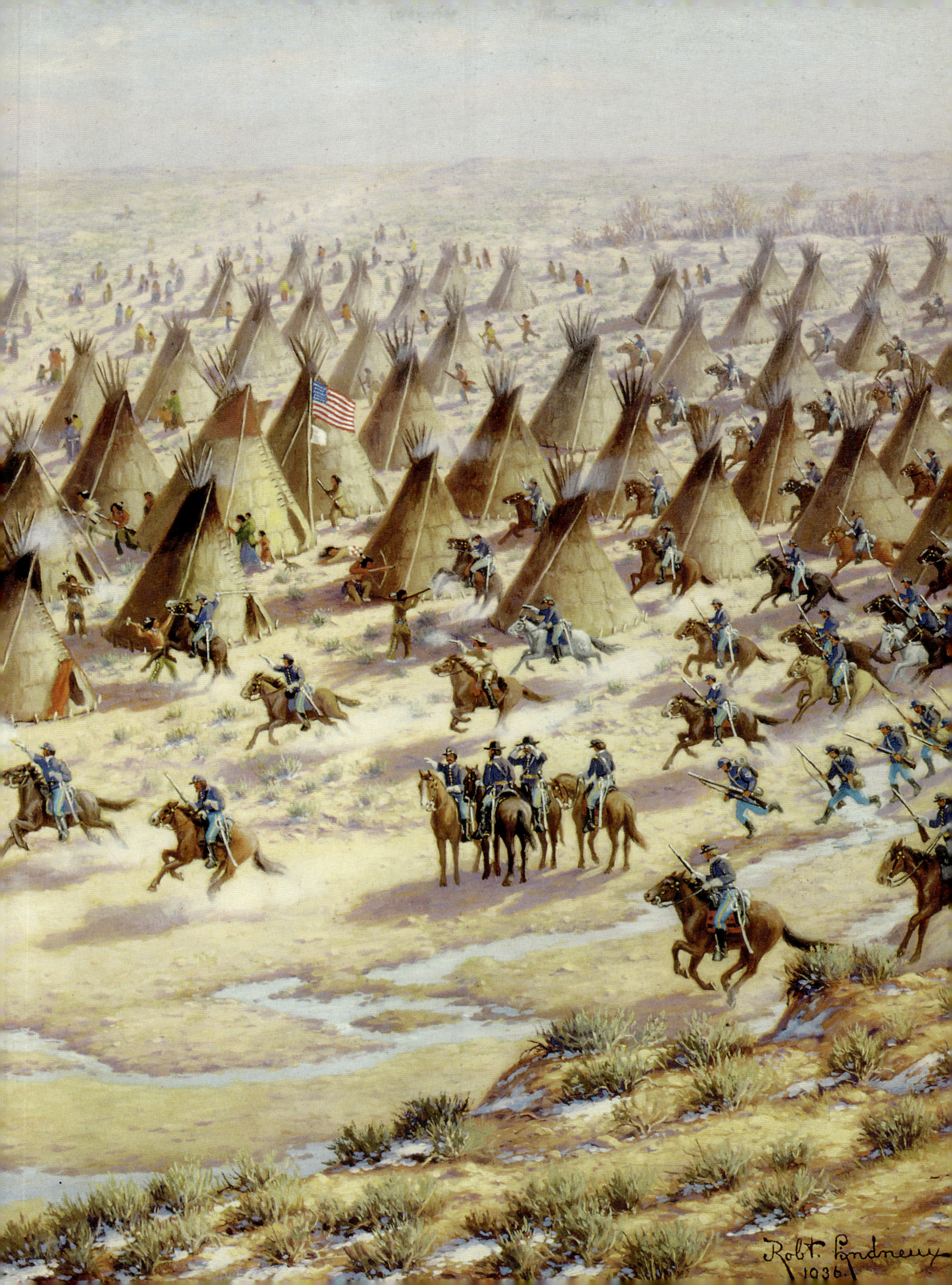
Robt. Lindneux
1936

THE NAVAJO LONG WALK

IN 1862, GENERAL JAMES H. CARLETON appointed his old friend Kit Carson to force the Navajos from their homeland in Arizona and New Mexico. Carson destroyed their crops and flocks and starved most of the tribe into surrender. They were then marched 350 miles (563 kilometres) to a concentration camp in New Mexico, where they endured four years of starvation and disease before being permitted to return to their homeland.

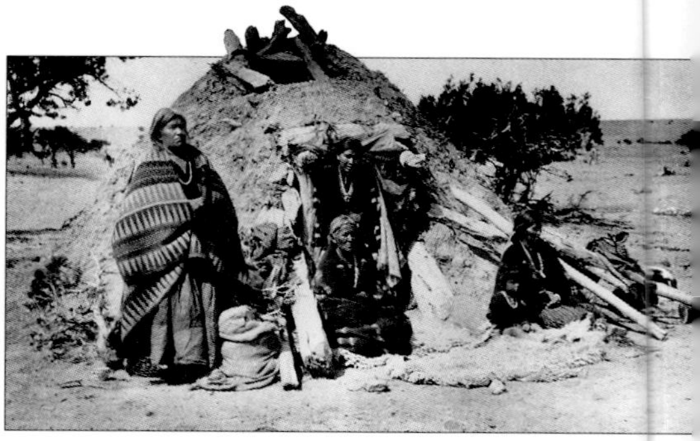

NAVAJO HOGANS
In 1863, the Navajos lived in hogans – well-insulated shelters of earth over a log framework, generally cone-shaped, but later built with six or eight sides. Hogan doorways always faced east.

LEGENDARY CARSON

Scout, guide, trapper, trader, and army officer, Christopher (Kit) Carson was also an Indian agent, once respected by the Indians he had served. Acting on the orders of General Carleton, he carried out a scorched-earth campaign against Navajos and Apaches.

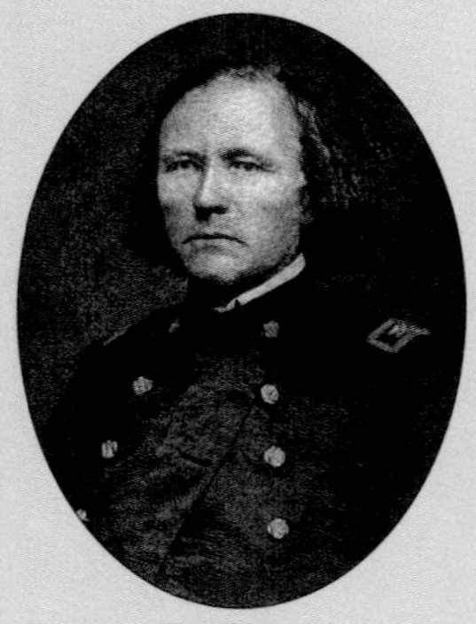

KIT CARSON

DURING THE CIVIL WAR, General James H. Carleton was appointed to defend New Mexico against invading Confederates. Arriving too late to confront the Confederates, who had withdrawn to Texas, he turned his attention to conquering Apaches and Navajos. Assisted by Colonel Kit Carson and five companies of New Mexico Volunteers, he set out to impose on the Indians the choice of going to a reservation outside the homeland, or fighting to the death.

In April 1863, after conquering the Mescalero Apaches and sending them to Bosque Redondo, a reservation in eastern New Mexico, Carleton met with Navajo chiefs Barboncito and Delgadito. He told them that they must go there, too, and become year-round farmers. When the Navajos resisted, Carleton appointed Kit Carson, a man the Indians had once called friend, to conquer them. Like good soldiers, Carson and his troops destroyed everything in their path – hogans, crops, stock, water holes, and carefully tended peach orchards.

By the middle of March 1864, more than 6,000 Navajos had surrendered and awaited deportation. The soldiers organized the "Long Walk," during which the Navajos marched the 350 miles (563 km) from Fort Defiance, Arizona, to the reservation on the Pecos River in New Mexico. Hundreds more Navajos were taken prisoner or surrendered to federal troops over the next few months. By late 1864, over 8,000 Natives – three-fourths of the tribe – had been moved to the fort.

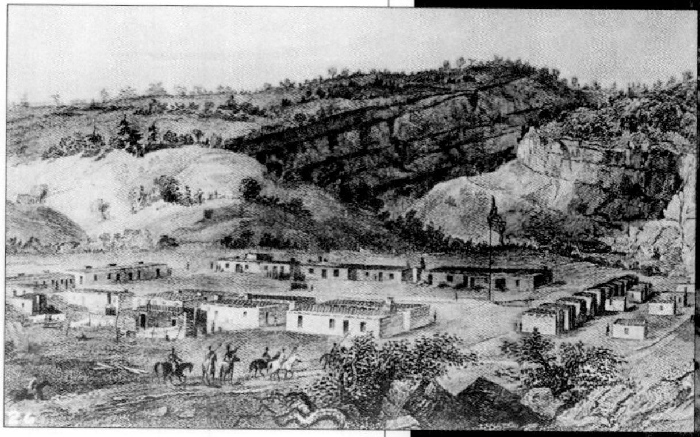

△ FORT DEFIANCE, ARIZONA
Established in 1851, Fort Defiance was located in the heart of Navajo country. It held Navajos who surrendered or were captured. In 1860, an attack by 1,000 Navajos, led by Manuelito and Barboncito, almost succeeded in capturing the fort.

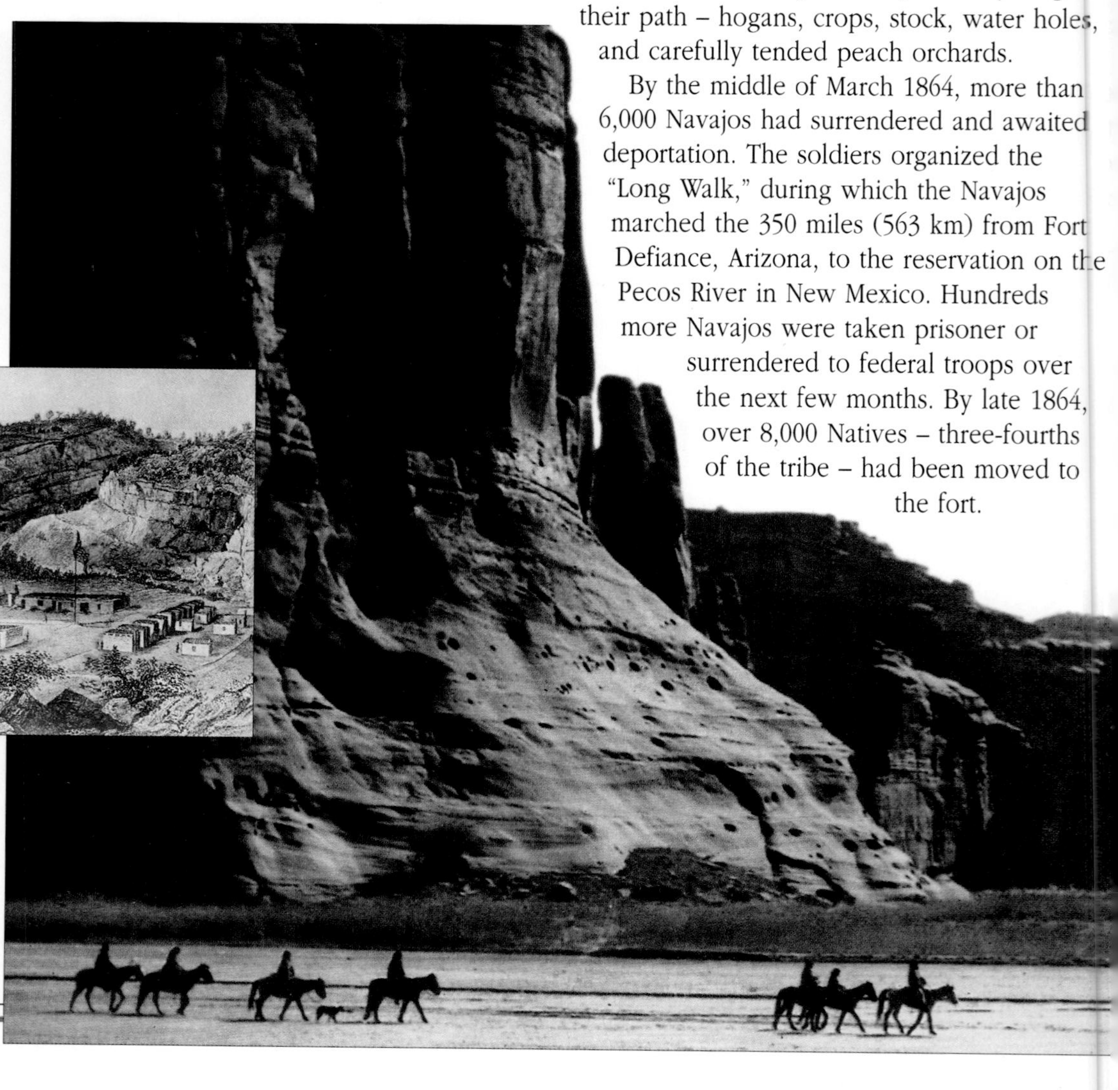

In 1866, Navajo chief Manuelito surrendered. With a remnant of the tribe, he had withdrawn far to the west rather than yield to Carleton. Manuelito's surrender marked the final triumph of Carleton's military campaign and, en route to Bosque Redondo, Manuelito was paraded as a prisoner through the streets of Santa Fe.

Wretched Conditions at Fort Sumner

Between 1864 and 1868, huge numbers of Navajos were crammed together into 40 square miles (104 square kilometres) of arid land incapable of supporting them. They willingly planted crops, but flood, drought, and pests destroyed them. Sheep and goats did not have enough grass to eat, and tribes from the plains raided the herds. Government rations were not sufficient to hold off starvation, alkaline water from the Pecos River caused gastro-intestinal problems, and government clothing failed to protect the prisoners from the winter's chill. Seriously weakened by malnutrition and exposure to the cold, about 2,000 prisoners at Bosque Redondo died of pneumonia, measles, and other diseases.

By 1868 it was clear that Carleton's plan to turn Navajos into farmers had failed. After tribal leaders signed a treaty giving up most of their land, the survivors were permitted to return to their beloved homeland.

▽ NAVAJO STRONGHOLD
Harried by Kit Carson, thousands of Navajos took refuge in Canyon de Chelly, Arizona, their tribal home for centuries. But, in January 1864, Carson marched defiantly through the canyon, corralling sheep and destroying fruit orchards. Eventually, thousands of Navajos were starved into surrender.

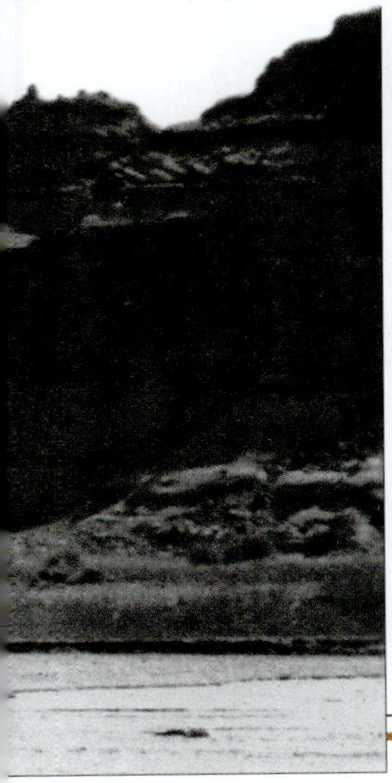

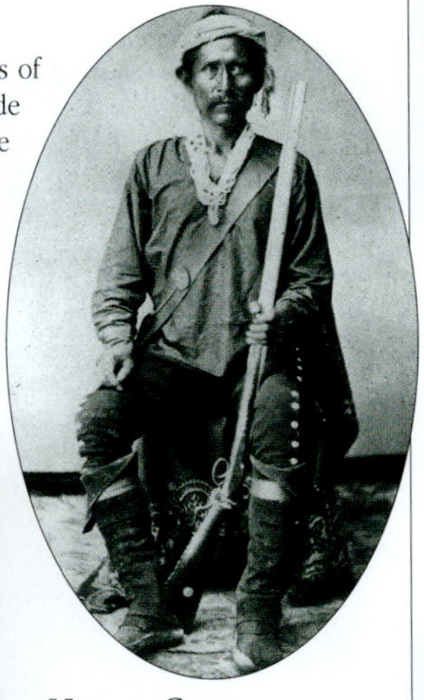

△ NAVAJO CHIEF
Barboncito resisted arrest after the Navajo defeat, but finally surrendered in 1864. On the tribe's return home in 1868, General William Sherman appointed both Barboncito and Manuelito chiefs of the Navajo Nation to lead and speak for the tribe on their reservation.

ROUTE TO DESPAIR

The Navajos' march to Bosque Redondo, over several hundred miles of frozen snow and rocky terrain, began in winter. Shocked by the forced removal and strange foods they ate along the way, hundreds became weak from diarrhea. Those who were too tired or sick to walk were shot. Stragglers were often taken captive and enslaved by Mexicans.

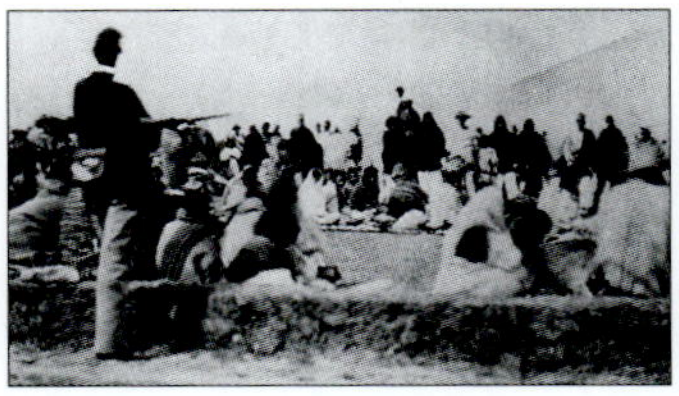

△ UNDER ARMED GUARD
Initially, guards at Fort Sumner kept close watch over the Navajos, but later they were allowed to roam up to 15 miles (24 km) in search of firewood.

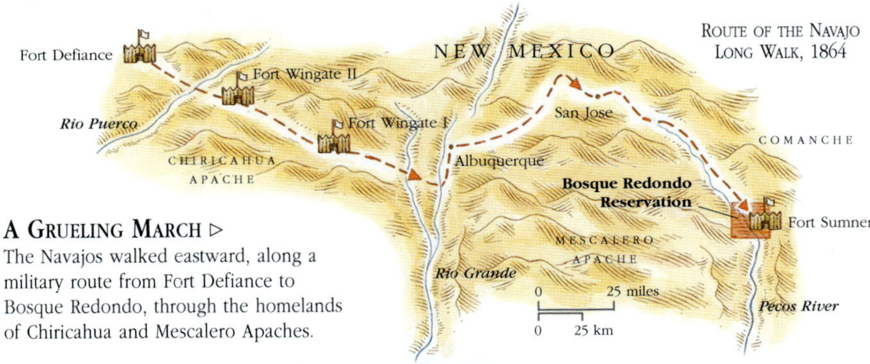

ROUTE OF THE NAVAJO LONG WALK, 1864

A GRUELING MARCH ▷
The Navajos walked eastward, along a military route from Fort Defiance to Bosque Redondo, through the homelands of Chiricahua and Mescalero Apaches.

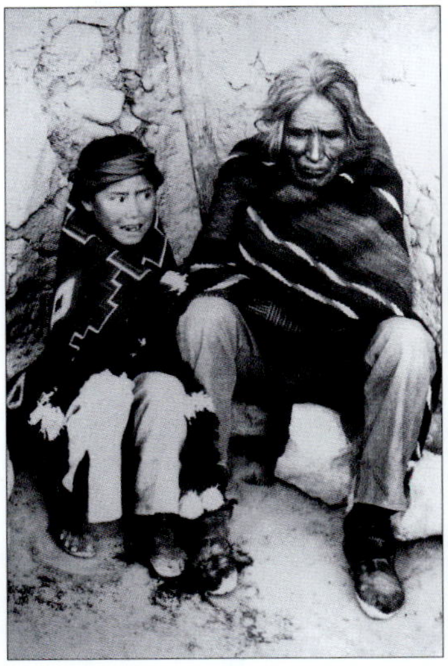

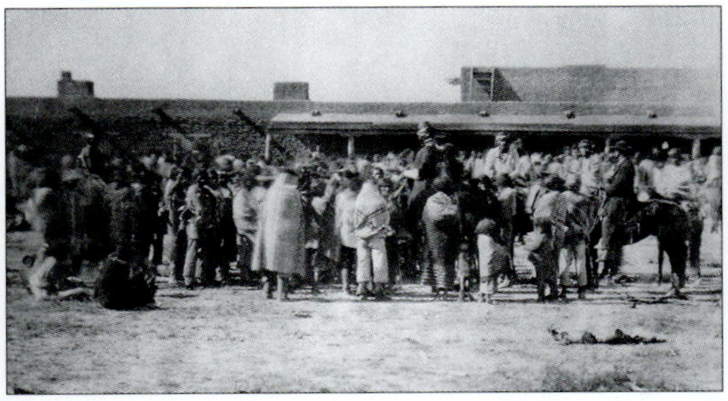

◁ BLEAK IMPRISONMENT
Prisoners at Bosque Redondo lived in crude shelters carved out of the earth and roofed with branches. They struggled to survive the cold winters, lacking firewood and with only gunnysacks for blankets.

△ SURVIVAL RATIONS
As crops failed and foods like grass seed, wild berries, and yucca fruit were inadequate to nourish them, the Navajos were provided with rations of unfamiliar foodstuffs such as bacon, flour, and coffee.

FORCED LABOR ▷
Under the watchful eyes of armed troops, Navajos were forced to construct large buildings for the use of the soldiers. In contrast to the dismal conditions in which the Navajos were forced to live, the soldiers lived in comfort, with fireplaces to warm them in winter.

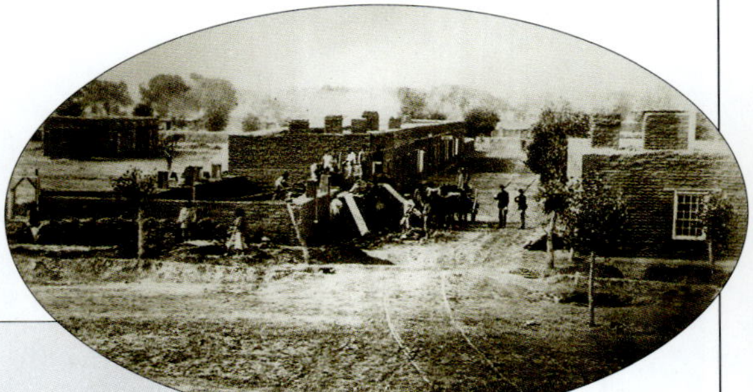

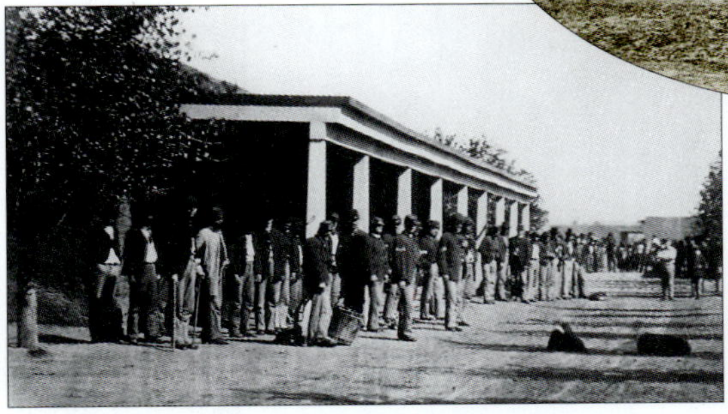

◁ HOSTILE GUARDS
Soldiers at Bosque Redondo permitted Comanches, enemies of the Navajos, to come into the area and steal Navajo livestock. Unarmed, the prisoners could not protect their stock. The guards also turned a blind eye to fights that broke out between Navajos and Mescaleros.

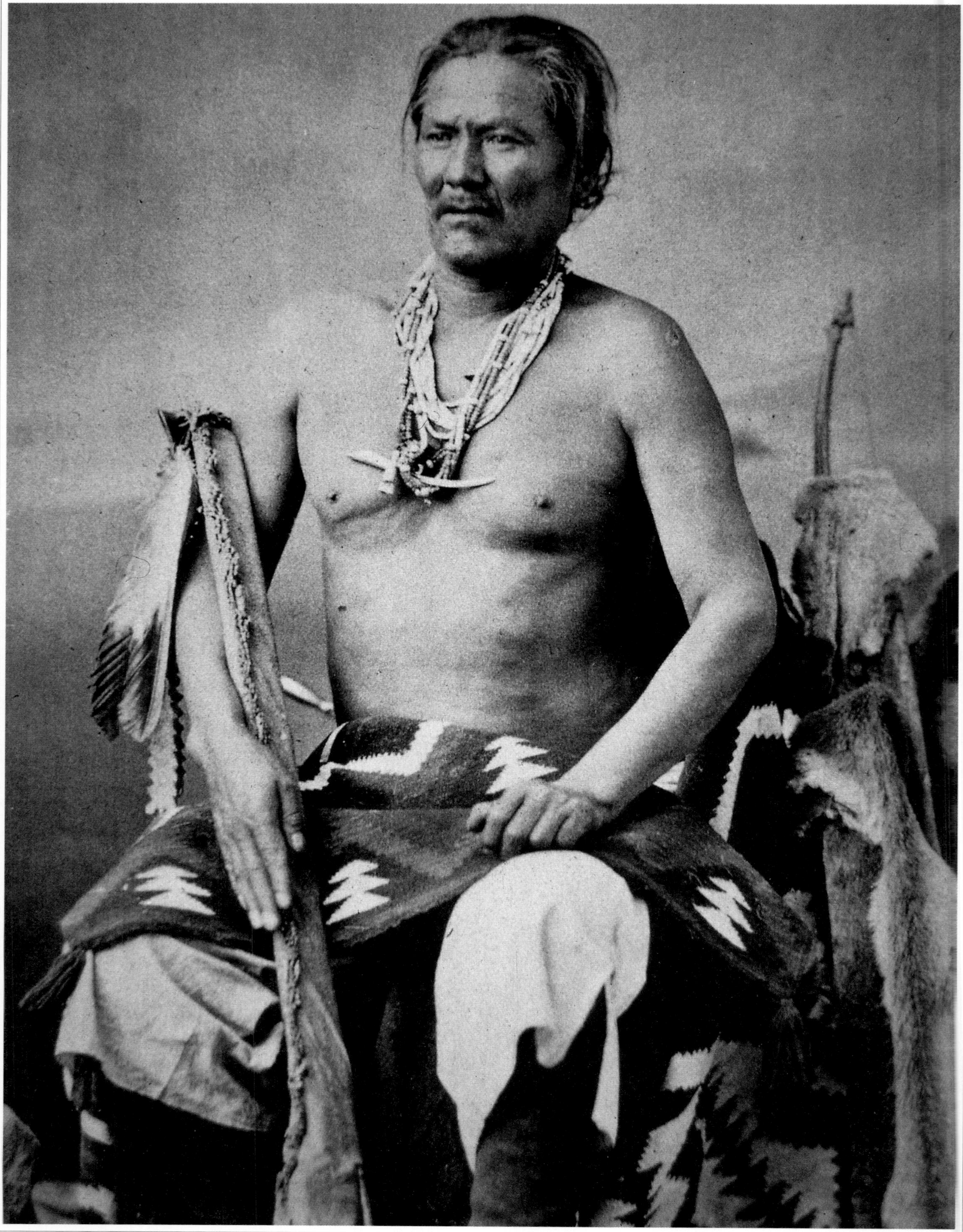

MANUELITO

1885: ON THE SIGNING OF THE 1868 TREATY AT FORT SUMNER

IN 1868, MANUELITO (*c.* 1818–94) and other Navajo chiefs traveled to Fort Sumner, New Mexico, to plead their case for a return to their homeland from the hated Bosque Redondo reservation. After the signing of the 1868 treaty at Fort Sumner, which permitted Navajos to return home, Manuelito was appointed principal chief of the Navajo Nation, a position he held until 1885. In 1876 he traveled to Washington, DC, where he met with President Grant to protest the opening of a portion of Navajo tribal lands to white settlement. In 1885, Manuelito gave this account of the June 1868 treaty signing at Fort Sumner.

"We promised to keep the treaty .... We promised four times to do so. We all said 'yes' to the treaty, and he gave us good advice. He was General Sherman. We told him we would try to remember what he said. He said: 'I want all you people to look at me.' He stood up for us to see him. He said if we would do right we could look people in the face. Then he said: 'My children, I will send you back to your homes.' The nights and days were long before it came time for us to go to our homes. The day before we were to start we went a little way towards home, because we were so anxious to start. We came back and the Americans gave us a little stock to start with and we thanked them for that. We told the drivers to whip the mules, we were in such a hurry. When we saw the top of the mountain from Albuquerque we wondered if it was our mountain, and we felt like talking to the ground, we loved it so, and some of the old men and women cried with joy when they reached their homes.

The agent told us here how large our reservation was to be. A small piece of land was surveyed off to us, but we think we ought to have had more. Then we began to talk about more land, and we went to Washington to see about our land. Some backed out of going for fear of strange animals and from bad water, but I thought I might as well die there as here. I thought I could do something at Washington about the land. I had a short talk with the Commissioner. We were to talk with him next day, but the agent brought us back without giving us a chance to say what we wanted .... I tell these things in order that you might know what troubles we have had, and how little satisfaction we got. Therefore we have told you that the reservation was not large enough."

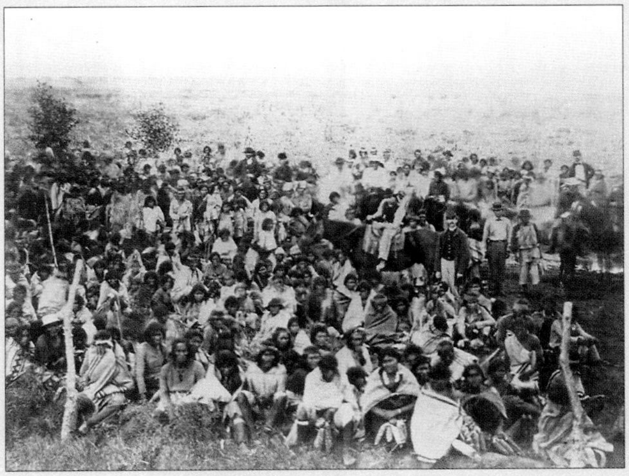

FAR FROM THEIR HOMELAND
In 1866, Navajo captives were photographed at Fort Sumner, New Mexico. After their release in June 1868, tribal chiefs led the survivors, many of them naked and barefoot, back to Navajo land. The journey took 15–20 days, during which many older people died; others simply gave up walking and settled down far from their homeland.

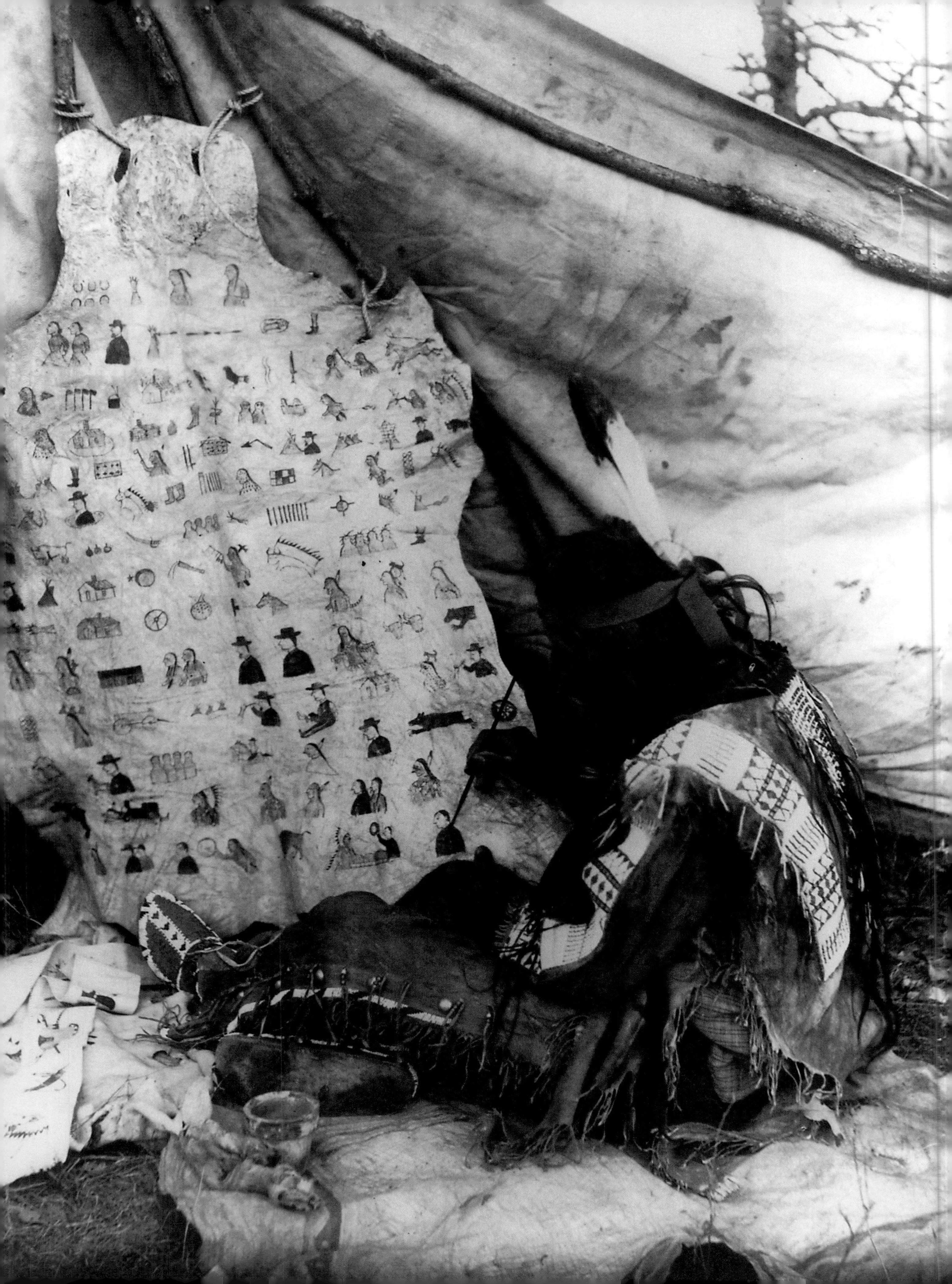

1860s to 1890s

WAR AGAINST NATIVE PEOPLES

In both the US and Canada, governments sought to eradicate Native cultures and identities both militarily and through the aggressive assimilation regimes of boarding schools.

The Winter Count

In 1910 Lakota tribal historian Sam Kills Two was pictured recording his winter count on an animal hide. Representing an outstanding event for each year, the pictographs show the impact of white people on the Lakota.

SOUTHERN PLAINS CONFLICT

THE VICIOUS ATTACK AT SAND CREEK in November 1864 (*see pp. 70–71*) poisoned relations between Indians and whites and reinforced Indian resistance. Hostilities continued from late 1864 until 1875, turning the entire Plains into a battlefield. As the war of attrition against Southern Plains tribes intensified and their buffalo diminished in number, most were forced to settle on reservations in Indian Territory. By 1875, the army had overwhelmed Indian resistance in the Southern Plains.

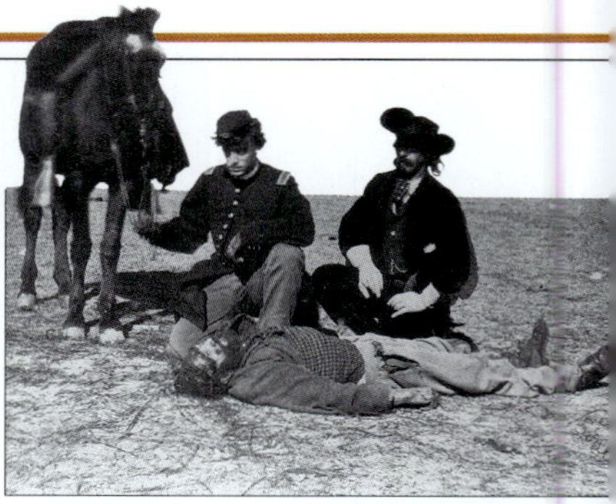

CHEYENNES' REVENGE
In the aftermath of the Sand Creek massacre, angry Cheyennes avenged Black Kettle's band by killing white people, including this hunter found near Fort Dodge, Kansas. Indians and whites regarded each other as enemies and killed indiscriminately.

HANCOCK'S CAMPAIGN

In 1867, Major General Winfield Scott Hancock became military commander of the Department of the Missouri. In April, he led a botched campaign against Cheyennes and Arapahos, which provoked months of retaliation by tribes on the Southern Plains.

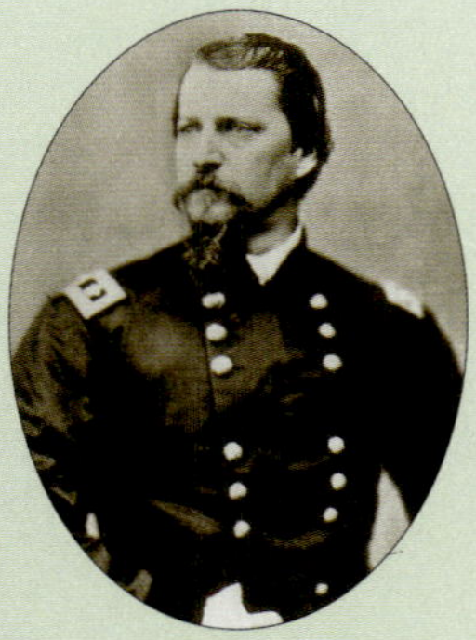

MAJOR GENERAL WINFIELD S. HANCOCK

AT THE END OF DECEMBER 1864 and in early 1865, angry Lakotas, Arapahos, and Cheyennes joined forces to avenge those slaughtered at Sand Creek. During 1865, thousands of warriors attacked the South Platte trail, burning ranches and stage-coach stations, plundering wagon trains, capturing livestock, and killing railroad workers and other people.

After the Civil War, the flood of travelers started to swell again. The 1862 Homestead Act and the Pacific Railway Acts of 1862–64 resulted in settlements springing up on the Plains, which the government made no attempt to restrain. Neither did they try to halt the buffalo slaughter: indeed, professional hunters were encouraged to kill the last great herds whose numbers had been dwindling since the late 1840s. With single hides going for as much as $3 each, hunters flocked to the Plains.

The US army returned to the Plains to provide protection for all white people in Indian country. In April 1867, Major General Winfield Scott Hancock announced his intention to subdue the Central Plains tribes, whom he suspected of planning an uprising. As his troops approached a Cheyenne-Lakota village at Pawnee Fork, Kansas, men, women, and children, seized by visions of Sand Creek, fled. Hancock sent Lieutenant Colonel George Armstrong Custer after the frightened Indians, who were later blamed for burning stage stations, running off stock, and butchering citizens. Hancock, who concluded that the Indian village harbored "a nest of conspirators, torched their tipis. His action provoked fierce retaliatory attacks by Cheyennes and Arapahos in western Kansas and eastern Colorado.

Hancock's expedition was considered a fiasco that discredited the purely military solution to Indian resistance, prompting the government to shift gears and pursue the more practical treaty approach. Calling for a peace council, it invited tribes from across the Southern and Central Plains to a meeting in October 1867; some 5,000 Indians gathered at Medicine Lodge Creek in Kansas. Hoping to avoid confrontation, almost every chief of importance on the Southern Plains signed treaties that established two large reservations in western Indian Territory – one for the Cheyennes and Arapahos, the other for Kiowas Comanches, and Kiowa-Apaches. The signatories represented only a portion of each

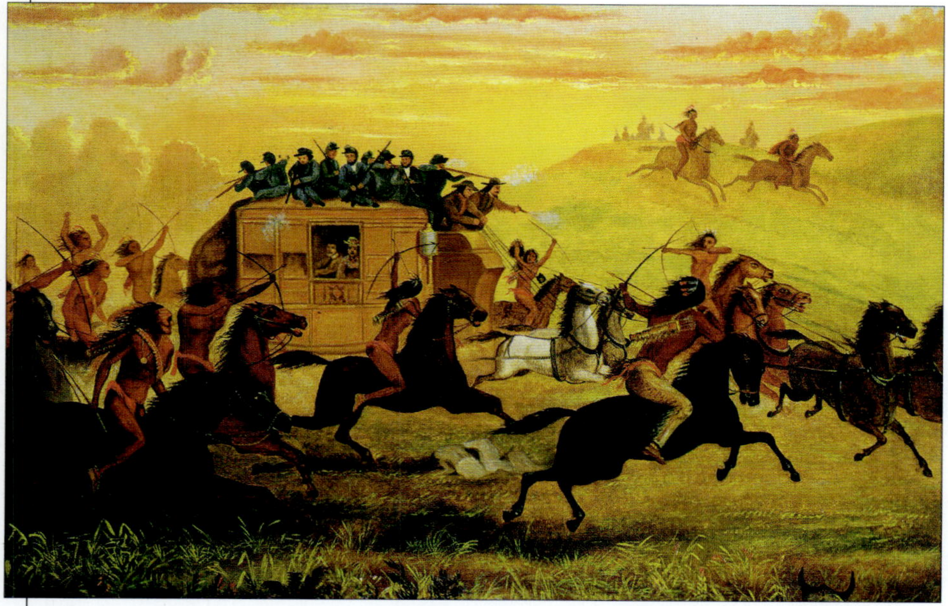

◁ STAGECOACH ATTACKS
The 1864 Sand Creek massacre and the 1867 burning of the Cheyenne-Arapaho village at Pawnee Fork by Major General Hancock sparked Indian raiding parties that struck at stage coaches and stage-coach stations on well-traveled routes.

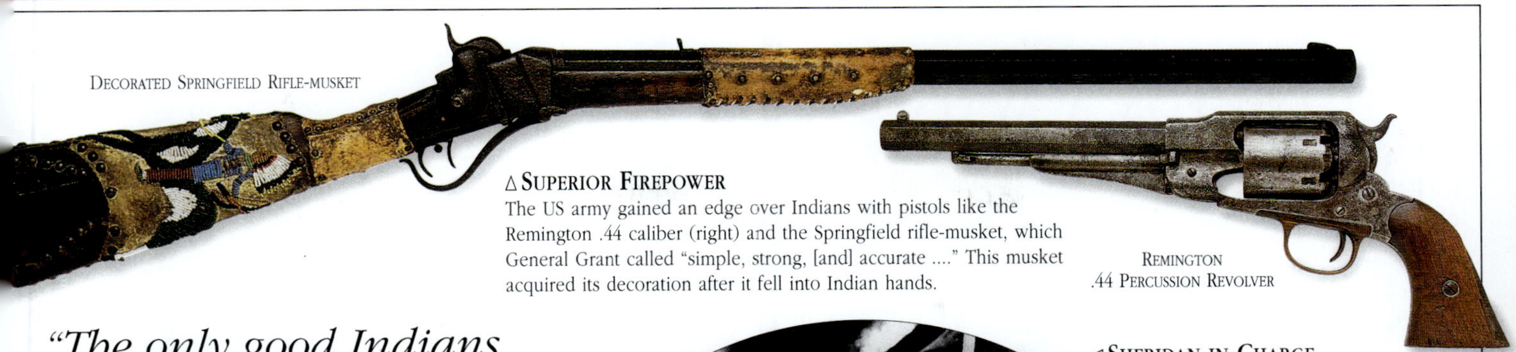

DECORATED SPRINGFIELD RIFLE-MUSKET

REMINGTON .44 PERCUSSION REVOLVER

△ **SUPERIOR FIREPOWER**
The US army gained an edge over Indians with pistols like the Remington .44 caliber (right) and the Springfield rifle-musket, which General Grant called "simple, strong, [and] accurate ...." This musket acquired its decoration after it fell into Indian hands.

"The only good Indians I ever saw were dead."

GENERAL PHILIP HENRY SHERIDAN, FORT COBB, 1869

ribe, but the US considered the deal binding on all bands and claimed the right to force esisters onto their reservations at gunpoint.

The reservations, out of the way of principal and routes, came from the holdings of the Five Tribes, forfeited as part of their punishment for choosing the wrong side in the Civil War. The government promised the Indians rations and presents; in return the Indians relinquished all rights to territory outside the reservations, promised to withdraw all opposition to railroads and military posts, and to refrain from harming white people or their property.

The End of Direct Resistance

Despite signing the treaty, few Indians had any intention of being confined to reservations. The Comanches and Kiowas used their reservations as bases for bloody forays into Texas, and, during 1868, young militant Indians struck repeatedly at farms, ranches, and travelers. In a winter campaign led by Lieutenant Colonel George Custer, severe defeats were inflicted upon the Southern Plains Indians in the battles of the Washita, Soldier Spring, and Summit Springs. During the Red River War of 1874–75, the army pursued the Indians in a campaign organized by General Philip Sheridan.

The relentless pursuit broke the spirit of the Indians. A number of their leaders were tried, and 70 were sentenced to detention in Fort Marion, Florida. The Southern Plains tribes mounted no further direct armed challenge.

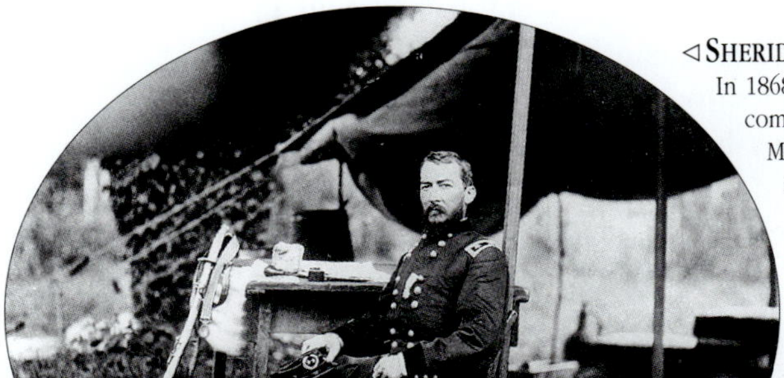

◁ **SHERIDAN IN CHARGE**
In 1868, Philip H. Sheridan, then commander of the Department of the Missouri, organized winter campaigns against Southern Plains Indians. He also directed later campaigns against them in 1874–75.

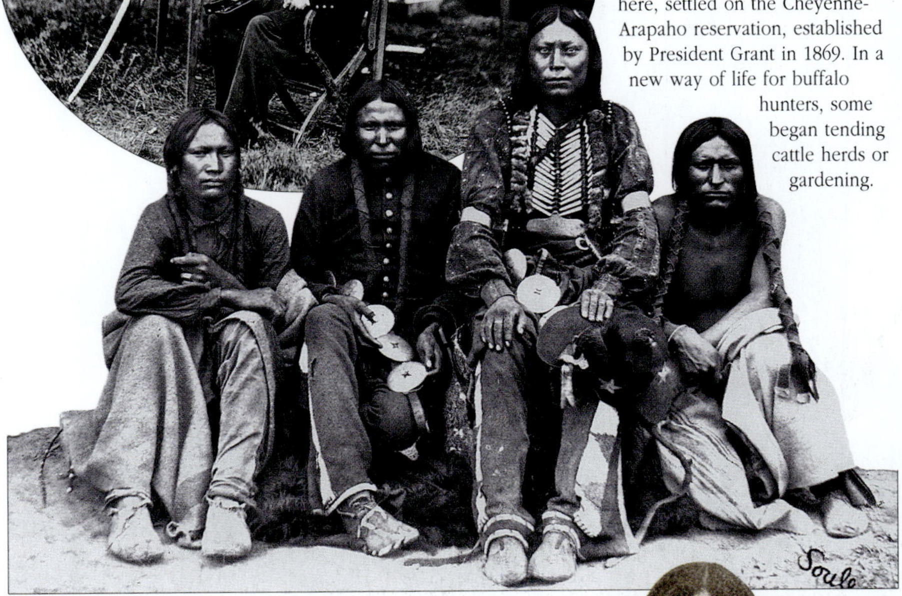

▽ **STARTING OVER**
Arapaho men, like the four seen here, settled on the Cheyenne-Arapaho reservation, established by President Grant in 1869. In a new way of life for buffalo hunters, some began tending cattle herds or gardening.

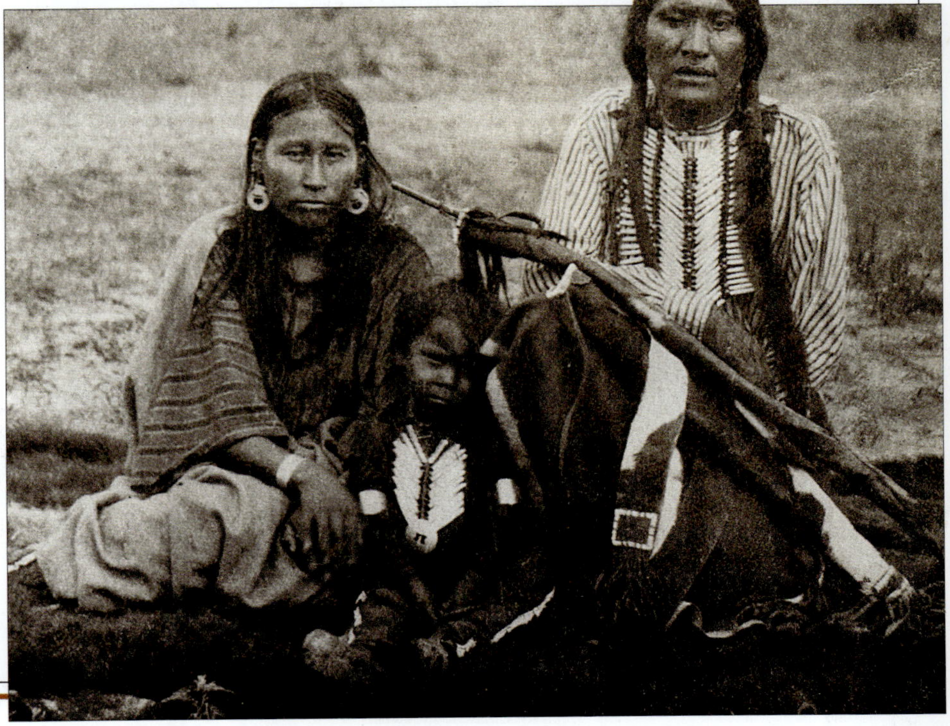

PEACEFUL INCLINATIONS ▷
The Southern Arapaho were more inclined than most Plains tribes toward peace with the whites, preferring trading to war. In 1868, however, they joined in the Cheyennes' raids because the loss of their lands threatened their survival.

FIGHTING FOR A WAY OF LIFE

Throughout the Southern Plains, from 1864–75, Arapaho, Cheyenne, Comanche, Kiowa, and Lakota Indians fought hard to save their way of life, despairing over the railroad building, the shrinking buffalo herds, and their confinement to small reservations. But US soldiers, well equipped with rifles and ammunition, were led by officers determined to crush the Indians into submission during winter campaigns when the Natives' food supplies were low and their horses weak from hunger.

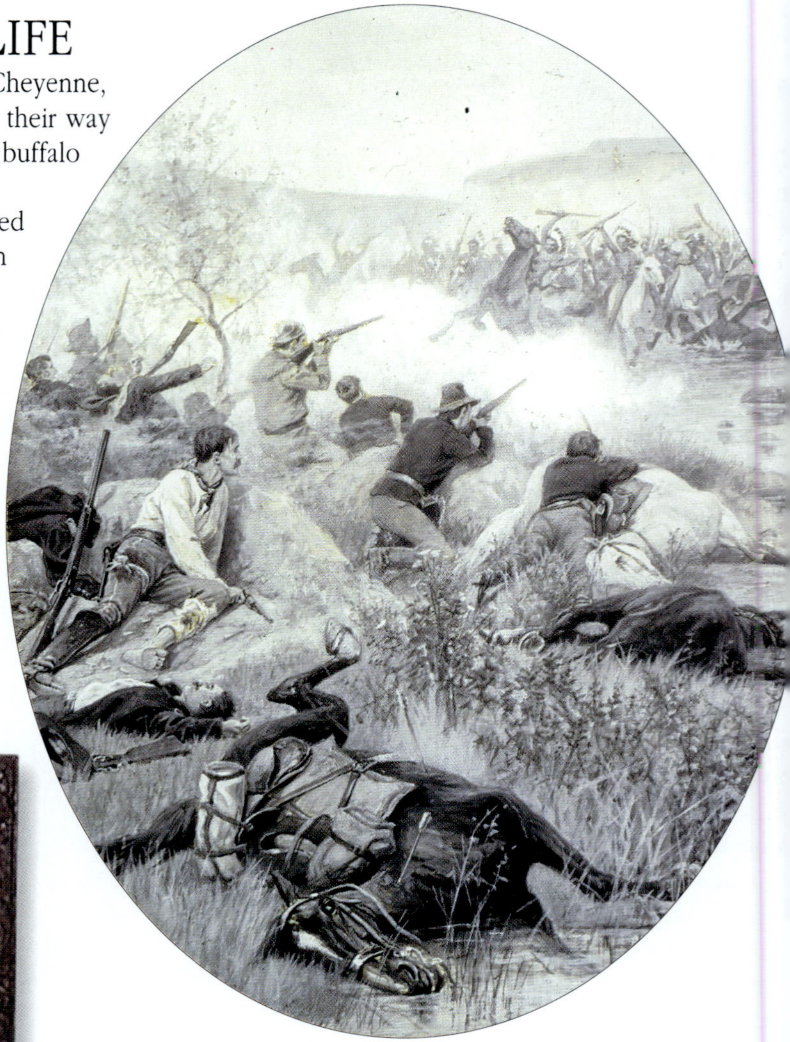

BATTLE OF BEECHER ISLAND ▷
In September 1865, under attack by a large Indian war party, Major George A. Forsyth led 50 frontiersmen to a small island in a river in northeastern Colorado. In one of the most famous battles in Great Plains history, Forsyth's small force held off its Indian attackers for nine days until, sighting a relief column, the Indians withdrew. During the battle, Cheyenne chief Roman Nose was killed.

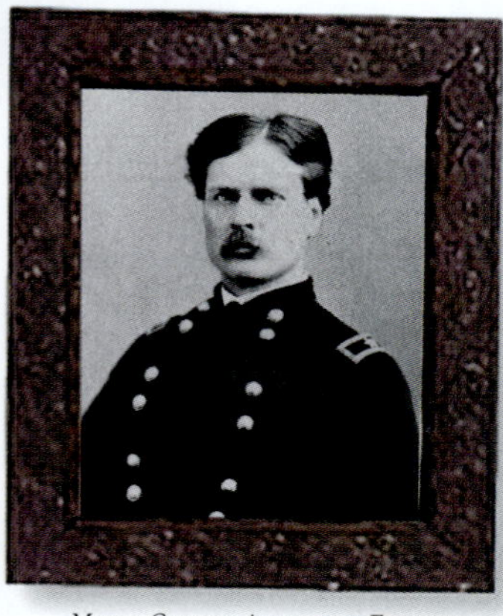

MAJOR GEORGE ALEXANDER FORSYTH

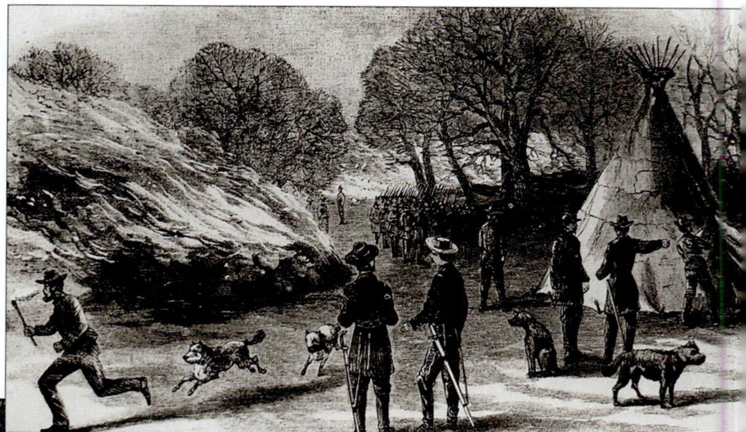

ARMY TORCHES PAWNEE FORK ▷
In April 1867, Major General Winfield Scott Hancock decided to bully a village of Cheyennes and Lakotas located at Pawnee Fork, Kansas, whom he suspected of planning an uprising. Fearing another Sand Creek, the Indians fled the village, which the soldiers looted before setting fire to the 252 tipis.

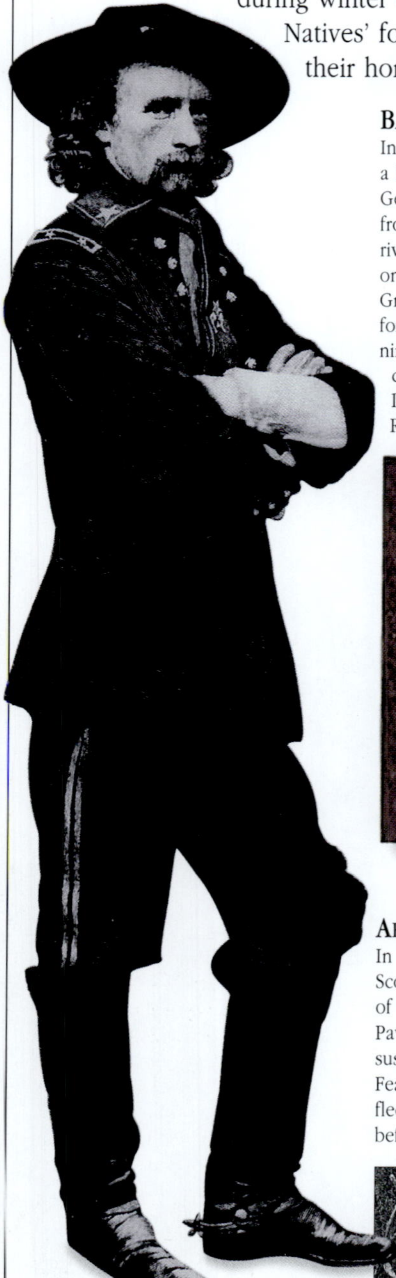

△ HARSH LEADER CUSTER
George Armstrong Custer's career as an Indian fighter began in 1866. During the 1867 Hancock campaign, he drove his men so hard and treated deserters so harshly that he was court martialed and suspended from duty for a year.

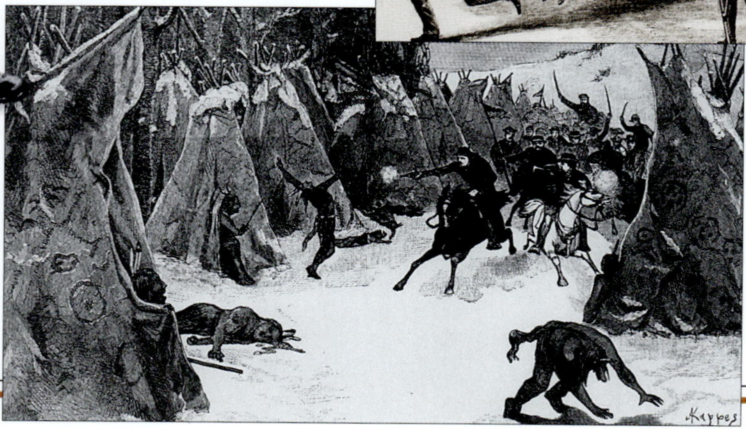

◁ BLACK KETTLE'S CAMP ATTACKED
On 27 November 1868, during a blizzard, Lieutenant Colonel George A. Custer led the Seventh Cavalry to Black Kettle's camp on the Washita River in Oklahoma, where the Sand Creek survivor had led his people for sanctuary. Taking the Indians by surprise, Custer's men set out to avenge Cheyenne raids on Kansas settlements. Chief Black Kettle was killed, along with mostly women and children.

RED RIVER WAR

'he so-called Red River War of 1874–75 refers to series of campaigns directed at Comanches, :heyennes, and Kiowas who had left their eservations in Oklahoma and Kansas to raid ettlements and ranches in northwestern 'exas. Huge numbers of troops were lispatched from forts in New Mexico, Texas, nd Oklahoma to pursue the Indians. By 1875 he last of the Indians had returned to their eservations, their will to resist shattered after t least 14 engagements.

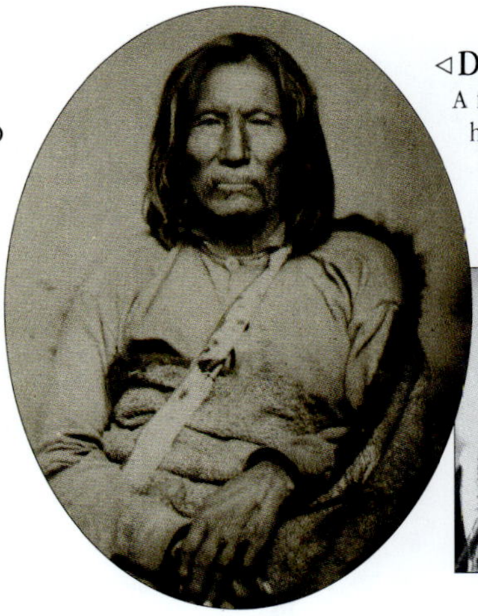

◁ DEFIANT KIOWA LEADER SATANK

A fierce enemy of white intruders on Kiowa land, Satank redoubled his determination to destroy the hated Texans after his son was killed during a raid in 1870. Convicted of the murder of wagon-train teamsters, Satank was given a prison sentence. On his way to penitentiary, Satank attacked a guard, and was shot dead.

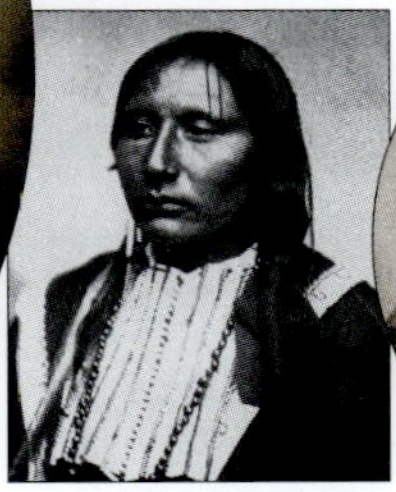

BIG TREE

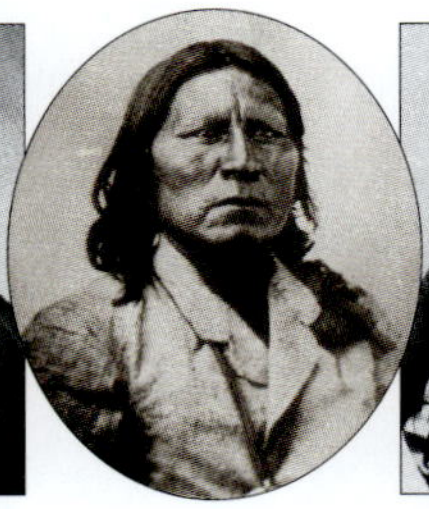

SATANTA

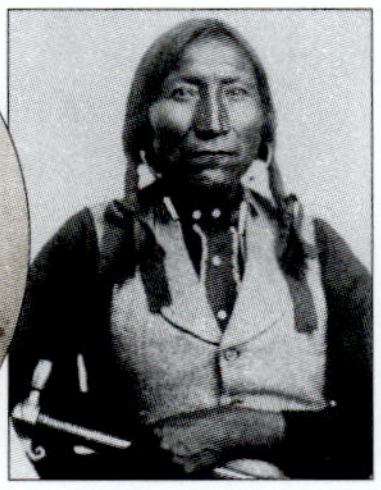

LONE WOLF

△ KIOWA CHIEFS WAGE WAR

During the wars on the Southern Plains, Kiowa chiefs Big Tree, Satanta, and Lone Wolf waged war on buffalo hunters and wagon trains, and participated in raids on Texas settlements. Big Tree and Satanta were sentenced to death but, following protests by humanitarian groups, the sentences were commuted. For his part in the Red River War, Lone Wolf was exiled to Fort Marion in Florida.

oldiers dug in to a 'efensive position are 'epicted firing at the :iowa fighters who ave encircled them

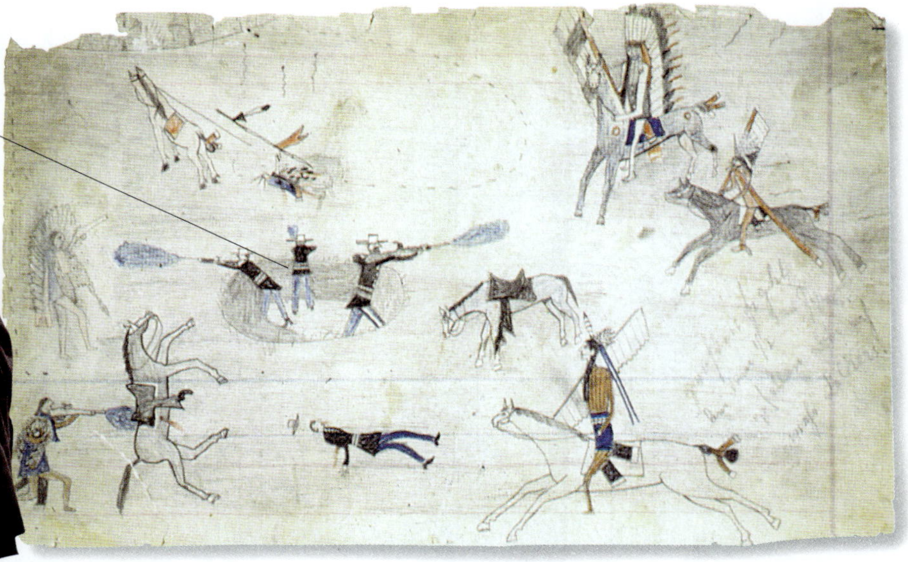

◁ A WARRIOR'S RECORD

This unidentified battle scene was recorded by a Kiowa warrior in a style known as "ledger drawing," because the drawings were executed on the pages of ledger books. The drawing documents the enduring pride of Kiowa warriors as they bravely face rifle-bearing soldiers.

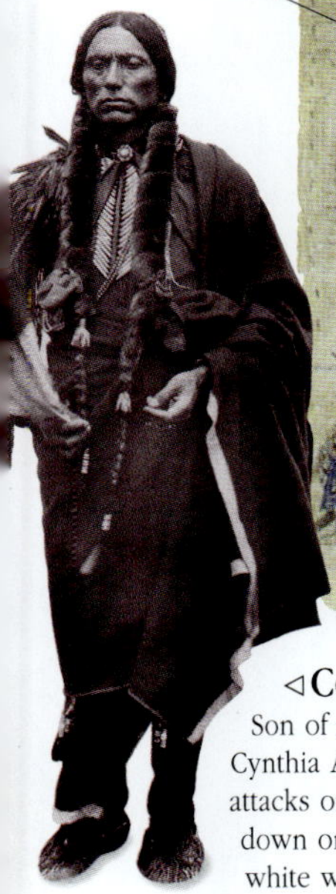

◁ COMANCHE CHIEF QUANAH PARKER

Son of a Comanche chief and a white captive, Cynthia Ann Parker, Chief Quanah Parker led attacks on the Texans until 1874, but later settled down on the Oklahoma reservation, adopting white ways and becoming a successful farmer.

"We have warred against the white man, but never because it gave us pleasure."

KIOWA LEADER SATANK, OCTOBER 1867

FLORIDA PRISON

in 1875, Brevet Captain Richard H. Pratt was assigned the job of rounding up Indian militants of the Red River War and escorting them to the Fort Marion Military Prison at Saint Augustine, Florida. For three years, this massive, medieval Spanish fortress, which was completed in 1695 and guarded the entrance to Saint Augustine harbor, held 72 Indians (Cheyennes, Arapahos, Comanches, and Kiowas) who were taken into custody and housed in miserably damp, stone rooms. Because the US was not officially at war with the tribes, the accused men were never tried by a military court.

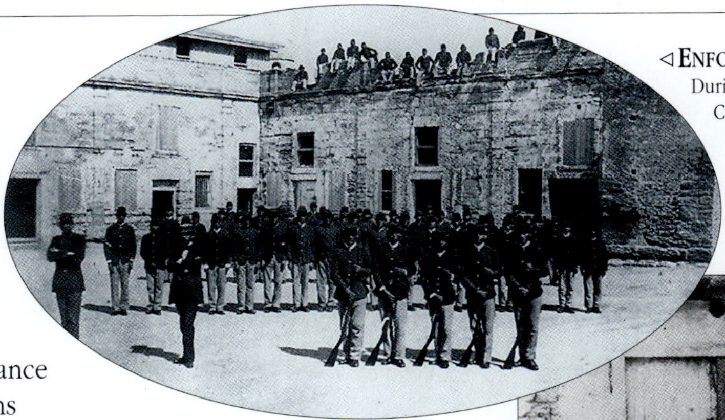

◁ ENFORCING WHITE WAYS

During their captivity at Fort Marion, Captain Pratt set about changing Indians into white men, cutting their hair and making them wear army uniforms. The pictures that the men drew in their free time were sold to tourists in the area.

SERVING TIME ▷

Many Indian prisoners, pictured here at Saint Augustine, spent their free time drawing pictographic images of camp and reservation life: ceremonies, hunts, and scenes of warfare on the Southern Plains.

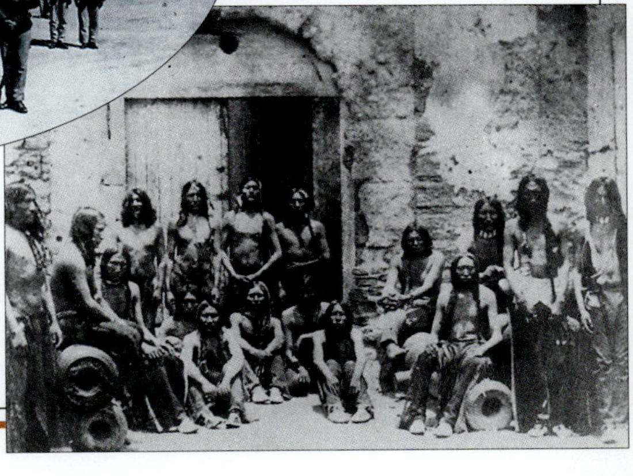

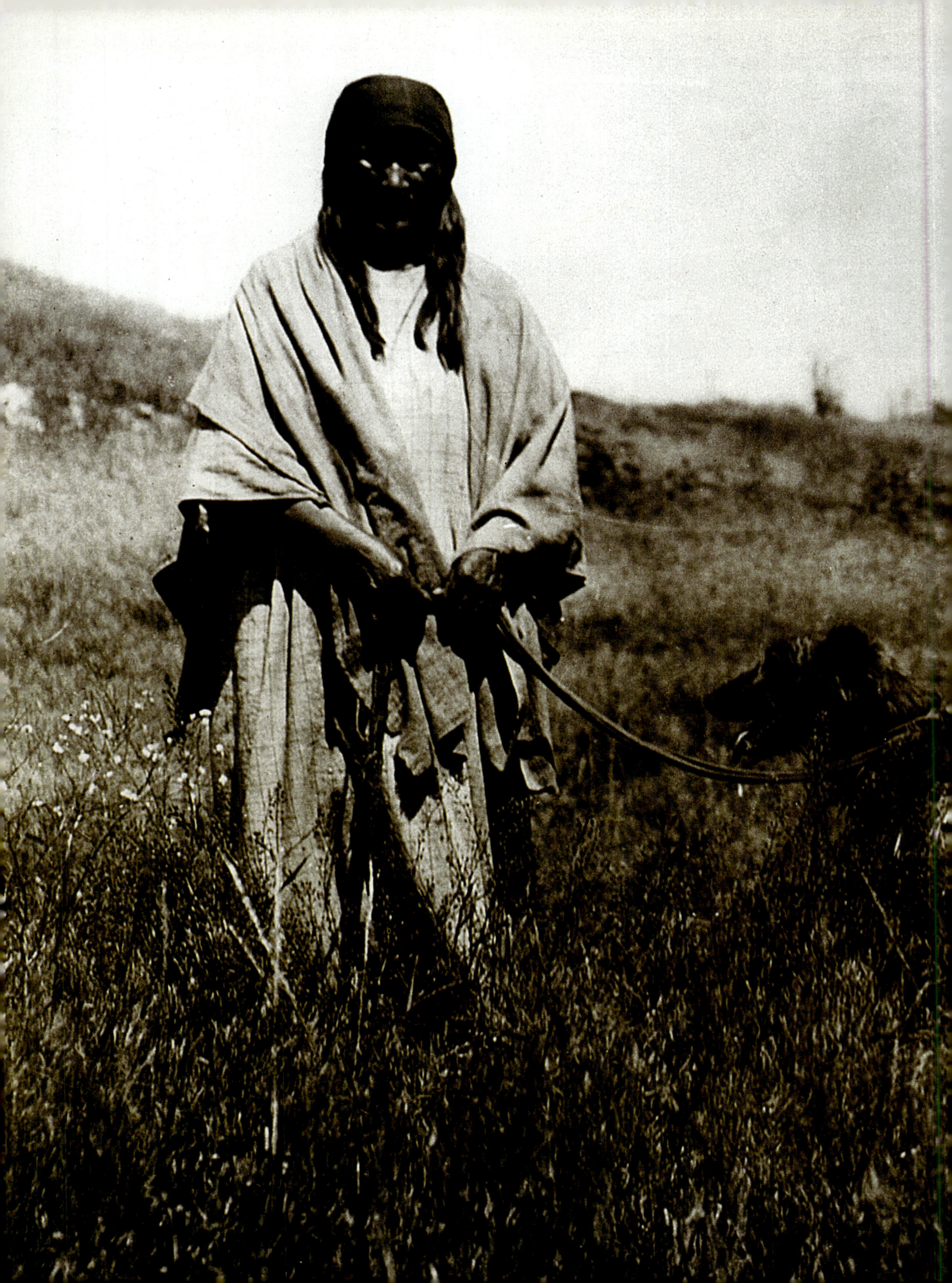

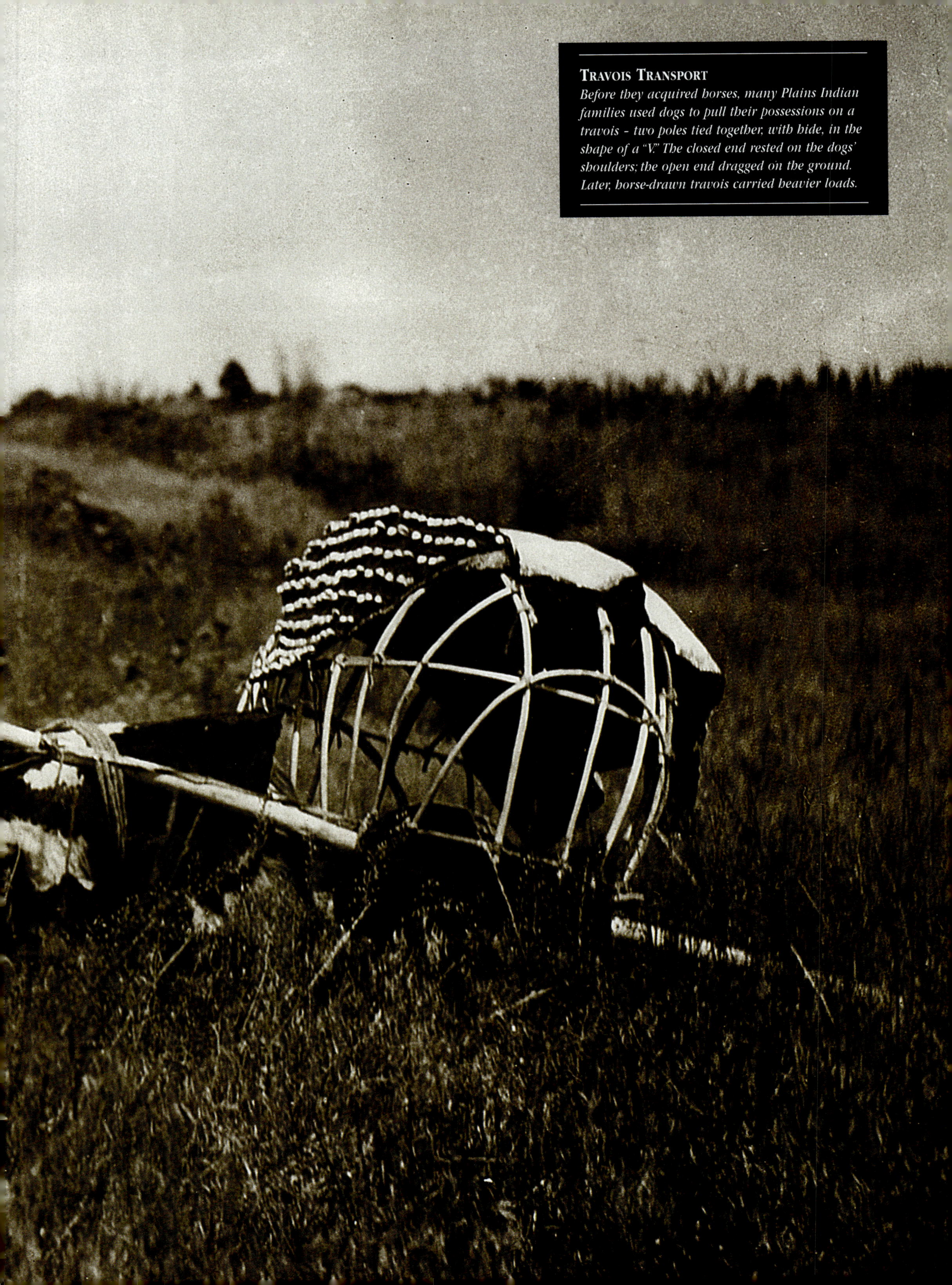

Travois Transport

Before they acquired horses, many Plains Indian families used dogs to pull their possessions on a travois - two poles tied together, with hide, in the shape of a "V." The closed end rested on the dogs' shoulders; the open end dragged on the ground. Later, horse-drawn travois carried heavier loads.

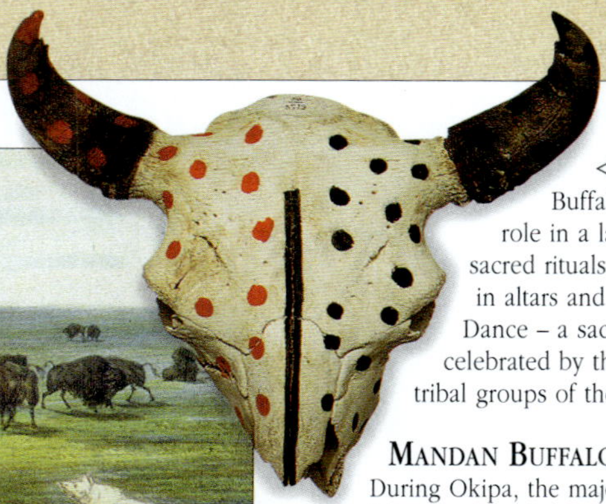

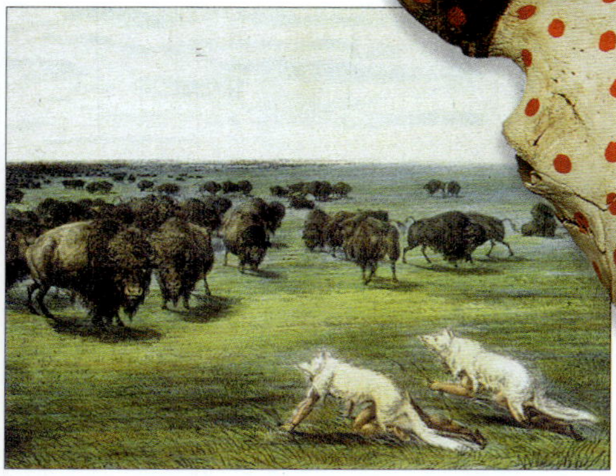

◁ SACRED SKULL
Buffalo skulls play a vital role in a large number of Plains sacred rituals. The skulls were used in altars and in the annual Sun Dance – a sacred religious ceremony celebrated by the buffalo-hunting tribal groups of the Plains region.

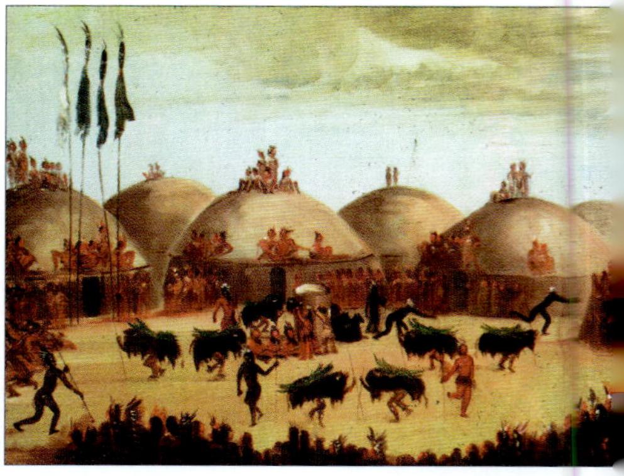

MANDAN BUFFALO DANCE ▷
During Okipa, the major religious ceremony of the Mandan of the upper Missouri region, participants prayed for the return of plentiful buffalo to sustain their people, while dancers performed bull dances and reenacted aspects of Earth's creation.

△ IN WOLVES' CLOTHING
Disguised under wolf skins or buffalo hides, one or two men would sneak close to a herd of buffalo and, when within range of the animals, take careful aim with their bows and arrows. In earlier times, hunters worked together to drive buffalo over cliffs called "buffalo jumps."

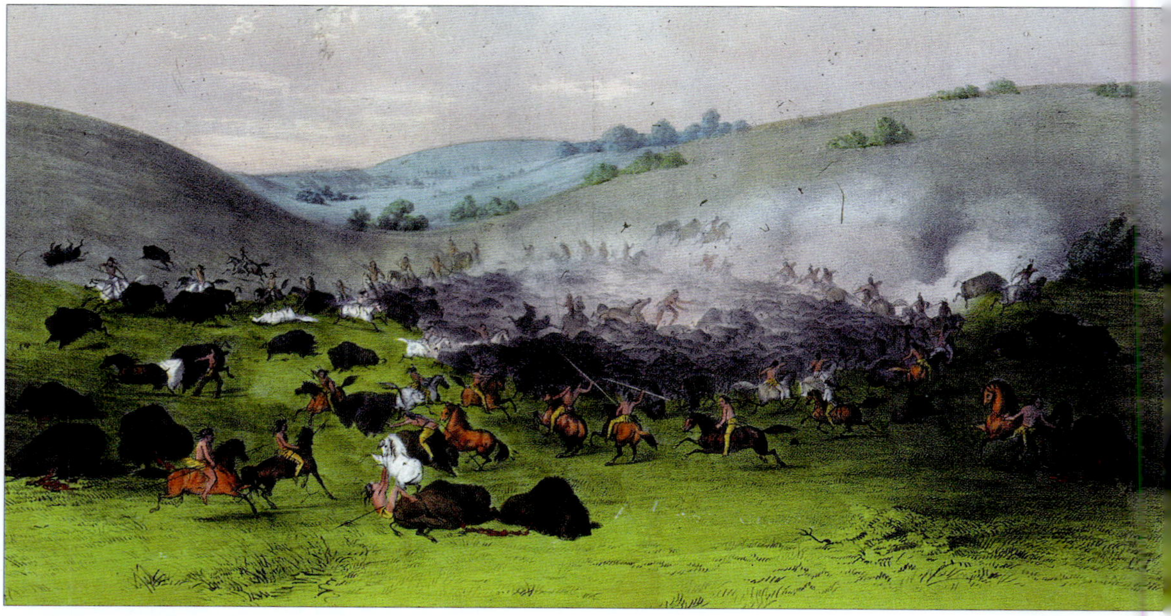

HORSEBACK HUNTING ▷
Horses transformed buffalo hunting for Indians. Instead of simply waiting for the animals to wander near to traps, hunters on horseback could now pursue them much farther and faster than was ever possible on foot. Hunters could follow the herds at almost any time of the year, and the best horses could outrun even a stampeding herd of buffaloes.

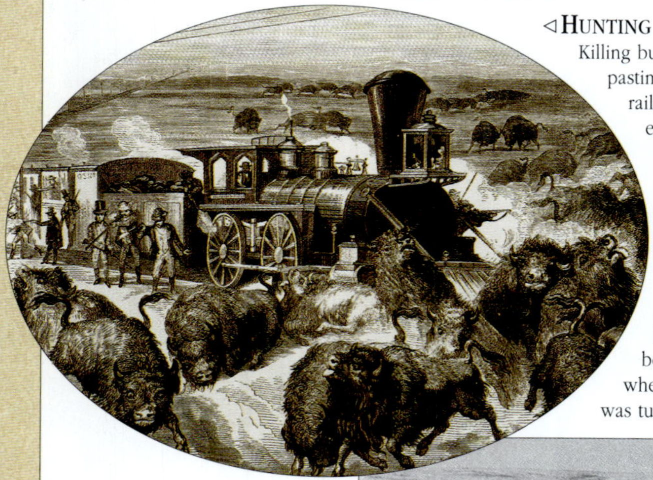

◁ HUNTING EXCURSIONS
Killing buffalo became such a popular pastime that, after the transcontinental railroad was built in 1869, special excursion trains were run to allow tourists to shoot buffalo through the open coach windows.

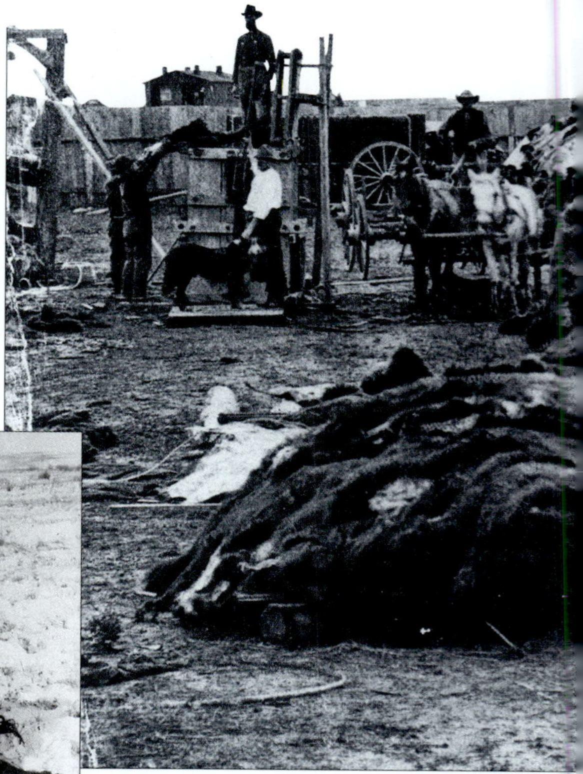

BUFFALO MOUNTAIN ▷
In 1874, these buffalo hides, which had been purchased by R.M. Wright of Dodge City, Kansas, lay piled up, waiting to be shipped to processing centers where even the poorest buffalo hide was turned into usable leather.

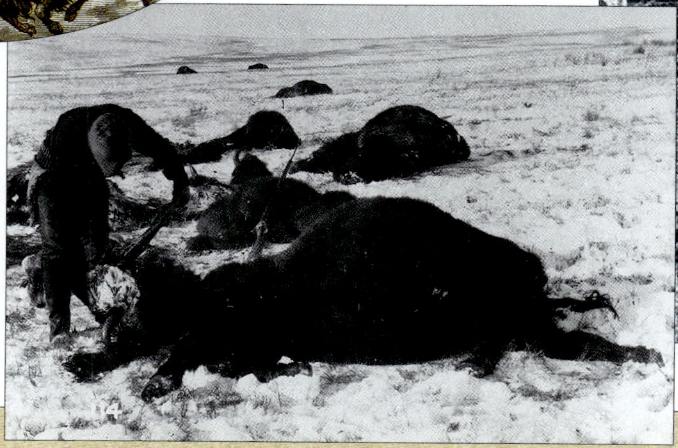

THE KILLING FIELDS ▷
Between 1800 and 1895, the buffalo population fell from an estimated 40 million to fewer than 1,000. Professional and sports hunters were largely responsible for the slaughter, which shattered the Plains Indians' way of life. Once the buffalo were killed off, the Indians faced starvation, homelessness, and despair.

The Staff of Life

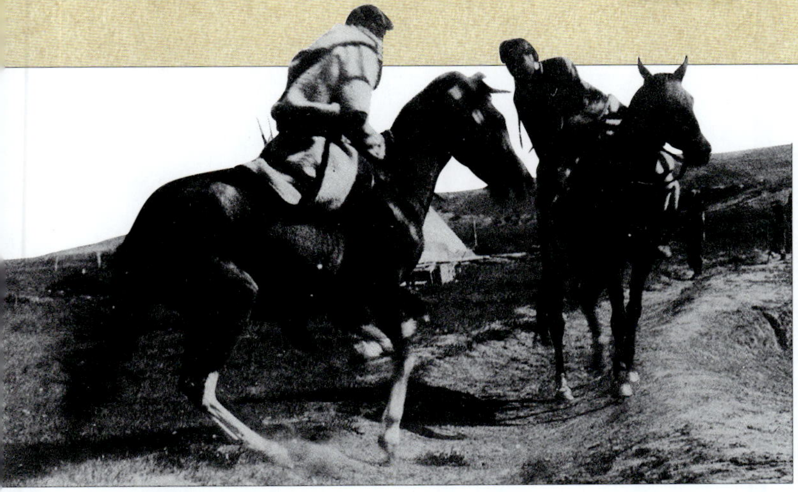

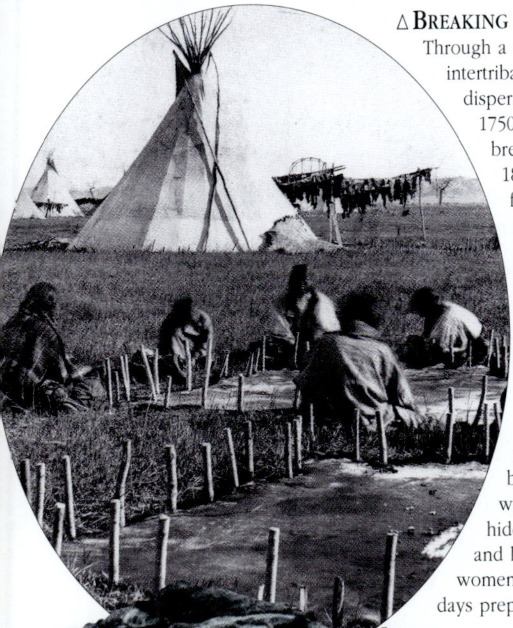

△ Breaking in the Horses
Through a combination of stealing and intertribal trading, Native peoples rapidly dispersed horses across the Plains. By 1750, the Blackfeet in Alberta were breaking in horses and, by the early 1800s, almost every Plains Indian family owned a few horses. Two Blackfeet men are pictured in Montana, in 1891, with the animals they called "big dogs."

◁ Women's Work
In most tribes, the task of butchering and skinning the buffalo fell to women. After scraping off fatty tissue, they stretched and dried buffalo hides by pegging them to the ground with stakes. Women tanned buffalo hide with a mixture of buffalo brains and liver, grease, and soaproot. The women might spend as many as ten days preparing each buffalo hide.

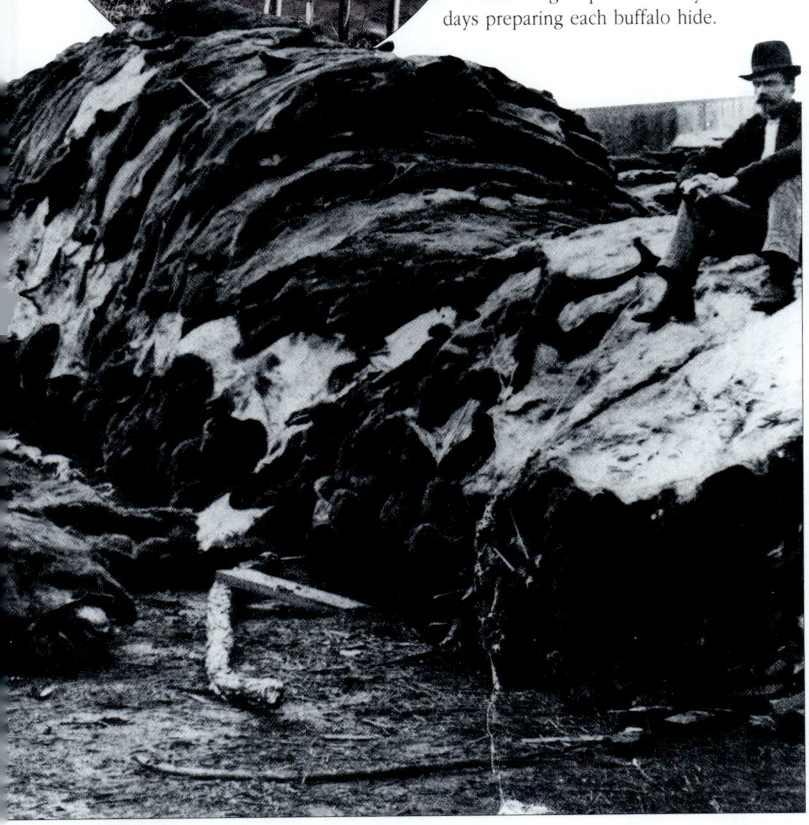

For the Plains Indians, the buffalo provided virtually all the requirements of human existence – from food and fuel to robes and tipi covers, knives, shields, drums, and playthings for the children. This huge animal was honored in ceremonies at which hunters thanked the animal's spirit for offering up its body.

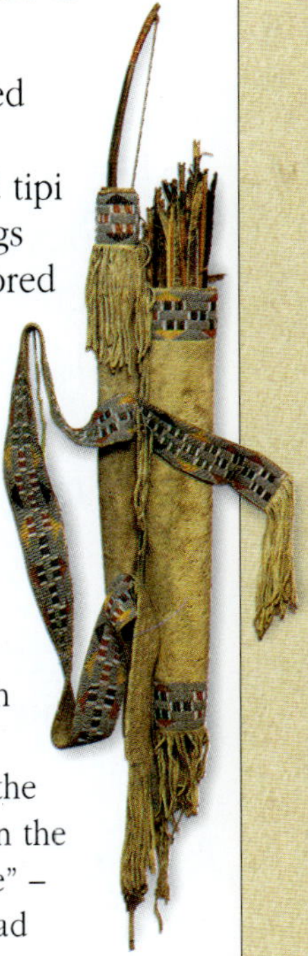

Dakota Hide Quiver and Bow Case

A Nourishing Food Source

Buffalo supplied a tasty, nourishing, year-round food for all ages. Mothers gave their infants choice pieces of meat to suck, and toothless old people sucked the juices in the same way. A favorite dish was a soup made with buffalo fat, buffalo blood, and berries.

When meat was plentiful, large quantities of the lean flesh were cut into long, thin strips, dried in the sun on racks of poles, then packed in "parfleche" – envelopes made of buffalo rawhide (hide that had been fleshed, washed, and dried). Dried meat was made into pemmican: the meat was cooked, then pounded with a stone hammer and mixed with boiled marrow grease and sometimes berries. It was then stored in bags made from buffalo rawhide.

The Many Uses of Rawhide

Plains Indians found countless uses for buffalo rawhide. Lodge covers were made from dressed skins – hides that had been fleshed, washed, and tanned with the brains and liver of the animal; the covers were sewn together with sinew, also from buffalo. In the winter, people wrapped themselves in heavy winter hides with the thick, shaggy hair side turned in. They also made mittens, caps, and moccasins from winter hides.

The long-wearing, waterproof qualities of buffalo rawhide made it the preferred material for containers in which to transport and store food, clothing, and camp equipment. Rawhide's flexibility and durability also made it useful for repairing the bottoms of worn, soft-soled moccasins. Most horse equipment was made of rawhide: picket lines, bridles, cruppers, whips, saddles, shoes for sore-footed horses, and portable watering troughs. Shields were made from the thick hide of the buffalo's neck, while green rawhide was used to bind knives and berry mashers to wooden handles. Buffalo horns were turned into spoons and drinking cups.

"Kill every buffalo you can. Every buffalo dead is an Indian gone."

Colonel R.I. Dodge, US Army, *c.* 1870

WAR FOR THE NORTHERN PLAINS

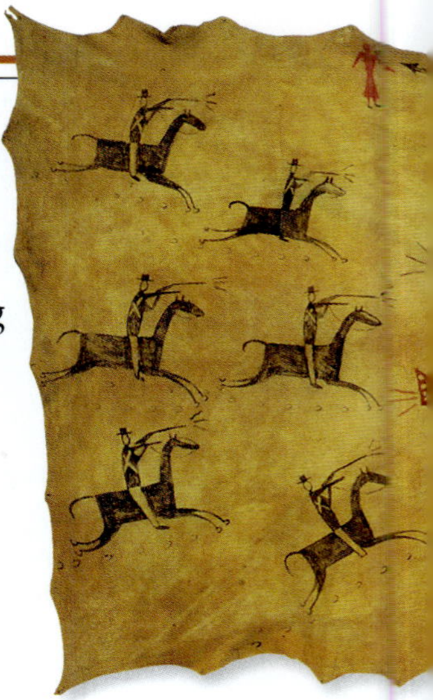

IN THE 1860S, GOLD MINERS poured into Montana along the Bozeman Trail, trespassing on the lands of the Northern Plains tribes. Red Cloud's War – a response to the intrusions – ended with the 1868 Fort Laramie Treaty, which closed the trail and dismantled the three forts set up to protect prospectors. When the 1874 discovery of gold in the Black Hills brought yet more miners to the region, the Sioux and Cheyenne who had not signed the 1868 treaty attacked Fort Abraham Lincoln (established in 1872 near Bismarck, North Dakota), provoking further hostilities.

BATTLES OF THE NORTHERN PLAINS

JULY 1865
General Patrick Connor's Powder River Expedition – a campaign against the Sioux and Cheyenne

21 DECEMBER 1866
Captain William J. Fetterman and his entire command of 80 men killed in Sioux attack

1866–68
Red Cloud's War: Lakota Sioux and allied Cheyenne and Arapaho warriors fight to close the Bozeman Trail

1 AUGUST 1867
Cheyenne and Sioux attack small group of haycutters near Fort C.F. Smith

2 AUGUST 1867
Sioux strike woodcutters near Fort Phil Kearny in Wagon Box fight

23 JANUARY 1870
Major Eugene M. Baker attacks Blackfeet in Montana

17 MARCH 1876
Lieutenant Colonel George Custer attacks Cheyenne village at Powder River

17 JUNE 1876
Sioux and Cheyenne, led by Crazy Horse, attack General George Crook at Rosebud Creek

THE DISCOVERY OF GOLD in southern Montana during the early 1860s attracted prospectors and opportunists to the area. Between 1863 and 1865, John Bozeman pioneered a road that led from what is now Casper, Wyoming, to the gold camps of Virginia City, Montana – a much shorter route than the journey by steamboat up the Missouri River followed by a trek overland. The new road passed through the Powder River country of the Sioux and Cheyennes, who retaliated against intrusions into their land by attacking travelers. In response, the army established three forts along the trail in 1866.

In 1865 and 1866, some chiefs signed treaties agreeing to "withdraw from the routes overland ... through their country" – but they did not represent all tribal bands; nor did they understand everything to which they agreed. Some of the Lakotas had no intentions of withdrawing from the Bozeman Trail, vowing to fight whites who used it. In a conflict known as Red Cloud's War, Sioux and allied Cheyenne and Arapaho warriors attacked wagon trains, army patrols, and civilians stationed at the forts from 1866 to 1868, aiming to drive out the army and close the trail.

One of the worst disasters for the army occurred on 21 December 1866, when Lakotas wiped out Captain William J. Fetterman and his command near Fort Phil Kearny, in present-day Wyoming. This was offset in 1867 by army victories at the Wagon Box and Hayfield fights.

End of the Trail

The Bozeman Trail remained in use until the 1868 Fort Laramie Treaty, which ended Red

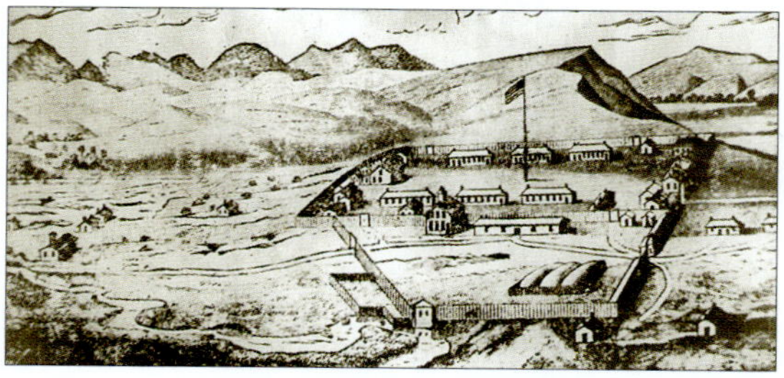

GUARDING THE TRAIL ▷ Fort Phil Kearney was built, in 1866, at the foot of the Big Horn Mountains and garrisoned with troops to guard travelers on the Bozeman Trail. The fort was harassed by Lakotas and Cheyennes, who hated its presence in their homeland.

"With eighty men I could ride through the whole Sioux nation."

CAPTAIN WILLIAM J. FETTERMAN, FORT PHIL KEARNY, 1866

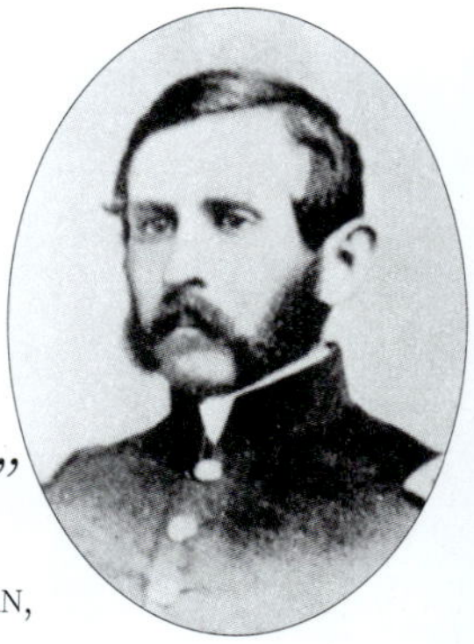

CAPTAIN WILLIAM J. FETTERMAN

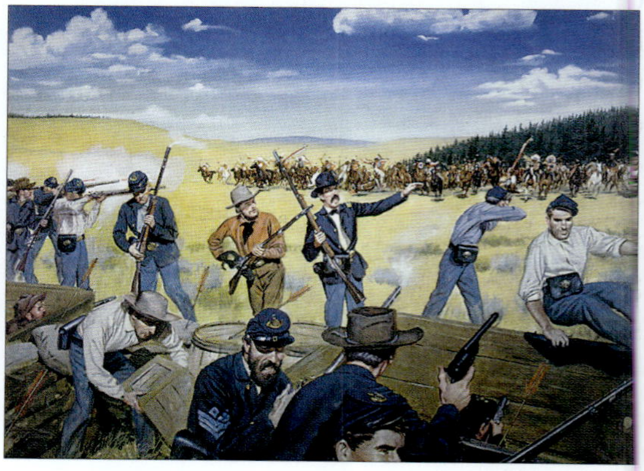

▽ WAGON BOX FIGHT On 2 August 1867, Lakota leader Red Cloud attacked 26 infantrymen guarding a group of woodcutters near Fort Phil Kearny. Armed with new, rapid-fire rifles, the soldiers took refuge behind a circle of wagon beds and held off the Indians until a relief party arrived.

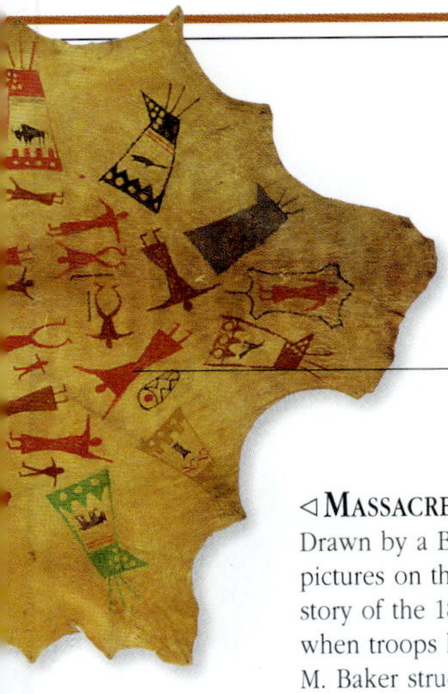

A Blackfeet artist, Percy Bull Child, depicted the dead – including many women and children. Stricken with smallpox, the Piegans offered little resistance

◁ **MASSACRE RECORDED**
Drawn by a Blackfeet elder, the pictures on the buffalo hide tell the story of the 1870 Baker massacre, when troops led by Major Eugene M. Baker struck a village of Piegans on the Marias River in Montana.

Cloud's War and closed down the forts and the rail itself. The treaty guaranteed that a portion of land would be "set apart for the absolute and undisturbed use" of the Sioux. The Great Sioux reservation included the Black Hills, which were declared off-limits to white development. In return, the tribes who signed agreed to stop attacking settlers and forts and to allow passage across the hunting grounds.

The treaty divided the Lakotas: Red Cloud honored the agreement, but Lakotas under Sitting Bull and Crazy Horse refused to sign.

Gold in the Black Hills

The 1874 discovery of gold in the Black Hills led to a "gold rush." The army and government did nothing to keep miners off tribal lands and the Indians retaliated with raids. In 1875, the Grant administration offered to purchase the Black Hills from the Sioux, who protested against incursions into their sacred lands. In December, the government ordered that all Indian bands return to their reservations by 31 January 1876 or be considered hostile. When the "hostile" bands failed to return, the War Department took over. On 17 June 1876, General George Crook was ordered into the field to force bands of Northern Plains tribes to return to their respective reservations. Crook's command of 1,000 cavalry and infantry, miners, civilians, and 300 Crow and Shoshone warriors was attacked, unexpectedly, along the Rosebud River near present-day Kirby, Montana, by a Sioux war party led by Crazy Horse. The troops suffered numerous casualties and were forced back to the base. The battle took place eight days before the even greater army disaster at the Little Bighorn (*see pp.94–97.*)

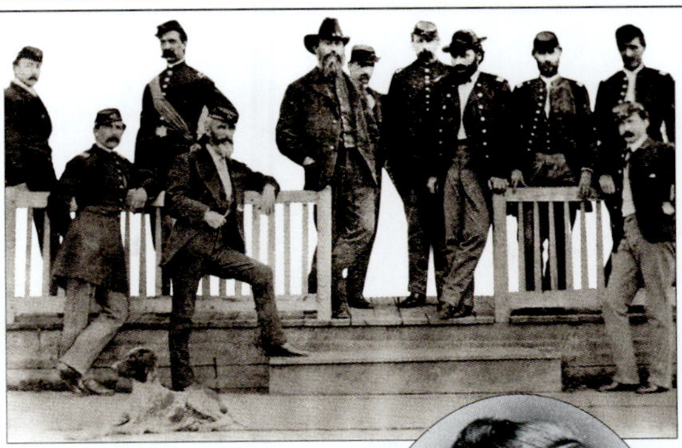

△ **BAKER'S STAFF**
In January 1870, Major Eugene M. Baker was ordered to punish Piegans, a Blackfeet Confederacy tribe in Montana, for raids against ranchers and miners. Baker destroyed their village and killed 173 Piegans in the controversial attack.

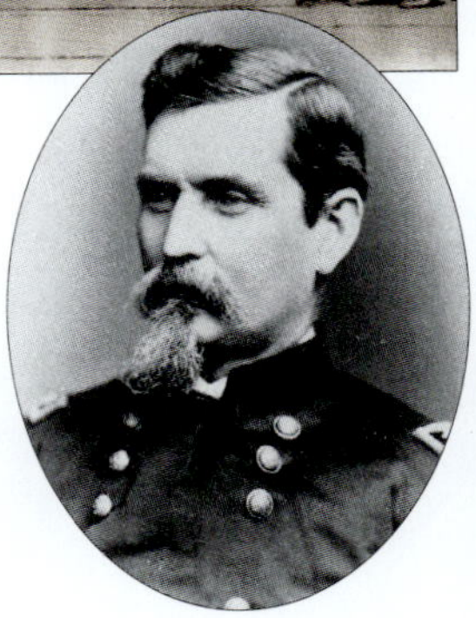

△ **GIBBON IN MONTANA**
Assigned to Fort Ellis, Montana, in 1866, Colonel John Gibbon commanded the military district of Montana during the 1870s, leading troops against Sioux and Cheyenne warriors.

▽ **CUSTER STRIKES GOLD**
An 1874 expedition led by Lieutenant Colonel George Armstrong Custer discovered gold in the Black Hills, part of the Great Sioux reservation. The US government made only a token attempt to deter miners from swarming into the area.

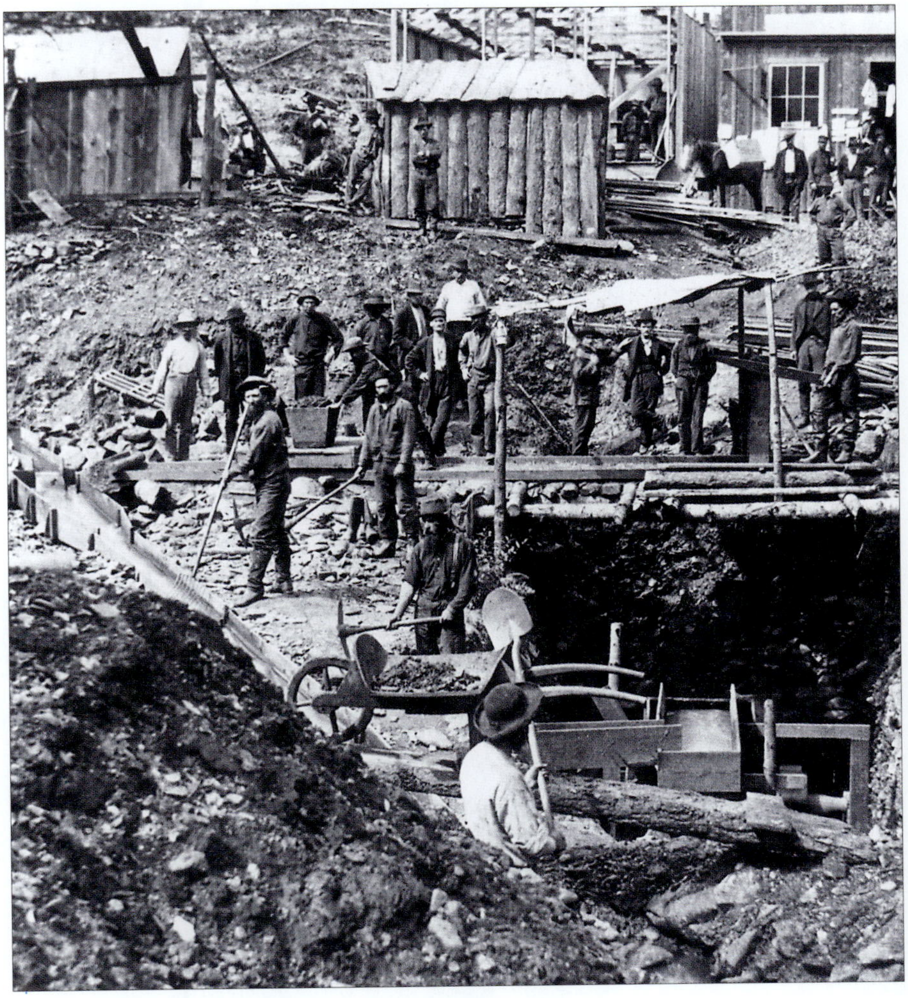

HUNKPAPA SIOUX LEADER

A prominent Hunkpapa Sioux leader, and a giant of a man, Gall earned a reputation as a warrior early in his career. During the winter of 1865–66, he was bayoneted by a soldier and left for dead; but Gall survived and, over the next decade, killed many US troops in revenge. In 1880, he abandoned warfare and settled on a reservation.

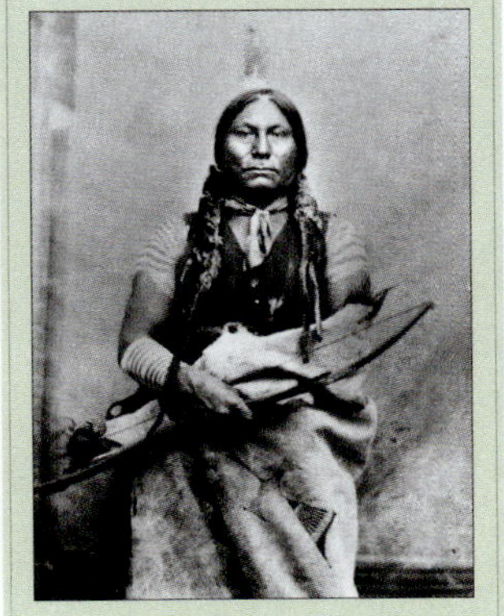

CHIEF GALL

INTO THE BLACK HILLS

Regarded by the Sioux and Cheyenne as sacred and the dwelling place of spirits, the Black Hills in western South Dakota were declared off-limits to whites by the 1868 Fort Laramie Treaty. After Lieutenant Colonel George Armstrong Custer had discovered gold there, however, the area was overrun by prospectors, whom the army and government did nothing to stop.

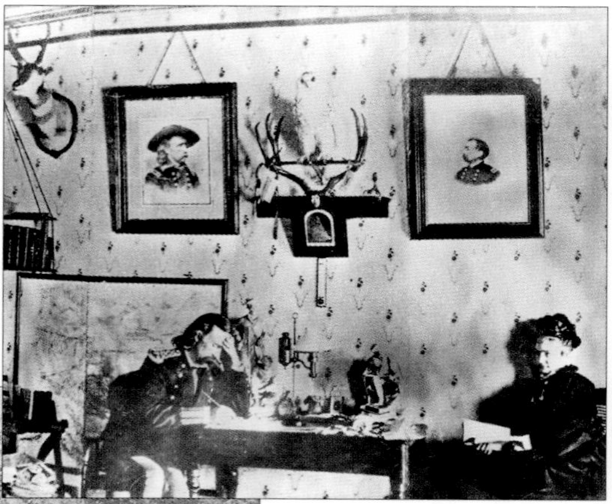

△ **PLANNING AN EXPEDITION**
Lieutenant Colonel George A. Custer was photographed at work in his office at Fort Abraham Lincoln, Dakota Territory, in 1873, shortly before he found gold in the Black Hills. His portrait hangs on the wall behind him.

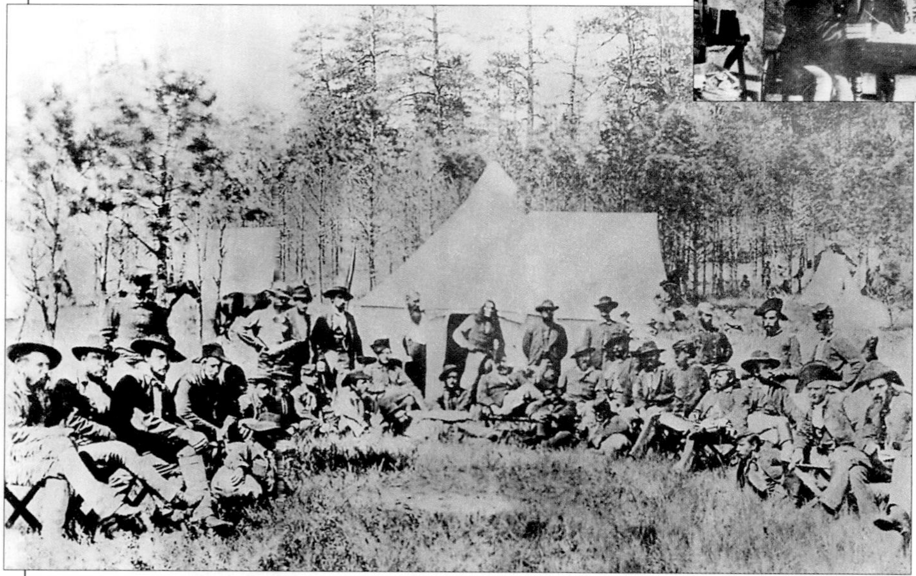

◁ **SCIENTIFIC STAFF**
Under orders from President Ulysses S. Grant, Custer and his staff embarked, in 1874, on an expedition to map the interior of the Black Hills. Although justified as a scientific enterprise, the group set out to locate a suitable site for an army post in the area.

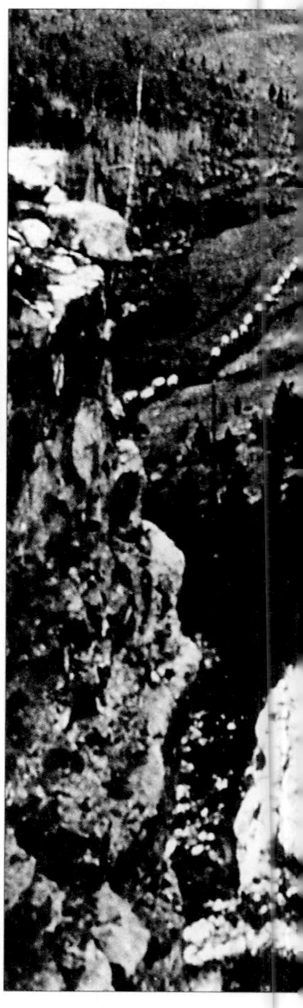

CUSTER'S SCOUTS

Bloody Knife, an Arikara-Sioux, was one of the US army's most effective scouts on the Great Plains. So great were his skills that Custer persuaded Bloody Knife to transfer to his command, and the two men reportedly became great friends. Bloody Knife was killed during the battle of the Little Bighorn.

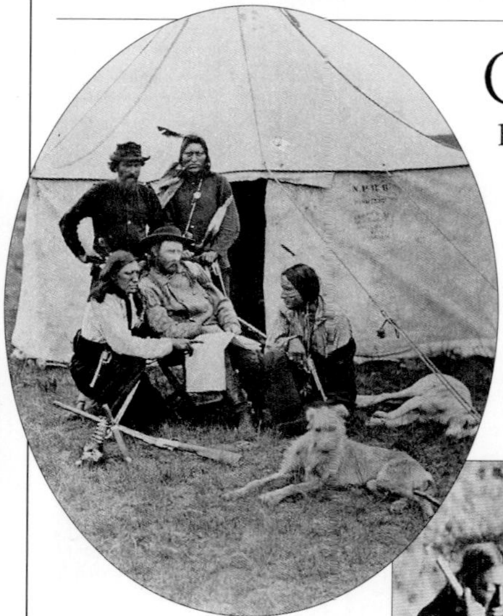

△ **VALUED SCOUTS ASSIST**
Indian scouts were on the army payroll as enlisted personnel. Pictured here with Custer are the scouts who guided his expedition to the Black Hills in 1874 and to the Little Bighorn in 1876.

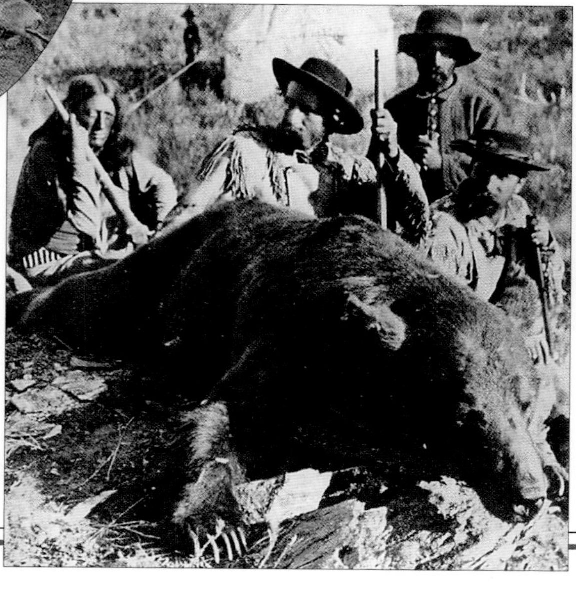

ASSISTING ON A HUNT ▷
Scouts such as Bloody Knife, who killed a grizzly bear on the Black Hills expedition, were hired to hunt game to feed the troops.

ROSEBUD BATTLE

On 17 June 1876, the Lakota and Cheyenne, who camped together in southeastern Montana for mutual protection, attacked General George Crook's unsuspecting column along the Rosebud Creek. The battle lasted for most of the day before the warriors, led by Crazy Horse, retreated. Crook, who lost many of his troops, withdrew to his base camp rather than pursue the Indians.

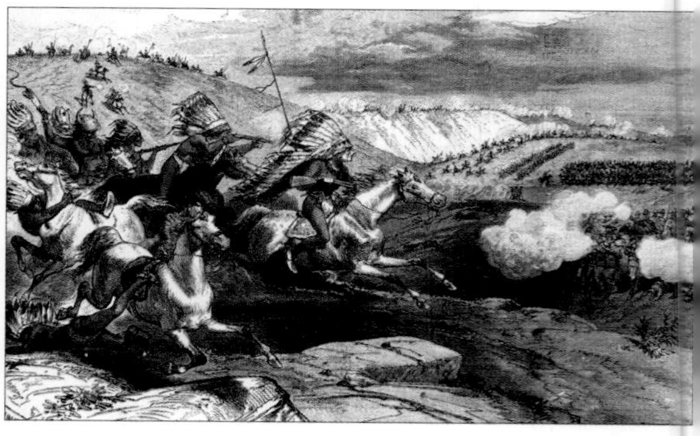

△ **A CHARGE AT ROSEBUD CREEK**
The Rosebud battle, which involved as many as 1,500 warriors and more than 1,000 soldiers, was fiercely fought on the high, open land above Rosebud Creek. The battle consisted largely of charges and countercharges by the two sides, both of whom claimed victory.

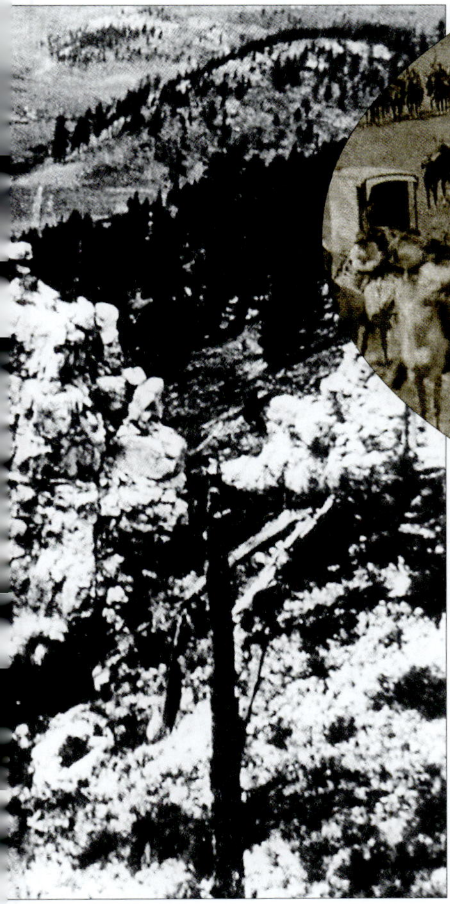

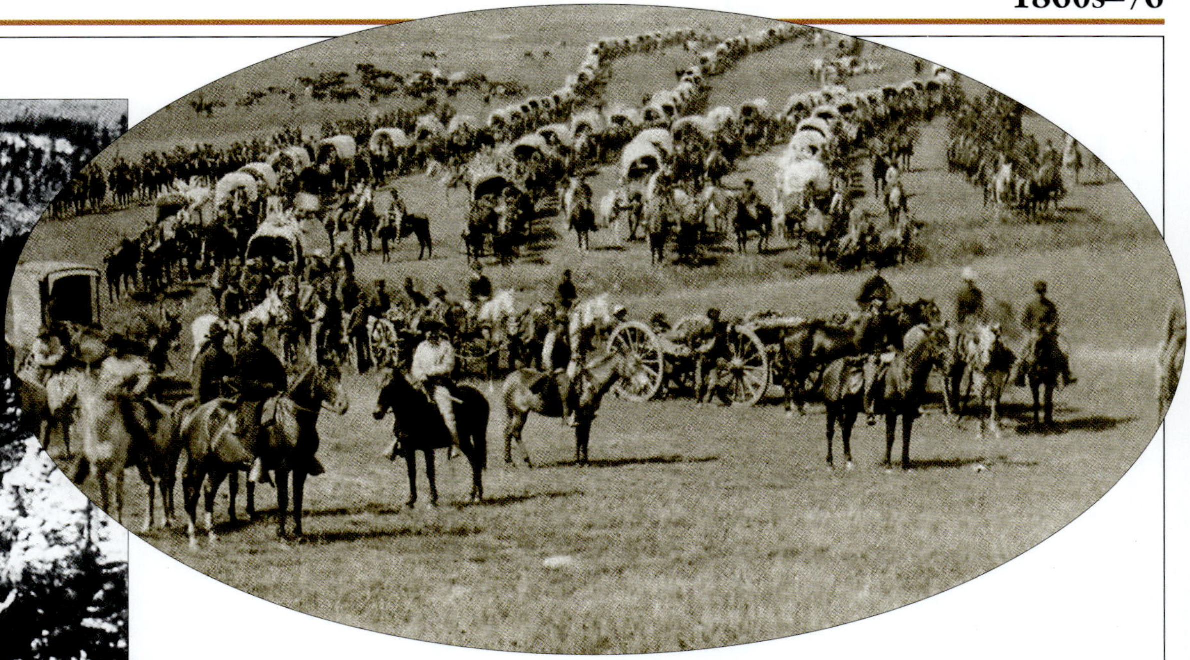

△ **Wagons Haul Supplies**
Army personnel, such as on Custer's 1874 Black Hills expedition, sometimes traveled in huge convoys with wagons carrying supplies. Military interests favored exploration of the Black Hills area in order to find suitable land on which to establish a fort.

◁ **Troops in the Black Hills**
More than 1,000 troops of the Seventh Cavalry, with 100 supply wagons, made their way through a pass in the Black Hills during Custer's Black Hills expedition. The press circulated Custer's report that there was "gold among the roots of the grass."

> *"The land known as the Black Hills is considered by the Indians as the center of their land."*
>
> Running Antelope, Lakota, following Custer's 1874 Black Hills expedition

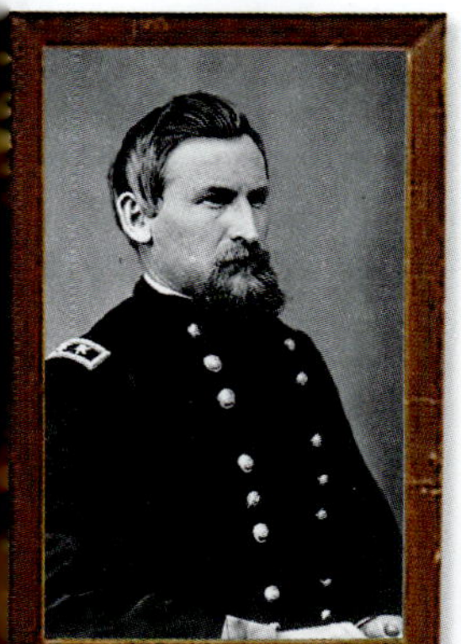

△ **Crook Claims Victory**
General George Crook's troops were sipping coffee when Crazy Horse's warriors attacked. Crook claimed victory since he remained on the field; his foes departed after six hours of fighting.

Rosebud Heroine ▷
A Cheyenne warrior named Comes in Sight had his horse shot from under him during the battle at Rosebud Creek. Saved by his sister, the rescue was recorded in a ledger book by a Northern Cheyenne artist.

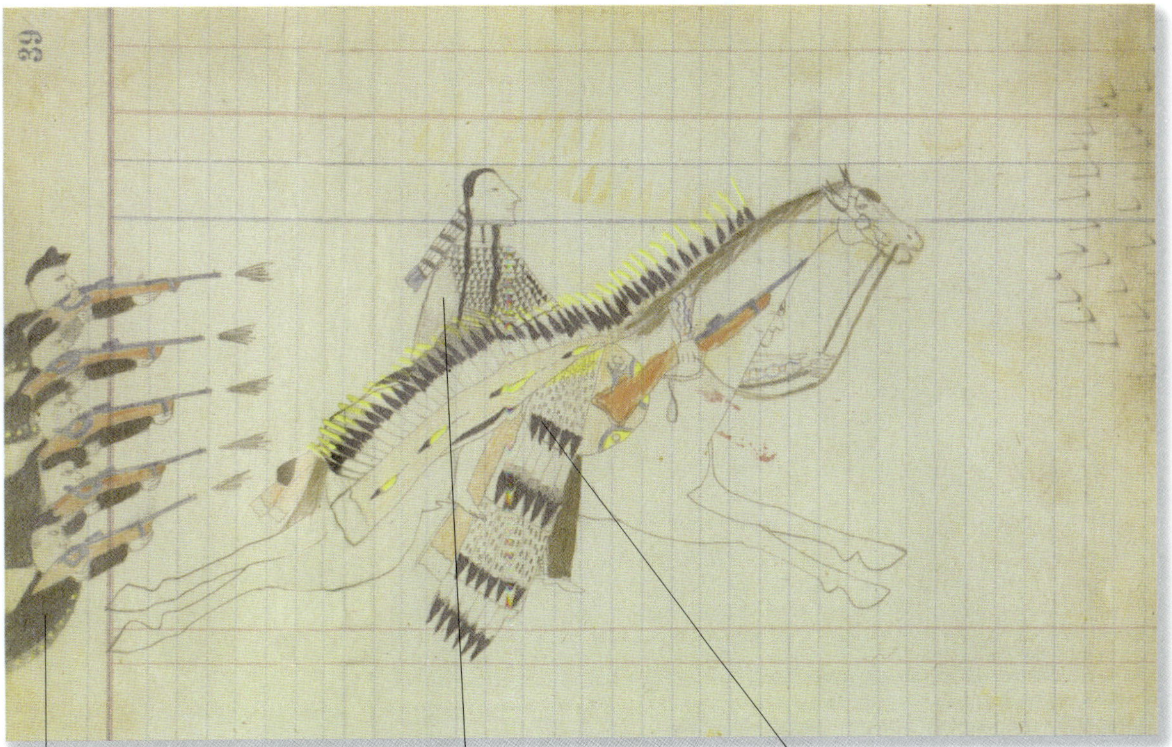

Crook's blue-coated troops are pictured firing their rifles at Buffalo Calf Road Woman and her brother, who rode to safety through a hail of bullets

Buffalo Calf Road Woman is depicted reaching down from her horse to help swing her brother onto the horse's rump

In the artist's ledger-book drawing, Comes in Sight is shown draped over his sister's horse, rifle still in hand

BATTLES FOR THE WEST

FOR MOST OF THE NINETEENTH CENTURY, as the US expanded westward, and squatters, homesteaders, and miners took over Native homelands, Indian tribes struggled with whites in an area that stretched from the Mississippi River to the Pacific Coast. During the 1850s and 1860s, when white expansion increased dramatically, wars spread to most of the West. It is estimated that between 1865 and 1890 the US took part in nearly 1,000 battles with Indians throughout the West, including the legendary battle of the Little Bighorn in 1876 (*see pp.94-97*). The location of some of these conflicts is shown on the map.

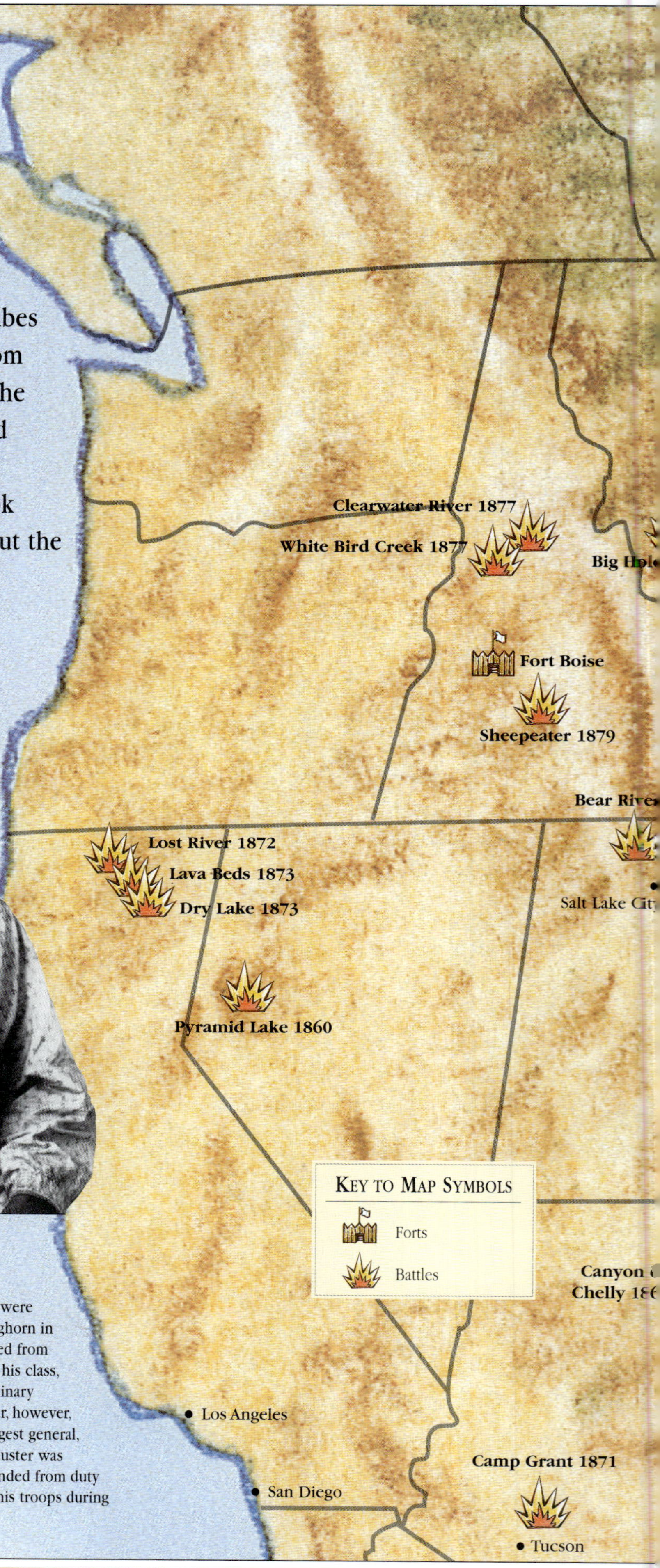

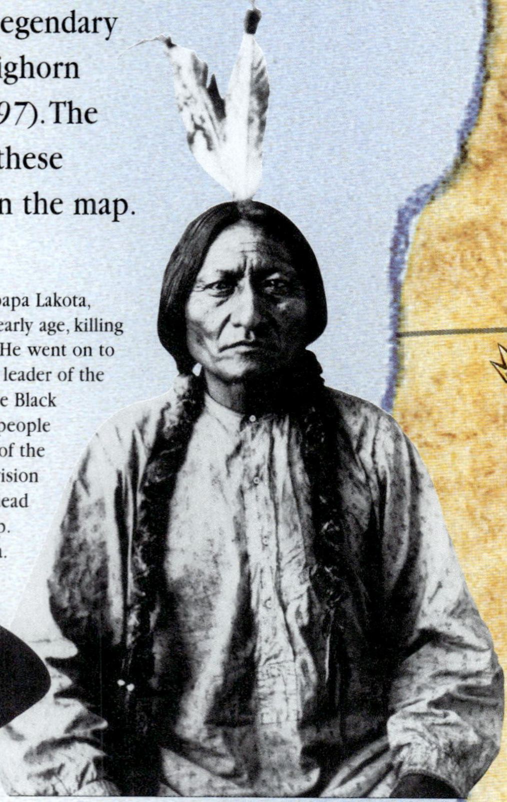

SITTING BULL ▷
Chief and holy man of the Hunkpapa Lakota, Sitting Bull proved himself at an early age, killing his first buffalo at the age of ten. He went on to become the spiritual and military leader of the resistance to white invasion of the Black Hills and the confinement of his people to reservations. Before the battle of the Little Bighorn, Sitting Bull had a vision in which he saw soldiers falling dead from the sky into the Indian camp. After the battle, he fled to Canada.

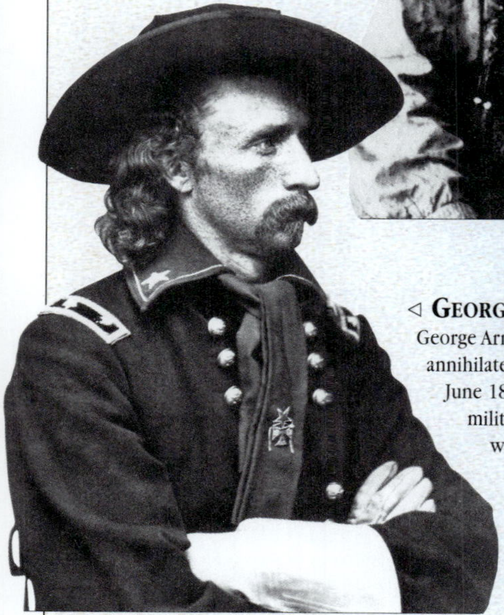

◁ GEORGE ARMSTRONG CUSTER
George Armstrong Custer and his forces were annihilated at the battle of the Little Bighorn in June 1876. Ohio-born Custer graduated from military academy at the bottom of his class, with a record number of disciplinary demerits. During the Civil War, however, he became the army's youngest general, at the age of 23. In 1867, Custer was court-martialed and suspended from duty for his harsh treatment of his troops during the Hancock campaign.

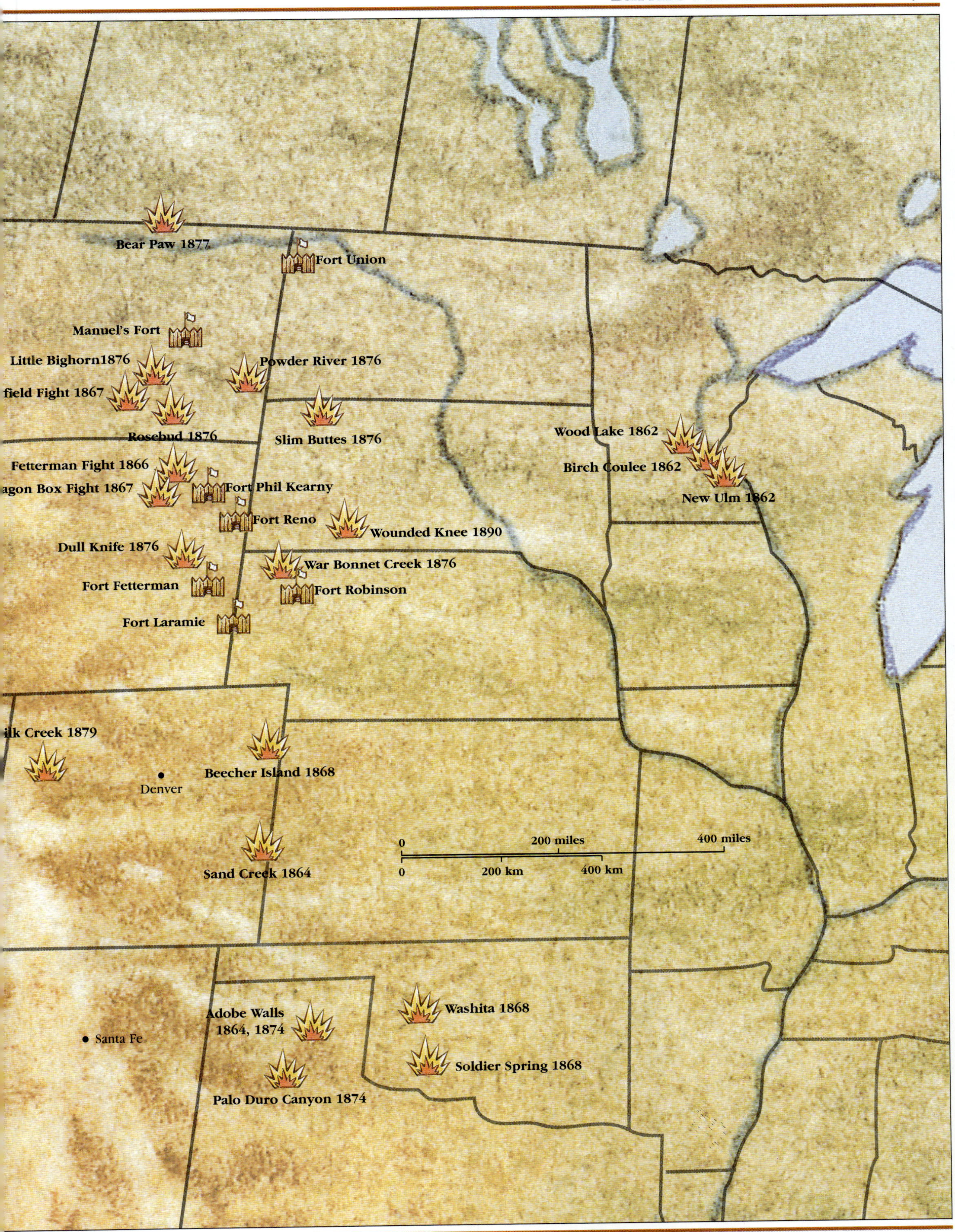
Bear Paw 1877
Fort Union
Manuel's Fort
Little Bighorn1876
field Fight 1867
Powder River 1876
Rosebud 1876
Slim Buttes 1876
Fetterman Fight 1866
agon Box Fight 1867
Fort Phil Kearny
Fort Reno
Wounded Knee 1890
Dull Knife 1876
War Bonnet Creek 1876
Fort Fetterman
Fort Robinson
Fort Laramie
Wood Lake 1862
Birch Coulee 1862
New Ulm 1862
ik Creek 1879
Beecher Island 1868
Denver
Sand Creek 1864
0
200 miles
400 miles
0
200 km
400 km
Adobe Walls
1864, 1874
Santa Fe
Palo Duro Canyon 1874
Washita 1868
Soldier Spring 1868

BATTLE OF THE LITTLE BIGHORN

THE PLAINS INDIANS' GREATEST VICTORY over the US Cavalry, and one of the worst disasters in American military annals, the battle of the Little Bighorn was fought on 25 June 1876 on the Little Bighorn River in Montana. That day Lieutenant Colonel George Armstrong Custer and his 200-odd officers and soldiers were killed in what is now called "Custer's Last Stand." The Indians won the battle, but their victory proved to be their defeat: Custer's death outraged Americans and brought a flood of soldiers to Indian country, where they pursued and crushed the Lakota and Cheyenne Indians.

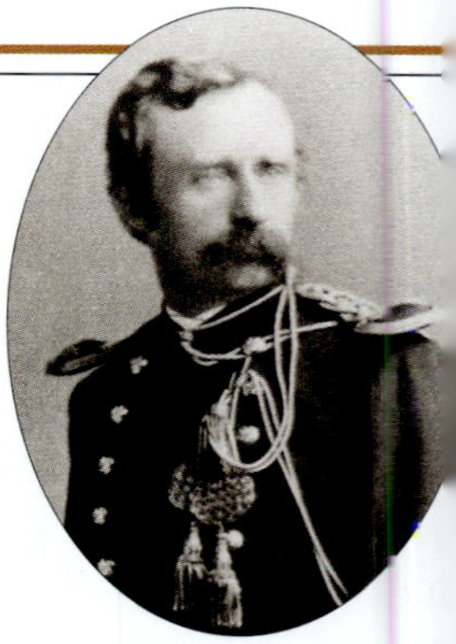

DOOMED COMMAND
Lieutenant Colonel George Cust led an attack that resulted in th destruction of the five compani under his command.

1876: BATTLE OF THE LITTLE BIGHORN

25 JUNE: DAWN
Custer's scouts detect large Indian village in distance

25 JUNE: MIDDAY
Custer splits command between Reno, Benteen, and himself

25 JUNE: *c.* 3 P.M.
Reno charges southern end of village and is driven back to defensive position on river bluff

25 JUNE: *c.* 3.30 P.M.
Custer sends message: "Benteen, Come on. Big village, be quick, bring packs."

25 JUNE: *c.* 4.15 P.M.
Benteen joins Reno on bluff

25 JUNE: AFTER 4.10 P.M.
Custer approaches northern end of village. Within an hour, he and all his men are dead

25–27 JUNE
Reno and Benteen withstand siege

27 JUNE
Indians retreat when General Terry and Colonel Gibbon arrive

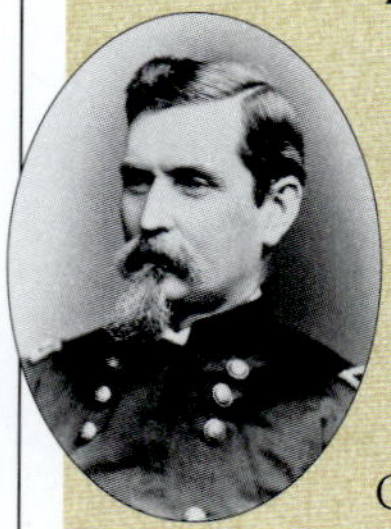

COLONEL JOHN GIBBON

AFTER THE BATTLE OF THE ROSEBUD (*see p.90*), many Sioux (the popular name for Lakota/Dakota people) and Cheyennes settled along Montana's Little Bighorn River (also known as Greasy Grass) to hunt buffalo. Their leaders, including Sitting Bull and Crazy Horse, refused to be confined permanently to reservations: they believed that the 1868 Fort Laramie Treaty gave them the right to range the buffalo grounds of the upper Missouri as long as the buffalo survived, and they were prepared to defend their hunting camp against the US army. The government responded by declaring all who refused to settle on reservations as "hostile" and subject to military action.

Commanding the operation, General Alfred H. Terry believed that Custer's Seventh Cavalry could overpower the Indians, and decided to split his forces. Terry marched west then south of the Bighorn River to seal any northern exit from the valley. He ordered Custer's force of 600 men to approach the Bighorn from the south to block any escape. Along the route, Custer's favorite scout, Bloody Knife, warned that more Indians lay ahead than there were bullets in the soldiers' belts; but Custer forged ahead, ignoring Terry's instructions to wait for his and Colonel John Gibbon's arrival.

Around noon on 25 June 1876, Custer sent Captain Frederick Benteen with three companies to scout the bluffs southwest of the Indian village. He ordered Major Marcus A.

> *"This is a good day to die. Follow me."*
>
> LOW DOG, OGLALA SIOUX LEADER, BATTLE OF LITTLE BIGHORN (GREASY GRASS), 25 JUNE 1876

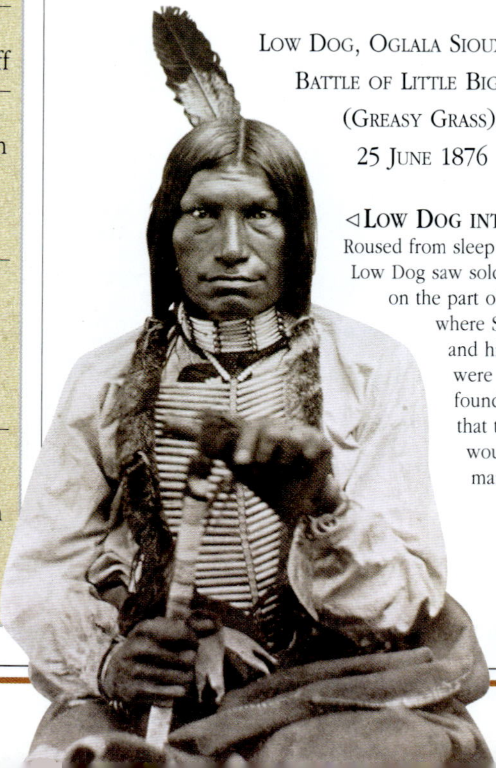

◁ **LOW DOG INTO BATTLE**
Roused from sleep by the noise, Low Dog saw soldiers firing on the part of the camp where Sitting Bull and his people were situated. He found it incredible that the troops would attack so many Indians.

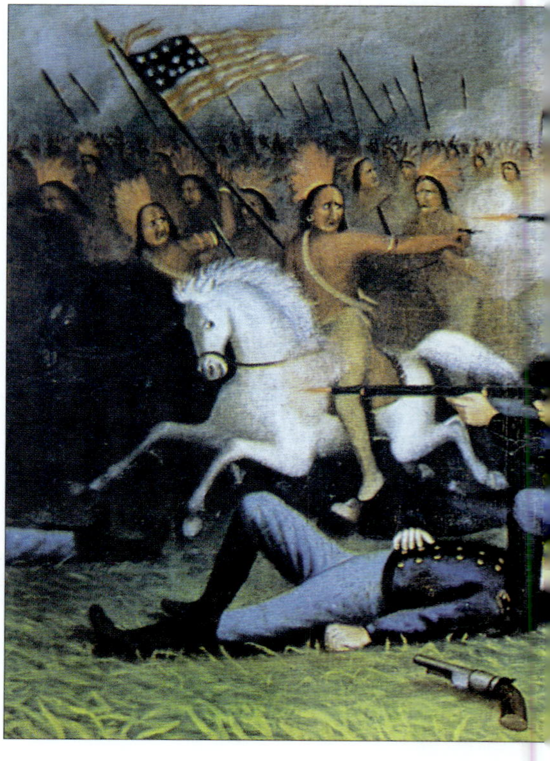

eno to charge the southern end f the encampment with three ompanies, while he led five ompanies around the camps to ttack from the north. Reno, vhose charge was rebuffed by ioux and Cheyenne warriors, ook refuge on a bluff, where he vas joined by Benteen's men. here they fought a defensive ction for two days until the ndians withdrew at the approach f General Terry's and Colonel ibbon's troops on 27 June.

Custer failed to reach the orthern end of the Indian ncampment and, his precise ctions a mystery, he came under ttack from a huge Indian force f as many as 2,500 men. He rdered a retreat up a hill, but the command ame too late to save his five companies.

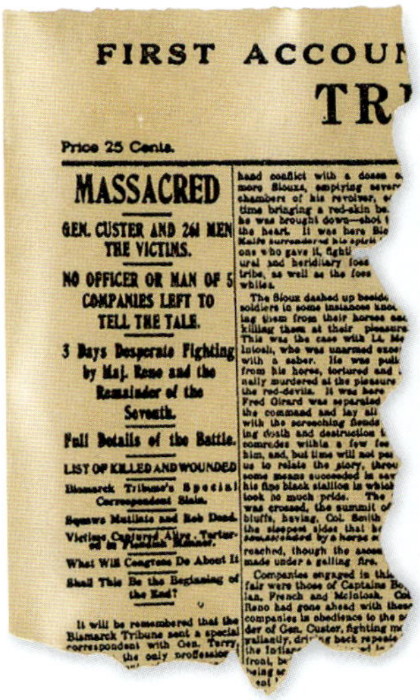
FIRST ACCOU
TR
Price 25 Cents.

MASSACRED

GEN. CUSTER AND 261 MEN THE VICTIMS.

NO OFFICER OR MAN OF 5 COMPANIES LEFT TO TELL THE TALE.

3 Days Desperate Fighting by Maj. Reno and the Remainder of the Seventh.

Full Details of the Battle.

LIST OF KILLED AND WOUNDED

Bismarck Tribune's Special Correspondent Slain.

Squaws Mutilate and Rob Dead.

Victims Captured Alive, Tortured in Fiendish Manner.

What Will Congress Do About It

Shall This Be the Beginning of the End?

It will be remembered that the Bismarck Tribune sent a special correspondent with Gen. Terry, the only professior

hand conflict with a dozen o more Sioux, emptying sever chambers of his revolver, e time bringing a red-skin be he was brought down—shot the heart. It was here Blo Knife surrendered his spirit one who gave it, fighti ural and heriditary foes tribe, as well as the foes whites.

The Sioux dashed up beside soldiers in some instances knoc ing them from their horses an killing them at their pleasure. This was the case with Lt. Mc Intosh, who was unarmed excep with a saber. He was pull from his horse, tortured and nally murdered at the pleasure the red-devils. It was here Fred Girard was separated the command and lay all with the screeching fiends ing death and destruction comrades within a few fe him, and, but time will not per us to relate the story, throu some means succeeded in sav his fine black stallion in which took so much pride. The was crossed, the summit of bluffs, having, Col. Smith the steepest sides that h surmounted by a horse reached, though the ascen made under a galling fire.

Companies engaged in this fair were those of Captains Bo lan, French and McIntosh. Co Reno had gone ahead with these companies in obedience to the or der of Gen. Custer, fighting mo gallantly, driving back repeate the Indian front, be being

NEWS OF THE MASSACRE
The first account of the Custer "massacre" appeared in the 6 July 1876 issue of the Bismarck (Dakota Territory) *Tribune*.

Sioux Relentlessly Pursued

After Custer and all his men were killed, the ndians broke up into smaller groups, but they vere pursued relentlessly by the army. In early August, General George Crook drove his men o exhaustion in pursuit of Sioux who had ought at the Little Bighorn. On 9 September, Crook's detachment of 150 cavalry captured a Lakota camp at Slim Buttes in South Dakota.

Until the first snows of winter, the Sioux and Cheyennes were able to elude the armies that chased them, but winter made them vulnerable and their resistance weakened. The final blow of the campaign to crush resistance on the Northern Plains came on 25 November 1876. Lieutenant Colonel Ranald Mackenzie, sent from Texas to punish the Indians who had annihilated Custer's command, mustered a force of 1,100 men. At dawn, he burst into the village of Dull Knife and Little Wolf, killing 40 Cheyennes, and destroying tipis, clothing, and food supplies.

After the victory over Custer, Sitting Bull led his followers to Canada. Year after year, as the buffalo dwindled, they grew hungrier and hungrier. Finally, in 1881, they returned home and Sitting Bull surrendered at Fort Buford, in present-day North Dakota.

Crazy Horse and his people remained in the Bighorn Mountains, continuing to evade the army who were sent to crush their resistance.

WHO KILLED CUSTER?

No one knows with certainty who killed George Armstrong Custer. Some attribute the deed to One Bull, a Hunkpapa Sioux warrior and the adopted son of Sitting Bull, but his personal account of the battle did not mention killing Custer.

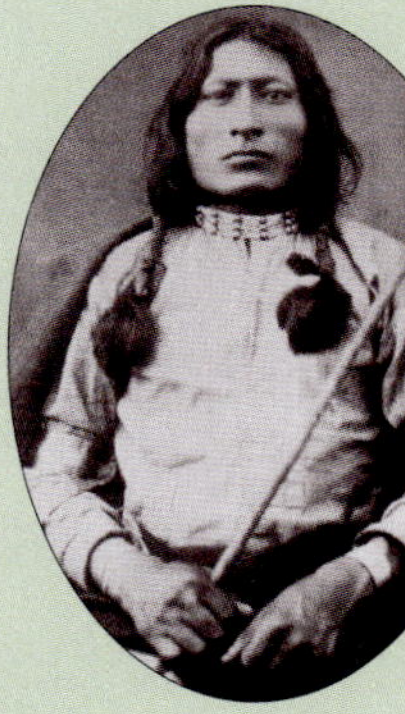
ONE BULL

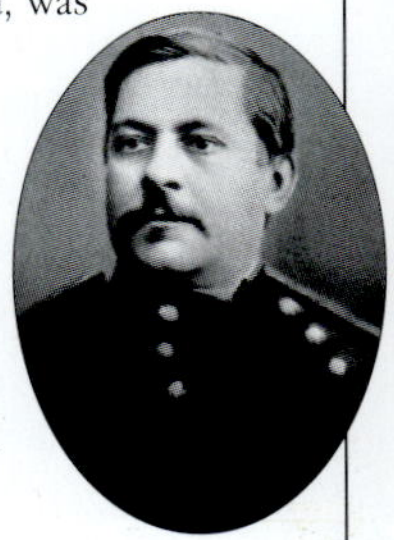
SECOND-IN-COMMAND RENO ▽
Major Marcus A. Reno, Custer's second-in-command, was criticized for his handling of the retreat from the valley. When tried for cowardice at a court of inquiry in 1879, however, he was cleared of direct responsibility for the defeat.

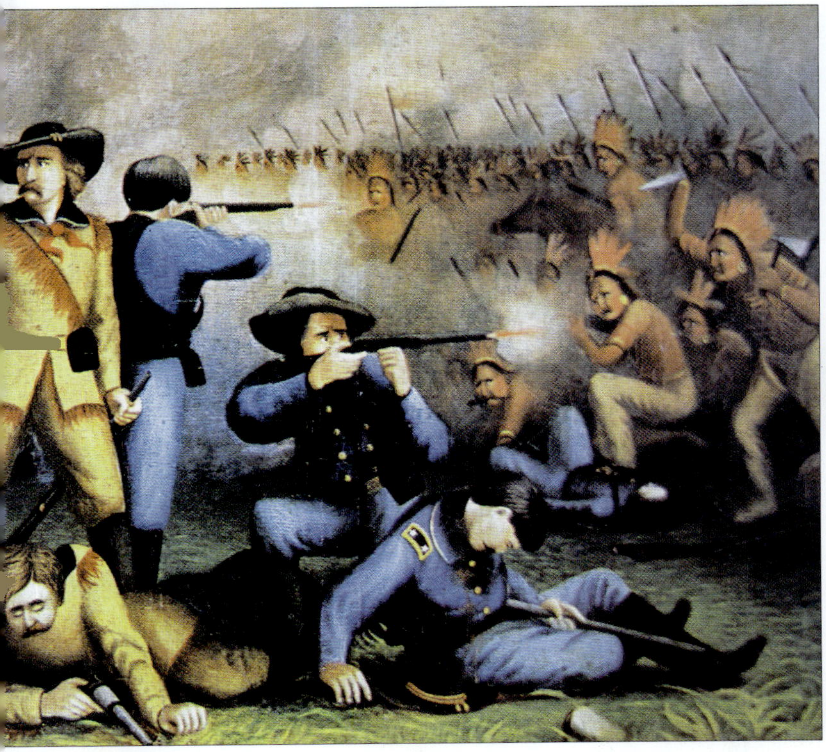
◁ CUSTER'S DEFEAT
Over 1,000 artists have made paintings of "Custer's Last Stand." Most, as in this folk-art depiction, show a heroic Custer, with weapon in hand, holding off Indian attackers. This artist leaves out the sickening horror of blood and gore that covered the battlefield.

▽ CAPTAIN'S HORSE SURVIVES
Captain Miles W. Keogh of Company I was one of Custer's officers slain at the battle of the Little Bighorn. His horse Comanche survived, but other horses were not so fortunate. Many horses, belonging to both Indians and soldiers, were killed during the battle. Some of the carcasses provided troops with temporary cover from bullets and arrows.

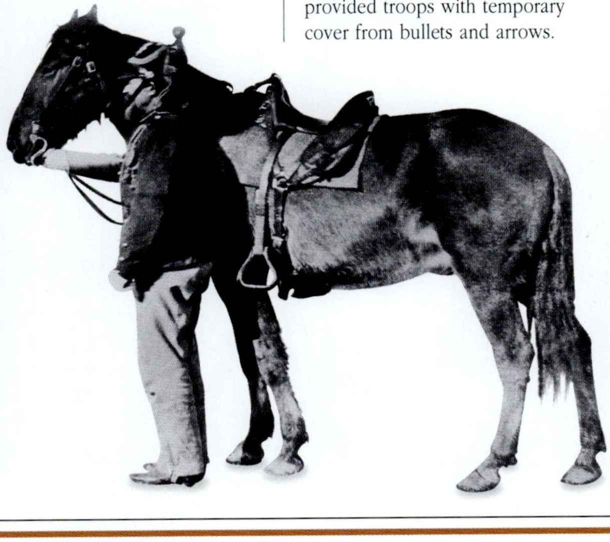

A Good Day to Die

At least 2,500 warriors defended their villages at the battle of the Little Bighorn, charging the soldiers and sometimes taking weapons off the dead to use against others. Some rode into the river in order to kill the retreating troops, while others rode among the troopers, unhorsing them. "There never was a better day to die," shouted Red Horse, a Lakota warrior who later made 41 pictographic drawings of the battle.

"They say we massacred [Custer], but he would have done the same thing to us had we not defended ourselves and fought to the last."

Crazy Horse, Sioux Leader, Battle of the Little Bighorn, 1876

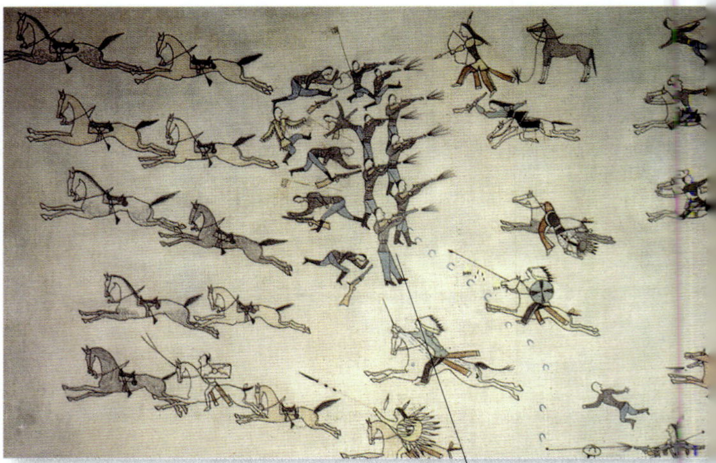

△ **An Eyewitness Depiction**
White Bird, a Northern Cheyenne who took part in the Little Bighorn battle when he was 15, painted his depiction of the event about 18 years later. Drawing on tribal knowledge, he showed Custer's final position on the hill where the soldiers died.

White Bird's drawing shows Custer's men under attack by a large force of Indians on horseback, armed with rifles and other weapons

Pursuit to Slim Buttes

After the Indians' victory over Custer, the various Lakota bands headed north and east to hunt buffalo. One small band, under American Horse, encamped beneath a rock formation called Slim Buttes. At dawn, on 9 September 1876, a detachment of soldiers, sent out by General Crook, attacked the camp, taking the Indians by surprise. The battle of Slim Buttes reversed the result of the earlier defeat, raising morale among the soldiers.

▽ **Mills Leads Attack**
The attack at Slim Buttes was led by Captain Anson Mills. American Horse defended women and children who had taken refuge in a cave until, mortally wounded, he had to surrender.

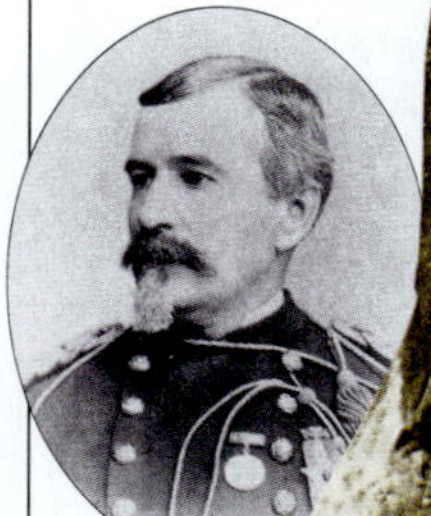

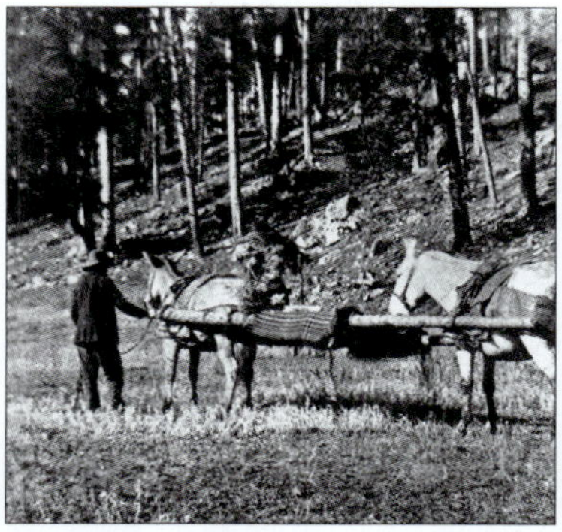

△ **Casualties of War**
Fifteen Lakota men and women trapped in a cave inflicted severe injuries on the troops and took heavy losses themselves before having to surrender. Here, a horse-drawn stretcher carries one of the wounded soldiers from the battle.

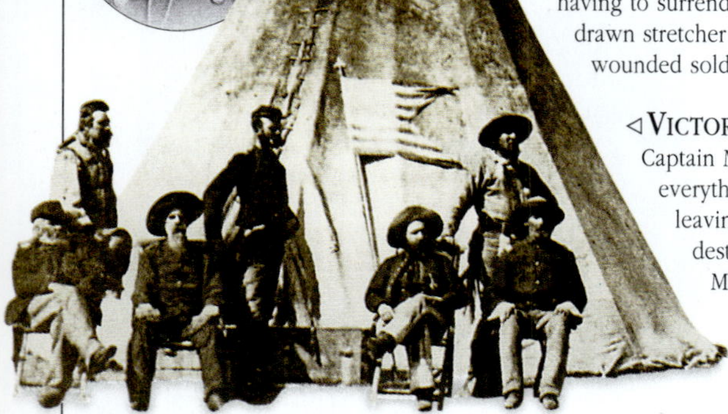

◁ **Victors Pose**
Captain Mills' men burned everything in the village, leaving the Lakotas destitute. Here, some of Mills' soldiers pose in front of a tipi before it was destroyed.

Army Seeks Vengeance

After the battle at Slim Buttes, the army continued to persecute the Lakotas and Cheyennes. In the late summer and fall of 1876, General Crook pursued Lakotas, while General Miles and his men attacked Lakota villages all winter and well into 1877. On 8 January 1877, Crazy Horse attacked Miles' troops, but the Indians were forced to retreat. In May 1877, freezing and out of ammunition, Crazy Horse and his followers surrendered.

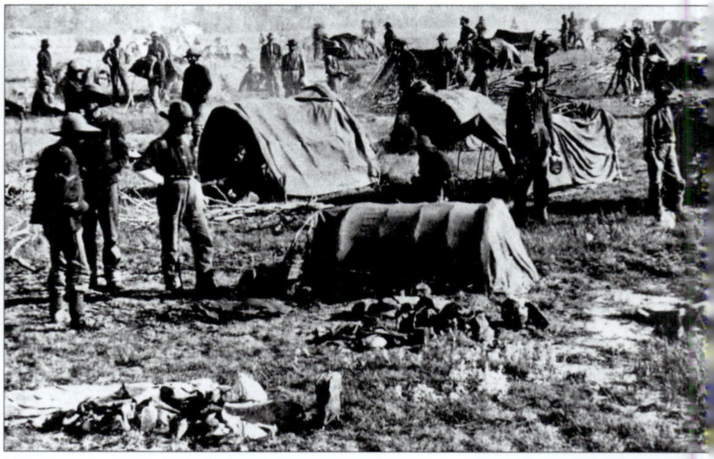

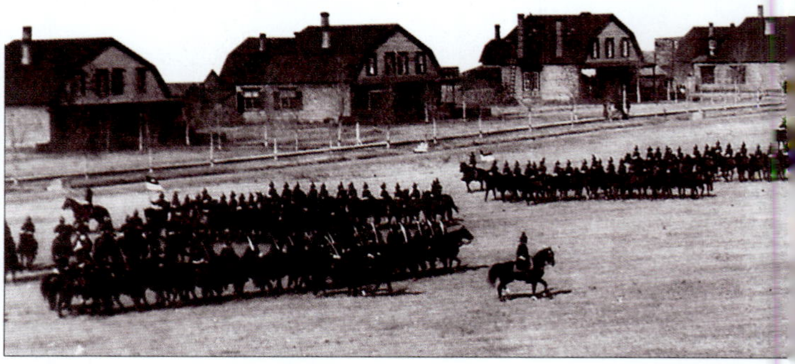

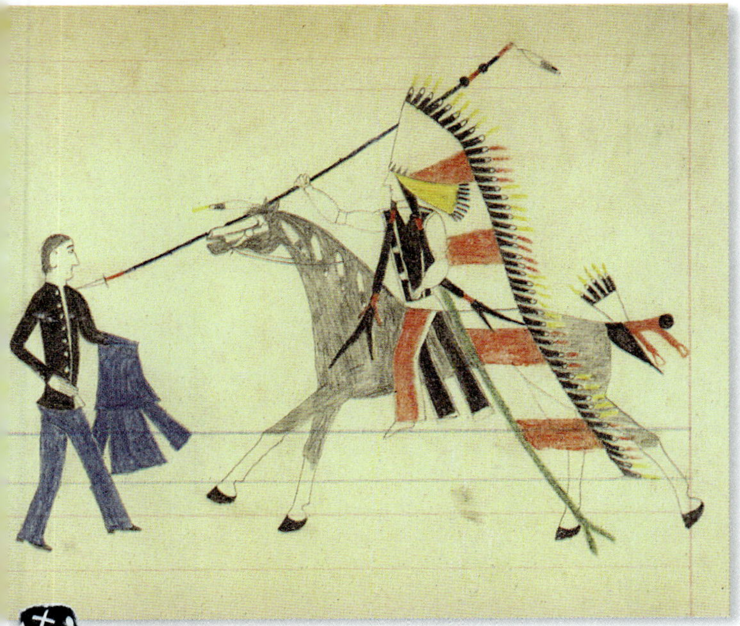

◁ PURSUING THE ENEMY
In this picture, a mounted Lakota warrior, his feathered war bonnet drawn in meticulous detail, may be spearing his enemy or "counting coup" (touching an enemy with a coupstick without being killed), which was a high honor for Plains Indians.

AFTERMATH OF BATTLE ▷
On 27 June, Terry and Gibbon found the bodies of Custer's men littering the ridge where they had fallen. The following day, they were buried at or near the places where they had fallen. Cheyenne and Sioux warriors killed in the battle were removed from the field by relatives and friends.

Red Horse's drawing depicts the field of dead cavalrymen. Women from the attacked villages stripped and mutilated the bodies

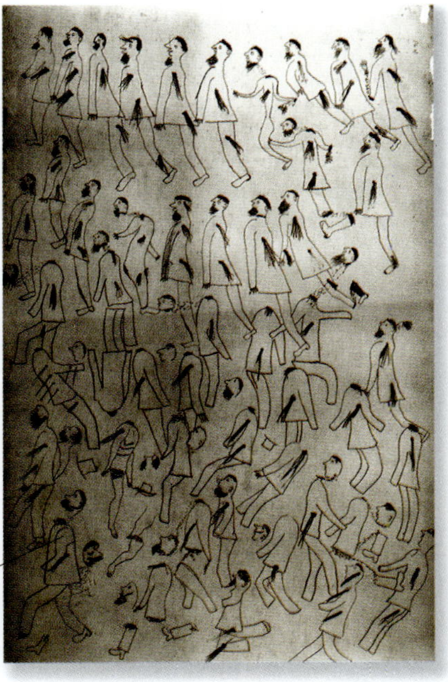

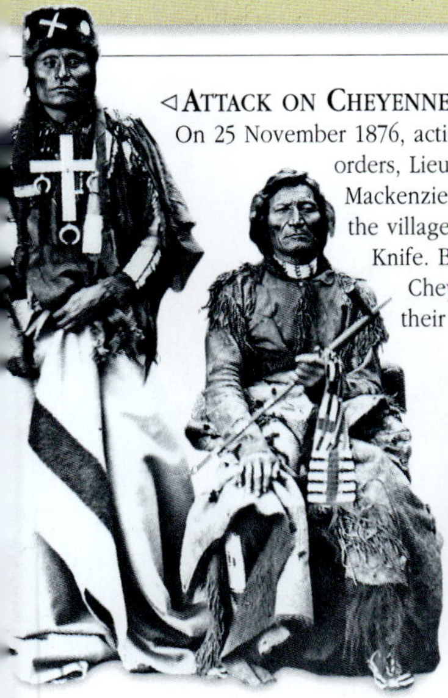

◁ ATTACK ON CHEYENNE LEADERS' VILLAGE
On 25 November 1876, acting on General Crook's orders, Lieutenant Colonel Ranald Mackenzie launched an attack on the village of Little Wolf and Dull Knife. Both escaped, but 40 Cheyennes were killed and their village destroyed.

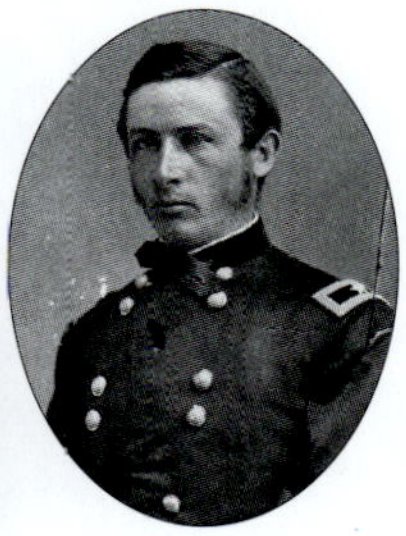

LITTLE WOLF DULL KNIFE LIEUTENANT COLONEL RANALD MACKENZIE

TROOPS MOBILIZED
On hearing of a large Cheyenne village in present-day Wyoming, General Crook ordered an army of nearly 2,200 men to mobilize. The soldiers had to put all their equipment on the pack train of 00 mules and 168 supply wagons that went along on the march.

▽ ARMY EXPANSION
In 1877, the US army built Fort Custer just a few miles from the site of the battle of the Little Bighorn, in the heart of Lakota country in Montana. This picture shows the unprecedented size of the outpost and the massive scale of the new cavalry units.

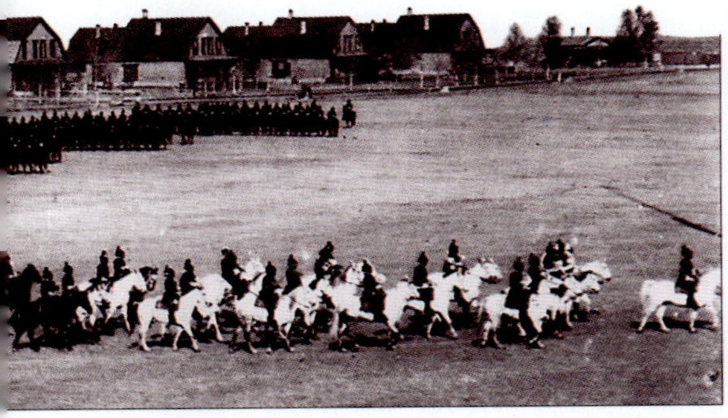

SITTING BULL'S SURRENDER

After the victory over Custer, Sitting Bull and his followers fled to Canada, receiving asylum in Saskatchewan. Over the years, Sitting Bull's people drifted back to the US. When his following had dwindled to fewer than 1,000, Sitting Bull returned also. In July 1881, he surrendered at Fort Buford, in present-day North Dakota.

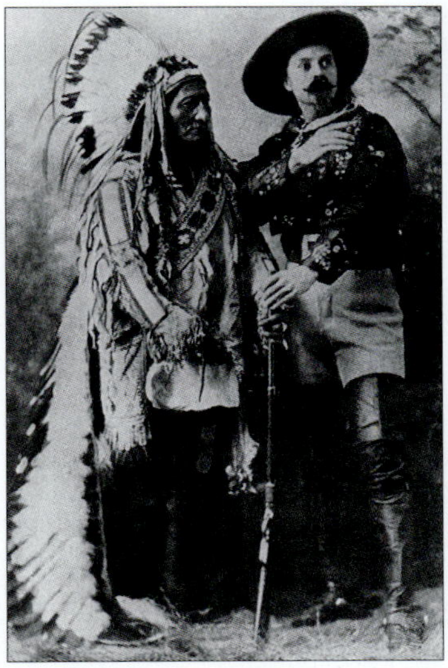

▽ FAMILY IN CUSTODY
Along with an army officer's daughter, Sitting Bull was pictured, in 1882, with one of his wives and four of his children outside their tipi at Fort Randall, Dakota Territory, where they were confined for two years.

A PUBLIC SPECTACLE ▷
In 1885, Sitting Bull toured the US and Canada with Buffalo Bill's Wild West Show. Sitting Bull, pictured here with the showman, told a missionary that he had become a public spectacle against his will.

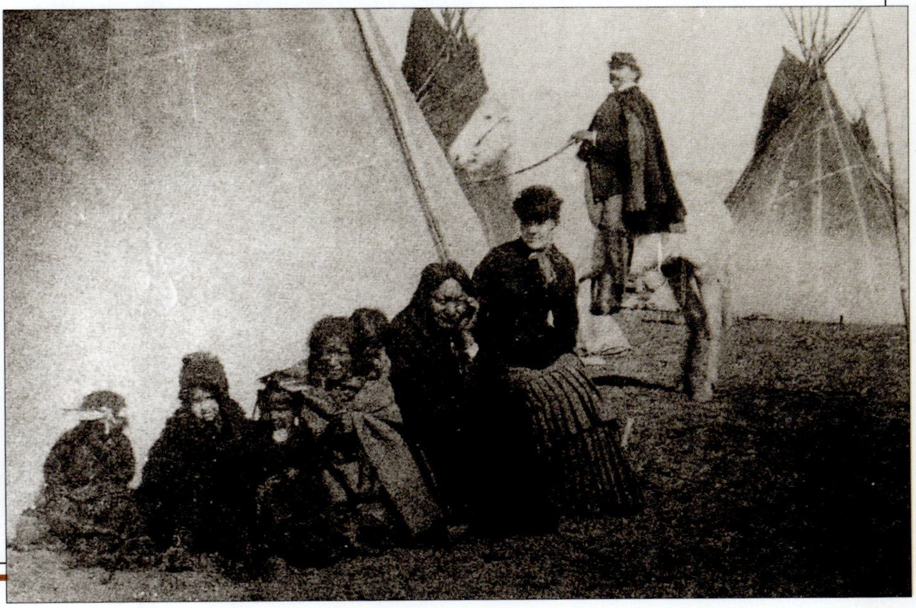

THE CUSTER LEGEND ▷

Artists, writers, and film-makers have constructed a heroic legend around Custer's role at the battle of the Little Bighorn in June 1876. Within 24 hours of receiving news of the battle, Walt Whitman mailed his poem "A Death Song for Custer" to the *New York Tribune*. Edgar S. Paxson painted this version of the disaster in 1899.

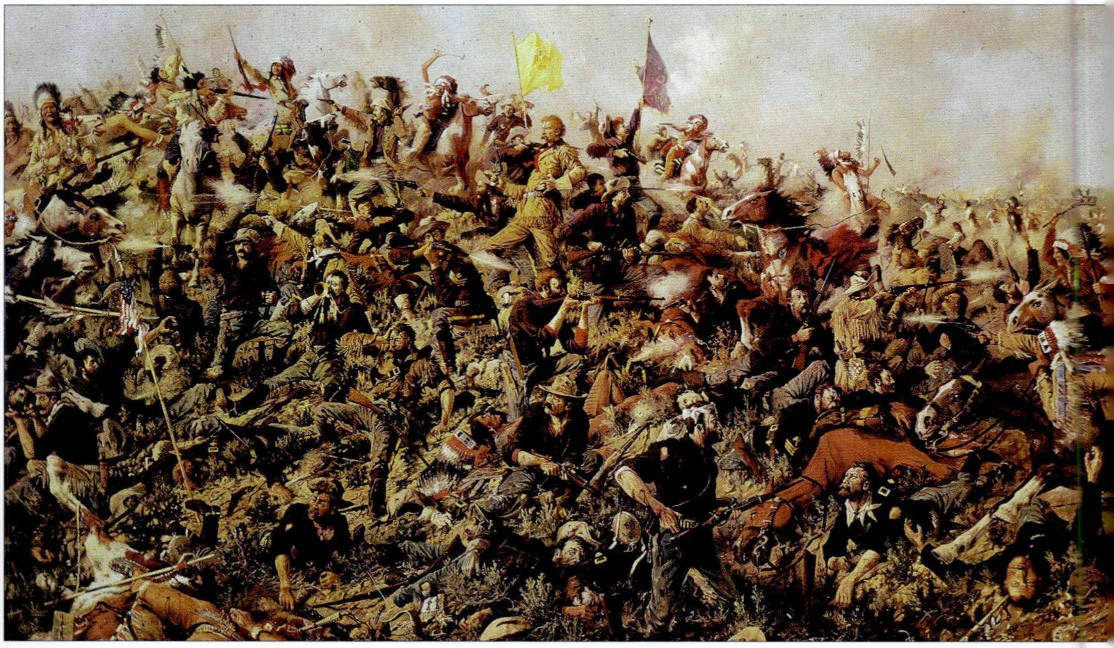

▽ WESTERN HEROES

Kit Carson (left card) and "Wild Bill" Hickok are immortalized for their roles in America's Indian wars. In the 1860s, Kit Carson led assaults on Navajos, Comanches, and Kiowas, while Hickok served as a scout with Custer.

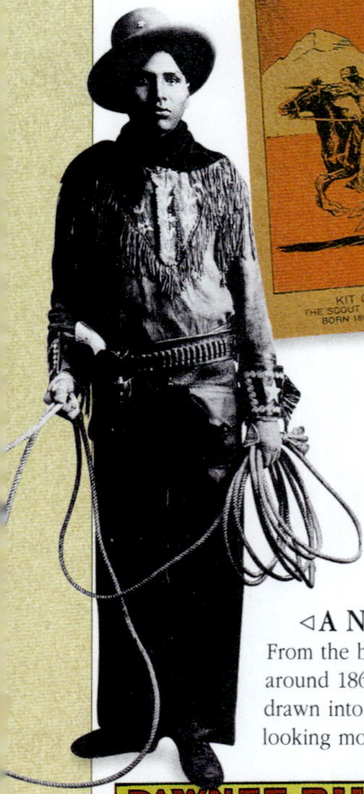

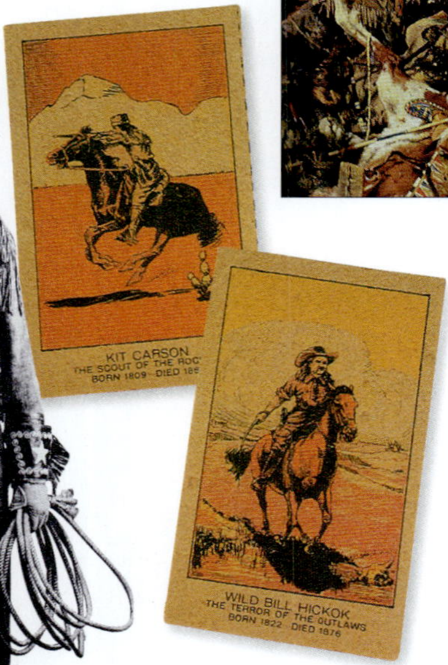

◁ A NATIVE AMERICAN COWBOY

From the beginning of the cowboy period, around 1865, Native Americans were drawn into the "cowboy culture," often looking more like cowboys than Indians.

▽ BRINGING MYTHOLOGY ALIVE

Between 1883 and 1913, Buffalo Bill's Wild West Show performed throughout North America and Europe. The show, which reenacted Indian attacks on the Deadwood Mail Coach and the demise of Custer, drew huge audiences. With galloping horses, hand-to-hand combat, gun powder, and pyrotechnics, the spectacle made Cody's mythological West seem real to audiences.

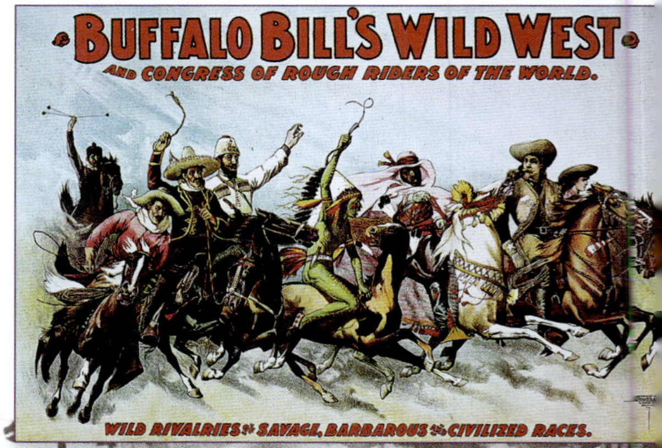

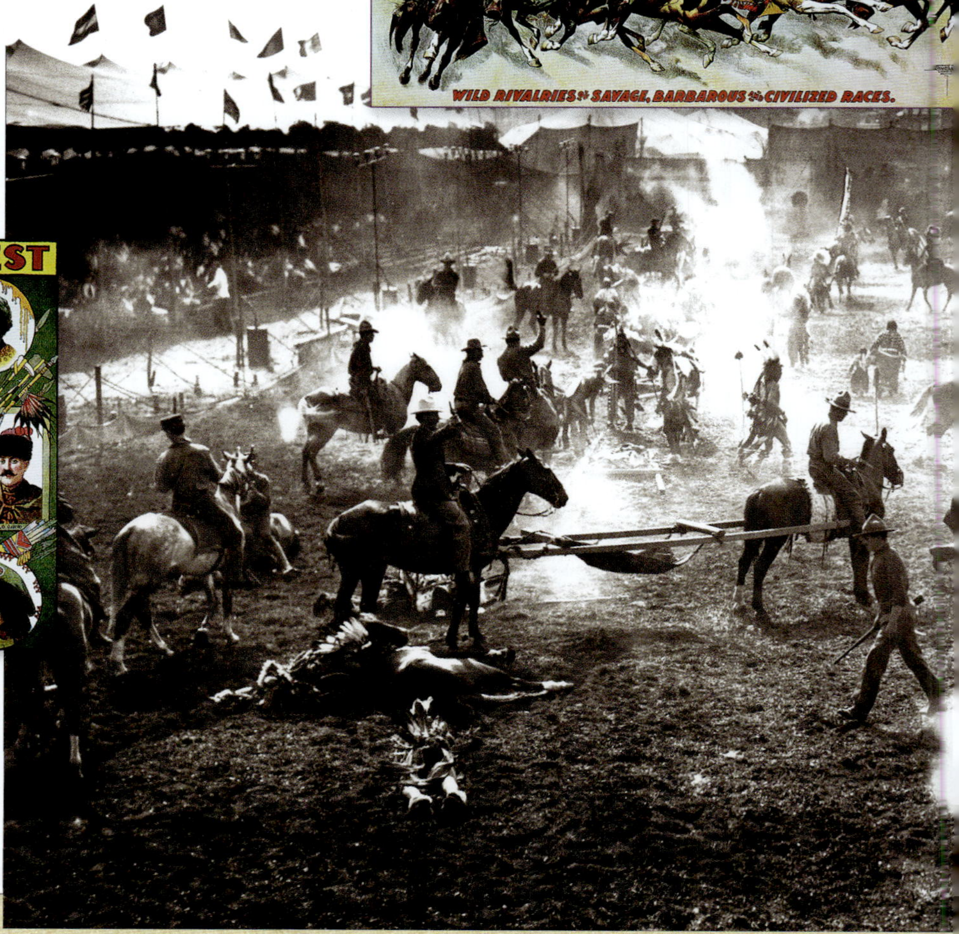

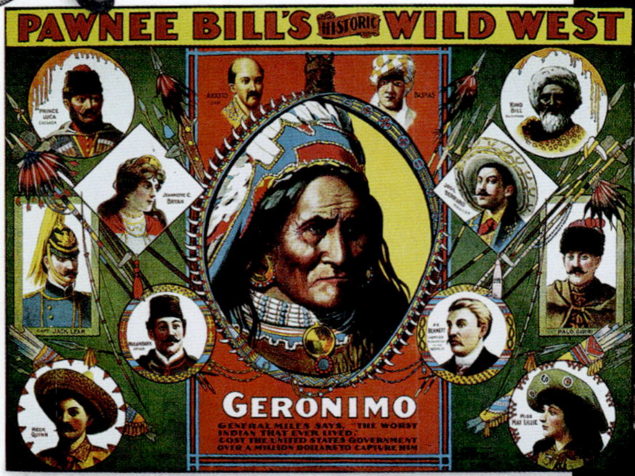

△ A LIVING LEGEND

Chiricahua Apache Geronimo starred in Pawnee Bill's Wild West Show, organized by showman Gordon W. Lillie. His was one of many shows that exploited the popularity of the Wild West. Large, color lithographed posters, like this one, advertised the show's arrival in town.

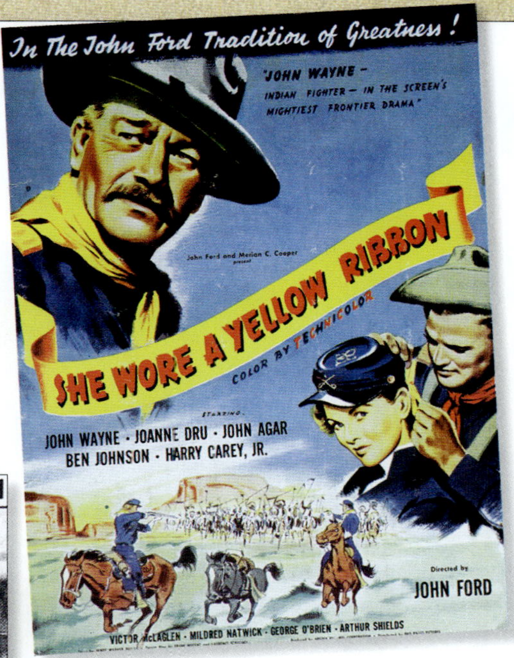

OLLYWOOD WESTERNS ▷
nce 1903, Hollywood has ade Westerns that perpetuate ages of Indians as bloodthirsty lains or noble-but-doomed vages – both emphasizing the periority of the white heroes. ages of Indians as too good too bad, but never real, have en repeated in thousands of ms, especially those starring hn Wayne, who acted in John rd's famous trilogy of films: *rt Apache*; *She Wore a Yellow bbon*; and *Rio Grande*.

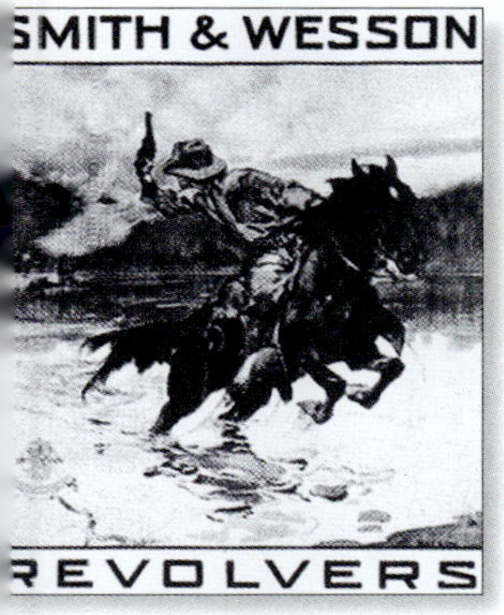

LIFE ON THE RANGE
hite or Indian, real cowboys ere not just gunfighters. They ere wage earners whose jobs tailed 16–18 hours each day of ueling, monotonous labor unding up cows – not outlaws.

"Ask any child ... what he would most like to see in the United States and the answer is likely to be 'Cowboys and Indians'."

LUCIA LEWIS, *THE CHICAGO DAILY NEWS*, 1961

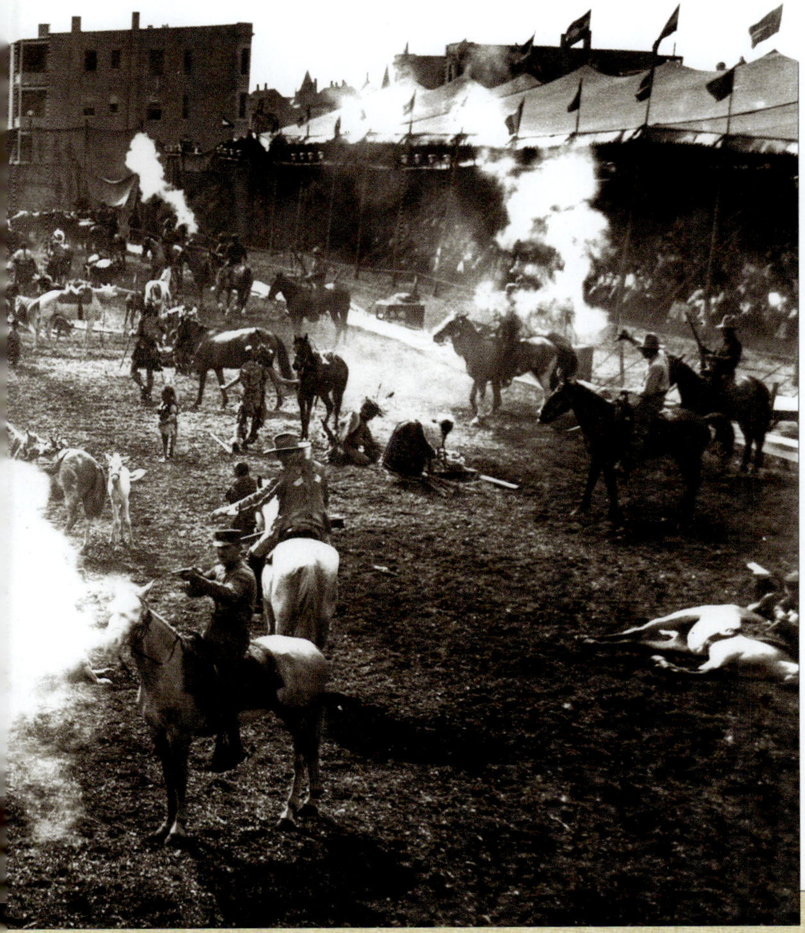

Wild West Myths

THE WORLD'S INFATUATION with the American West started with Buffalo Bill's Wild West Show, a cowboy and Indian spectacular starring real Plains Indians, cowboys, horses, and buffalo, produced by William F. Cody. Cody, a Pony Express rider, army scout, buffalo hunter, and showman, opened his traveling show in 1883, and it continued performing for 30 years before huge audiences in the US, Canada, England, and Europe. Cody treated audiences to blood-curdling reenactments, with Indians riding bareback, whooping and hollering, while they pretended to attack a settler's cabin, ambush a wagon train, or take part in realistic battle scenes.

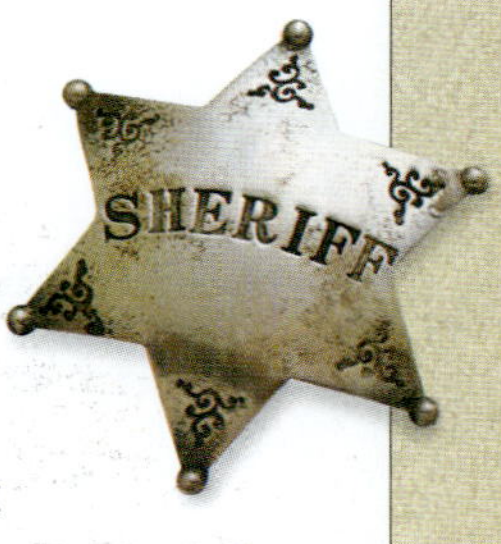

SHERIFF'S BADGE

Creating a Myth

These successful spectacles branded people's minds with the image of wild Indians and helped to perpetuate the Wild West myth for the millions who saw them. When the show was performed in London in 1887, the Kings of Belgium, Greece, Denmark, and Saxony were passengers in the Deadwood Stagecoach while the Indians "attacked" it. The show was also the hit of Queen Victoria's Golden Jubilee celebration in 1887. In the summer of 1889, a "Western" fashion sensation swept Paris after the Wild West Show performed there: Indians were taken up the Eiffel Tower in full regalia. Hundreds of Western Indian clubs sprang up in Germany as a result of the mania created by the Wild West shows and, in Italy, during an 1890 tour, Cody's Indians were blessed by Pope Leo XIII.

Myths and Distortion

Cody's Wild West shows inspired Hollywood film-makers and television writers who filmed ferocious Indians, speaking bad English, attacking forts, settlements, troops, and wagon trains until the Cavalry came to the rescue.

Just as countless novelists and Hollywood film-makers have fabricated stereotyped Indians, toy manufacturers have also invented Indian playthings that have little to do with real Indians, past or present. Armed and war-painted plastic dolls, dressed in ersatz headdresses and beaded buckskin, fill toy chests around the globe. These toys homogenize Native cultures, obliterating their enormous diversity of clothing traditions, jewelry, hairstyles, headdresses, and footwear.

The "Buffalo Bill" Indian stereotype seriously distorts the role of Natives in North American history. In the Wild West Shows, Indians are portrayed as threats to the onward march of Euro-American civilization and technological progress, whereas, in fact, Native people were defending their homes, families, lands, and way of life from white invasion.

CANADA PAST AND PRESENT

THIS MAP SHOWS the present-day locations of Inuit communities and a few of the 600 plus bands of Canadian Indians. Band members live on one of over 2,400 reserves - tracts of land set aside for their exclusive use. The reserves are located within areas the tribes had long occupied, but greatly reduced in size from the original territory. Approximately two-thirds of the Métis population dwell in the provinces of Manitoba, Saskatchewan, Alberta, and the Northwest Territories, with the rest scattered throughout Canada. In 1990, legislation gave the Métis in Alberta 1.25 million acres (500,000 hectares) of land - a protected land base now divided into 8 Métis settlements. The map also indicates areas of Canada affected by Indian treaties signed between 1850 and 1923.

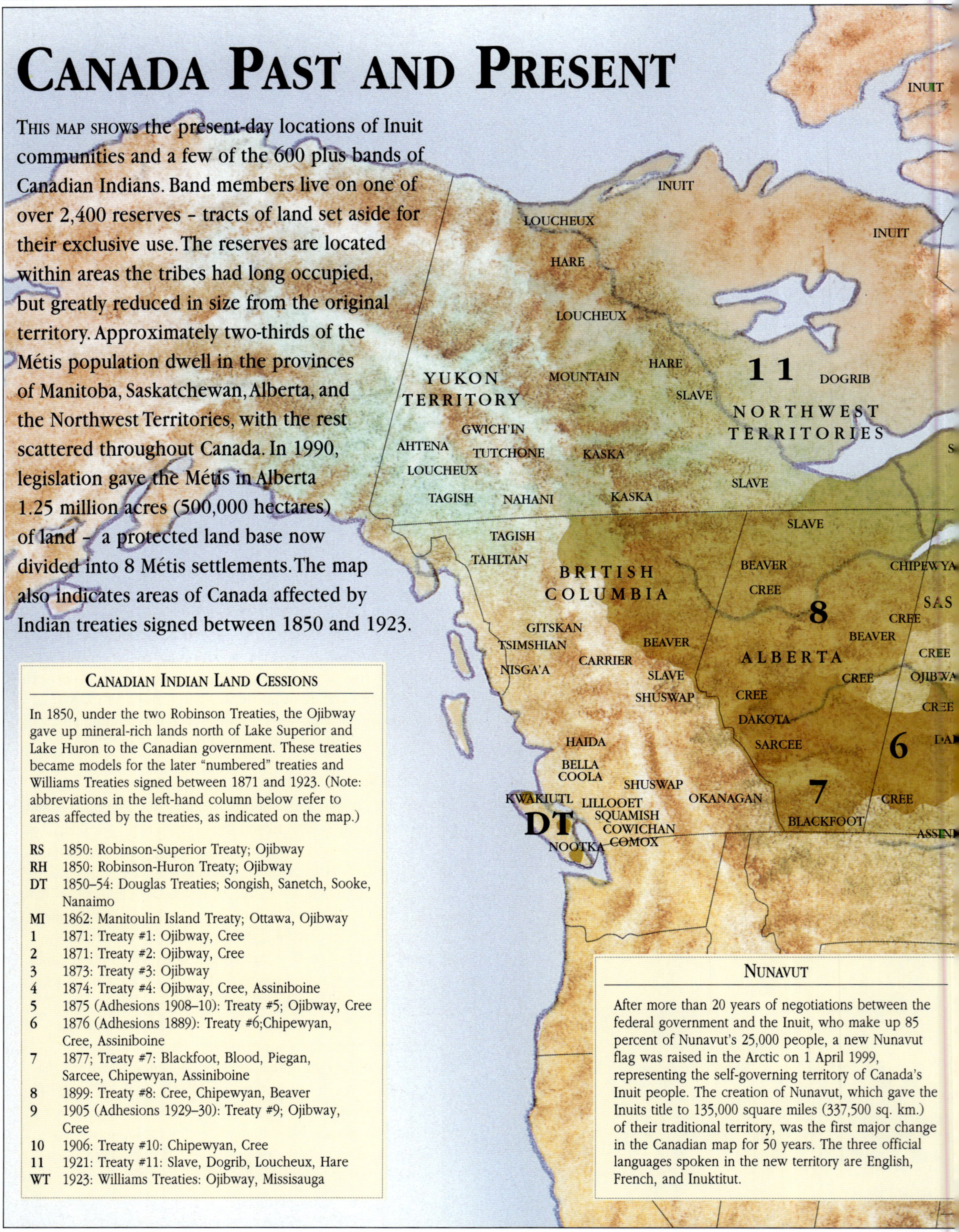

CANADIAN INDIAN LAND CESSIONS

In 1850, under the two Robinson Treaties, the Ojibway gave up mineral-rich lands north of Lake Superior and Lake Huron to the Canadian government. These treaties became models for the later "numbered" treaties and Williams Treaties signed between 1871 and 1923. (Note: abbreviations in the left-hand column below refer to areas affected by the treaties, as indicated on the map.)

RS	1850: Robinson-Superior Treaty; Ojibway
RH	1850: Robinson-Huron Treaty; Ojibway
DT	1850–54: Douglas Treaties; Songish, Sanetch, Sooke, Nanaimo
MI	1862: Manitoulin Island Treaty; Ottawa, Ojibway
1	1871: Treaty #1: Ojibway, Cree
2	1871: Treaty #2: Ojibway, Cree
3	1873: Treaty #3: Ojibway
4	1874: Treaty #4: Ojibway, Cree, Assiniboine
5	1875 (Adhesions 1908–10): Treaty #5; Ojibway, Cree
6	1876 (Adhesions 1889): Treaty #6;Chipewyan, Cree, Assiniboine
7	1877; Treaty #7: Blackfoot, Blood, Piegan, Sarcee, Chipewyan, Assiniboine
8	1899: Treaty #8: Cree, Chipewyan, Beaver
9	1905 (Adhesions 1929–30): Treaty #9; Ojibway, Cree
10	1906: Treaty #10: Chipewyan, Cree
11	1921: Treaty #11: Slave, Dogrib, Loucheux, Hare
WT	1923: Williams Treaties: Ojibway, Missisauga

NUNAVUT

After more than 20 years of negotiations between the federal government and the Inuit, who make up 85 percent of Nunavut's 25,000 people, a new Nunavut flag was raised in the Arctic on 1 April 1999, representing the self-governing territory of Canada's Inuit people. The creation of Nunavut, which gave the Inuits title to 135,000 square miles (337,500 sq. km.) of their traditional territory, was the first major change in the Canadian map for 50 years. The three official languages spoken in the new territory are English, French, and Inuktitut.

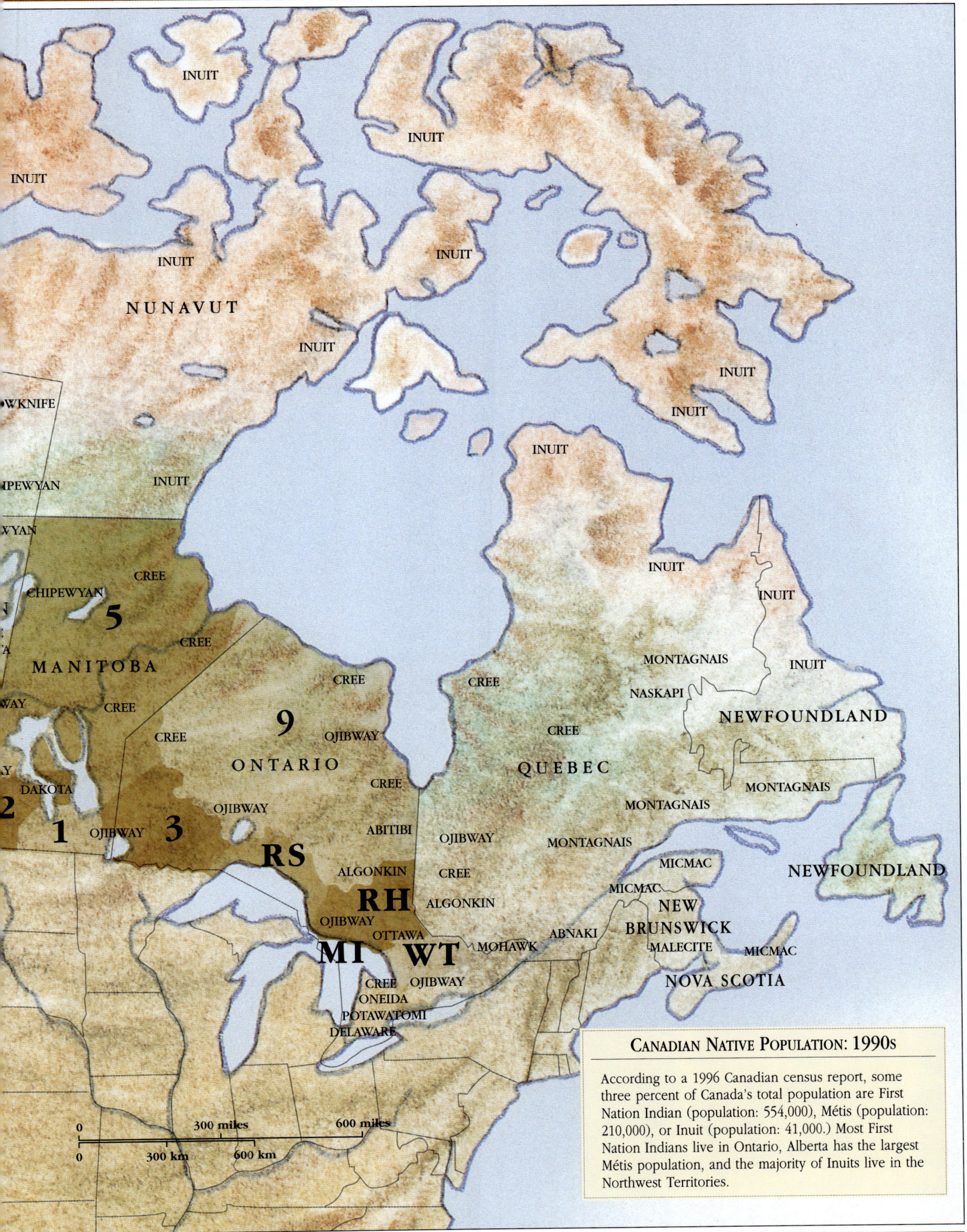

CANADIAN NATIVE POPULATION: 1990S

According to a 1996 Canadian census report, some three percent of Canada's total population are First Nation Indian (population: 554,000), Métis (population: 210,000), or Inuit (population: 41,000.) Most First Nation Indians live in Ontario, Alberta has the largest Métis population, and the majority of Inuits live in the Northwest Territories.

THE RIEL REBELLIONS

MÉTIS LEADER LOUIS RIEL led two rebellions against the Canadian government's indifference to his people's grievances. The First Riel Rebellion (1869–70), also known as the Red River Resistance, arose from the Canadian government's refusal to recognize Métis land rights and Riel's legitimate provisional government. Riel fled after a military force was sent to take control of the area. In the Second Riel Rebellion, in 1885, the Métis and their Cree allies won some battles, but the rebellion was again crushed by Canadian troops.

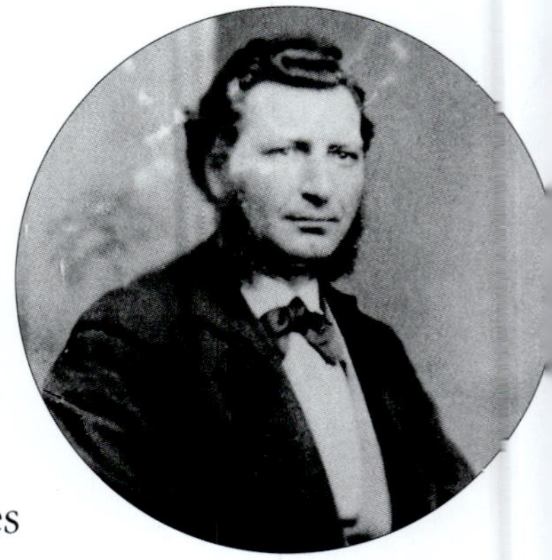
LOUIS RIEL

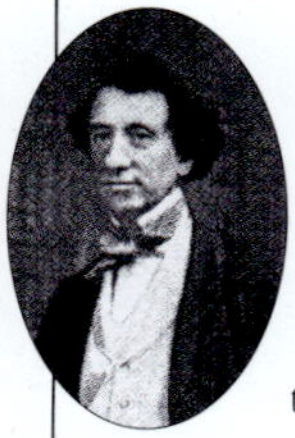
◁ PREMIER INTERVENES
Canada's first premier, John A. MacDonald, sent troops via the US during the First Riel Rebellion to avoid upsetting Quebec, which supported the French-speaking Métis.

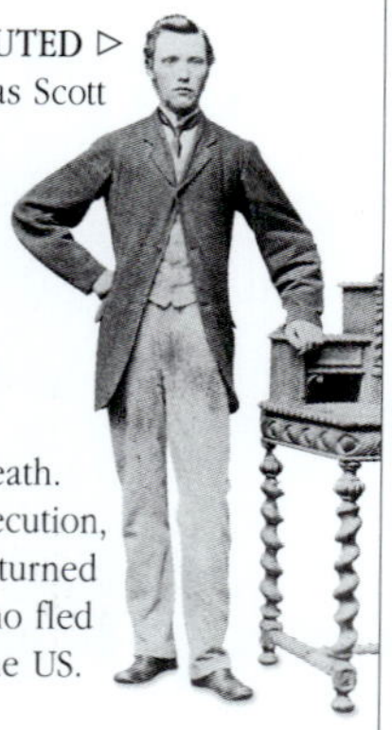
SCOTT EXECUTED ▷
In 1870, Thomas Scott organized two attacks against Riel. At a trial called for by Riel, Scott was found guilty of treason and sentenced to death. After Scott's execution, public opinion turned against Riel, who fled for his life to the US.

▽ MOUNTED POLICE
Pictured here is a group of Major Boulton's Mounted Infantry – part of the Northwest Mounted Police. During the Second Riel Rebellion, some of his men were ambushed by rebel Métis forces led by Gabriel Dumont.

IN 1869, THE CANADIAN government purchased Rupert's Land from the Hudson's Bay Company and encouraged settlement of the area, with no regard to the rights of the Métis, whose homeland it formed. When a party of surveyors began marking out boundaries on the settlement, the Métis rebelled, choosing 24-year-old Louis Riel to lead them.

During 1869–70, when the charismatic Riel headed the provisional government, he drove out the surveyors and executed a troublesome agitator named Thomas Scott. Enraged by the execution, the British in Ontario sent an army to the settlement and deposed Riel, who fled to the US. The confrontation became known as the First Riel Rebellion. Negotiations between the Métis and the Canadian government ensued and, in the Manitoba Act of 1870, many of the Métis' demands were met.

Over the following years, however, white settlers arrived and disrupted the Métis way of life. The completion of the Canadian Pacific Railway in 1885 displaced more Métis, pushing them north and west and opening up huge tracts of land for white settlement.

Many of the Métis trekked westward and settled near the village of Batouche, where they organized their homesteads in strips along the Saskatchewan River. The government then sent surveyors to divide the land into square lots, disrupting traditional Métis patterns of land use. The absence of buffalo, failure of crops, and drastic cuts in Indian food rations left the Métis starving and aggravated matters

Second Riel Rebellion

Urged by Métis leaders, Louis Riel returned from the US to Canada in July 1884 to lead a protest. Riel was undermined, however, by Prime Minister MacDonald's distribution of supplies to his Indian supporters, and only two Cree chiefs – Poundmaker and Big Bear – fought with him. The outnumbered forces of Métis and Indians were defeated after a series of battles. Riel surrendered and was hanged for treason on 16 November 1885.

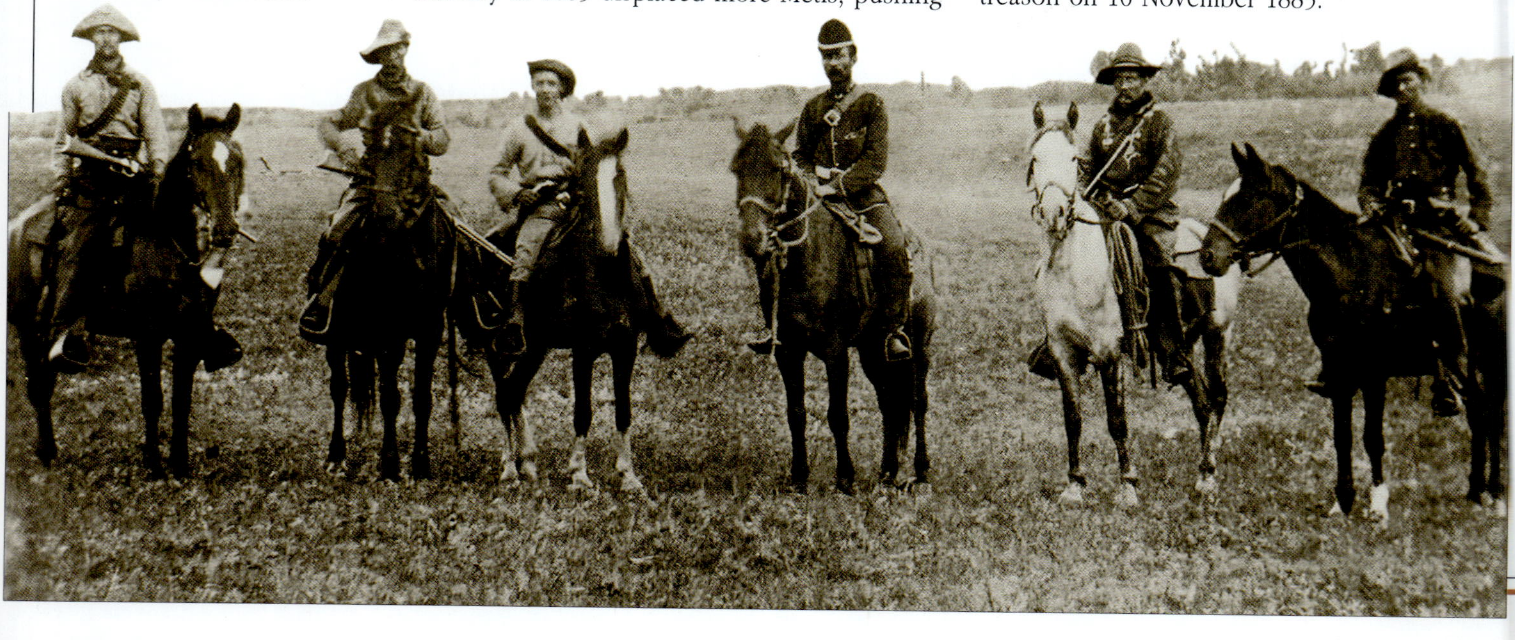

Crees Side with Riel

Only Poundmaker and Big Bear – Plains Cree leaders who hated reservation life and felt that whites had destroyed their way of life – participated in the Second Riel Rebellion. Hearing of Riel's surrender, they gave themselves up to the authorities and were convicted of treason. Both were sentenced to three years' imprisonment, but were released after becoming ill.

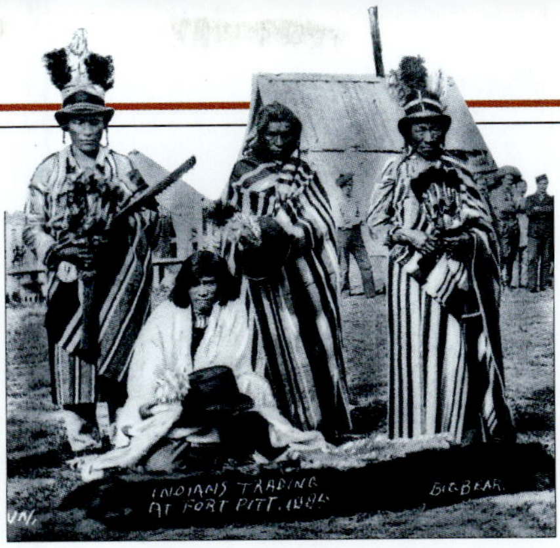

◁ **Cree Chiefs Trade Furs**
Only a few months before they joined Riel's rebellion, Big Bear and other Cree chiefs traded furs at Fort Pitt, in the center of Cree country. In April 1885, Big Bear and his men attacked the fort and took 44 civilians prisoner, but they allowed the hated police to get away.

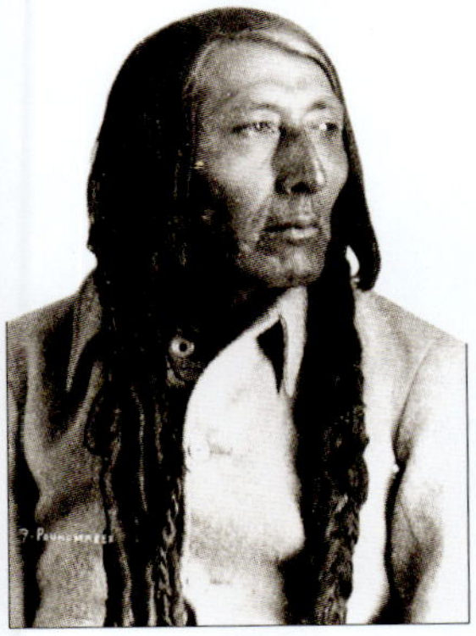

Chief Poundmaker

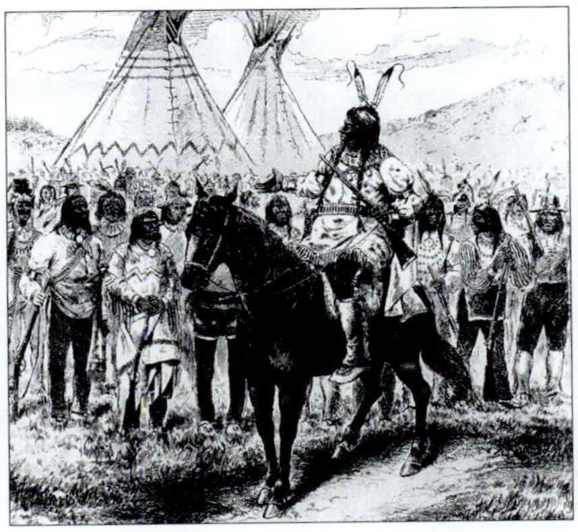

◁ **Poundmaker's Attack**
In March 1885, Chief Poundmaker and 200 Cree warriors attacked the town of Battleford on the North Saskatchewan River. The residents held out for three weeks in a police stockade.

Cut Knife Hill Battle ▷
In May 1885, after relieving the town of Battleford, a battalion led by Colonel William Otter attacked Poundmaker's camp at Cut Knife Hill. The Crees counterattacked and Otter's men withdrew.

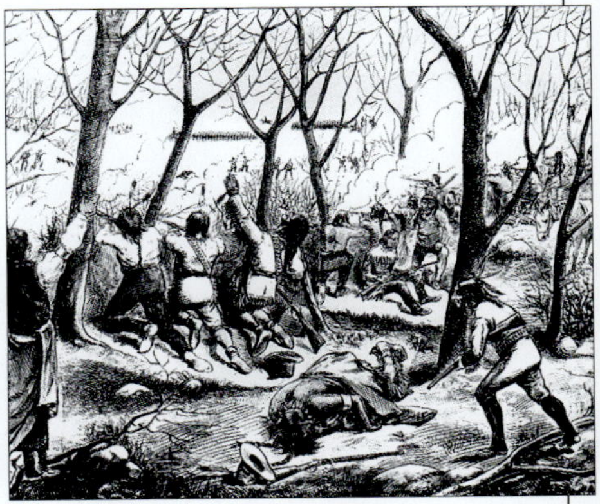

Defeat at Batouche

In May 1885, Major General Frederick Middleton, the leader of the Canadian army, attacked Batouche, Northwest Territories, with about 850 soldiers. Some 275 Métis, led by Gabriel Dumont – Riel's general in the field – defended the village from rifle pits they had dug around it. Fire was exchanged for three days, until the Métis ran out of bullets and surrendered.

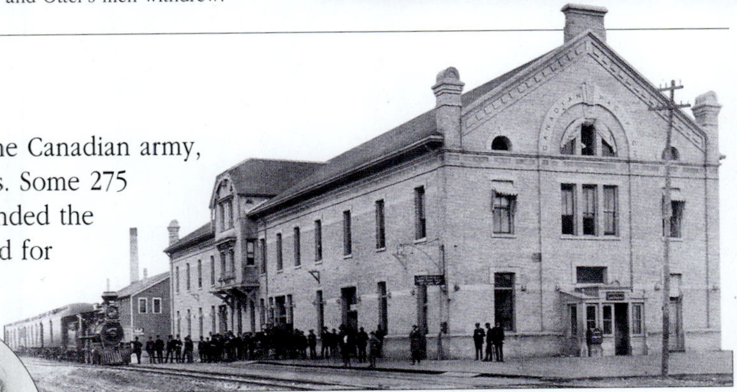

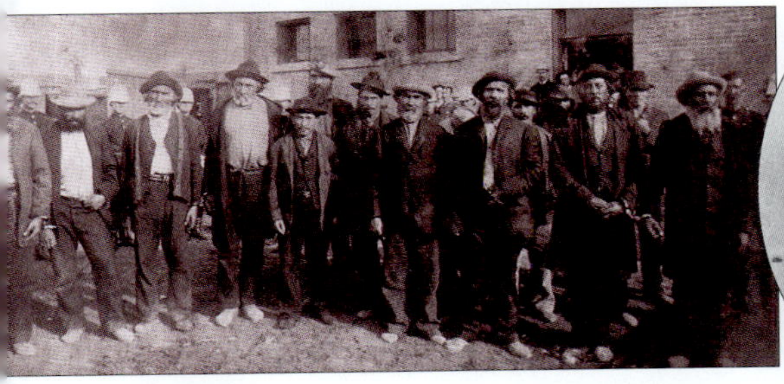

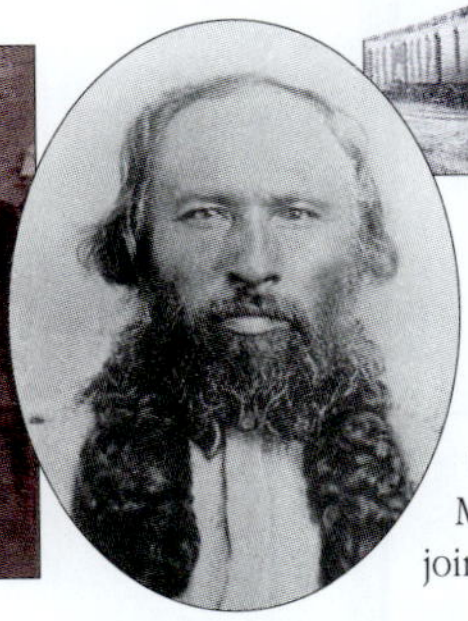

◁ **Militant Métis Leader**
Gabriel Dumont, elected chief of his Métis band at the age of 25, became the leader of some 300 Métis during the Second Riel Rebellion. After the Métis' defeat, he fled to the US and joined Buffalo Bill's Wild West Show.

△ **Troop Transport**
Soldiers from eastern Canada were transported to the Northwest by the new railroad. It took four weeks for the troops to travel to the halfway staging points west of the Winnipeg railroad station, pictured here.

△ **Métis Government**
In 1884, the Métis elected their own government led by Louis Riel, whom they regarded as a prophet. Many of the council also shared Riel's belief that God would work a miracle to help the Métis win the next battle.

Batouche Attacked ▷
When Middleton and his soldiers attacked Batouche, the Métis were dug in to their rifle pits, firing metal buttons and stones when they ran out of bullets. One of Middleton's men launched an attack that forced the Métis to retreat from trench to trench and finally to surrender on 12 May.

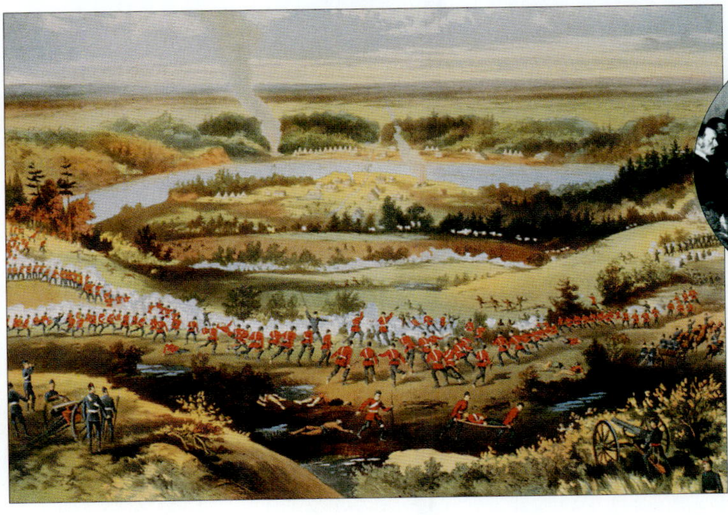

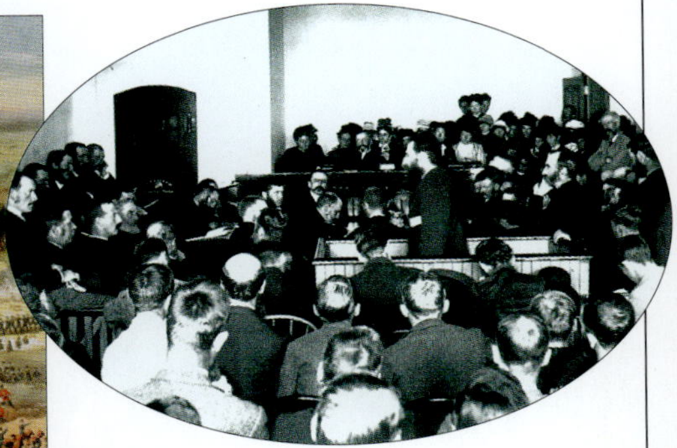

△ **Riel on Trial**
After the battle of Batouche, Riel gave himself up. He was tried for high treason, sentenced to death, and refused mercy. The day after he was hanged, thousands of Québecois marched through the streets of Montreal in protest.

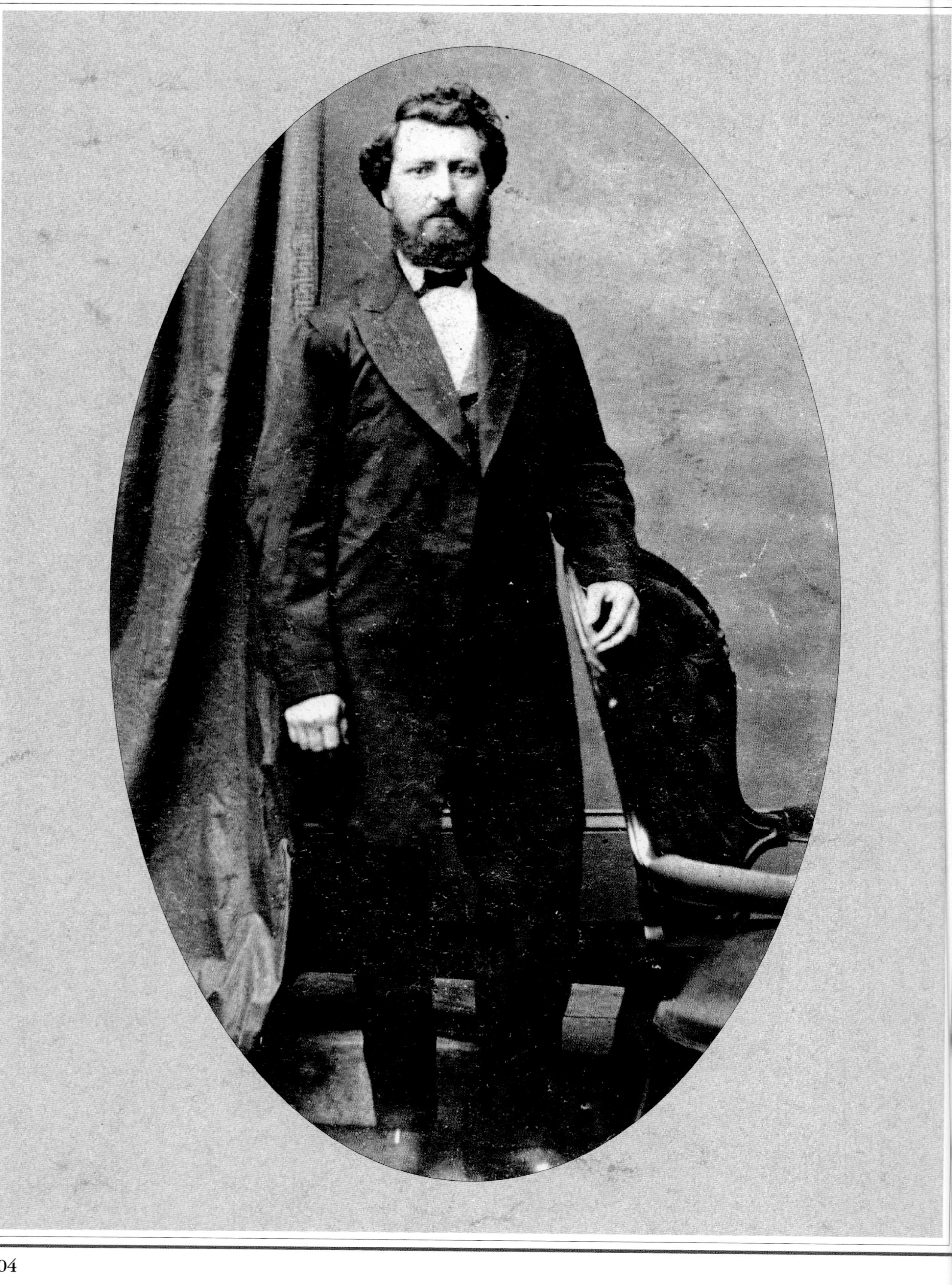

LOUIS RIEL

1885: STATEMENT AT HIS TRIAL FOR TREASON

BORN TO A FRENCH-OJIBWAY (MÉTIS) FATHER and French mother, Louis Riel (1844–85) was raised as a Catholic. Abandoning studies for the priesthood, he returned to his Red River home and, in 1869–70, led the Métis rebellion against the transfer of Northwest land from the Hudson's Bay Company to the Canadian government. Riel went into hiding in the US but returned, in 1884, to lead the Saskatchewan Métis' short-lived protest against the government's indifference to their grievances. Louis Riel made this plea at his trial in Regina, Saskatchewan, in 1885, but he was found guilty of treason and hanged.

"I have reasons why I would ask that sentence should not be passed upon me, against me ....

The troubles of the Saskatchewan are not to be taken as an isolated fact. They are the result of fifteen years' war. The head of that difficulty lies in the difficulty of Red River. Seven or eight hundred from Canada came to Red River, and they wanted to take possession of the country without consulting the people. True, it was the Halfbreed people. There were a certain number of white pioneers among the population but the great majority were Halfbreeds.

We took up arms against the invaders from the East without knowing them. They were so far apart from us, on the other side of the Lakes, that it cannot be said that we had any hatred against them. We did not know them. They came without notification. They came boldly. We said: Who are they? They said: We are the possessors of the country. Well, knowing that it was not true, we done against those parties coming from the East what we used to do against the Indians from the South and from the West, when they would invade us .... We took up arms, as I stated, and we made hundreds of prisoners, and we negotiated. A treaty was made. That treaty was made by a delegation of both parties."

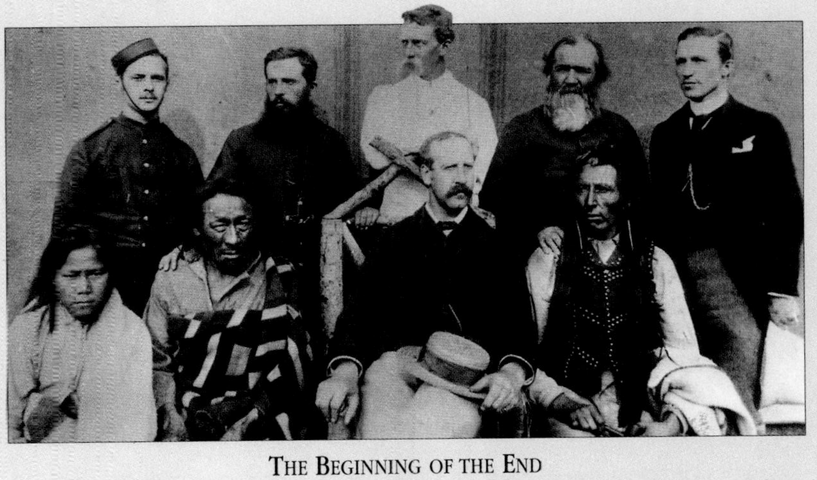

THE BEGINNING OF THE END

A group photograph taken in May 1885, at the start of Riel's trial, includes (front row, left to right) Horse Child, the youngest son of Big Bear, Big Bear, Alexander Stewart, the Chief of Police who signed the indictment charging Riel with treason, and Chief Poundmaker.

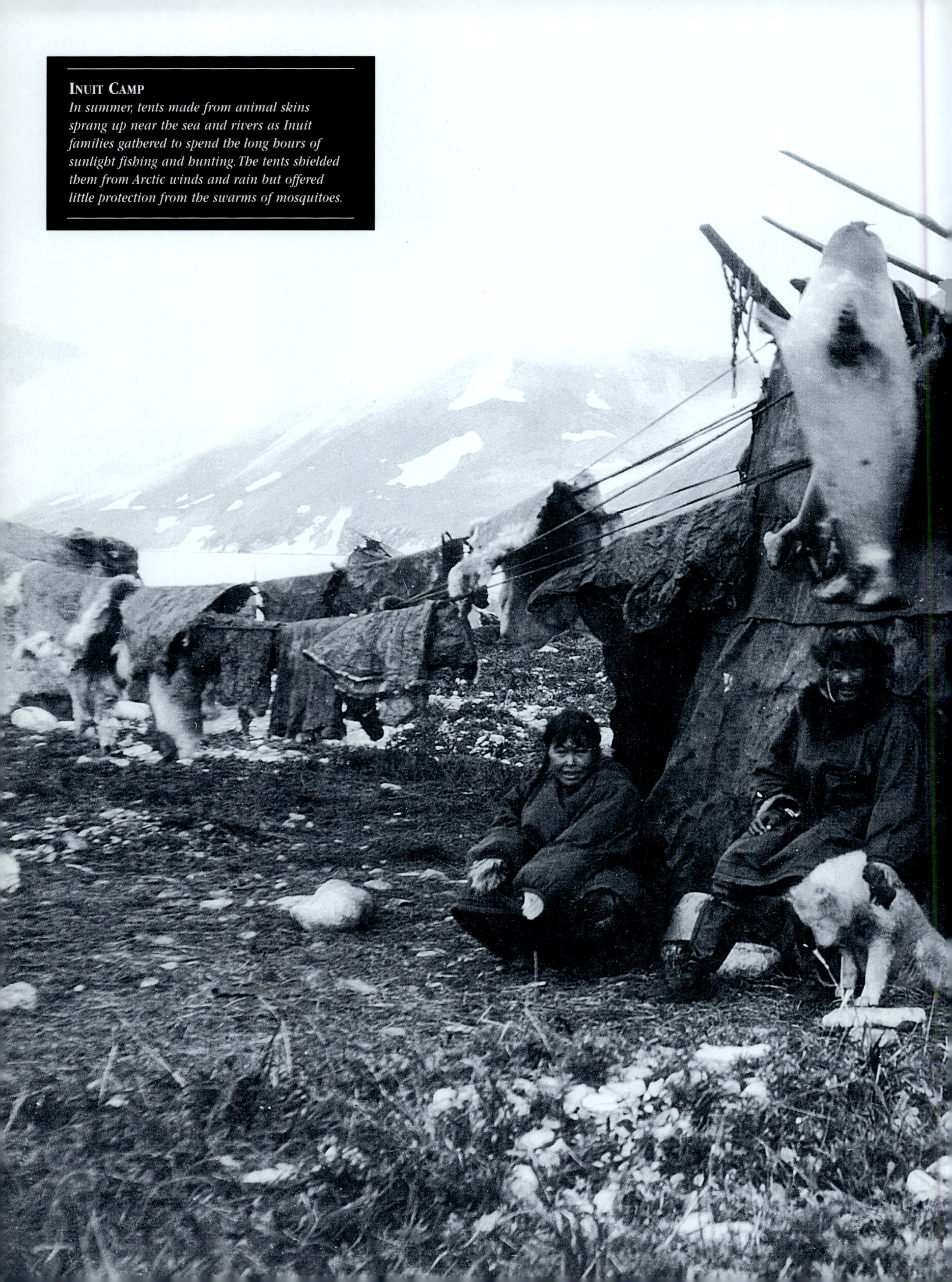

Inuit Camp

In summer, tents made from animal skins sprang up near the sea and rivers as Inuit families gathered to spend the long hours of sunlight fishing and hunting. The tents shielded them from Arctic winds and rain but offered little protection from the swarms of mosquitoes.

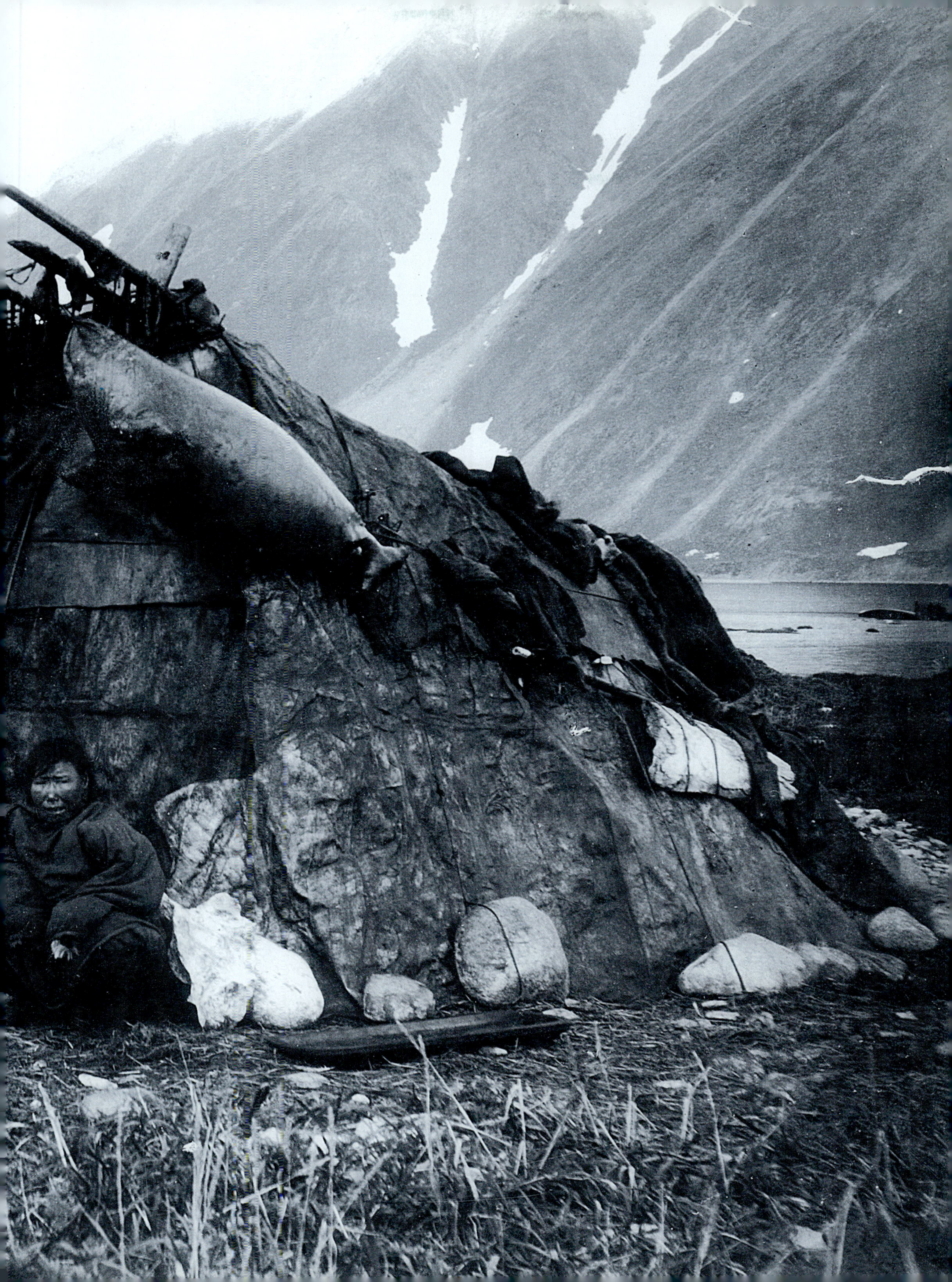

WARS FOR THE WEST

CONFLICT BECAME EVEN MORE COMMON during the 1860s and 1870s as white settlements spread out across the Great Basin, Plateau, and California. Ranchers, farmers, and fortune-seekers looking for gold and silver established settlements that crowded out Indian villages and increased the pressure on Indians to give up their land. The Paiutes, Shoshones, Modocs, Bannocks, Nez Percé, and Utes fought hopeless battles to hold on to their homelands.

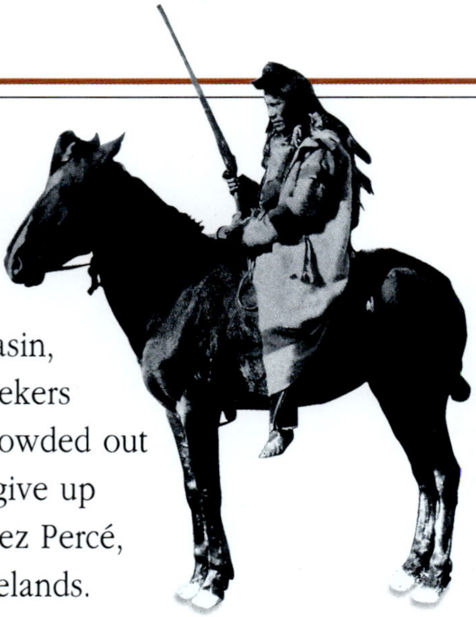

MOUNTED SHOSHONES
Many bands of Shoshones acquired herds of ponies that helped them pursue buffalo, deer, and elk. Horses were regarded as tokens of success: chiefs, religious leaders, and midwives claimed their earnings in ponies, which were also used for important gifts.

WAR DIARY

1860
Southern Paiute War in Nevada

1863
Shoshone War in Utah

1866-68
Northern Paiute (Snake) War in Oregon and Idaho

1872-73
Modoc War in California

1877
Nez Percé War in Idaho and Montana

1878
Bannock War in Idaho

1879
Sheepeater War in Idaho

1879
Ute War in Colorado

ALTHOUGH THE INDIANS who were living in present-day California, Oregon, Idaho, Nevada, Utah, and Colorado were willing to accommodate white settlers so they could remain in their homelands, the US government forced them onto reservations.

In 1860, a series of tensions culminated in the Paiute – or Pyramid Lake – War. Hungry Paiutes, angry at the intrusion of silver miners and settlers, raided small settlements for food. Paiute chief Numaga tried to stop his people from going to war, but had no choice after two young Paiute girls were abducted. After two furious battles, the conflict ended and Paiutes were forced to settle on reservations.

During the Civil War, Shoshone Indians living in the Great Basin region resisted white expansion by attacking wagon trains and stage coaches, riders on the Pony express trail, and crews stringing new telegraph lines. To keep the westward routes open, a company of volunteers under Colonel Patrick E. Connor was sent to the region. In January 1863, Connor marched a force of 300 men to Bear Hunter's village of Shoshones in present-day Utah. The volunteers killed over 200 Shoshones

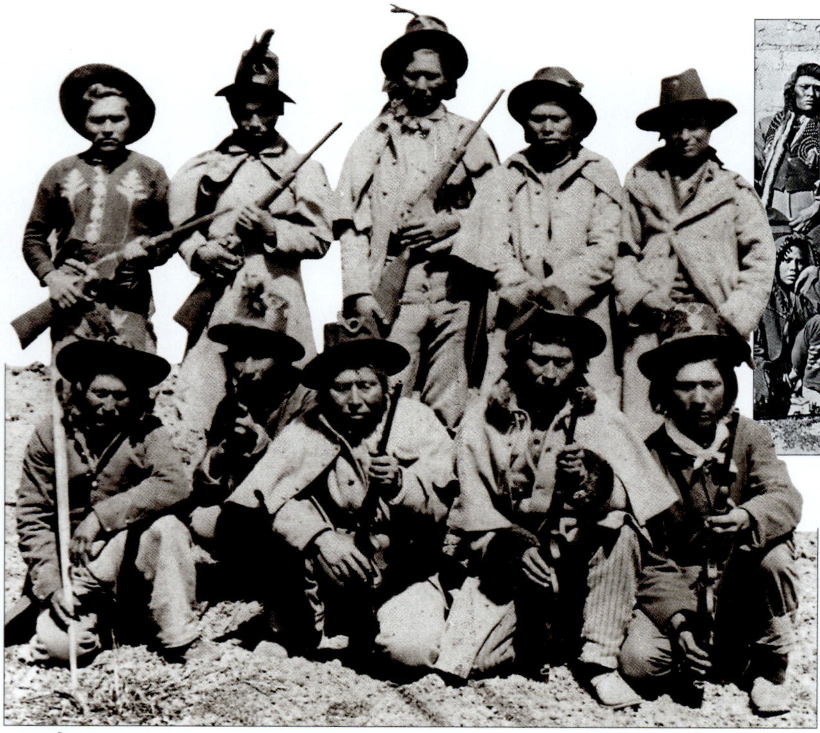

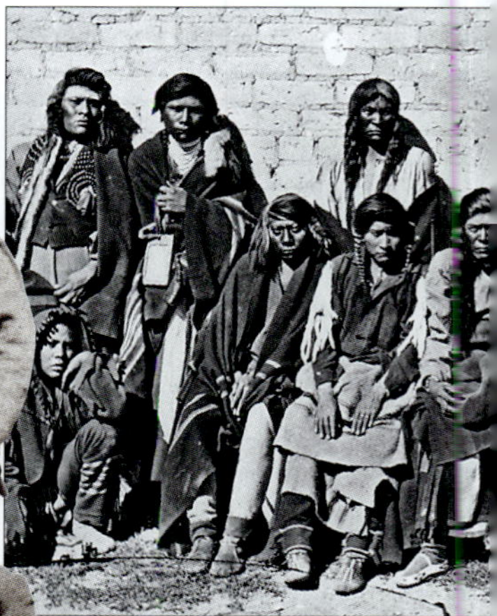

◁ **THE CAPTURERS**
At least 100 Warm Springs Indians from Oregon joined the army as scouts. Led by Donald McKay (center front), the scouts were ordered to hunt down Captain Jack and his followers. Soon after they had successfully located his hiding place, Jack was captured.

▽ **SUPERIOR WEAPONRY**
Springfield rifles were introduced by the US army for its infantrymen in 1873. A single-shot weapon with an exceptional 3,500-yd (3,200-m) range, the Springfield outdistanced Indian weapons – rifles as well as bows and arrows. By 1879, however, some Ute warriors had acquired Springfields.

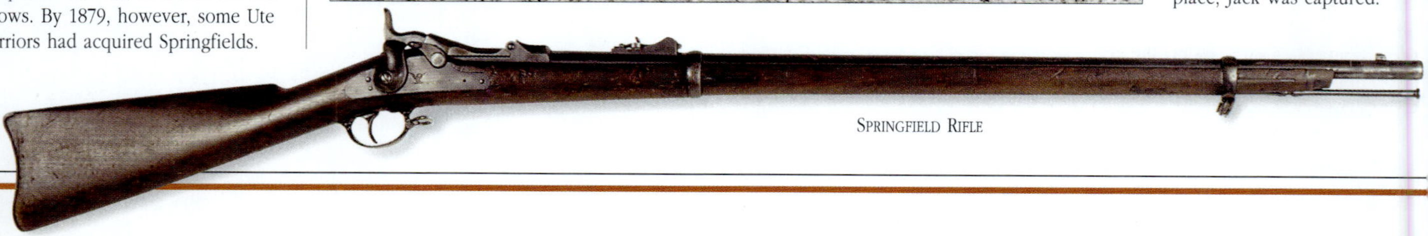

SPRINGFIELD RIFLE

including Bear Hunter, and took more than 150 women and children prisoner. That year the Indians were forced to sign a treaty ceding much of the Great Basin.

Like the Shoshones, the Northern Paiutes, under their leader Paulina, carried out raids on mining camps, stagecoaches, ranches, and farms. In what is called the Snake War, Colonel George Crook engaged Paiutes in about 40 skirmishes before the war ended. After Paulina was killed, Weawea led the militants until June 1868, when they surrendered to Crook.

Continuing Conflicts

The Modoc Indians were moved from their homeland in northeastern California to share a reservation in Oregon with longtime rivals, the Klamaths. Outnumbered and bullied, the Modocs, led by Kintpuash (Captain Jack) and Hooker Jim, returned to their homeland in 1870. The Modocs' refusal to remain on the reservation ignited a bloody war in the treacherous lava beds of northern California. When the war ended, Modoc leaders were executed and the tribe relocated to Oklahoma.

In the atmosphere of tension following the Nez Percé war (*see pp.114–15*), Bannocks and Paiutes living in Idaho and Oregon, infuriated that hogs belonging to white ranchers had destroyed the camas roots that were a staple in their diet, threatened the settlers. The incident, in 1878, sparked a war led by Bannock leader Buffalo Horn and later by Paiute chief Egan. Both were killed. Troops under General Oliver Howard, who had fought the Nez Percé the year before, captured some 1,000 militants, ending the war in September.

In 1879, a band of angry Shoshone and Bannock Indians in Idaho raided settlements. Tracked down by Lieutenant Edward S. Farrow's Umatilla Indian scouts, the Indians surrendered. Since the Indians lived primarily on sheep, the brief conflict became known as the Sheepeater War.

After lead deposits were discovered in 1878, Ute reservations were overrun by whites. In 1879, Utes in Colorado revolted, killing the reservation agent and several other whites, and fighting the soldiers sent to quell the uprising. The event, called the Meeker Massacre, ended when the Ute chief Ouray ordered his people to stop fighting. After the conflict ended, a commission of inquiry debated whether or not to punish the Utes, but none was tried in court.

PAIUTE LEADER NUMAGA

Recognizing the superior military power of whites, Paiute leader Numaga counseled against war. He also regarded Major William Ormsby, the military commander stationed at Pyramid Lake, as a friend. But when it was reported that two Paiute girls had been abducted, angry warriors rescued the girls and burned a trading post – and Numaga reluctantly assumed his role as war leader.

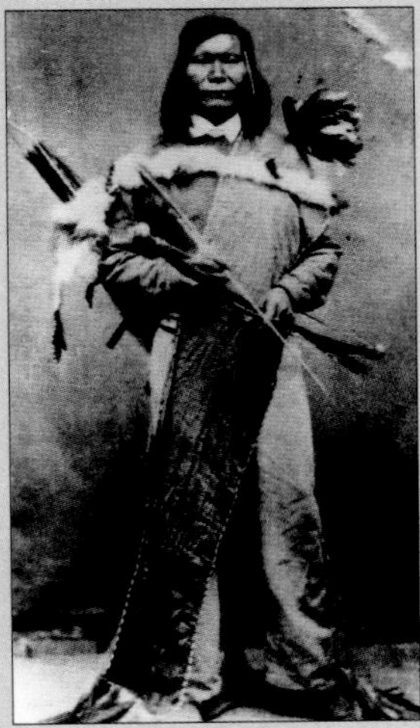

CHIEF NUMAGA

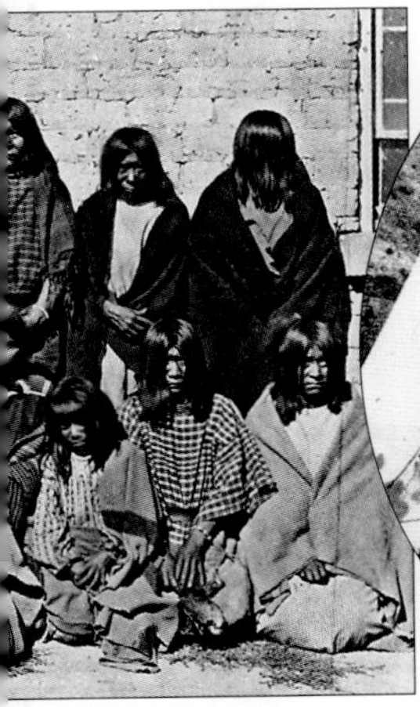

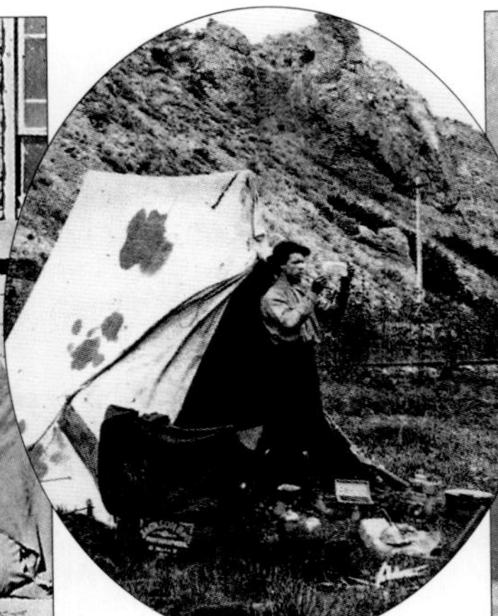

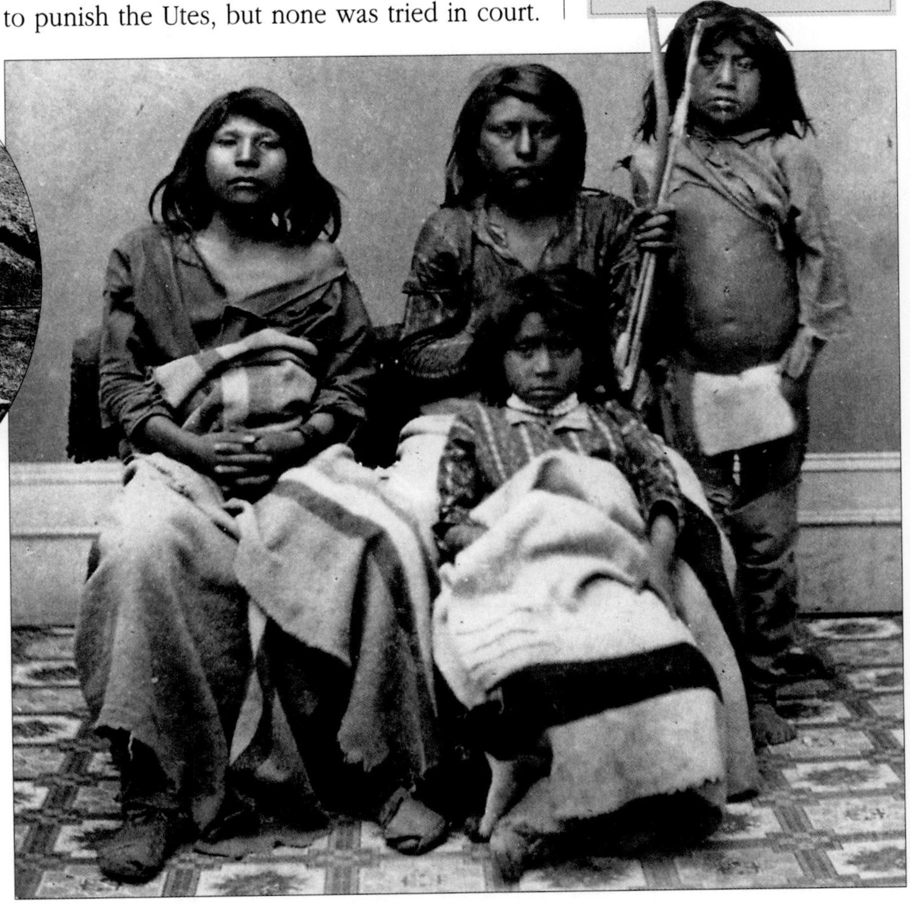

△ **BANNOCKS IMPRISONED**
Friction with settlers in 1878 provoked a war with Bannock and Paiute Indians in Idaho. The uprising ended with the surrender and capture of 131 Bannocks who were held as prisoners through the winter.

△ **PHOTOGRAPHIC RECORD**
William Henry Jackson, pictured with his equipment in Echo Canyon, Utah, in 1869, photographed Indians who lived in the Great Basin and Plateau. These were exhibited in Philadelphia in 1876.

UTE HOMELANDS OPENED TO SETTLEMENT ▷
After the 1879 Ute war ended, Utes from the northern part of the Colorado reservation, including the group pictured here, were moved to a reservation in Utah. Utes from the southern part of the reservation had their lands allotted in severalty, and a portion of the reservation was opened to settlement.

MODOCS HIDE IN LAVA BEDS

In November 1872, soldiers attempted to return Kintpuash's followers to the Klamath reservation. Kintpuash led his people to the lava beds south of Tule Lake, where he held off a force of over 1,000 soldiers for six months. Another band of Modocs, led by Hooker Jim, also took refuge there.

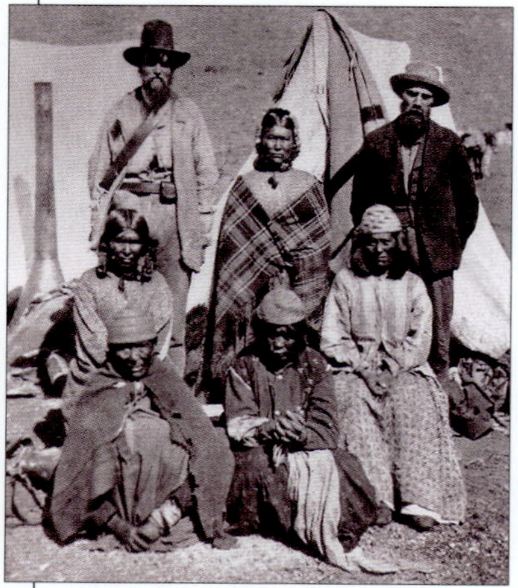

◁ PEACE TALKS
Aided by interpreters Frank Riddle (top left) and his Modoc wife Winema – or Toby – (top center) at peace talks set up by Brigadier General Canby, Kintpuash asked for the lava beds as a reservation and refused to hand over Hooker Jim to the authorities.

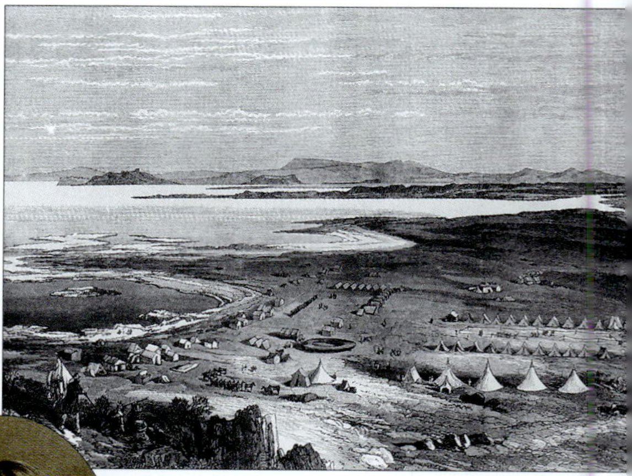

ARMY AT TULE LAKE ▷
Lieutenant Colonel Frank Wheaton, the army's district commander, built up the military presence at Tule Lake with regular army troops reinforced by companies of volunteers from California and Oregon.

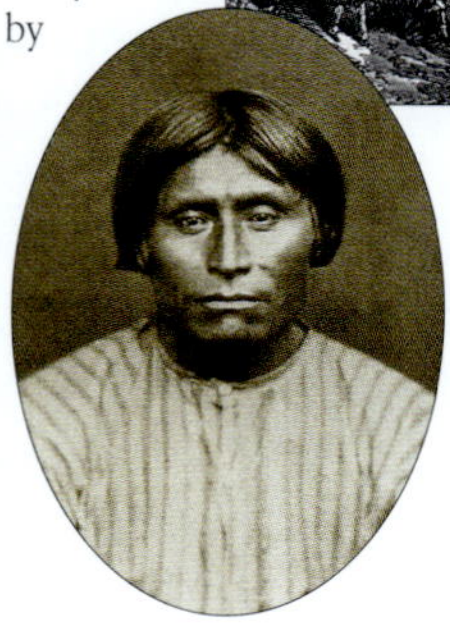

MODOC LEADER KINTPUASH ▷
Kintpuash, nicknamed Captain Jack by local settlers, was friendly toward white settlers and miners until 1864, when he was forced to move to the Klamath reservation in Oregon. There, his people were bullied by the rival Klamath tribe.

"All I wish is that my side of the story may be told."

CAPTAIN JACK (KINTPUASH), 1873

MURDER OF CANBY

In April 1873, General Canby traveled to the lava beds to confer with Modoc leaders in an attempt to end the war. Trying to deal fairly with the Modocs, and realizing that the tribe had been mistreated, he delayed sending his forces to attack them. When fighting began and the Modocs took refuge in the lava beds, he ordered a suspension of hostilities so that peace talks could take place on neutral ground.

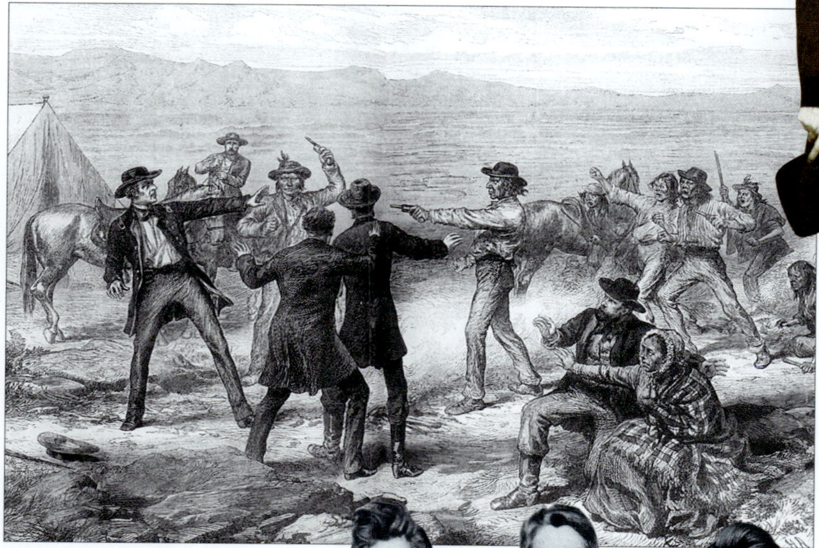

△ KINTPUASH TAKES AIM
Persuaded by Modoc militants to kill Brigadier General Edward R. Canby at the second set of peace talks, Kintpuash drew a hidden revolver and shot Canby, who became the first and only US general to die in an Indian war.

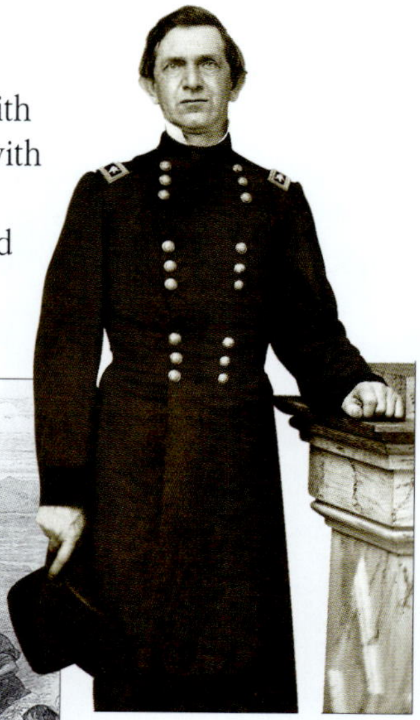

△ CAREER OFFICER SHOT
Brigadier General Edward R. Canby was murdered by Kintpuash on 11 April 1873, during peace talks with the Modocs. West Point graduate Canby had spent his career fighting Seminoles in Florida, Apaches in Arizona, and Confederates in Texas.

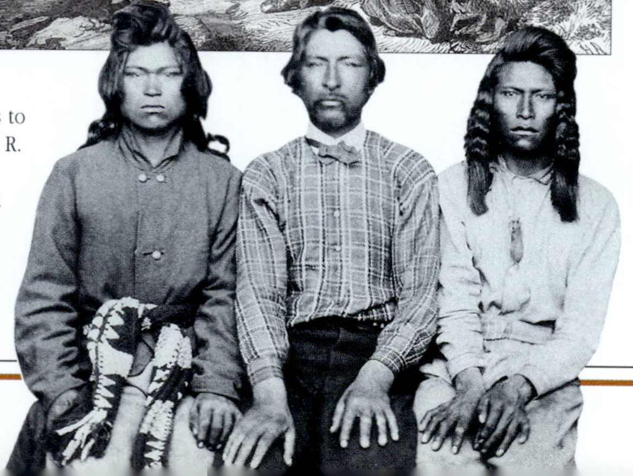

◁ TRIED AND CONVICTED
On 1 June, the army finally tracked down Kintpuash with the help of Hooker Jim, who had been captured earlier. After a military trial, Kintpuash was hanged for the murders of Canby and peace commissioner Eleazer Thomas.

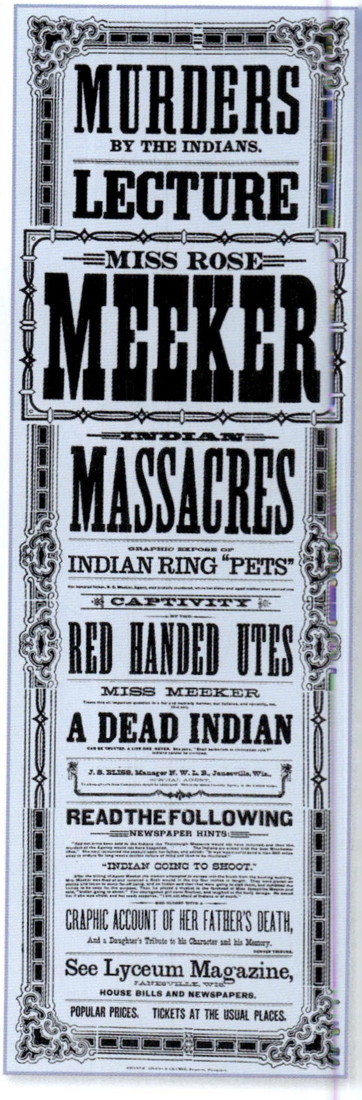

VOLCANIC HIDING PLACE

he lava beds proved an excellent place ɔ hide. High cinder buttes, long chasms nd fissures, zigzags, towers, bastions, nd parapets were all constructed of solid ɔck, and hard as iron. The Indians threw ı rocks to fill up the gaps, completely overing themselves so that they could ot be seen by the attacking soldiers.

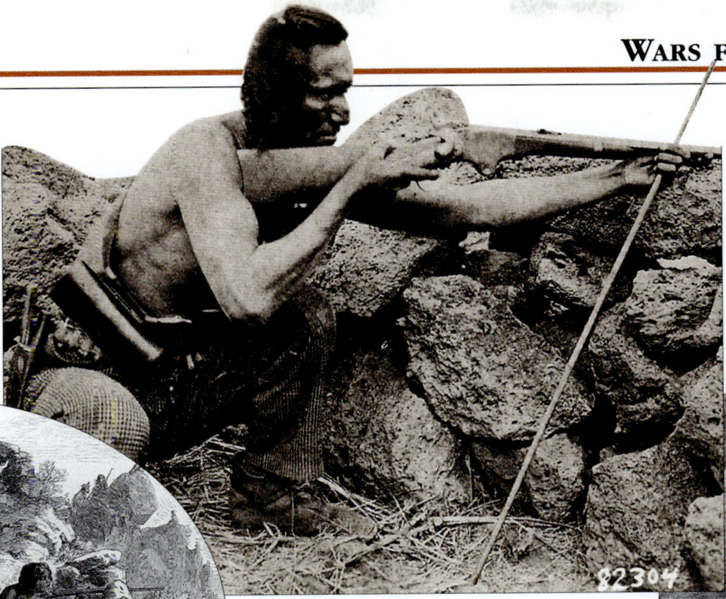

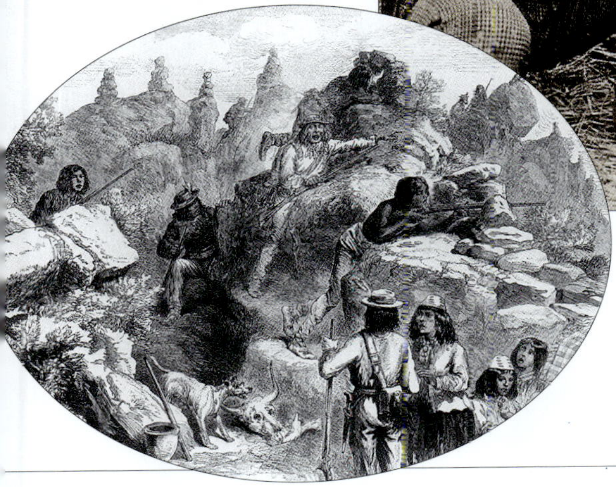

◁ DIVERSIONARY TACTICS

The Modocs, many of whom were armed with breech-loading rifles and were good shots, distracted their enemies by placing stones on top of any projecting points to appear like men, causing the soldiers to fire at scarecrows instead of real Indians. The troops also had the disadvantage of having to charge over open ground.

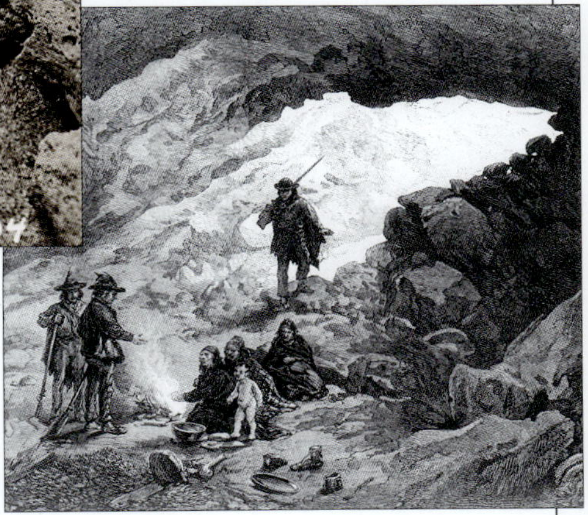

CAVE HIDEOUT FOR KINTPUASH ▷

For over three months, Kintpuash and his family lived in one of the caves in the lava beds. Sagebrush and greasewood covering the terrain provided fuel, while patches of grass afforded pasture for the herd of cattle the defenders brought in. Water was lacking, but the Modocs secured it from Tule Lake.

UTES RESENT AGENT MEEKER

As Indian agent to the Utes of the White River reservation, Nathan C. Meeker tried to apply his experience in cooperative farm management to Indians. He faced resistance in his efforts to transform the hunting-based economy to one of conventional agriculture. Meeker insisted that the Utes plow up their ponies' grazing lands, which would have starved the horses, and he made little attempt to remove prospectors from Ute lands.

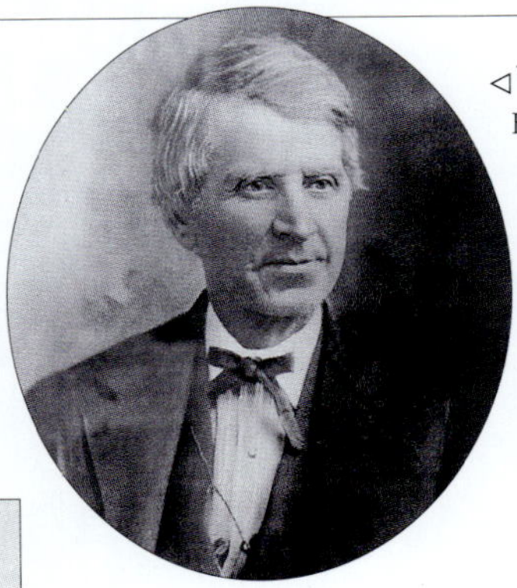

◁ WHITE RIVER AGENT

Frightened by a confrontation with a medicine man, Meeker sent for troops to quell an imaginary uprising. When troops approached their reservation on 29 September 1879, Chief Douglas and his followers killed Meeker and other agency employees.

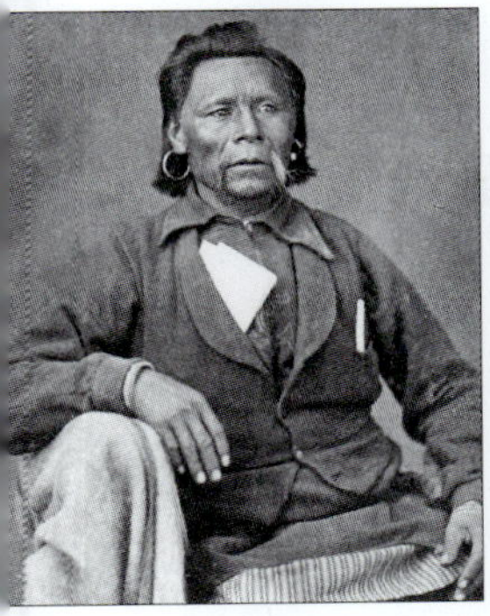

△ MEEKER'S EXECUTIONER

Ute Chief Douglas, dressed in a suit for this portrait, participated in the 1879 uprising, during which he killed agent Nathan Meeker. Douglas captured Mrs Meeker and others and was accused of raping her, but no public charge was ever made.

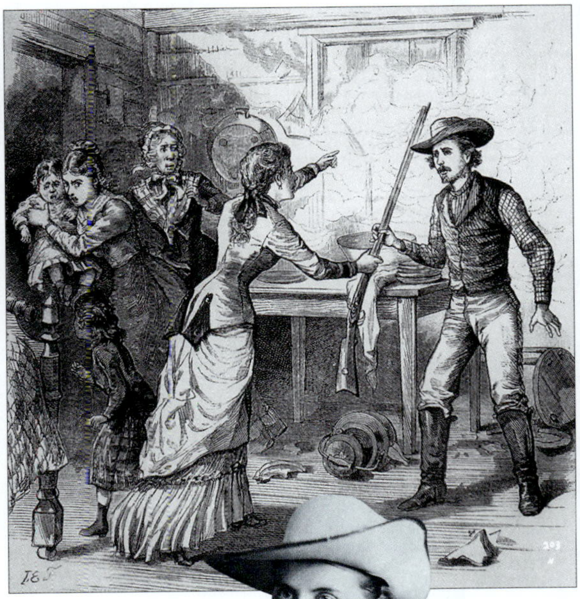

◁ THORNBURGH SPARKS ATTACK

Ute leaders had warned Major Thomas T. Thornburgh to keep away from the Milk Creek reservation. His approach sparked an attack on reservation employees and the capture of Meeker's wife and daughter, pictured here.

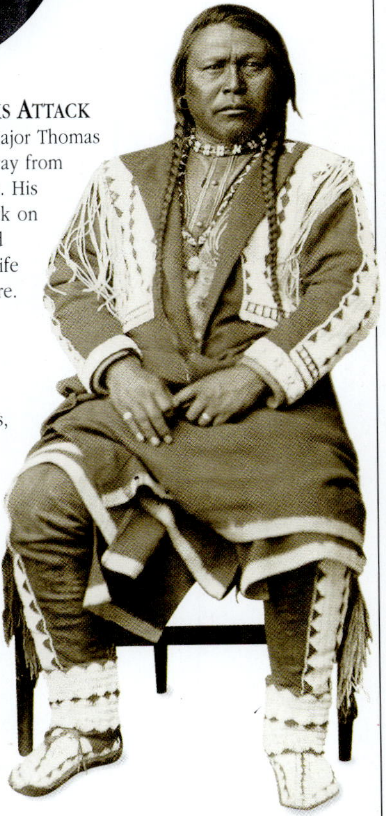

DIPLOMAT OURAY ▷

Although army generals wanted to launch major offensives against the Utes, a peace mission was sent to meet with Ute Chief Ouray. He defused the situation and the white hostages held at Milk Creek were released unharmed.

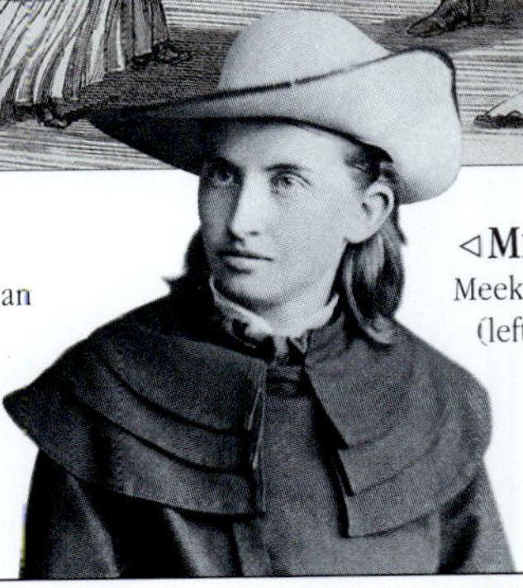

◁ RECALLING THEIR ORDEAL

Meeker's daughter, Josephine, wrote of her ordeal in an 1879 book entitled *Brave Miss Meeker's Captivity! Her Own Account of It.* She and her mother, Rose, who were rescued on 23 October, took to the lecture circuit and spoke of their ordeal at the hands of their Ute capturers and of Meeker's death.

◁ MISS MEEKER HELD HOSTAGE

Meeker's wife and his daughter Josephine (left) were held hostage for 23 days by Chief Douglas and his followers. A delegation of 13 Utes located the fugitive's camp and convinced Douglas to free the hostages to avoid a confrontation.

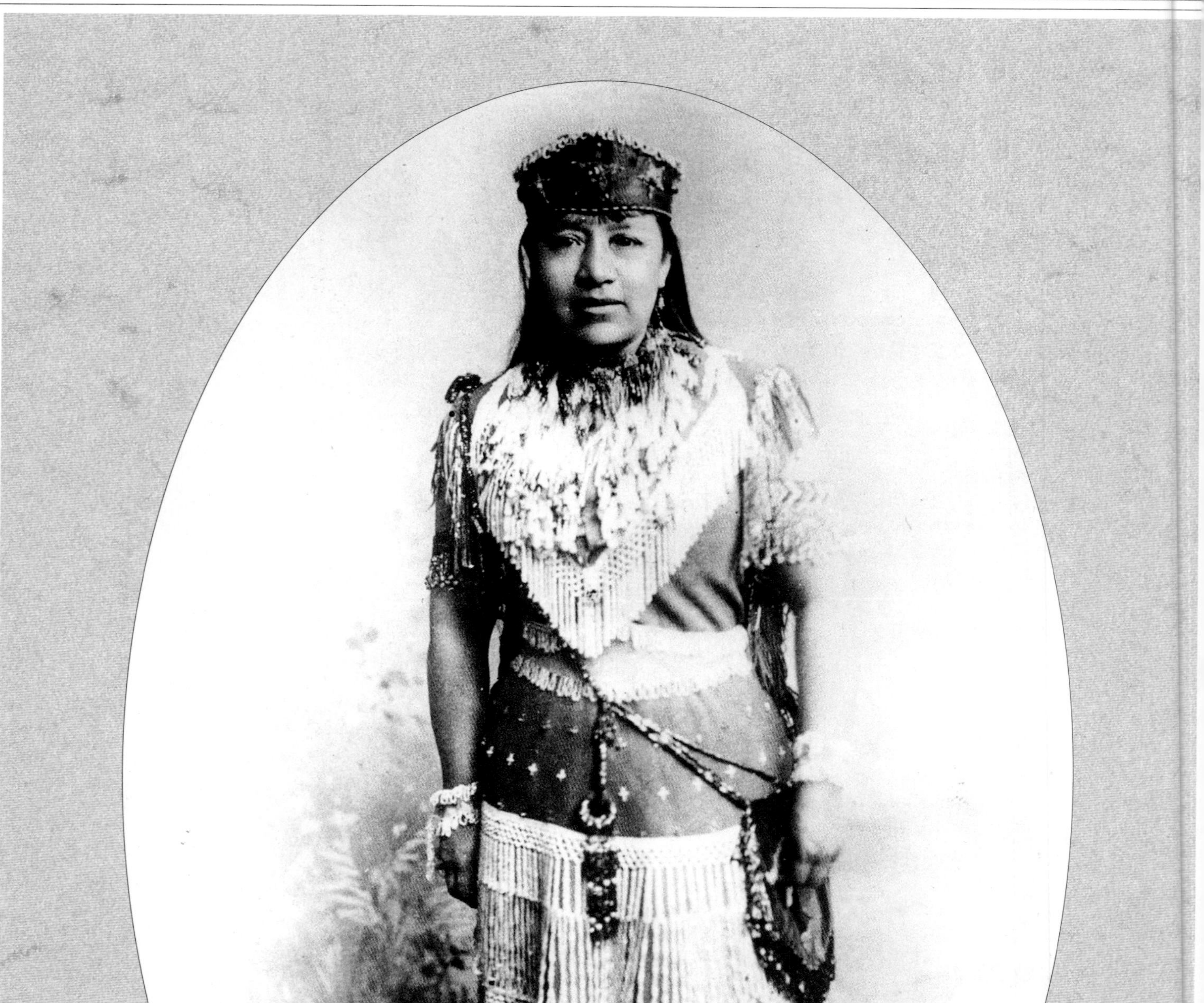

SARAH WINNEMUCCA

1883: ON THE CAUSES OF WARFARE BETWEEN PAIUTES AND WHITES

SARAH WINNEMUCCA (*c.* 1844–91) SERVED as an army interpreter and peace negotiator during the Paiute wars of the 1860s, having mastered, by her teens, English, Spanish, and three Indian languages, along with an understanding of both white and Paiute customs. After the war, Sarah aroused sympathy for Indian rights by lecturing extensively and critically on Indian agents. This extract is taken from *Life Among the Paiutes, Their Wrongs and Claims,* which she published in 1883 under her married name, Hopkins. In the late 1880s, Sarah taught at a school for Indian children that she established in Nevada.

"In 1865 we had another trouble with our white brothers. It was early in the spring, and we were then living at Dayton, Nevada, when a company of soldiers came through the place and stopped and spoke to some of my people, and said, 'You have been stealing cattle from the white people at Harney Lake.' They said also that they would kill everything that came in their way, men, women, and children .... The days after they left were very sad hours, indeed. Oh, dear readers, these soldiers had gone only sixty miles away to Muddy Lake, where my people were then living and fishing, and doing nothing to any one. The soldiers rode up to their encampment and fired into it, and killed almost all the people that were there. Oh, it is a fearful thing to tell, but it must be told. Yes, it must be told by me. It was all old men, women and children that were killed; for my father had all the young men with him, at the sink of Carson on a hunting excursion, or they would have been killed too. After the soldiers had killed all but some little children and babies still tied up in their baskets, the soldiers took them also, and set the camp on fire and threw them into the flames to see them burn alive. I had one baby brother killed there. My sister jumped on father's best horse and ran away. As she ran, the soldiers ran after her; but, thanks be to the Good Father in the Spirit-land, my dear sister got away. This almost killed my poor papa. Yet my people kept peaceful ....

About two weeks after this, two white men were killed over at Walker Lake by some of my people, and of course soldiers were sent for from California, and a great many companies came. They went after my people all over Nevada. Reports were made everywhere throughout the whole country by the white settlers, that the red devils were killing their cattle, and by this lying of the white settlers the trail began which is marked by the blood of my people from hill to hill and from valley to valley. The soldiers followed after my people in this way for one year .... These reports were only made by those white settlers so that they could sell their grain, which they could not get rid of in any other way. The only way the cattle-men and farmers get to make money is to start an Indian war, so that the troops may come and buy their beef, cattle, horses, and grain. The settlers get fat by it."

THE NEZ PERCÉ WAR

THE NEZ PERCÉ WAR began in June 1877, 14 years after a treaty that severely reduced the size of the Nez Percé reservation in Idaho was signed by some of their chiefs. After a skirmish between young Nez Percé warriors and white settlers, Chief Joseph joined the rebels and led the group in one of the most remarkable stories of pursuit and escape in military history, outsmarting and outfighting for four months the white army that pursued them.

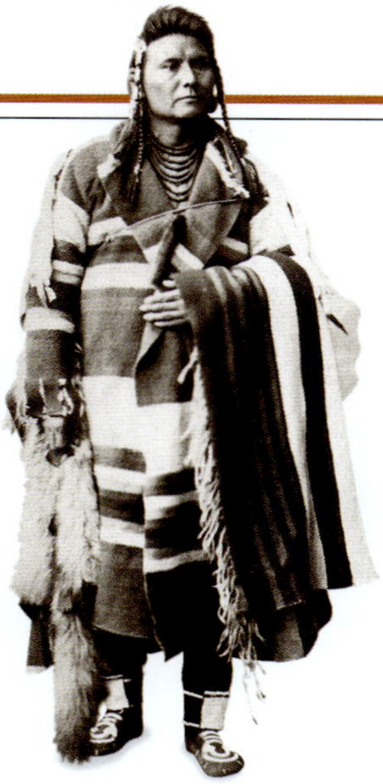

LEADER CHIEF JOSEPH
In 1871, Joseph became principal chief of the Nez Percé of the Wallowa Valley of Oregon. Like his father, he passively resisted relocation to the Nez Percé reservation near Fort Lapwai, Idaho. He was determined never to sell the Wallowa Valley because it contained the bones of his Nez Percé ancestors.

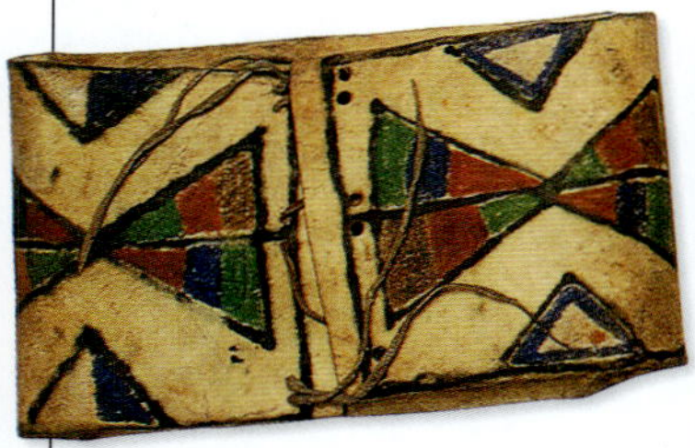

△ SIMPLE CARRYALL
Brightly painted geometric designs decorated Nez Percé parflèche – folding containers in all shapes and sizes, made by the women from tanned buffalo hide, and used to store food, clothing, and sacred objects.

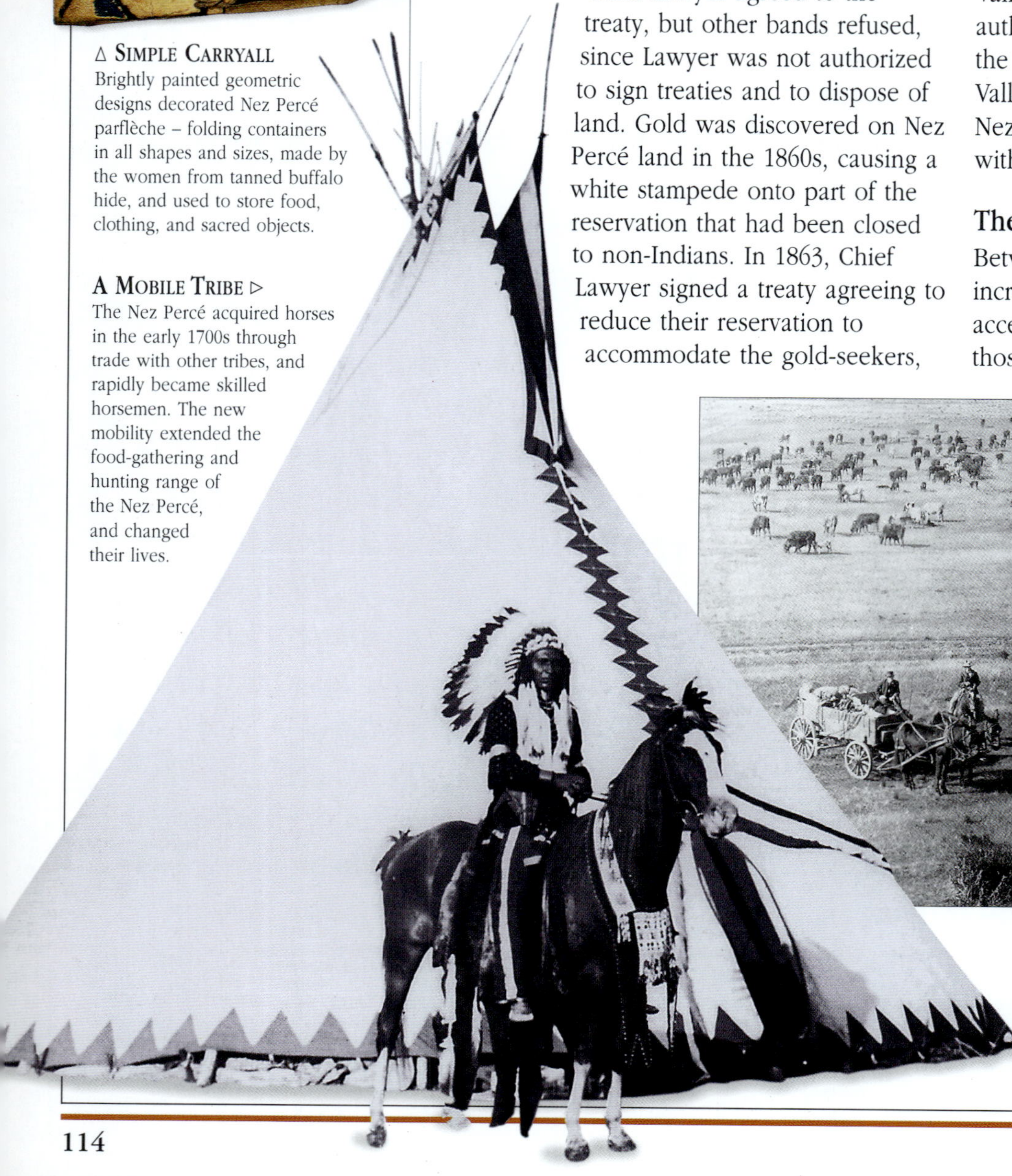

A MOBILE TRIBE ▷
The Nez Percé acquired horses in the early 1700s through trade with other tribes, and rapidly became skilled horsemen. The new mobility extended the food-gathering and hunting range of the Nez Percé, and changed their lives.

IN 1855, THE NEWLY APPOINTED governor of Washington Territory, Isaac I. Stevens, negotiated a treaty with the Nez Percé that created a 7.5 million-acre (3 million-hectare) reservation in Idaho. Followers of Nez Percé Chief Lawyer agreed to the treaty, but other bands refused, since Lawyer was not authorized to sign treaties and to dispose of land. Gold was discovered on Nez Percé land in the 1860s, causing a white stampede onto part of the reservation that had been closed to non-Indians. In 1863, Chief Lawyer signed a treaty agreeing to reduce their reservation to accommodate the gold-seekers, but resisters, led by Joseph and White Bird, refused to recognize the new boundaries or to live on the shrunken reservation. Chief Joseph insisted that his father had never signed the 1863 treaty and had never sold the Wallowa Valley, where Joseph made his home. Oregon authorities declared that Joseph had to go to the Idaho reservation, and opened the Wallowa Valley to white settlement. Realizing that the Nez Percé could not win an armed conflict with the US army, Joseph finally complied.

The Start of War

Between 1863 and 1877, the tribe became increasingly divided between those who accepted the new, diminished reservation and those who did not. In June 1877, a band of

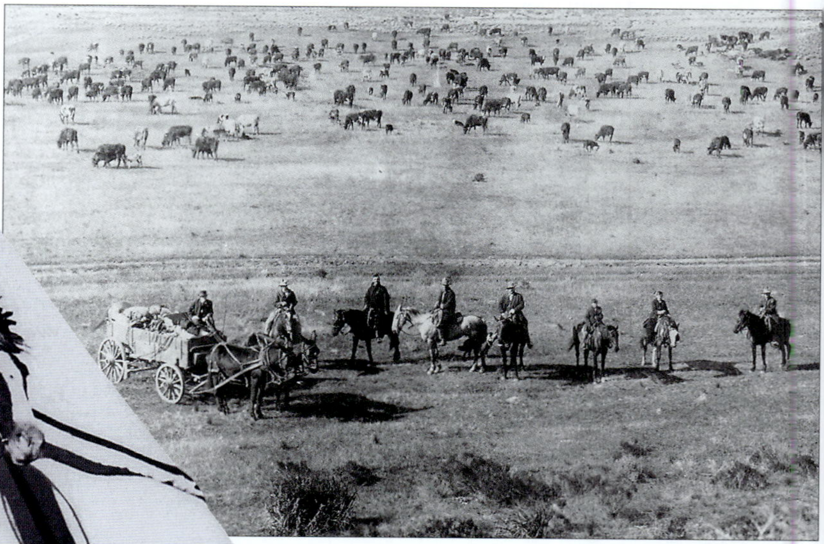

△ BELOVED WALLOWA VALLEY
Joseph's people lived in Wallowa Valley, a stretch of rich grazing land bordered by mountains. On his deathbed, Joseph's father told him: "Always remember that your father never sold his country ... stop your ears whenever you are asked to sign a treaty selling your home ...."

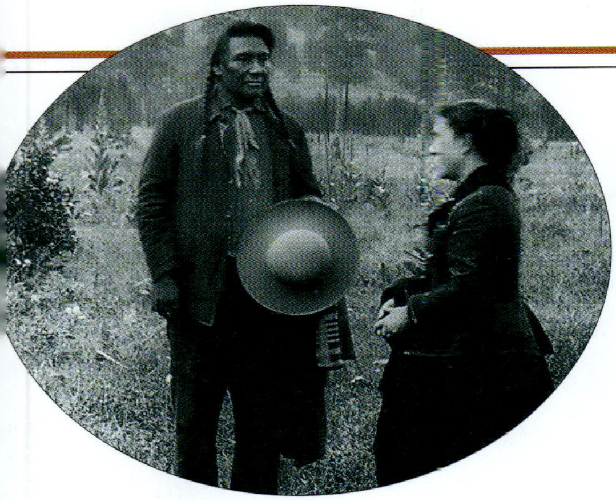

◁ CHIEF JOSEPH IN EXILE
Chief Joseph, seen here with government allotting agent Alice C. Fletcher, was exiled to the Colville reservation in Washington state in 1884. He was allowed only a short visit to his ancestral homeland before his death "from a broken heart" in 1904.

young Nez Percé killed four white settlers then took refuge in White Bird Canyon. The First Cavalry was mobilized and charged into the canyon, where Nez Percé warriors killed 37 soldiers and forced the survivors to retreat in a humiliating defeat for the military.

This fight at White Bird Canyon made war inevitable, and General Oliver O. Howard ordered his troops to march against the Nez Percé. Led by Chief Joseph, Looking Glass, White Bird, Toohoolhoolzote, and Joseph's brother Ollokot, some 650 Indians fled eastward, then headed north for the Canadian border, with General Howard hard behind them. Four months and 1,700 miles (2,736 km) later, the chase ended when Looking Glass told his people they had to rest. On 30 September, in the Bear Paw Mountains, less than 40 miles (64 km) from Canada, Colonel Nelson A. Miles, ordered by General Howard to intercept the Nez Percé before they escaped into Canada, besieged the Indians' camp for five days.

White Bird and 300 of the Nez Percé people slipped though the cordon to Canada but, on 5 October 1877, Chief Joseph, tired of fighting and concerned that his people were starving and freezing, surrendered to Colonel Miles.

Broken Promise

Miles promised that the Indians could return to the Idaho reservation in the spring, but the government failed to honor his promise. After Joseph's surrender and imprisonment, most of the tribe resettled within the boundaries of the 1863 reservation; but Joseph and his loyal followers were forbidden to return to Idaho and were forced instead to settle on the Colville reservation in central Washington State.

NEZ PERCÉ RETREAT

Joseph and other chiefs led their group from the Lapwai reservation, Idaho, almost to the Canadian border, with 1,900 soldiers in pursuit. During an epic journey, they fought battles at Clearwater Creek (Idaho), Big Hole (Montana), Camas Creek (Idaho), Canyon Creek and Cow Island (Montana), and finally at Bear Paw Mountain (Montana).

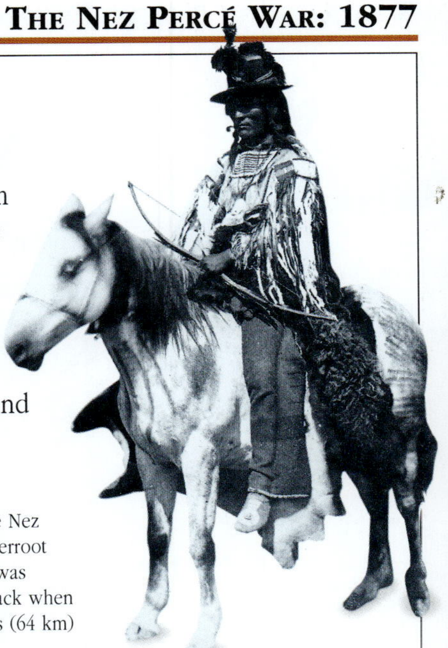

LOOKING GLASS KILLED ▷
Principal war chief during the Nez Percé flight through the Bitterroot Mountains, Looking Glass was killed during a cavalry attack when encamped within 40 miles (64 km) of the Canadian border.

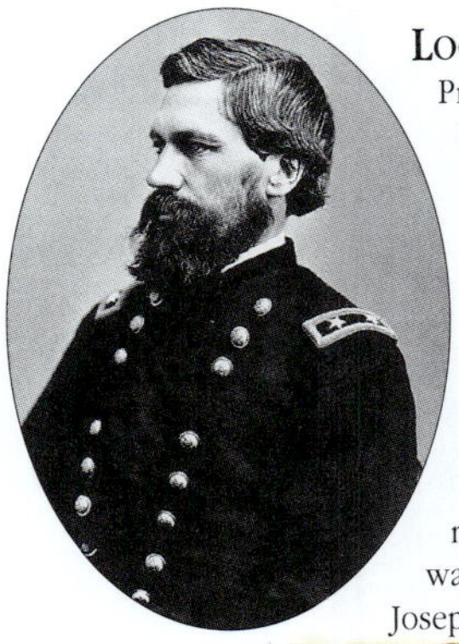

◁ HOWARD IN PURSUIT
General Oliver O. Howard led 400 soldiers against the Nez Percé, but never caught up with them. Howard was present, however, when Chief Joseph surrendered in October 1877.

▽ ROUTE OF RETREAT
During their long, winding flight through parts of present-day Idaho, Wyoming, and Montana, the Nez Percé had to traverse mountains, canyons, rocky plains, and rivers.

FLIGHT OF THE NEZ PERCÉ, 1877

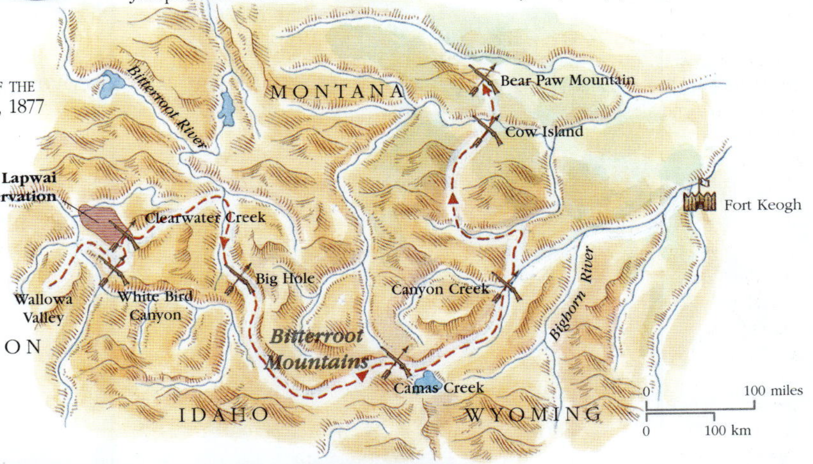

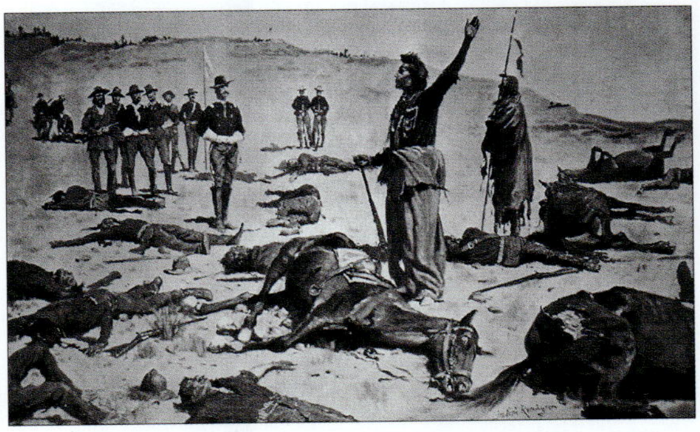

◁ SURRENDER AT BEAR PAW
The battle of Bear Paw Mountain was fought, on 30 September 1877, between the Nez Percé and almost 600 soldiers, led by Colonel Nelson A. Miles. The battle cost the lives of Joseph's brother, Ollokot, medicine man Toohoolhoolzote, and Looking Glass. Finally, on 5 October, Joseph surrendered to avoid any more suffering. In this painting, Chief Joseph faces Colonel Miles with General Howard looking on.

"Hear me, my chiefs, I am tired. My heart is sick and sad. From where the sun now stands, I will fight no more forever."

CHIEF JOSEPH AT HIS SURRENDER, 1877

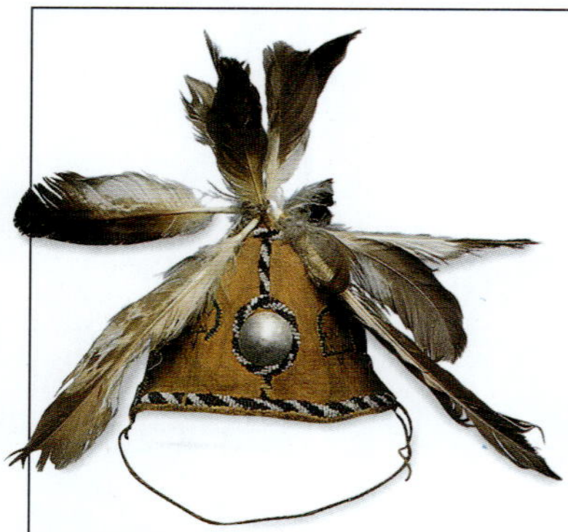

APACHE BUCKSKIN CAP
This Apache buckskin cap is decorated with glass beads and metal discs; eagle feathers adorn the top. Apaches wore war caps with similar designs.

APACHES HOLD OUT

FROM THE 1860S TO THE 1880S, relations between Apaches and the steadily increasing numbers of miners and settlers who were moving to the Southwest became hostile. Warfare was ignited when Apaches were killed by treacherous Americans, who ignored Apache land rights. Under the leadership of warriors such as Mangas Coloradas, Cochise, Victorio, and Geronimo, the Apaches struck back at settlements in present-day Arizona and New Mexico. The wars ended in 1886 when Chiricahua Apache Geronimo surrendered to General Nelson A. Miles.

WARM SPRINGS FIGHTERS

Mimbres Apache leaders Victorio and Loco initially refused to move from their Warm Springs reservation in New Mexico to San Carlos in Arizona. After Victorio was killed in battle, in 1880, Loco took his people to San Carlos, leaving Mangas, son of Mangas Coloradas, to lead the Warm Springs Apaches. After the remaining chiefs had surrendered, Mangas was captured, in 1886, and sent to a Florida prison.

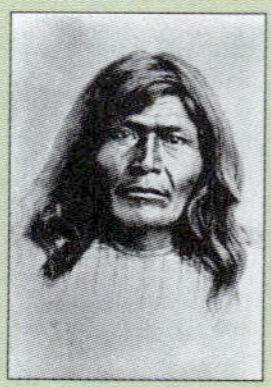

VICTORIO

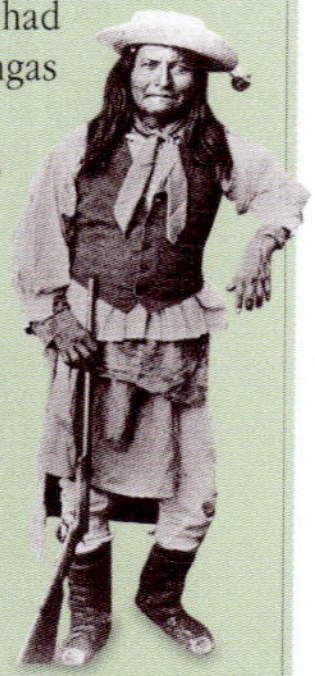

LOCO

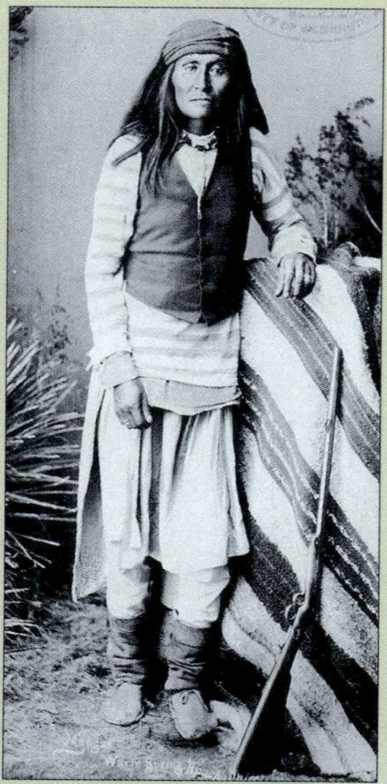

MANGAS, SON OF MANGAS COLORADAS

HOME OF THE APACHES, the Southwest became part of the United States as a result of the 1848 Treaty of Guadalupe Hildago and the Gadsden Purchase of 1853. At first, Apache contacts with Americans were peaceful, but this changed in the 1860s when miners and settlers failed to recognize the Natives' land and water rights and their hunting and gathering patterns. A series of incidents, in which Americans killed Apaches, ignited the Apache wars, which lasted until the 1880s.

Violence erupted in 1861 when Lieutenant George Bascom wrongfully accused Chiricahua Apache chief Cochise of cattle theft and kidnapping. Attempts to capture the chief resulted in a war with Cochise and his father-in-law, Mimbreno Apache chief Mangas Coloradas. In 1863, Mangas Coloradas agreed to meet a military detachment under a flag of truce. He was seized, imprisoned, and killed by guards, who claimed that he tried to escape.

Cochise retreated to the Dragoon Mountains, raiding settlements at every opportunity and refusing to submit to demands to move to a reservation. He fought until 1872, when he was persuaded to make peace.

Apache Reservations Set Up

Army posts were gradually established in Apache territory and, by 1870, the first Apache reservation had been set up in areas shunned by Americans. Many Apaches voluntarily

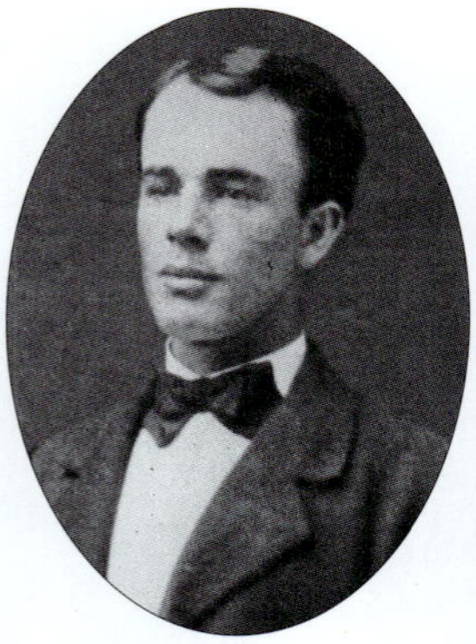

△ AGENT CLUM
Agent to the Apaches at the San Carlos reservation, John P. Clum brought Indians under civilian control, employing Indian police to enforce law and order.

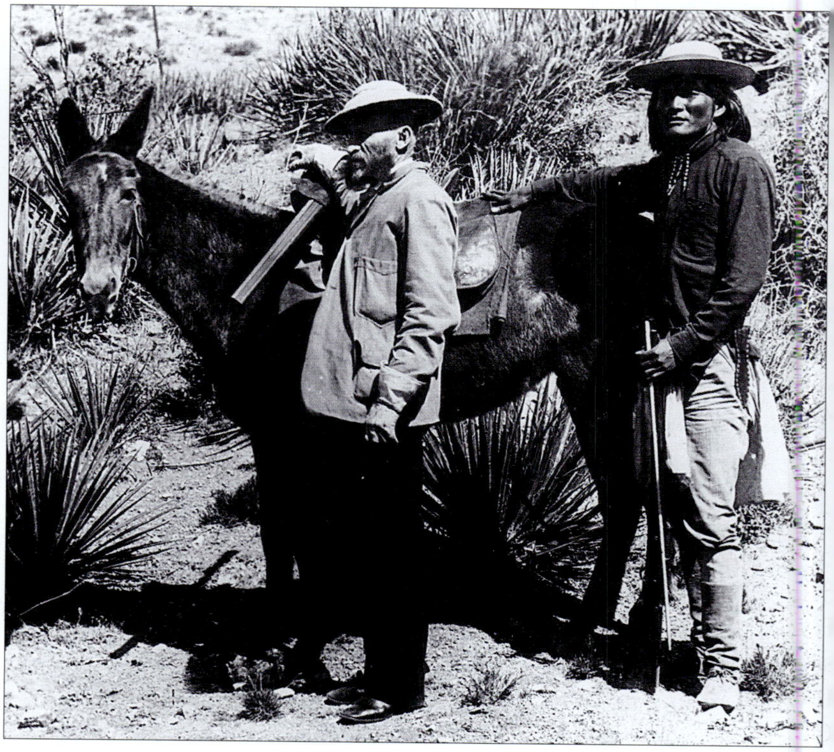

CROOK'S SCOUTS ▷
General Crook mounted several attempts to return escaping Apaches to their reservations, enlisting Apache scouts to trail them. He is pictured (left) with Apache scout Alchesay.

noved to these reservations because the lternatives were extermination or starvation. 'he rest were forcibly removed from their omelands by the military during the next few 'ears. In March 1871, settlers from Tucson, rizona, massacred over 100 Arivaipas, most of them women and children. The killing onvinced President Grant that a reservation ystem was needed to separate Apaches from ettlers. By 1886, the government had placed ll Apaches on reservations or in prison.

Resistance to San Carlos

Pressure by white settlers and miners hungry or Arizona's resources led the US government, n early 1875, to begin consolidating Apaches t the San Carlos reservation – located on bleak desert land of searing heat, dusty winds, and nsects. The Tonto, White Mountain Mimbreno, and other Apache groups (who preferred nountains and cool, timbered locations) were uprooted and moved to San Carlos, where farming was impossible. Victorio's Mimbreno band bolted and, in 1877, began an uprising on both sides of the Rio Grande. In 1879, Victorio attacked a Ninth Cavalry camp, prompting a US and Mexican campaign against him. He was killed in battle with Mexican troops in 1880.

Chief Geronimo Pursued

Between 1876 and 1886, Chiricahua Apache chief Geronimo (Goyathlay) repeatedly broke out of the hated San Carlos reservation. With a band of warriors, he fled to Mexico and raided settlements on both sides of the border from a stronghold in the Sierra Madre. Although Mexicans and whites had been killing Apaches for years, land-hungry settlers and government officials branded the Apaches as murderous renegades, and especially targeted Geronimo. His resistance lasted until September 1886 when, pursued by thousands of Mexican and American troops and Apache scouts who knew his hiding places, he surrendered to General Nelson A. Miles, who had replaced General George Crook, following Crook's failure to bring the chief to terms. Geronimo and over 300 of his followers were shipped to prisons in Florida and Alabama. In 1892, he and the surviving Chiricahuas were sent to Fort Sill, Indian Territory (present-day Oklahoma). Geronimo died there in 1909.

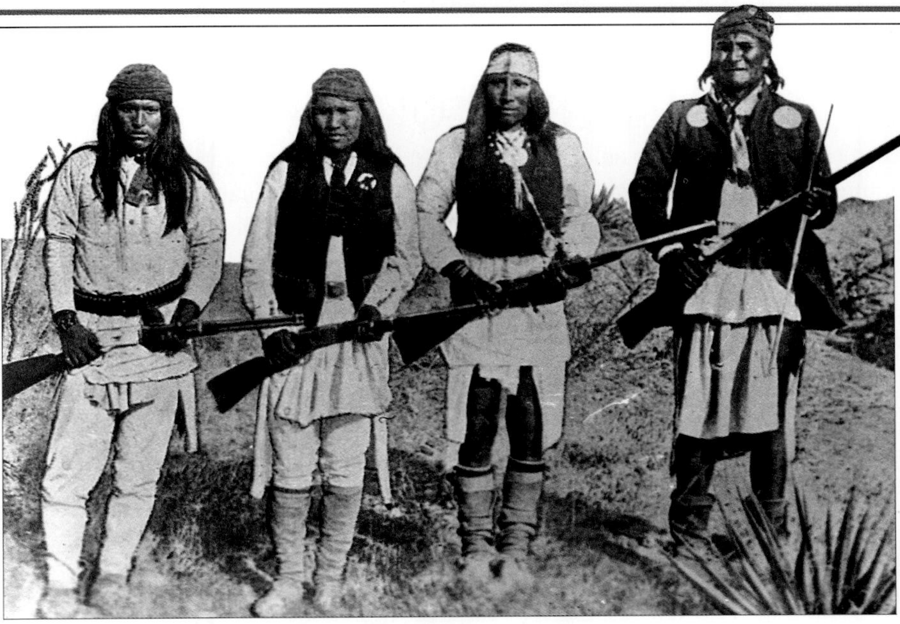

△ GERONIMO'S RENEGADES
About six months before his final surrender in Skeleton Canyon, on 4 September 1886, Geronimo (far right) is pictured with three of his warriors in Mexico's Sierra Madre. To capture Geronimo and the 24 renegade Apaches, General Nelson A. Miles ordered 5,000 soldiers, assisted by Apache scouts, into the field.

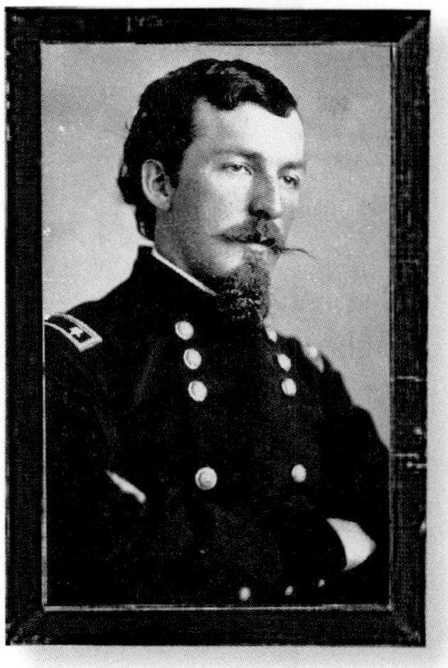

◁ MILES'S PROMISE
US President Cleveland wanted the renegades handed over in unconditional surrender but, at a meeting with Geronimo on 4 September 1886, General Miles (left) accepted conditional surrender and promised that the prisoners' lives would be spared. The warriors were sent to a military prison in Alabama.

▽ CROOK OUTWITTED
General George Crook led his troops into Mexico, where he obtained Geronimo's surrender at Canyon de los Embudos in March 1886. Geronimo escaped, however, and Crook was relieved of his Arizona command. Crook is pictured here (second from right) in council with Geronimo (third from left) and his band.

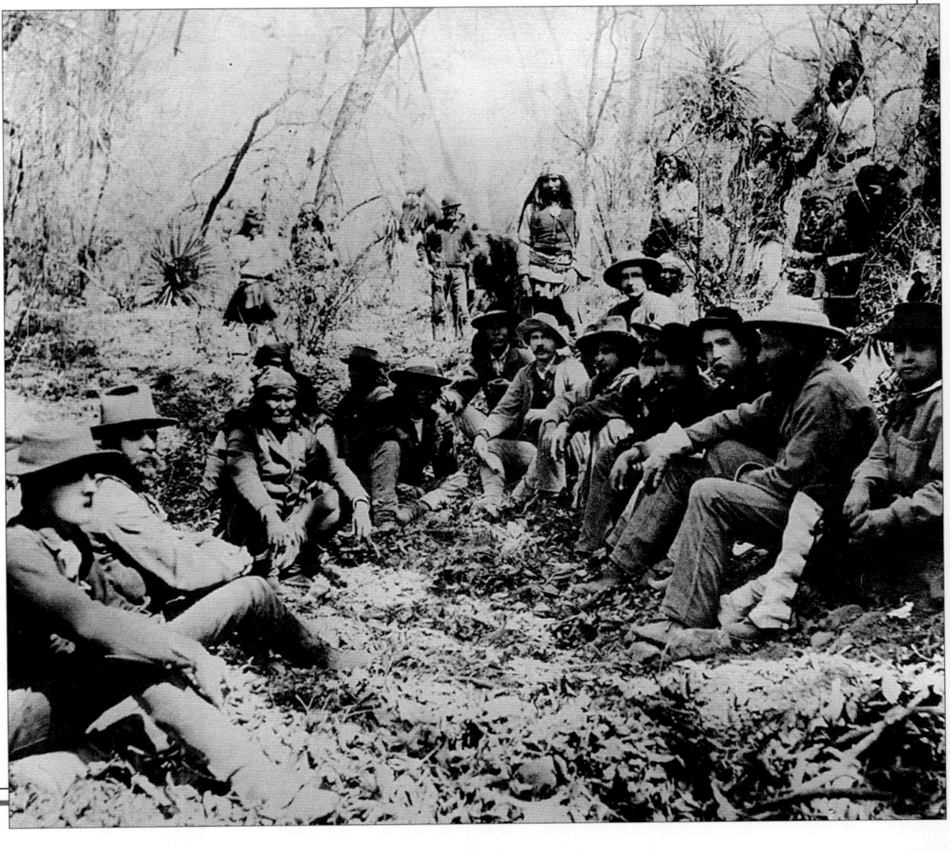

USING APACHE SCOUTS

General George Crook enlisted Apaches to scout and to fight other Apaches. Having studied the Indians' technique of rapid movement, he replaced slow-moving wagon trains with the use of mules to carry supplies. He also cut supplies to enable his troops to move faster, like the scouts who carried very little.

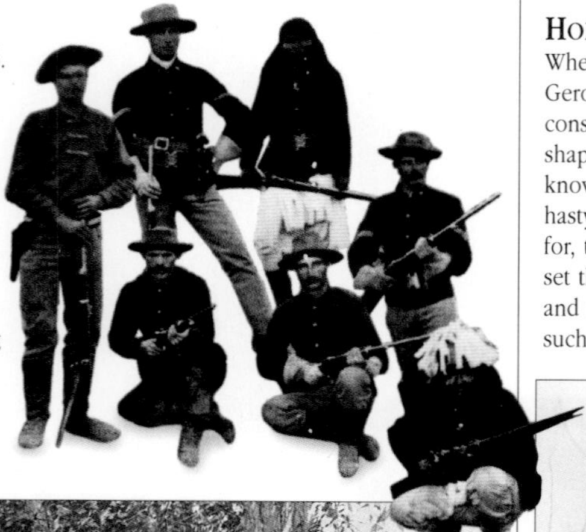

US AND APACHE SCOUTS ▷
US and Apache scouts pose in 1886. Hired mainly to trail Apache insurgents, the scouts, who had weapons, were issued a few cartridges. Scouts who fought were issued with additional weapons.

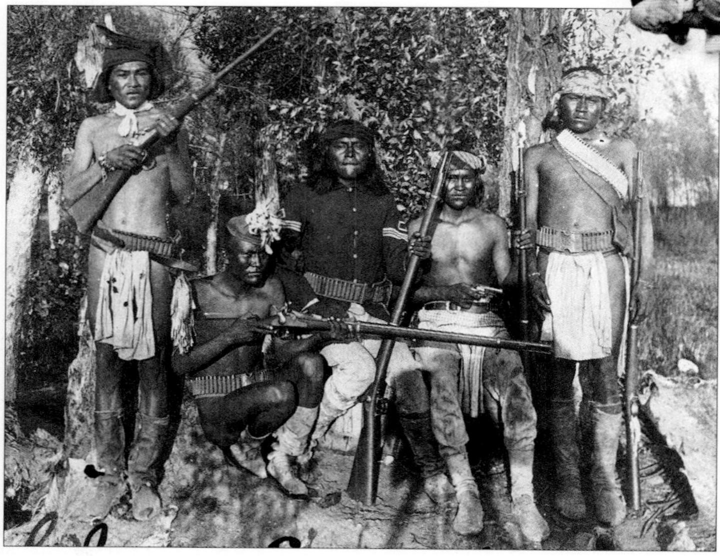

▽ SETTLING OLD SCORES
Apache scouts were easy to hire, for various bands had long-standing animosities and were keen to settle old scores. When one band raided another, Crook would go and enlist from those who had been attacked.

ESCAPE ACROSS THE BORDER

In 1885, Geronimo and about 150 members of the Chiricahua and Warm Springs Apaches made one of many escapes from the San Carlos reservation and headed for the Sierra Madre in Mexico. In the rugged mountain terrain, cut by seemingly impassable ravines, they evaded capture until September 1886.

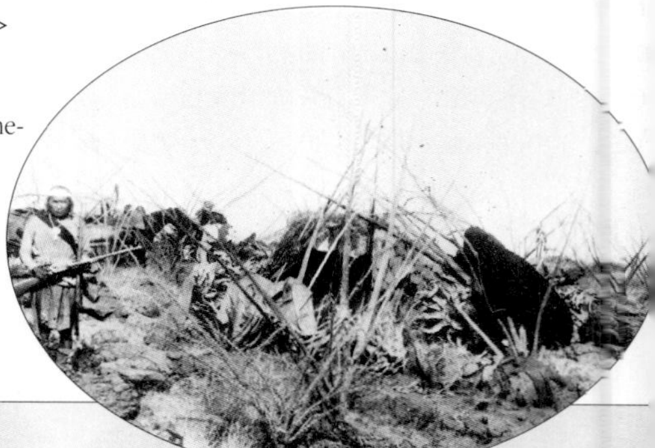

HOME ON THE RUN ▷
Wherever they camped, Geronimo and his men constructed circular, dome-shaped brush dwellings known as wickiups. If a hasty escape was called for, the Apaches would set the wickiups on fire and retreat. Here is one such camp in the 1880s.

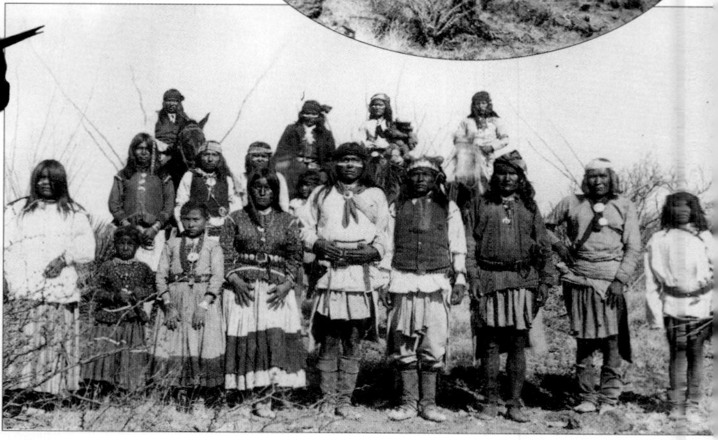

△ SMALL BANDS ELUDE CAPTURE
When General Miles replaced Crook, his scouts tracked down the Apaches and skirmished with them almost every day. To elude the troops, Geronimo divided his followers into small bands. Pictured here is a small group of Geronimo's followers in the Sierra Madre in 1886.

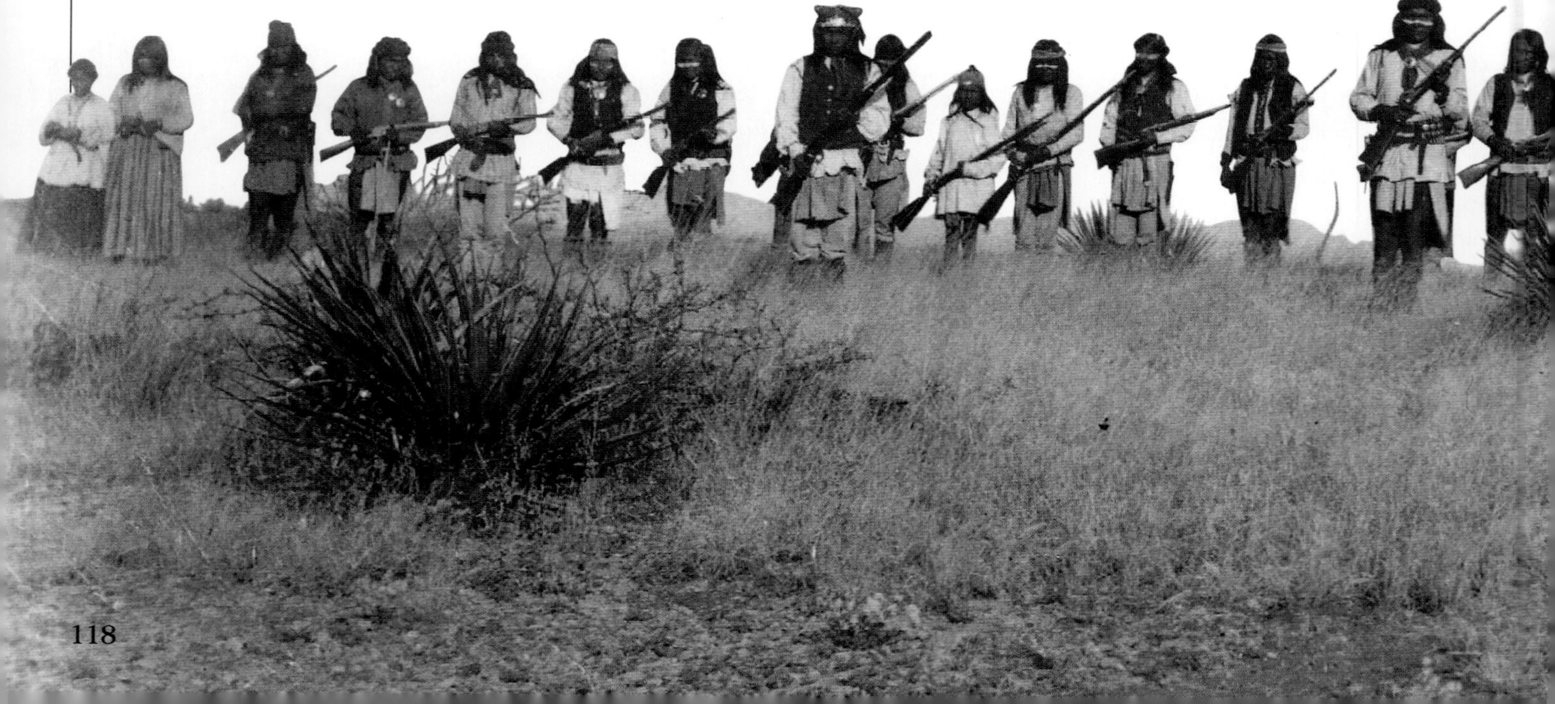

▽ GERONIMO'S ARMY
C.S. Fry, an Arizona photographer, took this dramatic photograph of Geronimo with his band of warriors in Mexico's Sierra Madre in March 1886. By the time he finally surrendered in September of that year, Geronimo's army consisted of only two dozen men.

PRISONERS OF WAR

Vhen Geronimo surrendered in September 1886, Jeneral Miles promised him a reunion with his amily, some land, a house, stock, and farming ools. The reality was different: Geronimo and his ollowers were treated as prisoners of war and hipped to prisons in Florida and Alabama, where nany died of tuberculosis. In 1894, Geronimo was ent, not to the homeland he longed for, but to 'ort Sill in Indian Territory, where he remained ıs a prisoner of war until his death in 1909.

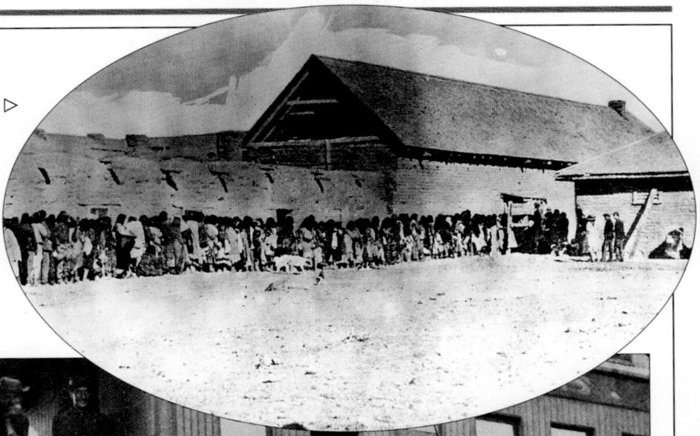

SAN CARLOS RATION LINE ▷
A line of Apaches wait for rations at the barren San Carlos reservation in Arizona. In 1876, in the first of many escapes, Geronimo protested the Chiricahuas' removal to the reservation by fleeing with his family.

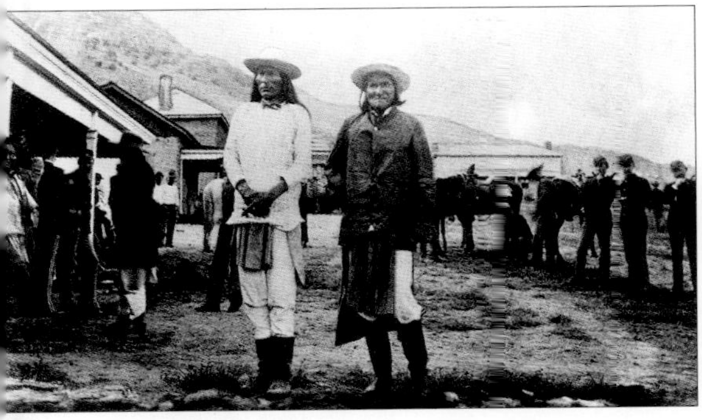

△ SURRENDER AT FORT BOWIE
Geronimo (right) and Naiche are pictured on the parade ground at Fort Bowie, Arizona, four days after their surrender to General Nelson A. Miles. As a band played *Auld Lang Syne*, the prisoners were escorted to Bowie Station and loaded onto a train for Florida.

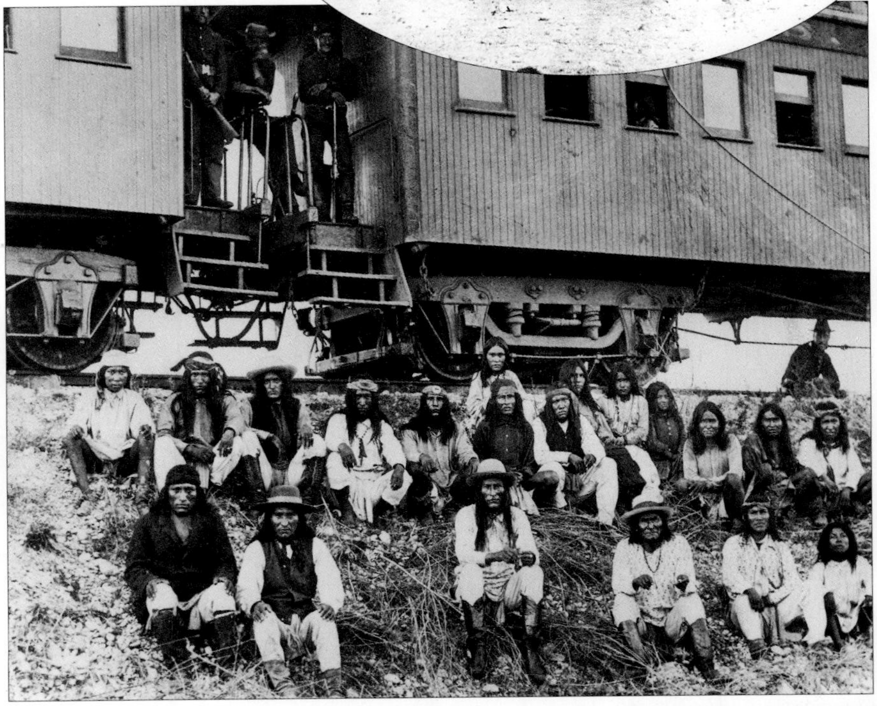

△ EN ROUTE TO PRISON
In 1886, Chiricahua Apache prisoners, including Geronimo (first row, third from right), were pictured on an embankment beside the railroad car that took them to prison in Florida. They had left behind their personal belongings, horses, and dogs.

"I surrender. Once I moved about like the wind. Now I surrender to you and that is all."

GERONIMO, 1886

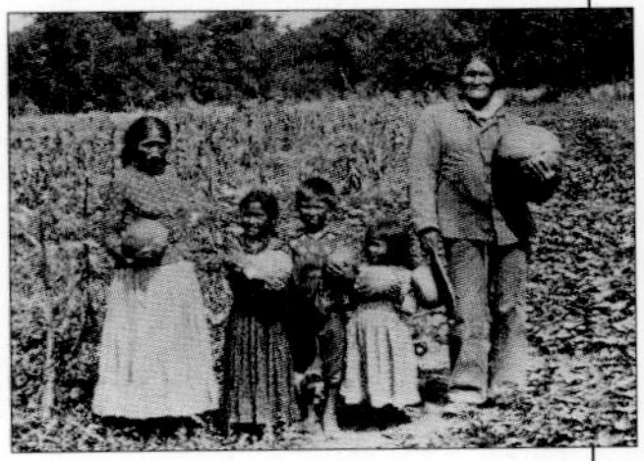

FARMING AT FORT SILL ▷
Geronimo is pictured, posing in a watermelon patch, at Fort Sill with his sixth wife, Zi-yah, and their children. While at Fort Sill, Geronimo became a farmer and joined the Dutch Reformed Church. He made money by selling photographs of himself.

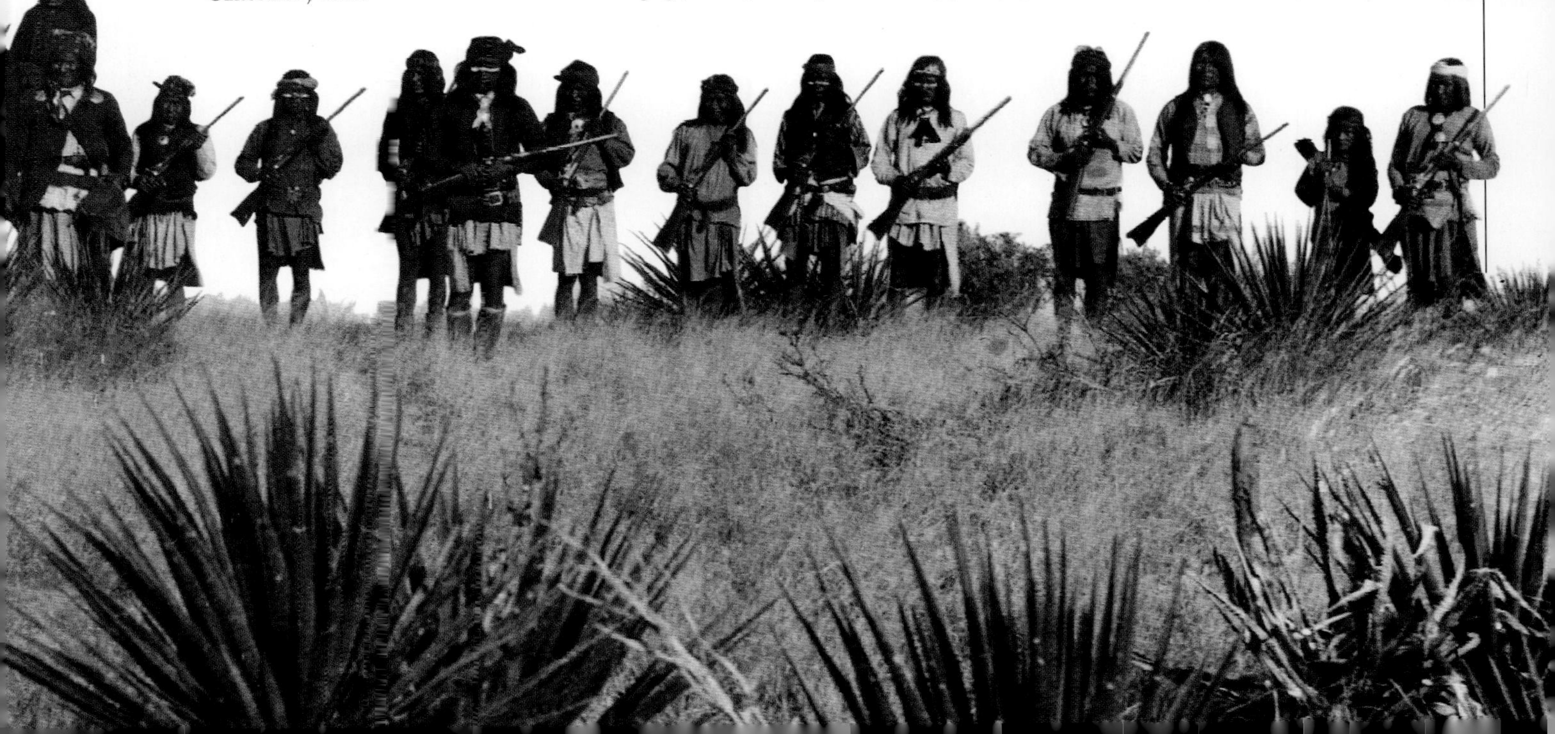

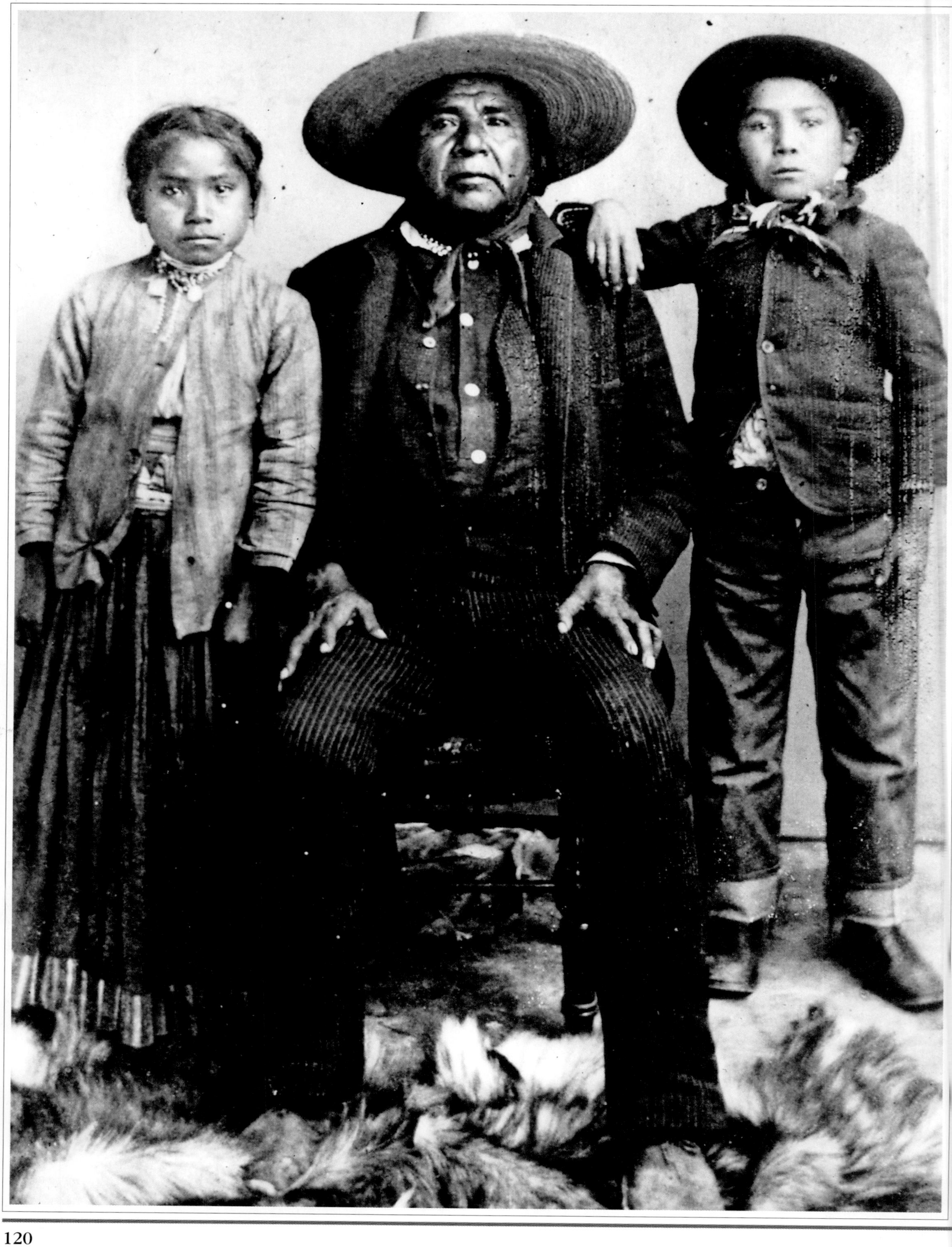

ESKIMINZIN

1871: ON THE MASSACRE OF HIS PEOPLE BY CITIZENS OF TUCSON

ESKIMINZIN (*c.* 1825–90), a Pinal Apache, married into the Aravaipas and eventually became their principal chief. In 1871, his band established a village near the army post at Camp Grant, near Tucson, Arizona, planting fields of corn and gathering agave. On 30 April 1871, after a series of raids that they blamed on Eskiminzin's band, citizens of Tucson organized a vigilante force and attacked Camp Grant, killing as many as 150 of the chief's people, including two of his wives and five of his children. This account of the massacre is taken from a report of the Board of Indian Commissioners to the US President in 1871.

"I was the first to come in and make peace before and was happy in my home here. I got my rations every three days. I was not living far from here. I was making tiswin [a drink] in peace, when one morning I and my people were attacked, and many of them were killed. The next day after the massacre I came into this camp because I knew it was not the people here who had done it; it was the people from Tucson and Papagos. I then continued to live here in the valley for nearly thirty days, when my people were again attacked; this time it was by a squad of military men, and although none of my people were killed, yet that made me mad, and I went on the warpath. I now admit I did wrong, but I was grieved and angry, and I could not help it. The one who first breaks the peace is the one who is to blame. I believe Commissioner [Vincent] Coyler [Board of Indian Commissioners secretary] has come to make peace .... The commissioner has sent out for me ... and probably thought he would see a great captain, but he only saw a very poor man, and not very much of a captain. Then I had a band of seventy men, but they had all been massacred; now I have got no people. Ever since I left this place I have been in the neighborhood; I knew I had friends here, but I was afraid to come back; but as soon as I heard the commissioner was here then I came in. I never had much to say, but this I could say – I like this place. I have said all I ought to say, since I have no people anywhere to speak for. If it had not been for the massacre, there would have been a great many more people here now; but after that massacre, who could have stood it? ... When I made peace with Lieutenant [Royal E.] Whitman my heart was very big and happy. The people of Tucson and San Xavier [Papagos] must be crazy. They acted as though they had neither heads nor hearts ... the people of Tucson and San Xavier must have a thirst for our blood ... these Tucson people write for the papers and tell their own story. The Apaches have no one to tell their story ...."

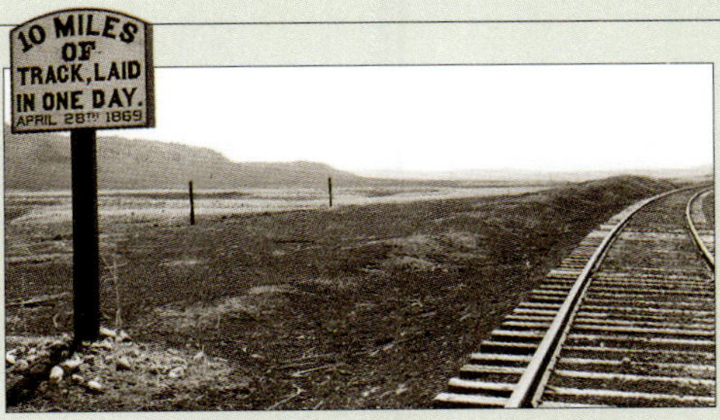

ENCROACHING ON NATIVE LANDS
In 1869, two years before Tucson citizens massacred the Aravaipa, the Natives lived on an isolated reservation at nearby Camp Grant. But, as this sign shows, Southern Pacific was rapidly laying railroad tracks into the area, bringing ever more land-hungry people to Arizona.

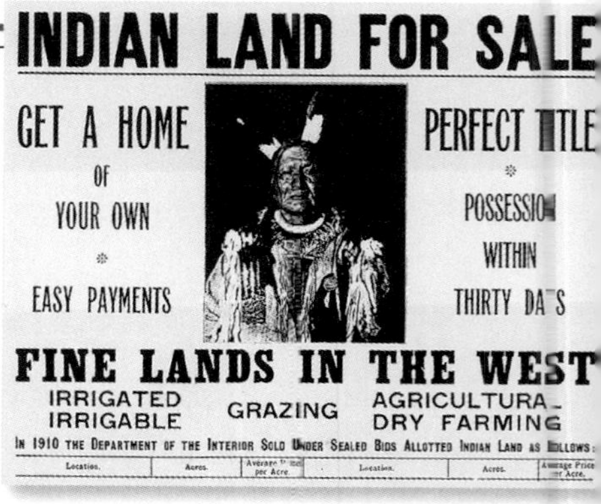

"SURPLUS" LAND FOR SALE
After reservations were divided up, the government purchased huge tracts of "surplus" land and sold them at bargain prices. This advertisement features a Yankton Dakota (Sioux) named "Not Afraid of Pawnee."

CARVING UP RESERVATIONS

IN THE 1880s, government policymakers looked for alternative ways of assimilating Natives into white society. Violence between the two races had not been resolved by isolating Indians on reservations, where they continued to hold onto tribal ways. By carving up the reservations and forcing individual tribal members to accept parcels of land, it was hoped to undermine the tribe as a cultural and territorial unit and replace it with the white system of private land ownership.

ALLOTMENT SPONSOR

Henry Dawes, principal sponsor of the General Allotment Act, believed that a drastic reduction in reservations was essential if Indians were to be assimilated into white civilization.

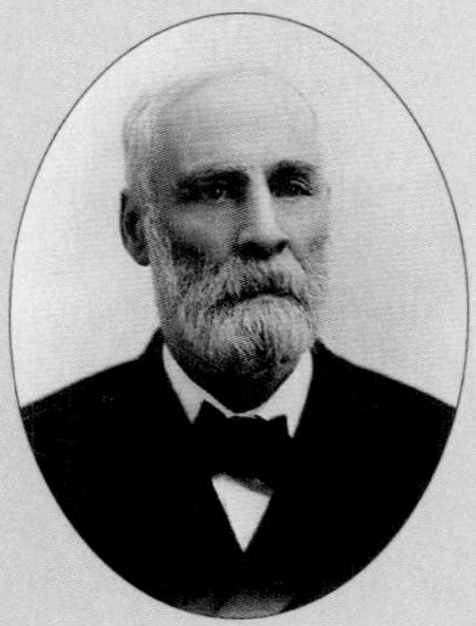

SENATOR HENRY DAWES

FOR THOUSANDS OF YEARS, Indian tribes sustained their lives and cultures within a system of common land ownership that ensured the use of land to citizens as long as they did not infringe on the rights of others. Individuals could not give away what belonged to the group; nor could land be bought, sold, or developed. White people misunderstood or despised a land tenure system so different from their own. Most felt that private ownership was the only basis for civilization. An "allotment in severalty" policy (or chopping up Indian reservation land) was suggested at various times, from the earliest days of white settlement. In 1633, the Massachusetts General Court authorized the settling of Indians on plots "according to the custom of the English," and, from 1850, severalty provisions were written into a number of treaties. But the discovery of gold, the completion of the transcontinental railroad in 1869, and demands for farms and homesteads by whites resulted in pressure to break up reservation lands and clear the way for westward settlement.

Allotment and private ownership

In 1887, Congress passed the General Allotment Act (or Dawes Severalty Act), a law that created private property for individual Indians out of tribal land. The law authorized the President to allot specific amounts to heads of families, single Indians, and orphans. The federal government retained trusteeship over the individual's allotment for 25 years, during which time the plot could not be sold, taxed, or leased. After the trust period ended, allottees

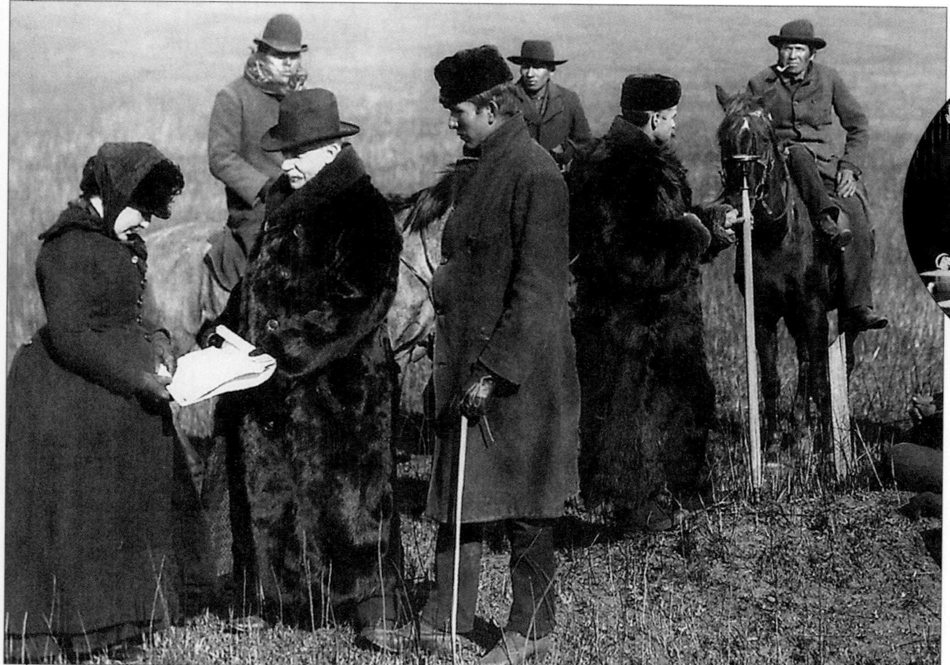

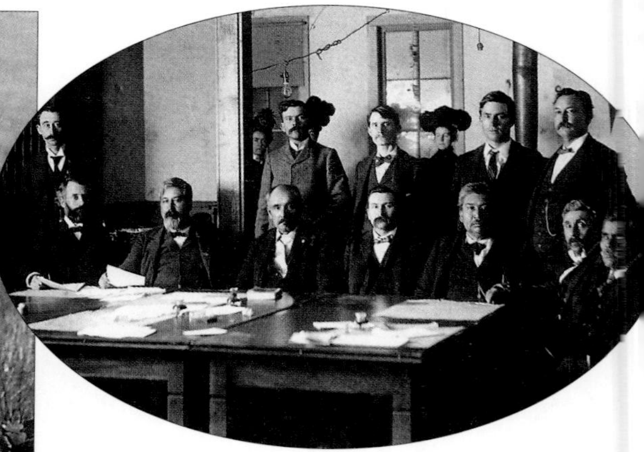

△ REACHING AGREEMENT WITH THE FIVE TRIBES
Members of the Dawes Commission, seen here with Cherokees, negotiated allotment agreements with the Five Tribes (Cherokee, Chickasaw, Choctaw, Creek, and Seminole) in Indian Territory.

◁ ALLOTTING TRIBAL LANDS
Alice Fletcher, photographed with boundary surveyors and several Nez Percé, believed that dividing tribal lands into individual homesteads would spur Indians on to "civilization." She acted as allotting agent for the Nez Percé from 1889 to 1893.

vere required to pay property taxes and were ɔermitted to sell their land and keep the ɔroceeds. "Surplus" tribal land was put up for ɔublic sale or sold to the US government.

Tribal lands were not all allotted mmediately and not all reservations were equally affected, but the tribal lands that went nto white ownership were the most valuable. As a matter of policy, government agents avoided allotting to Indians any land that was ɔotentially rich in water, minerals, or timber.

The allotment of the Sisseton Dakota 918,000-acre (372,000-hectare) homeland demonstrates the way the policy dramatically reduced Indian land area: the 2,000 members of the tribe collectively retained 300,000 acres (121,000 hectares), leaving roughly 600,000 "surplus" acres (250,000 hectares). These were then bought up by white homesteaders.

Resistance and persistence

Many tribal people resisted allotment. At a gathering in Indian Territory in 1887, representatives from 19 different tribes voted unanimously against it, to no avail. However, some tribes circumvented the law by selecting their plots in a block so they could try to continue the communal way of life.

Some whites believed that allotment would fail: even before the Act was passed a minority of the House Committee on Indian Affairs protested, "The real aim of this bill is to get at the Indian lands and open them up to settlement ...."

Allotment succeeded in separating Indians from their land. But Indians did not become carbon copies of white people: traditional tribal values, attitudes, and ways of life persisted.

"They made us many promises, more than I can remember, but they never kept but one; they promised to take our land and they took it."

SIOUX ELDER DESCRIBING THE WHITE MAN'S DEALINGS WITH INDIANS, *C.* 1890

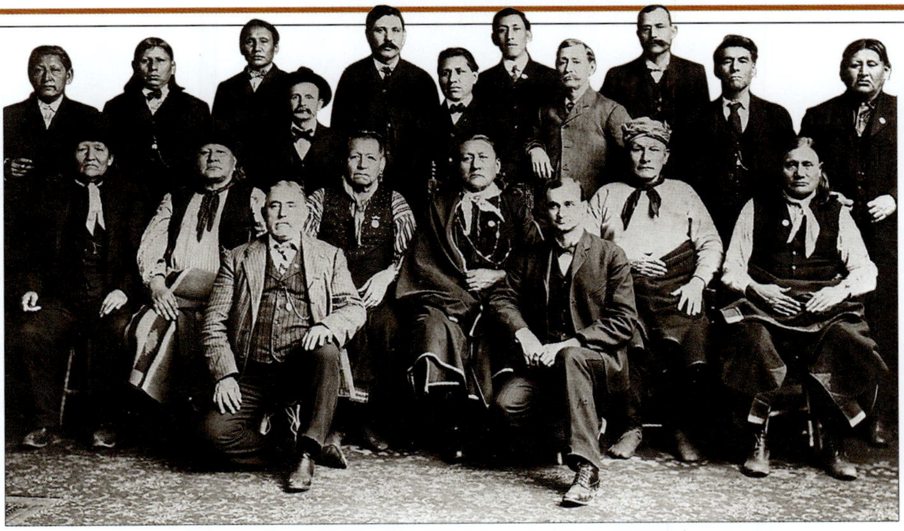

△ FORESIGHT OF OSAGE DELEGATION
In the early 1890s, an Osage delegation went to Washington, DC, to insist that all mineral resources remain communal tribal property. When oil was discovered in 1920 on former reservation land, the Osage, as a group, benefited from royalties.

▽ UNITY UNDER PRESSURE
Although a minority of Creeks resisted allotment, by 1890 – the time of this Creek Council meeting – Congress had bowed to pressure from white farmers, adventurers, and railroad promoters and opened the "unassigned lands" in Indian Territory to settlement.

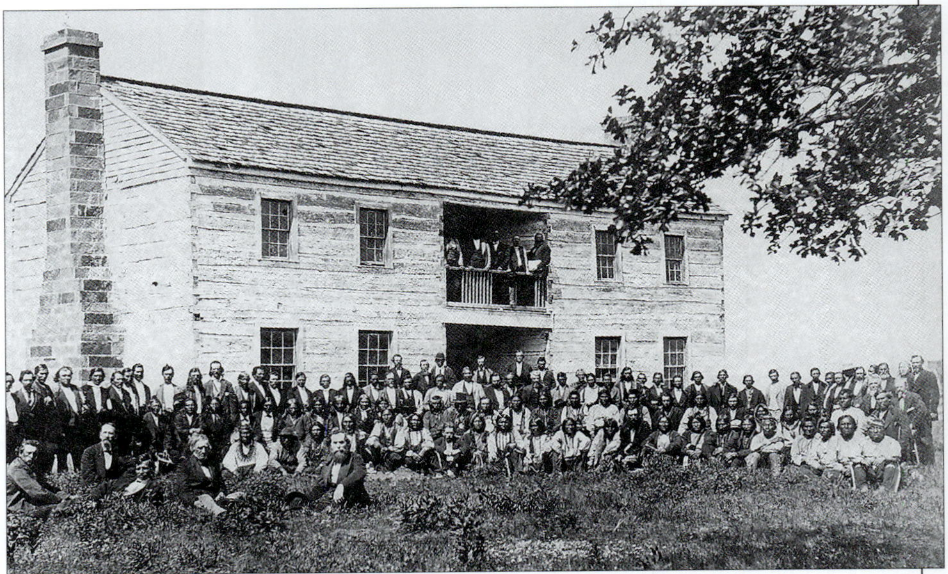

ANTI-ALLOTMENT LEADER ▷
Chitto Harjo, alias Crazy Snake, led the anti-allotment fight amongst Oklahoma Creeks. Jailed in 1901 for leading a short-lived uprising, he continued his fight legally on his return home. By the time of his death in 1912, all of Indian Territory was allotted.

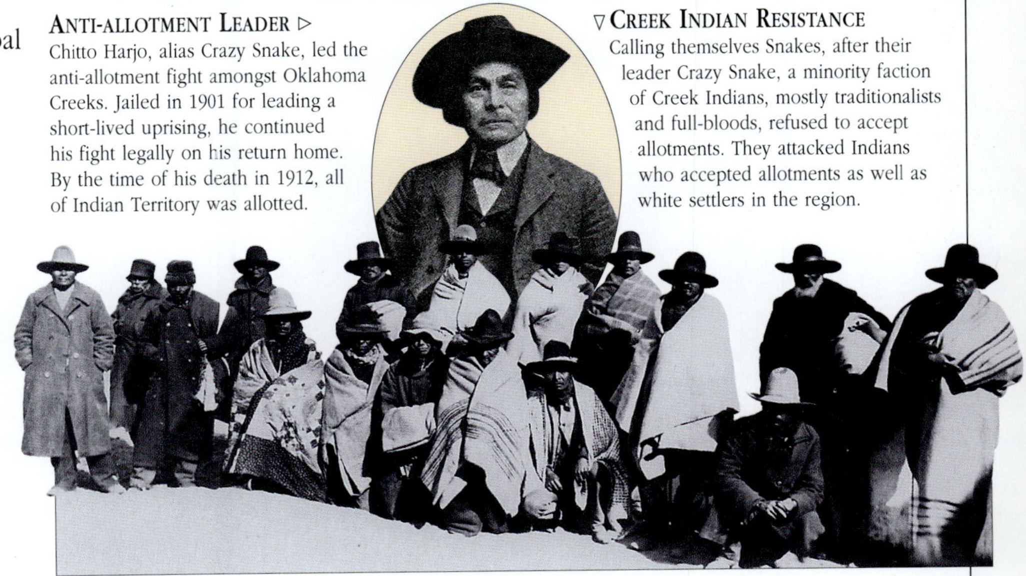

▽ CREEK INDIAN RESISTANCE
Calling themselves Snakes, after their leader Crazy Snake, a minority faction of Creek Indians, mostly traditionalists and full-bloods, refused to accept allotments. They attacked Indians who accepted allotments as well as white settlers in the region.

INDIAN ALLOTMENT

Under the 1887 General Allotment Act, most tribal heads of Indian families (male and female) received allotments of land. Managed by the Indian Office, the allotment process reviewed lists of members on tribal rolls to decide who was eligible to receive allotments. Agents were responsible for surveying land, dividing it up, and allotting plots.

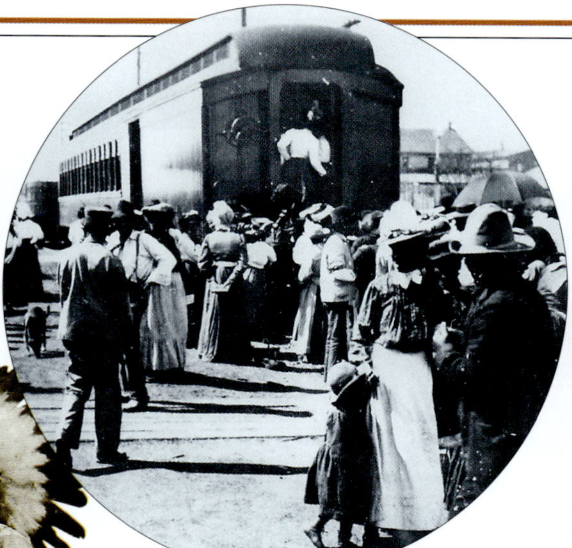

△ CHOCTAW AND CHICKASAW REGISTRATION
In 1893, Congress authorized the Dawes Commission to survey and allot the land of the Five Tribes. Choctaw and Chickasaw Indians, who signed an allotment agreement in 1897, are seen here lining up to register for plots of land.

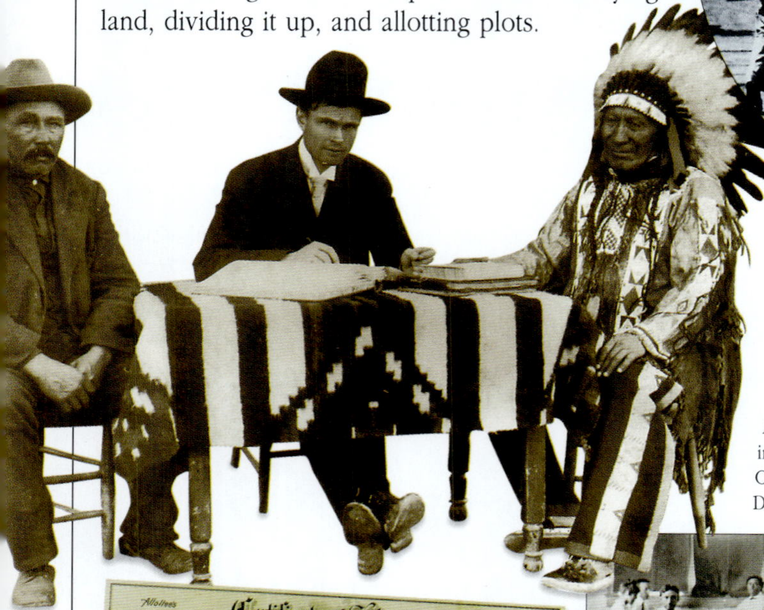

◁ ALLOTMENT PROCEEDINGS
A government allotment officer (center), assisted by an interpreter (left) takes information from American Horse, an Oglala Sioux leader from the Pine Ridge reservation in South Dakota, as they negotiate his personal allotment of land.

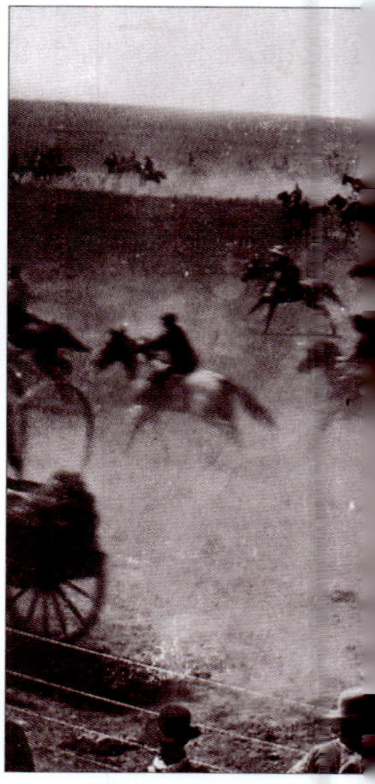

△ STAMPEDE FOR LAND
At a starting signal at high noon on 16 September 1893, over 100,000 whites raced to claim a piece of the Cherokee Outlet – Cherokee land that was previously leased to cattle ranchers, and coveted by settlers.

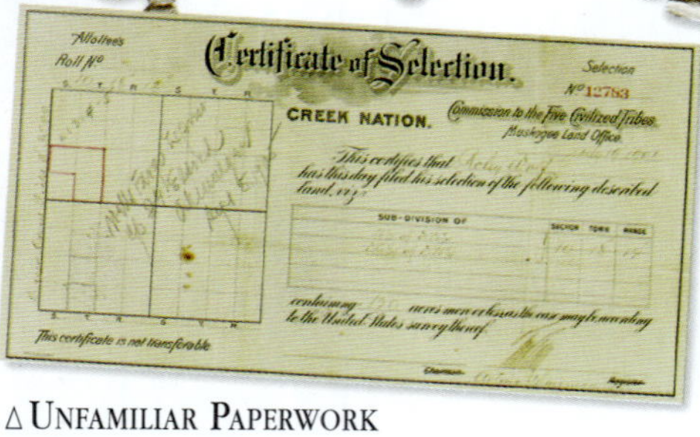

Allotee's Roll No

Certificate of Selection.

Selection No 12783

CREEK NATION.

Commission to the Five Civilized Tribes
Muskogee Land Office

This certifies that ... has this day filed his selection of the following described land, viz:

SUB-DIVISION OF | SECTION | TOWN | RANGE

containing ... acres more or less, as the case may be, according to the United States survey thereof.

This certificate is not transferable

Chairman

△ UNFAMILIAR PAPERWORK
Land transactions by white people required written documents, a concept that was foreign to Indians. This certificate spells out the location of one Creek Indian's allotted tract following the tribe's allotment agreement.

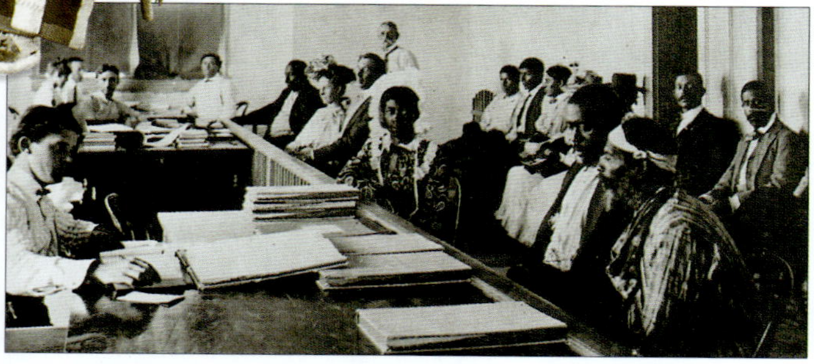

△ CHICKASAW FREEDMEN FILE CLAIMS
An 1866 treaty with the US required the Chickasaws to share their tribal lands, including allotments, with their former slaves. Each of the 4,607 freedmen was entitled to an allotment of 40 acres (16 hectares.) Here Chickasaw freedmen file claims for their plots at Tishimingo, the tribal capital.

▽ OPEN FOR BUSINESS
Federal land offices were hastily constructed at Guthrie Station in Oklahoma and at the Kingfisher stage stop 30 miles (48 km) further west, so homesteaders could file their claims for land.

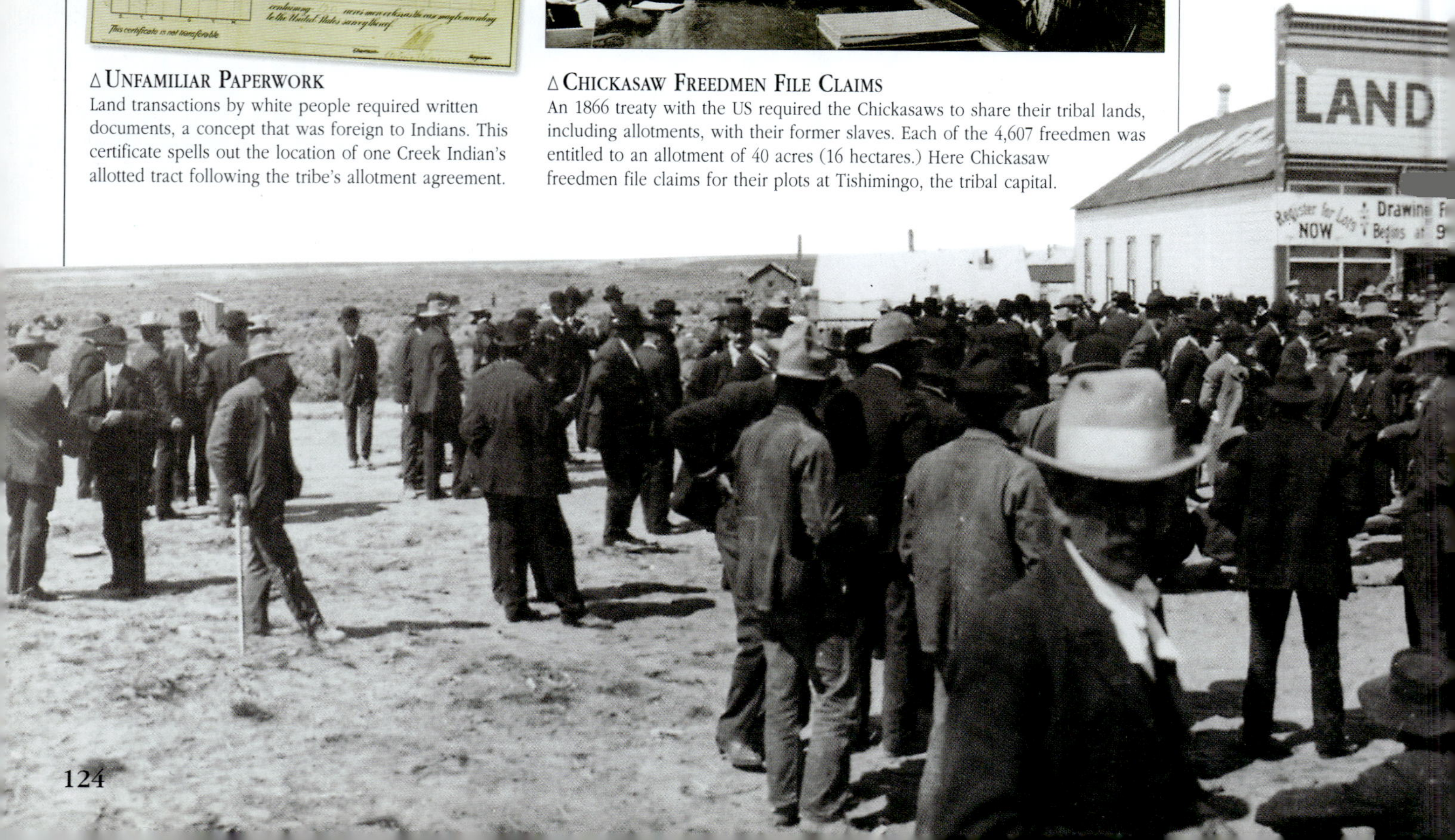

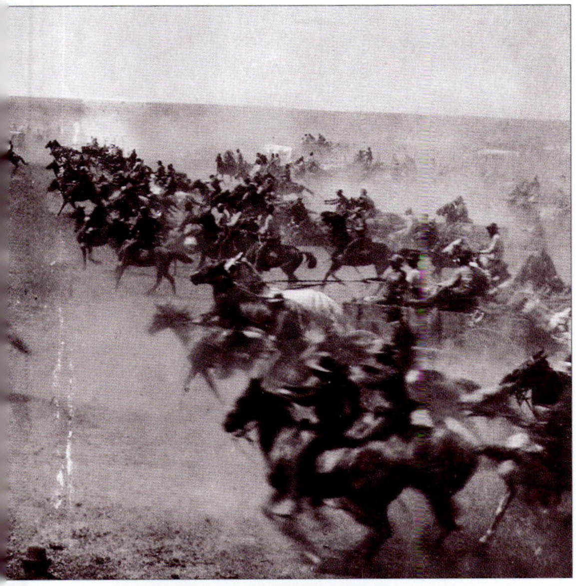

A RUSH FOR TERRITORY

On 27 March 1889, President Benjamin Harrison issued a proclamation opening the "unassigned" lands of Indian Territory for settlement, and set the stage for one of the most dramatic land rushes in US history. Land-hungry people came from all over the US and from other nations to stake out claims on the unused portions of the area inhabited by the Five Tribes.

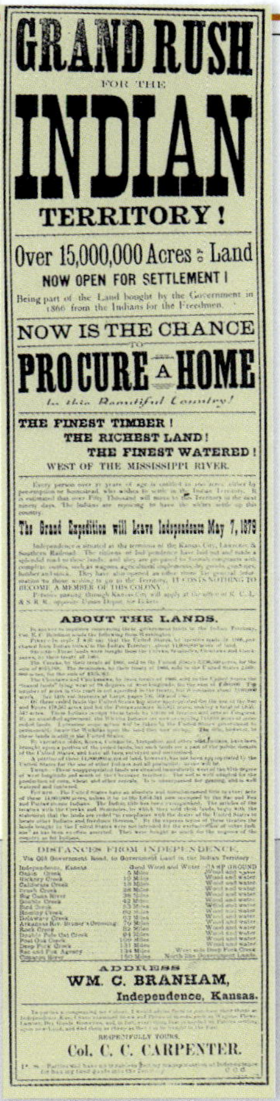

▽ THE BIRTH OF GUTHRIE
At 4 p.m. on the afternoon of 22 April 1889 – the day of the first Oklahoma land rush – a young photographer, William S. Prettyman, captured this picture as the city of Guthrie, Oklahoma, began to emerge. By the end of the day, a city of tents had been established, with stores and banks doing business.

MARKETING A MYTH ▷
Despite the rhetoric in this 1879 poster, the only whites permitted in Indian Territory at that point were hired hands working Indian farmland, cattlemen in the Cherokee Outlet, traders, and workers on railroads, mines, and forests. Homesteaders were officially barred until 1889.

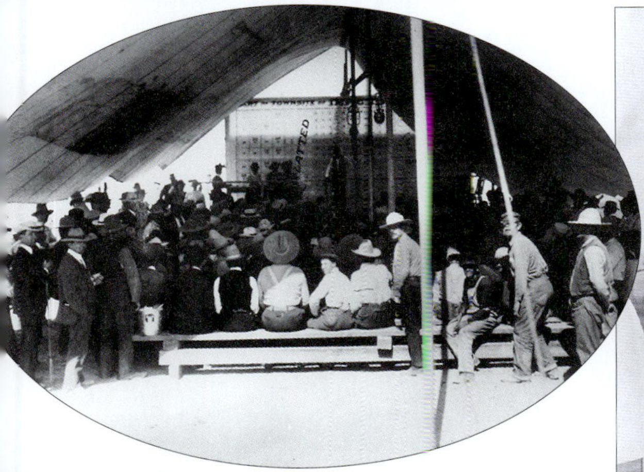

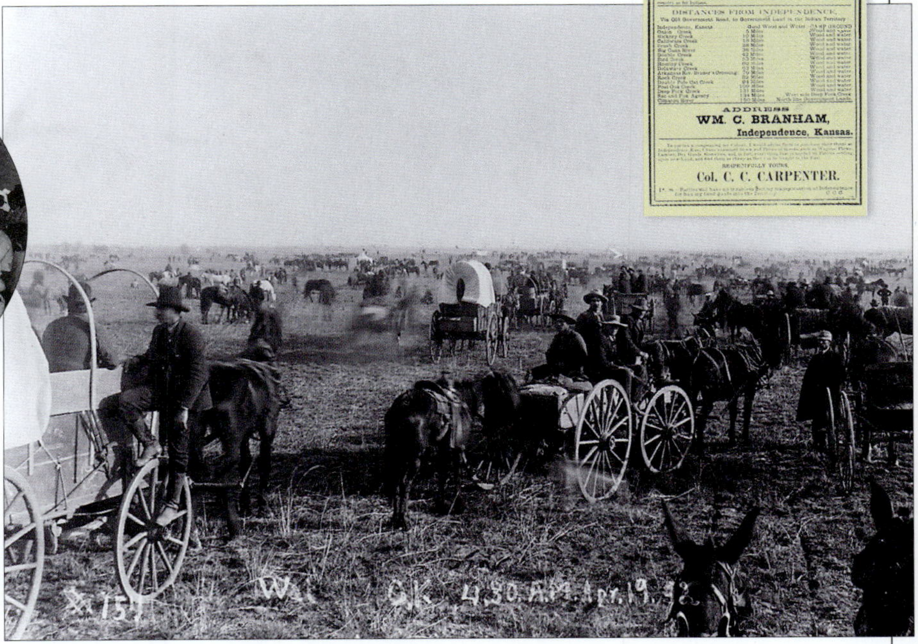

△ CALIFORNIAN LAND AUCTION
After increasing numbers of whites streamed into California, non-Indian squatters moved onto reservations in southern California. Angry Indians were eventually forced to accept allotments and to move off their land. Here, hopeful land purchasers attend a California development company auction.

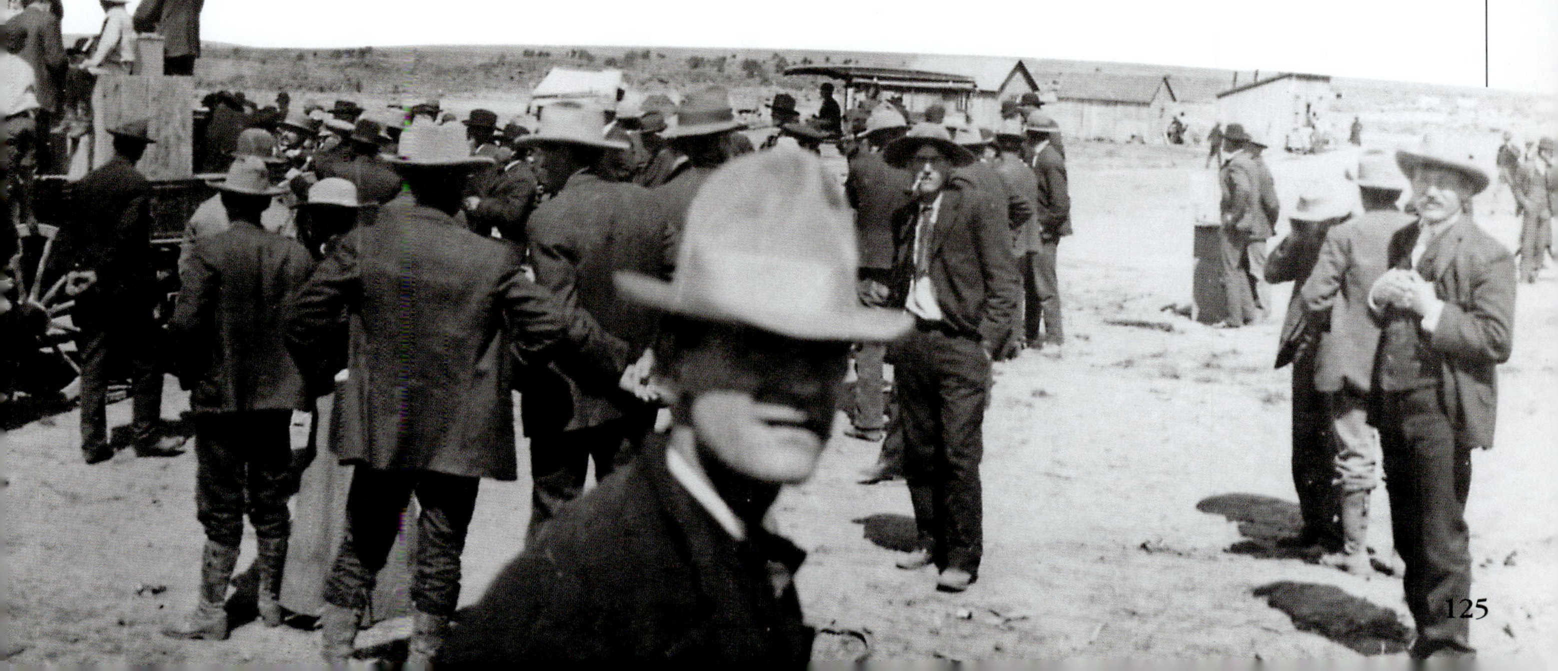

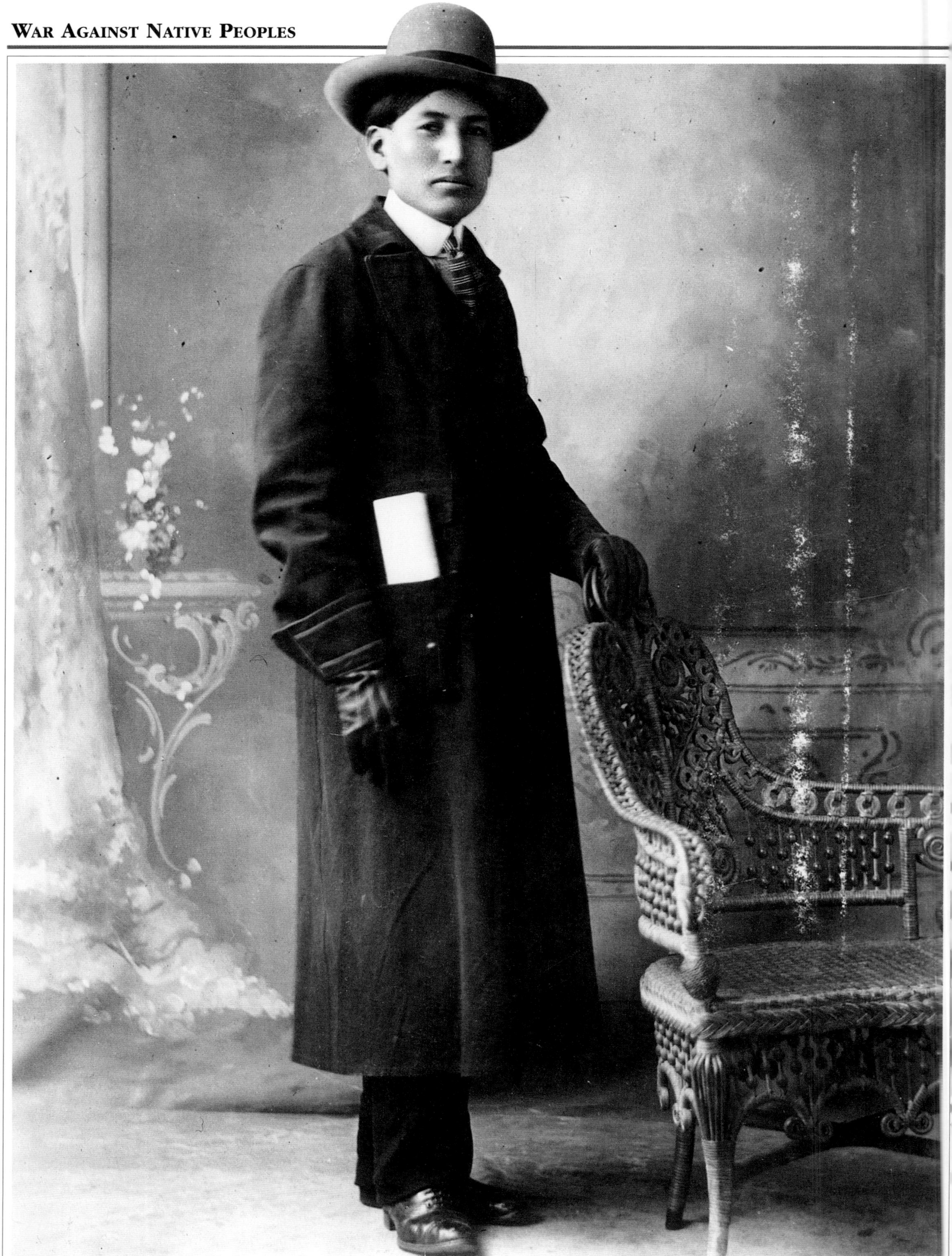

CARL SWEEZY

c. 1953: ON RECAPTURING THE THRILL OF THE BUFFALO HUNT ON RESERVATION ISSUE DAYS

BORN IN INDIAN TERRITORY, Arapaho Carl Sweezy (*c.* 1881–1953) took great pride in his Indian heritage and achieved fame as an artist, painting everything he knew about the traditional Arapaho way of life. He did not sign his early paintings or keep a record of his sales, but his works hang in institutions and private collections throughout the US. Sweezy's conversations with Althea Bass are recounted in *The Arapaho Way: A Memoir of an Indian Boyhood*, published in 1966 – 13 years after his death. The book, from which this extract is taken, provides a good deal of tribal history as well as an account of his life.

"Issue days were big times for all of us. The men who were to do the killing painted their faces and rode their fastest horses and brought along their best bows and arrows, or their guns. The women followed along usually with a pony travois to carry the smallest children and to bring home the beef. People all put on some of their finery, and braided some colored cloth into the manes and tails of their horses, and made a holiday out of the work they had to do. All across the prairies, on Monday mornings, people in bright colors and high spirits came riding to the issue station. There were visiting and excitement and work and feasting ahead for everyone. One by one, as the clerk stamped the ration tickets of the heads of families, the men in the corral drove a beef from the pen and sent it down the chute. Yelling and racing his pony and with his family coming along behind as close as they could manage to do, the man rode after his wohaw as it bellowed and plunged and tore across the prairie, trying to escape. Wohaw could run almost as fast and bellow and turn almost as wildly as the buffalo once did. For a few hours, the Arapaho knew once more some of the excitement of the old buffalo hunt. And when at last the beef was shot down, the women moved in with their knives and kettles, skinning the hide off and cutting up the meat to take back to their lodges. Everybody had a piece of the raw liver, fresh and warm, before the families set out for home. Then, in tipis or outside, fires were kindled; some of the beef was cooked, and the feasting began. Lodge walls were lifted at the sides if the weather was good, and the skins at the entrance were propped up overhead, so that lodges could be thrown together during the feast. It was a time of plenty and of hospitality for everyone."

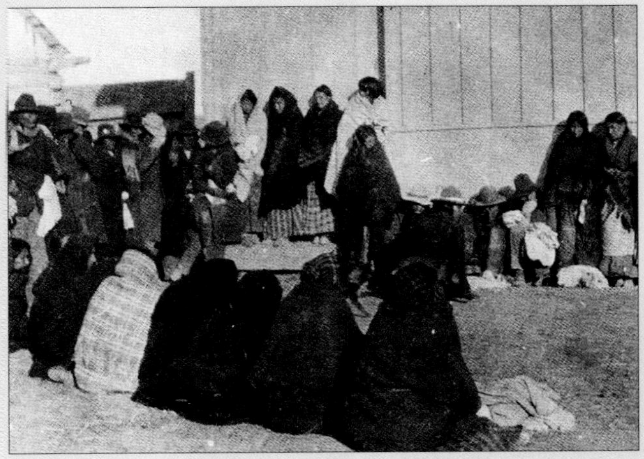

QUEUING FOR BEEF RATIONS
After the wohaw "hunts" described by Carl Sweezy were banned, slaughterhouses for butchering cattle were constructed. On ration days, such as the one pictured here in 1890 on South Dakota's Cheyenne River reservation, people were forced to wait in the bitter cold for beef rations.

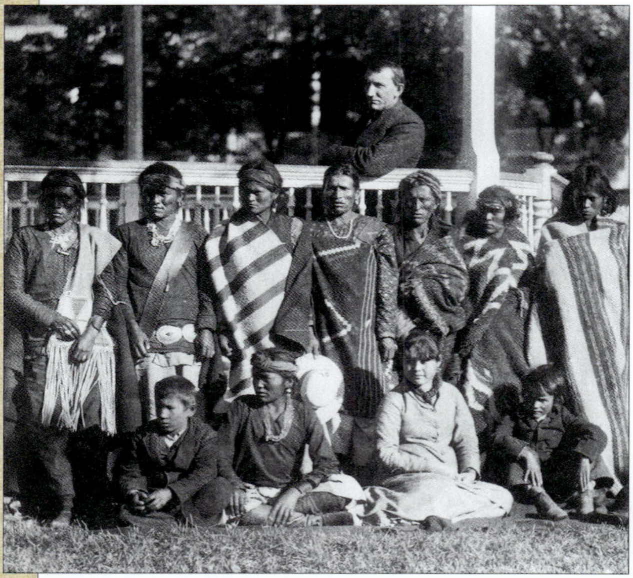

△ FATHER OF THE US BOARDING SCHOOL MOVEMENT
Captain Richard Henry Pratt established the first federally funded off-reservation boarding school in 1879, in an abandoned military barracks in Carlisle, Pennsylvania. Pratt, who advocated sudden and total immersion of Indians in white culture far from the reservation, wanted to establish enough Carlisle-style schools to enroll, by force if necessary, every Indian child in the US.

BEFORE ... ▷
In 1878, Samuel Armstrong, the founder of Hampton Institute – forerunner of the off-reservation boarding school – and Captain Pratt began photographing Indian children before and after their institutionalization. Pratt used these photographs to prove that Indians could be induced to abandon their traditional ways.

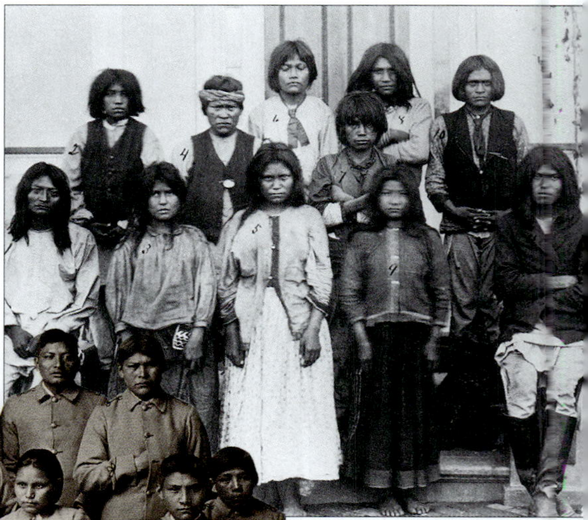

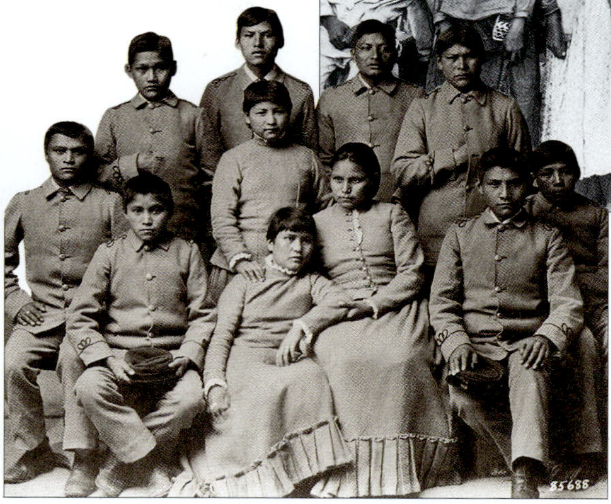

◁ ... AFTER
When Indian children arrived at boarding schools, they were photographed in school uniform and shirtwaist dresses, hard sho in place of soft moccasins, and with their long hair cropped. Th cultural transformation was completed by giving the children new Euroamericanized names.

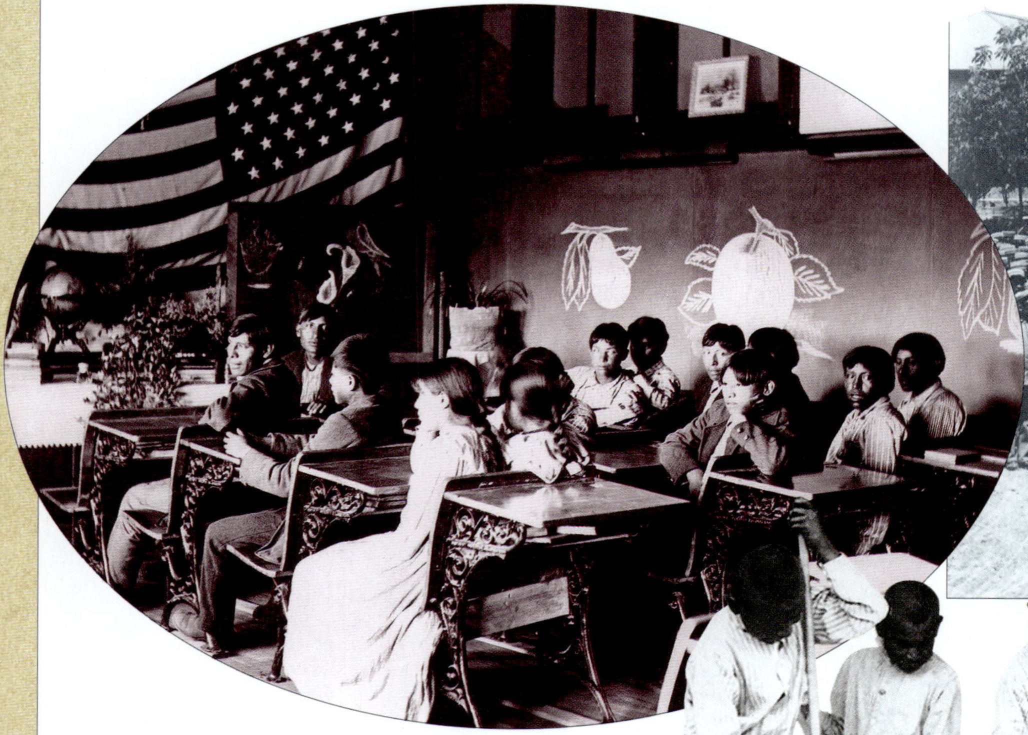

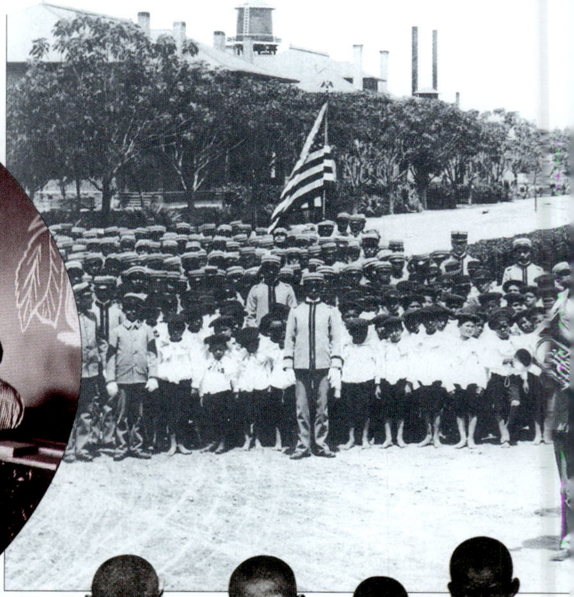

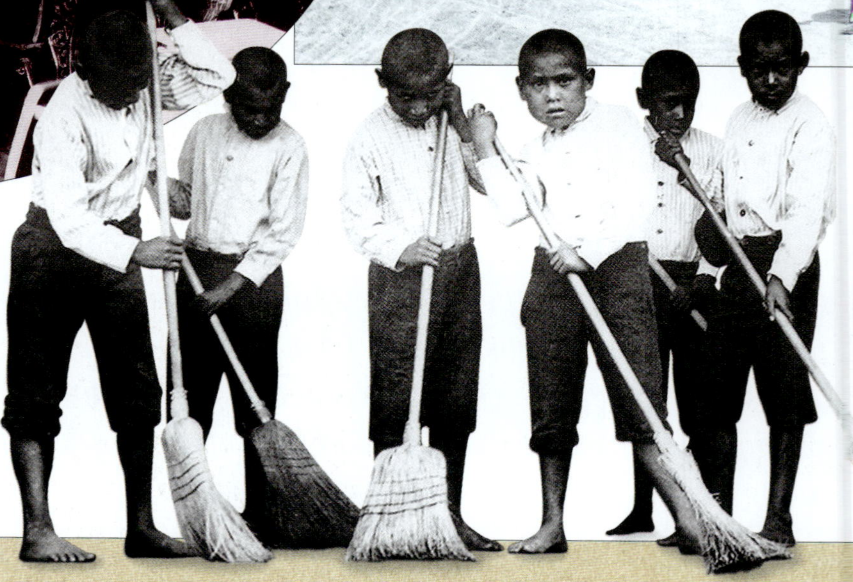

△ THE THREE RS
For half the day, boarding school teachers taught formal academic subjects; the other half was spent on "vocational skills." Boarding school education also covered religious instruction and worship and citizenship training, which included US history courses and patriotic singing.

CHEAP LABOR ▷
Because the federal government never provided enough money or staff, student labor was used to maintain the schools, with the result that children spent more hours cleaning, cooking, sewing, laundering, farming, and doing maintenance work than they did in classroom learning.

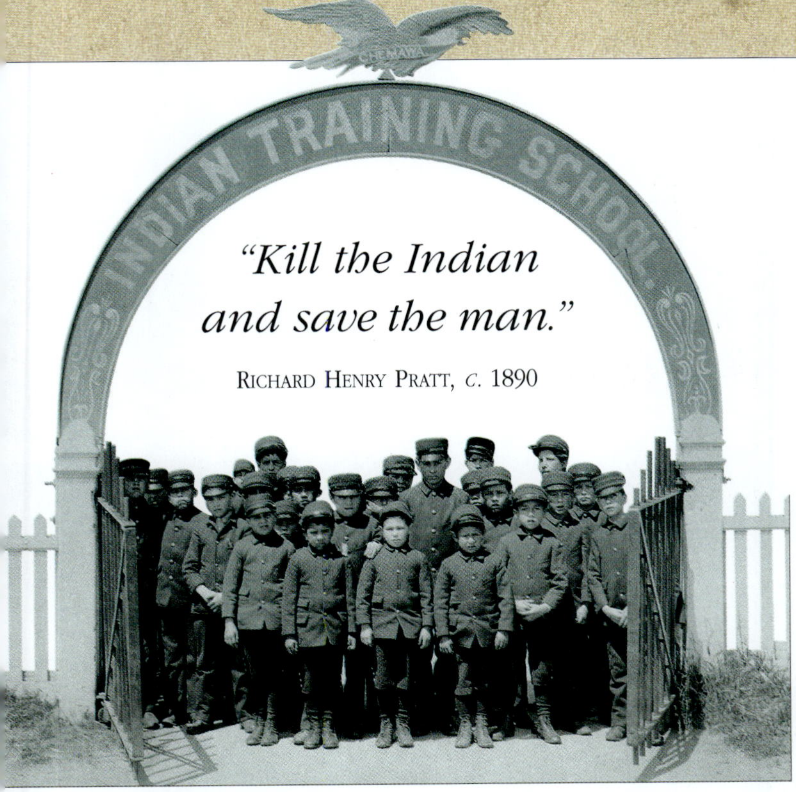

"Kill the Indian and save the man."

Richard Henry Pratt, c. 1890

Boarding Schools

In the late 1800s, federal policy makers in North America moved aggressively to "civilize" Indians according to Euroamerican/Canadian standards. They believed that one of the greatest barriers to assimilation was the Indians' attachment to tribal life. By separating Indian children (some only four years old) from their kinspeople and sending them to boarding schools, preferably located far from their homes and communities, it was hoped that assimilation would be finally achieved. If parents refused to let their children go, Indian agents on reservations threatened to withhold food rations until they cooperated. Some parents tried to hide their children, but agency police tracked them down and dragged them from their hiding places.

Destroying Indian Identity

Most boarding schools separated children and families for at least eight to nine months. During this time, a twofold assault on Indian children's identity took place: the schools stripped away all outward and inward signs of the children's identification with tribal life, at the same time instructing them in the values and behaviors of white culture.

Breaking rules in boarding schools led to punishments: in some institutions, bedwetters had to carry their mattresses around with them all day. Children caught speaking their Native language or performing religious rituals had to stand on tiptoe for hours, with their arms stretched over their heads. Disobedient girls were ordered to lift their dresses while they were spanked in front of their classmates. A runaway boy might be forced to wear a girl's dress, or be whipped with a rubber hose, or forced to wear a ball and chain around his ankle. A more common punishment was confinement in a dark basement on a bread-and-water diet.

At the close of the school year, many Indian students were sent to live with Euroamerican families, to undertake farm work and household chores, become immersed in the English language, and to absorb non-Indian Christian values. These summer programs ensured that some students did not return home for years.

Chemawa Indian Schoolboys
e success of Carlisle Indian School led to an expansion of off-reservation, industrial boarding hools like Chemawa Indian School, established in Oregon in 1880. By the turn of the century, reservation and 25 off-reservation schools had been created. Although some schools were uated near reservations, students were discouraged from ving direct contact with relatives.

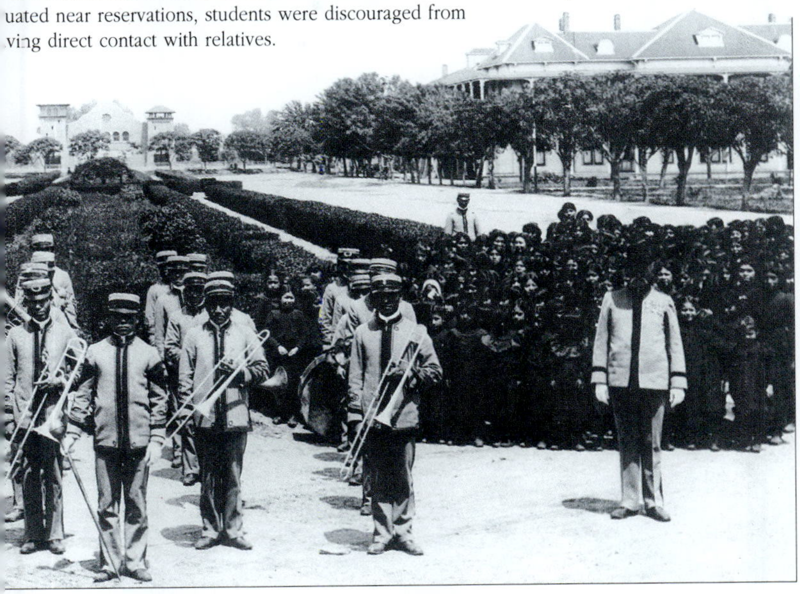

Strike up the Band
he Phoenix (Arizona) Indian School band rovided an outlet for students with good rades. Besides being relieved of ordinary hores so they could practice, band members aveled regularly to different cities where they erformed at parades and fairs.

Iilitary Regimen ▷
ntil the 1930s, life in boarding schools, which ere often housed in unused army barracks, as run along military lines. Children were equired to march in uniforms, in military ormations, to meals and classes – and in their ee time, to keep them out of trouble.

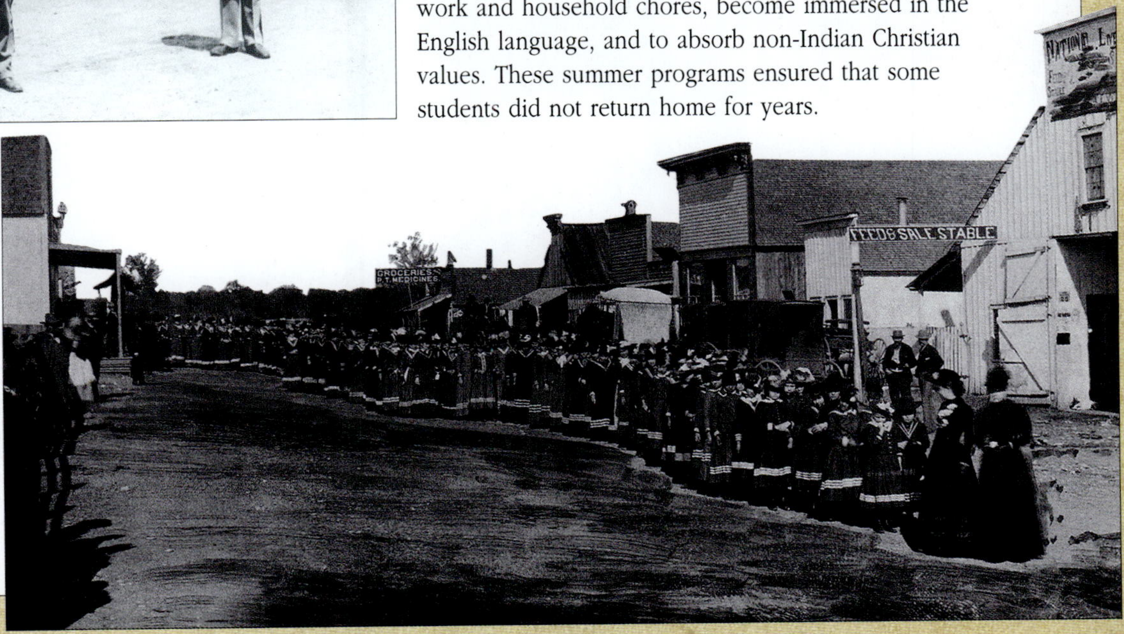

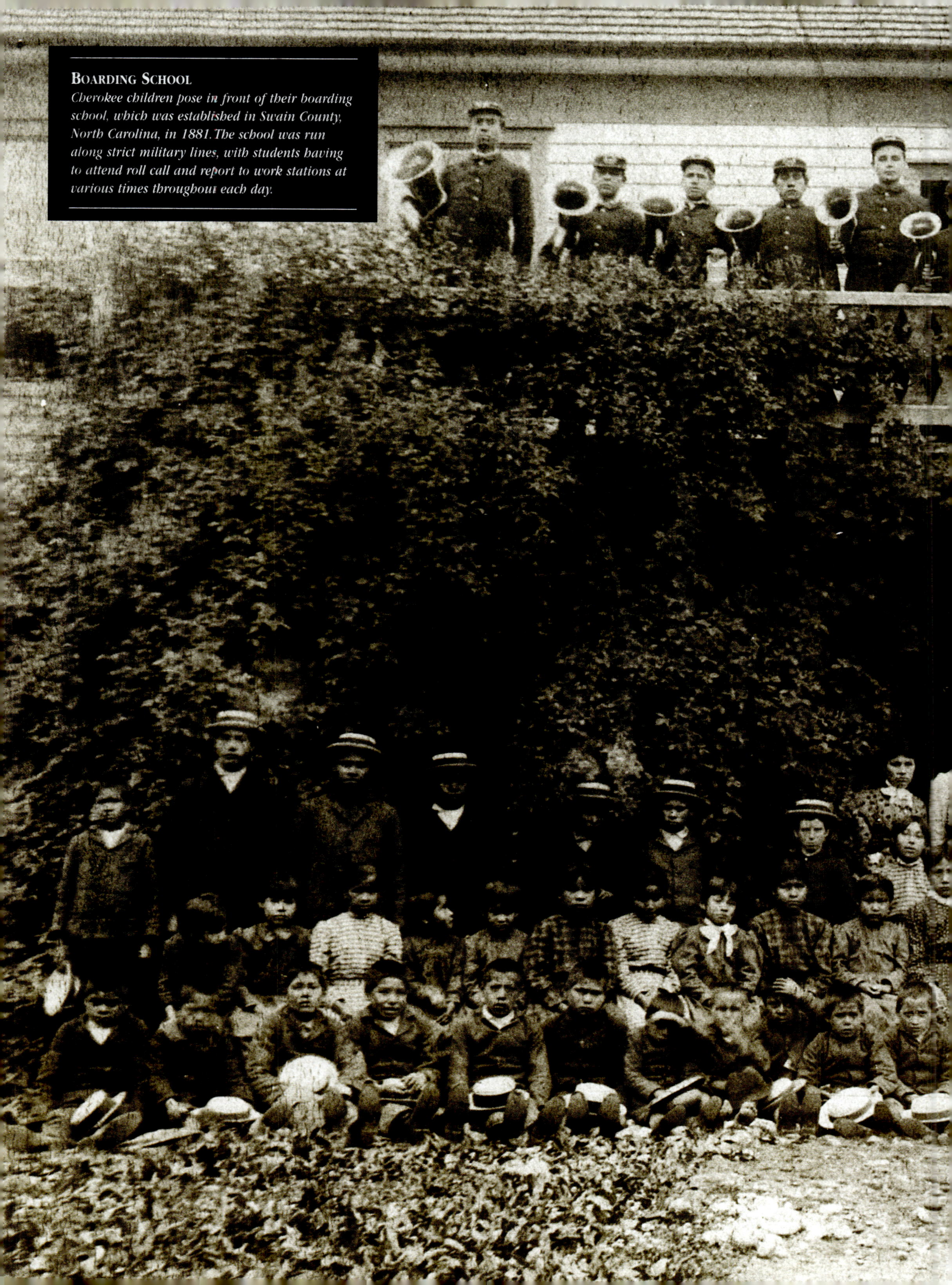

Boarding School

Cherokee children pose in front of their boarding school, which was established in Swain County, North Carolina, in 1881. The school was run along strict military lines, with students having to attend roll call and report to work stations at various times throughout each day.

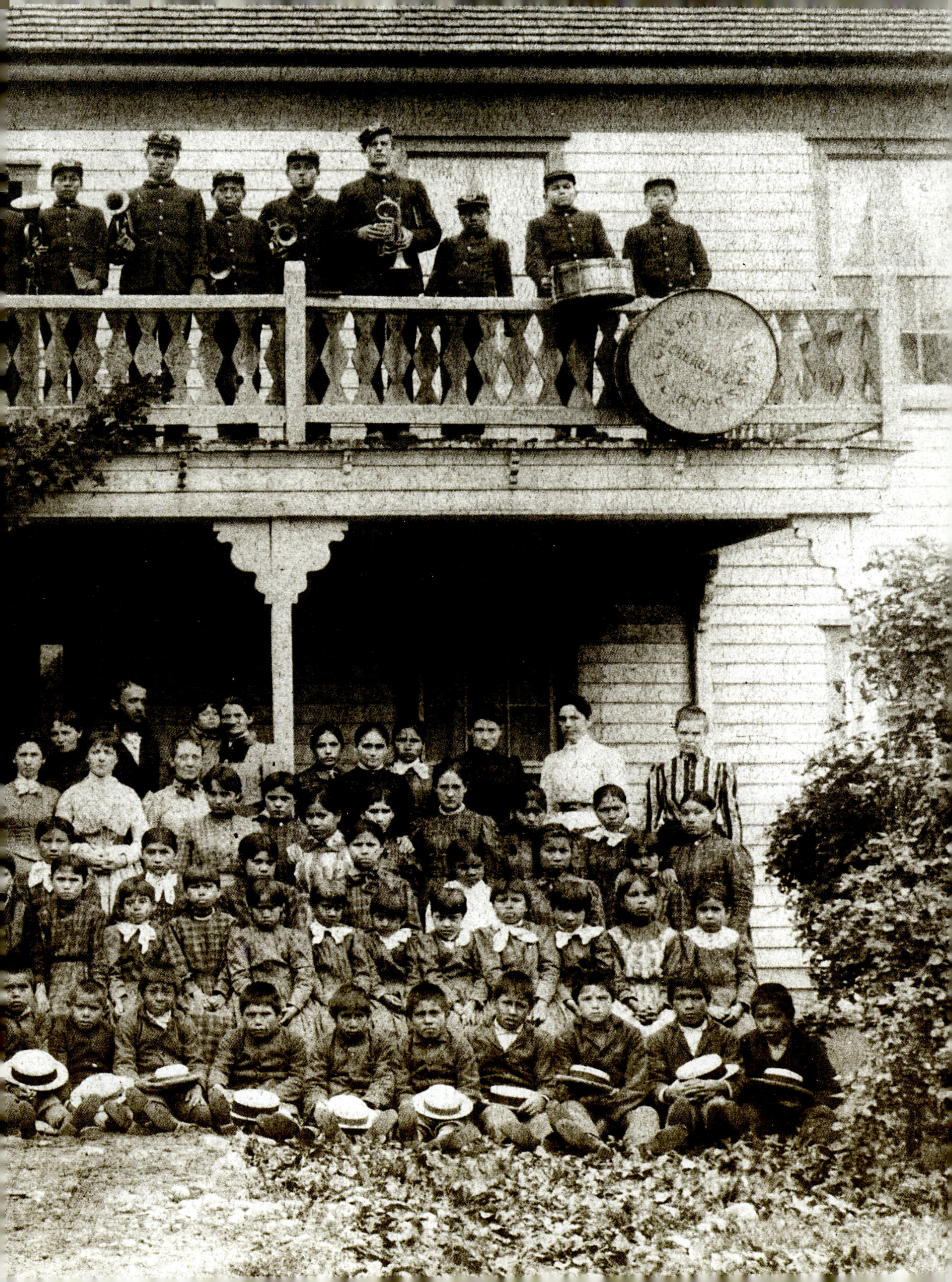

THE END OF ARMED RESISTANCE

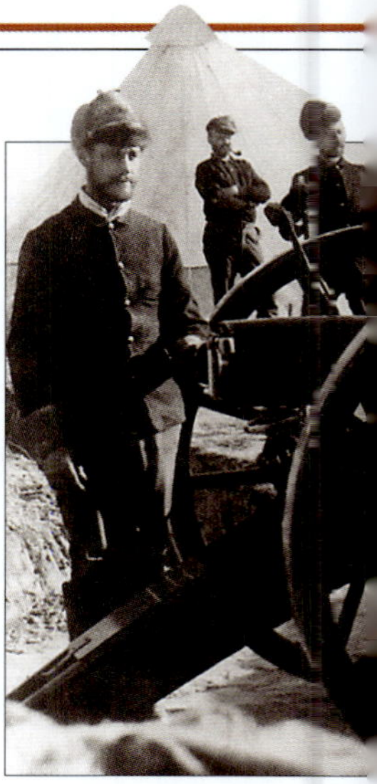

IN 1890, THE WRETCHED SITUATION on the Lakota reservations led Indians to embrace the Ghost Dance religion, based on a vision received by the Paiute prophet Wovoka. The dance frightened many whites in Dakota Territory and the US government responded by sending over half the US army to the reservations. A disastrous chain of events led to Sitting Bull's murder and to the massacre of Big Foot's band of Lakotas at Wounded Knee, South Dakota. This was the last significant armed conflict between the US army and American Indians, and one of the most appalling tragedies in US history.

BIG FOOT KILLED

A Lakota war chief throughout the 1870s, Big Foot initially accepted the Ghost Dance religion but after concluding that it preached nothing but desperation, he gave it up. Seriously ill with pneumonia, Big Foot was shot down at the Wounded Knee massacre.

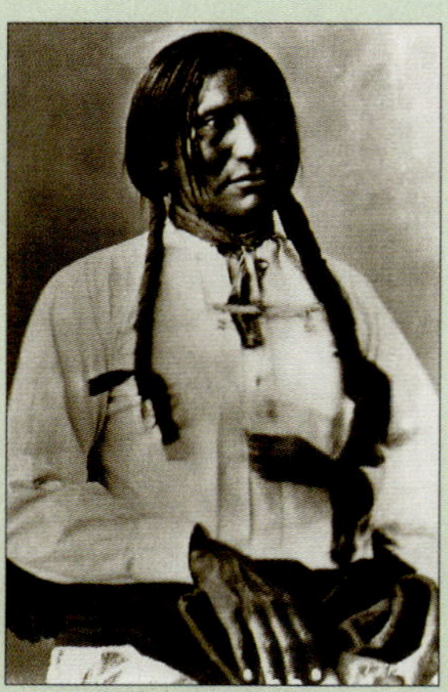

BIG FOOT

IN THE YEARS PRECEDING Wounded Knee, the Lakota were overwhelmed by the flood of settlers onto their lands. A gold rush in the 1870s intensified efforts by whites to claim the sacred Black Hills, which formed part of the reservation area assigned to the Lakota by the 1868 Fort Laramie Treaty. The sale of the Black Hills would have allowed whites to mine there legally, but the Lakota refused to sell.

In 1876, frustrated by the Lakota's refusal to part with the Black Hills, the government ordered their confinement to the reservation, declaring that Indians found off the reservation would be considered combatants and forced to return. Subsequent military attacks against off-reservation Indians were a success for the army, apart from the defeat of Custer's Seventh Cavalry troops on 25 June 1876. In reaction to Custer's defeat, the US government forced the Lakotas to sell the Black Hills.

In 1889, the situation on the reservation was desperate. The US failed to honor its promise of increased rations in return for the Lakotas' agreement to reduce Sioux treaty lands by half and create six separate and smaller reservations (Pine Ridge, Cheyenne River, Rosebud, Standing Rock, Crow Creek, and Lower Brulé). Conditions were ripe for the Ghost Dance religion on Lakota reservations.

Emergence of the Ghost Dance

The Ghost Dance originated in Nevada about 1888, under the leadership of Wovoka, a Paiute prophet. He prophesied that if Indians sang and danced to certain songs, the buffalo and deceased relatives and friends would return and the white man would disappear. A delegation of Plains tribal leaders, who had visited Wovoka, brought the dance back and taught it to others. By the fall of 1890, Ghost Dancing was taking place regularly in various locations on Lakota reservations.

At this time, the loss of the buffalo, drought, famine, influenza, and the prohibition of their traditional religious rites were decimating the Lakotas. Starving Indians were forbidden to

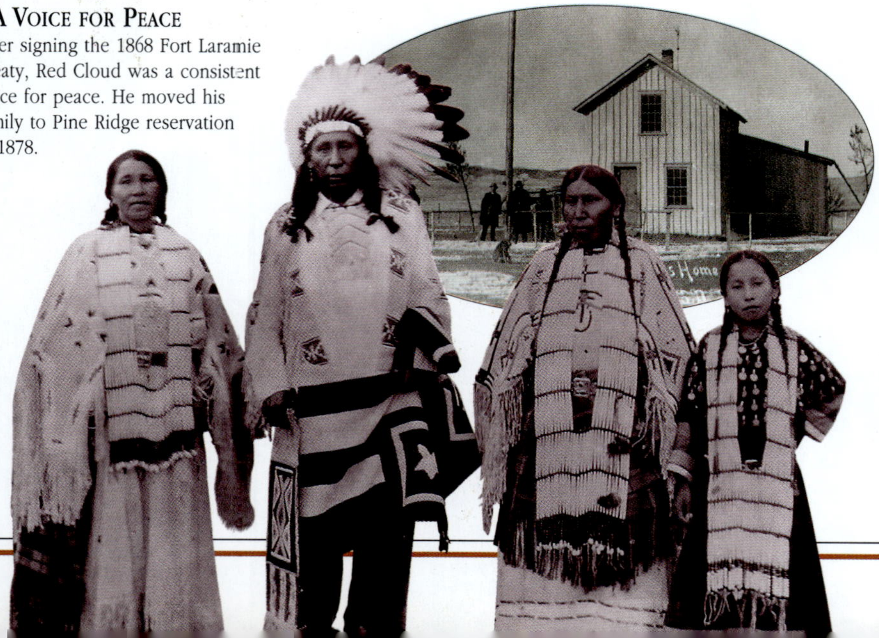

▽ A VOICE FOR PEACE
After signing the 1868 Fort Laramie Treaty, Red Cloud was a consistent voice for peace. He moved his family to Pine Ridge reservation in 1878.

◁ HOME AT PINE RIDGE
Red Cloud stands in front of his two-story frame house at the Pine Ridge reservation agency. The Bureau of Indian Affairs built the house in 1879, hoping that others would follow him and abandon their tipis to live in log or frame homes.

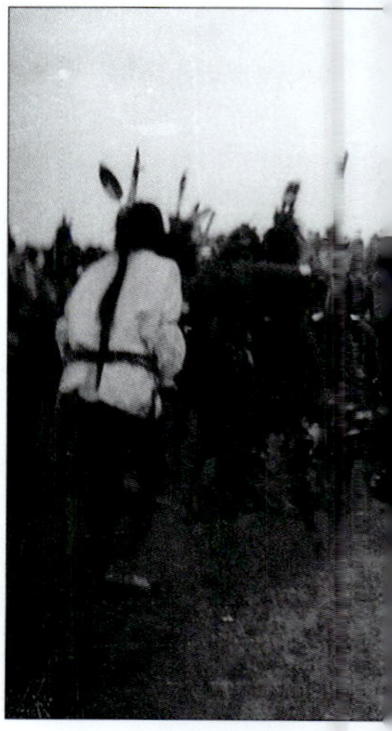

THE DANCE CONTINUES ▷
On Christmas Day 1890, a photographer caught Lakota Indians dancing on the Pine Ridge reservation. Agency officials sent Indian police to persuade them to discontinue, but no amount of threats could induce them to stop.

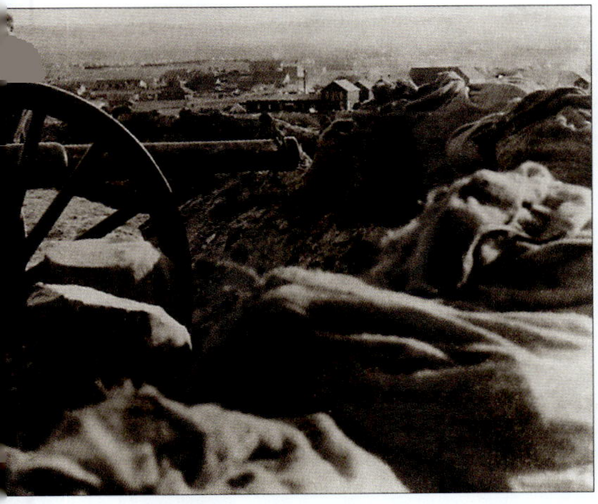

◁ WEAPONS OF WAR
Forsyth's troops positioned Hotchkiss cannons on a rise overlooking Big Foot's camp at Pine Ridge. From a distance of less than 100 yards (91 meters), the troops unleashed a hail of explosive shells on the camp, with devastating effects.

SCOUTS IN DEMAND ▷
Oglala Lakota scouts are seen drilling at South Dakota's Pine Ridge reservation in 1890. White commanders prized the services of the scouts, who had enlisted as regular troops.

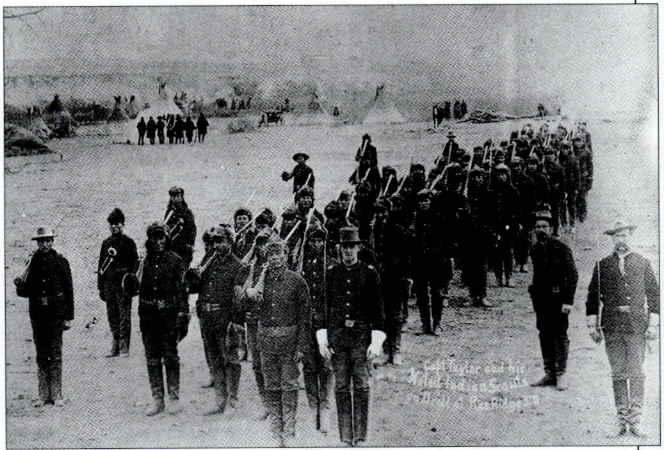

hunt game, and subsistence rations had been cut in half – or, due to corruption in the Bureau of Indian Affairs, were non-existent. Ghost dancing offered the Indians hope.

In October 1890, the Lakotas of Pine Ridge and Rosebud defied their agents and danced themselves to pitches of excitement that frightened government employees. In mid-November, Lakotas, dancing in shirts they believed to be bulletproof, set off a panic among white settlers. Pine Ridge agent Daniel F. Royer, fearful of an uprising, called for military help to restore order. Observers at the time held newspapers accountable for creating a genocidal frenzy and an unwarranted fear in the settlers that could only lead to bloodshed.

Massacre at Wounded Knee

On 15 December, an event occurred that set off a chain reaction ending in the massacre at Wounded Knee. Sitting Bull was murdered at his cabin on the Standing Rock reservation by Indian police who were trying to arrest him, on government orders. Refugees from Sitting Bull's camp, who had fled in fear, joined Big Foot at the Cheyenne River reservation. Unaware that Big Foot had renounced the Ghost Dance, General Nelson A. Miles ordered him to move his people to a nearby fort. On 28 December, Big Foot, seriously ill with pneumonia, set off to seek shelter with Chief Red Cloud at Pine Ridge reservation. Big Foot and his band were intercepted by Major Samuel Whitside and his detachment of the Seventh Cavalry, and were escorted to Wounded Knee Creek where Colonel James W. Forsyth assumed command.

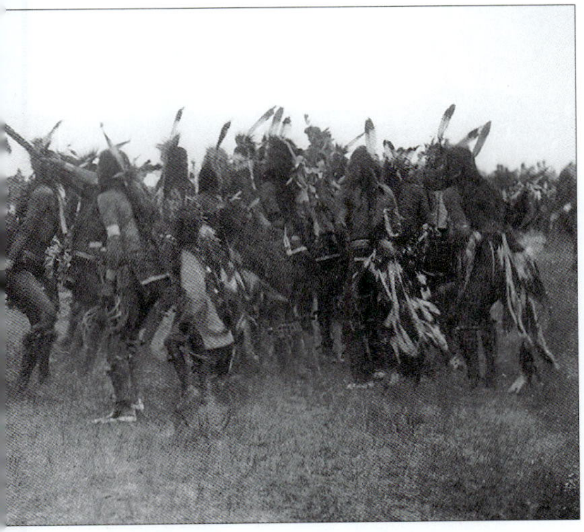

On 29 December, surrounded by troops and with Hotchkiss cannons positioned above Big Foot's camp, the Indians were informed that it was necessary to disarm them to prevent violence. A search was ordered, which turned up only a small number of weapons. As tension mounted, a scuffle broke out between a soldier and an Indian, during which a gun discharged. As troopers shouldered their rifles, a few warriors produced concealed weapons. The soldiers opened fire on the Lakotas, their Hotchkiss guns shredding tipis and killing some 300 men, women, and children. As they were firing, many of the soldiers were said to have yelled repeatedly, "Remember the Little Bighorn," or "Remember Custer."

After the shooting stopped, US army personnel gathered up their 25 dead and 39 wounded soldiers (some of whom died later) who had been caught in their own crossfire. Soldiers stripped the bodies of dead Lakotas, keeping as souvenirs Ghost Dance shirts and other clothing and equipment belonging to the Lakota people.

INFANT SURVIVOR

An infant named Lost Bird, orphaned by the massacre, was found alive under the slain body of her mother, who had shielded her from gunfire with her own body. Brigadier General Leonard W. Colby, pictured here, rode into the Indian camp and took Lost Bird, by force, from the elderly Lakota woman to whom she had been entrusted. He adopted the child, naming her Marguerite Colby, and later described her as a "living curio" of the massacre. Initially, Colby spoiled Lost Bird but then ran off with his housemaid, leaving his wife to raise the child.

BRIGADIER GENERAL LEONARD W. COLBY WITH LOST BIRD

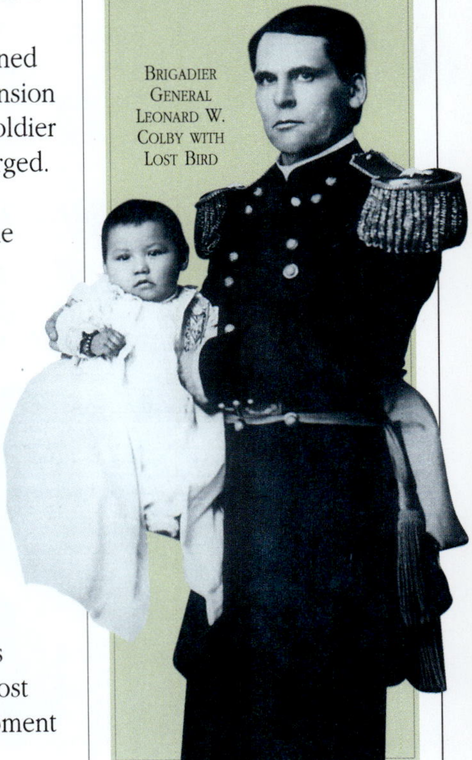

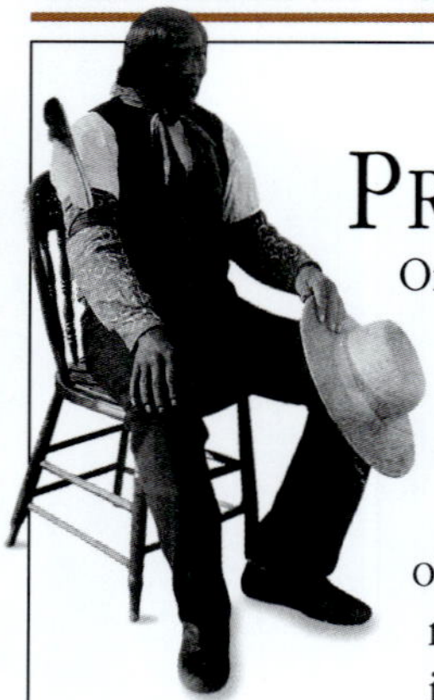

PRAYER OF SUFFERING

Originated by Wovoka, who was influenced by earlier visionaries among his people, the Ghost Dance found followers among the Lakotas at a time of great suffering and deprivation. Widespread hunger was a major cause of the unrest. Through the winter of 1889–90, many Lakotas lived close to starvation: not only had the government made deep cuts in beef provisions but, in the summer of 1890, a drought caused many crops to fail.

PAIUTE PROPHET WOVOKA

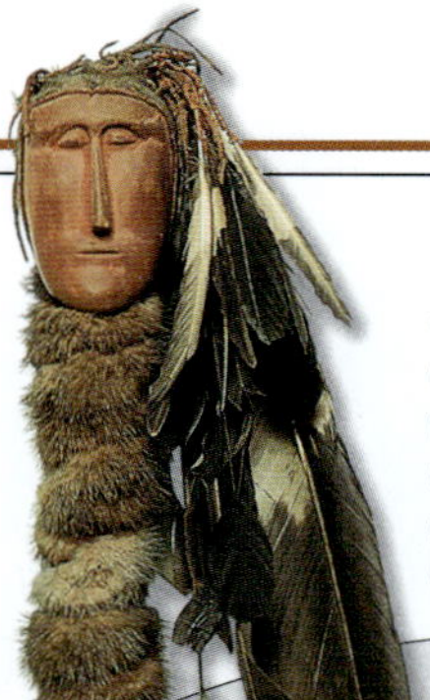

◁ SACRED WAND SEEN IN A VISION
Ghost Dancers sought visions in which they visited the spirit world. In later dances, they carried objects that they had seen in visions. The owner of this sacred wand saw his spirit helper during a Ghost Dance and carved his face on the wand.

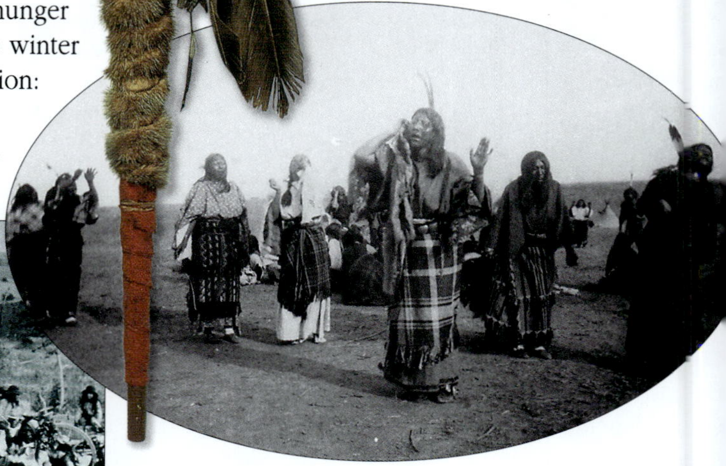

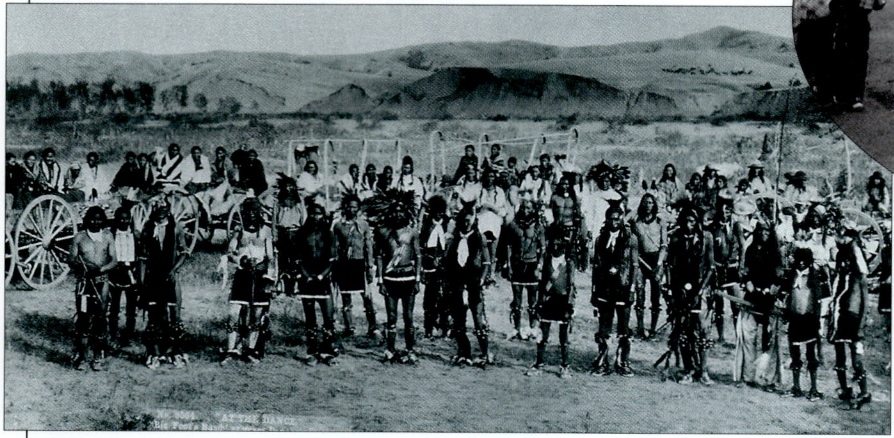

◁ GRASS DANCE ASSEMBLY
Members of Big Foot's band assembled for a "grass dance" on the Cheyenne River reservation on 9 August 1890. Some months later, most of those photographed were killed at Wounded Knee.

△ POWER OF THE DANCE
Arapaho men and women took part in the Ghost Dance, singing and dancing until they were exhausted and entranced. In their trances, their spirits visited with departed relatives and friends.

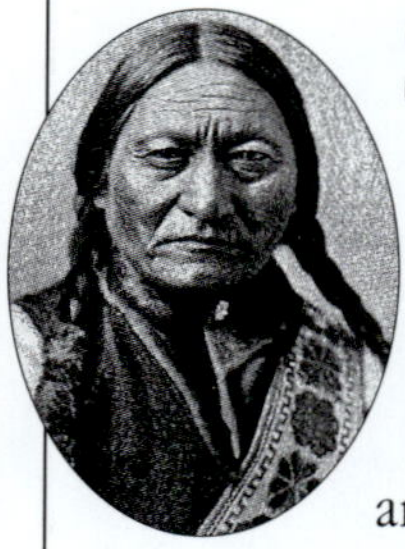

SITTING BULL KILLED

Sitting Bull, who had been living since 1883 on the Standing Rock reservation in Dakota Territory, became interested in the Ghost Dance religion in the fall of 1890. Alarmed by the chief's interest, General Miles wanted him arrested and, just before daylight on 15 December 1890, Indian police surrounded Sitting Bull's cabin.

SITTING BULL

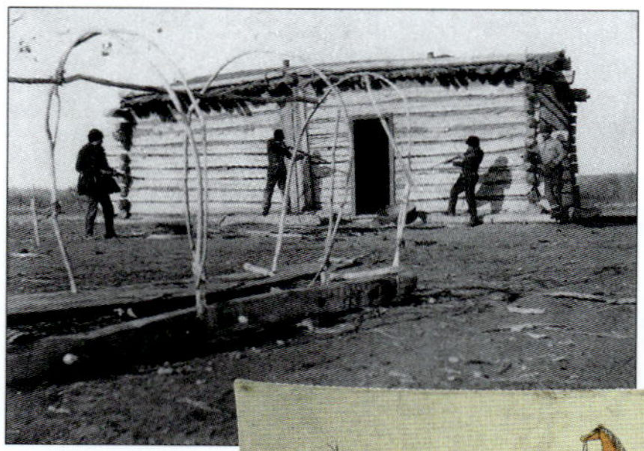

◁ THE ARREST REENACTED
George W. Scott, a Fort Yates photographer, staged a reenactment of Sitting Bull's arrest for the camera. Others dismantled Sitting Bull's cabin and shipped it to Chicago, where it was rebuilt and exhibited during the 1892 Columbian Exposition.

"I wish it to be remembered that I was the last man of my tribe to surrender my rifle."

SITTING BULL, HUNKPAPA LAKOTA, 1881

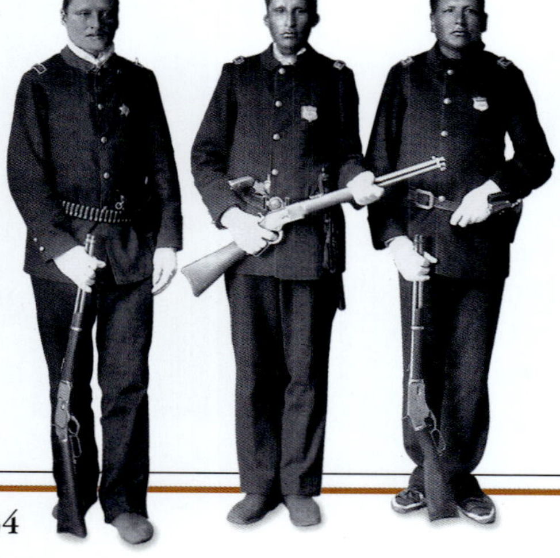

SITTING BULL'S DEATH ▷
After Sitting Bull was arrested, one of his followers shot at one of the Indian police sent to arrest him. The wounded officer fired back, striking Sitting Bull instead. This Native depiction shows the scene outside Sitting Bull's cabin.

◁ THE ARRESTING POLICE
Red Tomahawk (center), the sergeant of the Indian police at Standing Rock reservation, led the police sent to arrest Sitting Bull. He also fired at Sitting Bull, hitting him in the head, and claimed that his bullet killed the chief.

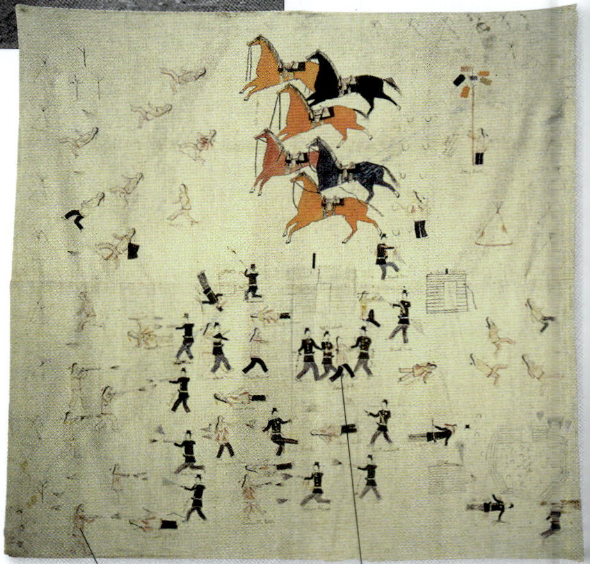

Over 150 Ghost Dancers tried to prevent Sitting Bull's arrest; seven of them were shot dead

Sitting Bull is dragged from his cabin by three of the 40 Indian police sent to arrest him

WOUNDED KNEE

Surrounded by troopers, and with Hotchkiss guns trained on the Indian camp, Big Foot's band had no escape. On the morning of 29 December, Colonel Forsyth told the Indians that they were safe and that the soldiers were their friends, but he wanted the Lakotas to hand over their guns to prevent any fighting. A search of the camp turned up a number of axes, hatchets, butcher knives, tent pegs, and fewer than 40 rifles, many in bad shape.

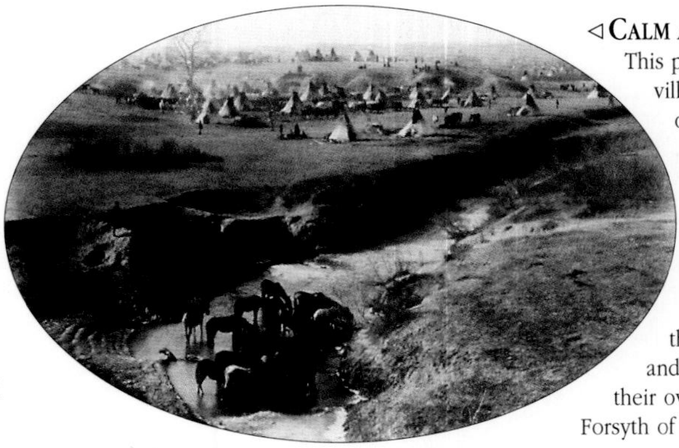

◁ **CALM AFTER THE STORM**
This peaceful scene of a Brulé (Lakota) village encamped, in 1891, on the site of the Wounded Knee massacre is in stark contrast to the carnage of the previous year.

▽ **COLONEL FORSYTH'S MEN**
Although General Nelson A. Miles condemned Forsyth for allowing the killing of women and children and for the death of soldiers killed by their own fire, a court of inquiry absolved Forsyth of any negligence or wrongdoing.

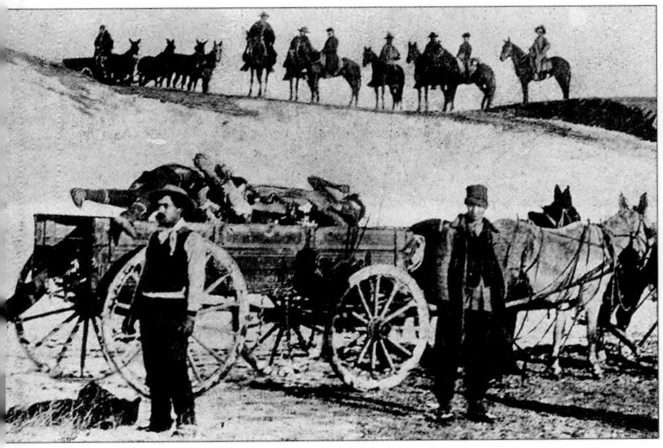

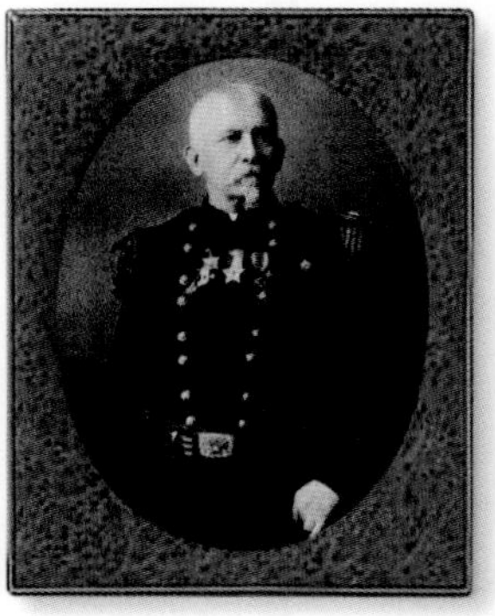

COLONEL JAMES W. FORSYTH

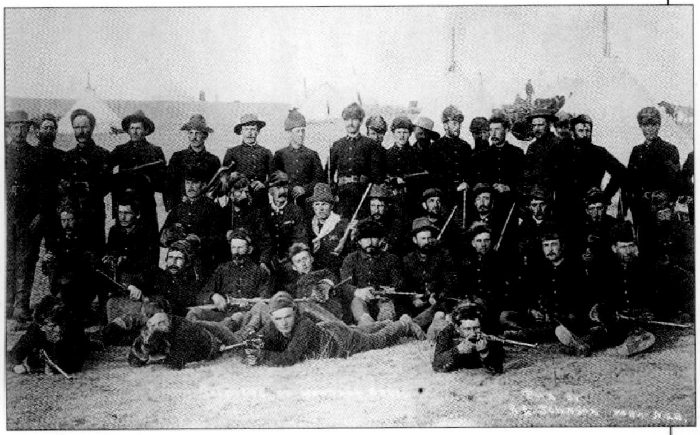

△ **GATHERING THE DEAD**
US army personnel are pictured here gathering the frozen bodies after the massacre. Some of the dead had been taken away by Indians from Pine Ridge, while other mortally wounded Indians crawled off to die elsewhere.

FROZEN AFTERMATH ▷
By the time the smoke cleared, an estimated 300 Indians lay dead. A blizzard developed and the Indian dead were left on the field. Many bodies, like that of a medicine man pictured here, froze into grotesque positions.

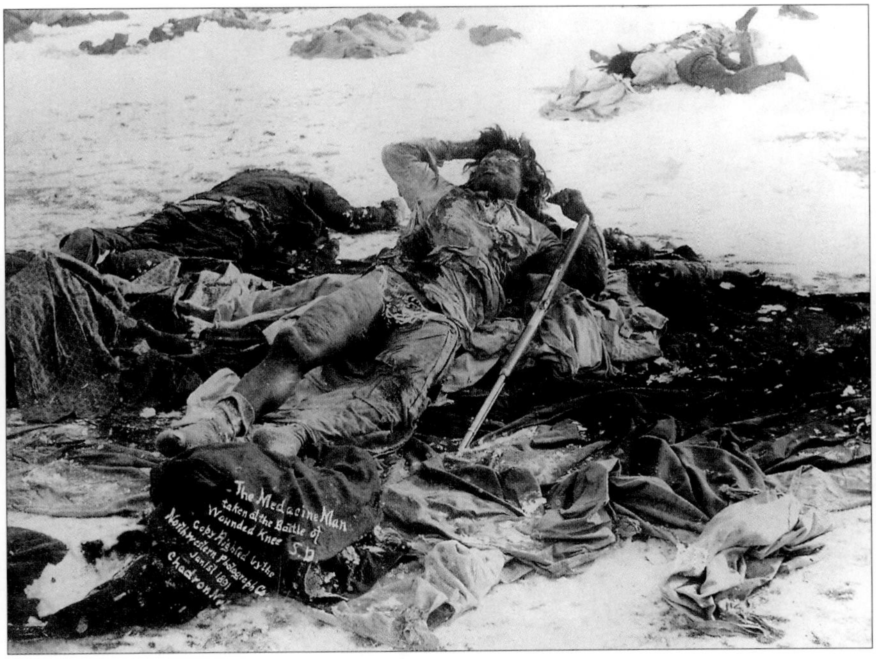

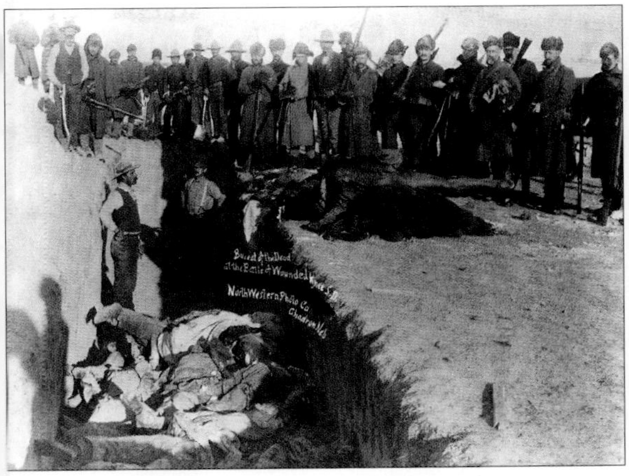

△ **MASS BURIAL**
On 1–2 January 1891, a US army burial party returned to transport the frozen bodies to a mass grave on the hill from where Hotchkiss guns had been fired.

LAKOTA WOUNDED ▷
51 Lakotas, mainly women and children, were wounded in the massacre. A few, including Lost Bird, survived the blizzard and were found several days later.

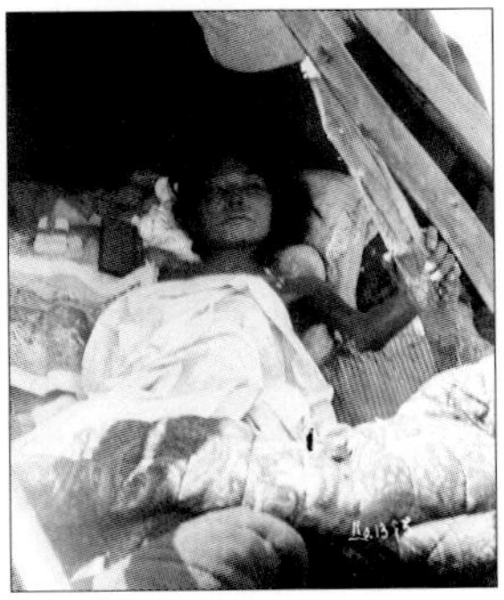

THE CAVALRY DEPART ▷
Scouts-turned-troops are here shown leaving the bloody scene after the massacre. One Indian combatant said later that it was as if the soldiers were crazed by the sight of blood and had appeared wild eyed as they shot again and again into some of the bodies.

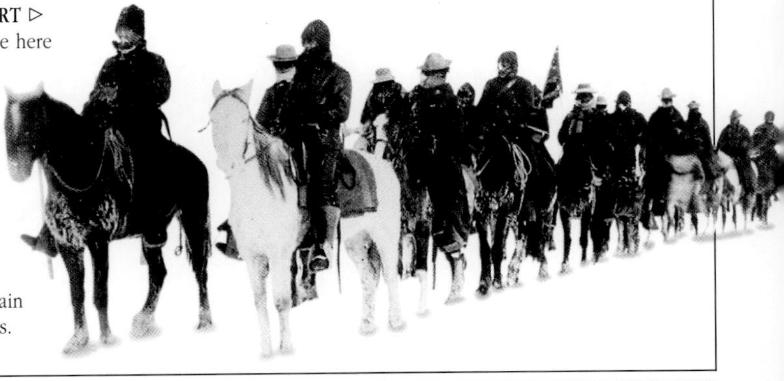

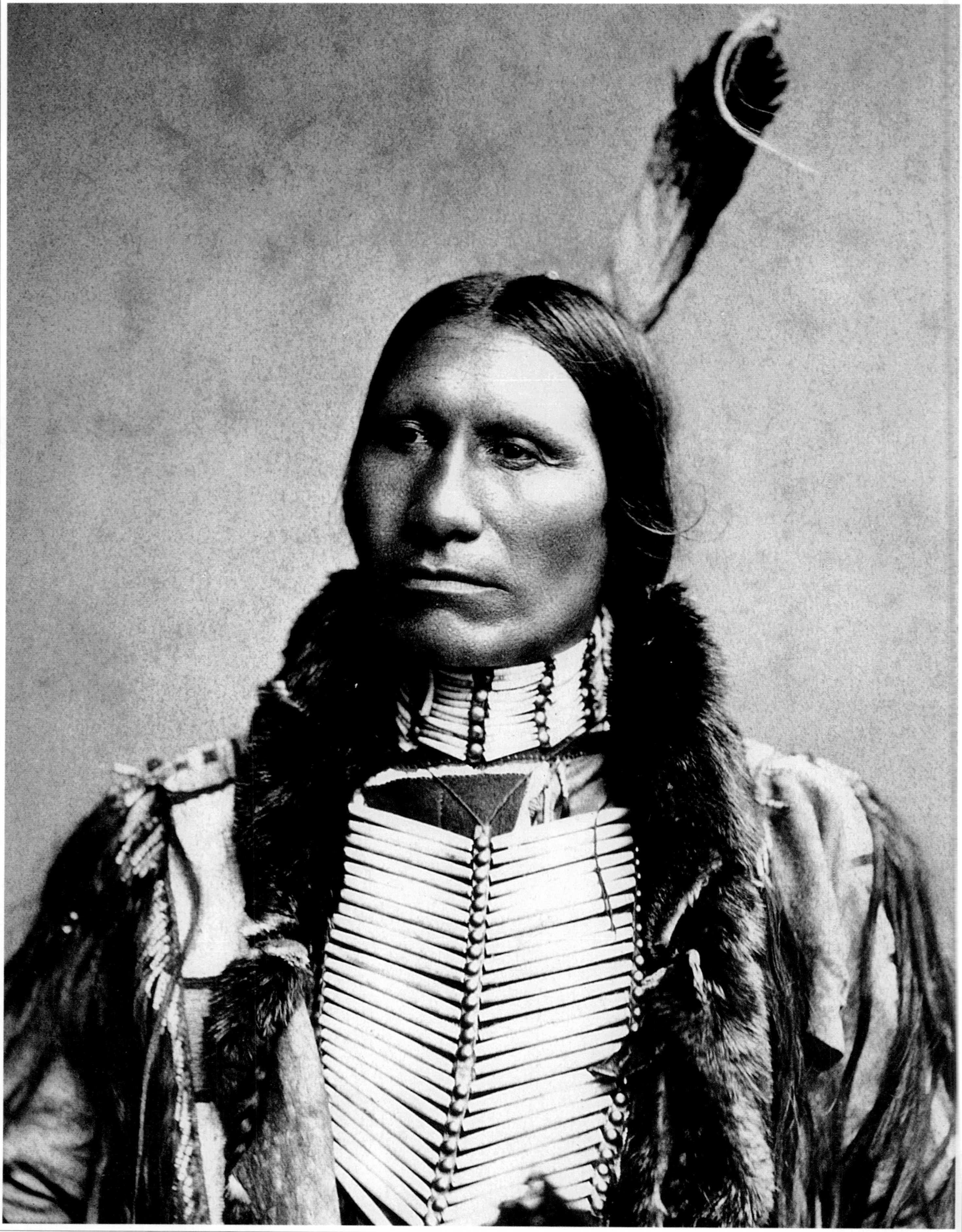

AMERICAN HORSE

1891: ON THE WOUNDED KNEE MASSACRE

OGLALA LAKOTA AMERICAN HORSE (1840–1908) rose to leadership through his oratorical and negotiating skills. He was also a warrior and, during the war for the Bozeman Trail, participated in the Fetterman fight of December 1866 – one of the worst-ever US army defeats. In 1890, American Horse opposed the Ghost Dance religion and persuaded Big Foot's band to return to the Pine Ridge reservation, where they were massacred at Wounded Knee. In 1891, on one of several trips to Washington, DC, American Horse delivered this passionate speech about the massacre, which helped to improve conditions for his people.

"The men were separated, as has already been said, from the women, and they were surrounded by the soldiers. Then came next the village of the Indians and that was entirely surrounded by the soldiers also. When the firing began, of course the people who were standing immediately around the young man who fired the first shot were killed right together, and then they turned their guns, Hotchkiss guns, etc., upon the women who were in the lodges standing there under a flag of truce, and of course as soon as they were fired upon they fled, the men fleeing in one direction and the women running in two different directions. So that there were three general directions in which they took flight.

There was a woman with an infant in her arms who was killed as she almost touched the flag of truce, and the women and children of course were strewn all along the circular village until they were dispatched. Right near the flag of truce a mother was shot down with her infant; the child not knowing that its mother was dead was still nursing, and that especially was a very sad sight. The women as they were fleeing with their babes were killed together, shot right through, and the women who were very heavy with child were also killed. All the Indians fled in these three directions, and after most of them had been killed a cry was made that all those who were not killed or wounded should come forth and they would be safe. Little boys who were not wounded came out of their places of refuge, and as soon as they came in sight a number of soldiers surrounded them and butchered them there."

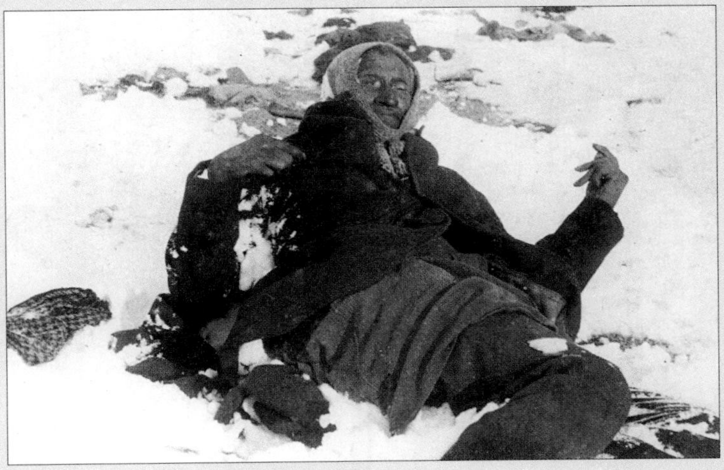

FROZEN INTO IMMORTALITY
American Horse was deeply affected by the carnage at Pine Ridge, as he had persuaded Miniconjou Lakota chief Big Foot to return to what turned into killing fields. On 29 December 1890, Big Foot, desperately ill with pneumonia, was shot to death by a soldier. This photograph of his contorted, frozen body in the snow is perhaps the most widely known image of the Wounded Knee massacre.

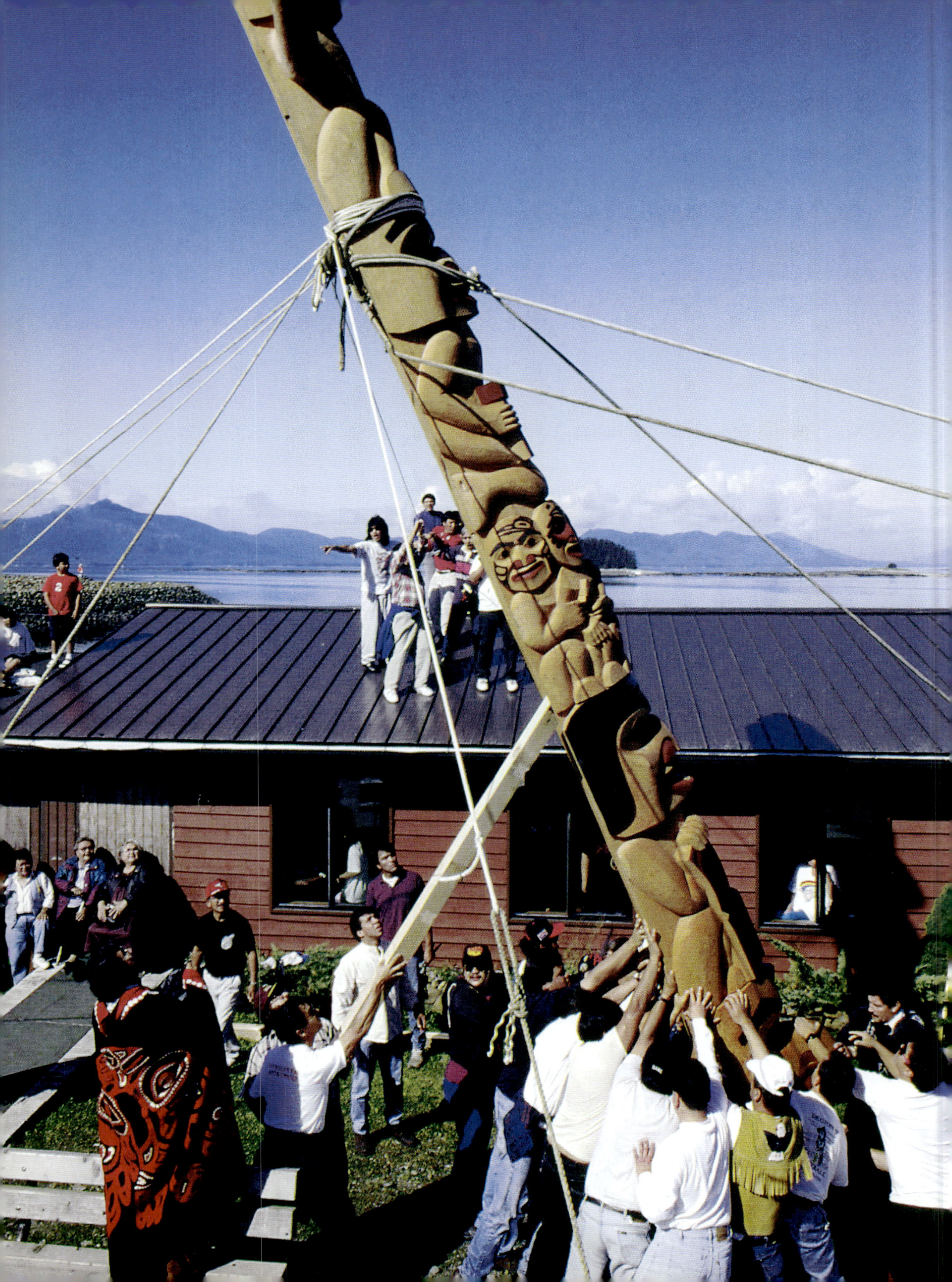

1900 TO PRESENT DAY

RESURGENCE AND RENEWAL

In the late 1950s, after decades of forced assimilation and disempowerment, Native peoples began to demand their sovereign rights. Today, Native leaders look forward to a revitalized future.

DECLINING TRADITION REVIVED

During the 1950s, a revival of totem-pole carving, which had declined at the end of the last century, emerged, and continues today. This Tsimshian totem pole was raised at Metlakatla, Alaska, in 1994.

LIFE ON THE RESERVATIONS

FROM THE 1890S INTO THE TWENTIETH CENTURY, the US and Canada pursued policies that tried to assimilate Native peoples into the mainstream culture. Confined to reservations, subject to bureaucratic controls that undermined their cultural identities, and forced into dependence on government rations or handouts for survival, Indian societies began to break down. In both countries, government agents held immense authority over the Indians' lives, effectively reducing them to the status of children.

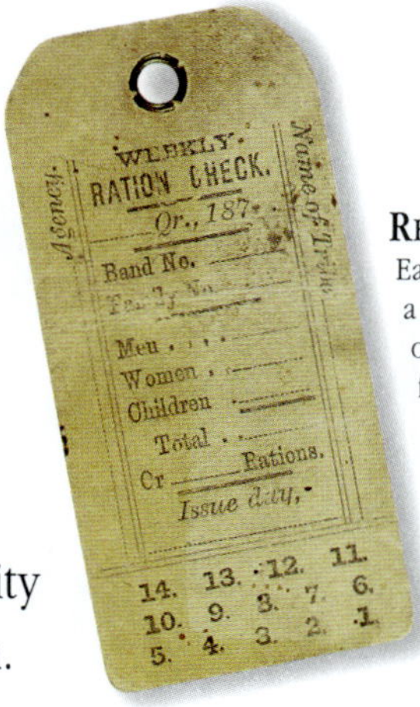

RESERVATION RATIONS
Each reservation family held a ration card – a certificate of eligibility to receive food and other goods issued by the reservation agent, who marked the card each time goods were received. Women stored these cards in hand-made beaded hide pouches.

ADOPTING WESTERN WAYS

Comanche war leader Quanah Parker, son of a Comanche chief and a white captive, Cynthia Parker, urged his people to make the most of reservation life. Photographed in the early 1890s, he stands beside Tonasa, one of his wives, on the porch of his 12-roomed house, complete with a white picket fence and stars emblazoned on the roof. Quanah adopted many white ways: he learned English and Spanish and was a successful rancher. But he never gave up his long twin braids, buckskin for everyday wear, or his many wives.

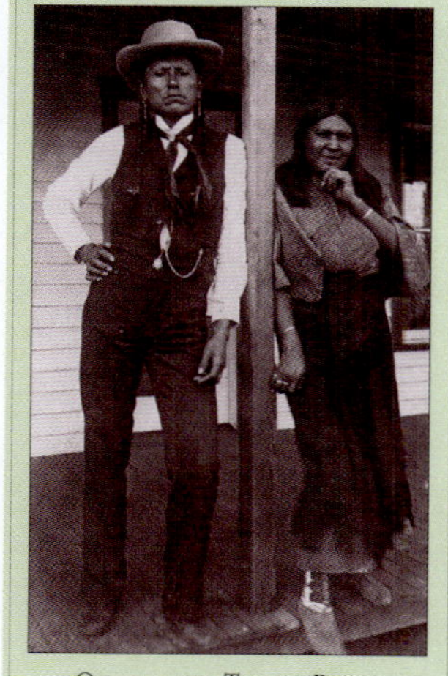

QUANAH AND TONASA PARKER

MOST US INDIAN NATIONS after 1890 were located on reservations, and Indians were subjected to the bureaucratic control of US Indian agents who enforced the law, controlled the use of land, administered tribal funds, and allocated treaty-guaranteed annuities. Distributing goods offered rich pickings for dishonest agents, and a series of scandals resulted in growing numbers of Indians being bullied, cheated, or bribed out of home and land. In 1905, however, the government, in a major overhaul of the Indian Service, succeeded in rooting out the widespread corruption.

Indian officials strictly regulated education and religious and cultural practices, targeting especially what they called "heathen" ceremonies. In 1883, traditional Plains tribal people were prohibited from worshiping in their sacred Sun Dance ceremony; penalties for those continuing to participate included the withholding of treaty rations and imprisonment. Indian agents also oversaw the forced removal of Indian children from their families to boarding schools, where the assimilation policies were intensified and children were taught to despise everything they loved – their parents, relatives, and cultures (*see pp.128–29.*)

Canadian Assimilation Policies

In Canada, the Indian Acts of 1876, 1880, and 1884 set forth a policy of assimilating Natives into Canadian society. The laws defined who was an Indian, confined Indians to reserves, controlled communities where Indian identity would be replaced with the "habits and ideas of a higher civilization," and imposed on them an alien bureaucracy. Government agents exercised near-dictatorial powers over the day-to-day life of communities, while the government supplanted traditional, consensus-based Indian leadership and decision-making with a system of elected band councils and chiefs, both of which ultimately depended on approval by the Minister of Indian Affairs in Ottawa.

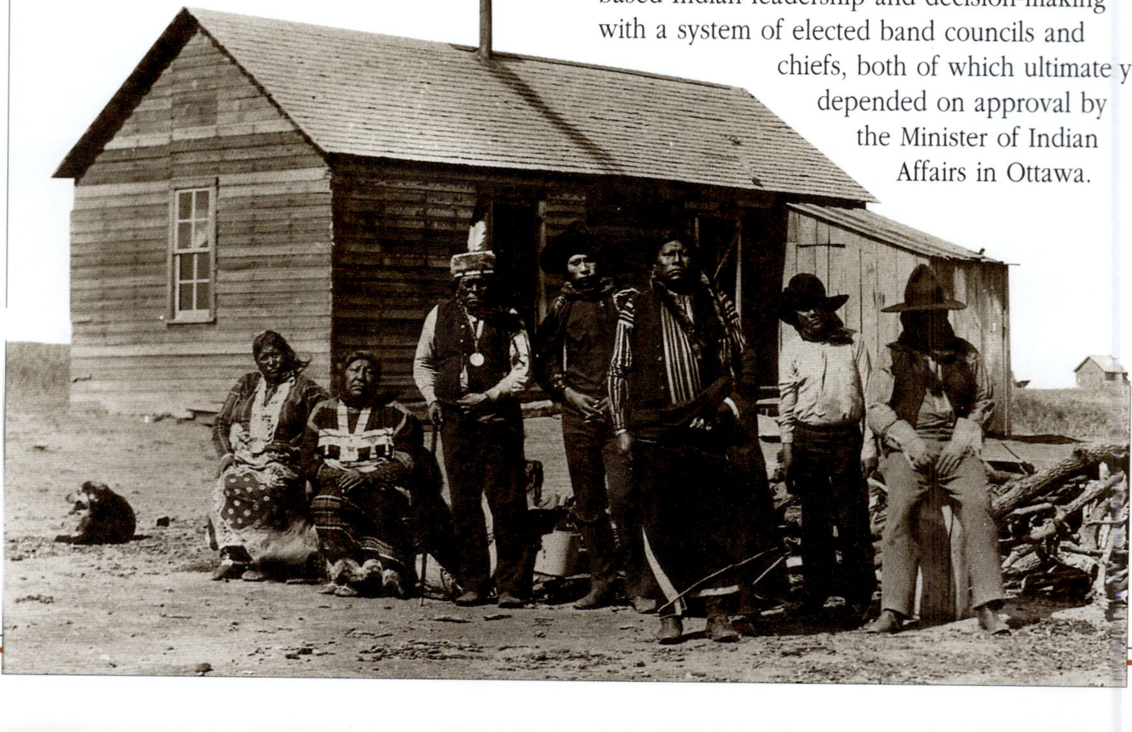

REJECTED HOUSING ▷
Indian agents forced Plains Indians to exchange their circular tipis for log houses. But Comanches, Lakotas, Osages, and others left the houses empty while they continued living in tipis pitched alongside. Medicine man Black Elk explained that log houses were "a bad way to live, for there can be no power in a square."

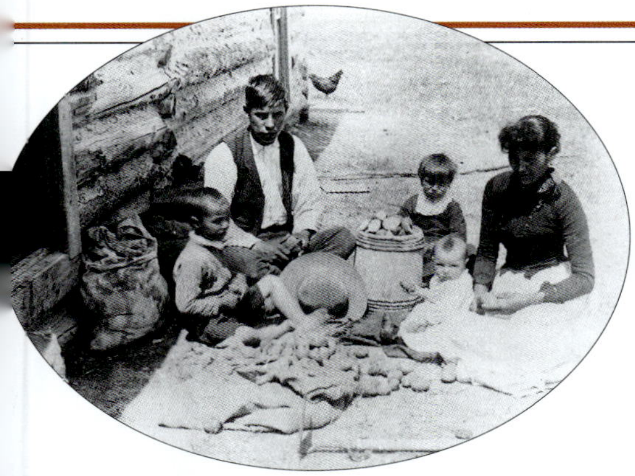

LEARNING TO BE FARMERS
A Blackfeet family in Montana, in 1891, prepares seed potatoes as they had been taught by government advisers. Agents expected Plains Indians to become self-supporting farmers, but growing crops was an alien activity to buffalo-hunters like the Blackfeet.

Native ceremonies and rituals, deplored as heathen superstitions, were banned, and Indian children, like their counterparts in the US, were sent to boarding schools where they were forced to discard their native cultures. The treaties, Indian Acts, and reservation system transformed Indians almost overnight from free hunters into impoverished prisoners in their own country, forced to cooperate with the authorities out of fear that their meager food supplies and money would be cut off.

Resistance and Divisions

Throughout the early twentieth century, many Indians in both the US and Canada resisted government efforts to assimilate them. The Lakotas conducted their outlawed Sun Dance in remote parts of their reservations while, in British Columbia, Indians figured out ways to potlatch in spite of Canadian law.

The assimilation process generated bitter social and political divisions that undermined the cohesion of Indian communities and continued old conflicts between Indians who had accommodated or resisted white settlement.

By the 1920s, the bulk of the most valuable US Indian farming and grazing lands had passed into the hands of non-Indians, and Natives were no longer seen as a military threat.

"Indians must conform to 'white man's ways,' peaceably if they will, forcibly if they must."

THOMAS MORGAN, COMMISSIONER OF INDIAN AFFAIRS, 1889

INDIANS POLICED

In 1878, Congress funded Indian reservation police as a means of keeping order without calling on the army. Within six years, small and badly equipped Native police forces were established at most reservations. Their major problem was that they were caught between the demands of white agents, to whom they were accountable, and the complaints of unhappy Indians.

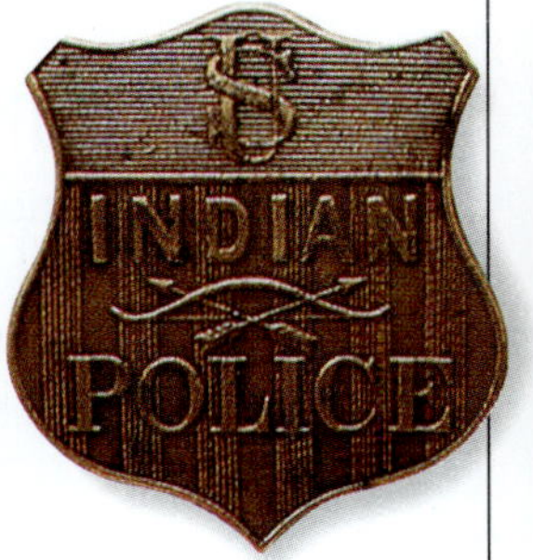

INDIAN POLICE BADGE

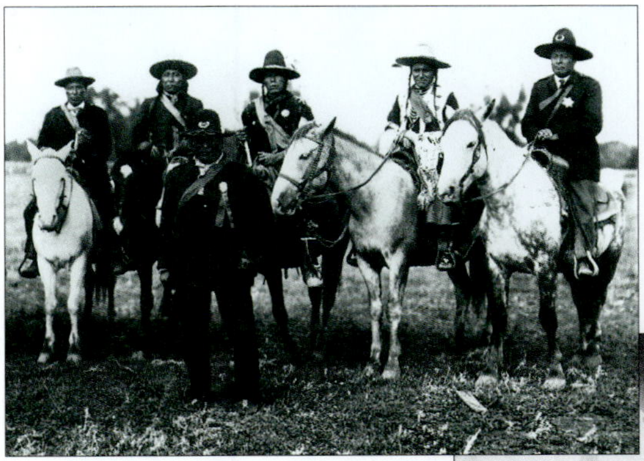

◁ INDIAN POLICE PATROL
Crow warrior societies traditionally maintained order within camp circles and regulated the buffalo hunt. Mounted police patrols, like these men on the Crow reservation in Montana, echoed tribal tradition and helped make police service popular. The Crow police were generally loyal to the agent and carried out their responsibilities.

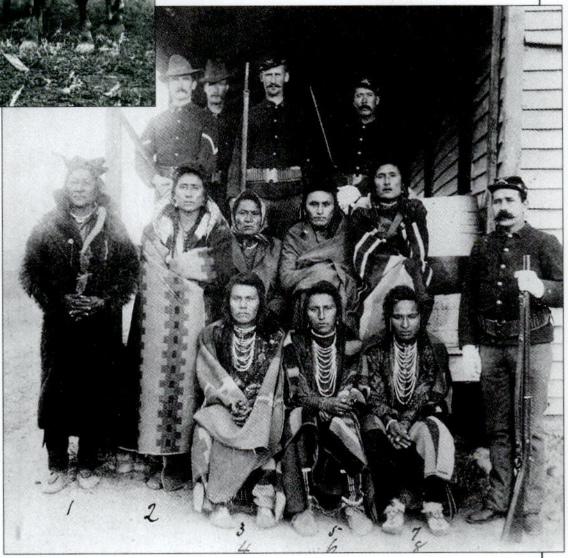

UNDER ARMED GUARD ▷
Despite the appointment of Indian agency policy, the cavalry were brought in to deal with unrest on reservations. These Crow men, pictured in 1887, were seized in Montana for an assault on government troops and buildings during an abortive uprising sparked by Sitting Bull.

▽ SETTING AN EXAMPLE
Assiniboine Sioux Indian police at Fort Belknap agency, Montana, pose in 1890, wearing badges, sidearms, hats, and kerchiefs. Indian police were expected to set an example by practicing monogamy, cutting their hair, and by wearing white man's clothing when off duty.

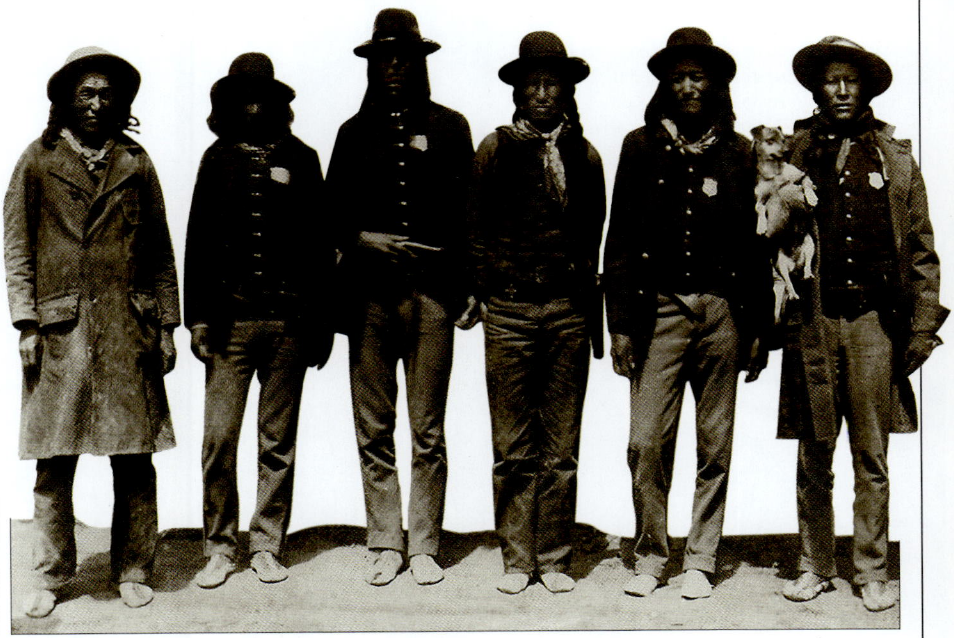

LIVING ON HANDOUTS

Indians on reservations continued to hunt, fish, and gather, but neither these activities nor their attempts at cultivating the land and investing in livestock were sufficient to sustain them. They thus became economically and politically dependent on the Office of Indian Affairs and its field agents for food, clothing, and tools.

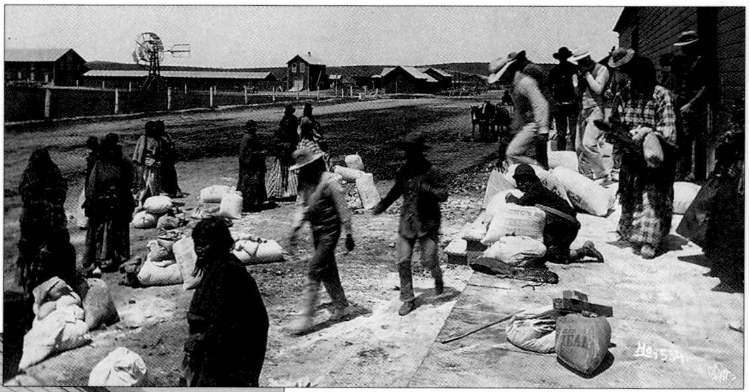

PAYMENT DAY ▷
Reservation Indians are pictured here lining up at the agency store on annuity payment day. Often, the beef ration was inadequate: Congress slashed the funds for food at a time when more, not less, food was needed. An agent on the Cheyenne reservation reported that "the issue of beef once a month and other stores twice a month, does not keep them from suffering from a lack of food."

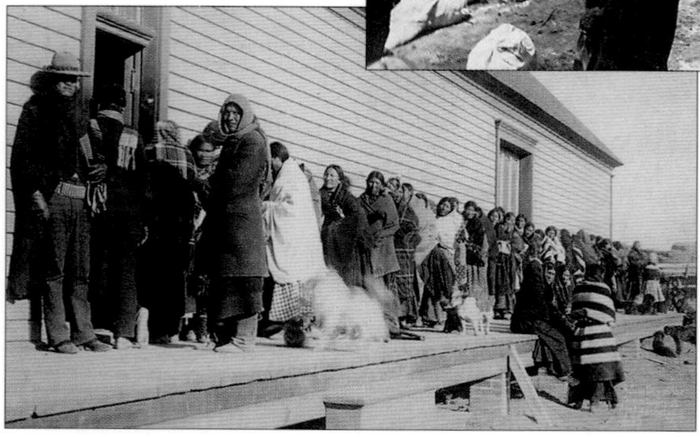

△ AT THE AGENCY STORE
This picture shows Sioux women collecting rations for their families from the store. Blankets, yards of cloth, shoes, and farming equipment were provided by the federal government, as well as food supplies.

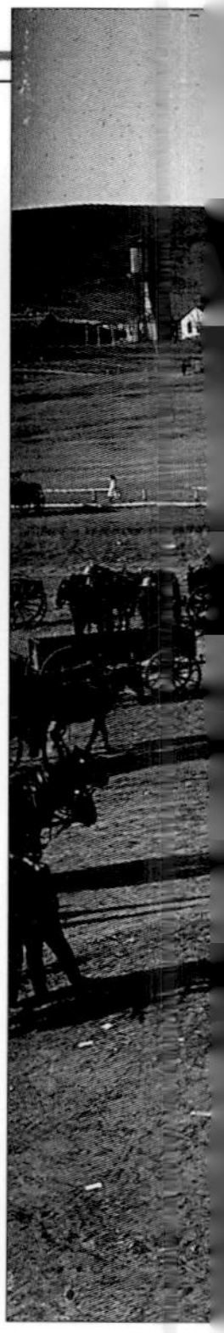

MAKING A DAY OF IT ▷
All across the plains and prairies, Indian families rode to the issue station on issue day. Turning it into a special occasion, they visited friends and relatives and traded articles they did not need.

LEARNING WHITE WAYS

Indian Office officials expected Indians to learn stock raising and modern methods of planting, cultivating, harvesting, and rotating crops. The officials also expected Indians to learn to speak English like white people, to wear the same clothes, eat the same food, go to the same churches, salute the US flag, and to patriotically celebrate the Fourth of July.

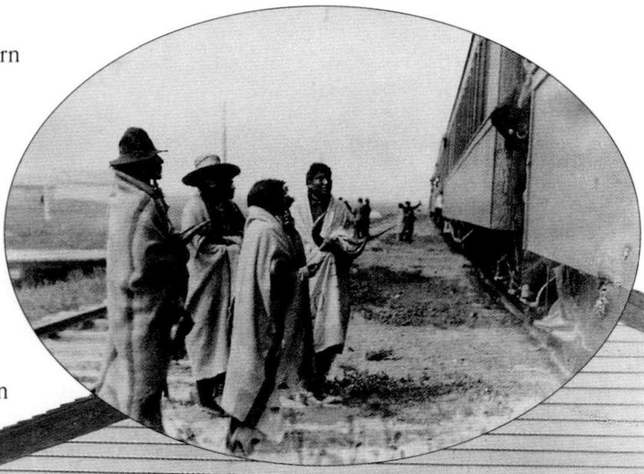

TRACKSIDE TRADING ▷
After the completion of the Great Northern Railroad in 1895, the hungry Blackfeet, without game to chase, were reduced to selling tokens, such as buffalo horns, to tourists alongside the railroad tracks.

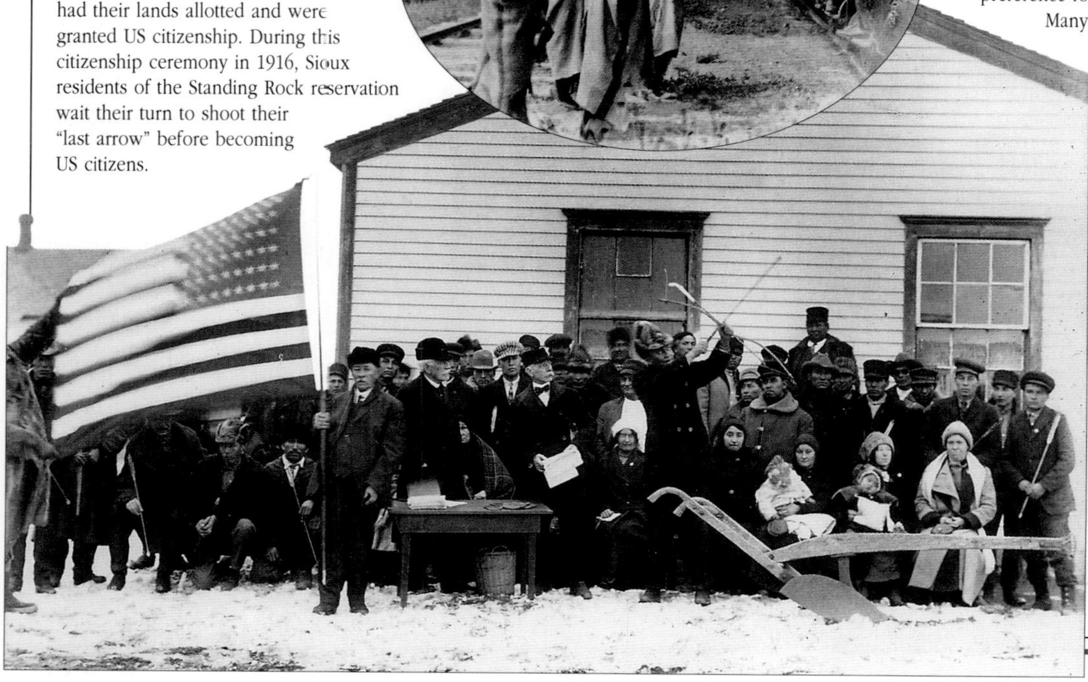

▽ SHOOTING THE LAST ARROW
From 1916 to 1917, some Sioux Indians had their lands allotted and were granted US citizenship. During this citizenship ceremony in 1916, Sioux residents of the Standing Rock reservation wait their turn to shoot their "last arrow" before becoming US citizens.

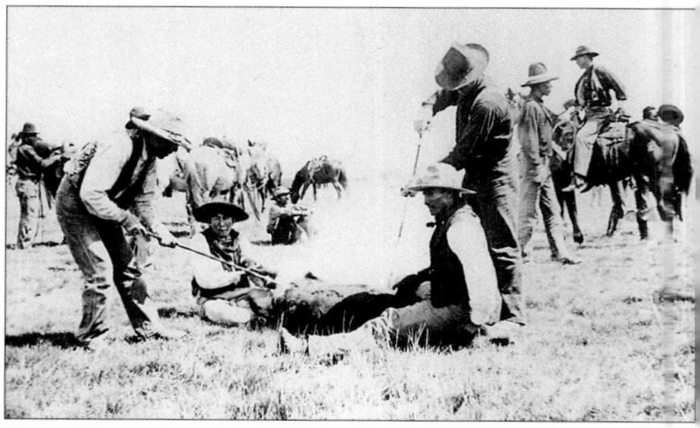

△ INDIAN COWBOYS ON THE PLAINS
The late nineteenth and early twentieth centuries saw the heyday of cattle ranching in the Northern Plains country. Indians, looking more like cowboys than Indians, took to ranching in spite of the federal preference for farming, and became skilled at branding cattle. Many Indian cowboys worked for non-Indian ranchers.

▽ PLOWING A NEW FURROW
The US government sent "government farmers" to reservations to train Indians in modern farming practices, including the study of soil, climate, and water condition, use of fertilizers, weeding procedures, and crop rotation.

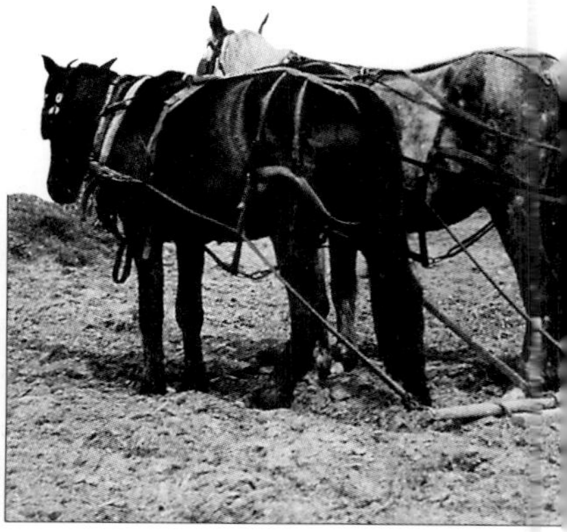

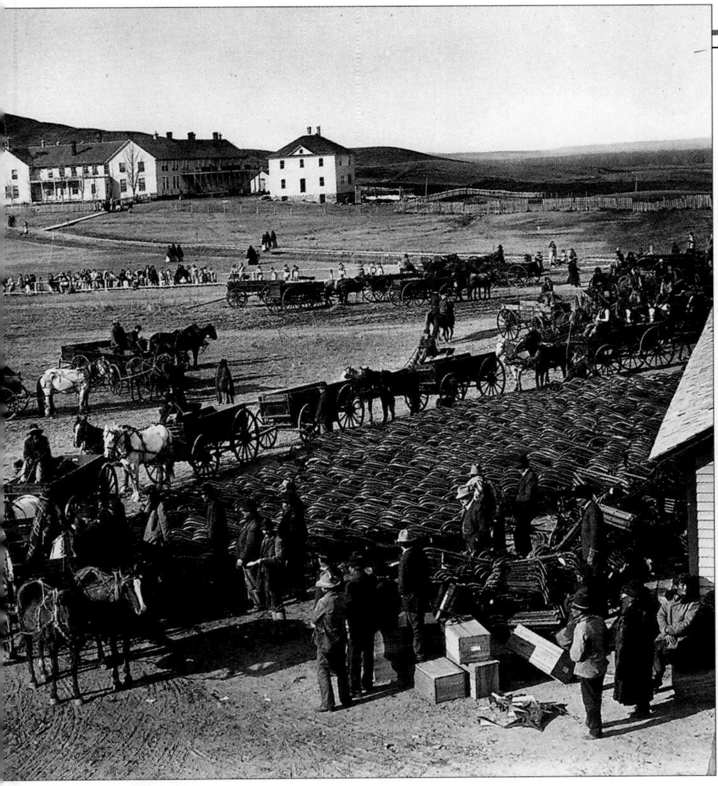

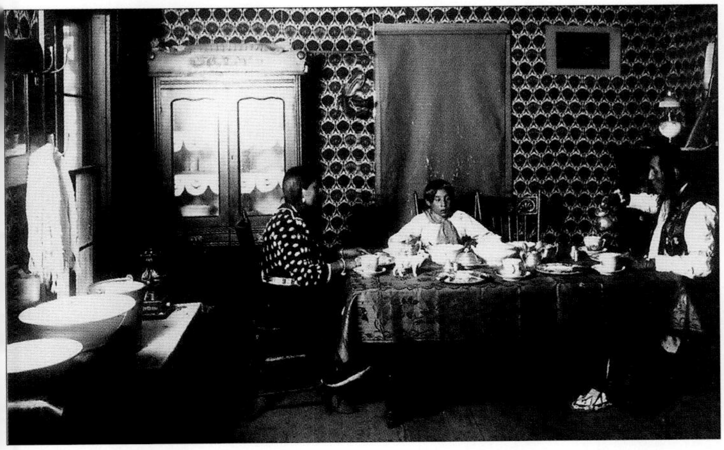

△ **A MODEL FAMILY**
A Montana family demonstrates, in 1910, how they have acquired the food rites of a "civilized" society. They sit at a table complete with tablecloth, napkins, and china, using knives, forks, and spoons to eat the meal, while the head of the family pours a beverage from a pitcher into a cup.

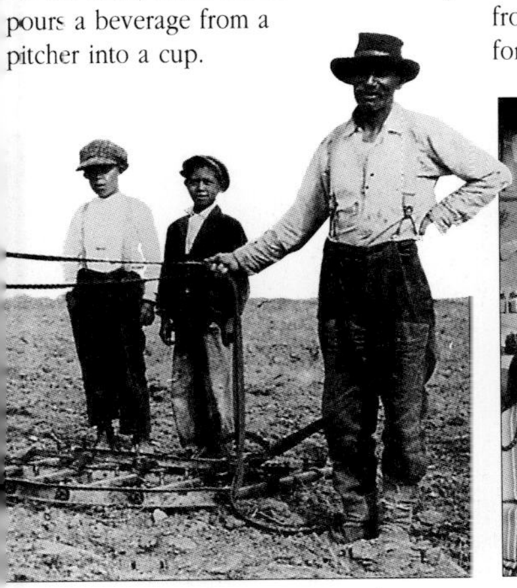

▽ **FARMING INSTRUCTION**
After buffalo were almost exterminated, the US government sent experts to teach the Blackfeet how to raise wheat. Here, during the Blackfeet winter fair, an annual event organized by the Indian Office, a group of women receive advice from Ignatius O'Donnell, a farm advisor for the Northern Pacific Railroad.

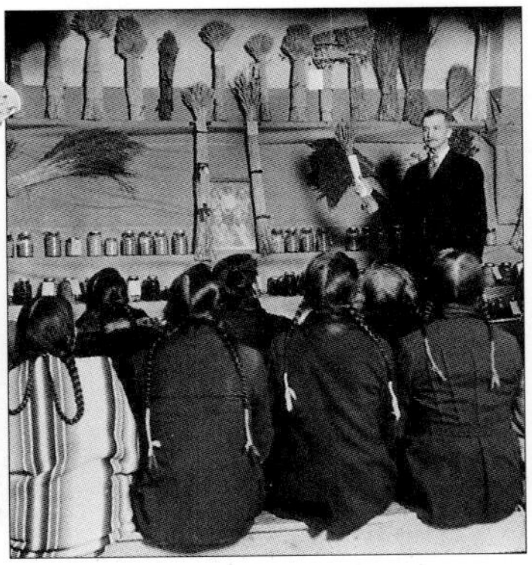

CLINGING TO THE PAST

Despite forced assimilation policies, many Indian communities in North America clung to their ancestral beliefs and traditions, resisting the white bureaucrats and the soldiers and Indian police who were sent to intimidate them. Many resorted to fasting, praying, and worshiping secretly in sacred ceremonies.

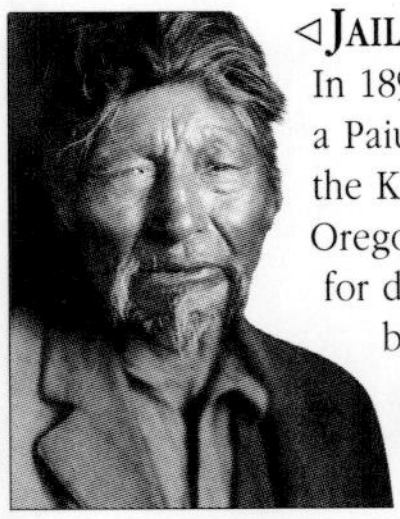

◁ **JAILED FOR "CURING"**
In 1897, Chief Tom Chocktoot, a Paiute religious leader from the Klamath reservation in Oregon, was jailed for a week for disobeying a government ban on Native curing practices. Disobedient practitioners could be jailed up to six months.

▽ **DANCING PROHIBITED**
Three Coast Salish initiates of the outlawed Spirit Dance, a major winter ceremonial in southern British Columbia and northern Washington, are pictured wearing their ceremonial clothing *c.* 1920. Enforcing the ban was costly: funds were required for policing, jails, lawyers, and court actions.

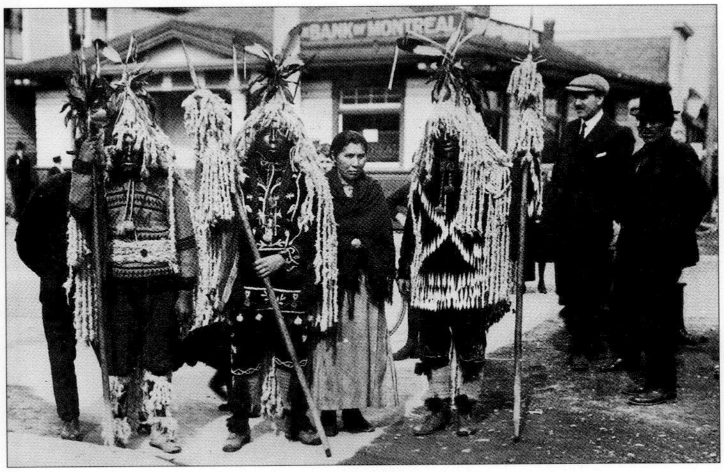

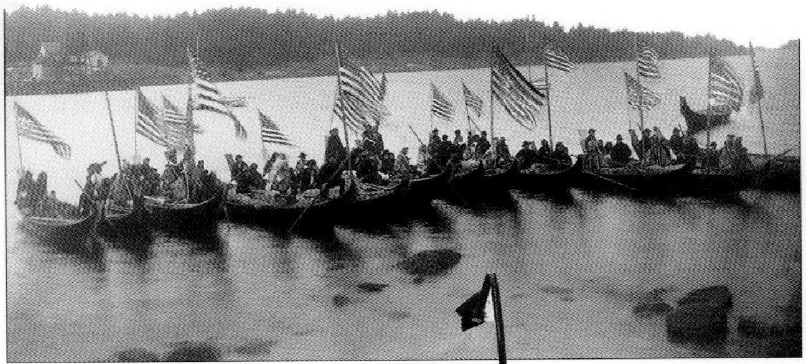

△ **ILLICIT CEREMONIES**
A group of Tlingit Indians approach the shore at Sitka, Alaska, in 1904 to attend a potlatch. Although potlatching was banned by the 1884 Canadian Indian Act, British Columbian Indians continued the tradition, often under the guise of celebrating national holidays.

IGNORING THE BANS ▷
Finding Indian religious practices repugnant, Major A.E. Woodson, the Indian agent at the Cheyenne reservation, banned them. Members of the Lance Society, seen here, and other tribal members ignored the ban and held Sun Dances anyway.

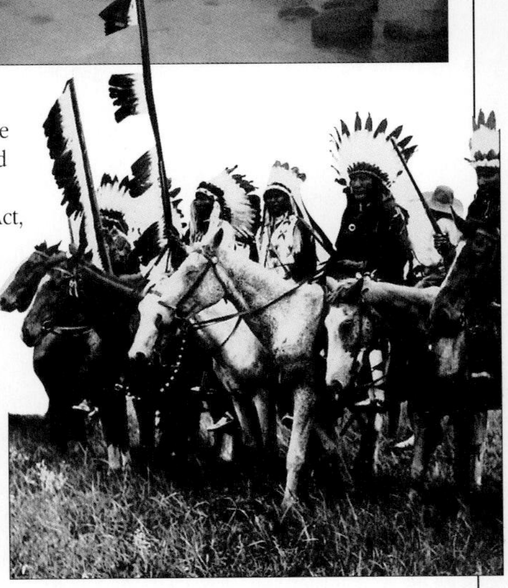

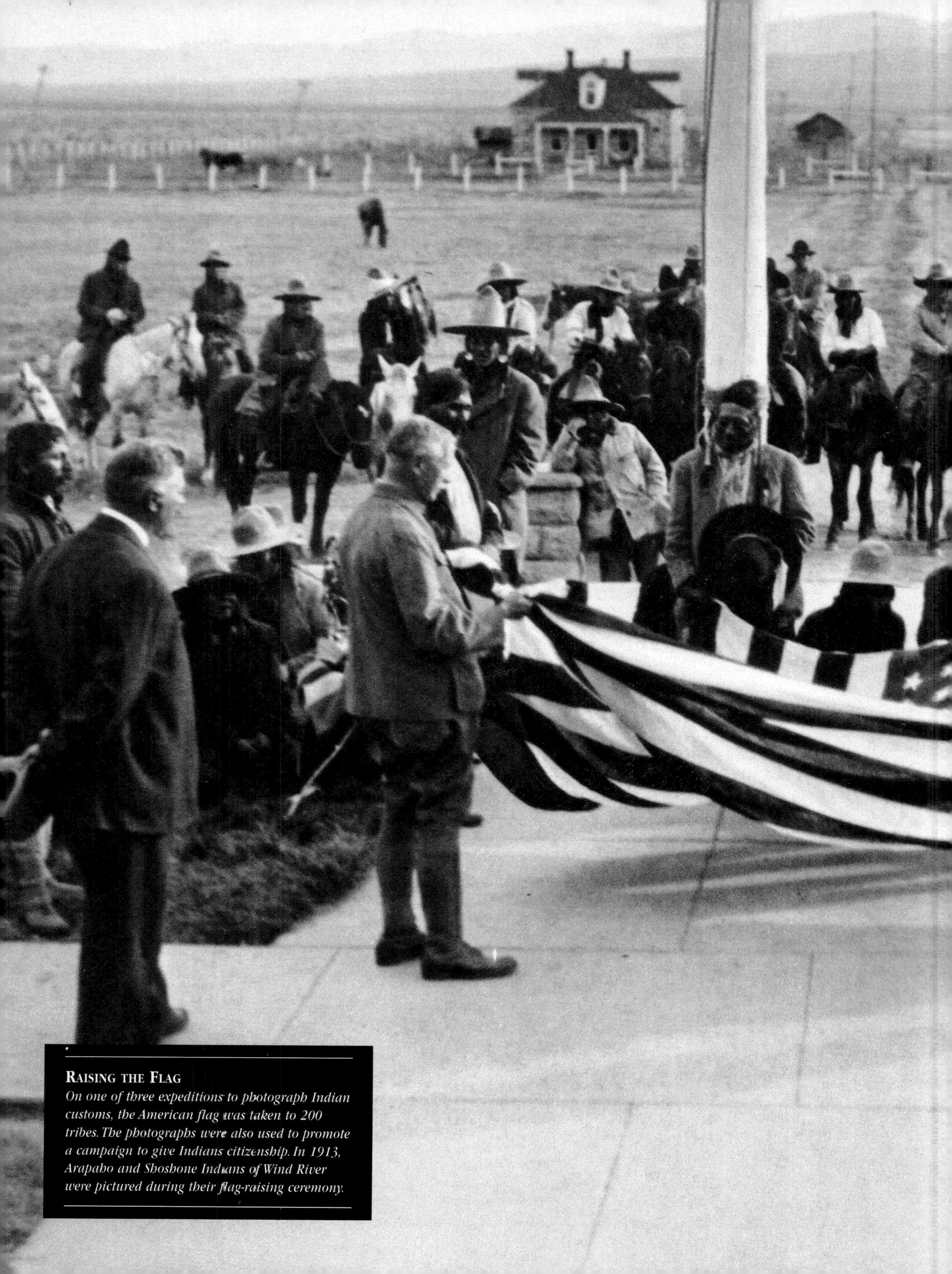

Raising the Flag

On one of three expeditions to photograph Indian customs, the American flag was taken to 200 tribes. The photographs were also used to promote a campaign to give Indians citizenship. In 1913, Arapaho and Shoshone Indians of Wind River were pictured during their flag-raising ceremony.

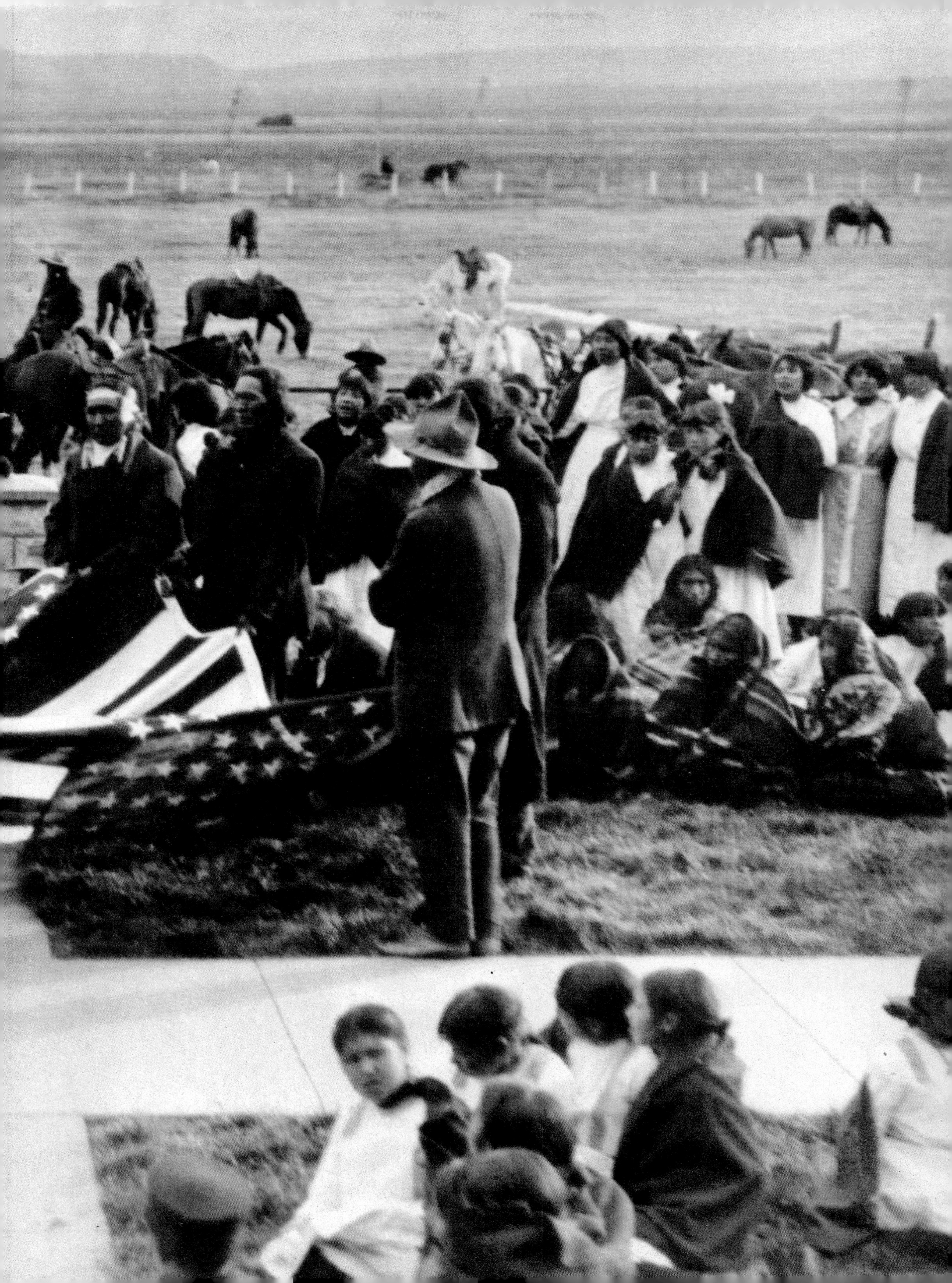

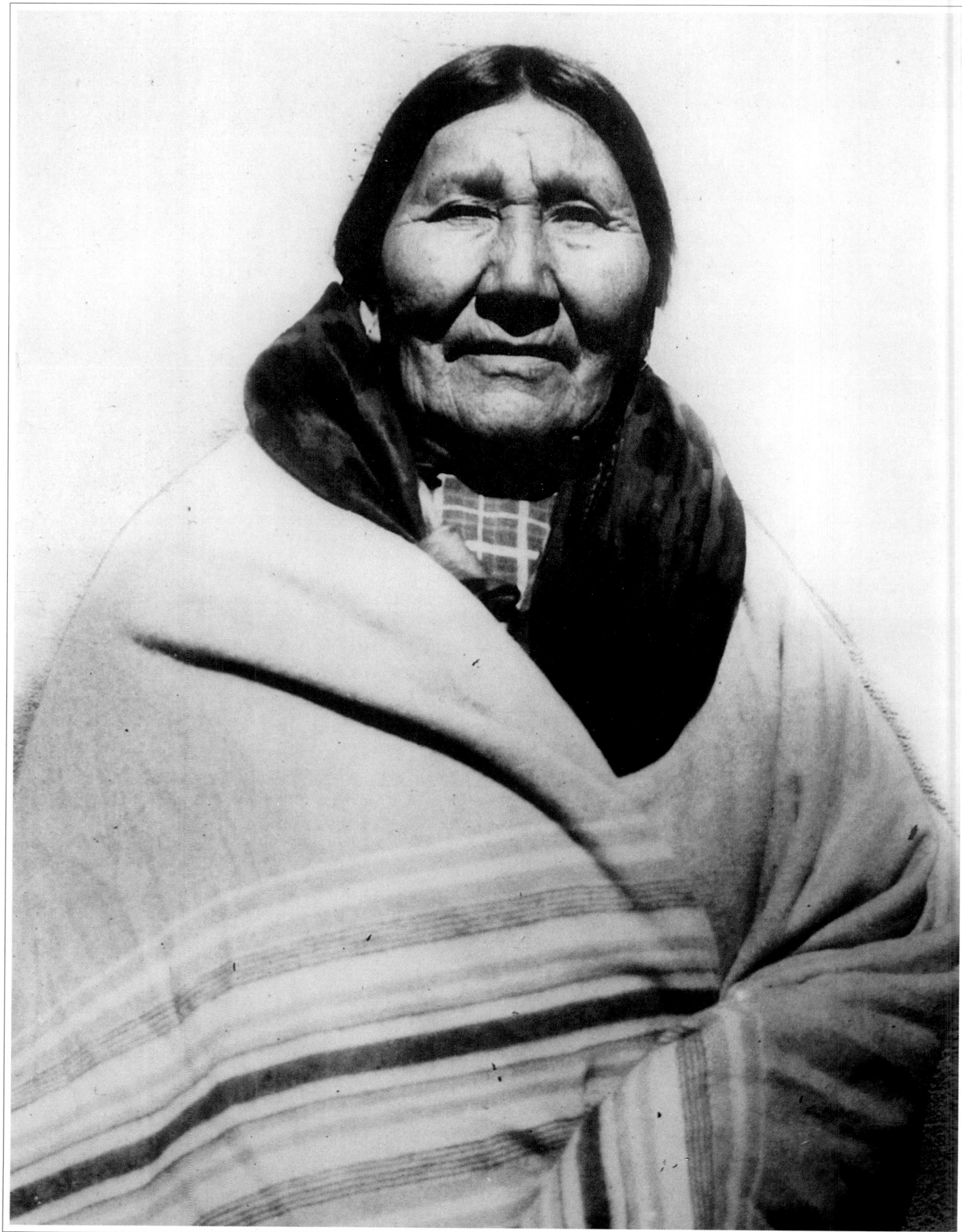

PRETTY-SHIELD

c. 1932: ON THE END OF THE BUFFALO WAY OF LIFE

CROW PRETTY-SHIELD (BORN *C.* 1857) derived her name from her paternal grandfather, who owned a medicine shield. She became a medicine woman through the spiritual guidance she received in a vision after the death of a baby daughter. Around 1932, Pretty-Shield told her life story to author Frank Linderman and, in her account of the female side of Native life, she recalls her vision as well as the traditional ways of the Crow people before European contact. This extract is from her book *Red Mother,* which was published in 1932, and later reprinted as *Pretty-Shield: Medicine Woman of the Crows.*

"Ahh, my heart fell down when I began to see dead buffalo scattered all over our beautiful country, killed and skinned, and left to rot by white men, many, many hundreds of buffalo. The first I saw of this was in the Judith basin. The whole country there smelled of rotting meat. Even the flowers could not put down the bad smell. Our hearts were like stones. And yet nobody believed, even then, that the white man could kill all the buffalo. Since the beginning of things there had always been so many! Even the Lacota, bad as their hearts were for us, would not do such a thing as this; not the Cheyenne, nor the Arapahoe, nor the Pecunnie; and yet the white man did this, even when he did not want the meat.

We believed for a long time that the buffalo would again come to us; but they did not. We grew hungry and sick and afraid, all in one. Not believing their own eyes our hunters rode very far looking for buffalo, so far away that even if they had found a herd we could not have reached it in half a moon. 'Nothing; we found nothing,' they told us; and then, hungry, they stared at the empty plains, as though dreaming. After this their hearts were no good any more. If the Great White Chief in Washington had not given us food we should have been wiped out without even a chance to fight for ourselves.

And then white men began to fence the plains so that we could not travel; and anyhow there was now little good in traveling, nothing to travel for. We began to stay in one place, and to grow lazy and sicker all the time. Our men had fought hard against our enemies, holding them back from our beautiful country by their bravery; but now, with everything else going wrong, we began to be whipped by weak foolishness. Our men, our leaders, began to drink the white man's whisky, letting it do their thinking. Because we were used to listening to our chiefs in the buffalo days, the days of war and excitement, we listened to them now; and we got whipped. Our wise-ones became fools, and drank the white man's whisky. But what else was there for us to do? We knew no other way than to listen to our chiefs and head men. Our old men used to be different; even our children were different when the buffalo were here."

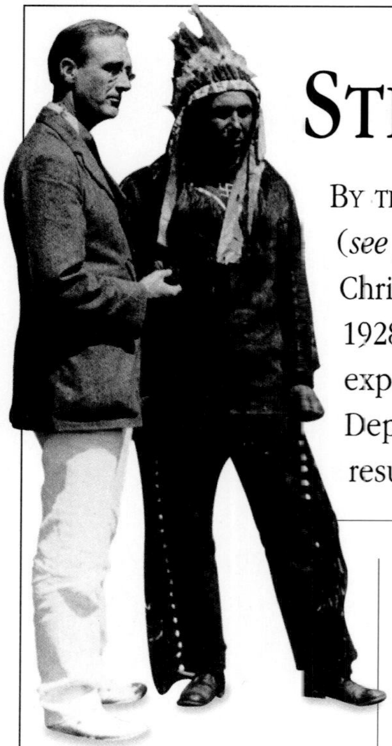

STRUGGLE FOR A NEW DEAL

BY THE EARLY TWENTIETH CENTURY, it was clear that repressive measures, such as allotment (*see pp.122–25*) and boarding schools, had failed to transform Indians into prosperous Christian farmers. The problems of Native peoples attracted little national attention until 1928, when a shocking study (named the Meriam Report after its editor, Lewis Meriam) exposed the poverty on reservations and severely criticized programs run by the US Department of the Interior agency, the Bureau of Indian Affairs (BIA) (*see p.187.*) The result was the passage, in 1934, of reform legislation known as the "Indian New Deal."

△ ROOSEVELT MEETS THE CHIEF
In 1921, New York lawyer Franklin D. Roosevelt met with Iroquois Chief Neptune. During his presidency of the US (1933–45), Roosevelt demonstrated his commitment to reforming Indian affairs by appointing men, such as John Collier, who shared his beliefs.

THE FIRST DECADES of the twentieth century saw some Native activism: in 1911, a group of well-educated Indians, concerned by the deplorable state of US reservation life, formed a pan-Indian reform group – the Society of American Indians. As the first prominent, national, Indian-controlled rights organization in the country, the Society offered individual (not tribal) membership and "associate" membership to non-Indians. United on the goals of better education and securing US citizenship for Indians, but divided over self-determination versus assimilation and whether to abolish the Bureau of Indian Affairs (BIA), the organization disbanded in the mid-1920s. Its brief existence presaged the eventual founding, in 1944, of the National Congress of American Indians, a multitribal, national organization.

The administrations of Warren G. Harding (1921–23) and Calvin Coolidge (1923–29) made few changes in federal Indian policy, despite the creation, in 1923, of the Committee of One Hundred to investigate Indian affairs. In 1924, a federal law gave US citizenship to all Indians not already enfranchised through treaties, but the act did little to improve Indians' well-being.

Instigating Change

A renewed interest in reform was generated by the release, in 1928, of the Meriam Report. This major investigation into the inadequacy of the BIA health care, education, and housing programs culminated in the so-called Indian New Deal, which was instigated by the Secretary of the Interior, Harold Ickes, and Commissioner of Indian Affairs, John Collier. Collier and others formulated the Indian Reorganization Act (IRA) of 1934 – the focal

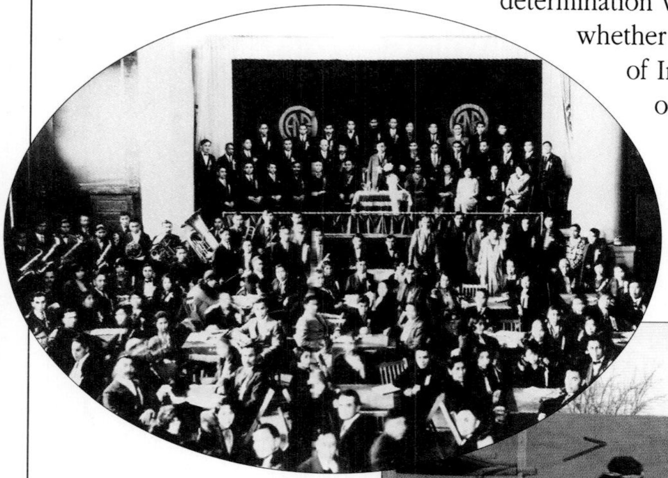

△ ALASKAN BROTHERHOOD
Founded in 1912, the Alaska Native Brotherhood (pictured in 1928) had Native officers and almost exclusive Native membership. The Alaska Native Sisterhood, a companion civil rights organization, was founded in 1915.

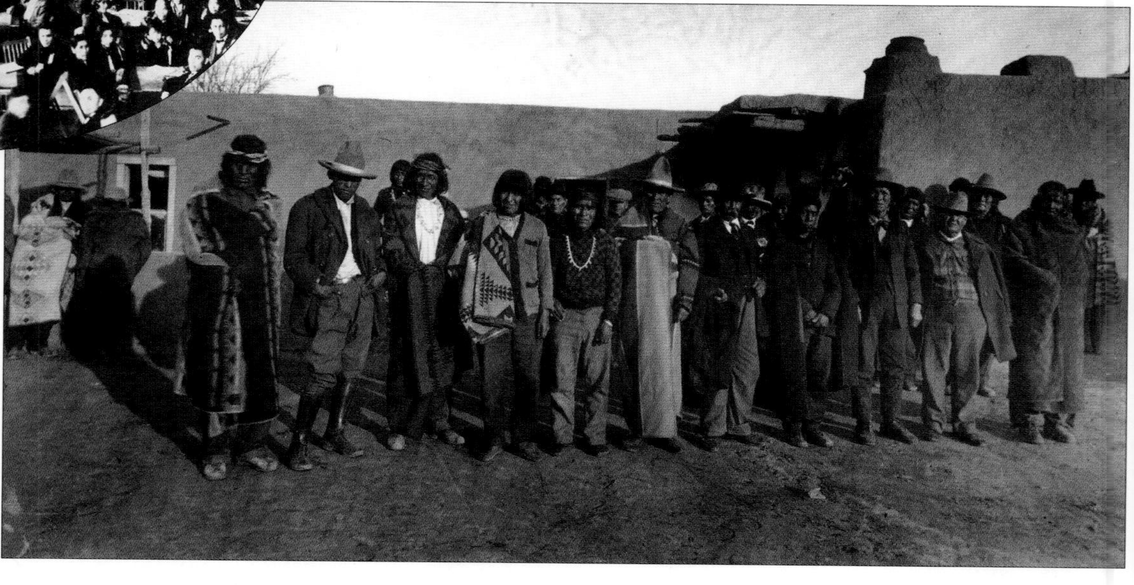

PUEBLOS FORM COUNCIL ▷
Governors of the All Indian Pueblo Council (AIPC), pictured in 1926, help Pueblo communities to protect their sovereignty. In 1922, the AIPC defeated a Bill granting rights to non-Native squatters on Pueblo lands.

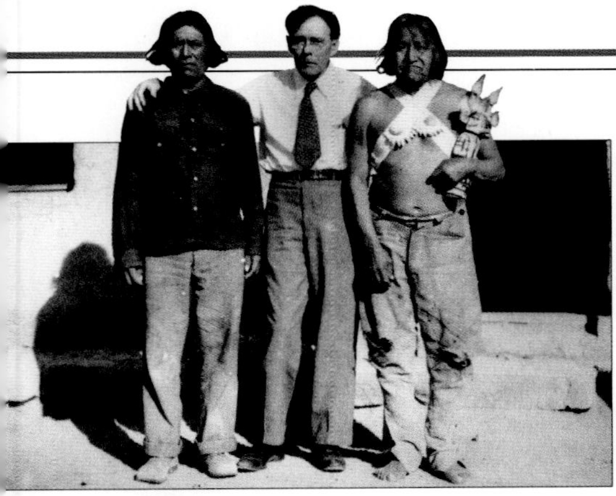

△ NEW DEAL BY COLLIER
As head of the BIA, John Collier (center) initiated sweeping reforms in Indian policy. Instead of "getting the Indian out of the Indian," he sought to preserve tribal cultures and heritage, which he considered essential to Native survival.

point of the New Deal, which repealed allotment, restored surplus land to some reservations, and introduced federal programs supporting Indian agriculture, vocational education, economic development, and Indian employment preference in the BIA. The Act also aimed to revive tribal governments by allowing reservation communities to set up governments patterned along majority-rule lines. Critics, however, claimed that the law limited the self-governing powers of tribes, imposed alien political systems on Natives, and gave the Interior Secretary too much power. Some of the new tribal governments aroused little support among the people they were supposed to represent.

When the US entered World War II in 1941, government support for Indian relief programs dwindled. John Collier, by then under attack from the government for his Indian policies, resigned from office in 1945.

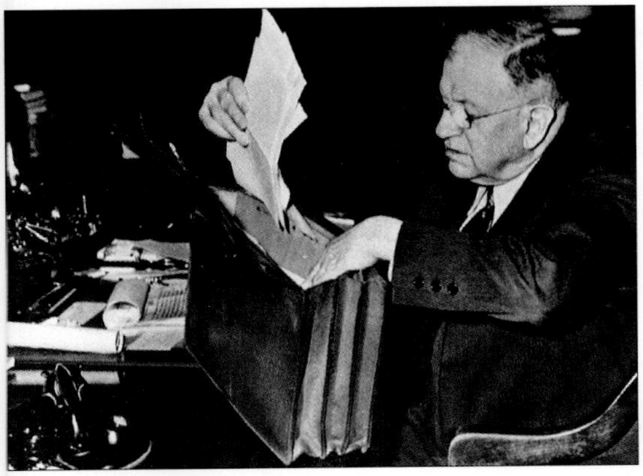

△ ICKES APPOINTED INTERIOR SECRETARY
In 1933, President Franklin D. Roosevelt appointed Harold Ickes Secretary of the Interior. The following year, Ickes, a founding member of the lobbying group, the American Indian Defense Association, and a critic of the BIA, formed a committee to study ways of protecting and marketing Native arts.

A SIGNAL OF CHANGE

From 1916 to 1922, Yavapai physician Carlos Montezuma wrote, edited, and published a monthly newsletter, *Wassaja: Freedom's Signal for the Indians*, in which he argued that the BIA should be abolished.

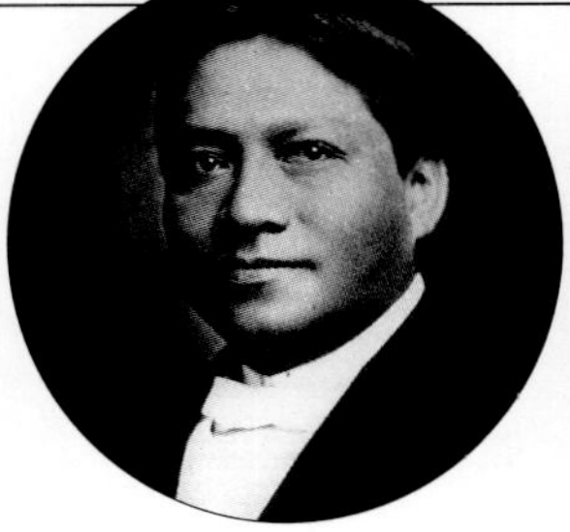

△ CRUSADING EDITOR
Carlos Montezuma, whose Indian name was Wassaja, helped to form the Society of American Indians, but ended up attacking it in his monthly newsletters.

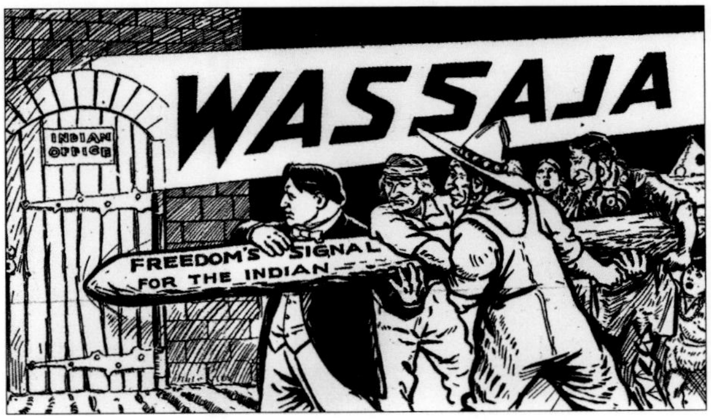

◁ PRESSING FOR FREEDOM
The May 1918 cover of *Wassaja* illustrates Montezuma's belief that Indian people must throw off the imperialistic shackles of the BIA if they were to survive Many Indians shared this view.

NEW DEAL ACHIEVES SOME SUCCESS

The Indian New Deal helped some tribes to increase their land base, created a loan program for students, guaranteed religious freedom, limited Christian instruction in BIA schools, and, in 1935, established an Arts and Crafts Board to promote Indian creative work as art rather than as ethnographic curiosity.

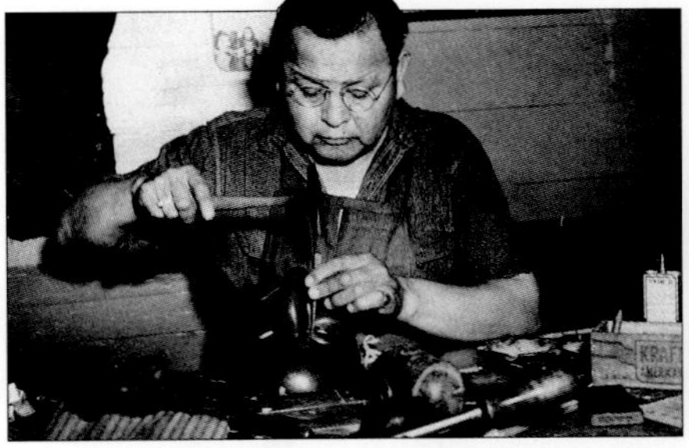

△ ART AND CRAFT SKILLS PROMOTED
The Indian Arts and Crafts Board promoted modern arts as an aid to economic independence, creating craft guilds, sponsoring art classes, and mounting exhibitions of Native work. Seneca artist Jesse Cornplanter is pictured, in 1940, working on a mask.

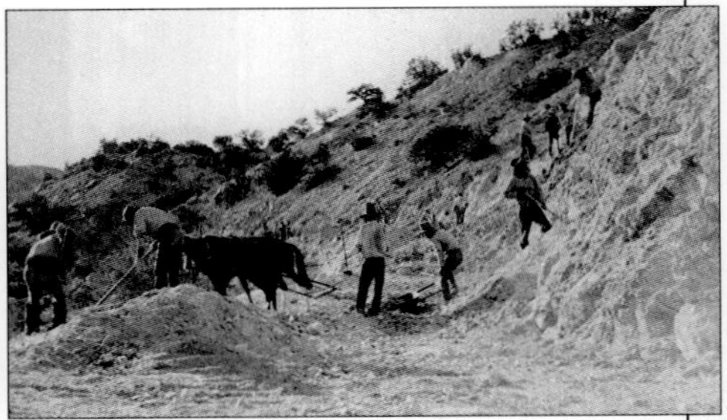

△ CONSERVATION WORK BEGINS
Before the Indian Reorganization Act was passed in 1934, John Collier pushed through legislation to provide funding for jobs in conservation work on Native lands. Navajo workers were pictured, in 1933, building a road in Tohatchi Canyon, New Mexico.

INDIANS WORK THE LAND ▷
The Indian New Deal gave impetus to rural projects. Imogene Lincoln Mosqueda, a Southern Arapaho, was pictured farming tribal lands in Oklahoma, probably during the late 1930s.

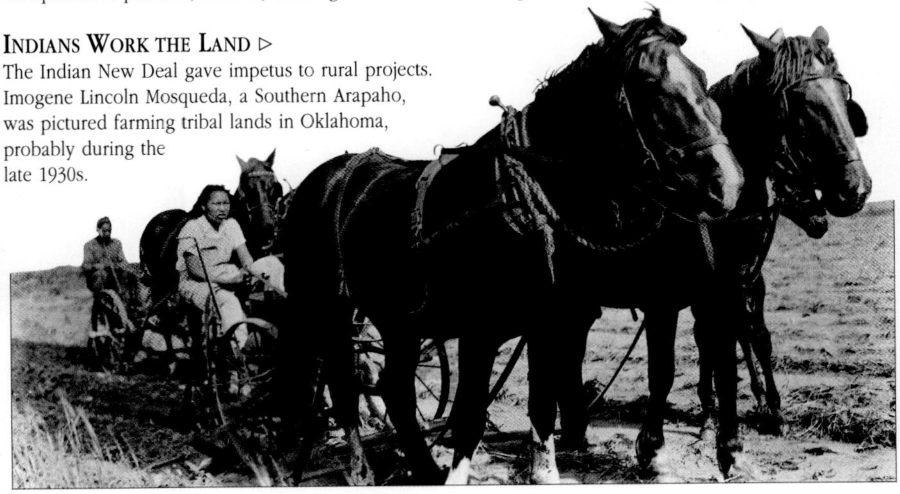

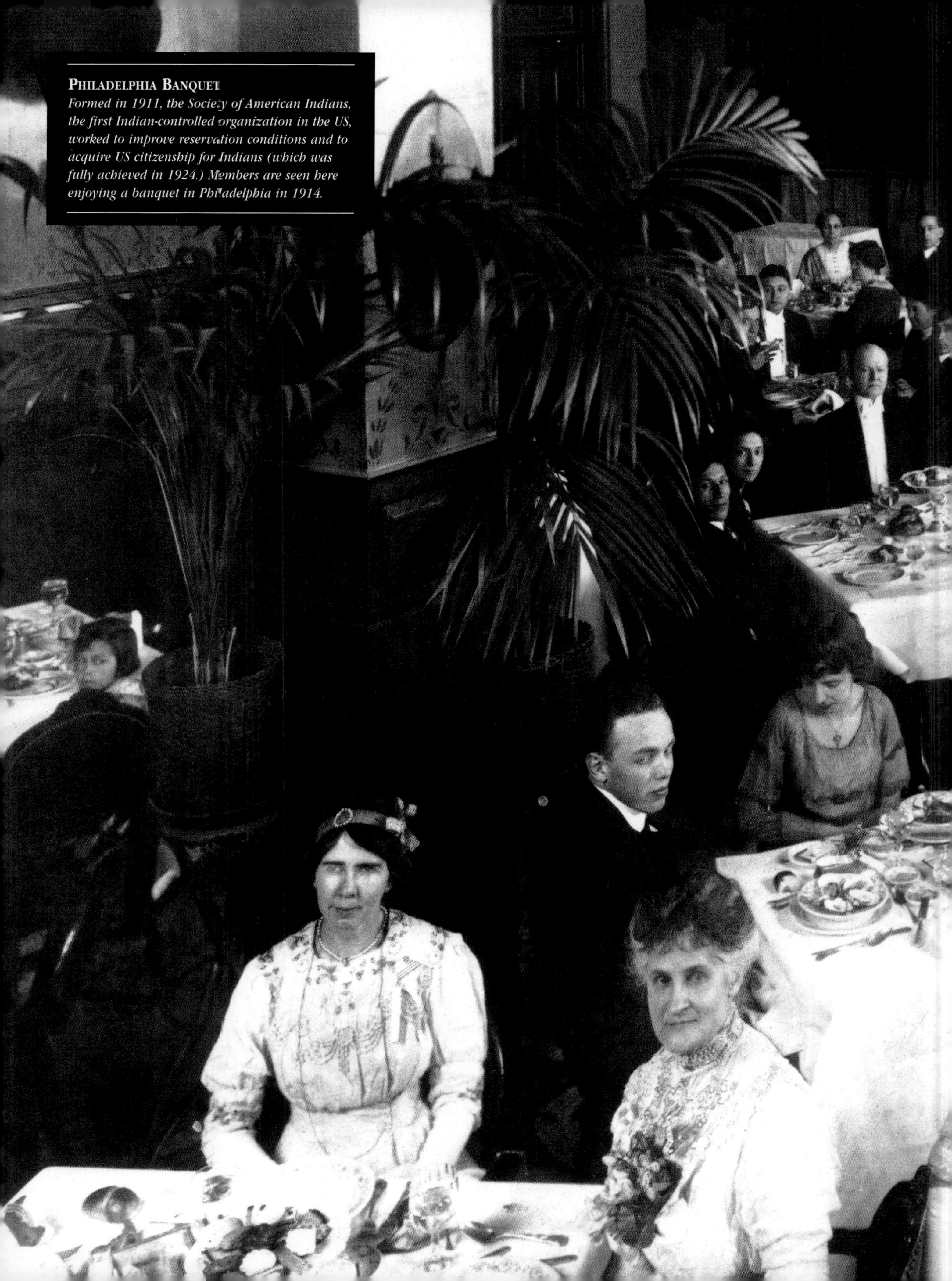

PHILADELPHIA BANQUET

Formed in 1911, the Society of American Indians, the first Indian-controlled organization in the US, worked to improve reservation conditions and to acquire US citizenship for Indians (which was fully achieved in 1924.) Members are seen here enjoying a banquet in Philadelphia in 1914.

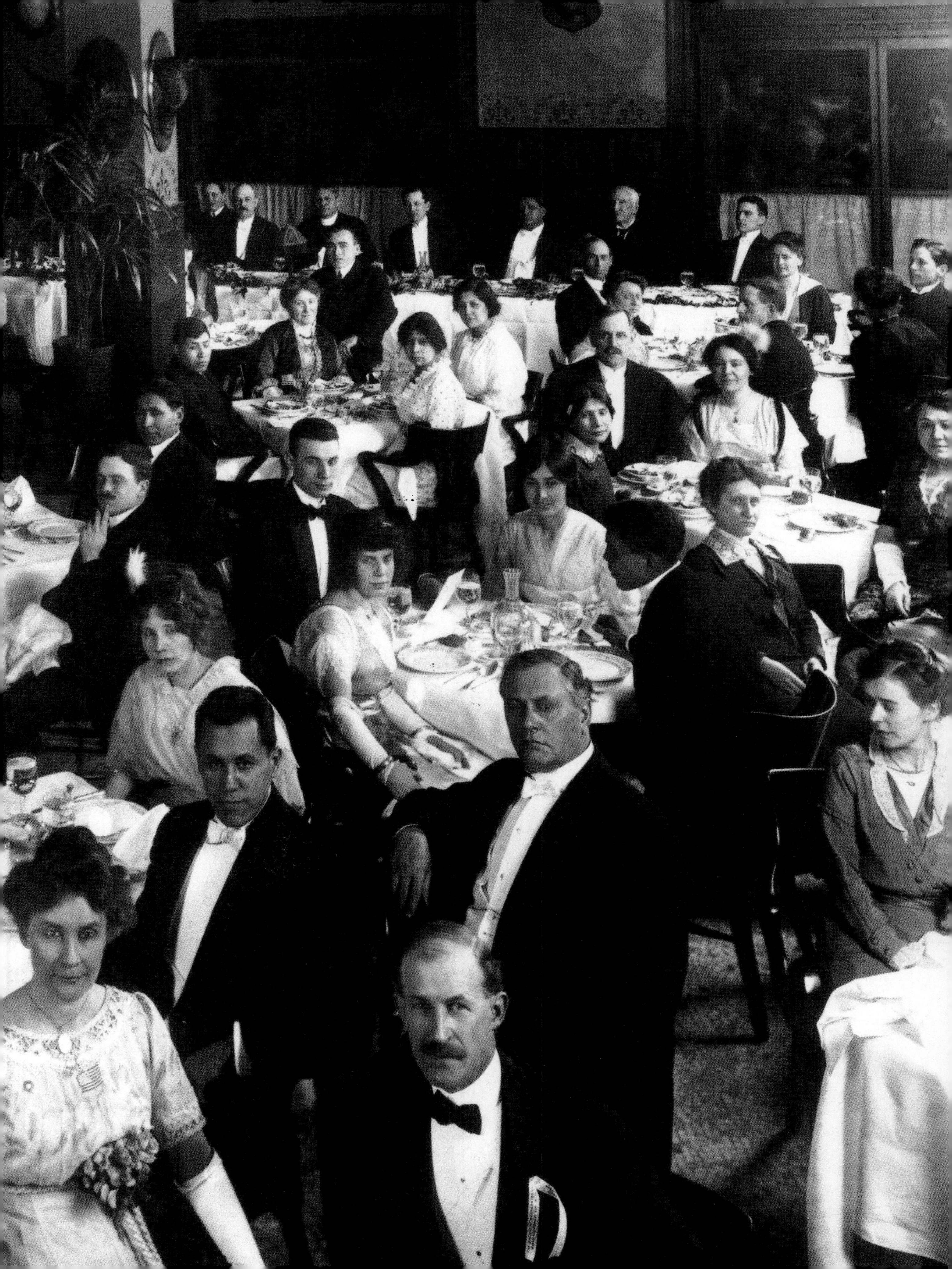

ON MILITARY SERVICE

AMERICAN INDIANS have a long history of serving in the US military. They have fought in all the American wars, serving in the armed forces of the US to protect their country, community, lands, and the dignity of their tribes. In the tradition of Indian cultures, the way to manhood and to an honored position in the community was to serve in warrior societies, where ceremonial status could be earned. At powwows and Indian ceremonies today, Indian veterans and those currently in the military are honored for serving their country.

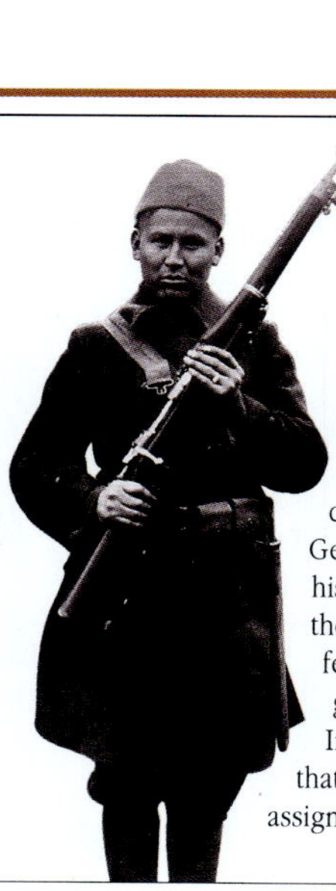

KEEN RECRUIT
Too old to enlist but eager to do his part during World War I, George Miner lied about his age so he could join the US army. He and fellow Winnebagos were grouped with other Indians and, in the belief that they had unique gifts, assigned to special duties.

TWENTIETH-CENTURY INDIAN WAR DIARY

WORLD WAR I: 1914–18
12,000 Indians serve, nearly all as volunteers

WORLD WAR II: 1939–45
25,000 Indians serve

KOREAN WAR: 1950–53
10,000–15,000 Indians serve

VIETNAM WAR: 1961–75
42,500 Indians serve

PERSIAN GULF WAR: 1990–91
3,000 Indians serve in operation "Desert Storm"

▽ TRAINING FOR WAR
A crew of Sioux, Comanche, and Apache Indians, manning a horse-drawn reel-cart, lays communications wire in a training exercise at Fort Riley, Kansas, during World War I.

LONG BEFORE Congress granted them citizenship in June 1924, Native peoples fought loyally in every one of the American wars. During the American Revolution (1775–83), the Tuscarora and Oneida nations sided with the Americans, while the Cayugas, Onondagas, Mohawks, and Senecas supported the British. During the Civil War (1861–65), some Indians fought for the Union, while others joined the Confederacy. Indians fought in the Spanish-American War (1898), some joining Teddy Roosevelt's Rough Riders in the charge at San Juan Hill.

12,000 Indians men and women served in World War I, nearly all volunteers since they were not yet citizens of the US. That number doubled in World War II. It has been estimated that between 10,000 and 15,000 Indians saw action in Korea, and over 42,000 Native military personnel were stationed in Vietnam.

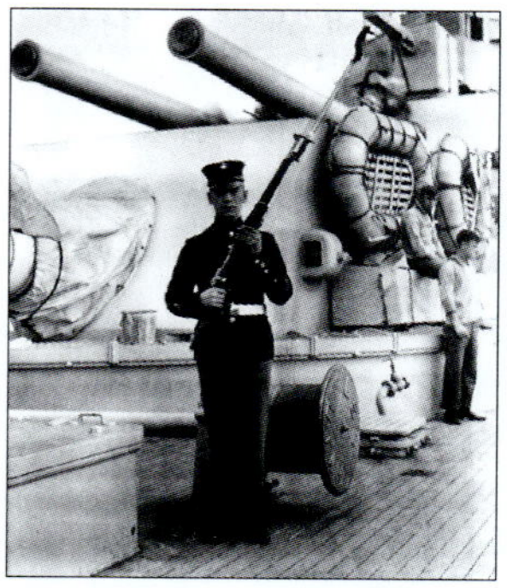

INDIAN MARINE
Corporal Roy La Valle, a Cree serving with the US Marine Corps, is pictured here on board the battleship *USS Utah* on 29 April 1919.

Indian communities support their men and women warriors regardless of the policy that sends them into battle. Relatives, who sponsor ceremonies, send soldiers into war armed with eagle feathers, sacred bundles, prayers of protection, and ceremonial sweats to prepare them for battle.

Indian Code-talkers

During both World War I and II, the US military used Indian languages as secret codes. The Indians transmitted and received tactical messages in their Native languages by radio and telephone. During World War I, the Choctaws were the first Indians to use their language as an unbreakable code. The language was again used in World War II, along with the Comanche, Creek, Hopi, Lakota, Menominee,

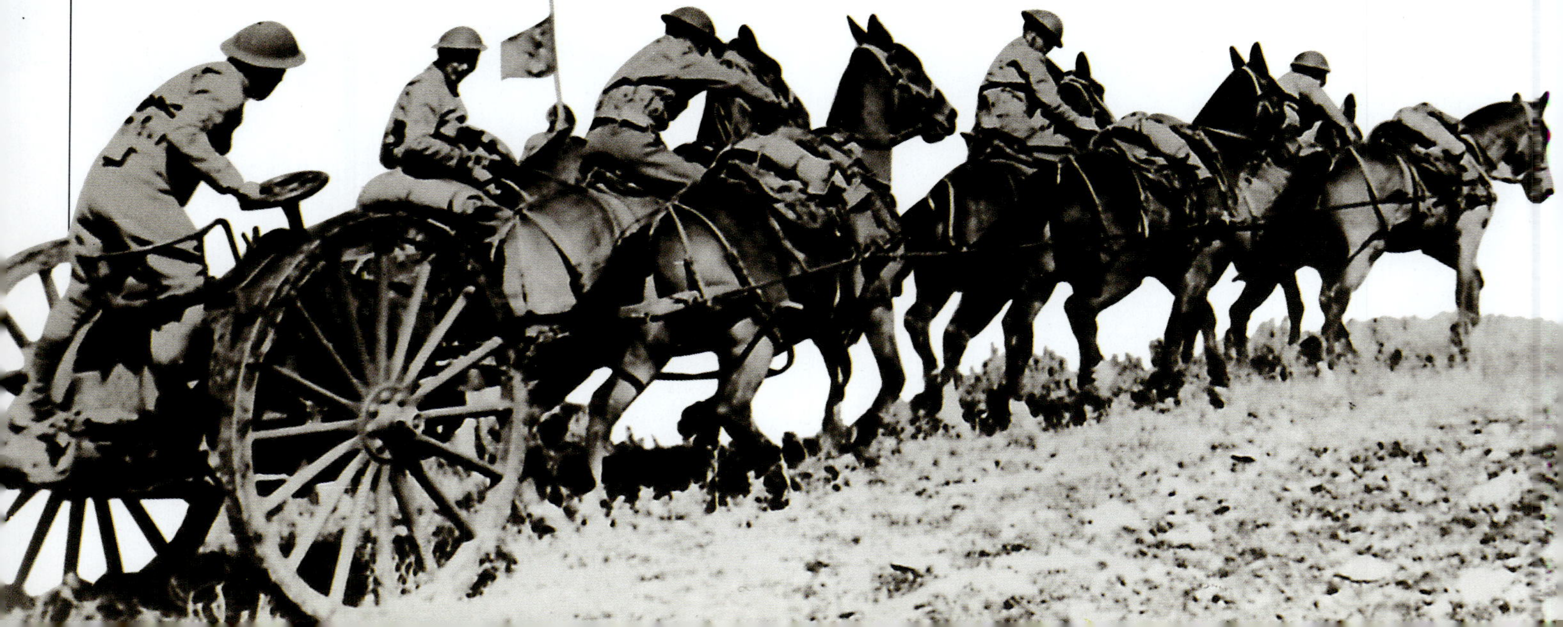

and Ojibways languages. The Comanche phrase *posah-tai-vo*, meaning "crazy white man," was used for Adolf Hitler. Since the Comanches had a word for airplane but not for bomber, the code-talkers came up with the Comanche phrase for "pregnant airplane."

During World War II, a Navajo code played a crucial role in the US victory in the Pacific. Although they usually broke codes as fast as they were created, Japanese cryptographers never broke the code based on the Navajo language. The idea originated with Philip Johnston, an engineer raised on the Navajo reservation. Confident that few people in the world understood the complex syntax and tonal qualities of Navajo, he suggested that the Marines use the language as a basis for a code. Twenty-nine Navajos fluent in Navajo and English, some only 15 years of age, constructed and mastered the code, which they transmitted in simulated battles. Eventually over 400 Navajos served in the code-talker program. Several hundred words were used that either corresponded to a particular military expression (for example, the Navajo word for "potato" meant grenade) or to a letter in the English alphabet, since difficult words had to be spelled out. A 1982 presidential proclamation eventually informed the world about the invaluable contributions of the Navajos.

In November 1989, the French government honored both the Comanches and the Choctaw code-talkers for their vital work in World War II by presenting the *Chevalier de l'Ordre National de Merité* (Knight of the National Order of Merit) to Choctaw Chief Hollis Roberts and Comanche Chairman Kenneth Saupitty at a ceremony at the Oklahoma State Capitol. Three surviving Comanche code-talkers attended the ceremony.

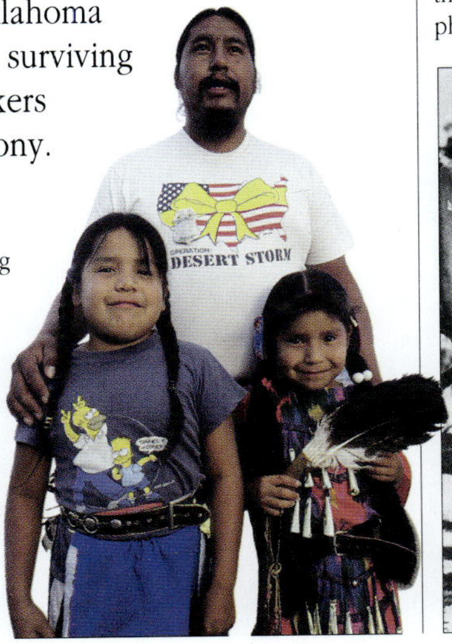

RECENT CAMPAIGNS ▷
This Arapaho veteran, along with 64 Crow men and women, 22 Mohawks from Canada's Kahnawake tribe, and thousands of other Native soldiers, took part in operation "Desert Storm" during the 1990–91 Persian Gulf War. Many of them felt they were better treated than Vietnam veterans on their return home.

TALKING IN CODE

During World War I, Choctaw soldiers transmitted messages in their own language so the German code-breakers could not decipher them. The Indian for "big gun" was used to indicate artillery; "little gun shoot fast" was substituted for machine gun.

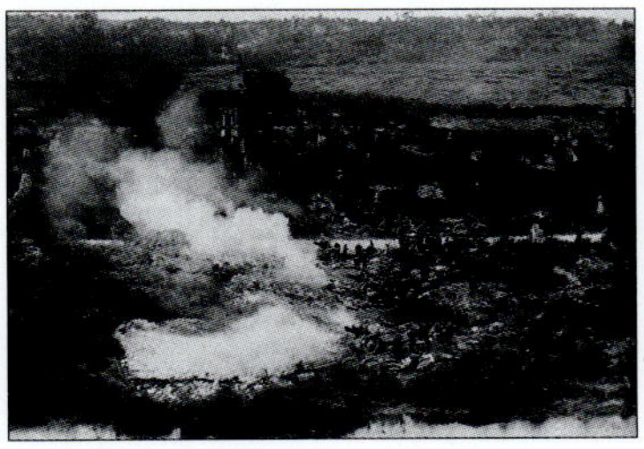

△ INDIANS IN FRENCH CAMPAIGN
Trained to use their language as a code, 14 Choctaw men in the US army's Thirty-sixth Division helped the American Expeditionary Force win several key battles in the Meuse-Argonne campaign in France, the final big German push of the war.

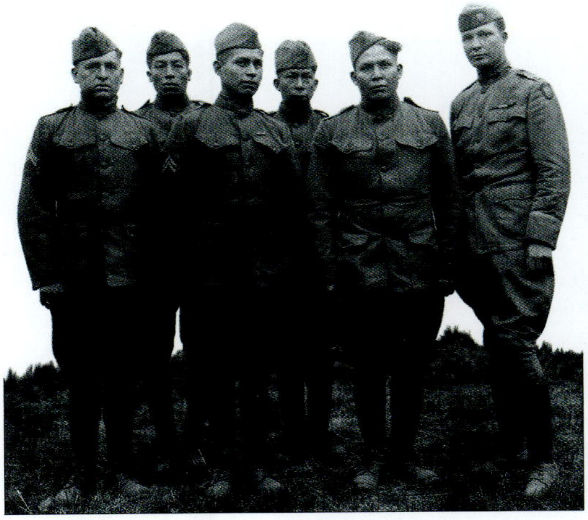

◁ POSTHUMOUS AWARD
A highly praised Choctaw phone squad pose at Camp Devons, Massachusetts. The code-talkers were promised medals for their contribution to ending the war, but these were never received. In 1986, Chief Hollis Roberts presented posthumous Choctaw Nation Medals of Valor to the families of the original code-talkers.

THE WAR EFFORT

When the United States entered World Wars I and II, American Indians became involved in the war effort in many ways. As well as serving directly in combat, Indian men and women worked in technical support positions. During World War II, a large number of Indians worked at home in defense plants and related industries.

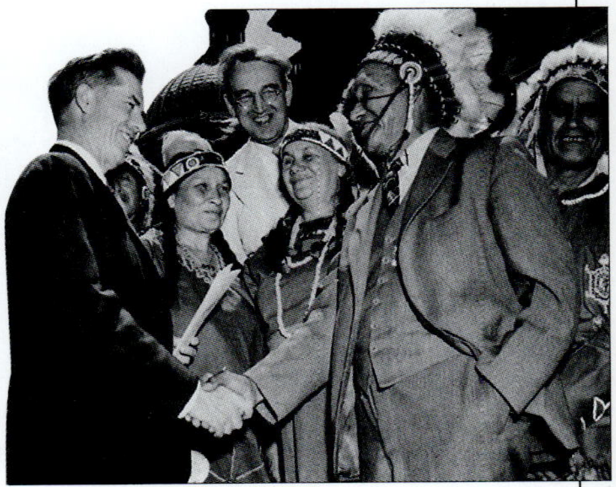

△ IROQUOIS DECLARE WAR
Onondaga Chief Jesse Lyons and one faction of the Iroquois declare war against the Axis (Germany, Italy, and Japan) in June 1942. The declaration was never endorsed by the full Six Nations leadership.

▽ WOMEN'S WAR SERVICE
As well as serving in US armed services, an estimated 12,000 Indian women were involved in the US war effort in 1943, working in defense industries. Here, three Marine Corps women reservists pose for a photograph at Camp Lejeune in North Carolina.

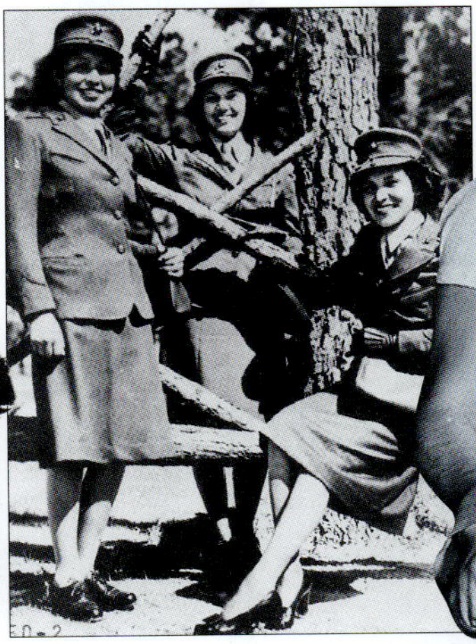

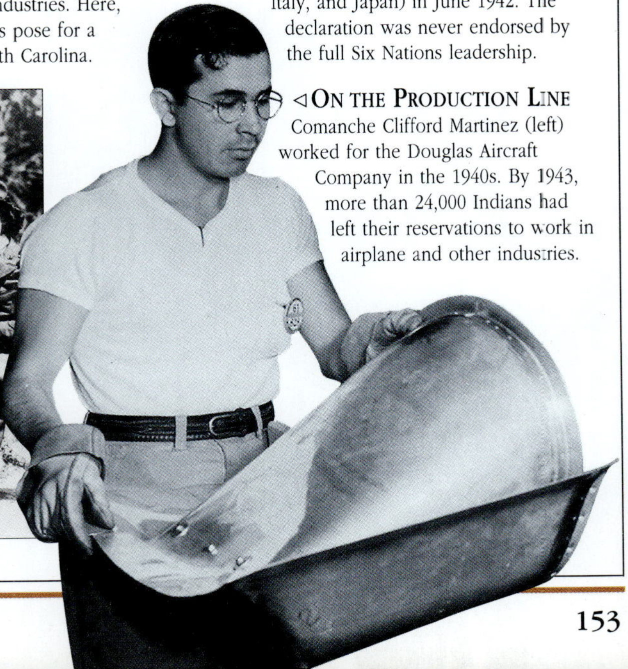

◁ ON THE PRODUCTION LINE
Comanche Clifford Martinez (left) worked for the Douglas Aircraft Company in the 1940s. By 1943, more than 24,000 Indians had left their reservations to work in airplane and other industries.

INDIANS IN WORLD WAR II

During World War II, American Indians carried out some of the most difficult and dangerous assignments, including scouting on long-range reconnaissance missions. In 1943, Navajos Corporal Henry Bake, Jr., (below, left) and Private First Class George H. Kirk (below, right) were photographed operating a portable radio close behind front lines in the Solomon Islands.

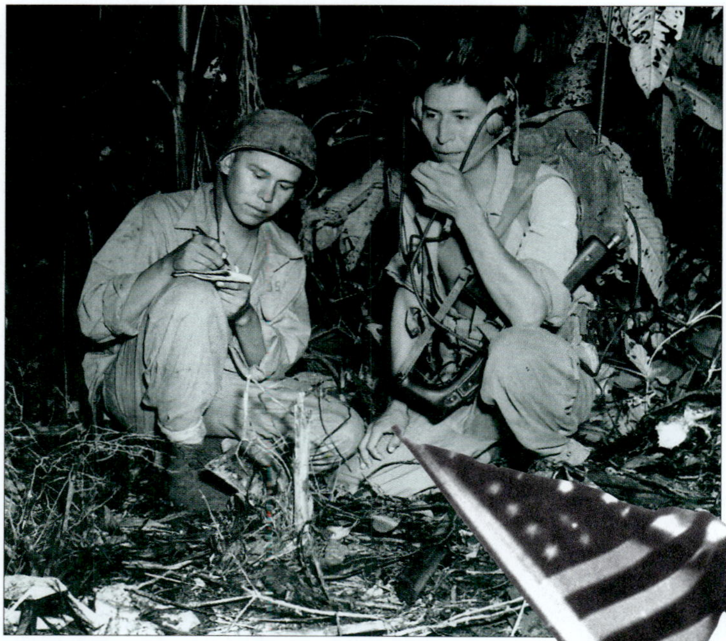

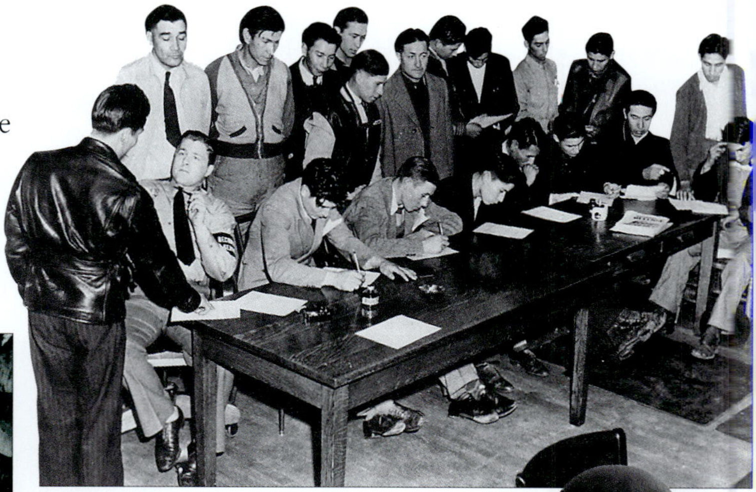

△ **SIGNING UP FOR ACTION**
During World War II, 22 members of the Crow Creek reservation registered for enlistment at a South Dakota recruiting station. Occasionally Indians opposed the draft on religious grounds. The Tuscarora, Seneca, and Mohawk claimed that it did not apply to them since they refused to recognize the 1924 Citizenship Act.

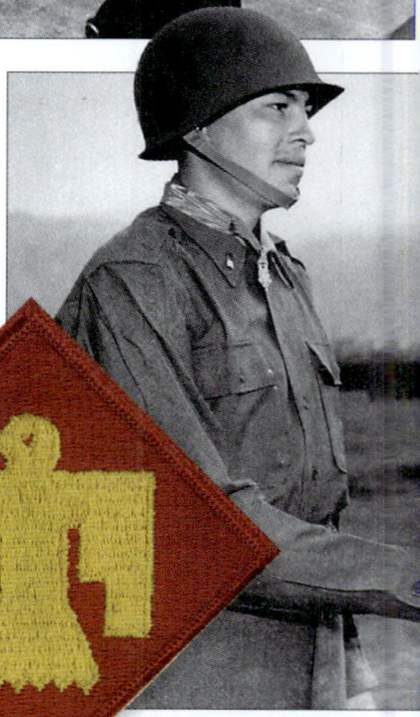

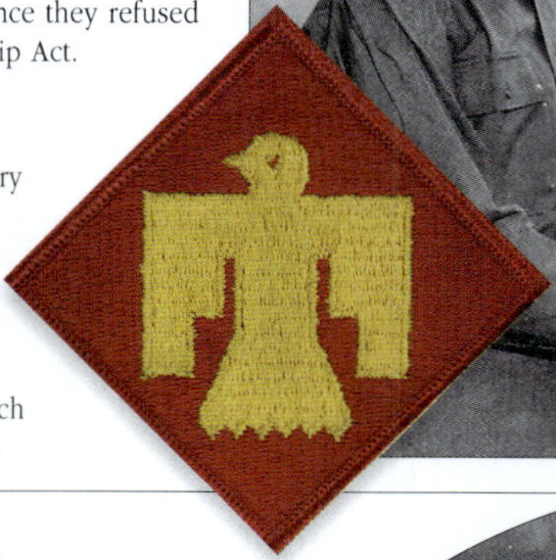

WORN WITH PRIDE ▷
The acclaimed Forty-fifth Infantry enlisted Indian troops from Oklahoma, New Mexico, Arizona, and Colorado. The troops' Indian heritage was reflected in the unit shoulder patch depicting a thunderbird.

THE IRA HAYES STORY

Ira H. Hayes, a Pima from Arizona, enlisted in the US Marines in 1942. He saw action throughout the Pacific and earned the rank of corporal following campaigns at Vella Lavella and Bougainville. In 1945, Hayes took part in a forward attack on Mount Suribachi on the Japanese island of Iwo Jima, during which he and five other Marines raised the US flag on the summit, in the midst of heavy fire.

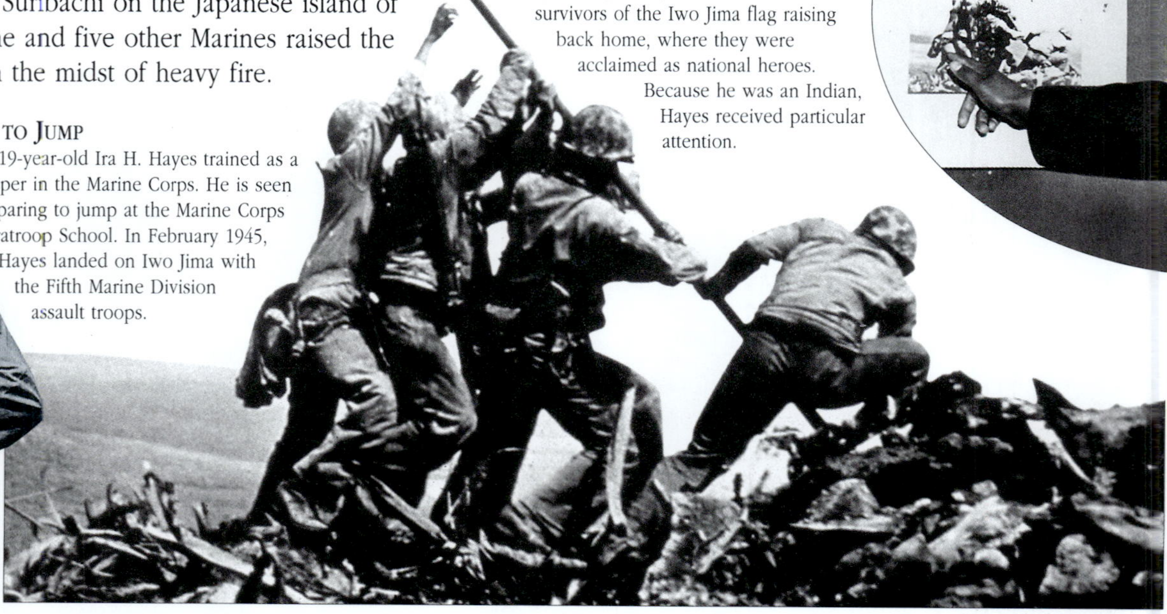

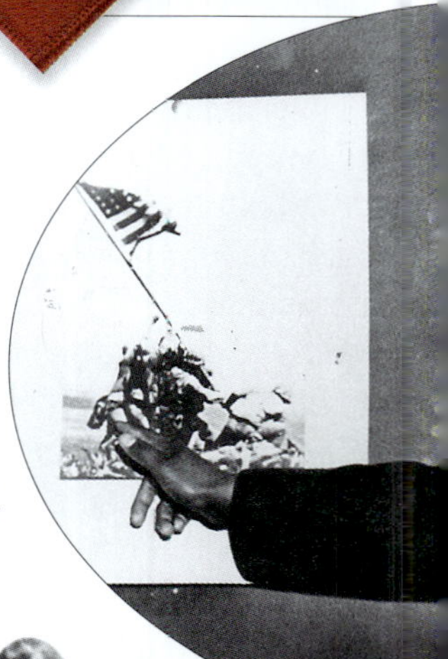

▽ **MARINES RAISE THE FLAG**
Joe Rosenthal, an Associated Press photographer, captured the moment when Hayes and five other Marines raised the flag on Mount Suribachi. Recognized as one of the most inspiring war photographs ever taken, it was published in newspapers throughout the US. The Marine Corps brought Hayes and two other survivors of the Iwo Jima flag raising back home, where they were acclaimed as national heroes. Because he was an Indian, Hayes received particular attention.

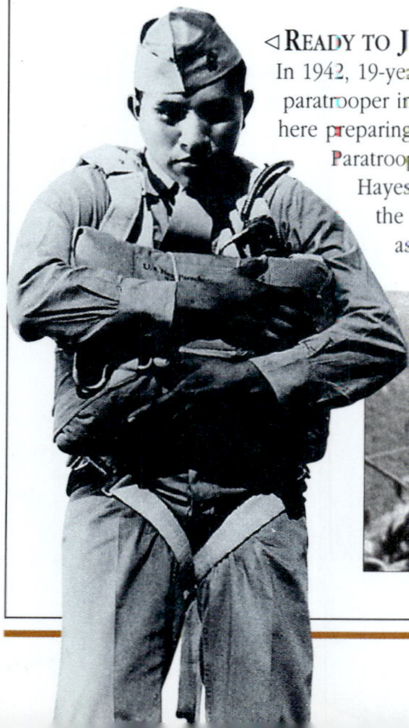

◁ **READY TO JUMP**
In 1942, 19-year-old Ira H. Hayes trained as a paratrooper in the Marine Corps. He is seen here preparing to jump at the Marine Corps Paratroop School. In February 1945, Hayes landed on Iwo Jima with the Fifth Marine Division assault troops.

Today's Warriors

Powwows frequently recognize and honor Indian veterans of twentieth-century conflicts as well as those who are serving in the armed forces today. Such servicemen are considered the modern equivalent of warriors of the past, and much of the clothing worn by men at powwows – such as the roach headdress, feathered bustles, and eagle feathers – has evolved from insignia that was once worn by proven warriors.

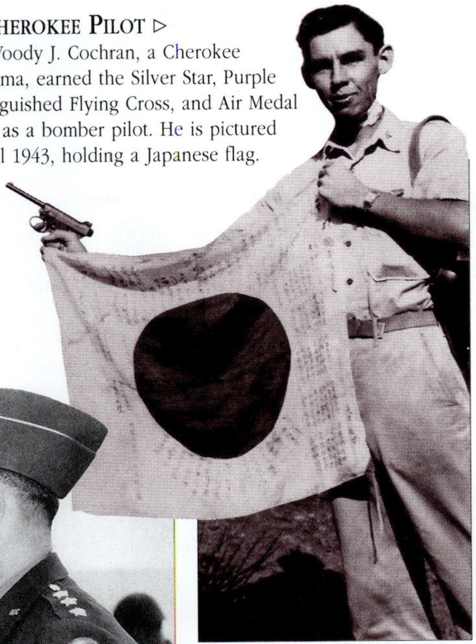

Lauded Cherokee Pilot ▷
Lieutenant Woody J. Cochran, a Cherokee from Oklahoma, earned the Silver Star, Purple Heart, Distinguished Flying Cross, and Air Medal for his valor as a bomber pilot. He is pictured here, in April 1943, holding a Japanese flag.

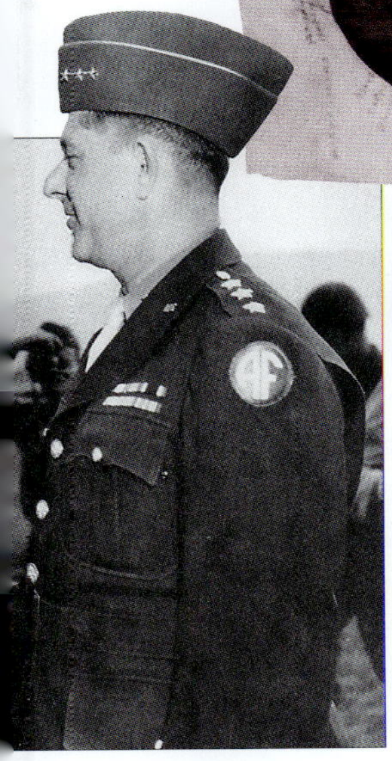

◁ Medal of Honor
Lieutenant Ernest Childers, an Oklahoma Creek, is seen here being congratulated by General Jacob L. Devers on receiving the Congressional Medal of Honor in July 1944 for wiping out two machine gun nests. Several fellow Indians also received the medal for acts that "exceeded any just demand of duty."

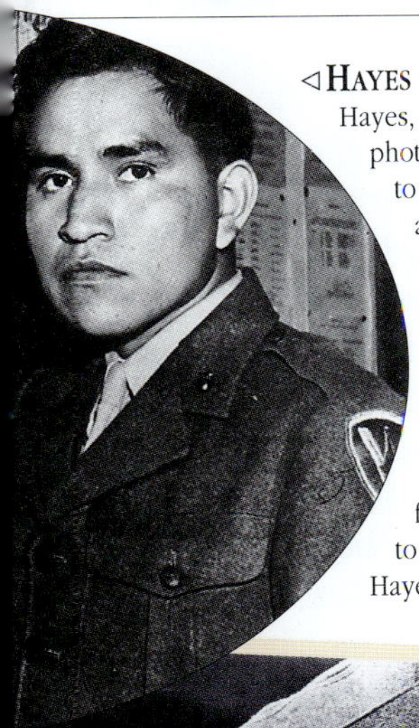

◁ Hayes the Hero
Hayes, pointing to himself in Rosenthal's photograph, was sent around the US to appear at patriotic celebrations and rallies. He struggled with the unwelcome attention brought by the memorable picture.

▽ Man and Legend
Hero and symbol, Ira Hayes died in January 1955 on the Pima reservation, destitute and suffering from alcoholism and over-exposure to the cold. Tony Curtis played Ira Hayes in the 1961 movie *The Outsider.*

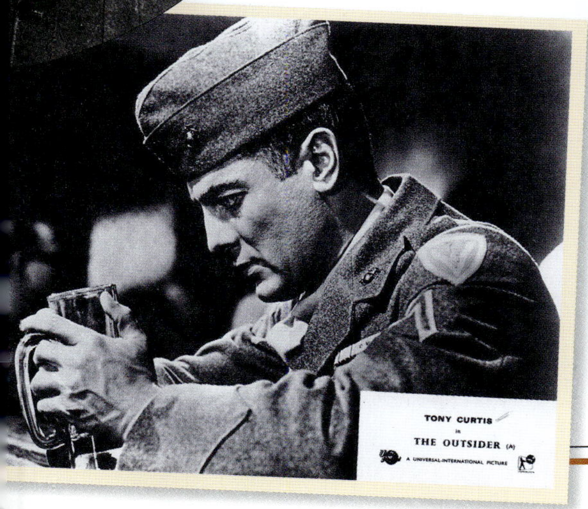

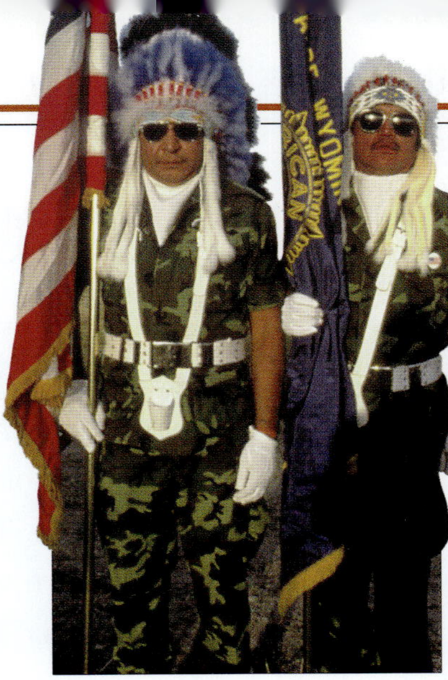

△ All Flags Honored
National and Indian flags "lead the way" at powwows. Nearly every tribe has a flag song that is dedicated to people who have served in the armed forces. During the singing of flag songs, the audience stands.

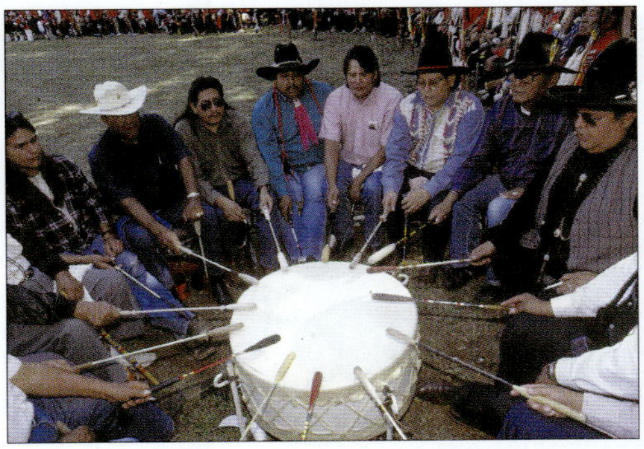

△ Heartbeat of a Nation
Representing the heartbeat of an Indian nation, the drum is treated as a sacred object: nothing is set on a drum and no one reaches across it. The term "drum" also refers to the group itself, which sings songs for the dance contests.

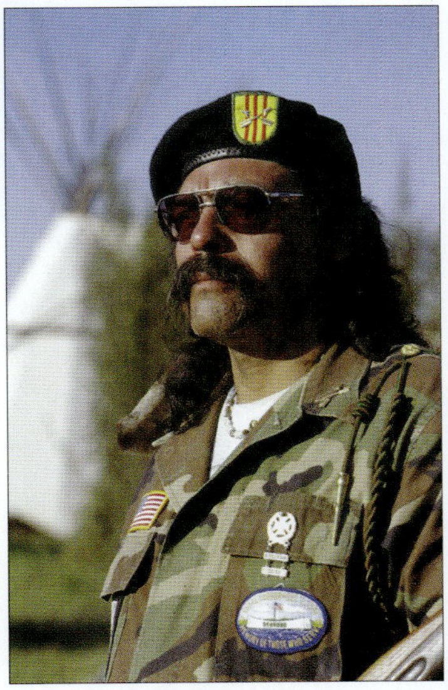

Vietnam Veterans ▷
Indian Vietnam veterans were not treated as heroes when they returned home, leading many to reexamine their status. Some joined the American Indian Movement (*see p.162.*)

▽ The Grand Entry
During the Grand Entry – the opening ceremony of a powwow – flag bearers (Indian veterans) carry the eagle staff, US and Canadian flags, and state and tribal flags into the arena.

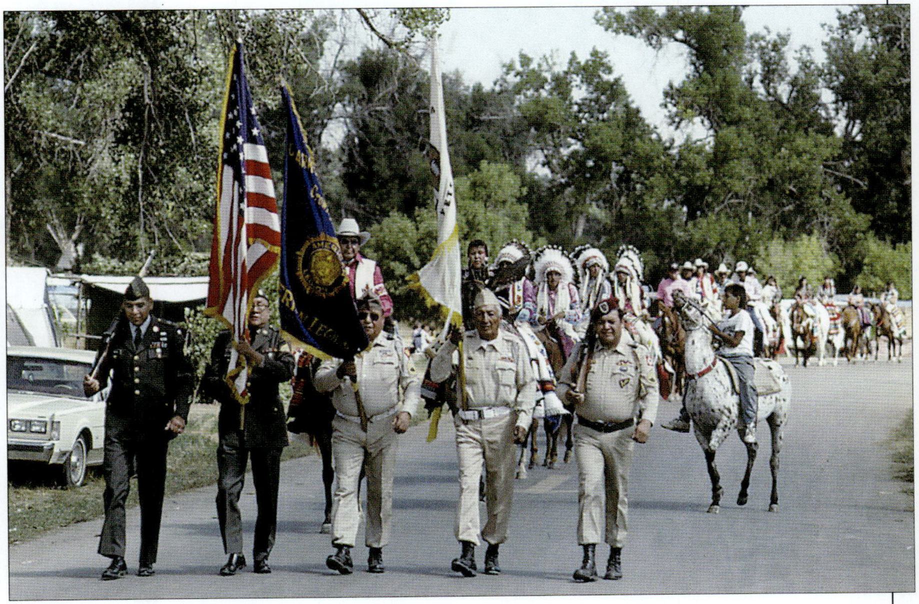

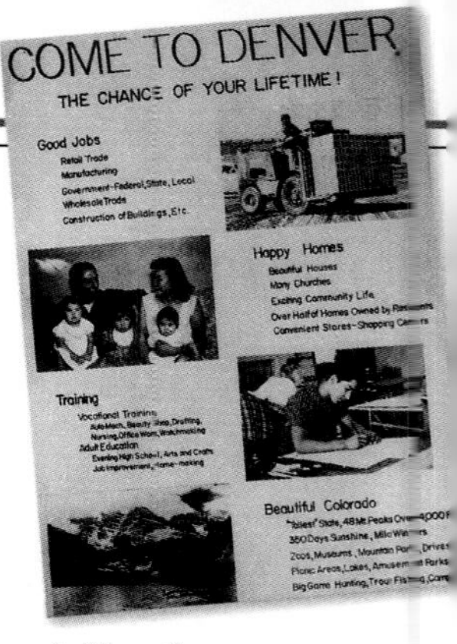

A NEW START
The BIA believed the solution to reservation unemployment lay in persuading large numbers of Indians to relocate to urban areas like Chicago and Denver.

TERMINATION AND RELOCATION

DURING THE 1950s, the US government, without the consent of Indians, tried to end its special relationship with Native tribes and shift the financial cost of assimilation policies to states. Triggered in part by pressures from non-Indian interests seeking to acquire commercially valuable Indian lands, policymakers had little concern for the wellbeing of affected tribes. Termination involved a huge Bureau of Indian Affairs (BIA) program to relocate reservation Indians to cities, as well as the construction of dams in the US and Canada, which caused serious social and cultural disruptions.

TRIBAL TERMINATORS

In 1950, Dillon S. Myer became Commissioner of Indian Affairs. Myer, who believed that the Indian-land relationship had to be dissolved, was assisted by Utah Senator Arthur V. Watkins, who dominated the hearings on the termination bills, and helped minimize opposition by Congress and Indians.

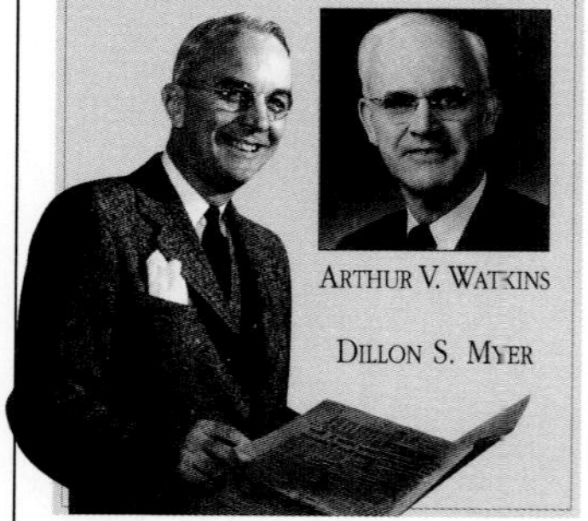

ARTHUR V. WATKINS

DILLON S. MYER

UNHAPPY WITH REORGANIZATION policies during the 1940s, Congress criticized the costs of BIA operations and the slow pace of Indian assimilation. A new policy took shape, aimed at solving the "Indian problem" by terminating the special relationship between Indians and the federal government, regardless of whether or not Indians wanted or were prepared for it. In 1953, Congress defined official congressional termination policy in House Concurrent Resolution 108, and singled out certain tribes for immediate withdrawal of federal support.

Although Indian opposition to termination was substantial, Congressional opposition was meager and the consent of affected Indian groups was not considered necessary. Between 1954 and 1964, Congress passed 13 termination acts affecting over 100 tribes, some quite small and some large. Land was removed from trust and often sold; assets were distributed to tribal members, who were subject to state laws and taxes and ineligible for federal Indian services. States were given broad authority over terminated Indians in education, child adoption, and land use. Criminal and civil cases were turned over to state courts without Indian consent, and federal and tribal law were no longer applicable. After terminated tribes relinquished their lands, large amounts of Indian land once again passed into non-Indian hands. Eventually, after the loss of their land base, tribes were unable to exercise their governmental powers.

Relocation to Urban Centers

In the early 1950s, the federal government launched an extensive program of relocating reservation Indians to urban centers. World War II had already prompted some Indians to head for cities, where many became wartime factory workers. After the war, when Indians returned to reservations, jobs were few. Some went to school on the GI Bill, which authorized educational and other benefits for veterans. The BIA, capitalizing on the lack of opportunities, offered employment assistance to Indians who would relocate to distant cities; once there, they were cut off from BIA services. The tactic became another way for the government to get out of the Indian business. One third of Indians, lonely and isolated, went back to their reservations, but more moved to cities in search of work.

The construction of dams during the 1950s flooded large areas of Indian land, and this also played a role in forcing many Indians to relocate their homes and communities.

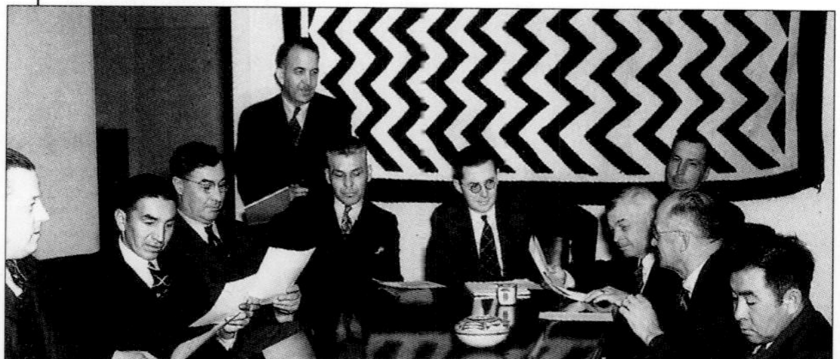

△ **CHIPPEWAS CLAIM COMPENSATION**
A delegation from the Minnesota Chippewa tribe is seen here with federal officials in Washington, D.C. Robbed of a vast amount of acreage since 1889, the tribe filed claims with the Indian Claims Commission (ICC), established by Congress in 1946.

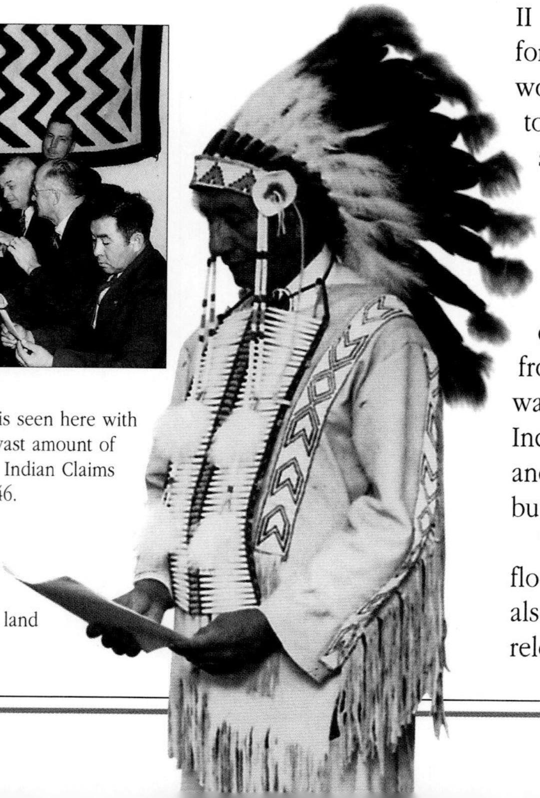

SIOUX TRIBAL LAND CLAIM >
Oglala Sioux Tribe Vice President David Long reads a statement before the ICC in 1957. Some legislators felt that it was necessary to settle tribal land claims before beginning the termination process.

Homelands Flooded

Dam construction in the 1950s, most of which provided water for huge commercial interests, devastated Indian lands and communities throughout North America. Besides forcing Indian families to relocate, waters flooded rich agricultural grounds, Indian fishing grounds, villages, sacred sites of major cultural importance, and ancestral burial grounds. Dams caused the loss of game, grazing lands, timber, and traditional plants of cultural and nutritional value.

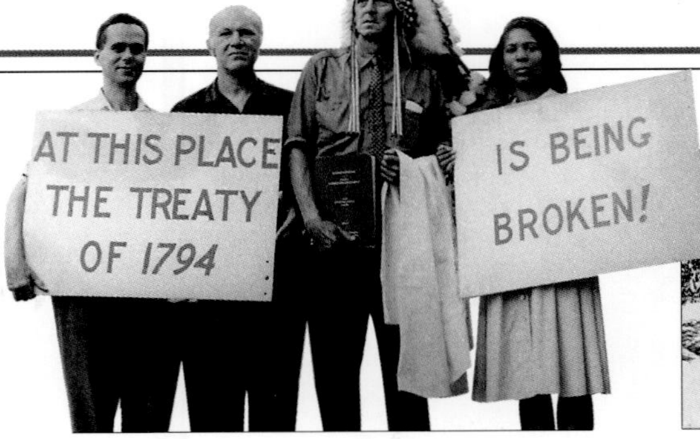

△ **Kinzua Protesters**
In the 1950s, Seneca people protested against the construction of the Kinzua dam, which flooded some 10,000 acres (4,050 hectares) of reservation lands in New York State, forcing 130 Indian families to relocate.

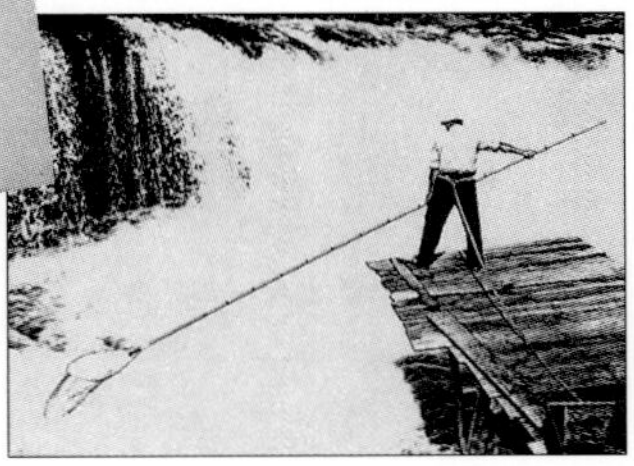

△ **The End of a Tradition**
In 1957, the Dalles dam flooded Celilo Falls, an ancient place of worship on the Columbia River, and ended traditional dip-net fishing.

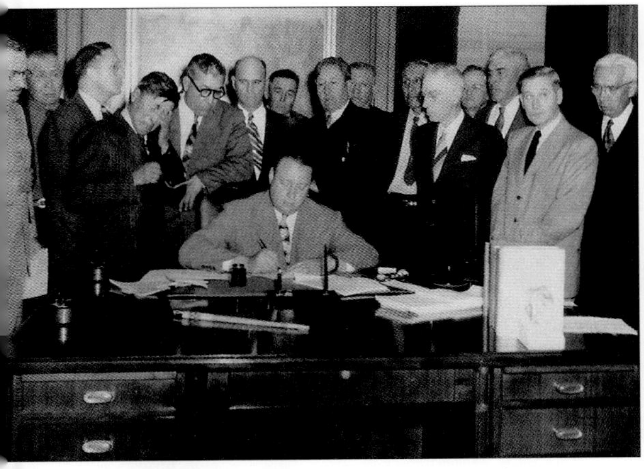

△ **From Reservation to Reservoir**
George Gillette (fourth from left), a member of the Fort Berthold Tribal Business Council, is overcome with emotion as Interior Secretary Julius Krug signs a 1948 contract ceding 155,000 acres (63,000 hectares) of the North Dakota reservation to the government for construction of the Garrison reservoir on the Missouri River.

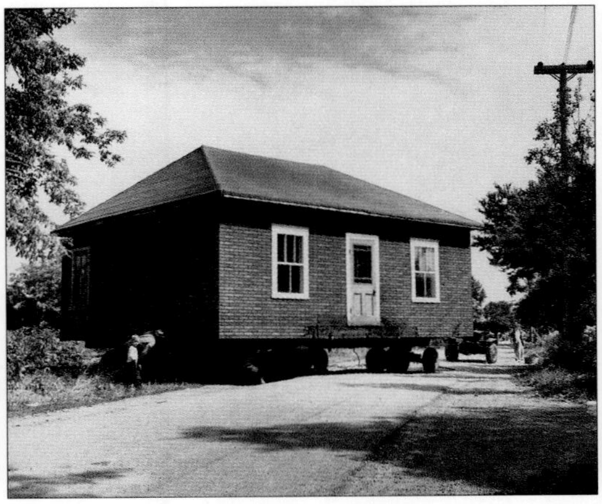

△ **Caughnawaga Homes Relocated**
The construction of the St. Lawrence Seaway began in 1954, seriously affecting the Mohawk Indians of Caughnawaga in Quebec, who lost 1,260 acres (510 hectares), despite their refusal to surrender the land. In 1956, their homes were hauled to new sites and fitted onto new foundations.

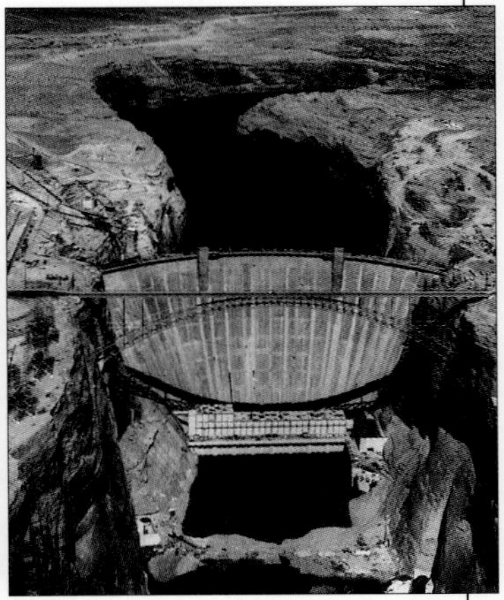

△ **Sacred Site Flooded**
The completion of the Glen Canyon dam across the Colorado River in Arizona and the creation of Lake Powell flooded Rainbow Natural Bridge, a Navajo sacred site.

Indians Relocated to Cities

Relocation went hand in hand with termination. The BIA's Voluntary Relocation Program encouraged Indians to move, with unrealistic promises of a prosperous urban life. Along with one-way bus tickets and moving expenses, the BIA provided housing, free medical care for a year, and a 30-day subsistence allowance. Once Indians left the reservation, they were cut off from Indian Bureau services.

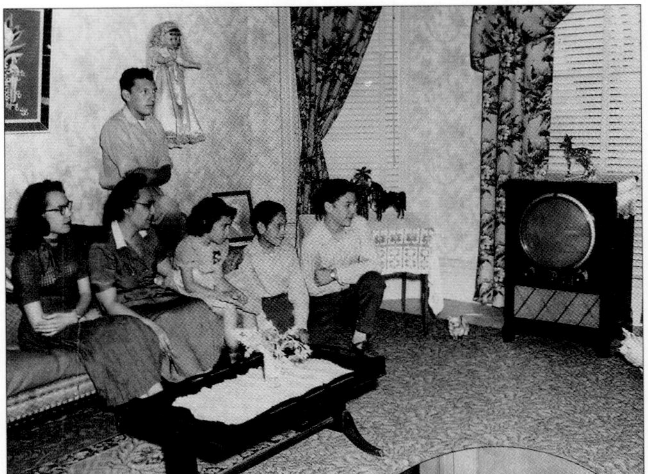

Urban Indian Ideal ▷
An Ojibway family, pictured here in 1955 in their new home in Oakland, presents the white ideal of the urbanized Indian. But families were resettled as far away from their reservation homes as possible in order to weaken family and tribal ties, and were scattered throughout cities to prevent them forming cohesive Indian neighborhoods.

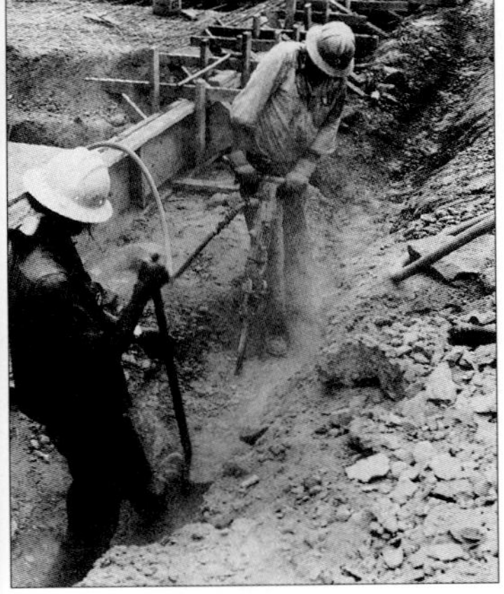

◁ **Training for Industry**
In 1956, Congress passed a law that authorized the BIA to provide adult vocational training and on-the-job training for Indians between the ages of 18 and 35, and to provide relocated Indians with subsistence for six months. These Navajo workers were trained in skills that prepared them for industrial work in cities, not on reservations.

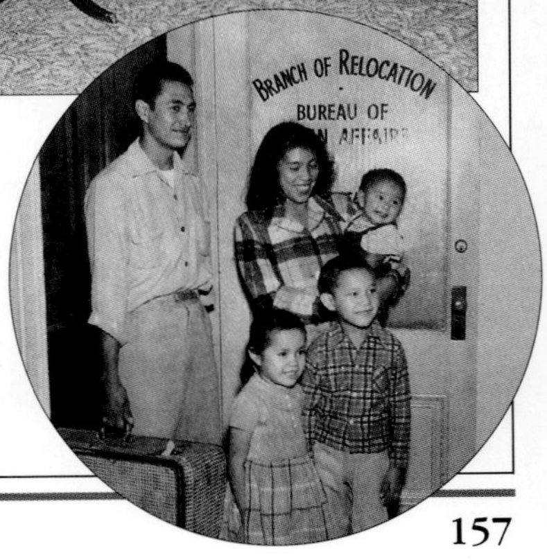

Aiding Relocation ▷
The first relocation centers were established in Chicago and Los Angeles. By 1958, there were 12 relocation field offices, but these were not adequately staffed to handle the number of relocated Indians looking for work.

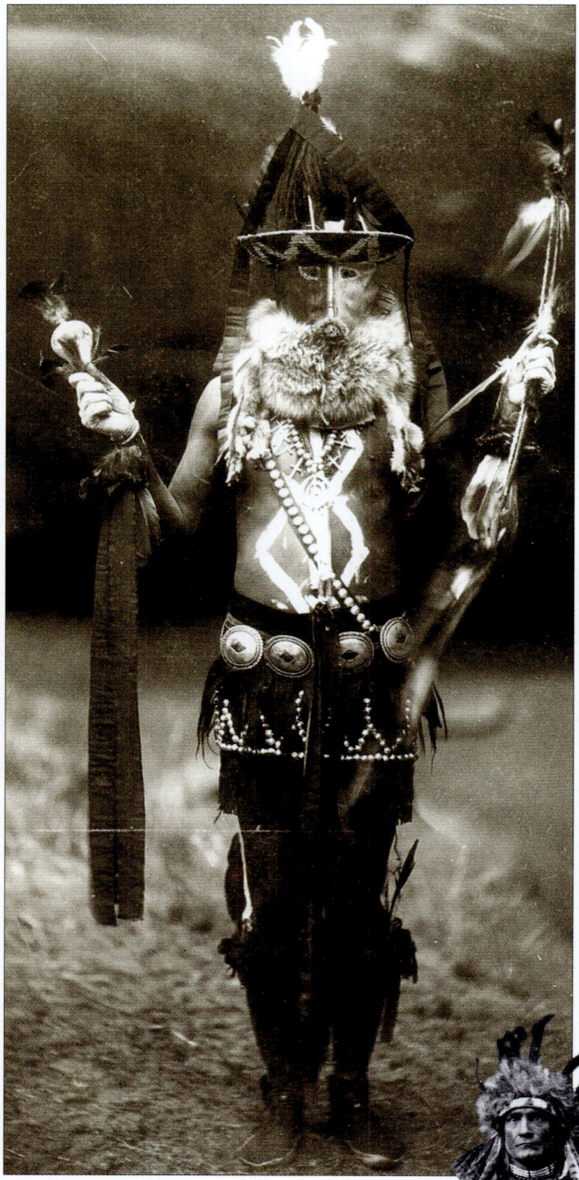

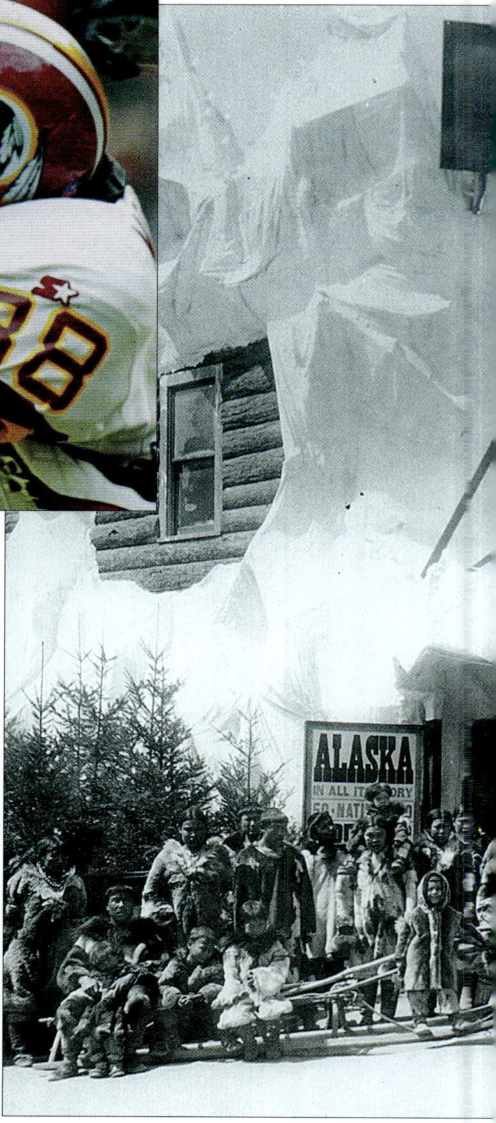

SKILLS DISPLAYED ▷
The Seminoles in Florida publicly display their talent at wrestling alligators. The five men pictured here, wearing trademark Seminole appliqué jackets, have passed the final test at an alligator-wrestling school in Musa Isle Village near Miami, Florida.

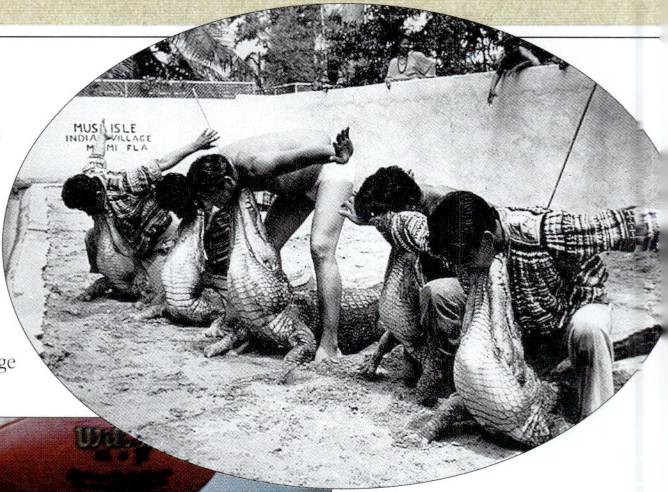

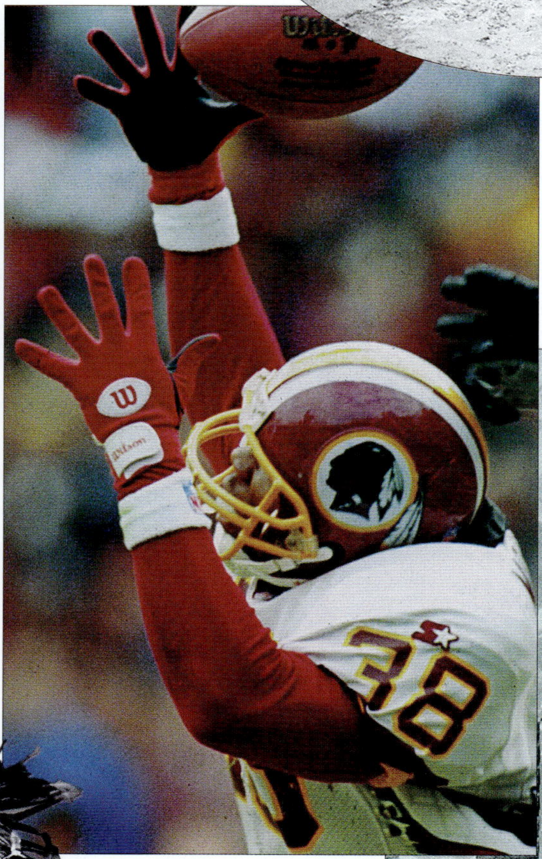

◁ ON THE WRONG TEAM?
Indian petitioners have long argued that Indian mascots, nicknames, and logos offend Natives. In 1998, the US Patent and Trademark Office canceled seven registered Washington Redskins trademarks for being disparaging to Native Americans, but other teams still use stereotypical Indian images.

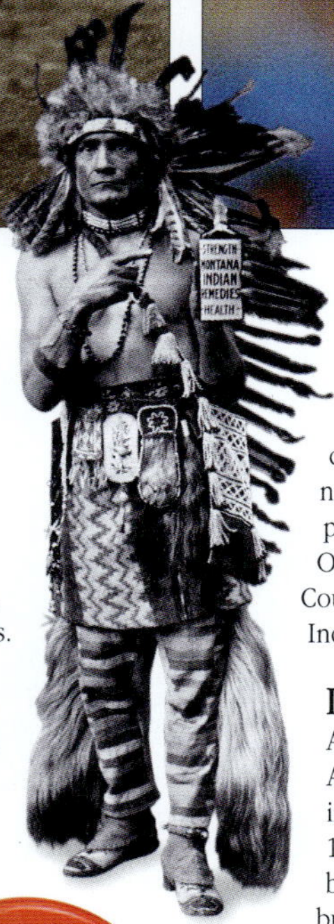

△ THE CURTIS CAMERA LIES
Edward S. Curtis photographed American Indians for 30 years and used every trick of the camera and the darkroom to fabricate a romanticized image of Indians. Curtis made the costume for this Navajo Yeibichai dancer who was nervous about being photographed in his own sacred clothing.

▽ TWO-WHEELED HORSE POWER
A stylized Indian profile adorns the Indian Motorcycle, first manufactured in 1902 in Springfield, Massachusetts. The Indian theme and logo are carried on models called the Scout, the Chief, and the Warrior, as well as on toy motorcycles and the company's other products.

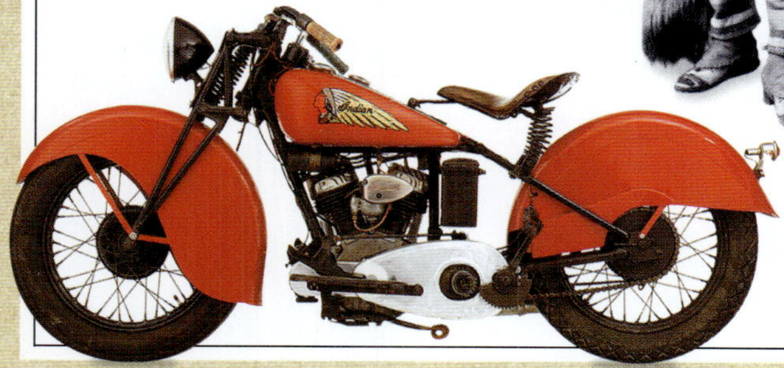

◁ SELLING HEALTH
Many people perceived Native people to be strong and long-lived, and these ideas were exploited by pharmaceutical companies, who used Native names or pictures of real Native people to sell products such as Old Sachem Bitters, Seminole Cough Balsam, or the Montana Indian remedy pictured here.

IMPORTED ESKIMOS ▷
An Eskimo village at the 1909 Alaska-Yukon-Pacific Exposition in Seattle, Washington, exhibited 100 Eskimos (described in the brochures as "strange people") – but none from Alaska. Instead, the promoters imported Siberian Yupik Eskimos, who were displayed in a gigantic papier mâché igloo – the dwelling of Canadian Inuits (*see Note on Names, p.15.*)

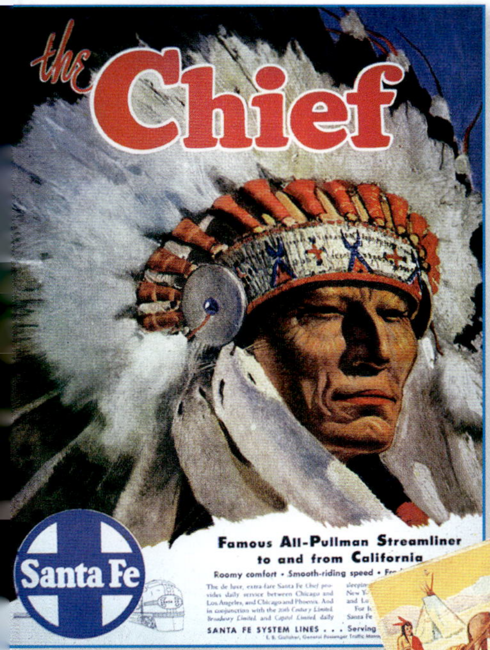

◁ PART OF THE SCENERY
At the turn of the century, the Santa Fe Railway set out to lure travelers into its Southwestern territory. They commissioned artists to present the area in a picturesque fashion and to capitalize on the dramatic scenery and Indian tribes. Romanticized Indian images were used in their advertising material.

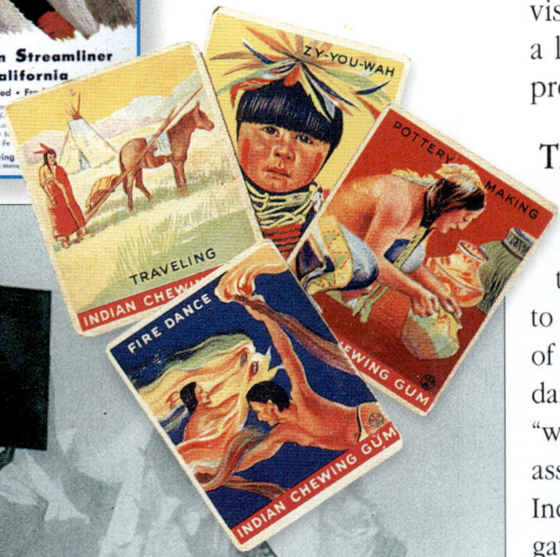

▽ INDIAN COLLECTIBLES
Gum manufacturers, in a marketing ploy, inserted small picture cards bearing colorful Indian images in packets of gum. The sketchy information on the back of the cards perpetuated the idea that Indians were primitive and quaint.

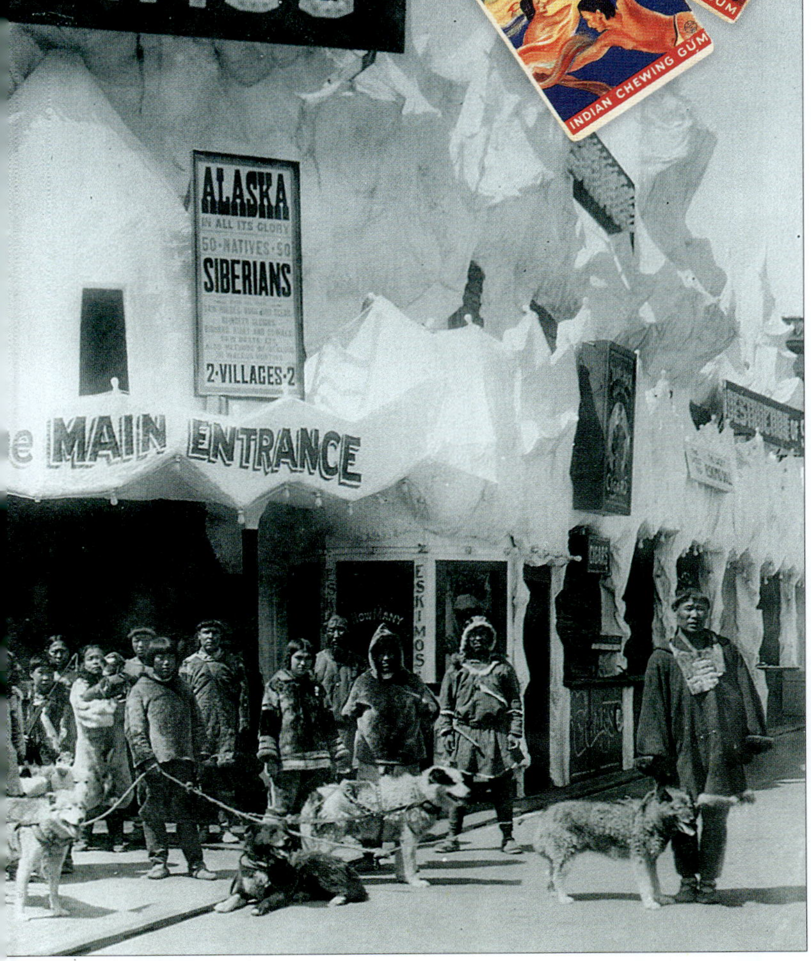

Trading an Image

RED INDIAN MOTOR OIL, Red Man Chewing Tobacco, Calumet Baking Powder, General Motors Pontiac cars, Mutual of Omaha Insurance (whose symbol is a stylized Indian), Land-O-Lakes Margarine, Mohawk Carpet, Indian Head Cornmeal, Cherokee of California clothing, Crazy Horse Malt Liquor, the Washington Redskins, Cleveland Indians, and Atlanta Braves, Trail Chief thermal socks, Chippewa Shoes, Lawn Chief mower, and Iroquois brands. None of these products has anything to do with authentic Indian cultures, yet the images have been used to create high product visibility, say something quickly about an item, create a lasting impression, sell merchandise, and to increase profit. Anything "Indian" sells.

The Selling Power of Indian Imagery

Products have used Indians as part of their advertising and packaging since the days of the nineteenth-century traveling medicine shows. Kickapoo Indian Salve, claiming to cure "all skin diseases," was promoted by traveling troupes of Indians (rarely Kickapoos) who demonstrated Indian dances and crafts. Indians were used to lend credibility to "wonder cures" and herbal preparations because they were associated with a special knowledge of plants and animals. Indian Woman's Balm, with a drawing of an Indian woman gathering roots, was advertised to cure "female ailments." "Red Mac: King of Tonics," was another popular patent medicine, used in Canada, which featured a drawing of an Indian in headdress on the label.

Since the 1880s, countless products and sports team mascots have sported Indian profiles and nicknames. People have been conditioned to associate the image of Indians with nature, the outdoors, the wilderness, wildness, bravery, ruggedness, physical prowess, and medicinal knowledge. These associations are difficult to shake off.

Indian Images Mock Reality

Indians care about how they are portrayed. They care because these invented images prevent people from understanding authentic Native America. They care because they are singled out like no other human group, and labeled in ways that serve to enrich others and that are culturally harmful. They are relegated to the past, displayed as museum exhibits, and misrepresented by countless manufacturers.

In 1992, seven Native American leaders filed a lawsuit challenging the Washington Redskins' trademark. They argued that "redskin" is offensive to Native people and should not enjoy federal registration protection. In 1998, the Patient and Trademark Office ruled that "redskin" was a racial slur and canceled the trademarks. The Redskins appealed the decision.

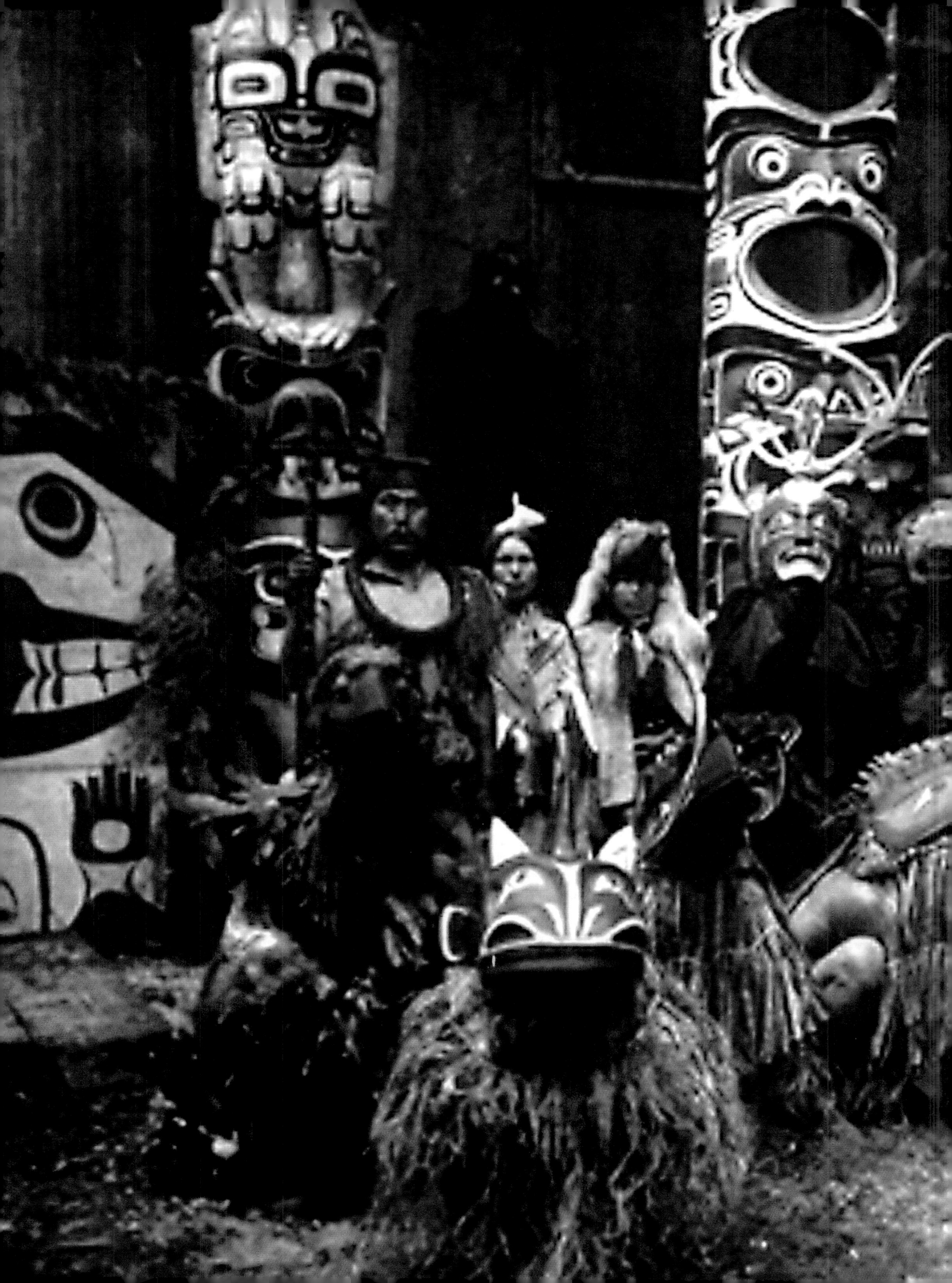

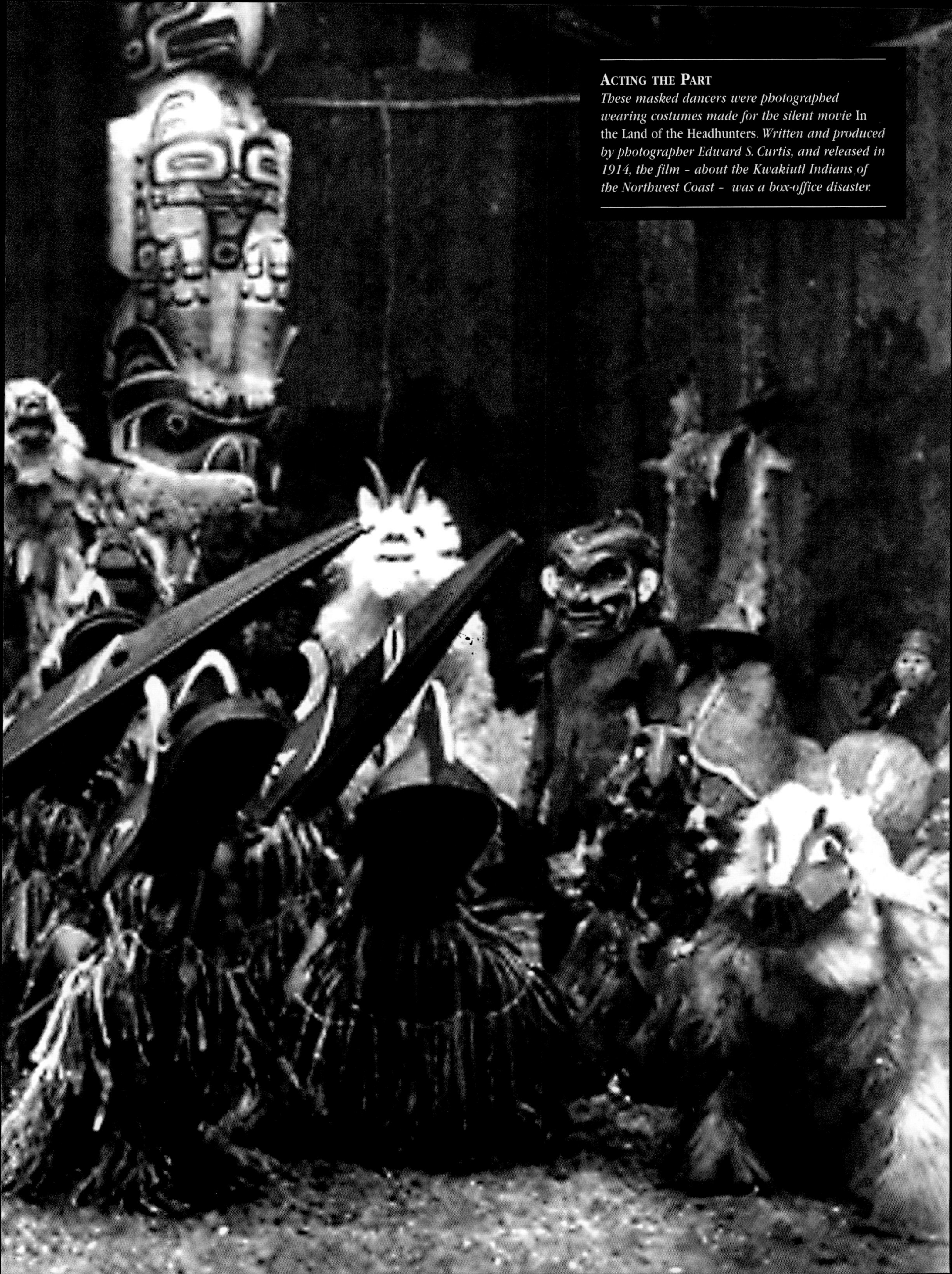

Acting the Part

These masked dancers were photographed wearing costumes made for the silent movie In the Land of the Headhunters. *Written and produced by photographer Edward S. Curtis, and released in 1914, the film - about the Kwakiutl Indians of the Northwest Coast - was a box-office disaster.*

THE MARCH OF RED POWER

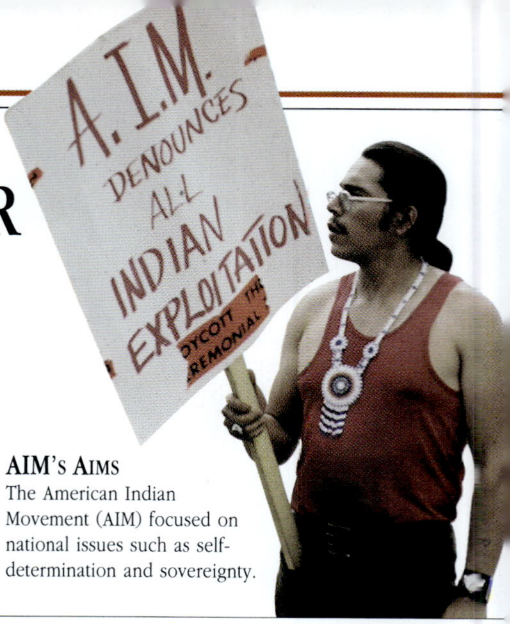

AIM'S AIMS
The American Indian Movement (AIM) focused on national issues such as self-determination and sovereignty.

IN THE 1960S AND 1970S, as a result of a long history of oppressive federal policies, the Red Power movement swept through the cities and reservations where Native people lived. Activists decried the wretched circumstances of Indians as the poorest, the least educated, the most disempowered, most malnourished, and most disease-ridden section of US society, and used direct action to fight discrimination and political oppression and to demand their lawful rights.

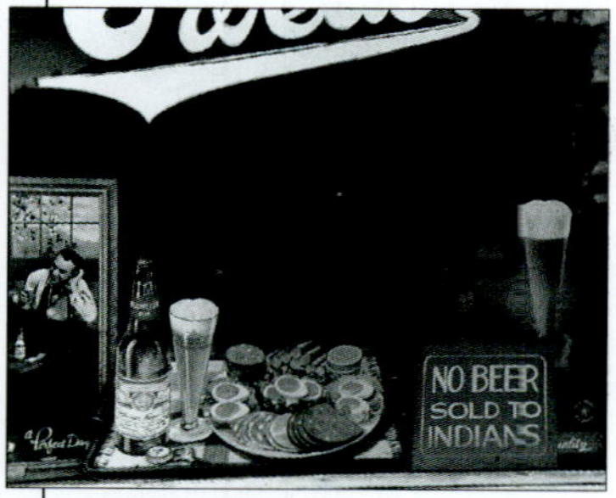

△ **RACIST RESTRICTIONS**
A notice in a tavern near a Sioux reservation denies the sale of beer to Natives, who were also barred from restaurants and other public places.

▽ **POVERTY TRAP**
In the 1960s, too many Indians lived in shoddily constructed government dwellings or tar shacks without toilets, electricity, or running water. The average age of death was 43 years.

THE RED POWER MOVEMENT that emerged in the 1960s was, in part, a response to the devastating impact of termination policies. Ironically, one consequence of the relocation of Indians to cities was a drive for pan-Indian unity, an emphasis on self-determination, and a sense of militancy. Youthful Indian militants also responded to the successful example of the Black civil rights movement. In the summer of 1961, college-educated Native youths who favored direct political action founded the National Indian Youth Council (NIYC).

In 1964, in defiance of Washington State regulations, NIYC leadership organized a "fish-in" on a river in Washington State to support the treaty rights of small, almost landless Native nations. The event led to more fish-ins on several other rivers. This new method of challenging state regulations involved Indians in risking their boats, nets, and fish – and sometimes their own safety – in confrontations with game wardens. The fishing rights struggle continued until 1974, when a federal district judge ruled that the Native nations of Washington State not only held the right to fish, but were entitled to one half of the annual fish harvest in the State.

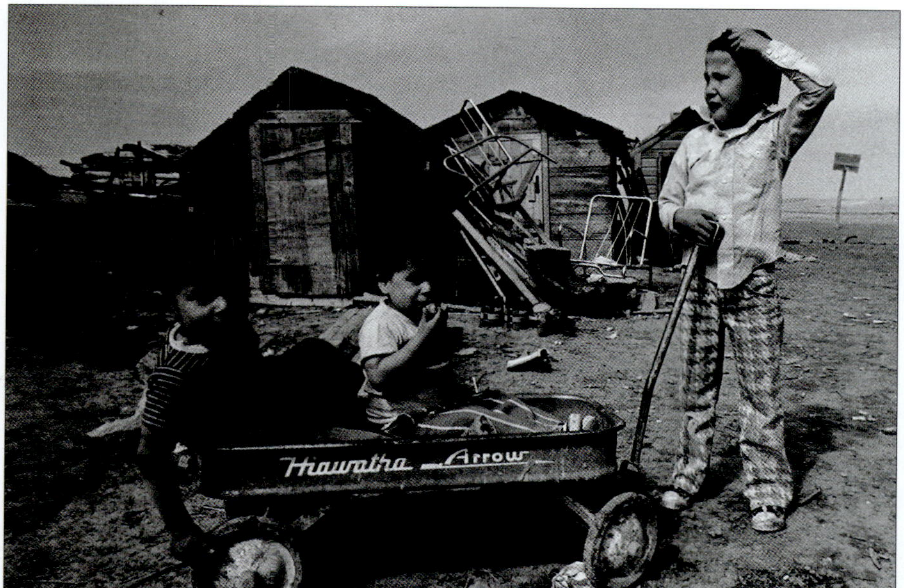

From Alcatraz to Wounded Knee

Between 1968 and 1978, the NIYC style of Red Power politics caught on with other Native peoples. In 1969, boatloads of AIM members and other Indians, many of them college students, seized and occupied Alcatraz Island in one of the most successful Indian protest actions of the modern era. The 19-month occupation heightened public awareness of their people's grievances.

AIM, along with several other Indian groups, mobilized a mass demonstration that came to be known as "The Trail of Broken Treaties." A protest for sovereignty and treaty rights, it took the form of a march from San Francisco to Washington, DC, in the fall of 1972. The march turned militant on 2 November 1972 when some 500 demonstrators occupied the Bureau of Indian Affairs building in Washington, DC.

The following year, hundreds of traditional Lakotas and others asked for AIM's help in addressing the reactionary tribal government headed by Oglala Lakota Richard Wilson on the Pine Ridge Sioux reservation in South Dakota. On 28 February, AIM members and supporters took over the hamlet of Wounded Knee. For 71 days, the world's attention was captured by a historic standoff between tribal people and the

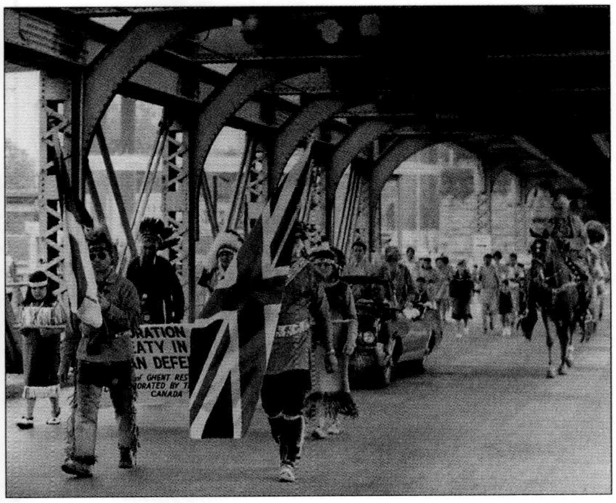

◁ **TREATY RIGHTS COMMEMORATED**
On 20 July 1969, members of the Indian Defense League crossed the Whirlpool Bridge, at Niagara Falls, to commemorate their rights under the 1794 Jay Treaty, which gave Indians in the US and Canada free and unrestricted passage and trade across the US-Canadian border.

MAYFLOWER PROTEST ▷
On Thanksgiving Day 1972, members of United American Indians of New England protested against the holiday by climbing into the rigging of the Mayflower II (a replica of the ship that brought the Pilgrims to Massachusetts) and replacing British flags with their own banner.

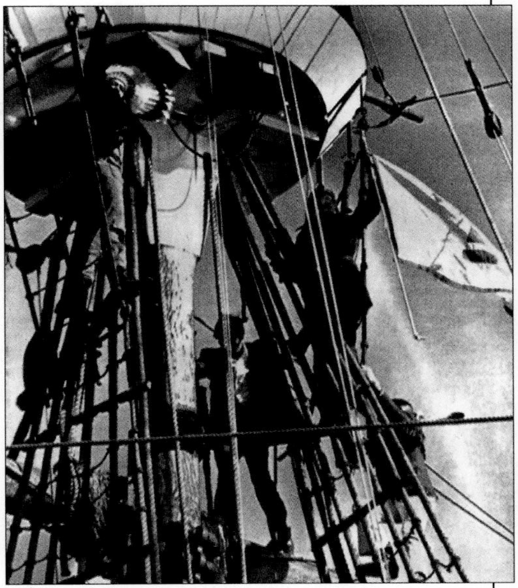

▽ **OCCUPATION OF BIA BUILDING**
In November 1972, protestors occupied the Bureau of Indian Affairs building in Washington, DC, demanding that issues laid out in "Twenty Points" – a list of unfulfilled, earlier treaty rights – be negotiated. The protest ended when the government agreed to consider the issues.

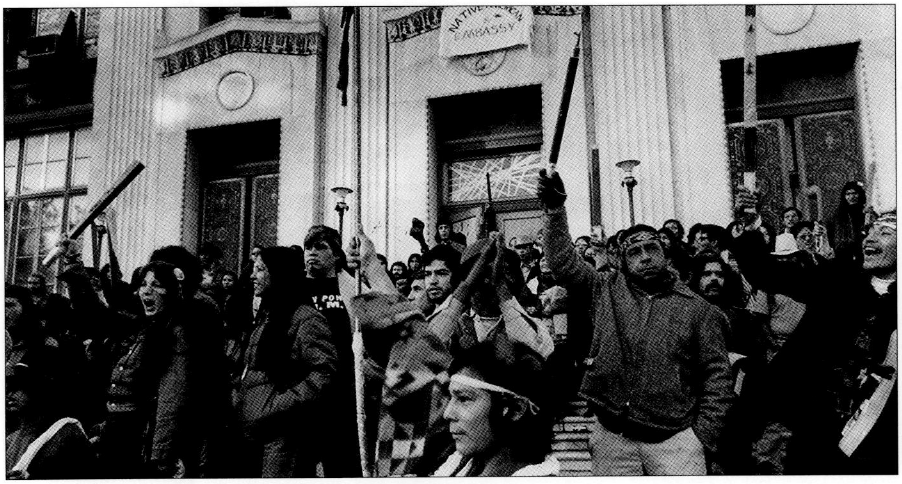

federal government and Wilson's "goons" (the term is allegedly an acronym for "Guards of the Oglala Nation.") By the time a settlement was reached, two Indians had been killed, a federal marshal wounded, and 300 Indians indicted.

Protests in Canada

During the 1960s and 1970s, Canada's Native peoples also pursued tribal sovereignty and self-determination, with Ottawa the scene of many protests. In 1974, Shuswap George Manuel, President of Canada's National Indian Brotherhood, announced that activist groups were opposed to an agreement between the James Bay Cree and the Quebec government to settle their land claims in northern Quebec. In 1976, the Inuit began their campaign for sovereignty in Nunavut, their homeland.

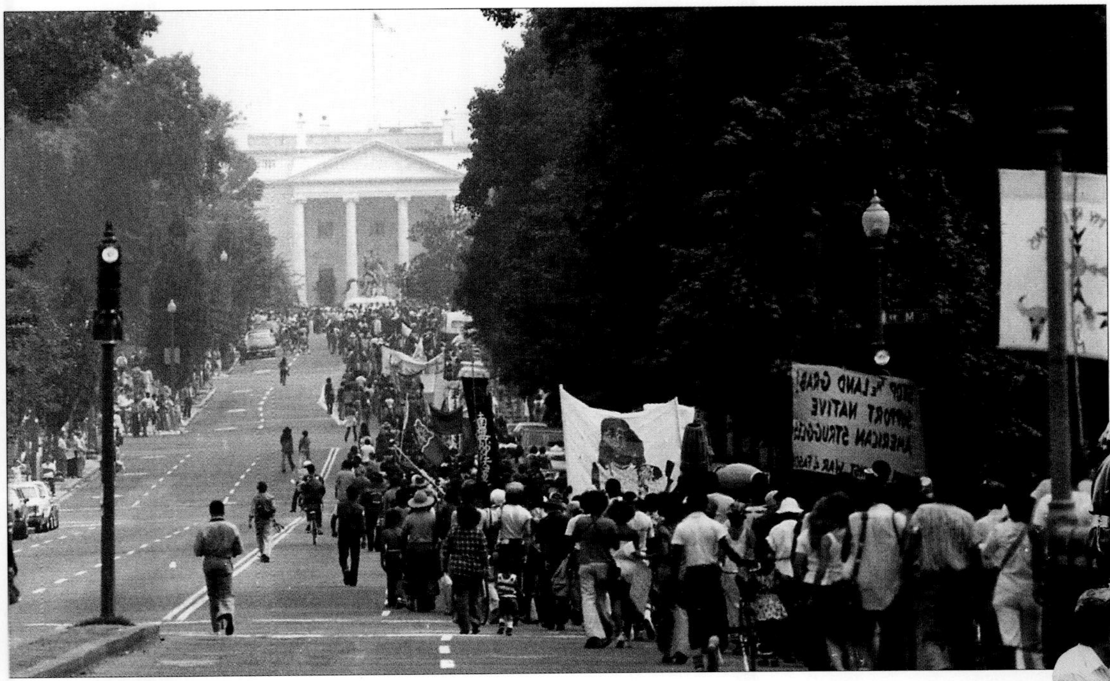

◁ **THE LONGEST WALK**
In 1978, more than 200 Native Americans marched on a seven-month 3,000-mile (4,828-km) pilgrimage from Alcatraz to Washington, DC, to protest BIA attempts to exploit Native American land. The marchers are pictured going down 16th Street toward the Washington Monument.

▽ **A LEADER SPEAKS OUT**
On 15 July 1978, Chief Oren Lyons of the Iroquois Confederacy addressed a crowd in Washington, DC. At a rally ten days later, a manifesto enlarging the sentiments of the "Twenty Point" program was read out.

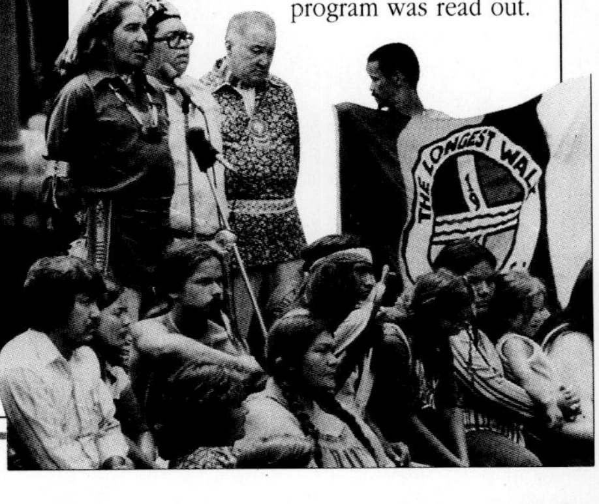

THE FISHING PROTESTS

Indians were permitted to fish on and off reservations in their usual fishing sites, which were identified in 1850s' treaty negotiations. However, state game wardens, under pressure from commercial fishermen, harassed the Natives, seizing their boats and cutting their nets. In 1964, this led to fishing protests organized by the National Indian Youth Council.

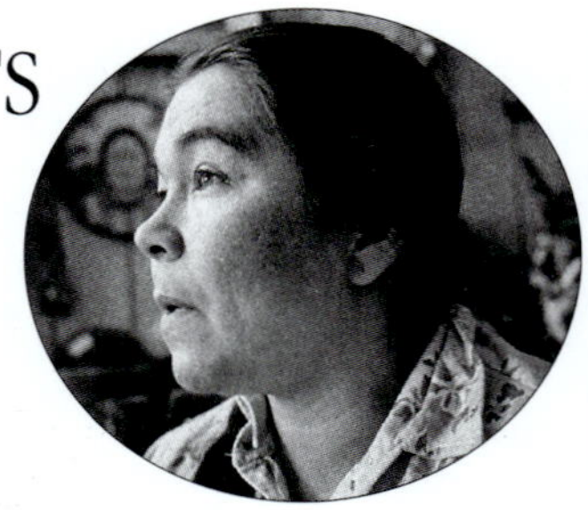

△ **LEADER MCCLOUD**
Tulalip Janet McCloud led a major march and demonstration on the Washington State Capitol in Olympia on 23 December 1963.

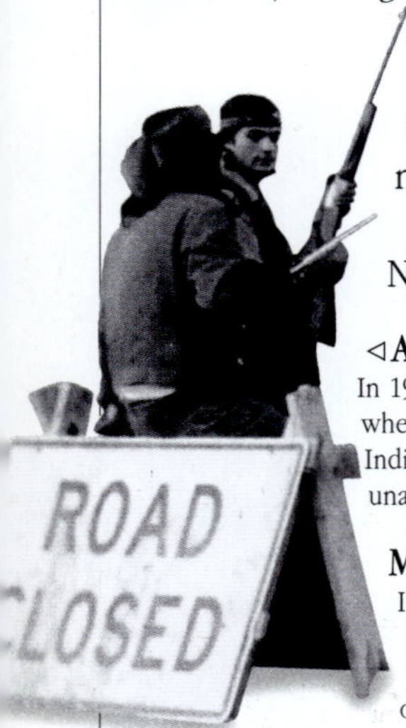

◁ **ARMED ROAD-BLOCKS SET UP**
In 1971, armed Indians protected roads leading to rivers where fish-ins were taking place. In preceding years, Indian fishermen reported that thieves had destroyed unattended Indian nets and stolen fish.

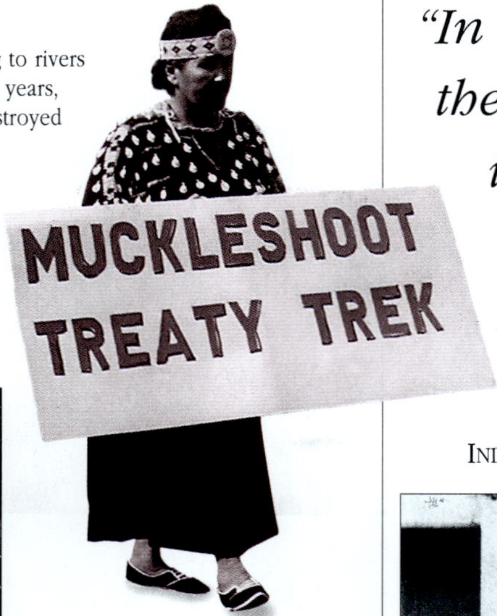

MARCHING IN SEATTLE ▷
In May 1966, Muckleshoot Indians marched in Seattle for their treaty fishing rights. The tribe, from the southern end of Puget Sound, received legal support from the American Civil Liberties Union.

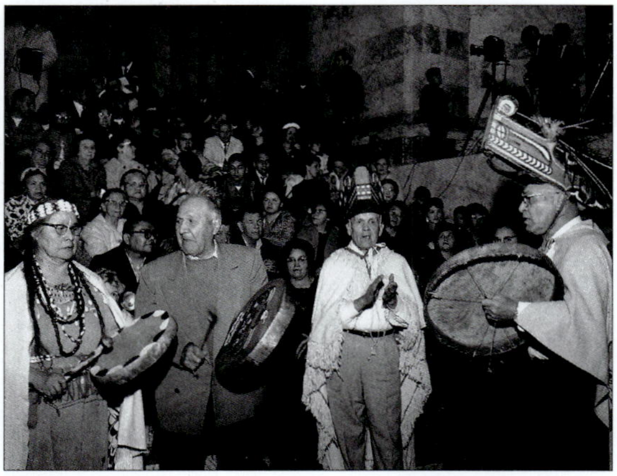

◁ **RIGHTS DEMONSTRATION**
Native Americans from around Washington State are pictured at a demonstration for treaty fishing rights at the Washington State Capitol building in Olympia on 3 March 1964. Several celebrities helped to publicize their struggles.

▽ **BRANDO ARRESTED**
In 1964, actor Marlon Brando, who lent his support to the Indians in their fishing protests, was arrested for net fishing in the Puyallup River. He was released on a technicality, and was not tried.

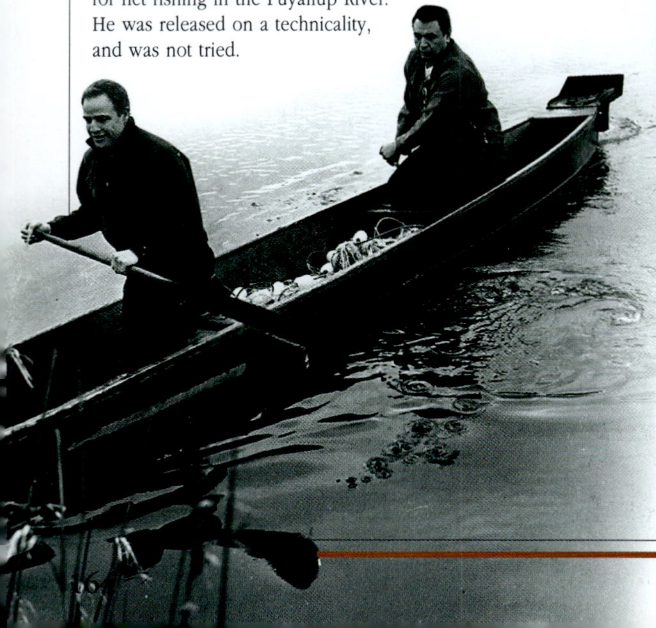

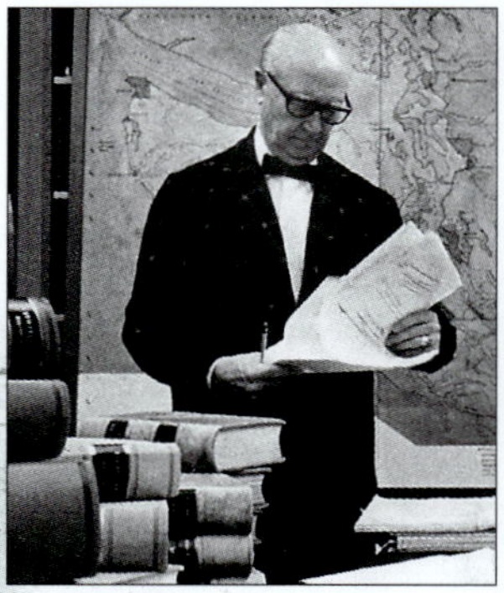

△ **A LANDMARK JUDGMENT**
Federal District Judge George W. Boldt made a landmark decision affirming the fishing rights of 14 Indian tribes in Washington State. He ruled that they were entitled to half of the harvestable salmon and steelhead (rainbow trout) passing through their usual fishing grounds.

ESCAPE TO ALCATRAZ

On 20 November 1969, members of Indians of All Tribes (IAT) occupied Alcatraz Island, an abandoned federal prison in San Francisco Bay. They claimed the right of possession under an 1868 Sioux treaty that gave surplus federal land to Indians. During the course of the occupation, hundreds of Indian protestors controlled the "rock" but, eventually, enthusiasm dwindled and their numbers fell to a token group of 15, who were finally ousted by federal marshals.

"In the name of all Indians, therefore, we re-claim this island for our Indian nations .... We feel this claim is just and proper."

INDIANS OF ALL TRIBES, ALCATRAZ ISLAND, 1969

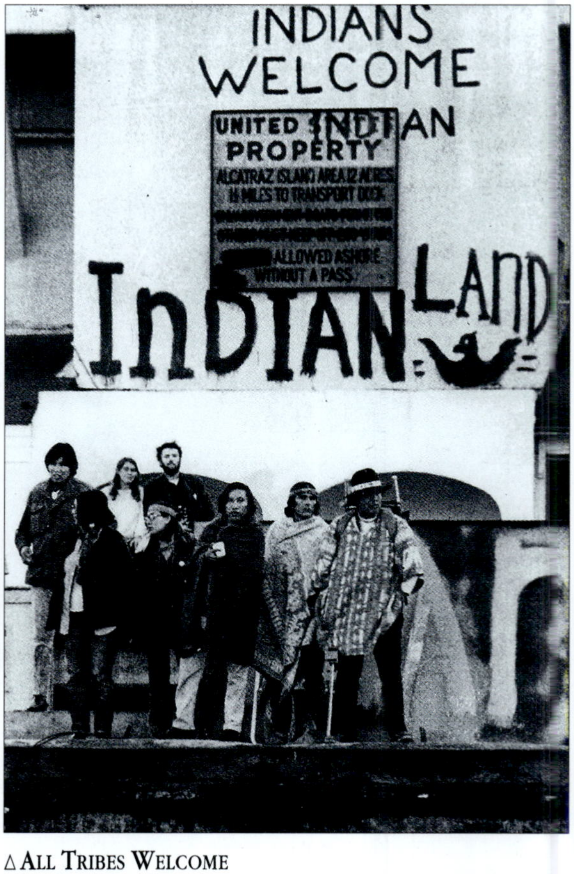

△ **ALL TRIBES WELCOME**
IAT invited all tribes throughout North America and Mexico to gather on Alcatraz. On 25 November 1969, Indians were pictured standing under a sign on which the word "States" was changed to "Indian."

WOUNDED KNEE, 1973

In February 1973, after the failure of attempts to remove Pine Ridge tribal chair, Richard Wilson, from office, the traditional Council of Elders and Oglala Sioux Civil Rights Organization requested the American Indian Movement's assistance in publicizing Wilson's repressive tactics. On 28 February, protestors took over Wounded Knee, but immediately found themselves sealed in by road blocks. After 71 days of battles, erratic negotiating sessions, ceasefires, and firefights, the protest ended peacefully on 9 May.

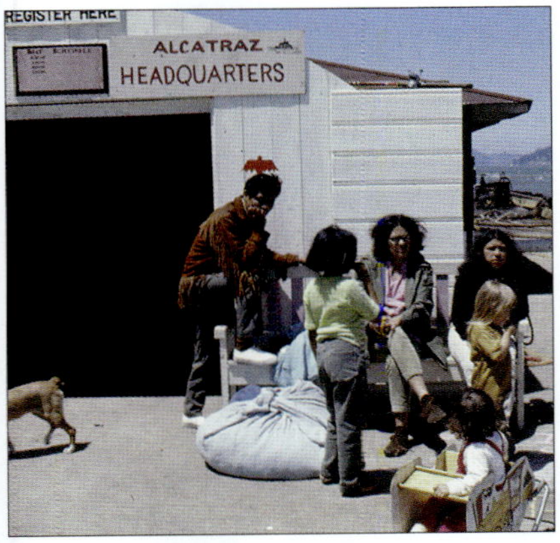

△ **MONITORING MOVEMENT**
The Indians monitored people coming onto and leaving Alcatraz, and the Press had to obtain passes, which gave them only limited access. They also set up a police force, public relations office, communal kitchen, clinic, nursery, and school.

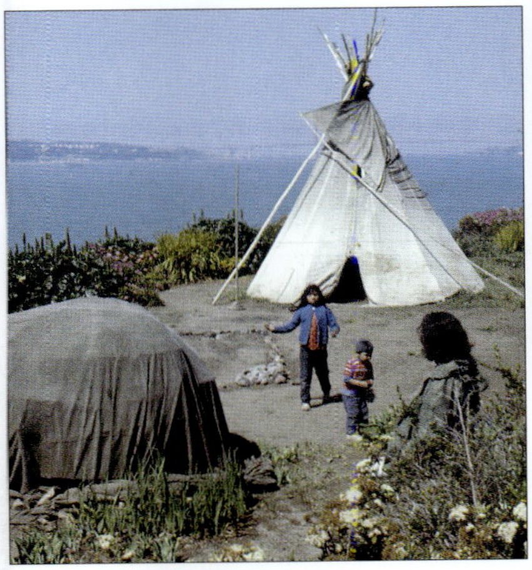

△ **ISLAND OF DREAMS**
During the first few months, amidst tremendous enthusiasm, a teenager built this 18 ft- (5.5 m-) tipi on the western edge of the island; nearby stands a ceremonial sweat lodge. The Indians tried, but failed, to negotiate turning Alcatraz into a cultural, ecological, and spiritual home.

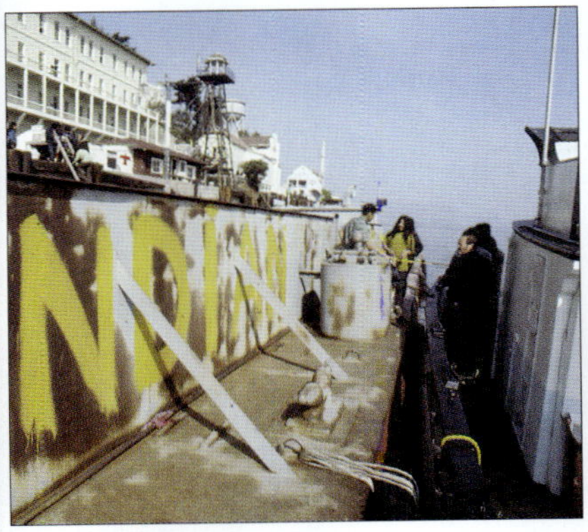

△ **BOATS BRING SUPPORT**
Before the Coast Guard blockade was lifted, donations of money, food, clothing, and medical supplies were smuggled onto the island by a variety of means. This photograph shows a boat delivering supplies during the occupation.

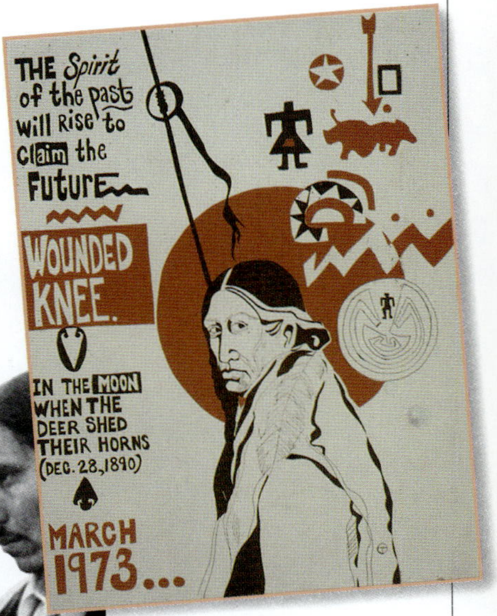

△ **"SPIRITS OF THE PAST"**
During the 1973 protest at Wounded Knee, on the site of the 1890 massacre, Sioux medicine men conducted unifying religious ceremonies, recalling the way the Ghost Dance united people in 1890.

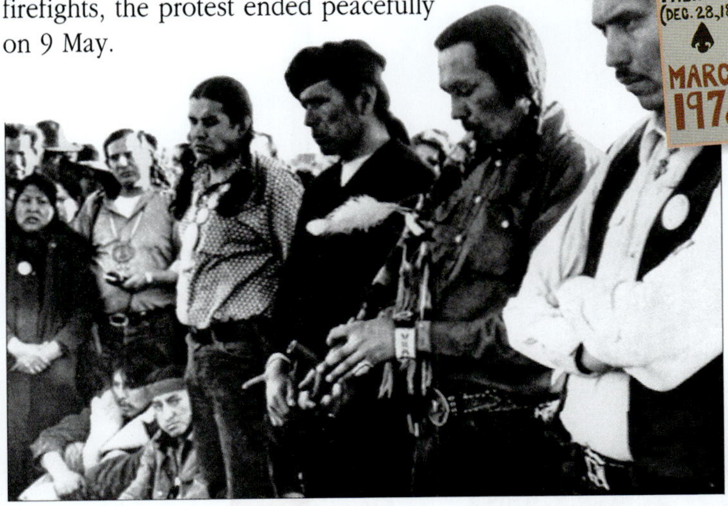

△ **SMOKING THE PEACE PIPE**
On 10 March, federal authorities lifted their road blocks. Hundreds of Native peoples poured in and declared themselves an "Independent Oglala Nation," separate from the Wilson regime. Here, AIM leaders celebrate the end of the road block by smoking a ceremonial peace pipe.

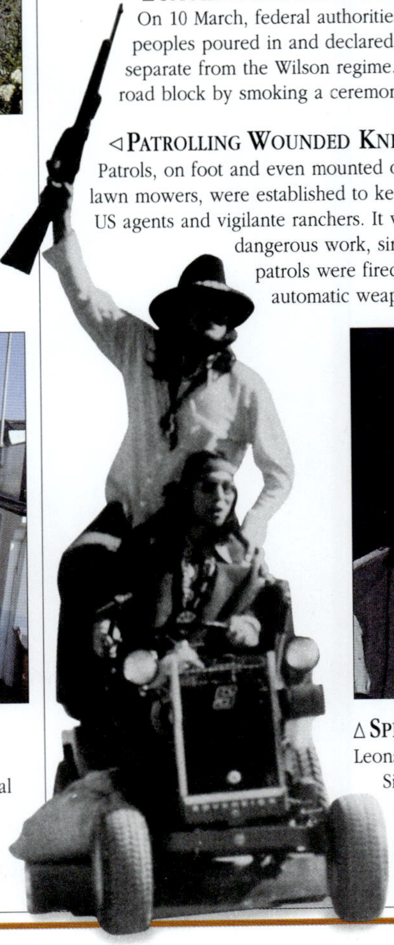

◁ **PATROLLING WOUNDED KNEE**
Patrols, on foot and even mounted on lawn mowers, were established to keep out US agents and vigilante ranchers. It was dangerous work, since patrols were fired on by automatic weapons.

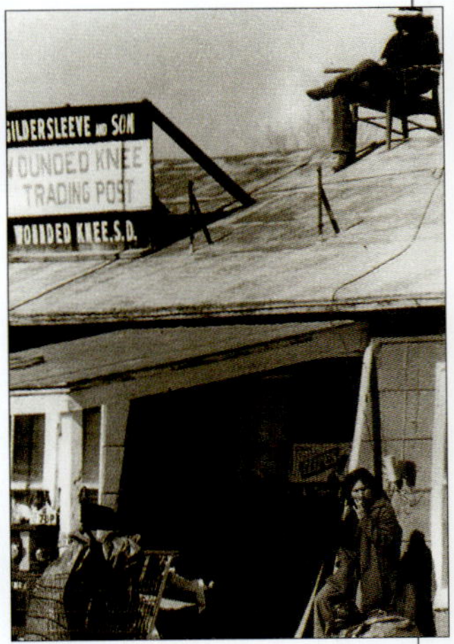

SOURCE OF ARMS ▷
Surrounded by tribal and federal forces, AIM members, who had gone to Wounded Knee unarmed, broke into the Gildersleeve trading post and armed themselves with the weapons on sale inside.

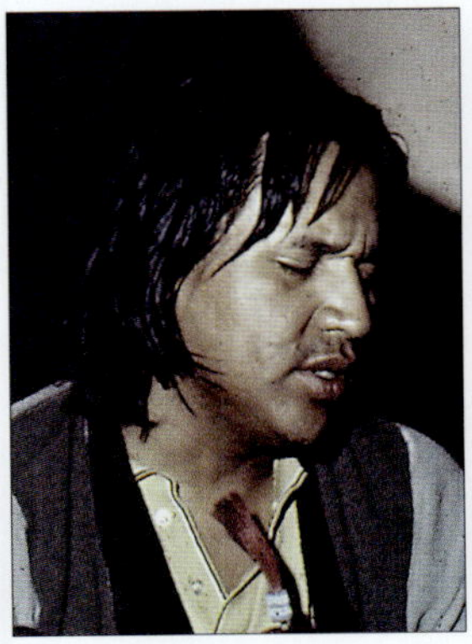

△ **SPIRITUAL WELCOME**
Leonard Crow Dog conducted Sioux ceremonies during the Wounded Knee siege: all were welcomed in the ceremonial circle.

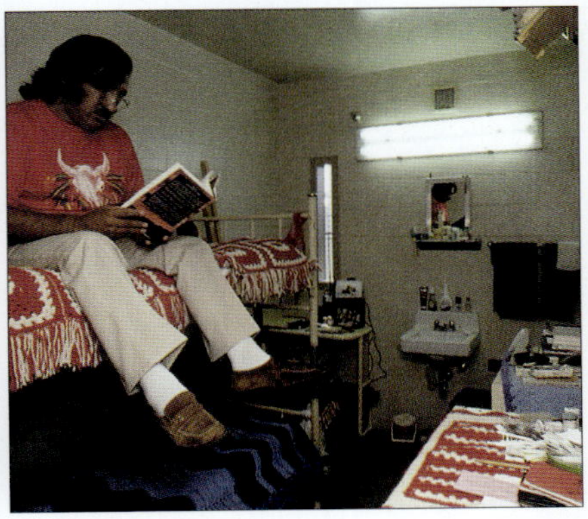

△ **LIFE IMPRISONMENT FOR LAKOTA PELTIER**
After months of repressive actions against AIM members, a fight in June 1975 between AIM and FBI agents led to the deaths of two agents and one AIM member. Leonard Peltier was sentenced to life imprisonment for his alleged role in the affair.

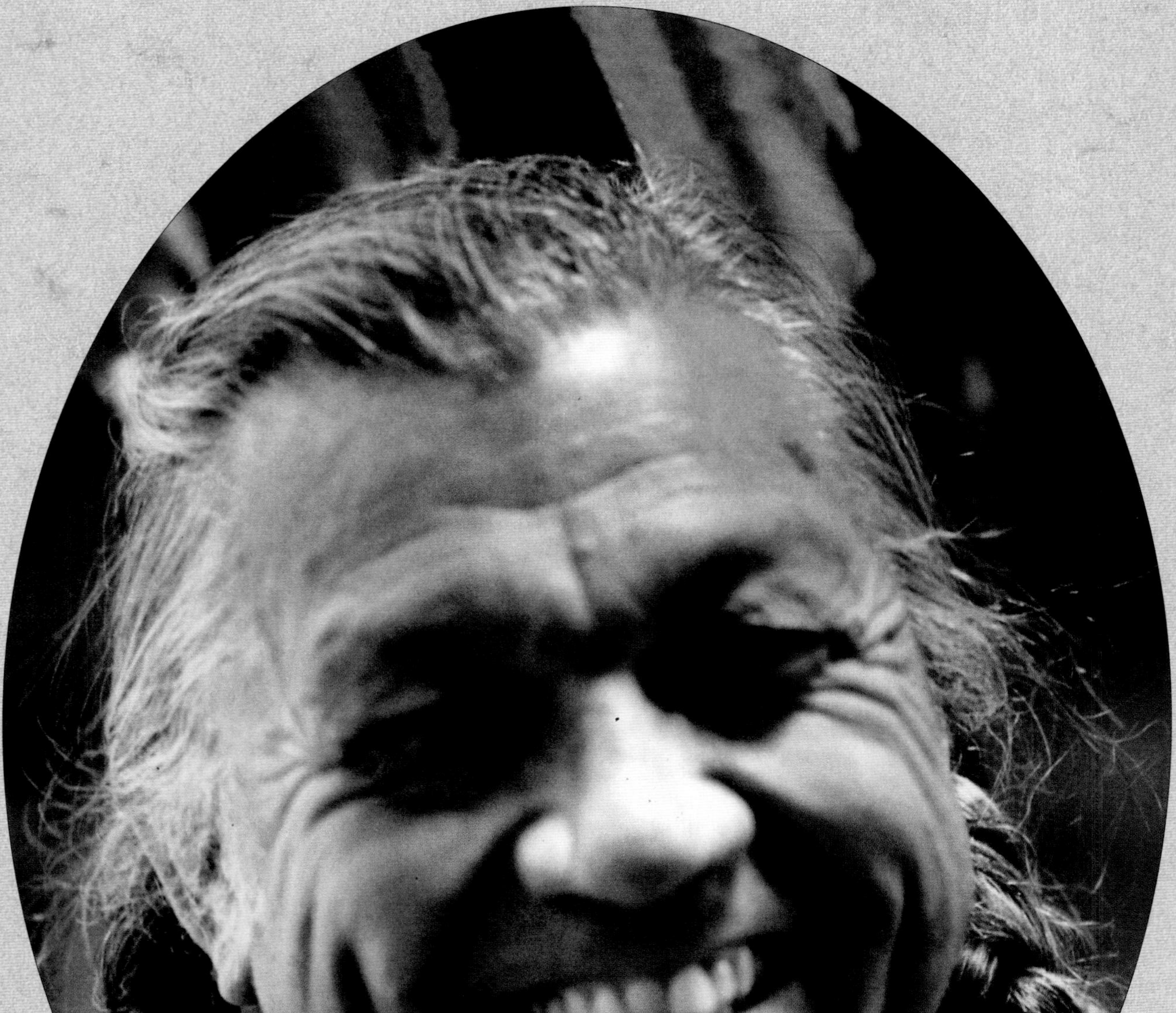

ADAM FORTUNATE EAGLE

1992: ON THE OCCUPATION OF ALCATRAZ ISLAND

BORN IN 1929, ON THE Red Lake Chippewa reservation in Minnesota, Adam Fortunate Eagle was a key figure in the 1969 Alcatraz occupation. This extract is taken from his book *Alcatraz! Alcatraz!: The Indian Occupation of 1969–1971*, which was published in 1992. Fortunate Eagle attracted worldwide attention in 1973 by stepping off a plane in Italy, driving a spear in the ground, and claiming Italy for Native American people, based on the same right of discovery as was used by Columbus to claim Hispaniola in 1492. He now lives with his wife on her Shoshone-Paiute reservation near Fallon, Nevada.

"We set out from San Leandro, my family and I, with our tribal outfits packed, and with $24 in beads and colored cloth arranged in a wooden bowl for the symbolic purchase of Alcatraz Island from the government. With a feel of optimism we were soon on the Nimitz Freeway, driving for Fisherman's Wharf in San Francisco, and Pier 39.

The weather on Sunday morning, November 9, 1969, was beautiful and calm. This was a pretty strange thing we were doing. Indian people, twentieth-century urban Indians, gathering in tribal councils, student organizations, clubs, and families ... with the intention of launching an attack on a bastion of the United States government. Instead of the horses and bows and arrows of another era, we were riding in Fords and Chevys, armed only with our Proclamation but determined to bring about a change in federal policy affecting our people ....

At Fisherman's Wharf we parked and joined a growing group of Indian students. When I learned that our scheduled boat was nowhere around I suggested they stall while I looked for another. Then I noticed this beautiful three-masted barque that looked like it had come right out of the pages of maritime history. Its name was the Monte Cristo, and its owner ... was Ronald Craig.

When I approached he said, 'Hey, I'm curious – what's going on over there with all those Indians?' I explained the fix we were in, pointing out the media contingent that had come to cover the landing. 'I'll take you,' he said, 'on condition we get permission from the Coast Guard and that we carry no more than fifty people ....'

After he counted to make sure we were only fifty, he fired off the little cannon on the bow. Here were Indians sailing on an old vessel to seek a new way of life for their people. I thought of the Mayflower and its crew of Pilgrims who landed on our shores. The history books say they were seeking new freedoms for themselves and their children which were denied in their homeland. Never mind that Plymouth Rock already belonged to somebody else. What concerned them was their own fate, their own hopes. Now, 350 years later, its original citizens, to focus national attention on their struggle to regain those same basic rights, were making landfall on another rock."

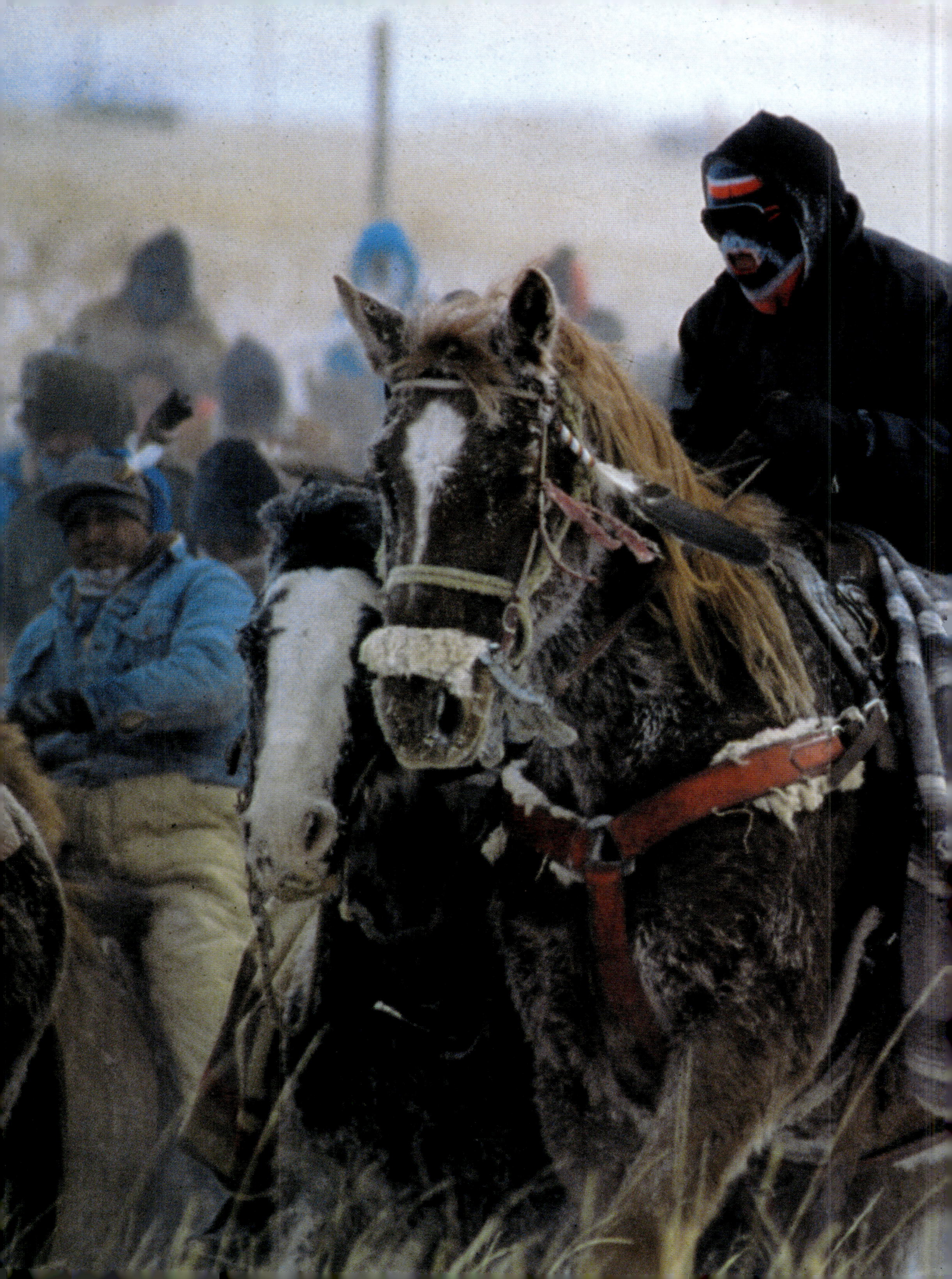

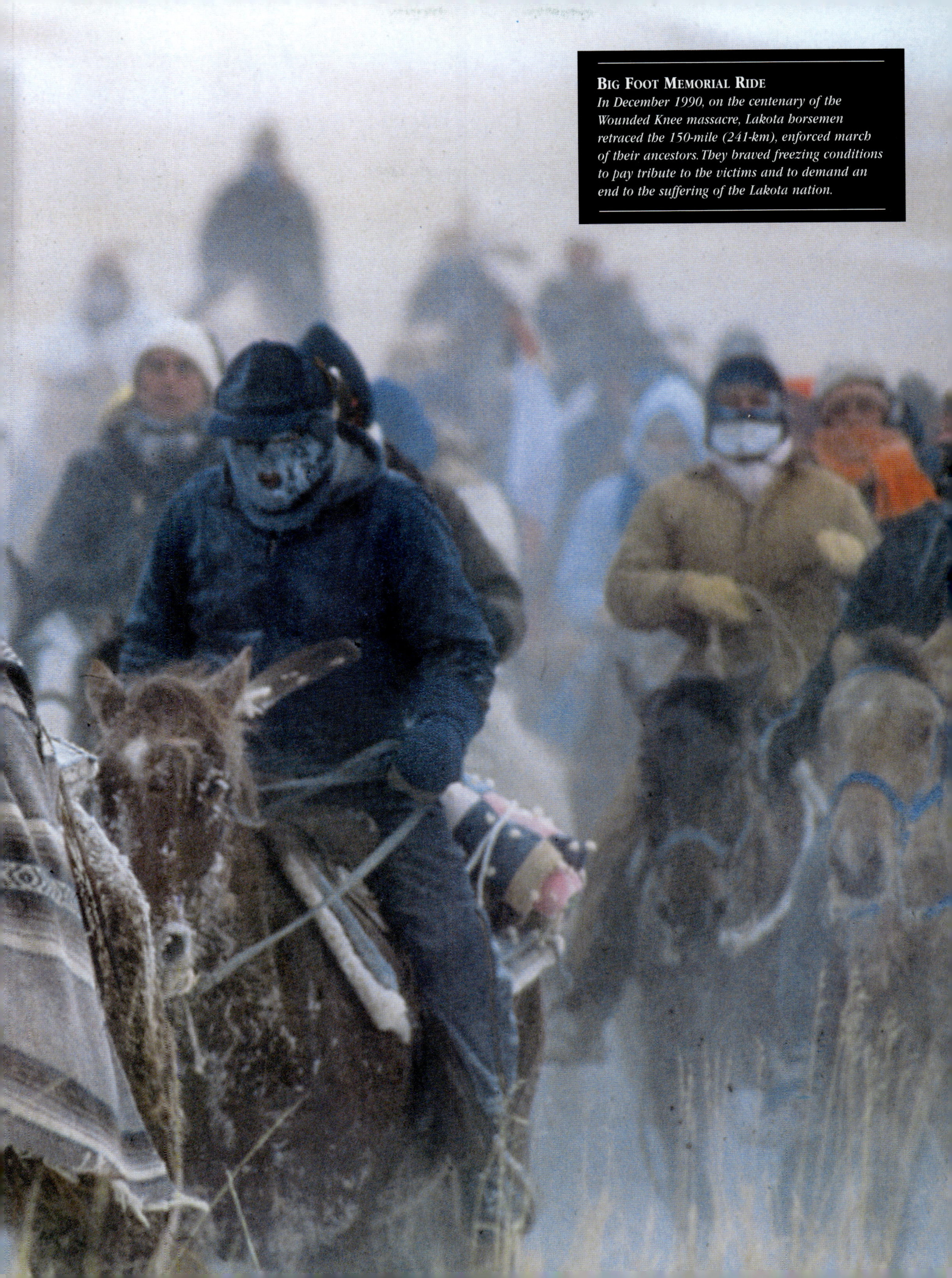

Big Foot Memorial Ride

In December 1990, on the centenary of the Wounded Knee massacre, Lakota horsemen retraced the 150-mile (241-km), enforced march of their ancestors. They braved freezing conditions to pay tribute to the victims and to demand an end to the suffering of the Lakota nation.

THE FIGHT CONTINUES

FROM THE 1970S THROUGH THE 1990s, North American tribal peoples have become more skilled at fighting in legislatures and courtrooms for the survival of their ancient cultures in a contemporary world. They have struggled to retain what is left of their tribal homelands, to preserve the right to practice their religion, and to protect their sacred sites and burial grounds; and they continue their fight to hold on to timber, minerals, and water resources, and to preserve their treaty rights.

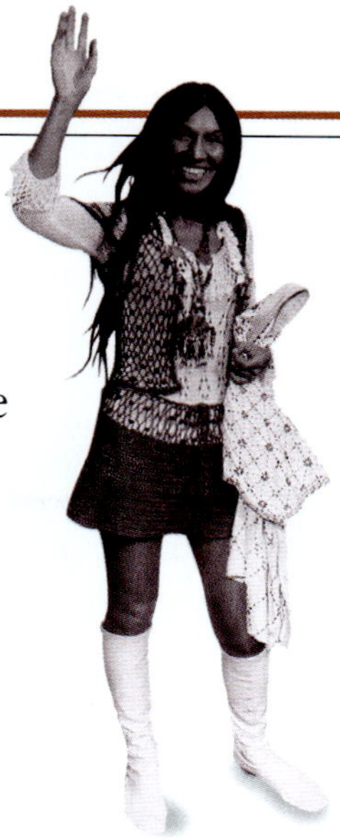

PROTEST SINGER
Canadian Cree musician and activist, Buffy Sainte-Marie was orphaned as an infant and raised by a Micmac couple. By the 1970s, she had become a world-famous star, singing her own songs and accompanying herself on guitar. Protest songs like "Now That the Buffalo's Gone" draw attention to the dire problems faced by Indians.

ACTIVIST DANN SISTERS

In 1973, Western Shoshone sisters Carrie and Mary Dann refused to pay trespass fees for grazing livestock on lands that the US Bureau of Land Management claimed were public, arguing that an 1863 treaty never ceded the land. Still not settled, their challenge set off over 20 years of legal battles to preserve their homelands in Nevada and California.

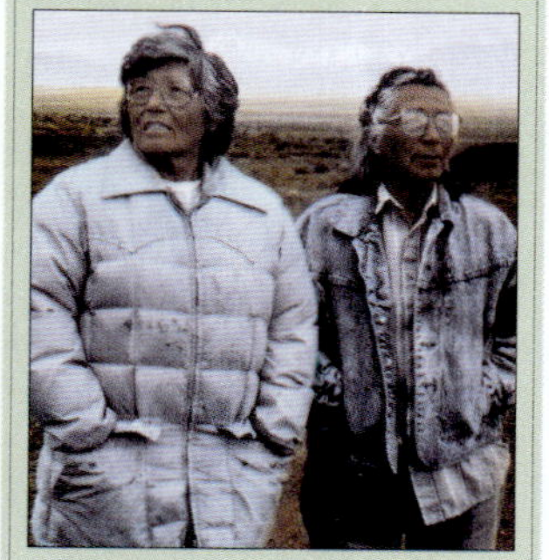

CARRIE (LEFT) AND MARY DANN

SINCE THE 1970s, Indian tribes and First Nations have fought legal battles in courts and legislatures to protect what is left of their lands – or to reclaim lands previously lost – and to practice their religions without intrusive regulation by government agencies. Hundreds of Native lawyers now use the judicial system and the legislative process to work on behalf of individual and tribal clients.

Deep-seated grievances by Indian nations in the United States over the destruction of Native burial sites, and the mistreatment of the dead by archaeologists, led to the 1990 Native American Grave Protection and Repatriation Act, which gives tribes the power to reclaim skeletal remains and sacred objects from museums and universities. Indian nations also grieve over the despoliation of off-reservation sacred sites that are central to Native religions. Many have been threatened by vandals, tourism, private developers, mining, logging, power lines, and hydro-electric plants. In a few cases, Congress has protected sacred sites. In 1970, Taos Pueblo in New Mexico recovered its sacred Blue Lake after six decades of lobbying. For the most part, however, congressmen from states with energy development and extraction industries show little interest in protecting Native sacred places.

Land Claim Victories

Successful lobbying by Indian peoples has led to a number of land claim victories. In January 1975, the Havasupai Tribe won its 66-year-old struggle for title to a portion of its ancient homeland along the Grand Canyon's south rim in Arizona; and, in 1980, Passamaquoddy and Penobscot tribes secured a land base in Maine. In a land claims case involving the Gitxsan in British Columbia in 1997, the Supreme Court of Canada validated Indian claims to land, even where no treaties or titles existed.

In 1993, after 20 years of lobbying, Inuit leaders won the largest Native land claim in

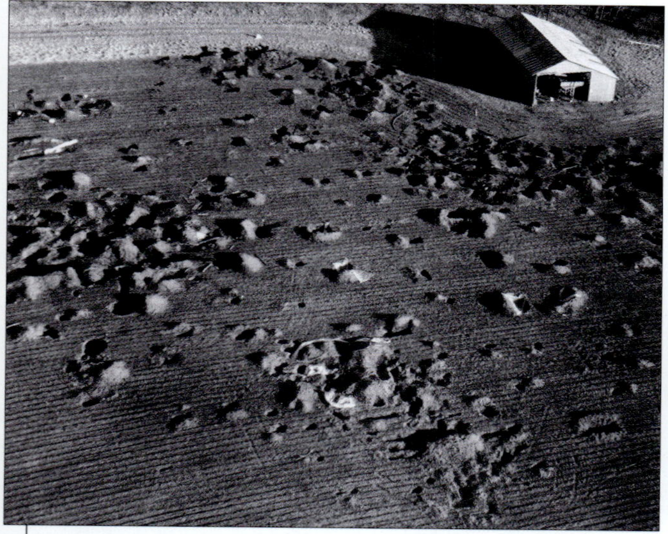

◁ **GRAVES DESECRATED**
In 1987, the graves of over 1,000 Indian men, women, and children were desecrated when potholers dug over 350 holes at a farm outside Uniontown, Kentucky, and used mining equipment to blow skeletal remains out of the ground.

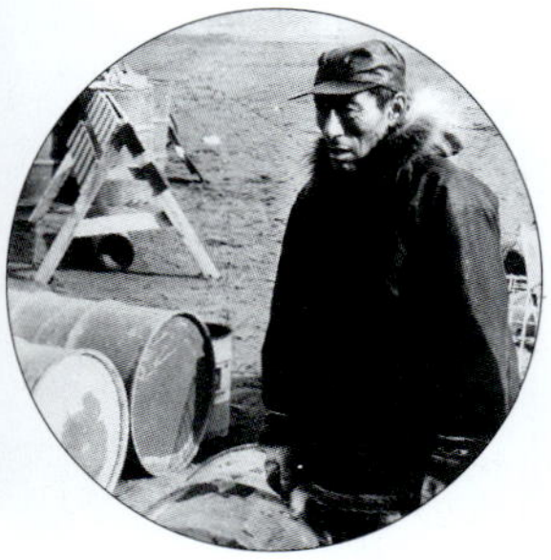

◁ **ALASKA SETTLEMENT**
Oil discoveries in 1968 on Alaska's North Slope increased interest by energy corporations in the state's resources. This resulted in a 1971 settlement act that terminated the Alaska Natives' title to nine-tenths of their land. Natives retained the remaining 44 million acres (17.8 million hectares.)

A CHIEF RETURNS ▷
Accompanied by a Lakota holy man, relatives of Lakota Chief Long Wolf, who died in London in 1892, traveled to the UK in 1997 for the repatriation of the chief's body. His remains were taken to the US for reburial on the Pine Ridge reservation.

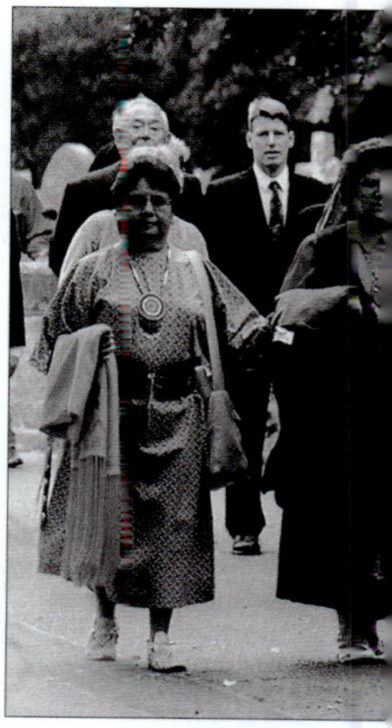

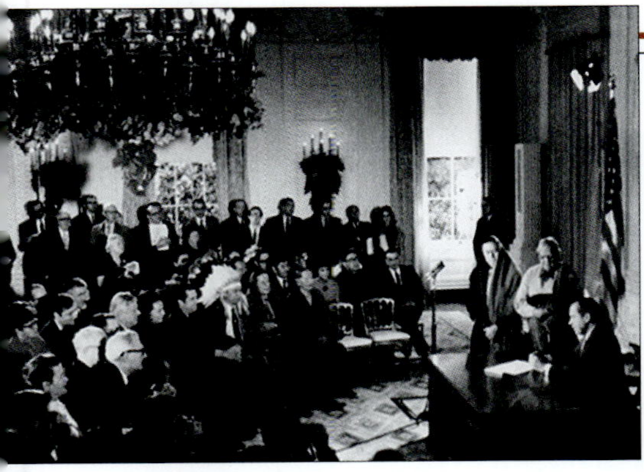

▲ SACRED BLUE LAKE RESTORED
In 1970, President Richard M. Nixon signed the law restoring the sacred Blue Lake to the people of Taos Pueblo in New Mexico, 64 years after it was taken from them. The people of Taos had battled with the US government until they recovered their holy site – a rare recognition of Native American ancestral rights.

Canada's history, gaining the right to about one-fifth of the country, carved out of the eastern 60 percent of the Northwest Territories. Nunavut came into existence on 1 April 1999: its 25,000 residents occupy an area as large as that of Western Europe.

Intertribal Conflicts

Sometimes struggles for land have pitted Indian against Indian, as in the case of the Navajo and their Hopi neighbors in Arizona. In 1974, Congress passed the Navajo-Hopi Indian Land Settlement Act, providing for the partition of 1.8 million acres (0.73 million hectares) of land between the two tribes, and decreeing that those who lived on the "wrong" side (mostly Navajo) would have to move. In 1992, after 20 years of conflict and legal battles, the tribes finally reached an agreement, which formed the basis for a 1996 federal law that halted the further relocation of Navajo who wished to remain in their homes.

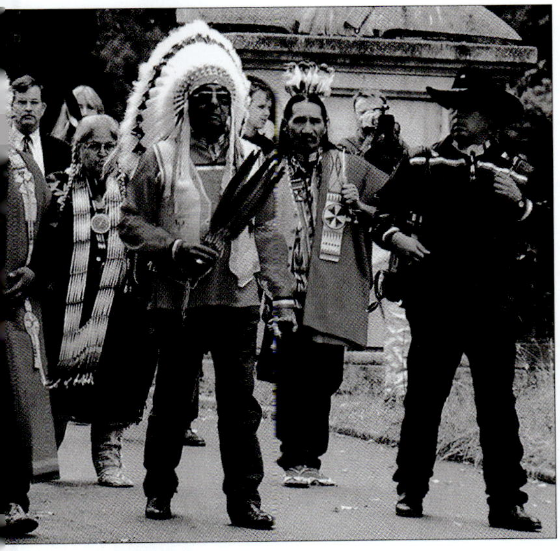

RESISTANCE AT OKA

In July 1990, a crisis at Oka (near Montreal) began when police tried to dismantle a road block set up by Mohawks to prevent the expansion of a golf course onto land regarded by Kanesatake Mohawks as their own. The golf course was never built.

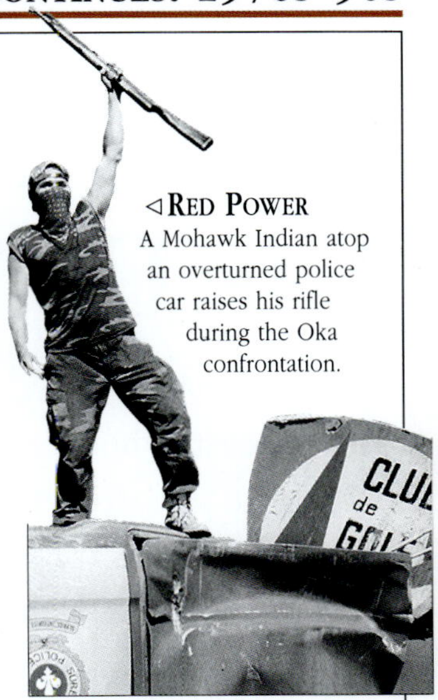

◁ RED POWER
A Mohawk Indian atop an overturned police car raises his rifle during the Oka confrontation.

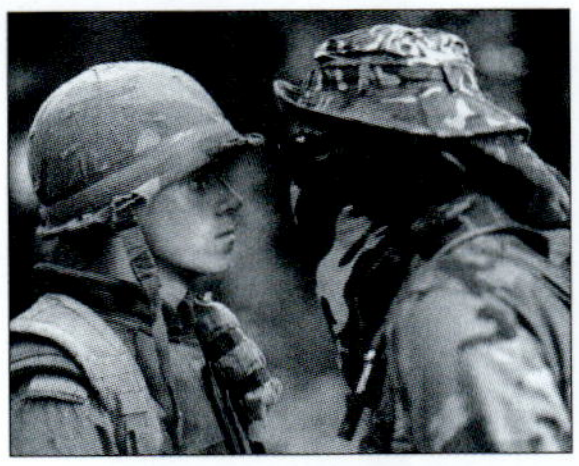

◁ CLOSE ENCOUNTER
A decision by the Quebec police to storm the Mohawk blockade resulted in the death of one officer in a gun battle. The Canadian government called in 1,400 army troops to surround the Mohawks, who surrendered after a 78-day standoff.

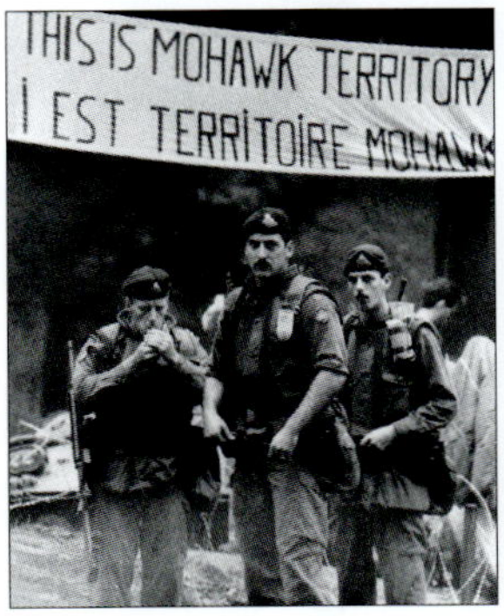

◁ THE MILITARY MOVES IN
Heavily armed troops, in armored personnel carriers, moved in to dismantle the barricades in Oka. The Mohawks resisted and the authorities backed down.

A WOMAN'S STRUGGLE ▷
In a scene from Abenaki film-maker Alanis Obomsawin's 1993 documentary *Kanehsatake: 270 Years of Resistance*, a woman and child raise their hands in victory before leaving the barricade.

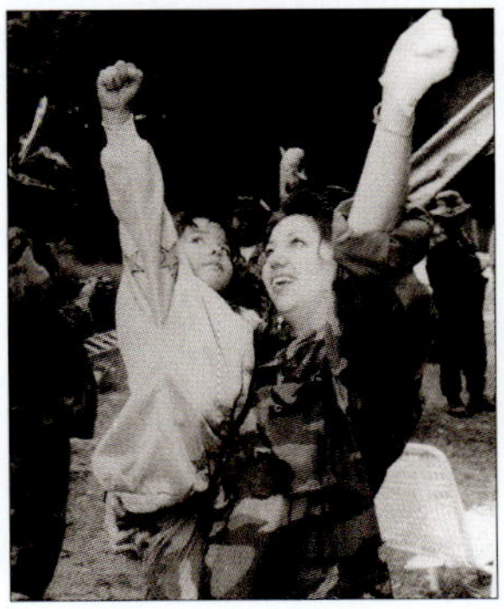

VICTORY AT JAMES BAY

In 1986, Quebec province planned to build the Great Whale River hydro-electric project as part of its plan to dam and divert most major rivers running into James and Hudson Bays. The Crees fiercely opposed the project, spending $8 million on their successful campaign to defeat it.

KENNEDY SPEAKS OUT ▷
Robert Kennedy, Jr., and Matthew Coon Come of the Crees, seen here carrying a canoe, spoke out against Hydro Quebec at a New York press conference in 1993.

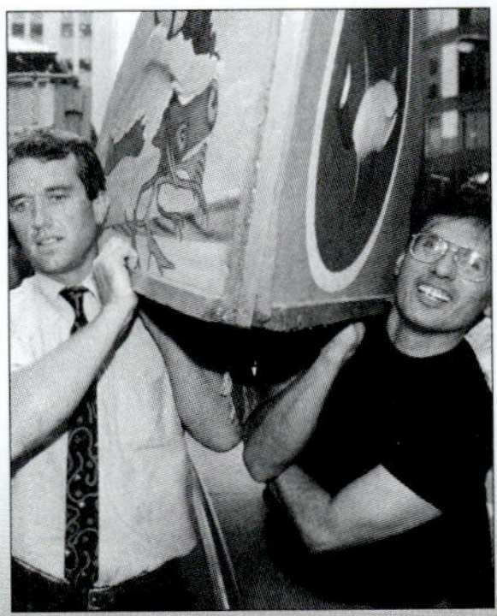

▽ PROTEST ON THE HUDSON
Cree Indians and Inuit paddled from Odeyak to New York City in 1990 to galvanize opposition to the Great Whale River hydro-electric project. The development was canceled.

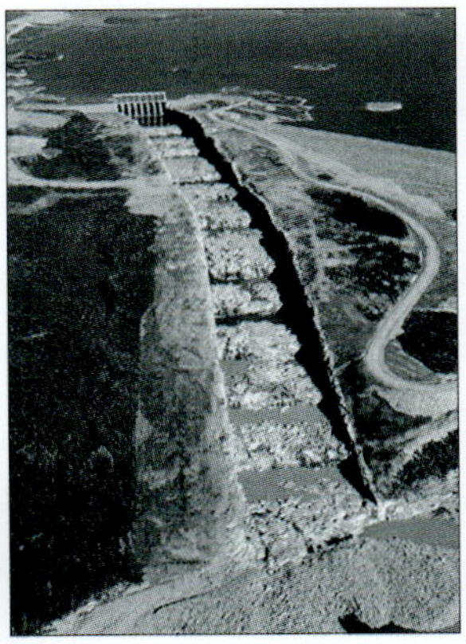

△ DAMS CONSTRUCTED
Over a period of 12 years, from 1973 to 1985, three reservoirs and powerhouses were built on the La Grande River to complete Phase One of the hydro-electric project. The 985-yard (900-meter) spillway of the LG2 reservoir, carved from solid rock, is pictured here.

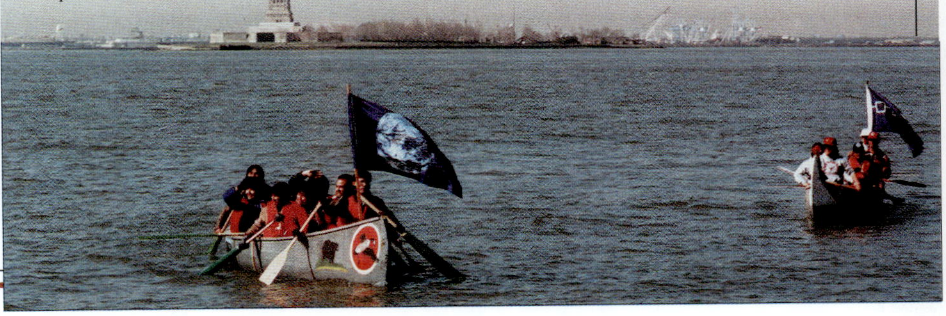

HOMELANDS IN THE US TODAY

NATIVE AMERICANS TODAY are a small minority in their ancestral homelands. According to the 1990 census, there were 1,959,234 Native people in the US - less than one percent of the total population. In that year about 35 percent of Native people lived on an Indian land base of approximately 54 million acres (22 million hectares). This land includes rancherias and colonies in California and Nevada, trust land, historic Indian areas (former reservations in Oklahoma), and Alaska Native villages. In total, there are over 500 federal and state recognized tribes in the US today. This map shows the location of the largest federally recognized reservations in the US.

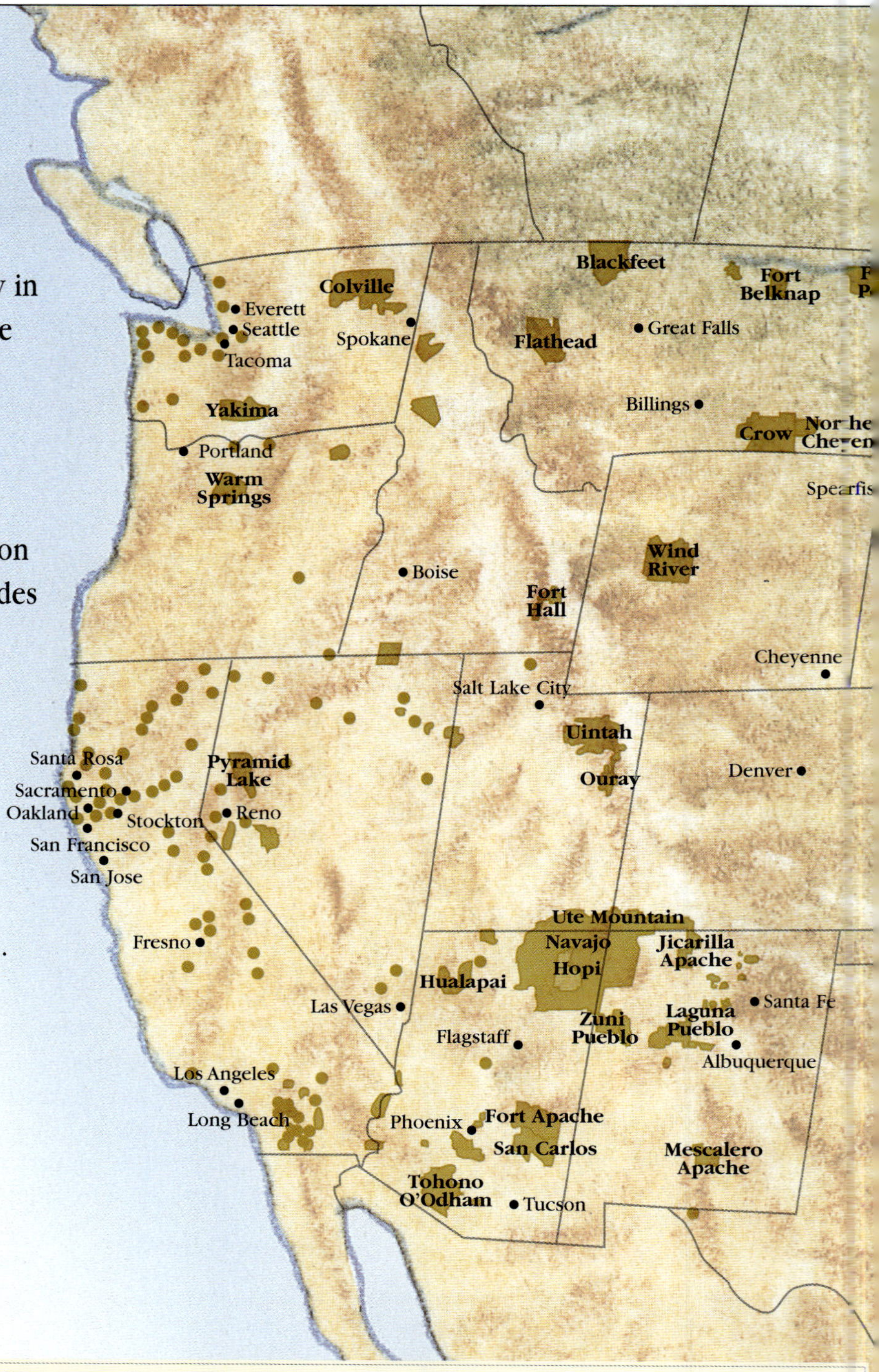

SHRINKING NATIVE HOMELANDS

In 1492, the homelands of American Indians and Alaska Natives extended uninterrupted from the Atlantic to the Pacific Ocean. Over the course of four centuries, the original inhabitants were stripped of most of their homelands by Europeans and Americans, their lifestyles were threatened by the white settlers, and the Native population shrank from 7–10 million to fewer than 250,000. Their population, however, is now on the increase.

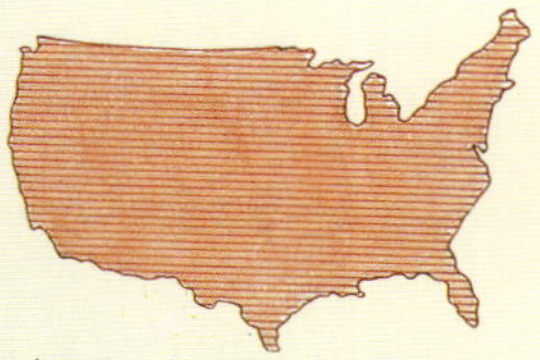

1492: PRE-CONTACT NATIVE AMERICA *Extensive civilizations and religions were established across the continent by North America's Native inhabitants.*

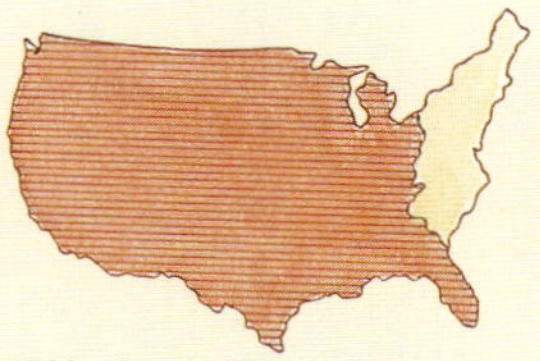

1790: NATIVES FORCED INLAND *As numbers of settlers increased (the US population was 4 million), demand for land forced Indians westward.*

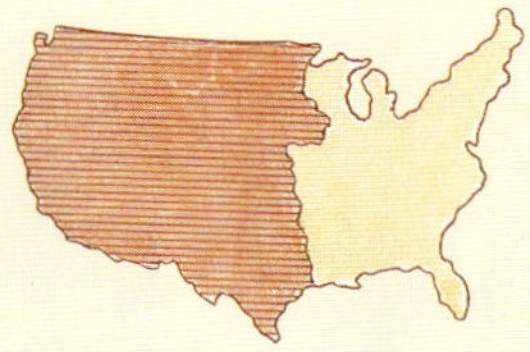

1830: REMOVAL TO THE WEST *The Indian Removal Act enforced the removal of Indians from east of the Mississippi River to the West.*

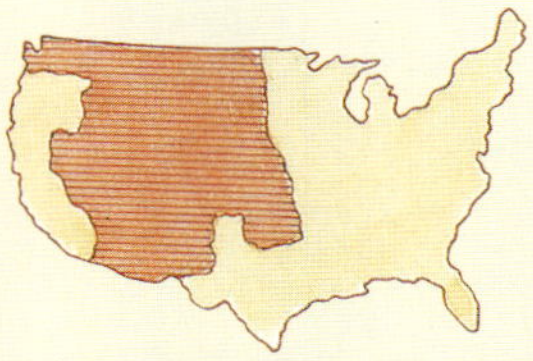

1860: IMMIGRANT STAMPEDE *Discovery of gold in the West and the establishment of reservations further diminished the Native land base.*

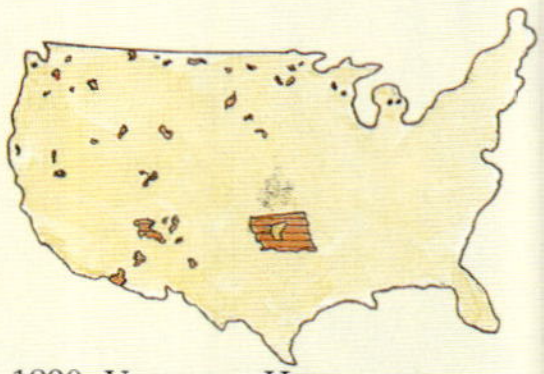

1890: VANISHING HOMELANDS *A further 90 million acres (36 million hectares) of Indian lands were lost as a result of allotment policies.*

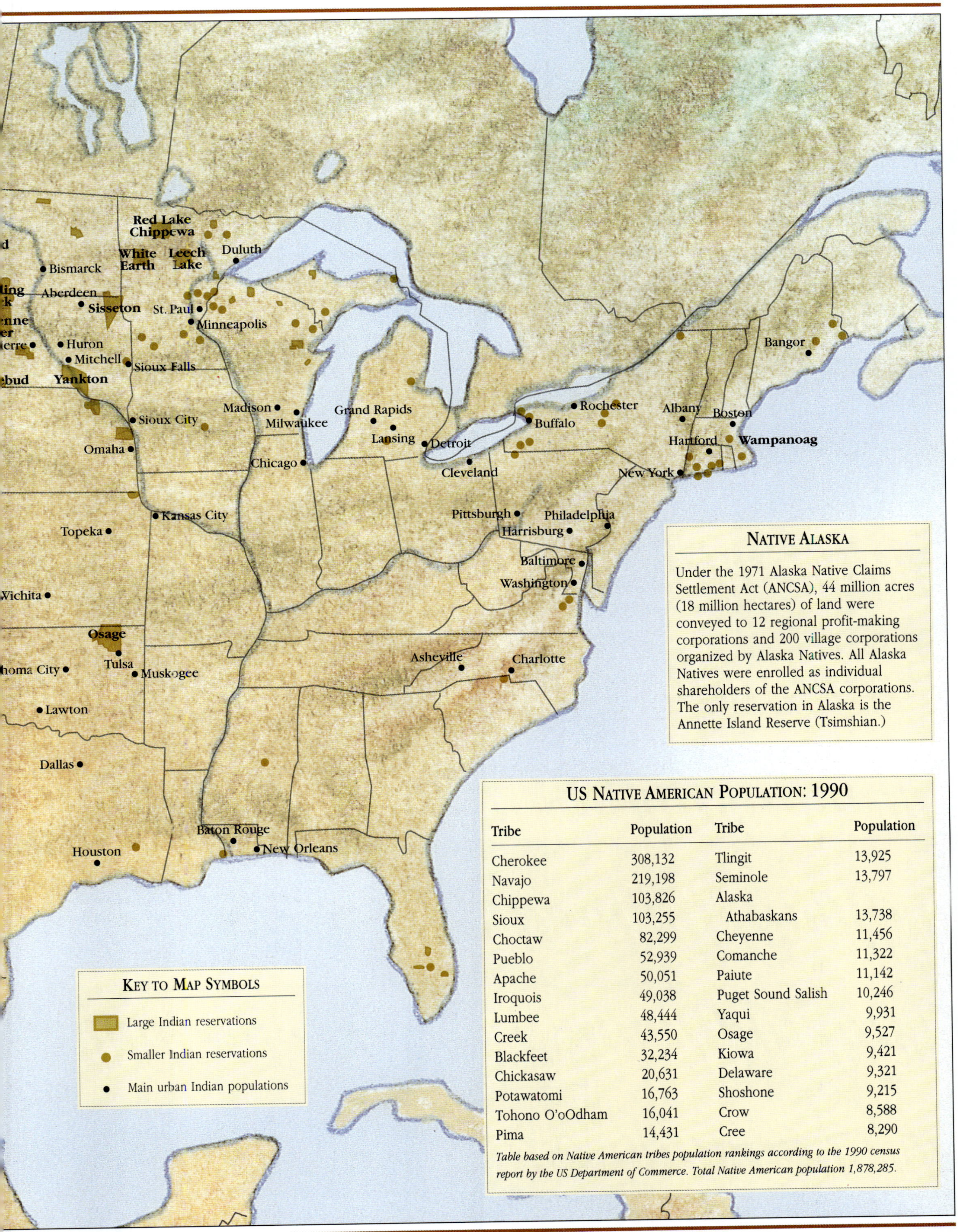

NATIVE ALASKA

Under the 1971 Alaska Native Claims Settlement Act (ANCSA), 44 million acres (18 million hectares) of land were conveyed to 12 regional profit-making corporations and 200 village corporations organized by Alaska Natives. All Alaska Natives were enrolled as individual shareholders of the ANCSA corporations. The only reservation in Alaska is the Annette Island Reserve (Tsimshian.)

US NATIVE AMERICAN POPULATION: 1990

Tribe	Population	Tribe	Population
Cherokee	308,132	Tlingit	13,925
Navajo	219,198	Seminole	13,797
Chippewa	103,826	Alaska Athabaskans	13,738
Sioux	103,255	Cheyenne	11,456
Choctaw	82,299	Comanche	11,322
Pueblo	52,939	Paiute	11,142
Apache	50,051	Puget Sound Salish	10,246
Iroquois	49,038	Yaqui	9,931
Lumbee	48,444	Osage	9,527
Creek	43,550	Kiowa	9,421
Blackfeet	32,234	Delaware	9,321
Chickasaw	20,631	Shoshone	9,215
Potawatomi	16,763	Crow	8,588
Tohono O'oOdham	16,041	Cree	8,290
Pima	14,431		

Table based on Native American tribes population rankings according to the 1990 census report by the US Department of Commerce. Total Native American population 1,878,285.

CONTEMPORARY INDIAN LIFE

AT THE TURN OF THE TWENTIETH CENTURY, many believed that Native Americans would disappear into US or Canadian society. But Native communities have survived and are revitalizing tribal governments, creating modern economies, attaining legal rights, and reviving the cultural traditions and ceremonies that nearly died out. To be sure, Native North Americans face serious economic, health, and educational problems, but a new generation of Native leaders is hopeful that their actions will strengthen Native identities and cultures.

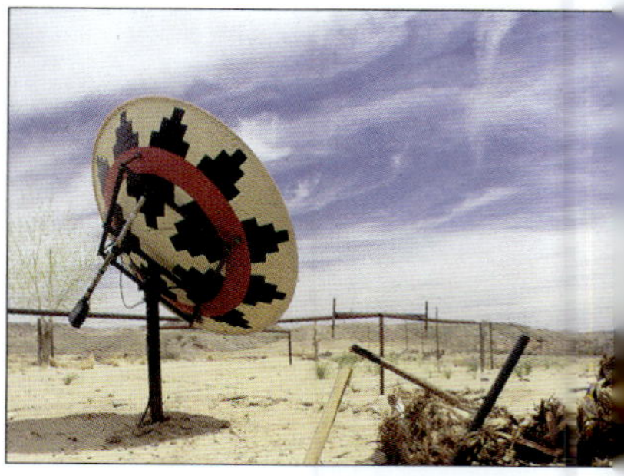

TRADITION IN A CHANGING WORLD
On the Navajo reservation, Hazel Merritt's satellite dish sports a traditional wedding-basket design, blending tradition with the modern age.

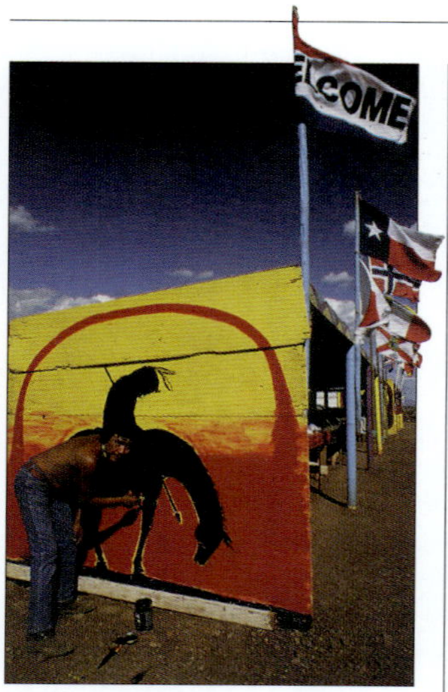

△ DISPROVED PREDICTION
At a trading post in Utah, a painter finishes his version of *The End of the Trail*, based on a sculpture originally created by James Earle Fraser and exhibited in San Francisco in 1915. Fraser believed that the Indian race was vanishing, but today the message is Indian resurgence, not extinction.

THOUSANDS OF NATIVE North American peoples today live in cities as well as in rural communities. Others live on reservations ranging in size from a few to thousands of acres. Almost half of the US Native population of 2.4 million live on over 550 reservations. In Canada, 60 percent of the 622,000 registered Indians live on over 2,407 reserves. This figure excludes Inuit, Métis, and Non-Status Indians (who are persons of Indian ancestry and cultural affiliation who have lost their right to be registered under the Indian Act, first passed in 1876 and amended in the twentieth century.)

Native people today strive to blend aspects of the traditional with the contemporary, without sacrificing the core of their identity. Blue jeans and powwow outfits, motor homes and tipis, hot dogs and corn soup typify Native American cultural life today. Tribal ceremonial practices, such as Sun Dances and potlatches, coexist with satellite dishes and cell phones. During the 1980s, the US government drastically cut social programs in the belief that state and local governments and the private sector would fill the gap. When that failed to happen, tribes were forced to look for other sources of revenue to bolster reservation economies. An emerging class of Indian executives set about creating Indian-owned businesses and educating tribes about market capitalism. Some tribes, blessed with abundant natural resources, began exploiting these for the first time. Depending on their assets, tribal leaders have chosen manufacturing, farming, ranching, tourism, mining, service industries, or even gambling to drive the tribal economies.

The Gambling Economy

In the US, about a third of the federally recognized reservations have turned to legalized gaming as a business activity, which, since the late 1980s, has created 125,000

◁ CULTURE ON DISPLAY
A five-year-old Navajo girl poses here for tourists who pay to take her photograph. The desperate poverty and social pain that marks their daily life have forced Indian families to "display" their culture for cash.

▽ TACKLING ALCOHOLISM
Burdened by poverty and suffering, many Indians try to escape their misery by drinking. A growing sobriety movement uses treatment programs that are steeped in ancient ways, including sweat lodges.

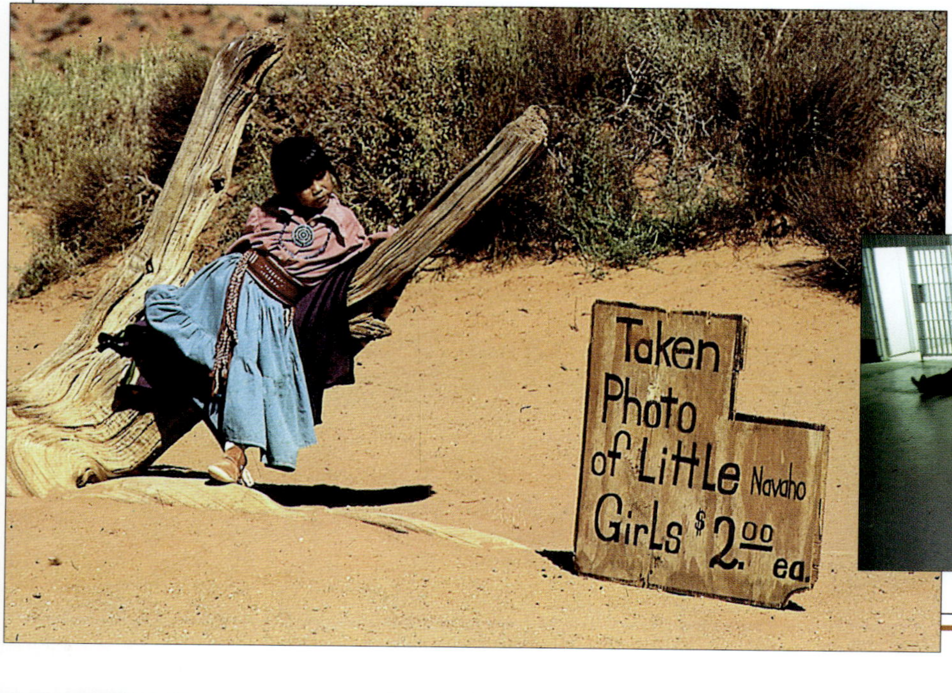

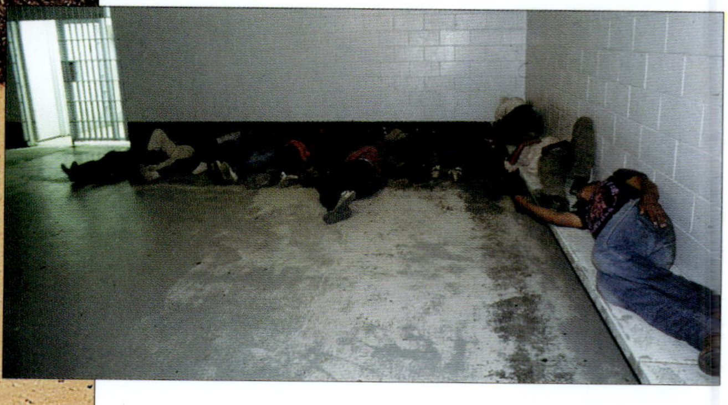

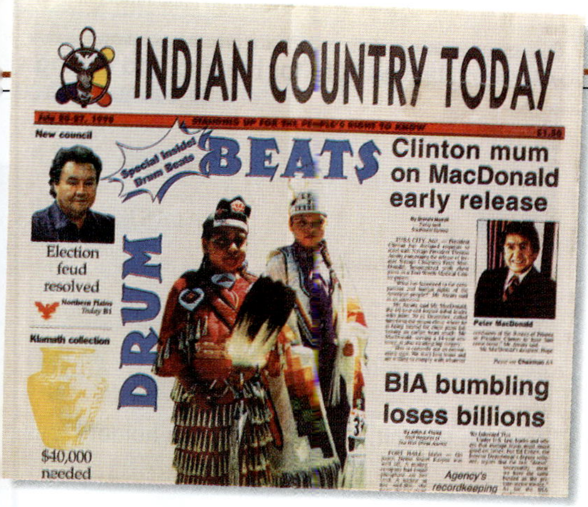
INDIAN COUNTRY TODAY
New council
Special inside! Drum Beats
DRUM BEATS
Clinton mum on MacDonald early release
Election feud resolved
Klamath collection
Peter MacDonald
BIA bumbling loses billions
Agency's recordkeeping
$40,000 needed

△ **READ ALL ABOUT IT**
Indian Country Today, a weekly newspaper published in Rapid City, South Dakota, since 1981, carries news relevant to Indian people throughout North America. Native journalists, frustrated by biased reporting, tell their stories from an Indian perspective.

reservation jobs in casinos, restaurants, and hotels, as well as an additional 160,000 jobs indirectly tied to gambling. In 1999, this $6 billion industry accounted for 2 percent of the $330 billion that Americans bet legally each year. For the first time, gaming tribes have the capital to provide employment, better schools, housing, roads, scholarships, health care, and other services for their people. Nevertheless, only a few Indian communities have reaped large profits from gaming enterprises.

Signs of Renewal

In Canada, aboriginal reserves located far from population centers have few job opportunities and unemployment rates run high, forcing people to move to cities. In response, many First Nations business leaders have fostered the growth of aboriginal businesses on or near reserves. Most are band- or community-owned retail operations, and include video stores, bush airlines, commercial art, and radio stations.

Despite such advances, Indian country continues to present a landscape of poverty and social problems. Many US and Canadian Natives live in poverty in cities and, on most reservations, unemployment rates hover around 50 percent. Indians have the lowest life expectancy of any population in North America. Rates of school dropout, alcoholism, suicide, murder, and crime are far above those for the US as a whole.

As a testament to the cultural and economic renewal taking place on reservations, however, many Indians are now leaving cities and returning home. They go for jobs, to attend college, or to participate in long-dormant ceremonies.

ECONOMIC PROGRESS

During the 1990s, in a serious effort to combat unemployment, a growing number of US Native tribes and individual Indians started up small businesses. These include home-based arts and crafts businesses, carpentry and tire-repair shops, video stores, restaurants, and hair salons. In Canada, the Council for Aboriginal Business offers business education internships for Natives.

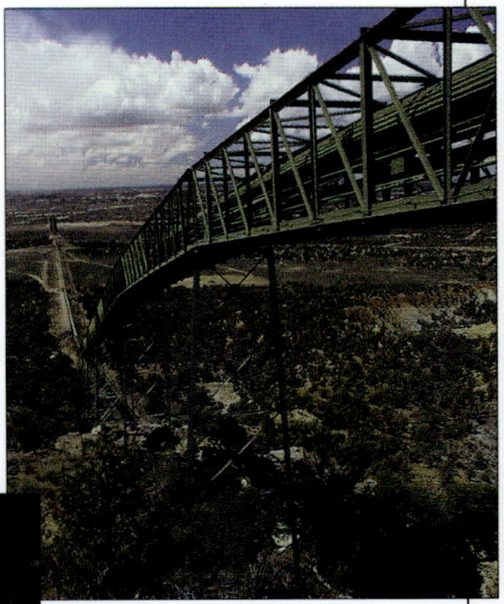

△ **BLESSING OR CURSE?**
Mineral wealth creates problems as well as benefits. The Navajo reservation's coal-slurry pipeline, for example, drains the arid region of scarce water resources.

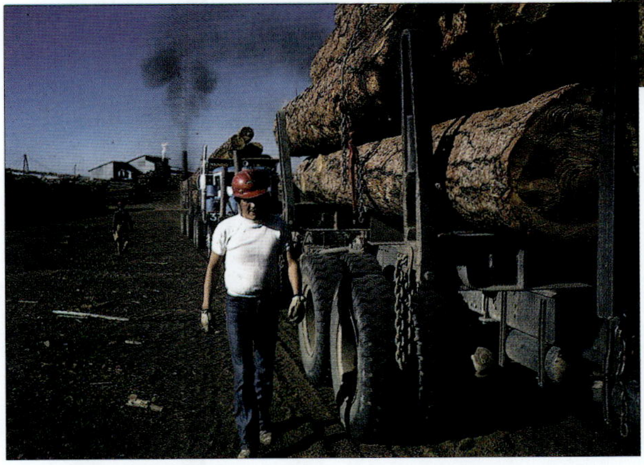

◁ **INCOME FROM TREES**
The Navajo tribe operates this lumber mill, manufacturing wood products from the pine-fir forest. Pacific Northwest tribes also log and market forest products.

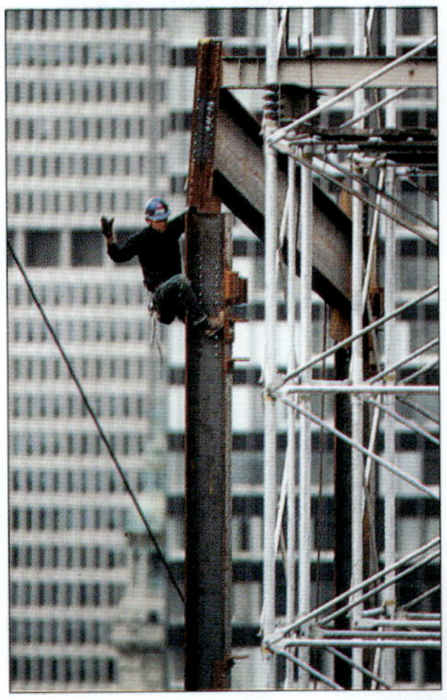

◁ **MOHAWK SKYWALKERS**
New York's Mohawks are famed for their highly skilled work in erecting bridges and skyscrapers. These high-steel workers are known as "skywalkers."

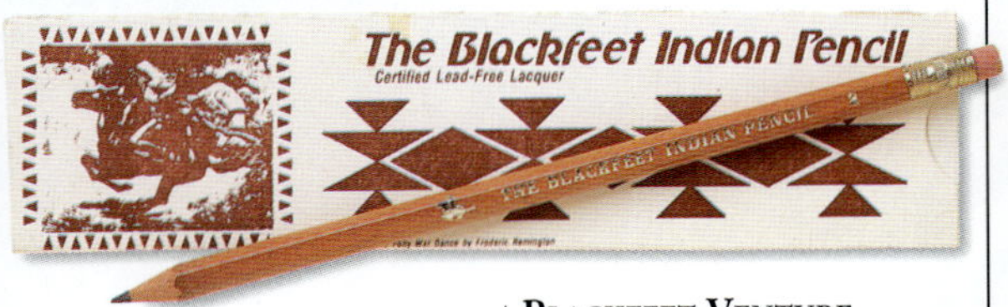

△ **BLACKFEET VENTURE**
The Blackfeet Indian Writing Company of Browning, Montana, has been producing pencils and pens since 1972, generating revenue and providing steady employment for tribal members.

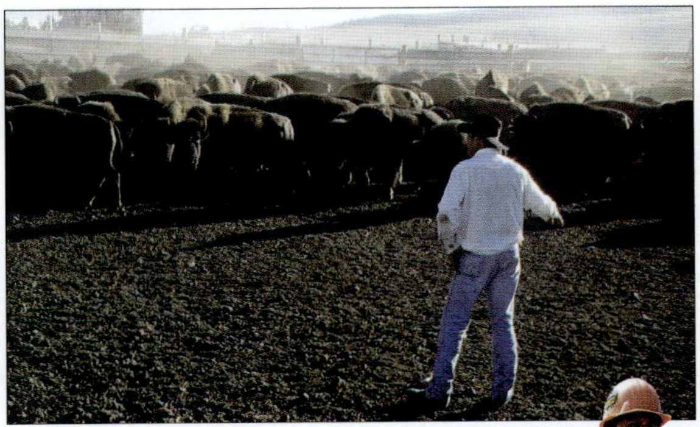

RETURN OF THE BUFFALO ▷
Since the Intertribal Bison Cooperative came up with the idea of raising bison (buffalo) as a cash crop, the buffalo have returned to Indian reservations, including the Crow reservation pictured here.

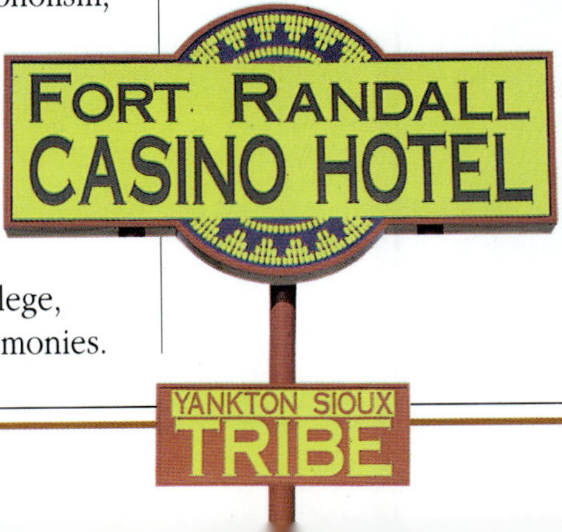

◁ **GAMBLING ON SUCCESS**
In 1998, more than 100 tribes in over 20 states ran high-stakes bingo parlors and casino operations, grossing $6 billion annually. Only a handful, however, have made substantial profits.

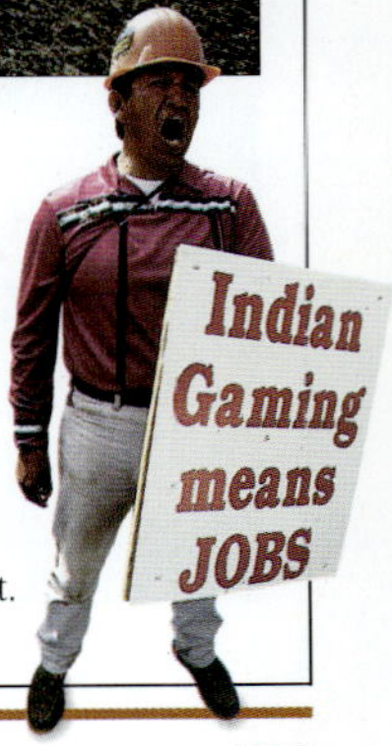

GAMING AND SELF-SUFFICIENCY ▷
In some areas, tribal games are a major source of jobs and revenue for tribal members and help the tribes and local communities to become self-sufficient.

LEARNING FOR THE FUTURE

Today tribes, educators, and parents want culturally responsive schools that maintain a strong commitment to the basics, as well as to tribal languages – an essential part of being Indian. Some elementary and high schools come under local Native control, as do over 30 colleges with tribe-specific curricula. Most Indian students attend mainstream colleges, and many graduate, going on to become successful professionals.

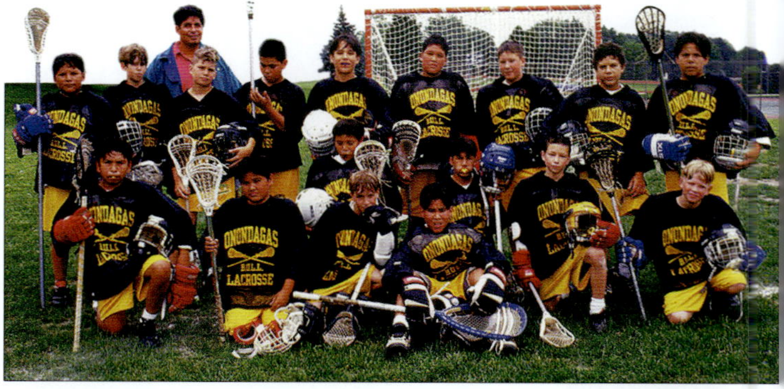

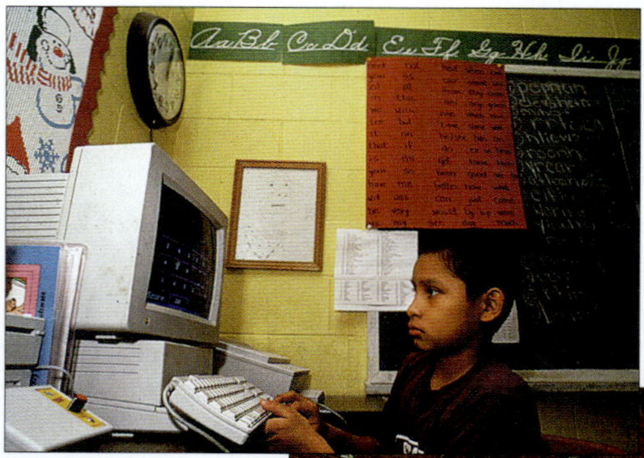

NEW TECHNOLOGIES EMBRACED ▷
In elementary and secondary schools run by Indian tribes and organizations, students use modern technology to help them with their academic studies.

▽ INDIAN-STYLE CAMPUS
Since the Navajo Community College (NCC) was established in 1969, many Indians have enrolled in higher education. The NCC administration building shown here is shaped like an eight-sided hogan.

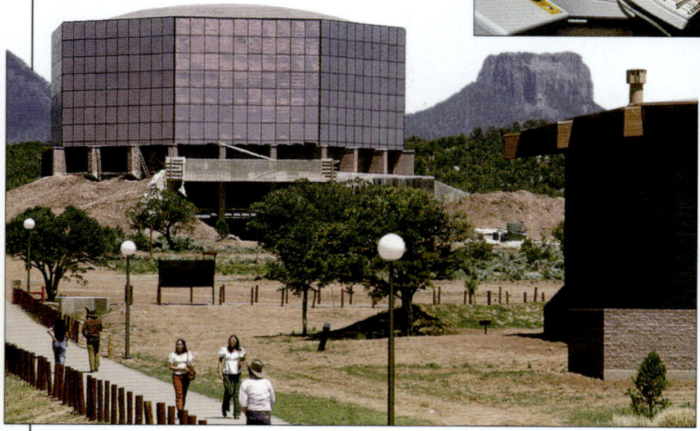

△ LACROSSE TRADITION
According to the Iroquois, the game of lacrosse is a gift from the Creator, and North American Indians consider the game part of their cultural and spiritual heritage. Here a lacrosse team, composed of Onondaga youngsters from New York, pose for the photographer.

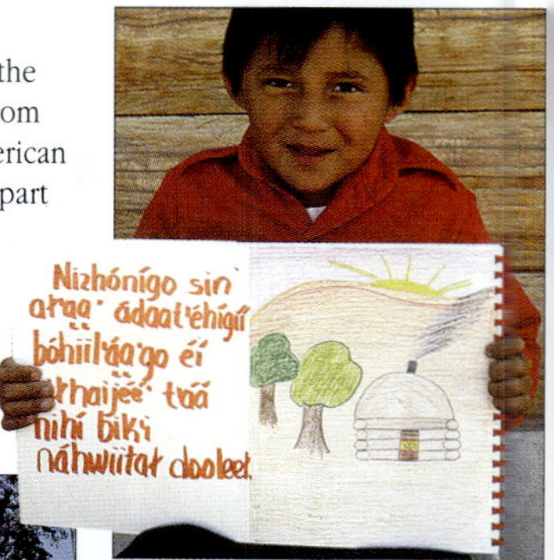

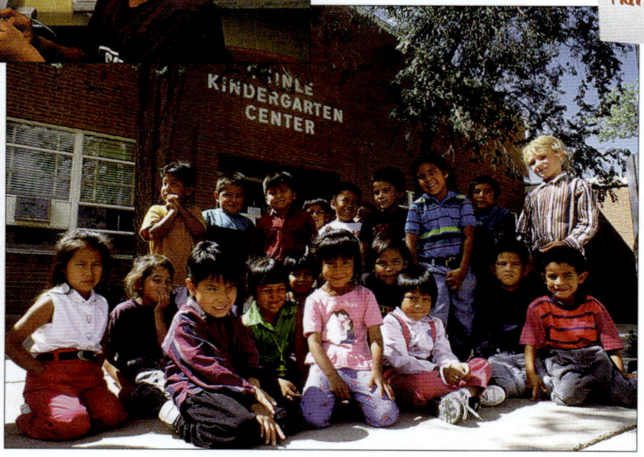

△ KEEPING CULTURE ALIVE
Once banned, ancestral tribal languages are now taught to schoolchildren. Navajo second-grader Pedro Lee shows how he uses the Navajo language.

◁ NAVAJO KINDERGARTEN
Kindergarteners pose in front of their school in Chinle, Arizona, where they are taught about their own culture as well as reading, writing, and arithmetic.

EVOLVING TRADITIONS

Despite all the government efforts to stamp out Indian cultures, many Native traditions have survived. Indeed, Indians have demonstrated a remarkable ability to adapt to new and changing circumstances and to adopt new ways while staying true to their cultural identity. Across North America, Native people have continued, renewed, or modified their traditions.

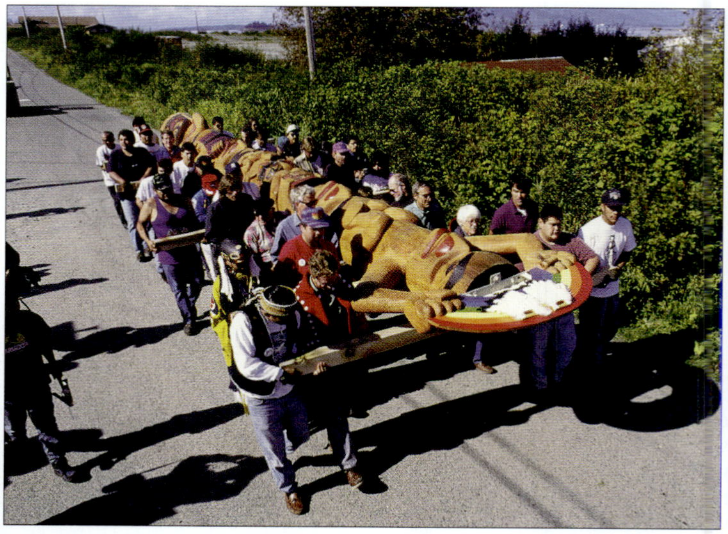

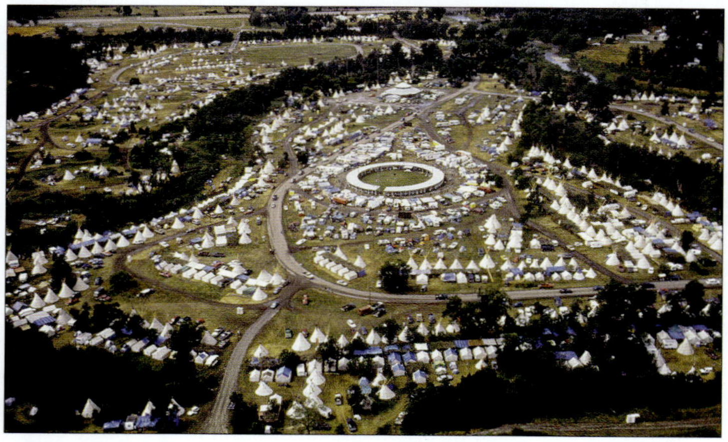

◁ CONTEMPORARY POWWOW
The honoring and gift-giving ceremonies of modern powwows exemplify active Indian resistance to cultural annihilation. Pictured here is an aerial view of the annual Crow Fair in Montana, one of the largest powwows in North America.

△ TOTEM TRADITION REVIVED
In a revival of a Northwest Coast Indian tradition, totem poles are again being raised in Haida villages in the Queen Charlotte Islands as well as at Alaska's Metlakatla reservation – home to the Tsimshian people pictured here.

ON THE RESERVATIONS

Indian people hold steadfastly to their reservation lands and constantly battle against those who want to acquire pieces of them – non-Indians, the federal government, ranchers, miners, the park system, and others. Reservations are where many Indians will return to end their days, even if they have been away from them for most of their lives.

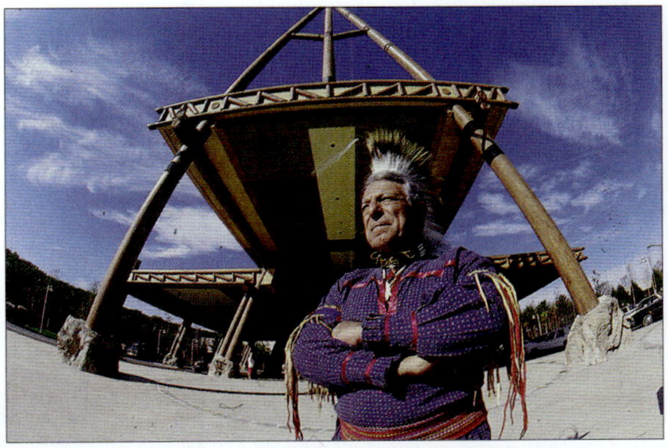

◁ **OWNING BUSINESSES**
In 1996, the Mohegan Indian Tribe of Connecticut opened its Sun Casino. The venture came about through a partnership between the tribe and a South African company, Sun International.

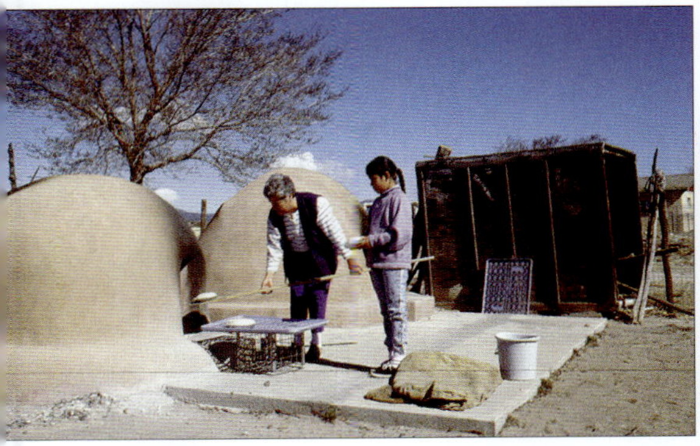

△ **PUEBLO BREADMAKING**
Cochiti pueblo village women bake bread in outdoor adobe ovens just as their ancestors did. After the wood fire inside burns out, the ashes are removed and the dough is placed in the oven, which retains enough heat to bake the bread.

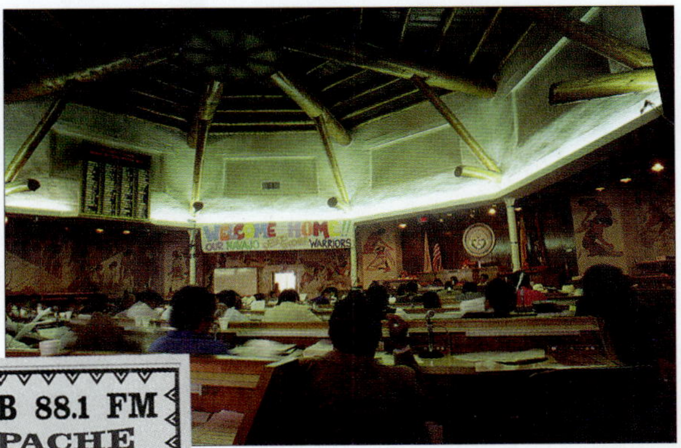

△ **COUNCIL MEETING**
Navajos were traditionally governed by clan leaders but today they have a more formal government that includes an elected council and president. Officials meet in the Navajo Council House at Window Rock, Arizona, an octagonal building meant to suggest a hogan although, unlike this building, hogans never had two stories.

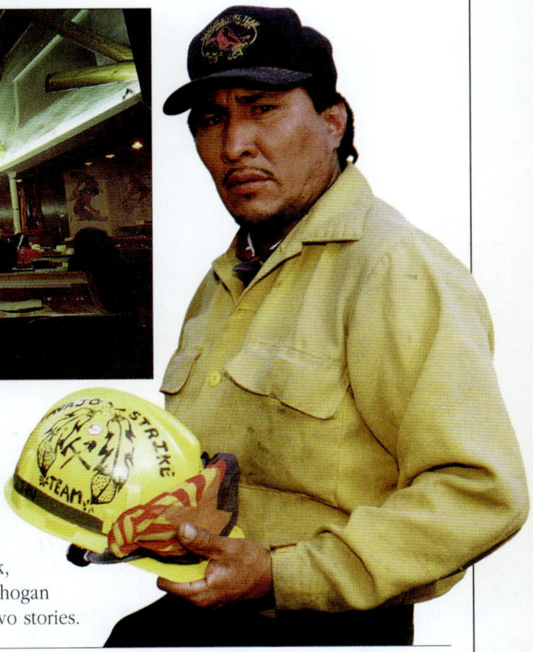

▽ **NAVAJO FIREFIGHTERS**
This firefighter belongs to the exclusively Navajo, Color Country III Navajo Firefighting Unit. For three weeks in 1996, the unit fought a blaze that spread from Colorado to Wyoming.

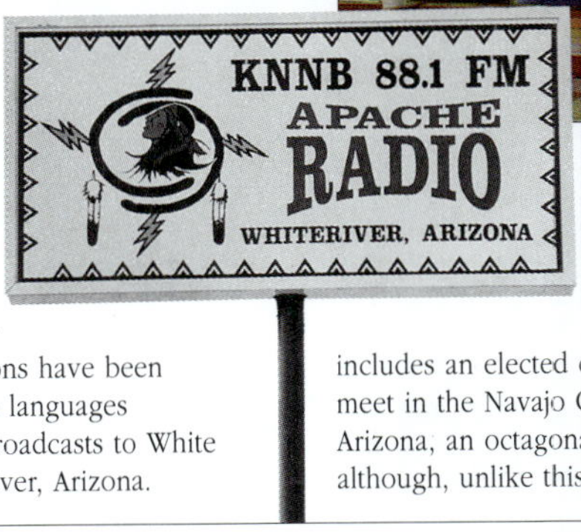

TUNE IN TO NATIVE BROADCASTING ▷
Since the 1970s, Native American radio stations have been broadcasting programs in English and Native languages throughout the US and Canada. KNNB-FM broadcasts to White Mountain Apaches from its station in Whiteriver, Arizona.

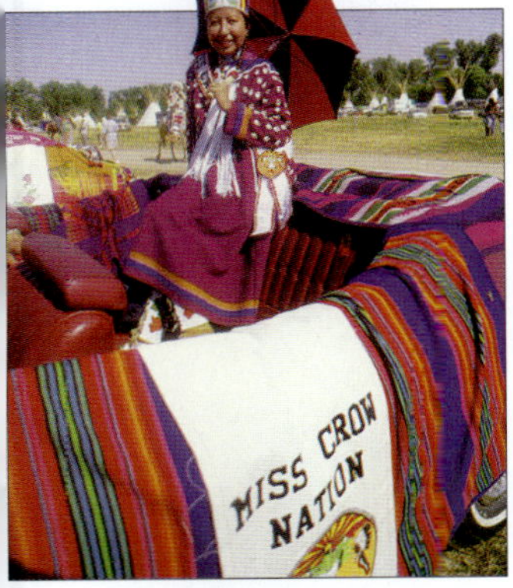

△ **MISS CROW NATION 1996**
Wearing a beaded crown, this young woman takes part in the 1996 Crow Fair. Beauty pageants are held on many reservations, although crowned royalty was never a Native concept.

NATIVE FESTIVAL ▷
With their tribal museum in the background, Kwakiutl Natives of Alert Bay, British Columbia, welcomed traditional canoe paddlers. Many Native nations have created museums that celebrate their cultures.

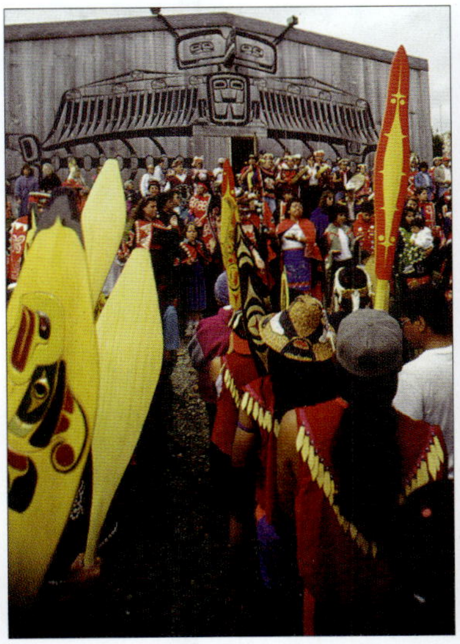

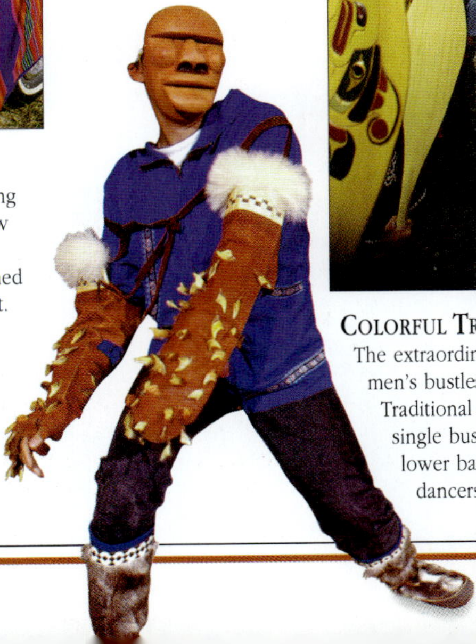

POWERFUL PERFORMERS ▷
In Anchorage, Alaska, a masked Inuit dancer performs on stage. Masks such as his represent the spirits portrayed in shamanic curing rites and in dance festivals

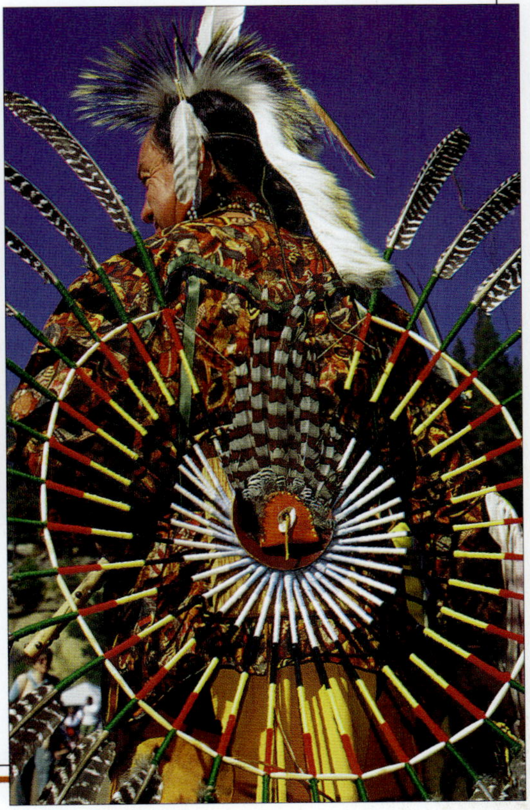

COLORFUL TRADITIONS ▷
The extraordinary color and design of the men's bustles amaze powwow visitors. Traditional straight dancers wear a single bustle of feathers tied to their lower back, while fancy feather dancers wear two bustles.

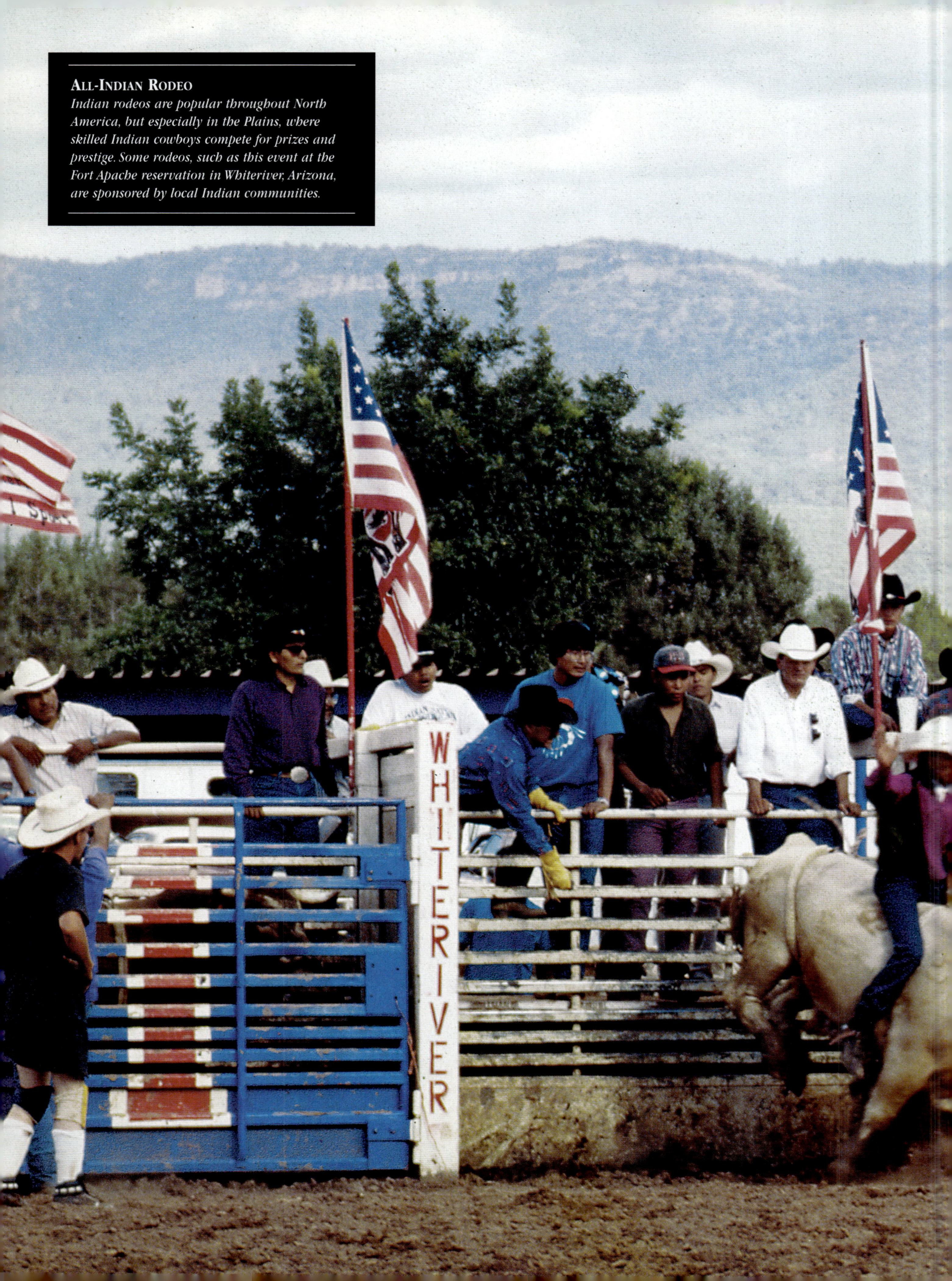

All-Indian Rodeo

Indian rodeos are popular throughout North America, but especially in the Plains, where skilled Indian cowboys compete for prizes and prestige. Some rodeos, such as this event at the Fort Apache reservation in Whiteriver, Arizona, are sponsored by local Indian communities.

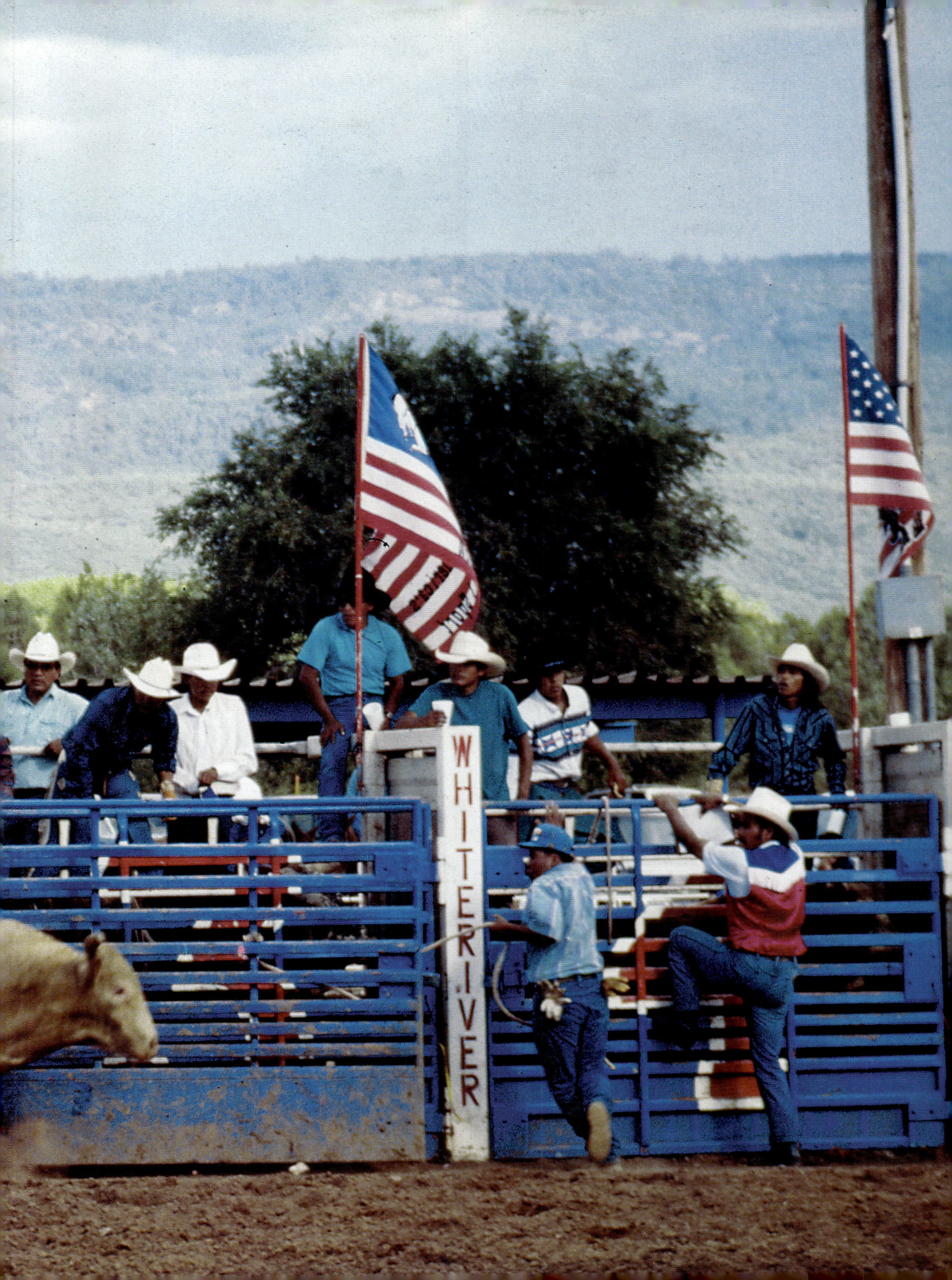
WHITERIVER

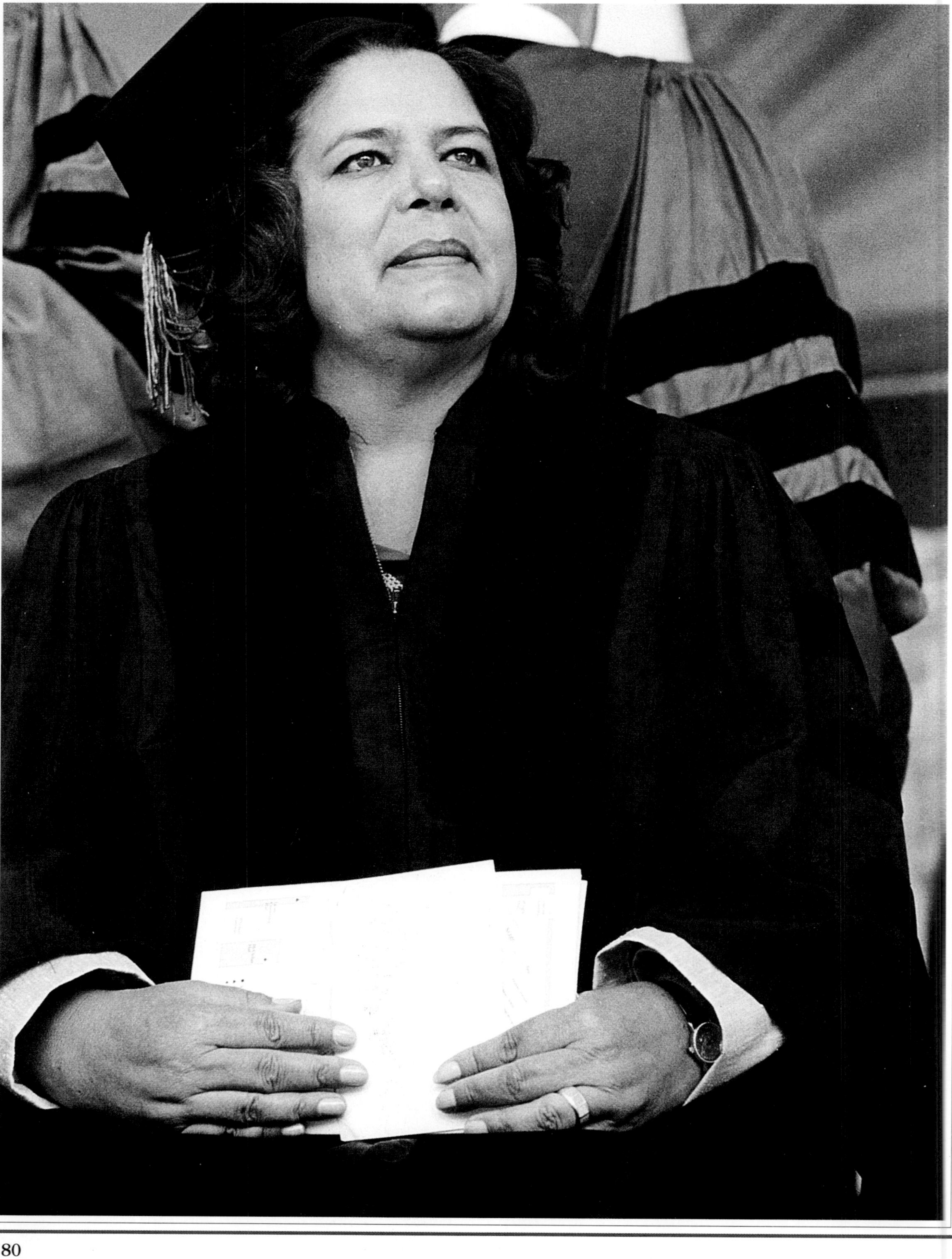

WILMA MANKILLER

1991: ON TRADITIONAL VALUES IN THE MODERN WORLD

BORN IN 1945 IN TAHLEQUAH, OKLAHOMA, Wilma Mankiller (whose name was originally an honored Cherokee title) was elected the first woman Deputy Chief in Cherokee history in 1983. In 1969 she joined the Alcatraz occupation, later becoming involved in grass-roots activities to improve the Cherokees' living conditions. Mankiller became Principal Chief in 1985, winning reelection in 1987 and 1991. Since giving up the leadership in 1995, Wilma Mankiller has written a memoir and taught at Dartmouth College, Hanover, New Hampshire. This extract is from an article published in *Native Peoples* magazine in 1991.

"Certainly I believe that ancient tribal cultures have important lessons to teach the rest of the world about the interconnectedness of all living things and the simple fact that our very existence is dependent upon the natural world we are rapidly destroying. Most non-tribal societies have a hierarchical, segmented world view. They appear not to understand or to ignore the impact of their decisions on everything around them ....

While it is indisputable that the traditional value systems native people held for centuries before European contact have been somewhat eroded, basic traditional values continue to exist, even in the most fragmented, troubled communities. The traditional value systems that have sustained us throughout the past 500 years of trauma are those value systems that will bolster us and help us enter the twenty-first century on our own terms.

Despite the last 500 years, there is much to celebrate .... Our languages are still strong, ceremonies that we have been conducting since the beginning of time are still being held, our governments are surviving and most importantly, we continue to exist as a distinct cultural group in the midst of the most powerful country in the world. Yet, we also must recognize that we face a daunting set of problems and issues – continual threats to tribal sovereignty, low educational attainment levels, double digit unemployment, many homes without basic amenities, and racism. To grapple with these problems in a forward-thinking positive way, we are beginning to look more and more to our own people, communities and history for solutions. We have begun to trust our own thinking again. If we are to look to our culture and history for solutions to problems, let us look at an accurate history, not the Columbus myth ... taught in every grade history class in America.

As native people approach the twenty-first century, we look into the faces of our youth and see ... hope. We would like to see that hope kept alive by doing everything possible to assure that our tribal communities continue to dig a way out of the devastation of the past 500 years. We look forward to the next 500 years as a time of renewal and revitalization for native people throughout North America."

REVITALIZED CULTURES

THROWING OFF THE SHACKLES of colonial government policies, Native peoples in North America in the 1960s started to define and shape their own art forms. Contemporary painters and sculptors, musicians, poets and novelists, and film- and videomakers began to create works that reflected the social, political, and economic upheavals that have decimated Native societies. Working in a variety of media, they show the texture of contemporary tribal and urban life as well as the disastrous effects of decades of assimilationist policies.

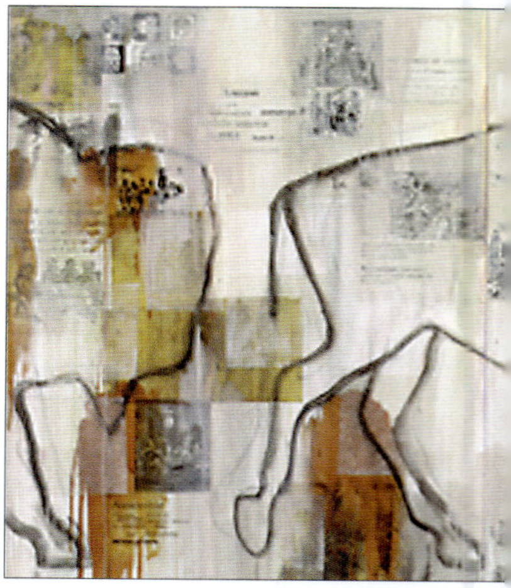

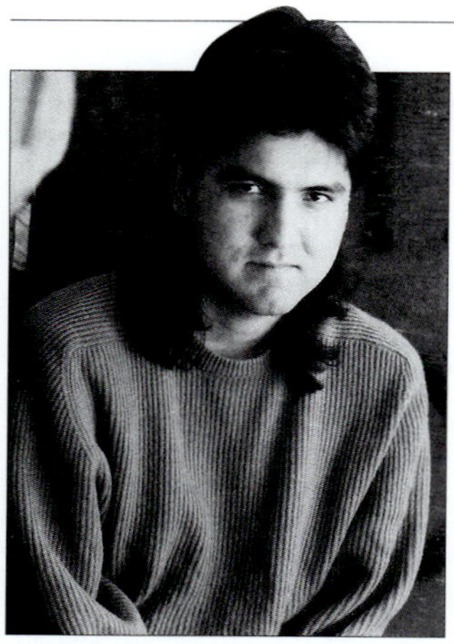

△ SPOKANE AUTHOR
Poet and novelist Sherman Alexie authored *The Lone Ranger and Tonto Fistfight in Heaven* (1993), a collection of short stories. One formed the basis of Alexie's screenplay for the movie *Smoke Signals*, which he also produced.

▽ WORDS AND MUSIC
Muskogee poet Joy Harjo plays saxophone and recites her poetry with her jazz/reggae band. A professor of creative writing, Harjo also writes screenplays and children's books, and compiles anthologies of Native writing.

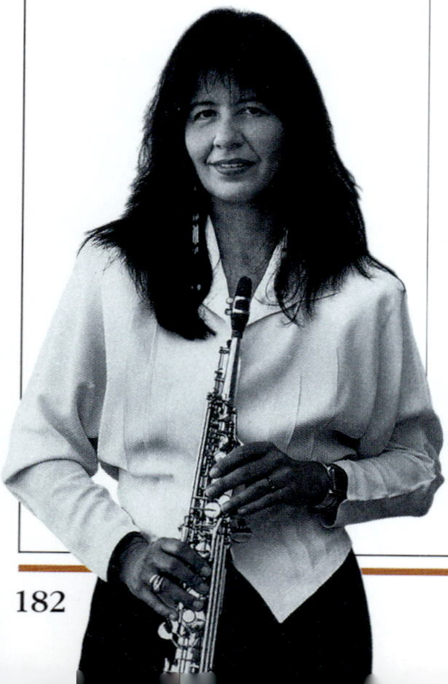

NATIVE AMERICAN WRITING is a relatively new medium but, since 1969, when Kiowa writer N. Scott Momaday won the Pulitzer Prize for Fiction for *House Made of Dawn* and Dakota lawyer-historian Vine Deloria, Jr. published his best-selling history *Custer Died for Your Sins*, scores of Native North American writers have published works. Drawing much of their power from the oral tradition, many Native writers use their own tribal world views as the vehicle to present modern themes about the Native cultural experience and struggles. Writers like Linda Hogan (Chickasaw), Leslie Silko (Laguna Pueblo), and James Welch (Blackfeet) tell of the power of old beliefs and the survival of Native American peoples, and write about the despair of living in two worlds, of people struggling with alcohol addiction, with dams that flood traditional fishing grounds, and tourist invasions of sacred sites.

Contemporary Indian artists, too, produce work that has a clear connection with their artistic forebears as well as incorporating western techniques and styles. Using new materials and tools, Native artists create work that affirms Native identity and defies the forces of assimilation, freeing themselves from the constraints imposed by non-Indian "experts." Influential Salish/Shoshone/Cree painter Jaune Quick-to-See Smith creates richly textured canvases by pasting down pieces of fabric and paper and rubbing layers of paint over all of it, a process she finds similar to the ancient method of smearing earth pigments and animal fat on animal hides. Celebrated Maidu

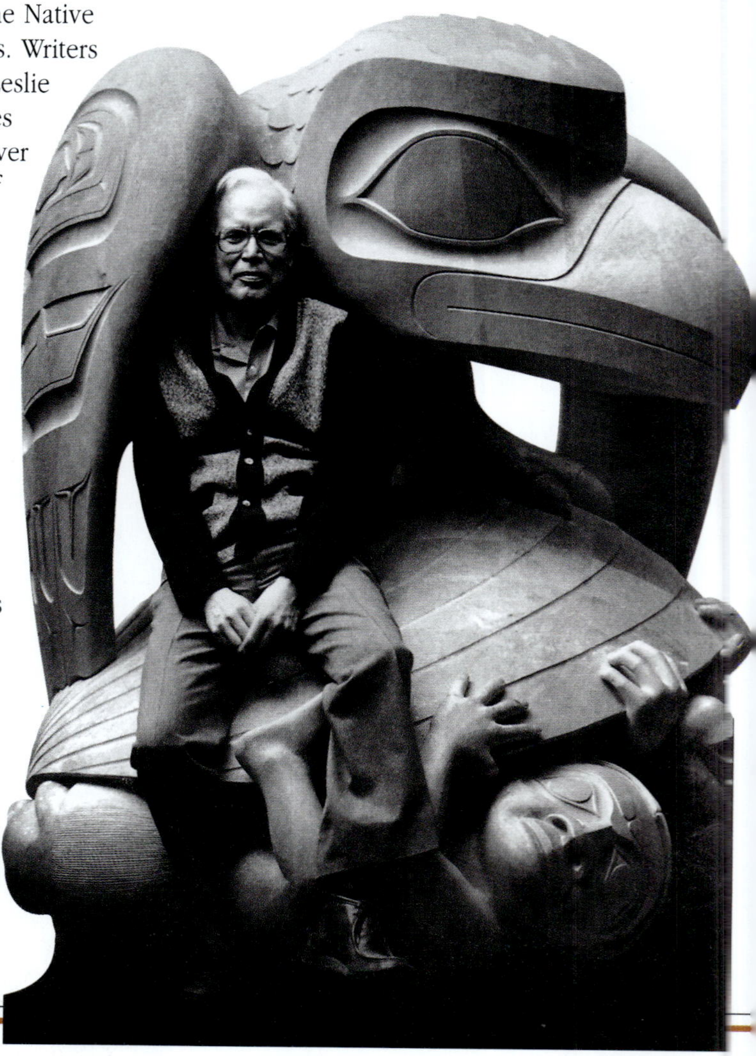

RENOWNED HAIDA SCULPTOR ▷
Bill Reid, from British Columbia, who died in March 1998, is pictured here with his sculpture *The Raven and the First Men*. Reid, who created art ranging from miniature brooches to huge wooden sculptures, won many awards and honors for his creativity and innovations and for his success in reviving and bringing recognition to ancient Northwest Coast art forms.

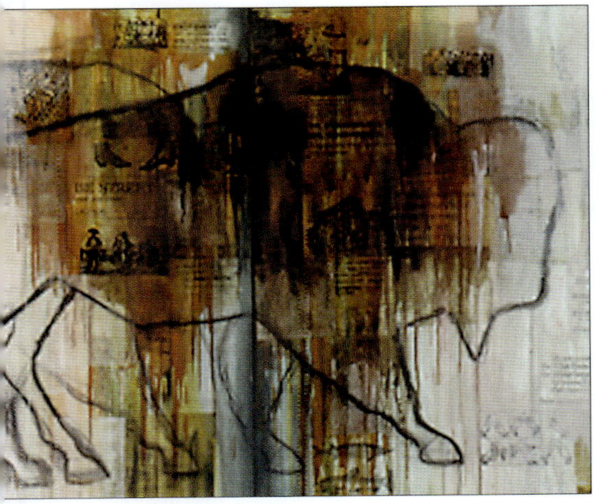

△ A MODERN EXPRESSION OF NATIVE IMAGERY
Entitled *Herd* (1998), this mixed media collage on canvas by Jaune Quick-to-See Smith, a Salish/Shoshone/Cree artist from Montana, demonstrates her love of combining Native American imagery with the styles of modernists and abstract expressionists.

painter Harry Fonseca, on the other hand, takes the traditional coyote out of the tribal world, eliminates his Maidu identity, and puts the playful figure in black leather jackets, blue jeans, high-top tennis shoes, and baseball cap.

Blending Styles in Music and Film

Since the late 1960s and early 1970s, there has been a steady increase in contemporary Native music. Native musicians combine their Native chants and instruments with folk, rock, reggae, country, New Age, or rap to convey their messages. Saxophonist Jim Pepper (Creek/Kaw), for example, developed a unique mix of jazz and tribal music, while members of the Canadian band Kashtin ("tornado" in the Innu language) blend folk-rock and Cajun. Native singers have been especially vocal in protesting against government mistreatment of Native people in songs like Cree Buffy Sainte-Marie's "Bury My Heart at Wounded Knee."

Although a handful of Indian film-makers were already making documentaries in the US and Canada, in the 1970s, hundreds of Natives began producing, directing, and acting in documentaries. Since 1991, a number of Native-organized festivals have resulted in wider opportunities for Native producers like Chris Ayer (Cheyenne/Arapaho) and Beverly Singer (Tewa-Navajo). In 1998, *Smoke Signals*, the first feature film written, produced, and directed by American Indians, was distributed by Miramax to theaters across the US.

NATIVES ON CAMERA

Indians have acted in movies since the silent-movie era. Although they were used primarily as extras and in bit parts, a few Indian actors became stars. In 1979, for example, Jay Silverheels was the first Native to receive a star in the Hollywood Walk of Fame. Since the 1970s, some Native actors, such as Irene Bedard (Inupiat/Cree) and Will Samson (Creek), have been cast in leading roles, gaining star recognition in Hollywood and in television movies.

WHITES PLAY INDIANS ▷
Throughout the twentieth century, Hollywood has churned out hundreds of movies about Indians but, until recently, Indian roles were not played by Natives: the major Indian roles were played by stars such as Burt Lancaster, Rock Hudson, and Loretta Young.

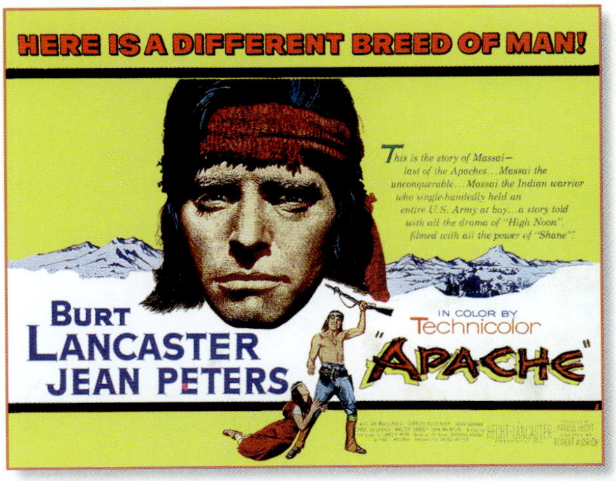

▽ SILVERHEELS AS TONTO
In 1960, Mohawk Harry Preston Smith, better known as Jay Silverheels, played Tonto in *The Lone Ranger*. In 1966, he and other Indians formed an Indian Actors' Workshop to bring more Native people onto the screen.

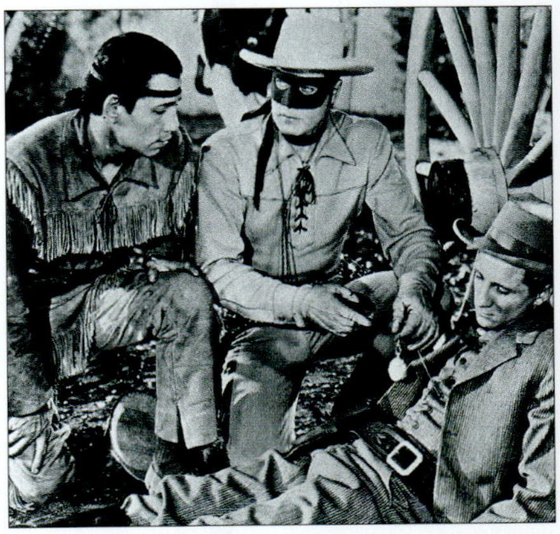

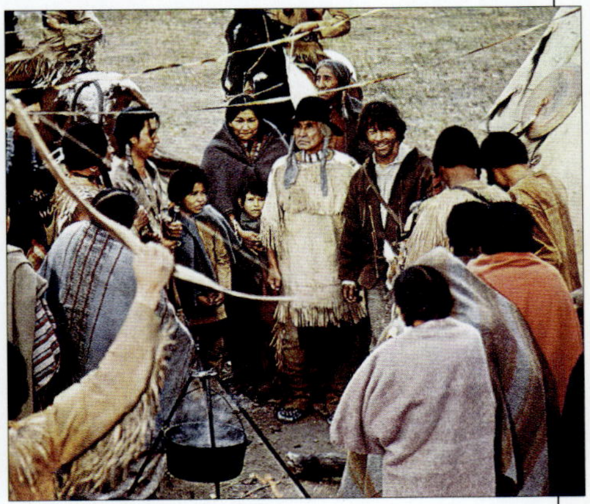

△ OSCAR-NOMINATED CHIEF
Chief Dan George, a Salish elder from British Columbia, was nominated for an Oscar (though he did not win it) for his role as Old Lodge Skins (man wearing hat, above) in the 1970 film *Little Big Man*.

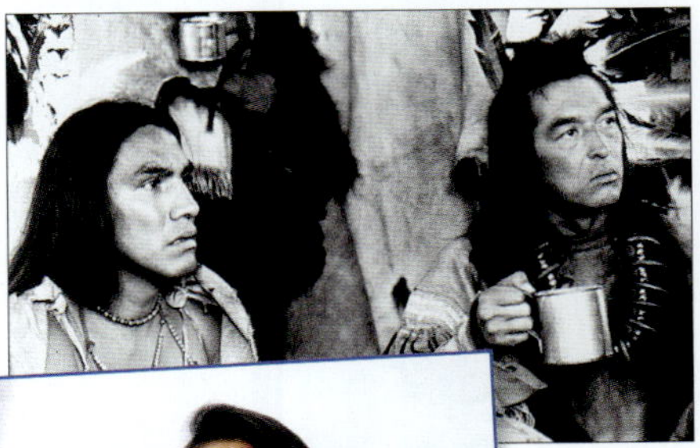

◁ MOVIE SUCCESS
Omaha actor Will Grant (left) and Oneida actor Graham Greene both acted in the 1990 film *Dances With Wolves*. Greene was nominated for an Oscar for Best Supporting Actor (but did not win it.)

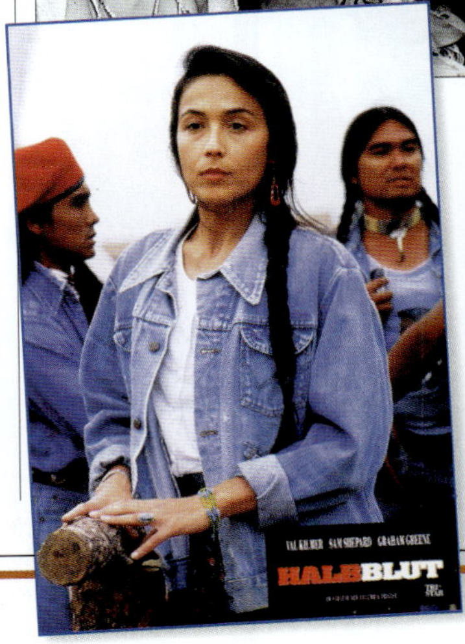

◁ EUROPEAN APPEAL
Films like *Thunderheart* (1992), which deal with real contemporary issues and the struggles of Native peoples, are popular in Europe. *Thunderheart* star Menominee-Stockbridge actor Sheila Tousey is pictured here.

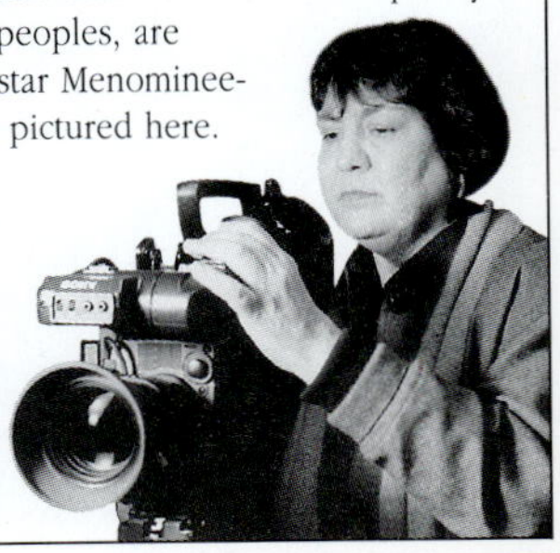

INDEPENDENT FILM-MAKER ▷
Dozens of independent Native film- and videomakers, like Sandra Johnson Osawa (Makah) now produce and direct works about Native experiences.

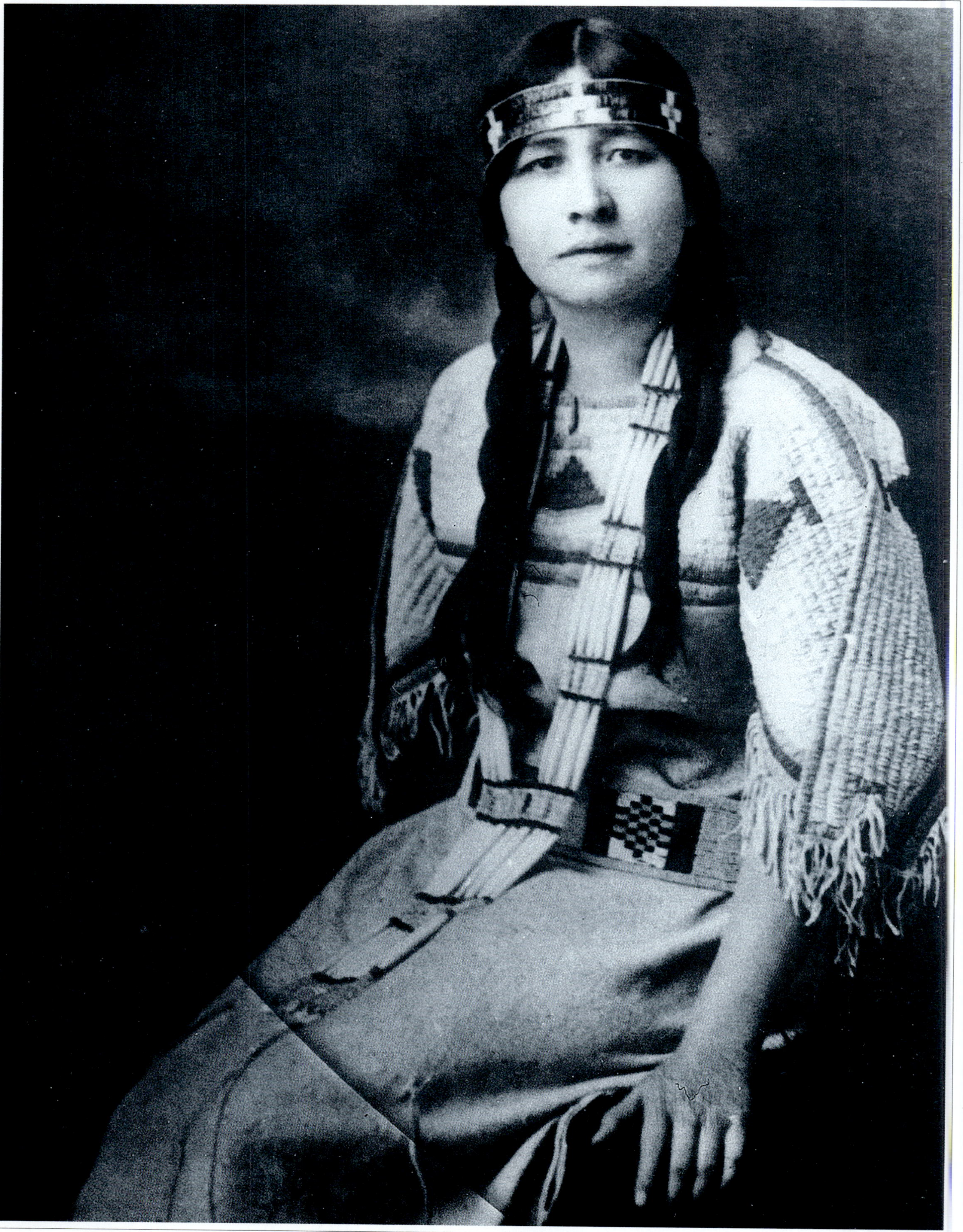

ELLA DELORIA

1944: ON THE PAST, PRESENT, AND FUTURE OF NATIVE AMERICANS

THE GRANDDAUGHTER OF A FRENCH FUR TRADER and a Dakota woman, Yankton Sioux Ella Deloria (1889–1971) became a renowned scholar of the Dakota language and culture. After receiving a BA from Columbia University in New York, she established a professional relationship with the anthropologist Franz Boas. Having overcome enormous difficulties to become a scholar in her own right, Ella went on to produce a huge body of work, including books about Dakota society and grammar and a Sioux dictionary. In 1944, Ella published *Speaking of Indians*, from which this extract is taken.

"Science tells us that the native Americans came from northern Asia and that they may have arrived here from ten to twelve thousand years ago. But they were not the first inhabitants of this continent. From archeological evidences we know that man-made implements of stone were left beside ancient campfires fifteen to eighteen thousand years ago, some even say twenty thousand. Man-made projectiles, too, have been found deep in the earth, together with the skeletons of a prehistoric species of bison. It is known from such remains that these earlier peoples lived by both hunting and seed-gathering. We cannot know what became of them – whether they had all vanished before the ancestors of the modern Indians arrived, or whether some were still wandering about and were absorbed by the newcomers. Of course, every bit of this is speculative; one guess is nearly as good as another, for we can never be sure of what actually took place.

And it doesn't really matter, does it? All that which lies hidden in the remote past is interesting, to be sure, but not so important as the present and the future. The vital concern is not where a people came from, physically, but where they are going, spiritually."

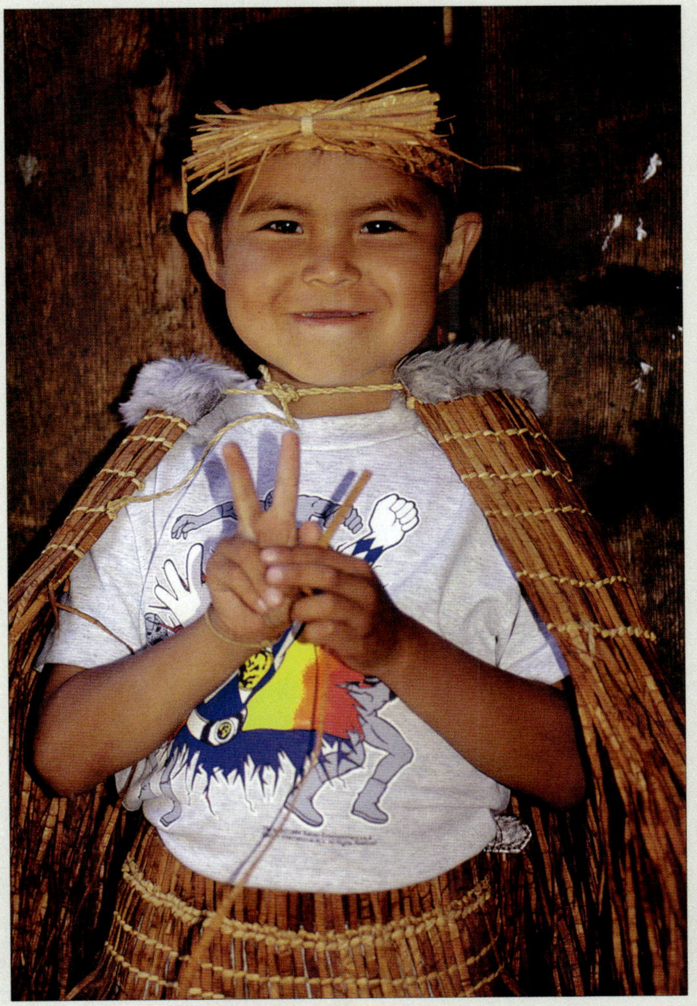

THE HOPES OF A NEW GENERATION

Native children represent the future: families and tribes want youngsters, like this young Yakima girl, dressed in traditional regalia, to take their place in the mainstream of US and Canadian society without severing their ancient tribal roots.

FURTHER INFORMATION

BIBLIOGRAPHY

Axelrod, Alan. *Chronicle of the Indian Wars: From Colonial Times to Wounded Knee.* New York, Prentice-Hall General Reference, 1993. The book portrays the history of 400 years of Indian-white warfare, based on hundreds of eyewitness accounts.

Cantor, George. *North American Indian Landmarks: A Traveler's Guide.* Detroit, Visible Ink, 1993. Arranged by region, 300 sites are described, including reservations, museums, recreated villages, battlefields, state parks, cultural centers, and festivals.

Champagne, Duane, editor. *The Native North American Almanac: A Reference Work on Native North Americans in the United States and Canada.* Detroit, Gale Research, Inc., 1994. This huge, well-illustrated volume, written by authorities, includes documentary excerpts and covers chronologies, demography, major culture areas, languages, administration, activism, environment, urbanization, religion, arts, literature, media, health, education, economy, plus 470 biographies of prominent Native North Americans.

* **Ciment, James.** *Scholastic Encyclopedia of the North American Indian.* New York, Scholastic, Inc., 1996. A lavishly illustrated A–Z guide to 149 tribes from the Arctic Circle to Central America.

Davis, Mary B. *Native America in the Twentieth Century: An Encyclopedia.* New York, Garland Publishing, Inc., 1994. Arranged in an A–Z format, the book's articles focus on every conceivable subject concerning Native peoples in the twentieth century.

Francis, Lee. *Native Time: A Historical Time Line of Native America.* New York, St. Martin's Press, 1996. Beginning in 200,000 BC, this chronological time line runs to the present day, illuminating History/Law/Politics; Literature/Art/Legends/Stories; Heroes/Leaders/Victims; and Elder Wisdom/ Philosophy/Songs. A calendar section gives a month-by-month listing of celebrations, events, and festivals that take place annually among Native nations in the US.

* **Griffin-Pierce, Trudy.** *The Encyclopedia of Native America.* New York, Viking, 1995. Divided into seven cultural and geographical areas, the volume explores Native cultures in these regions as well as the impact of European colonization.

Hirschfelder, Arlene and Molin, Paulette. *Encyclopedia of Native American Religions*, updated edition. New York, Facts on File, 1999. Over 1,000 entries describe traditional beliefs and worship practices in North America, consequences of contact with Europeans and other Americans/Canadians, and contemporary Native religions.

Hoxie, Frederick E., editor. *Encyclopedia of North American Indians: Native American History, Culture, and Life from Paleo-Indians to the Present.* Boston, Houghton-Mifflin Co., 1996. Written by over 260 authorities, many of whom are Native, this richly illustrated A–Z volume has articles on history and contemporary life as well as descriptions of more than 100 tribes in North America and treatments of numerous Native historical figures.

Josephy, Alvin. *500 Nations: An Illustrated History of North American Indians.* New York, Knopf, 1994. An introduction to hundreds of Native nations in the US and Canada as well as a story of conquest, displacement, genocide, forced assimilation, and survival. Over 450 illustrations, most in color.

Keenan, Jerry. *Encyclopedia of American Indian Wars: 1492–1890.* New York, W.W. Norton, 1997. In 450 entries, this volume analyzes battles, famous Native leaders, weapons, forts, treaties, and military officers and units in the US.

King, Thomas, editor. *All My Relations: An Anthology of Contemporary Canadian Native Fiction.* Norman, University of Oklahoma Press, 1992. The short fiction of 19 Canadian Native writers, including King himself.

Klein, Barry T. *Reference Encyclopedia of the American Indian*, eighth edition. West Nyack, Todd Publications, 1997. This huge resource contains listings of US and Canadian government agencies, national associations, schools, college courses, tribal councils, casinos, museums, audio-visual aids, events, web sites, and more, plus hundreds of biographies and an extensive bibliography.

Lesley, Craig and Stavrakis, Katheryn, editors. *Talking Leaves: Contemporary Native American Short Stories: An Anthology.* New York, Dell, 1994. Selections of short fiction by 35 Native writers capture the traditions of their cultures and struggles of the present.

* **Marra, Ben.** *Powwow: Images Along the Red Road.* New York, Abrams, 1996. Over 100 photos illustrate the powwow event, plus commentary from dancers.

Nabakov, Peter, editor. *Native American Testimony: A Chronicle of Indian-White Relations from Prophesy to the Present, 1492–1992.* New York, Penguin Books, 1992. A history of Indian-white relations, in all its complexities, is presented in over 100 documents, along with the editor's commentaries putting each selection in historical perspective.

* **National Geographic.** *1491: America before Columbus.* National Geographic, Volume 180, No. 4 (October 1991). This issue provides a close look at Native peoples on the eve of cataclysmic change.

* **Ortiz, Alfonso and Erdoes, Richard, editors.** *American Indian Myths and Legends.* New York, Pantheon Books, 1984. A collection of over 160 traditional stories from North American tribes.

* **Ortiz, Simon.** *The People Shall Continue.* Emeryville, Children's Book Press, 1977. Renowned Acoma poet tells the epic story of Native North American peoples from Creation to the present in traditional, oral narrative style. Full-color illustrations.

Riley, Patricia. *Growing Up Native American: An Anthology.* New York, William Morrow, 1993. 22 Native fiction and non-fiction writers discuss growing up.

Thomas, David Hurst. *Exploring Ancient Native America: An Archaeological Guide.* New York, Macmillan, 1994. This guidebook describes 400 accessible archaelogical sites in the US and Canada.

Thomas, David Hurst et al. *The Native Americans: An Illustrated History.* Atlanta, Turner Publishing, Inc., 1993. This history by five historians and anthropologists provides cultural information and details the devastating impact of the European invasion on Native peoples in the US. With almost 500 photographs, engravings, and Native paintings.

Tiller, Veronica E. Velarde, editor. *Tiller's Guide to Indian Country: Economic Profiles of American Indian Reservations.* Albuquerque, BowArrow Publishing Company, 1996. Profiles of over 550 federal and state-recognized reservations located in 36 states include maps, addresses, phone numbers, location, climate, culture and history, government, economy, tourism and recreation, and more.

Wade, Edwin L., editor. *The Arts of the American Indian, Native Traditions in Evolution.* New York, Hudson Hills Press, 1986. This book presents the arts of Native peoples across the Americas.

* **Waldman, Carl.** *Encyclopedia of Native American Tribes*, revised edition. New York, Facts on File, 1999. Guide to the history and cultures of more than 150 tribes in North America.

Waldman, Carl. *Who Was Who in Native American History: Indians and Non-Indians from Early Contacts through 1900.* New York, Facts on File, 1990. The book identifies Native leaders, fur traders, missionaries, explorers, and others who had an impact on Native history from 1492 to 1900.

Wall, Steve and Arden, Harvey. *Wisdomkeepers: Meetings with Native American Spiritual Elders.* Hillsboro, Beyond Words Publishing, Inc., 1990. The authors provide photographs and the words of 17 elders (men and women) from 13 Indian nations.

Weatherford, Jack. *Native Roots: How the Indians Enriched America.* New York, Crown Publishers, 1991. The author tells how the cultural, social, and political practices of Native peoples transformed the world, including the status of women, farming and hunting techniques, crafts, and language.

* Good for youngsters aged 10 years and up

NATIVE AMERICAN ORGANIZATIONS

For hundreds of years, Native peoples have organized into groups to promote their mutual welfare. One of the oldest organizations in North America, the Iroquois Confederacy, is still in existence after 500 years. Scores of other associations have been formed by Native peoples to represent their interests at all levels, with objectives ranging from political and economic aims to social, educational, cultural, and spiritual concerns. The following is a small sample of national organizations in the United States and Canada.

UNITED STATES

American Indian Science and Engineering Society (AISES), 2201 Buena Vista S.E., Suite 301, Albuquerque, New Mexico 87106. (505) 765-1052. Founded in 1977, AISES aims to integrate science and technology with traditional Native values. www.aises.org

First Nations Development Institute, 11917 Main Street, Fredericksburg, Virginia 22408. (540) 371-3505. Founded in 1980, the Institute promotes appropriate economic development by and for Native peoples. www.firstnations.org

National Congress of American Indians (NCAI), 1301 Connecticut Avenue N.W., Suite 200, Washington, DC 20036. (202) 466-7767. Founded in 1944, this political organization represents the interests of some 150 tribes. www.ncai.org

National Indian Education Association (NIEA), 700 North Fairfax Street, Suite 210, Alexandria, Virginia 22314. (703) 838-2870. Formed in 1970, NIEA aims to improve the educational status of Native peoples. www.europe.com/~nadm/pages/NIEA.html

Native American Rights Fund (NARF), 1506 Broadway, Boulder, Colorado 80302. (303) 447-8760. Established in 1970, NARF addresses major Indian legal problems and provides competent legal representation. www.narf.org

CANADA

The Assembly of First Nations (AFN), 1 Nicholas Street, Suite 1002, Ottawa, Ontario K1N 7B7. (613) 241-6789. Organized in 1982, this association of First Nations chiefs represents Status Indians. It succeeded the National Indian Brotherhood, which was founded in 1968. www.afn.ca/

Congress of Aboriginal Peoples, 867 St. Laurent Blvd., Ottawa, Ontario K1K 3B1. (613) 747-6022. Founded in 1971 as the Native Council of Canada, to represent Métis, off-reserve, and non-treaty Indians. www.abo-peoples.org

Inuit Tapirisat of Canada, 510 170 Laurier Avenue W., Ottawa, Ontario K1P 5V5. (613) 238-8181. Founded in 1971, this organization is dedicated to the needs and aspirations of all Canadian Inuit. www.tapirisat.ca

Métis National Council (MNC), 350 Sparks Street, Suite 201, Delta Hotel Office Tower, Ottawa, Ontario K1R 758. (613) 232-3216. Formed in 1983, the MNC represents Métis people, based in the western Canadian provinces of Alberta, Saskatchewan, Manitoba, and the Northwest Territories. www.sae.ca/mbc/mnc

The National Association of Friendship Centers (NAFC), 275 MacLaren Street, Ottawa, Ontario K2P 0L9. (613) 563-4844. Incorporated in 1972, NAFC aims to improve the quality of life for Native peoples in urban areas and represents the concerns of over 100 centers at national level. www.nafc-aboriginal.com

GOVERNMENT AGENCIES

UNITED STATES

Bureau of Indian Affairs (BIA), (Central Office), 1849 C Street N.W., Washington, DC 20245. (202) 208-3711. Established in 1834, the BIA is a division of the Department of the Interior and is the principal government agency carrying out the government-to-government relationship between the US and federally recognized tribes. www.doi.gov/bureau-indian-affairs.html

CANADA

Department of Indian Affairs and Northern Development (DIAND), (Central Office), 10 Wellington Street, North Tower, Ottawa, Ontario K1A OH4. (819) 853-3753. Established in 1967, the Department of Indian Affairs and Northern Development (also called Indian and Northern Affairs Canada) delivers authorized federal funds and programs to those aboriginal people who qualify under the Indian Act. The Northern Affairs branch is the primary conduit for fostering northern development. www.inac.gc.ca

NATIVE AMERICAN WEB SITES

Native American nations, tribes, communities, individuals, organizations, and others have created numerous web sites relating to Native cultures and issues. A selection of the most important sites are listed here. (Note: the Internet is an ever-changing universe and sites may disappear.)

Census data, 1990: US American Indians and Alaska Natives: http://www.census.gov/ Under "A" find American Indians and Alaska Natives [choose "Population"].

Census data, 1996: Canadian Native Peoples: http://www.statcan.ca/Daily/English/980113/d980113.htm

First Nations of Canada: http://fullcoverage.yahoo.com/Full_Coverage/Canada/First_Nations/ This site gives Native news and includes links to Provincial, Territorial, and other sites.

First Perspectives On Line: http://www.mbnet.mb.ca/firstper/ One of Canada's sources for Native news and events.

Home Pages of Native Artists and Authors: http://www.hanksville.org/ An index provides links to the home pages of Native artists and authors as well as Native American resources on the Internet, including culture, language, history, health, education, and indigenous knowledge.

Indian Country Today: http://Indiancountry.com/ The weekly national newspaper, *Indian Country Today*, covering national news and events and distributed in all 50 states and in 12 foreign countries, can be accessed online.

National Museum of the American Indian Resource Center: http://www.conexus.si.edu/ Conexus is a web site with a "window" through which people can view programs and exhibits at the George Gustav Heye Center, National Museum of the American Indian, New York City.

Native American Public Telecommunications: http://www.Nativetelecom.org/ This site is the national distribution system for AIROS (American Indian Radio on Satellite) – Native programming to tribal communities and to general audiences through Native American and other public radio stations as well as the Internet. "Native American Calling," the nation's first live one-hour call-in radio show geared toward a Native American audience, is also available at this site. This one-hour electronic talking circle can be heard on the Internet. Before listening on the computer, it is necessary to click onto the RealTime Audio web site and download its program (at no charge.) The site is www.realaudio.com/ This site also has several music programs, such as "Native Sounds-Native Voices," featuring traditional and contemporary Native American music.

Native Americas: http://nativeamericas.aip.cornell.edu/ – or http://www.news.Cornell.edu/general/July97/NatAm.Online/ *Native Americas* is the quarterly publication of Akwe:kon Press of the American Indian Program at Cornell University. The journal features articles that cover issues of concern to indigenous peoples throughout the western hemisphere. Visit the site for subscription information, Native happenings, and information on Akwe:kon Press.

Native Tech: http://www.nativeweb.org/NativeTech/ A wealth of information on the technology of Native American crafts including beadwork, clay and pottery, games and toys, metalwork, food and recipes, poetry, and much more. One section has articles dealing with contemporary issues about Native American art.

NativeWeb: http://www.nativeweb.org/ NativeWeb uses the Internet to educate the public about indigenous cultures and issues and to promote communications between indigenous peoples and organizations supporting their goals and efforts. The content of NativeWeb is predominantly about the Americas, from the Arctic to Tierra del Fuego. Lists Native-owned enterprises, deals with issues of cultural property, genealogy, and lots more.

Smithsonian Institution: http://www.si.edu/newstart.htm/ The Smithsonian Institution's searchable site contains a vast amount of information from all of the Smithsonian museums, including a section with resources for teachers. The site's Native American section includes a number of bibliographies and articles plus information on relevant Smithsonian exhibitions.

Windspeaker: http://www.ammsa.com/windspeaker/ This award-winning Native newspaper is one of Canada's best national aboriginal news sources. The site provides links to government and political sites as well as dozens of other excellent sites covering numerous subjects including health and economics.

INDEX

Page numbers in *italics* refer to entries with related illustrations

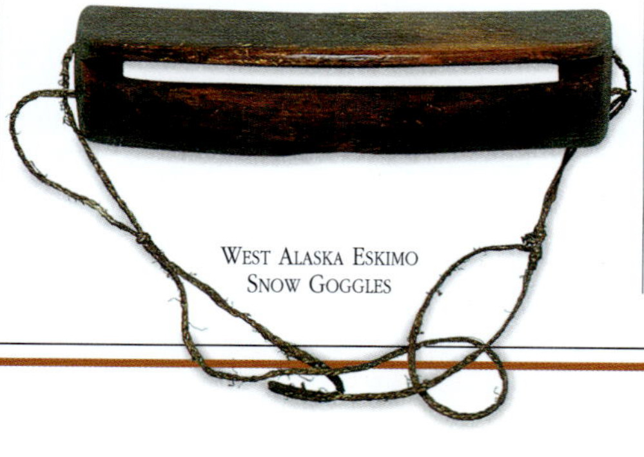
WEST ALASKA ESKIMO SNOW GOGGLES

F

G

H

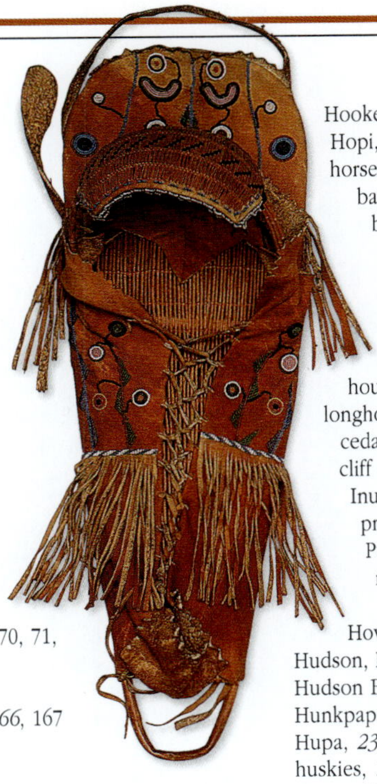
PAIUTE CRADLEBOARD

I

J–L

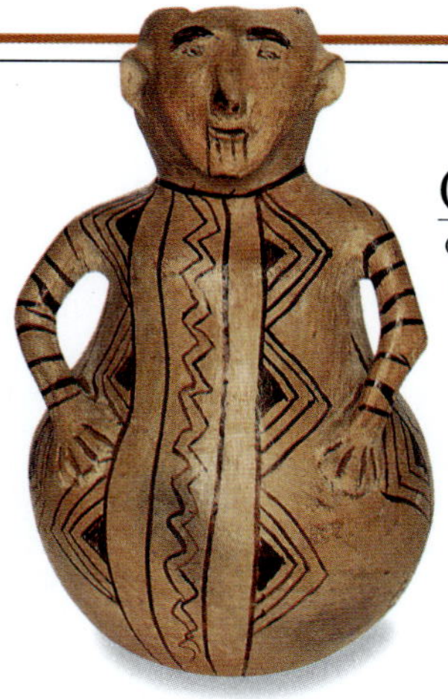

TOHONO O'ODHAM POTTERY VESSEL

O

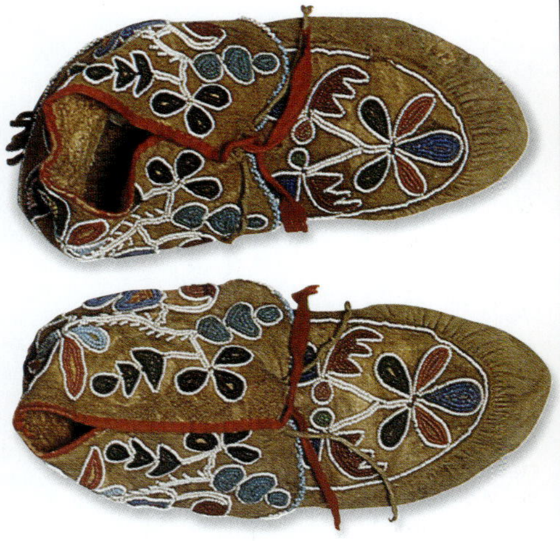

MENOMINEE MOCCASINS

ACKNOWLEDGMENTS AND CREDITS

AUTHOR'S ACKNOWLEDGMENTS

The author would like to thank: Mary-Clare Jerram, whose telephone call on 4 July 1997 set this project in motion. Thank you for your many kindnesses in London and the US. Martin Hendry: your laser-like eye for photographs that tell stories, for colorful accents, and for polished designs has made this history all the more accessible to readers. Irene Lyford: the only downside to finishing this book is not waking up to e-mails from DK's prized editor. For two years we've worked closely on this book, and she continually amazed me with her ability to fit square pegs into round holes and make sentences sing. Fiona Wilson: you not only quickly grasped Native history but you dealt effortlessly with scores of archivists in the US and Canada, remembering their names, collections, and where you filed hundreds of photographs. And to the numerous archivists who responded so graciously to Fiona's requests, thank you. My neighbors, Leslie and Jack McKeon, come to my aid every time I call, and bring their enthusiasm to every project. I treasure their intelligence, integrity, and, this time, their indexing ability. My dear friend Larry Pringle: you sprang into action at a moment's notice. Beverly Wright for writing the Foreword. I am honored to have your words grace this history.

PUBLISHER'S ACKNOWLEDGMENTS

Dorling Kindersley would like to thank: Hulton Getty Picture Collection and all the photographers, picture libraries, and archives who supplied images for the book; the American Museum of North American History for help with identification of artefacts; Murdo Culver, Phil Hunt, and Miranda Kennedy for work on the map spreads; Jenny Jones for dealing with permissions and picture credits; Polly Boyd for proofreading; Jane Cooke for editorial help with the index and map spreads; Anna Hayman and Georgina Earle for administrative support; Sean Hunter for additional picture research.

PICTURE CREDITS

Dorling Kindersley would like to thank the following for their kind permission to reproduce their photographs (key: l=left, r=right, b=below, c=centre, t=top)

Alaska State Library: Winter & Pond Collection (PCA 87–106): 54–5t; Case & Draper coll.: 143crb (photo no. PCA 39–15); Allen Memorial Art Museum, Oberlin College, Ohio: 70–1; Allsport: 158c; Arizona Historical Foundation: 128–9c; Arizona Historical Society Library: 118ac & cl; American Heritage Center, University of Wyoming: 141ac; American Museum, Courtesy Department of Library Services: 55bc (neg. No. 1520); American Museum of Natural History, Department of Library Services: 38bc; George Ancona: 155br; Associated Press: 163tr, bl & br, 164crb, 165ac; Kenny Barkley: 170bl; Alan Berner: 38br; British Columbia Archives and Records Service: 20–1c; Brown Brothers: 74cl, 156clr; Brown Country Historical Society: 65tr; Buffalo and Erie County Historical Society: 63bc, 157tc, 163tl; California State Library: 44cla; Colorado Historical Society: 70cl, clb & bc, 71, 72–3, 74tr, 108b, 110cr, 111c, clb, cb & bc, 140tr; Colorific/Peter S. Mecca/Black Star/Telegraph Colour Library: 175cb; Paul Conklin: 157bl, 163cr, 175ac, 176cl; CP Picture Archives: 60; Mario Cabreral: 171br; Tom Hanson: 171tr; Shaney Komulainen: 171ac; Quebec Hydro: 171crb; Chris Wahl: 171cb; Edward S. Curtis: 160–1; Dakota Indian Foundation: 184; Denver Art Museum: 88–9t; Denver Public Library:116br; Western History Department: 14b, 44cra, 45tl, 95cr, 124cla, 124–5b, 132–3b, 134bl, 142tr, 165cr & bc; DK Picture Library: 1, 9tc, 18tr, 20ac, cra & c, 21cl, 23cra, 32clb & cb, 39tr, 42 clr, cl, clrb, clb & bl, 46–7, 47crb, 54c, 55br, 59cr, 81tl & tr, 86tc, 87cra, 98cla, c & clb, 99cra, 114cla, 116tl, 134tc, 141tr, 149cr, 158bl, 159c & br, 175tl, tr & cr, 182tl & cb, 186, 188, 189, 190, 191, 192; Courtesy of Florida State Archives: 32–3bc; Adam Fortunate Eagle: 166; Gamma Liason: J. Pat Carter 155ac; Garth Dowling 177cr; Jeff Topping 175br; Hulton Getty: 4cra, 12tc, 16, 18cb & bl, 20 cla, bc & br, 21bl, 22tl & cr, 23cl, 30, 30–1, 31tr & ac, 32cla, cra, c & bl, 33tl, tr, cra, c, clb & bc, 34tr & cla, 36, 38tr, 42tl & ac, 43tl, bl & br, 44clb & bl, 45tr & cl, 54cr, 58bl, 62bl, 63clb, 64cl, 66tr (of President Lincoln) & cr, 68, 70tr, 81ac, 82tr, cl & bc, 83br, 86tl, c & clb, 90crb, 90–1, 92cb, 96–7b, 97c & cr, 98cl, 108tr & cb, 109br, 100tr, 110clb, 111tc, cla & cra, 114tr, 117br, 118–9b, 119crb, 121, 122tr, 123cr & crb, 125tr, 128tr & ac, 134cl, 135tc & clb, 141cr, 148tl, 149tl & clb, 150–1, 153tr, 154bl, 156tr & clb, 157cra, 158tr & cb, 162cla, 164cla, 165tr & cb, 170tr & bc, 174cl, 182crb & br; Glenbow Archives: 103cla, ac, cra, c & crb, 104–5; Ronald Grant Archive: 99tc, 155bl, 183cra, c, cr, bc & cb; Ernest Hass: 162tr; Hulton Getty Picture Collection 46-7tc, br; Idaho State Historical Society: 48cl (neg. no. 42), 48–9b (neg. no. 63.221.205/A), 115tl (neg. no. 3771), 122bl (neg. no. 63–221.24); Joslyn Art Museum: 80bl; Kansas State Historical Society: 69, 82crb, 86–7b, 132cb; Latter Day Saints Historical Dept., Archives: 51clb; Liaison 15; Liaison Agency: Michael Abramson: 162bl; Bill Gillette: 55tc; Stan Godlewski: 177tc; Mike Roemer 175bc; Renato Rotolo: 153bl, 155tr, 165crb, 174br; Michael Springer 168–9; A. Weiner: 176ac; Library of Congress: 19br, 39cl, 63ac & cb, 110ac, c & bc, 116bl, 118cr, 154br; Heirs of Frank Bird Linderman: 146; Courtesy Little Big Horn Battlefield National Monument: 88cb, 90clb & bc, 94tr, 96bl; Special Collections, McFarlin Library, University of Tulsa: 122cl & crb, 124cl; Massachusetts Commandery Military Order of the Royal Legion and the US Army Military History Institute: 82c; Medals of America Press: 154cr; Lawrence Migdale: 5cra, 138, 175crb, 176tr crb & bl, 177cla; Minnesota Historical Society: 39tl; 65bl & br: 66tcl, tc, tcr & ac; 67tr; I. Bennetto and Co: 67cl; Adrian Ebell, Whitney's Gallery, St. Paul: 64bl; Beaverhead County Museum Archives: 64crb; Simon & Shepherd: 65bc; B. F. Upton: 66–7, 67crb; Whitney's Gallery, St Paul: 65tl, 66cl & bl; Montana Historical Society, Helena: 86bc, 143bc; Museum of Cherokee: 63tr; Courtesy Museum of New Mexico: 74clb (neg. no. 14516); 75cr (neg. no. 44516), crb (neg. no. 1816) & bc (neg. no. 28537); T. Harmon Parkhurst: 19tr (neg. no. 55189), 40–1 (neg. no. 3984); National Archives: 14tc, 58br & t, 59br, 75tr, 80cl, 83tc & tr, 88cb, 89ac, cra & br, 91tr & clb, 94bl, 96clb, cb & crb, 110cla, 115ac, 117c, 119cra, 125cl, 127, 132cl, 134cla, 135br, 149c & bc, 152tr, 153cr, bc & br, 154tr & cla, 154–5c, 155tc, 156cl & bc, 157cla, crb & br, 171tl; National Archives of Canada: 103bc, 142cb (neg. no. C 16717), 157ac; National Film Board of Canada: John Kenney: 171c; Jonathan Wenk: 171cr; National Library of Canada: 49cr (neg. no. NLZ1831); Naturegraph 42cl; Nebraska State Historical Society: Front Jacket image, altered, 5c, 63cr, 133tr, 135cra, cr & bc, 136, 142ac; David Neel: 2–3, 177cb, 185; Nevada State Historical Society: 109cr, 112; Peter Newark's American Pictures: 62bc, 63crb, 86tr; Peter Newark's Military Pictures: 92bl, 98tr; Peter Newark's Western Americana: 64tr, 76–7, 88br, 94bc, 94–5b, 95cra, 98cr, 99cla, 115cb, 159tl; The Newberry Library: 149ac; New York Public Library (Special Collections): 74–5; The News Tribune, Tacoma, Washington: 164tc, cb & bl; North Wind Picture Archives 59tr; Oklahoma Historical Society: 5tl; 56; 123tr; Archives & Manuscripts Division: 123br; Oneida National Museum: 13tc; Oregon Historical Society: 43tr, 114crb (neg. no. CN020648), 129tl (neg. no. OrHi36112), 157tr (neg. no. OrHi65996); Phototheque des Musees de la Ville de Paris: 44cl; Press Association: Fiona Hanson 170–1b; Princeton University Libraries: 154–5cb; Laurence Pringle 6; Provincial Archives of Alberta: 61; Harry Pollard Collection: 47br, 50ac; Provincial Archives of Manitoba: Indians 9 31br (neg. 10970); 102; 103tr, cr & clb; Courtesy of the Royal British Columbia Museum, Victoria, B.C.: 22ac, 143cr; Royal Ontario Museum: 38cb; San Diego Museum of Man: 50–1c, 75c, 120; Santa Barbara Historical Society: 48bl; Scottish National Portrait Gallery: 49tr; Seattle Post/Intelligencer Collection, Museum of History and Industry: 164cl; The Seattle Times: 164ac; Jaune Quick-to-See Smith: Jeff Sturges, courtesy Steinbaum Krauss Gallery: 182–3t; Smithsonian Institution, NAA: 4bc; 8; 19cr; 20cr; 21tr & cr; 22tcr cl & b; 22–3c; 23bl 24–5; 26; 38tl & cra; 44br; 45br; 54tc, cla & b; 55cl; 59cb; 63cl; 67c & cr; 75clb; 81br; 83trl, cl & cb; 84–5; 87cl; 91br, 97tl, tr & cl, 106–7, 108–9cb, 109clb, 111br, 114bl, 115tr, 126, 128tl, 133br, 134tl & cra, 137, 140clb, 142–3c, 149tr, 158tl, National Numismatic Collection: 59bl; Photograph courtesy of National Museum of the American Indian: 59bc; Southwest Museum: 116cb, 148b; State Historical Society of North Dakota: 27, 97br, 134cr & crb, 142b, 142–3t; State Historical Society of South Dakota: 9b, 95tc, 132–3t 142cr; State Historical Society of Wisconsin: 59tc (Whi/X3/48063), 62clb (Whi/X3/51189), 142–3b; Stern: 165tl, cl & clb; General Sweeny's: 62tr, 63cla; Telegraph Colour Library/Colorific/Peter S. Mecca/Black Star 175c; Texas Memorial Museum: 83c; Tony Stone Images: 78, 177br; Charles Farciot 38cl; Sylvain Grandadam 174bl, 176c; Bobby Lane 155cr; Lawrence Migdale 178–9; David Neel 177clb; Chris Noble 48tr; Paul Sodders 177cb; Tom Till 19ac; Stephen Trimble: 174tr, 176cra, 177ac; Hulleah Tsinhnahjinnie: 170cl (courtesy from 1199 Bread & Roses Cultural Project); United States Military Academy, West Point: 135ac; University of British Columbia, Museum of Anthropology 182bl; University of Pennsylvania Museum, Philadelphia: 18–19b, 21: tl (neg. S4–142726), ac (neg. S4–142703), cb (neg. S4–142694) & br (neg. S4–142720), 38c (neg. S4–142700), 39clb & br (neg. S4–142684), 50c, 51tl (neg. no. S4–142705), 87tl (neg. S4–142682), 129br (neg. S4–142708), 130–1 (neg. S4–142706), 141tl & br, 148clb (neg. S4–142721); University of Washington Libraries, Special Collections Division: 50cra (neg. no. NA 3049); 50–1b (neg. no. NA 3048); 158–9b; photo by Hegg: 50cla (neg. no. 3093); Courtesy Upstream Productions: 183br; US Army Signal Museum: 152b; Victoria Library, Canada: 49br; Karen Warth: 177c; Washington State Historical Society: 45cr; Western History Collections, University of Oklahoma Libraries: 12–13b, 23tl, 49cb, 51cra & cr, 52–3, 80tr, 81cr, 83tcr, 89tc, 90tc & cla, 95br, 116cl & clb, 117tr, 118cra, 119tr & cla;, 124tc & c, 124–5t, 125cr, 128cl & br, 132bl, 135cla, 138br, 143br, 149crb. Stacy B. Weisfeld Back Jacket tc; West Point Museum/US Military Academy: 96tr; William Hammond Mathers Museum: 19cb; 22clb; 33crb; 143ac; 144–5; 152ac; 153ac; Indian University:152ac; Woolaroc Museum, Bartlesville, Oklahoma: 34b; Wyoming Division of Cultural Resources: 98–9b; Yale University: 180.

Maps: Aziz Khan (pp.10–11, 28–9, 34–5, 46–7, 94–5, 102–3); John Woodcock (pp.75, 115, 172–3); David Ashby (overlays)

Index: Leslie McKeon